H. C. Granger –

Dec. 9th
1824

A

COMMENTARY

ON THE

BOOK OF DANIEL.

BY

MOSES STUART,

LATELY PROF. OF SACRED LITERATURE IN THE THEOL. SEMINARY AT ANDOVER.

BOSTON:

PUBLISHED BY CROCKER & BREWSTER.

1850.

Entered according to Act of Congress, in the year 1850, by
CROCKER & BREWSTER,
In the Clerk's Office of the District Court of Massachusetts.

ANDOVER: JOHN D. FLAGG,
STEREOTYPER AND PRINTER.

PREFACE.

While engaged in writing my Commentary on the Apocalypse, I found myself so often remitted to the book of Daniel, for the sake of illustration, that I of necessity was obliged to study that book with more than ordinary care and diligence. It was natural for me, in the course of an often repeated study of the book, to contract a fondness for it, or at least to take a deep interest in it. When I had completed my apocalyptic labors, and acquitted myself of some engagements which followed them, I began the study of Daniel anew, and with a view to the writing of a Commentary on it. The labor was severe; for very much has been written upon the book, a considerable portion of which has much more of chaff than of wheat in it. Just as I had completed the exegetical part of my work, a typhoid fever took strong hold upon me, and brought me near to the grave. For two years and six months it was utterly beyond my power to write another paragraph. Toward the close of January last, I began slowly to mend, and after a while I ventured to resume my labor. But for several weeks subsequent to this, I could not venture beyond the effort of studying an hour in a day. The opening Spring brought some further relief; and thus I have been able to complete my original design.

In this personal history the public, I am aware, can take but little interest. But it has so often been published, in one way and another, that I was about to print a Commentary on the book in question, that I have deemed it not inapposite to state the ground of my delay.

As to the book of Daniel itself, I believe that no other of the scriptural books, the Apocalypse excepted, has called forth such a variety of discrepant opinions and interpretations. How can I agree with all of them? And yet the great mass of readers are ready to say, each one for himself, that I ought to agree with him. But why? my friend. You take the liberty to differ from others; and why should you refuse the same liberty to me? Besides, I have to ask: On what grounds have you based your opinion? Have you studied the book in its original languages; sought for light on every side, from history, and from antiquities; and above all, have you thoroughly and simply applied to it, irrespective of any favorite and preconceived notions about it, the established principles of historico-grammatical exegesis? And do you even know, with any certainty, what those principles are? If not, how much is your opinion worth, even in your own eyes, when you look candidly at such a difficult matter as the interpretation of the book before us?

If here and there a self-complacent critic of my Commentary on the Apocalypse, had asked himself such questions, before he sat down to write his *diatribe*, the public would have been spared a deal of *a priori* interpretation and spider-web theories. Some had written their book, on the same work of John, and mine disagreed with it. *Hinc illae lacrymae.* Some had read that *profound* work of Bishop Newton on the Prophecies; and because I did not agree with him, I must be in the wrong. The most confident of my condemning judges were, of course, those who could not read a word of the original, and would not be able to form any idea what one means, who talks about historico-grammatical interpretation. I have no defence to make against any such assailants.

What happened then, may and probably will happen now. I have not come to the conclusion, that Daniel has said, or knew, any thing about the *Pope* and his *Cardinals*. This will be enough to pass sentence of condemnation. *Do manus*. I can have no dispute with criticism like this. Of all the books in the Bible, except perhaps the Apocalypse, Daniel has been least understood, and most perverted and abused. I will bide my time, and wait with patience to see, whether this will be conceded and myself justified in the attempt to vindicate its true meaning.

For the rest, I have only a few things to say, as to the design and manner of the Commentary. I have kept in my eye, every where, the wants of a beginner in the study of Hebrew, and specially of the Chaldee. For the Chaldee part, the book is, as I trust, a complete *Chrestomathy*, i. e. it gives the solution of every difficulty respecting the forms and the syntax of words. The reader may depend on its being a sufficient introduction to the grammatical study of the Chaldee language. The references everywhere made in copious abundance to Prof. Hackett's translation of Winer's Chaldee Grammar, will familiarize him, if he is faithful in consulting that Grammar, with all the forms and peculiarities of the Chaldee dialect. All the Chaldee words are of course comprised in Gesenius' Hebrew Lexicon.

The few in our country, who are acquainted with the Chaldee, will take no offence at a brief space being occupied with the solution of grammatical questions. They can pass on and leave these, without any hinderance. If they once have studied the language, and let slip the memory of grammatical minutiae, they will thank me for rendering it quite easy for them to recal what they had lost.

Most heartily do I commend it to all Hebrew students, to go on and study the Chaldee. If they are well grounded in Hebrew, four or five weeks spent faithfully on the Chaldee, will enable them to read this with as much facility as they do the Hebrew. The study of the Chaldee in Daniel, will be sufficient to enable them to read the Chaldee in Ezra with entire ease; and from him they may go into the Chaldee Targums without any difficulty. The conquest is easy, and ought to be achieved by every valiant soldier of the cross.

Should the present volume prepare the way for a more extensive study of one of the sacred languages in our country, by young candidates for the ministry, the writer of it will not have labored in vain.

M. STUART.

ANDOVER, MAY 24, 1850.

CONTENTS

OF SUBJECTS SPECIALLY DISCUSSED.

Commentary.

Excursus.

Critical History and Defence.

COMMENTARY.

[CHAP. I. *Early history of Daniel.* Siege of Jerusalem by Nebuchadnezzar, capture of Jehoiakim, and deportation of a part of the vessels of the temple to Babylon; vs. 1, 2. Daniel with some of his companions is selected by the king's overseer to be trained up in the Chaldee manner, for the personal service of the king; Babylonish names are given to the young Hebrews, and they are supported from the king's table, vs. 3—7; Daniel makes earnest request that he and his companions may have liberty to adopt a simple vegetable diet, so that they may not defile themselves with the royal viands; he obtains liberty, and thrives remarkably well under his new regimen; vs. 8—16. All four of the Hebrew children make unusual progress in knowledge; but Daniel is endowed by God with uncommon sagacity and knowledge, and becomes able to interpret visions and dreams; v. 17. At the end of three years, Daniel and his companions are brought before the king, and they are found to be far more intelligent and sagacious than any of the Chaldean astrologers; vs. 18—20. The 21st verse contains an indication of Daniel's long continuance at court, even until the restoration of the Hebrews to Palestine, during the first year of Cyrus's reign. In other words, Daniel, in person, was a witness to the beginning and end of the Jewish exile.]

CHAP. I. 1. In the third year of the reign of Jehoiakim king of Judah, came Nebuchadnezzar king of Babylon to Jerusalem, and besieged it.

בִּשְׁנַת שָׁלוֹשׁ, lit. *in the year of three.* This is the usual method of expressing time in this book; see 1: 21. 2: 1. 7: 1 (Chald.). 8: 1. 9: 1. So frequently elsewhere; e. g. 2 K. 12: 2. 13: 1. 15: 1. al. The Hebrew usually employs *cardinal* numbers (1—10) for *ordinals*, when *years* or *days* are reckoned, Roed. Heb. Gramm. § 118, 4. e. g. the *construct* form of the noun designating *year*, etc. (as in the case before us), is often employed; comp. Gramm. § 118, 4. — לְמַלְכוּת, *of the reign*, the Gen. in such a case being ordinarily marked by prefixing לְ, when it is preceded by *numerals;* Roed. Gramm. § 113. 2. *c.* — יְהוּדָה, first the name of Jacob's oldest son, and (after the exile) employed also for the name of the

Jewish *country ;* as it is here. — בָּא *came.* Hengstenberg (Authent. Dan. p. 61) translates it *zog*, i. e. *proceeded*, or *set out*, viz. upon an expedition. But the sequel *(and besieged it)* shows, that the usual sense of בָּא (= ἔρχομαι) must here be attached to the word ; and so I have rendered it in the version above — The name נְבוּכַדְנֶאצַּר is probably composed of נְבוֹ = *Mercury*, who was worshipped by the Babylonians, خدان *(chodan)* = *deus*, and שַׂר = *prince*, i. e. the name means *prince of the god Nebo*, or Mercury, i. e. belonging to him, and so of high rank. — וַיָּצַר (either Imperf. Hiph. of the root צָרַר, or the Imperf. Kal of צוּר, the *Pattah* of the final syllable being adopted because of the final ר, Roed. Gr. § 22. 2. *a* and 5. Moreover, a shortened Imperf. and a retracted accent are normal here, Gramm.* § 48. b., 2. *b.* The עַל (with Suff. it becomes עָלֶי) lit. means *against ;* but here it qualifies the preceding verb, and the construction resembles Isa. 7: 1, הִלָּחֵם עָלֶיהָ. עַל is usually found after this verb in the sense of *besieging ;* Lex. צוּר No. 2. (the more probable stem.)

(2) And the Lord gave into his hand Jehoiakim king of Judah and a part of the vessels of the house of God, and he brought them to the land of Shinar, to the house of his god, and the vessels he carried to the treasure house of his god.

בְּיָדוֹ, *into* or *in his hand*, very frequently employed by the Hebrews to designate the idea of *putting in one's power* or *at his disposal.* As to the fact of the invasion itself, comp. 2 K. 24: 1. — מִקְצָת, *a part of*, (קְצָת is an abridged form of קְצָאת = קְצָאת, from קָצָה). It is disputed whether מִ is a *prefix-formative* here or a *preposition.* I regard it as being the latter, i. e. as derived from מִן, the Daghesh which we should expect in the ק being omitted, because it would make the Sheva vocal under this letter in case of its insertion ; Gr. § 20. 3. *b.* This usage of omitting Daghesh in such cases, is not unfrequent. Comp. the same word, although with a sense somewhat diverse, in Dan. 1: 15, 18. Here the *form* is the same, and מִ is unquestionably a *preposition* in both these cases. So in Neh. 7: 70, comp. Ps. 135: 7. In 2 Chron. 36: 7, the same idea as here is expressed simply by מִכְּלֵי, *a part of the vessels*, instead of מִקְצָת כְּלֵי as in our text. But the passage in 2 Chron., I cannot well doubt, describes the *second* invasion of Palestine by Nebuchadnezzar, at the close of Jehoiakim's reign, when this king was put in chains to be carried to Babylon, and probably died in this condition, Jer. 22: 18, 19. 36: 30. Still the occasion and the transaction are of the like nature with those which per-

* This abridged mode of citation always applies to my edition of Roediger's Hebrew Grammar.

tain to the first invasion. At the first invasion, Nebuchadnezzar, who made Jehoiakim the Jewish king tributary to him, rifled the temple of only a *part* of its treasures; at the second, he took away another portion of them, 2 Chron. 36: 7. At the third, he repeated the same thing on a more extensive scale, 2 K. 24: 13. At the fourth and final invasion under Zedekiah, when the temple was destroyed, all its treasures were carried away, together with king Zedekiah, his family, and his court, 2 K. 25: 6—20. A part of these treasures were brought back under Cyrus, Ezra 1: 7; and the rest under Darius, Ezra 6: 5.

וַיְבִיאֵם *and he brought them* — who? where? The vessels and Jehoiakim, (for the verb of itself with its suffix might easily have this meaning), or only the vessels? The latter only, as the sequel shows; for surely he did not bring Jehoiakim and *put him in the treasure-house of his god.* As the actual coming of Jehoiakim to Babylon is not here mentioned, it is probable that he died on the way, after he was taken captive and bound in fetters, 2 Chron. 36: 6; see and comp. Jer. 22: 18, 19. 36: 30. — *Land of Shinar* is the old name for the province of Babylon; see in Gen. 10: 10. 11: 2. Isa. 11: 11. Zech. 5: 11, the last two cases seem to be a kind of poetic use. The origin of the name has not yet been developed. — *And the same vessels did he bring to the house of his god,* is a literal rendering of the last part of the verse. As to the version above, we may render the second הֵבִיא by *deposited,* (Sept. ἀπηρείσατο, *safely conveyed* or *carried*), which will preserve the sense, and avoid a seeming tautology in case we here render it *brought.* In fact, הֵבִיא often means *introduced,* εἰσφέρειν (Sept.), and corresponds to וַיִּתְּנֵם, and *he put* or *deposited them,* in 2 Chron. 36: 7. The writer first designates, generally, the deportation of a part of the vessels to Babylon, and then he names the particular locality where they were there deposited. He had special reasons for so doing, in reference to a part of his subsequent history; see Dan. 5: 3, 4, 23. Besides, the clause in question leads us to see, that the vessels were in safe keeping, and that Nebuchadnezzar's motive was probably to make acceptable presents (*ἀναθήματα,* as the Greeks called them in such cases), to his god Belus — a thank-offering for the victories he had won, and at the same time an evidence of his glorying that Belus was more powerful than the God of the Hebrews. The famous temple of Belus, at Babylon, is known to all. That the vessels were put into the *treasure-house* shows, moreover, both the precaution taken for their safe-keeping and the value attached to them. All the temples of antiquity had treasure-houses, from which the priests were supported; see Num. 31: 48—54. Josh. 6: 19. Comp. Mal. 3: 10. Neh. 13: 5, 12, 13.

As to the time of the invasion by Nebuchadnezzar, neither Kings, Chron., or Jeremiah give any date; but the facts recorded by Berosus show, that it could not be later than the time named in v. 1, for it was not possible to subdue all those countries in less than two years. That the *first* year of Nebuchadnezzar was the fourth year of Jehoiakim (Jer. 25: 1. 46: 2), does not contradict this; for the *Jews* of Palestine (not Daniel) reckoned Nebuchadnezzar's first year as beginning *with* his mission upon the western invasion, and a small part of that year fell in with the closing part of Jehoiakim's third year, while probably the greatest part of that first year corresponded to the *fourth* year of Jehoiakim. For the full discussion of these disputed matters, and justification of this statement, I must refer the reader to the Excursus at the close of Chap. I.

(3) And the king commanded Ashpenaz, the chief of his eunuchs, to bring some of the sons of Israel, both of the royal seed and of the nobles,

The phrase וַיֹּאמֶר לְ means *to command;* see in Esth. 1:17. 4:13. 9:14. 1 Chron. 21:17; mostly in the later Hebrew. Sometimes אָמַר has this sense before a verb Imperf. with ו conversive, and even before the Acc. This meaning is the usual one in Arabic; and very frequent in the Chaldee, see Dan. 2: 12, 46. 3: 13, 19, 20. 4: 23. 6: 24. — *Ashpenaz* has been the subject of many conjectural etymologies; but none of them are satisfactory. — *The chief of the eunuchs.* In the later Hebrew, רַב (originally *much* or *great*) is equivalent to שַׂר, *prince* or *praefect;* in Chaldee, this is the usual sense of the word as a noun, e. g. in Rab-shakeh, Rab-saris, Rab-mag, etc. In the N. Test. ῥαββί, (our present *Rabbi*), seems specially to designate a *leader in teaching.* As to סָרִיסָיו (with Qamets under ס, sometimes treated as mutable and sometimes as immutable), there is every probability that the translation here given (*eunuchs*) is the true one. The οἰκονόμος of an oriental king had charge of his household, including his Harem and all his house servants, the male part of which of course were eunuchs. To such an one would belong the training up of servants who were to be the personal waiters of the king. That young persons of royal descent and of noble families should be chosen for such a service, is altogether in accordance with the pride and haughtiness of the Babylonian king, and the customs of the East. The proud title, *king of kings,* carries with it the implication that kings are servants of the great monarch. That *young* lads should be chosen for such a service, was almost a matter of course. They could easily become acquainted with the language and the customs of the court, and were specially capable of great personal activity. In some passages (see Ges. Lex.) it is difficult to say, whether the original idea סָרִיס (from סָרַס ܣܪܣ, *castravit*) is retained; e. g. Gen. 37: 36. 39: 1. At all events, the leading sense occasionally is *courtier* or *court-officer*. Among oriental kings, their greatest confidants have been of this class of persons. In the Turkish court, the *Kislar Aga* is an officer of the like kind. Comp. רַב בֵּיתוֹ in Esth. 1: 8. — לְהָבִיא, *to bring*, i. e. carry or convey, viz. from Jerusalem to Babylon. So C. B. Mich. and Ros.; but Lengerke understands the command as having respect to captives *already arrived* at Babylon. But if this were the case, why not employ לָקַחַת *to take*, rather than הָבִיא *to convey?* Yet in the particular sense of *bringing them into the place* of their training, this view of Leng. might be admitted.

Sons of Israel = Israelites, i. e. posterity of Jacob or Israel. This was the first meaning; the second was the *ten tribes*, who revolted with Jeroboam; and after the exile, the name was again used in its primitive sense, as it is here. The sequel designates the narrow limits of the choice to be made by Ashpenaz. That מִבְּנֵי is employed to designate *some of the sons*, is agreeable to common usage; see Ges. Lex. מִן. — *Both of the royal seed and of the nobles*. Such a translation makes this clause an epexegetical limitation of the preceding expression. C. B. Mich. makes three classes, by interpreting the three classes as *coördinate;* and so Rosenm. This is a possible, but not a probable, interpretation. — מִזֶּרַע הַמְּלוּכָה, lit. *seed of the kingdom* or *of the kingly power*, i. e. of royal descent; see the same idiom (which belongs to the later Hebrew) in 2 K. 25: 25. Jer. 41: 1. Ezek. 17: 13. — הַפַּרְתְּמִים, a word of foreign origin, Pehlvi *pardom*, Sanscrit *prathama* = primores, magnates, nobles. The Greek πρῶτος seems to be, originally, of the same origin. The word receives the form of the Heb. plural here; as transplanted words frequently do. Good is the version of Josephus (Archaeol. X. 10. 1), τοὺς εὐγενεστάτους; so Polychronius, τῶν εὐγενῶν. Comp. in this the fulfilment of Isa. 39: 7. The whole transaction is strictly in accordance with oriental customs.

(4) Young lads, in whom was no blemish, and of goodly appearance, and skilled in every kind of wisdom, and acquainted with knowledge, and discerning in science, and who were able to stand in waiting at the palace of the king; and to teach them the writing and the language of the Chaldees.

The word יְלָדִים is, in our English version, translated *children*. Of itself it does not determine the *age;* and it may be rendered *boys, youth*, or *young lads*, as above. The Persians began education, properly so called, at the age of fourteen, (Plat. Alcib. I. § 37); and the young man's age of action was seventeen, (Cyrop. I. 2). In all probability, the Hebrew lads in question were some twelve to fifteen years of age, when selected. The noun יְלָדִים is in the Acc., and depends on the Inf. לְהָבִיא;

which latter depends on וַיֹּאמֶר. This shows that the *Soph Pasuq* (׃) does not always divide the verses according to the sense or grammatical construction; comp. 2 Sam. 17: 27—29, where is a notable example of a similar nature. *No blemish*, etc.; such a custom still pervades the East, e. g. in the Turkish and Persian courts, as to the selection of personal servants. Everything is required to be beautiful or magnificent, which surrounds the person of the king. מְאוּם = מוּם = Greek *μῶμος*, which has the same sense. — וְטוֹבֵי מַרְאֶה, lit. *goodly of appearance*, Gramm. § 110, 2. — מַשְׂכִּילִים, Part. Hiph., but divested of its *causative* sense, in case we translate it *skilled, intelligent;* but if we revert to the original signification of the root (*to look*), we may see that it is used elliptically in Hiphil = *causing* [the mind] *to look* or *attend to*, and as a consequence *skilled.* — חָכְמָה, *wisdom*, is of widely extended meaning in Hebrew, importing (in its largest sense) a knowledge of all things, i. e. of what is true respecting them, and here employed as nearly equivalent to our English word *learning.* — וְיֹדְעֵי דַעַת, Part. Const. pl. Gramm. § 132, 1. *b;* *acquainted with knowledge* is a repetition of the preceding idea in another form, for the sake of intensity. So also is it with the clause, *discerning in science;* מְבִינֵי importing properly the power of *discriminating* between things, or of *discerning* their properties and relations. Construction as before. This accumulation of different phrases nearly equivalent in meaning, is after the common usage of the Hebrews, and plainly, as has been remarked, is intended to designate intensity of expression, being equivalent to the simple declaration, *skilled in knowledge of every kind.* — כֹּחַ, lit. *strength, force*, here *ability, power.* — לַעֲמֹד, *standing* was the position of waiters in readiness to do their master's will. Hence the secondary sense of the verb עָמַד, viz. *serve, minister to*, Ges. Lex. s. v. I. *a.* Usually it is followed, in such cases, by לִפְנֵי *before*, joined with the designation of the person served, as in v. 5. — הֵיכַל, *palace*, i. e. a large magnificent building; which corresponds to the Arabic verb هَيْكَلَ, *to be great* or *lofty.* The word is properly generic, and so may designate a *palace*, or (as often) the *temple* of Jehovah. — וּלְלַמְּדָם, *and to teach them*, which falls back, as to construction, upon the וַיֹּאמֶר of v. 3; for Ashpenaz was charged with the education of the Jewish lads. — סֵפֶר, lit. *writing.* The accent (*Tiphha*) separates it from the sequel, and shows that the Punctators took it as not in the const. state before כַּשְׂדִּים (implied), but as standing by itself, and meaning *books* or *literature.* This is made probable by בְּכָל־סֵפֶר in v. 17, which cannot mean merely *every kind of alphabetic characters*, but *every kind of literature.* Gesenius (in Lex.) understands it as meaning the *written characters* of the Chaldee; and this, at first view, seems the most facile interpretation; but v. 17 appears plainly to modify it. — *The tongue of the Chaldees* is differently interpreted. Lengerke says it designates the proper language of the original barbarian Chaldees from northern Mesopotamia; and Maurer (Comm. in loc.) appears inclined to this, and also Hävernick (Comm.). Also Winer (Chald. Gramm. p. 15, English version, ed. Hackett) seems disposed to think favorably of it. But in Dan. 2: 4, the Chaldees address Nebuchadnezzar in *Aramaean* (אֲרָמִית), and he replies in the same tongue. It would seem, therefore, to be the *court language* of that period. Comp. 2 Kings 18: 26. Isa. 36: 11. Ezra 4: 7, where the same appellation occurs. That it should here be called *the tongue of the Chaldees* is natural enough, since the court was principally made up of *Chaldeans*. That the Chaldees, in their original and barbarous state, (provided we admit that those northern barbarians had emigrated into Babylonia), had a written language, is very improbable. Rabshakeh, the commander of the *Assyrian* forces, addressed the Jewish courtiers in Hebrew, (Isa. 36: 11); and he is invited by them to speak in *Aramaean*. That the court of Nebuchadnezzar spoke the same language, Dan. 2: 4 seq. shows. But the young Jewish lads in question, probably were not acquainted with it so early in life as when they went into exile. Hence it was necessary that they should be taught it. That it was a *written* language, would appear from סֵפֶר being connected with it, in our text. With Ros. in loc., Ges. and Hitzig on Isa. 36: 11, and C. B. Michaelis (Comm. in Hagiog.), I deem it most probable, that the same language, i. e. *Aramaean-Chaldee*, is meant here, as in Dan. 2: 4.

(5) And the king assigned to them a daily allowance from the delicate viands of the king and from the wine which he drank, and that they should be nurtured three years, and after the close of them that they should stand in waiting before the king.

וַיְמַן, Imperf. Piel of מָנָה, Gramm. § 74. Note 9. — דְּבַר יוֹם, lit. *the thing of a day*, i. e. *quotidianum*, something belonging to the day; which is made still more specific by בְּיוֹמוֹ, *on each day*, lit. *during its day;* see Luke 11: 3, *τὸ καθ' ἡμέραν*. The English expression, used in the version above, gives the exact idea of the whole phrase. So the Hebrews say: שָׁנָה בְשָׁנָה = *each year;* פַּעַם בְּפַעַם = *once as before* or *one time as another*, etc. — מִפַּתְבַּג is evidently a foreign word, the meaning of which is probably given in the translation. The most facile etymology seems to be the old Persian پاد باه (pad-bah) *father's meat*, i. e. *king's food*, and so it designates figuratively delicate viands, costly bits, or choice food. This agrees well with the other passages where the word is employed, viz. in vs. 8, 13, 15, 16. 11: 26; and also with the Syriac ܦܬܒܓܐ, as employed by Ephrem Syrus (I. 382 F. 423 A.), and by

Bar Hebraeus (p. 331), to designate *dainties, luxurious food.* So Gesenius, Winer (in Lex.), Van Bohlen (Symb. ad interp. SS. e ling. Pers.), Rosenm., Maurer, and Lengerke (Comm.); but Lorsbach (Archiv. etc. II. s. 312 f.) prefers the etymology from پت (*pot*) *idol* and باه (*bah*) *food;* to which Hävernick and Fürst (Concord. Heb.) give their hearty assent. But the context (see v. 8, specially v. 10, where מַאֲכָל is substituted for פַּתְבַּג, with vs. 13, 15, 16) shows that the *ordinary food* of the king is assigned to the young Hebrews, and not merely such food as is presented to idols, on feast-days appropriate to the honoring of them. Of course, the former sense is preferable.

Very different conclusions are drawn from this passage, in respect to the alleged demeanor of Daniel. Lengerke (Comm.) and others argue, that it was only during the *Maccabaean* times that such superstition about food existed among the Jews, and therefore that the author of the book drew his views from that source, and must have lived at that time; while Hävernick and others, urging the view of Lorsbach as to etymology, strenuously vindicate the conduct of Daniel on the ground of avoiding participation in idolatrous feasts. Both parties seem to have made too much of the matter. Daniel needs no other vindication than the perusal of Lev. 11: 4 seq. 20: 25, and the consideration, that oftentimes the king's choice food would not only consist of animals forbidden to the Jews, but also that not unfrequently what had been presented before idols would be furnished for him. The same was the case with his *wine.* Of course, as conscientious Jews, Daniel and his companions were bound to avoid eating it indiscriminately, if it was in their power to shun it. Such demeanor was peculiar to no age, as it respected sincere disciples of Moses. To represent such abstinence as a grave argument for the composition of the book so late as the time of the Maccabees (so Lengerke), is little short of trifling. Even if Daniel's conduct was tinctured with superstition, was there no case of this nature before the time of the Maccabees?

The ·מִ before פַּתְבַּג means (as often elsewhere) *some of, a portion of;* and so also before the following יֵין. — מִשְׁתָּיו, lit. *of his drinking,* i. e. what he drank. The noun is *sing.,* although it appears to have a *plur.* suffix; for in nouns from roots לה, the original third radical (י) often returns before a suffix, when the noun is in the *singular,* and gives it the appearance of a plural; Gramm. § 91, 9, in Note. — וּלְגַדְּלָם, lit. *to grow them,* or *to make them grow large;* hence to *educate* or *nurture them.* — *Three years,* the Acc. of time, Gramm. §116, 2. For the plural שָׁנִים with a *numeral,* § 118, 2. — מִקְצָתָם, *from* or *after the termination of them,* viz. the years; Dag. forte omitted in the ק, § 20, 3. *b.* — יַעַמְדוּ, as before, *stand in waiting;* for the form of the vowels, see § 62. 3. This verb also depends on וַיְמַן at the beginning of the verse; so that we have here, first an Acc. case, then an Inf., and lastly a verb in the Subj.; all dependent on the same verb. Such changes in the construction of a sentence, i. e. such a mixture of different constructions after the same verb, are not uncommon in the Hebrew; comp. Isa. 32: 6.

(6) And there were among them some of the sons of Judah, Daniel, Hananiah, Mishael, and Azariah.

These names, like all other proper names in Hebrew, are significant. But I need not repeat here what the reader will find in his Lexicon. What the writer designs to say is, that while there was a number of Jewish captives, those named were selected from them, as having something in their appearance that was promising or prepossessing.

(7) And the chief of the eunuchs assigned names to them: to Daniel he assigned Belteshazzar; and to Hananiah, Shadrach; and to Mishael, Meshach; and to Azariah, Abed-nego.

These new names also are significant; and the Lexicon sufficiently develops their probable etymology. A custom, like this, of imposing new names when persons entered upon a new condition or new relations in life, is extensively developed in the O. Test.: see *Abram* and *Abraham*, Gen. 17: 5; *Joseph* and *Zaphnath-Paaneah*, Gen. 41: 45; comp. 2 Sam. 12: 24, 25. 2 K. 23: 34. 24: 17 (a case in which Nebuchadnezzar was concerned). Esth. 2: 7. Ez. 5: 14 comp. with Hag. 1: 14. 2: 2, 21. So in N. Test.: Mark 3: 16, 17. These names, thus imposed anew, generally designate something which is intended to honor the persons who receive them, or to honor the god that is worshipped by him who imposes them, or to commemorate some event that is interesting, etc. Thus *Belteshazzar* = *prince of Bel*, i. e. a prince to whom Bel is regarded as propitious, or to whom the giver of the name wishes Bel to be propitious, etc. — Of נְגוֹ no satisfactory explanation has yet been given. We have no knowledge, from any other quarter, of such a divinity among the Babylonians; but we find נְבוֹ, i. e. the planet *Mercury*, in many names. Gesenius supposes נְגוֹ to stand for נבו. C. B. Michaelis conjectures that the word comes from נָגַהּ *to shine*, so that it means *the splendid one.* This conjecture seems plausible.

(8) And Daniel anxiously sought that he might not defile himself with the delicate viands of the king and with the wine which he drank, and he made request of the chief of the eunuchs that he might not defile himself.

וַיָּשֶׂם . . . עַל־לִבּוֹ, lit. *put it to his heart* = the English *took it to heart*, i. e. was anxious, solicitous, concerned; Ges. Lex. שׂוּם 2. *h.* For the form of the verb, see § 71. n. 7. — אֲשֶׁר, conj. *that;* see Lex. B. — For the form of הִתְגָּאֵל (Hithp.), see § 63, 3. — מִשְׁתָּיו as above, in the *sing.* — יִתְגָּאָל, in Pause, § 29, 4. *a.* The probable ground of this request may be found in the precepts recorded in Lev. 11: 4 seq. 20: 25.

(9) And God made Daniel an object of kindness and compassion before the chief of the eunuchs. (Lit. God gave Daniel to kindness, etc.)

וַיִּתֵּן, § 65, 2.— The article before אֱלֹהִים is designed to be emphatic, *the God*, viz. of the Hebrews, or *the only true God.* — לְחֶסֶד etc. *to kindness*, etc., the literal form of expression we cannot successfully imitate in the English language. In the later Hebrew, לְ stands not unfrequently (see Lex.) before the Acc.; and verbs of *giving* govern two Accusatives, § 136, 2. But here, this is not a probable solution of the construction. — לִפְנֵי, *before* or *in the view of*, referring to the person from whom the kindness proceeded.

(10) And the chief of the eunuchs said to Daniel: I fear my master the king, who hath appointed your food and your drink; for why should he see your countenances sad, more than [the countenances] of the lads who are of your age, and you thus make me forfeit my head to the king?

וַיֹּאמֶר, § 67, 1. — יָרֵא Part. § 49, 2. *a*, § 131, 2. *a*, § 132, 1. *a*. — אֲדֹנִי, sing., different from אֲדֹנַי or אֲדֹנָי, which are in the plur. with suff. — מִשְׁתֵּיכֶם, sing. again, as in v. 5, although the suff. appears to belong to a plur. noun; see in § 91, 9. — אֲשֶׁר לָמָּה, *for why;* see אֲשֶׁר in Deut. 3: 24. Judg. 9: 17. and Lex. B. 3.; also שַׁלָּמָה in Cant. 1: 7. Gesenius and Lengerke render the two words as = *ne*, connecting the clause thus: *I fear . . . lest he should see*, etc., and they compare the Syriac ܕܠܡܐ, *lest, that not*, and the Syr., Chald., Ar., ܠܡܐ, מָא, لما, *ne, lest, not.* The sense of the passage is well enough developed by this interpretation, but not the shape of the phraseology. Doubtless לָמָּה is employed in questions that are tantamount to a negative or prohibition; but there is no need, in any case, of directly assuming the *negative* as the meaning of לָמָּה. Comp. moreover Neh. 6: 3. Ecc. 5: 5. 7: 16, 17. Rosenm. and Maurer defend the meaning first given. — זֹעֲפִים, Part., *sad, tetricus*, i. e. gloomy, sour, = σκυθρωπά, Matt. 6: 16. The idea of *scowling*, whether from anger or suffering, seems to be the true literal notion affixed to the word. — Before הַיְלָדִים there is an *implied* repetition of פְּנֵי (*face*), which breviloquence here omits; see the like in the Chaldee of 4: 13, 30. — כְּגִילְכֶם, lit. *according to your age*, i. e. your contemporaries, or those of the same age. גִּיל properly means *orbis, a circle;* and hence, both in Heb. and Arabic, *age*, γενεά. The secondary meaning of the word (*exultation*) would be inappropriate here. — וְחִיַּבְתֶּם, from חוּב, and forming a regular Piel, § 71, 7; lit. *and so ye will make guilty my head*, etc. The word רֹאשִׁי may have either a literal or a tropical sense. In the former case, the whole phrase means what the translation above expresses. Lengerke renders the verb by *verwirket*, i. e. forfeit. The idea is, that he would be exposed to decapitation, or to strangulation. The tropical sense would be: Endanger my life; for ראשׁ may be used in such a sense, 1 Sam. 29: 4; and so *head* is used with us.

(11) And Daniel said to Meltsar, whom the chief of the eunuchs had appointed over Daniel, Hananiah, Mishael, and Azariah;

הַמֶּלְצַר, probably a word from the old Persian, ملسر, *praefectus vini*, i. e. butler or steward, the derivation being from a foreign source like that of many other names in this book. Most, probably all, of the proper names were originally *appellatives;* and hence their significance. In the present case, the *name of office* seems to go over into, or to be used as, a kind of proper name; as is often the case with us. It might be rendered *chief butler* or *steward;* for the article prefixed to it seems to indicate such a meaning, inasmuch as the article is not usually prefixed to strictly proper names, § 108. 1. It would seem, from this verse, that the care of the young Hebrews, in respect to nutriment, was assigned by Ashpenaz, the head master of the king's household, appropriately to the steward; who in the present case was addressed by Daniel, because he sustained this office. What was said by Daniel (וַיֹּאמֶר) is related in the next verse; so that the division of the verses here by a *Soph Pasuq* is inappropriate, because the next verse properly constitutes the Acc. after the verb just named.

(12) Make trial now of thy servants, for ten days; and let them give us of the vegetables that we may eat, and water that we may drink.

נַס, Imper. Piel of נָסָה, § 48, 5. § 74. n. 9. — נָא, *now* or *I pray thee*, intensive, i. e. increasing the energy of the request. — *Thy servants*, i. e. the speaker uses the *third* person plural, in describing himself and his companions, instead of the first person, *us*. Such was the usual mode of courteous address to superiors, among the Hebrews, inasmuch as they avoided the use of *I* and *thou* in addresses of this nature; Ges. Lehrgeb. p. 742. — *Ten days*, Acc. of time, § 116, 2. On the special import of *ten*, see remarks on v. 20 below. — וְיִתְּנוּ, § 65, 2, lit. *and let them give*, § 125, 3. *c;* no definite subject to the verb being mentioned, it may be rendered either in the passive = *let there be given*, or in the active = *let some give*, § 134. 3. *b*. — מִן *of*, or *some of*, see Lex. — הַזֵּרֹעִים, lit. *things sowed*, i. e. vegetables in this case, such as pulse, lentiles, salads, etc. (not bread-corn); with the article, § 107, n. 1. *b*. — וְנֹאכְלָה, § 48, 3. וְ *that* conj., § 152. I. *e*. — מַיִם omits the מִן before it, § 151, 4, or else there is a change of construction. It omits the article also, as unnecessary for the sake of distinction. In the preceding case, the class of [eatable] vegetables is adverted to, by employing the article. Such occurrences as to the *use* and *omission* of the article before nouns apparently in the same predicament, are not unfrequent; see Ps. 104: 18. 105: 18. 107: 4. 114: 4, 6. 117: 1. 118: 8, 9. 121: 6. 125: 4, etc.

(13) And let our countenance and the countenance of the young lads who eat the delicate viands of the king be inspected before thee, and according to what thou shalt see, deal with thy servants.

וְיֵרָאוּ, Niph. Imperf. of רָאָה; *plur.*, because both מַרְאֵינוּ and the following מַרְאֵה are the subjects of the verb. Plainly מַרְאֵה is sing. in both cases, § 91, 9. The הָ before אֹכְלִים is a relative demonstrative = *who*, § 107 (at the beginning). — וְכַאֲשֶׁר תִּרְאֵה, not (with most translators), *as it shall seem good* (Sept. καθὼς ἐὰν θέλῃς), but *according to that which thou mayest see*, i. e. according to our appearance. So Theodotion: καὶ καθὼς ἐὰν ἴδῃς. The final vowel here in תִּרְאֵה (*Tsere*, and not the normal *Seghol*), is plainly after the analogy of the Aramaean, § 74. n. 17. — עֲבָדֶיךָ = *us*, as in v. 12.

(14) And he hearkened to them in respect to this matter, and he made trial of them ten days.

In לַדָּבָר, the article is so specific that it approaches very near to the demonstrative; as in הַיּוֹם. — The demonst. הַזֶּה renders still more intensive the specification. — יְנַסֵּם, § 74, n. 19, Piel Imperf. of נָסָה with suffix.

(15) And after the close of ten days their countenance appeared fairer, and [they were] fuller in flesh, than all the lads who ate the delicate viands of the king.

מִקְצָת as in v. 5. lit. *the cutting off*, and so it may mean *part* or *portion* as in v. 2, or *end*, *close*, as in v. 5 and here. The fem. ending ־ָת has a Qamets immutable; § 79. n. 2. *b*. § 84. V. 13. Dagh. in ק omitted as before in v. 5. — נִרְאָה, sing. (and so also the subject of this verb, viz. the following מַרְאֵיהֶם, which the sing. טוֹב plainly shows), lit. *showed itself* = appeared. וּבְרִיאֵי בָּשָׂר, § 110, 2. The pronoun הֵם *they were* (§ 119. 2), is implied here after בָּשָׂר, and seems to be omitted because the preceding noun has it, and so it might easily be supplied. בְּרִיאֵי lit. *fat;* the more comely mode of expression among us employs *full*, in such cases. I have translated *fuller*, because the מִן which follows, shows that the adjective is to be understood in the *comparative* sense, § 117, 1. This influence of מִן extends back also to טוֹב, and so we may translate *fairer*. The Part. הָאֹכְלִים appropriately denotes *continued* action, and such a Part. is of any tense demanded by the context; § 131, 1.

(16) And Meltsar took away their delicious viands and the wine which they drank, and gave them vegetables.

נֹשֵׂא, Part. = the Lat. Imperf. when joined (as here) with הָיָה, § 131, 2. *c; took away, removed*, Lex. s. v. 2. *d.* — מִשְׁתֵּיהֶם, lit. *the wine of their drinking;* sing. as before. — נֹתֵן as נֹשֵׂא above, וְהָיָה being implied, denoting continued or repeated action in the past, like the Greek and Latin Imperfect.

(17) And those four lads — to them God gave knowledge and intelligence in every kind of learning and wisdom; moreover, Daniel understood every kind of vision and dreams.

Heb. lit. *As to those lads, the four of them*, being in the case abs. here; § 142, 2. אַרְבַּעְתָּם, § 118, 1. *c*, in apposition here with the preceding noun, and epexegetical. See the like construction of the numeral in Ezek. 1 8, 10. 10: 10, 12. — הַשְׂכֵּל, Inf. Hiph. *nominascens*, i. e. it is used here as a noun in the Acc. § 128, 1. — סֵפֶר *learning*, see v. 4. As it has no article, and is preceded by כָּל, the whole phrase designates *every kind of learning.* — חָכְמָה as in v. 4. וְדָנִיֵּאל, the *Vav* here stands before a clause designating some *contrast* or *distinction*, which is also implied in our English *moreover*, i. e. something more may be said of Daniel, who is here distinguished from his fellows by some additional endowment. — הֵבִין (Hiph.), although it has often a *causative* sense = *teach, instruct*, i. e. make to know, here, like Kal, means *scivit, intellexit;* see in Lex. Nearly the exact sense is given in the version above. The meaning is, that Daniel was able to *discern* or *distinguish* (the proper sense of בִּין) the import of every kind of vision and of dreams; but according to Heb. usage, חָזוֹן is applied only to a *prophetic vision* divinely sent, i. e. to something seen in a kind of supernatural ecstasy; comp. Dan. 8: 1, 2, 13. 9: 24. חֲלֹמוֹת, on the other hand, may of itself mean *any kind of dream;* but its connection here with חָזוֹן shows it to be the intention of the writer to include only such dreams as are of the like character with prophetic visions. Jacob's dream, Gen. 28: 12—16; Joseph's dreams, Gen. 37: 5—11; Pharaoh's dream, Gen. 41:1 seq.; the dream of the Midianitish soldier, Judg. 7: 13—15; Nebuchadnezzar's in Dan. ii., iv.; Daniel's in Dan. vii., etc.; seem to be all of the character here intended. The seeming visions of a disordered brain, or the fugitive and ordinary dreams that proceed merely from a disturbed state of the physical system, cannot properly be supposed to come within the writer's design; for this would be merely to compare Daniel with the ὀνειροσκόπος or ὀνειρόφαντος of the heathen, and therefore it would not exhibit anything of importance in which this young Hebrew exceeded his companions. Nor

2

can it be said that the Hebrews, who so often appeal to the fugitive, unsubstantial, and trifling character of ordinary dreams, did not distinguish between them and such ones as the context bids us to suppose in the present case. חָזוֹן is *something seen* by the mind ἐν ἐκστάσει, whether in a sleeping or waking condition of the body; while חֲלוֹם is something which the mind conceives, while the body is asleep; and in cases like that before us, something conceived of by virtue of impressions from a superior power.

In reviewing the disclosures made by the narrative contained in vs. 12—17, it seems plain, that the writer meant to exhibit the thriving state of the lads upon their slender diet, as a special blessing of Providence upon their *pious resolution;* for so, in view of the Mosaic prescriptions, it would seem that it ought to be called. Yet it is not certain that the writer intends their thrift to be regarded by his readers as strictly *miraculous.* Certainly in a climate so excessively hot as that of Babylon, a vegetable diet, for many months in the year, would be better adapted to occasion fairness of countenance and fulness of flesh, than a luxurious diet of various highly seasoned meats. That the God of heaven *rewarded* the pious resolution and the persevering abstinence of the Jewish lads, lies upon the face of the narrative; and this is a truth adapted to useful admonition, specially to the Jews who dwelt among the heathen, and were under strong temptations to transgress the Mosaic laws. The uncommon and extraordinary powers, which were conferred upon those young Hebrews, are placed in such a light, as to show that their peculiar gifts were the consequence of their pious resolution and firmness.

(18) And at the end of the days, when the king had commanded to present them, then did the chief of the eunuchs present them before Nebuchadnezzar.

לְמִקְצָת = לְמִן קְצָת, Dagh. forte being omitted in the ק; see under v. 2. Gesenius (in Lex.) says that לְמִן = מִן לְ, and moreover that it is equivalent to מִן in signification. For substance this is true; for מִן and לְ both are used, separately, to mark the *terminus a quo* of time, and when combined they would seem to have merely an augmented force. More minutely examined, however, לְ = *at* a particular time, i. e. the time in which this or that is done; while מִן marks the *terminus* from which one begins to count the doing. Strictly considered, the combination לְמִן unites the two ideas of *at* and *from.* Lit. we might translate thus: *at from the close,* i. e. at the time from which the close is reckoned. In v. 5 above, the same word occurs without the לְ. It is easy, however, to see that the לְ in the present case gives additional significancy to the expression. — אֲשֶׁר *when,* as often elsewhere, i. e. *in which time,* in relation to the preceding designation of time. — אָמַר *had commanded,* see in v. 3 for this sense, and for Pluperf. § 124, 2. — וַיְבִיאֵם, *then brought he them,* Gramm. p. 99, 2d par. comp. § 152. B. 1. It is in the Imperf. form with the usual suff. ־ֵם; on the other hand, the preceding Inf. (apparently of the like form) takes the suff. ־ָם, see Par. of Inf. p. 292. These suffixes refer not merely to Daniel and his three particular friends, but to all the Jewish lads (see in v. 19) whom the king had originally commanded to select; see vs. 3 and 6, which show that there were others besides these. The subsequent distinction that had been made, was the work of Ashpenaz and his subordinate, and was not originally required by the king.

(19) And the king communed with them, and there was not found, among them all, the like to Daniel, Hananiah, Mishael, and Azariah; and they stood in waiting before the king.

לֹא נִמְצָא, *there was not found*, impers., § 134, 2. — מִכֻּלָּם, מִ׳, *out of*, here = *among*, as rendered above. The ־ָם plainly relates to the whole company of Hebrew lads, as mentioned above. — כְּ *the like to*, prep., see § 151, 3. *f*. The king, by his own personal examination, fixed upon the very individuals as his personal waiters, whom Providence had distinguished by peculiar gifts which rendered them superior to the other children.

(20) And as to everything [which was] matter of intelligent wisdom, concerning which the king made inquiry of them, he found them ten times superior to all the sacred scribes [and] the enchanters who were in all his kingdom.

כֹּל is not in the const. here, but in the case absolute; for the const. would demand a short vowel, כָּל (*Kŏl*). דְּבַר, etc., is in apposition with כֹּל and exegetical of it. The Heb. omits, as very often, the אֲשֶׁר, which would make the second clause a *relative* one, and idiomatically prefers simple apposition. Lit. the second clause runs thus: *matter of wisdom of intelligence* or *of distinguishing*. But חָכְמַת is put as *const.* before בִּינָה, while the latter qualifies the former by taking the place of an adjective, § 104, 1. For the meaning of חָכְמַת, see in v. 4; and בִּינָה specifically applies to the *discerning* and *discretive* powers of the mind, i. e. to those powers which make distinctions between different things, and thus arrive at accuracy of knowledge. By separating these two words, and putting *and* between them, (as nearly all the versions do), the intensity of the description here is destroyed; for the writer means to characterize the highest degree of acute discernment in matters abstruse and difficult. אֲשֶׁר is properly the Acc. governed by בִּקֵּשׁ, but I have conformed the translation more to our English idiom, by introducing a preposition before it. — וַיִּמְצָאֵם, with a *Vav consec.* before an *after-clause* or apodosis; Lex. 1. *e*. Gramm. p. 238. second N. B. *a*. The וַ might be rendered *so*; but our idiom rather rejects such a construction, and omits any particular sign of the apodosis. — *Ten times*, יָדוֹת = *parts*, *portions*, quasi *handfuls*.

This we express by the word *times*. עַל lit. *above* = *superior to.* — *Sacred scribes*, הַחַרְטֻמִּים, like to the *γραμματεῖς* of the N. Test. It seems evident that the word is from חֶרֶט *stylus* or *pen*, with the formative ־ֹם, as in פִּדְיוֹם from פָּדָה, and the like. So *pen-men* would be a literal translation. It designates, however, those who were busied with books and writing, and skilled in them; and designates *priests* or *sacred scribes*, because literature was confined almost entirely to such. To derive it from חֶרֶט and חָרַם, or to go to the Persian, as some have done (see Lex.), seems to be far-fetched. The word occurs often in Gen. and Ex. (see Lex.); and therefore a *Persian* origin is quite improbable. — הָאַשָּׁפִים, *the enchanters*, asyndic, i. e. without any וְ (conjunction) before it. Is it in apposition, therefore, with the preceding word? This circumstance looks rather like it; but a comparison of the usage of this writer as to the omission of וְ, as well as the nature of the case, rather leads us to doubt in respect to apposition, comp. 5: 15, and also 2: 27, 45, where some four or five different nouns are grouped together, without any *conjunction* between them. Still, *apposition* might be admitted there, if Dan. 2: 2 did not decide against it, for there the two words plainly belong to two different classes. See on 2: 2.

The number *ten* which is associated in this verse with יָדוֹת *times* or *portions*, is in unison with the custom of the Hebrews, who employed this definite number in cases where an indefinite number not inconsiderable was required.* In such a connection as in our text, *ten* is found in Gen. 31: 7, 41. Num. 14: 22. Neh. 4: 12. Job. 19: 3. The reader, who will take the pains to examine the examples throughout (and these are not all), will learn that the number *ten* may be classed with *three* and *seven*, as to the frequency with which it is employed by the sacred writers, in a kind of symbolical rather than literal sense. At times there may be difficulty in determining the question, whether *ten* is to be taken simply in a numerical way, or whether it is only a symbol of a moderate but not inconsiderable number. In the connection above, however, as *ten* is not compared with any *greater* number, but by implication only with a *unit*, it means an excess above that unit which is large. That the *ten days* of trial mentioned in v. 12, has a tacit reference to the custom of employing *ten* as already stated, there can hardly be room for doubt.

---

* See, for example, Gen. 18: 32. 24: 10, 22. 32: 15. Ex. 26: 1. 27: 12. Lev. 26: 26. Num. 11: 32. 29: 23. Josh. 21: 5. Judg. 6: 27. 17: 10. 20: 10. Ruth 4: 2. 1 Sam. 1: 3. 17: 17. 25: 5. 2 Sam. 18: 11. 19: 43. 1 Kings 7: 24, 27, 38. 11: 31. 14: 3. 2 Kings 5: 5. 2 Chron. 4: 7. Neh. 11: 1. Ecc. 7: 19. Isa. 5: 10. Dan. 7: 7. Amos 5: 3, 6: 9. Zech. 8: 23. Matt. 25: 1. Luke 15: 8. 19: 13. Rev. 12: 3. 13: 1. 17: 3, 7, 12, 16.

(21) And Daniel was until the first year of Cyrus the King.

And Daniel was — what? A question answered differently by different critics. One class, taking וַיְהִי as a verb absolute, translate *lived* or *remained.* The difficulty with this interpretation is, that הָיָה *to be* nearly always differs from חָיָה *to live.* The latter is opposed to מוּת *to die;* the former to אַיִן *there is not;* see in Acts 17: 28, Ζῶμεν καὶ κινούμεθα καὶ ἐσμέν, where the first and last verbs plainly have a different import. In fact, I can find no passage where הָיָה is employed directly in the simple sense of *living.* It is indeed sometimes used *absolutely,* and not as a mere copula; in which case it means simply *existed* or *came into existence,* Gen. 1: 3. 2: 5; or (with a little variation) *was made* or *formed = came into existence,* as in Gen. 1: 6. Isa. 66: 2, and so γεγονέναι in Heb. 11: 3. In very many cases, with a little more variation, it means *accidit, it came to pass, happened,* etc. = the καὶ ἐγένετο of the N. Test.; see Lex. But neither of the meanings just given suit the case before us. Other usual meanings of הָיָה are connected with it as a *copula,* and serve to express that *he* or *it was* something, or was for some person or thing, or was in some place or condition. There is an instance, however, in Jer. 1: 3, where וַיְהִי is employed exactly as in the present case, and is followed by עַד (*until*) before a limitation of time, as here. The case in Jeremiah is one which seems quite plain, and the analogy between that case and the present seems to be so striking as to make out a very strong probability, if not a certainty, of meaning in respect to וַיְהִי. In Jer. 1: 1, 2, the statement is made, that *the word of the Lord* came to Jeremiah in the 13th year of Josiah's reign. V. 3 plainly declares, that Jeremiah continued to receive the word of the Lord until the 11th year of Zedekiah's reign and the captivity of the Jews. But this declaration is made, as in Dan. 1: 21, simply by וַיְהִי prefixed to the verse, after which follows merely a designation of time. Just so in our text. Of course, וַיְהִי has respect to some person or thing, or to both, which is mentioned in the preceding verse. In Jer. 1: 3, the reference is to the prophet and to the word of the Lord before mentioned, so that the meaning is plain. And the like in Dan. 1: 21. The preceding context exhibits Daniel as possessed of חָכְמַת בִּינָה ten times more than that of the sacred scribes and enchanters; and verse 17 attaches to his *wisdom* the power of interpreting dreams and visious. V. 21, then, declares that this Daniel, preëminent for wisdom and skill, *was,* or rather *continued to be,* until the first year of Cyrus. Comp. the like force of ἐστί in Acts 17: 28. 1 Cor. 7: 7, 26. 2 Cor. 13: 5. The history of Daniel exhibits this. Shortly before Cyrus' reign, we find him in presence of Belshazzar, interpreting the hand-writing on the wall. Under Darius the Mede, he was made head of the princes, "because an excellent spirit was in him," Dan. 6: 3. It appears, indeed, that for a time he was neglected by the Babylonish king, Dan. 5: 11—13. But the וַיְהִי before us has respect more to the *qualities* of Daniel, than to the constant tenure of his court-offices. In this way the meaning seems to be plain, although the idiom is not a usual one. The case in Jer. is surely plain; is not the present one equally so? J. D. Michaelis, Hezel, and Bleek, explain thus: "Daniel was *in Babylon*, and in such relations." The words in italic are necessary, in their view, to explain the וַיְהִי. But as this idea is virtually implied in the whole connection of the sentence, it is unnecessary to supply it otherwise. I need only add, that the *first year of Cyrus* is named, because then the Babylonish monarchy ceased, and of course the relations of Daniel to it; and then the Jews were freed from exile, and Daniel survived so as to see the end as well as the beginning of it. Hence the designation of it in our text, as a period specially to be marked in respect to the condition and the hopes of Daniel. It is as much as to say: 'Daniel, as conversant with matters that pertained to wisdom and learning, lived to see the joyful day of Jewish freedom. The earliest in exile, 'he still lived to see the end of it.' Those who assail the credit of the book of Daniel, have not failed to make out a difficulty here. First, they render וַיְהִי *he lived*, just as if it were וַיְחִי. Next, they allege that the import of v. 21 is, that Daniel lived only until the first year of Cyrus's reign. Lastly they assert, that 6: 29, which declares that "Daniel prospered in the reign of Cyrus," is a contradiction of 1: 21. The first assertion, as we have seen, is not correct. The second is palpably without ground. In the case of Jeremiah, to whom the word of the Lord is said to have come, from the time of Josiah to the captivity, we are certain, from the book itself, that he frequently prophesied *after* this period. And so it might have been with Daniel, if he lived (as he did, see 10: 1), after the first year of Cyrus's reign. A *terminus ad quem* surely does not exclude all beyond it. If I say to a friend: "Farewell until my return from a journey," I do not mean that I wish him no prosperity after this. When the Messiah, in Ps. 110, is bidden to sit at the right hand of God until his enemies are made his footstool, the meaning is not that his seat shall then be vacated. As to 6: 29, Daniel may have prospered in Cyrus's reign, even in case he died near the close of the first year; which, however, did not happen, 10: 1. Nothing can be made out of these objections.

EXCURSUS I. — *On the alleged discrepancy between Daniel* 1: 1 *and Jer.* 25: 1, *and some other passages.*

The charge of *historical incorrectness* against the writer of the book of Daniel, rests partly upon some *dates of time*, and partly upon some *historical occurrences*. I shall first examine the allegation of error in respect to the designation of TIME.

In Dan. 1: 1 it is said, that Nebuchadnezzar, king of Babylon, came up against Jerusalem, besieged it, took Jehoiakim captive, and rifled the temple of a part of its furniture, *in the third year of Jehoiakim.* In Jer. 25: 1 it is explicitly said, that the *first* year of Nebuchadnezzar's reign was the *fourth* year of Jehoiakim's. Moreover, in Jer. 46: 2 it is said that king Nebuchadnezzar smote Carchemish on the Euphrates, then in possession of Pharaoh-Necho king of Egypt, in the same *fourth* year of Jehoiakim. Taking all these passages into view, it is alleged that the writer of the book of Daniel could not have lived in the time of Nebuchadnezzar, when the true date of the invasion of Palestine by that king must necessarily have been well known; but at a subsequent period, when the chronology of these events was more obscure, and when he might be misled by erring tradition. That period is placed, by most of the recent critics belonging to the so-called *liberal* School, near to the close of the Maccabaean times, with the history of which, as they aver, the book of Daniel concludes.

As this has been, of late, an almost uniform assertion among critics of the new School, and has been placed in the front rank of objections against the genuineness of the book of Daniel, it becomes necessary to give it an attentive examination. Lengerke says of it, in his recent Commentary on this book, that "all attempts to remove this objection have to the present hour been frustrated. . . . Not only is the *date* wrong, but the *deportation* [of captives] under Jehoiakim remains at least unproved;" p. 2 seq.

The documents which must guide our inquiries, are a fragment of Berosus (preserved by Josephus), and several brief passages in the Hebrew Scriptures. These are all the historical data on which we can place any reliance. All subsequent testimony is either a mere repetition of these, or a constructive exegesis of them, or if not, it is mere conjecture. In respect to the original documents, we have evidently the same right of interpretation as Abydenus, Megasthenes, Josephus, Eusebius, and others had. The native Greek historians, whose works are now extant, make no mention at all of Nebuchadnezzar; consequently, Josephus's quotations from the oriental writers, and the historical notices comprised in the Hebrew Scriptures, are all on which we can place any dependance as legitimate sources of testimony. These consist of the following particulars.

No. I. — The king of Egypt, Pharaoh-Necho, after having slain Josiah, and deposed his successor, Jehoahaz, made Eliakim (surnamed *Jehoiakim*), the son of Josiah, king over the Hebrews, and treated him as a tributary vassal; 2 Kings 23: 29—37. The sacred writer then proceeds thus, in 2 Kings 24: 1: "In his days came up Nebuchadnezzar, king of Babylon; and Jehoiakim became his servant three years; then he turned and rebelled against him. (2) And Jehovah sent against him bands of the Chaldees, and bands of Syria, and bands of Moab, and bands of the sons of Ammon; yea, he sent them against Judah to destroy him; according to the word of the Lord which he spoke by his servants the prophets.

No. II.—After relating events previous to Jehoiakim's reign, as in the book of Kings, the writer thus proceeds in 2 Chron. 36: 6: "Against him came up Nebuchadnezzar king of Babylon, and he bound him in fetters, to convey him to Babylon. (7) And a part of the vessels of the house of the Lord did Nebuchadnezzar take to Babylon, and he put them in his temple at Babylon.

No. III.—Jer. 25: 1. "The message which was to Jeremiah, concerning all the people of Judah, in the *fourth* year of Jehoiakim the son of Josiah king of Judah; the same was the *first* year of Nebuchadnezzar, king of Babylon."

No. IV.—Jer. 46: 1, 2. "The word of the Lord . . . against Egypt, against the army of Pharaoh-Necho king of Egypt, which was by the river Euphrates in Carchemish, which Nebuchadnezzar king of Babylon smote, in the *fourth* year of Jehoiakim king of Judah.

No. V.—Dan. 1: 1, 2. "In the *third* year of the reign of Jehoiakim, king of Judah, came Nebuchadnezzar, king of Babylon, to Jerusalem, and besieged it. And the Lord gave into his hand Jehoiakim, king of Judah, and a part of the vessels of the house of God; and he brought them to the land of Shinar, to the house of his God, and the vessels did he bring into the treasure-house of his God."

No. VI.—BEROSUS, as quoted by Josephus, Antiq. X. 11. 1, also Contra Ap. I. 19, "When his father Nabopolassar had heard, that the Satrap, who had been appointed over Egypt and the regions around Coelo-Syria and Phenicia, had rebelled, not being able himself to endure hardships, he committed to his son, Nebuchadnezzar, then in the vigor of life, certain portions of his forces, and sent them against him. And Nebuchadnezzar, falling in with the rebel, and putting his forces in order, gained a victory over him, and the country belonging to his control he brought under his own dominion. Now it came to pass, that Nabopolassar fell sick at that period, and died, *having reigned twenty-one years*. Not long after, having learned the death of his father, he arranged his affairs in Egypt and the other regions, and committed the captives of the *Jews*, the Phenicians, the Syrians, and the nations in Egypt, to certain of his friends, to conduct them to Babylon, with the most weighty part of his forces, and the remainder of his booty. He himself, accompanied by very few, went to Babylon through the desert. Then taking upon him the affairs which had been managed by the Chaldees, and the kingdom which had been preserved for him by their leader, becoming master of *the whole* (ὁλοκλήρου) of his father's dominion (ἀρχῆς), he assigned to the captives who had arrived, colonial dwelling-places in the most suitable regions of Babylon," etc. The passage goes on to show how Nebuchadnezzar used a part of the spoils as ἀναθήματα, i. e. votive offerings, in the temples of his gods, and the rest, in building and adorning the city of Babylon.

Preceding this passage, as quoted from Berosus (Cont. Apion. I. 19), Josephus gives a summary of the history of Nebuchadnezzar, as exhibited by the Chaldean historian. In this summary he says, that Berosus has related, "how Nabopolassar sent his son, Nebuchadnezzar, against Egypt and *against our land* [Palestine], with a large force (μετὰ πολλῆς δυνάμεως), who subdued them, burned the temple at Jerusalem, and, transplanting the great mass of the people, carried them away to Babylon." In a part of this summary, he seems to quote the words of Berosus, and represents him as saying, that "the Babylonian conquered Egypt, Syria, Phenicia and Arabia, and exceeded in achievements all of the Chaldean and Babylonian kings, who had reigned before him."

We have now before us all the documents on which any reliance can be safely placed. On these I would make a few remarks which may assist our further inquiries. (*a*) From a survey of these documents it is plain, at first sight, that no one of them is anything more than a mere *summary* sketch of Jehoiakim's reign; and so of Nebuchadnezzar's. The particulars of events, and even the order of them, in some respects, are not specified at all. Thus in No. I., *two* invasions of Nebuchadnezzar are made certain ; but no particular time of either is specified. In number II. only one (probably the final) invasion appears to be mentioned. In Berosus, there is a still more rapid *coup d' oeil* of events, without any effort to narrate particulars, much less to make out dates. (*b*) We are, therefore, at liberty to supply the omissions of one account, by that which another has furnished. An argument against more than one invasion, in the time of Jehoiakim, drawn from the fact that no more than one is mentioned in 2 Chronicles, would amount to nothing; for it need not be again proved, that the *argumentum a silentio* is in such cases of no value. So an argument drawn from the silence of Berosus as to more than one invasion of Palestine by Nebuchadnezzar, would prove nothing against the united testimony of Kings, Jeremiah, and Daniel, that there was more than one. (*c*) It follows, that we are at liberty to make out probabilities of time and order of succession in respect to events, from *circumstances* that are narrated, where the writers have omitted formally to make out these in their narrations. This, however, should always be done with caution, and we should keep strictly within the bounds of probability.

In respect to the main subject now before us I would remark, that there are some points so well settled, and of such controlling influence, that nothing can be safely admitted which is inconsistent with them. (1) It is now a matter of nearly universal agreement, that Nabopolassar, the father of Nebuchadnezzar, in union with the Median king Astyages, destroyed the Assyrian empire, and began his independent reign in Babylon, in 625 B. C. (2) It seems to be certain, from the testimony of Berosus (No. VI. above) and Syncellus, that he reigned *twenty-one* years. Of course his death was near the close of 605 B. C., or at the beginning of 604. At this period, then, Nebuchadnezzar by inheritance became sole king of Babylon. (3) *Previously* to this period, Nebuchadnezzar had invaded and subdued Carchemish, and overrun and brought under subjection to himself Syria, Palestine, Moab, the country of the Ammonites, Phenicia, and lower Egypt. This is clear from a comparison of No. I. and No. VI. with its sequel above. When these achievements and conquests were completed, Nebuchadnezzar received tidings of his father's death, hastened to Babylon, and left the captives and the booty to be forwarded by his subordinate officers ; No. VI. above. These are *facts* which we must either admit, or else renounce the credit of historical testimony which we are unable fairly to impeach.

The question then, whether Nebuchadnezzar came into the regions of hither Asia *before* 604 B. C., is settled. But — how long before? Long enough, at any rate, to overrun and subdue all these countries. Less than some two years for such achievements, no one who looks at the extent of those countries, and knows the slowness with which armies formerly moved in the East, will venture to fix upon. The book of Daniel (1: 1, 2) says, that Nebuchadnezzar came up and besieged Jerusalem in the *third* year of Jehoiakim, i. e. in 607. That this was near the close of that third year, would seem probable from two circumstances; first, the fast kept by Jehoiakim and his people, on the *ninth* month of the fifth year of this king, i. e. Dec. 605. This was no legal or ritual fast, (for none belonged to this period), but one either commemorative of some great evil, e. g. the capture of the city by Nebuchadnezzar, (comp. Zech. 8: 19, where four fasts of a like kind are specified); or anticipative of some great and dangerous struggle, e. g. Jehoiakim's rebellion against Nebuchadnezzar. Moreover, as Nebuchadnezzar is called *king*, while on this expedition, both in Daniel, Kings and Chronicles, and Jeremiah, and as we know (see Nos. III. IV.), that Jehoiakim's *fourth* year corresponded with the *first* year of Nebuchadnezzar, as viewed by the Hebrews, it would seem to follow of course, allowing the historical verity of Daniel, that the invasion by Nebuchadnezzar must have been late in 607. If so, then of course the greater part of his *first* year, as counted by the Hebrews, corresponded to the *fourth* year of Jehoiakim, as Nos. III. IV. declare. Later than the time which Daniel designates, Nebuchadnezzar's expedition could not well have been, if we admit the great extent of his conquests already made at, or a little before, the beginning of 604. Cyrus and Cyaxares were about ten years in subduing Asia Minor; could Nebuchadnezzar have overrun all hither Asia and Egypt in less than *two?* All those then, who, like Lengerke, Winer, etc., make the fourth year of Nebuchadnezzar and the eighth of Jehoiakim, i. e. 602 or 601, to be the time when the king of Babylon first invaded Palestine, are obliged to dishonor the credit of Berosus, who (No. VI.) says, in so many words, that 'when Nebuchadnezzar heard of his father's death, he left the spoil and the captive *Jews*, Syrians, Phenicians and Egyptians, to be conducted to Babylon by his officers.' The same is also asserted by Alexander Polyhistor, Euseb. Chron. Arm. I. p. 45. All agree that this must have been in 604; and scarcely a doubt can remain, that it was near the *commencement* of this year. Lengerke says, in respect to what Berosus asserts, that "it may appear to be doubtful;" p. 6. He refers to Jer. 29: 10, comp. v. 2, for proof that the exile of Jechoniah was the *first* deportation of Jews by Nebuchadnezzar. But I can find no proof of such a nature there. The simple truth is, that events are everywhere related, in respect to Jehoiakim's reign, *without any dates* of time, with the exception of Dan. 1: 1, 2. But still, these events are plainly such as to show the entire probability of what is declared by Daniel.

"But Nebuchadnezzar took Carchemish in the *fourth* year of Jehoiakim (No. IV. above); how could he do this, and yet send Daniel and his compeers into exile, in the *third* year of the same Jehoiakim?"

One may well reply, that there is no impossibility, or even improbability, in this. Where is the passage of history to show that Nebuchadnezzar did not besiege and take Jerusalem, *before* he went against Carchemish? Babylon, Carchemish, and Jerusalem, are at the extreme points of a triangle, the shortest side of which is indeed the distance from Babylon to Carchemish. Why then did not Nebuchadnezzar go directly from Babylon to Carchemish? The probable answer seems to me not to be difficult. Jehoiakim was placed on the throne by Pharaoh Necho, and consequently was his hearty ally and tributary. Nebuchadnezzar, by marching first against him, and then subduing all the countries under Egyptian sway, through which he passed on his march to Carchemish, avoided the possibility of aid from Egypt being given to the city in question, or from the allies of Egypt. Carchemish was the strongest place in all that region; and such a plan showed the expertness of Nebuchadnezzar as a warrior.

The whole course of events, in this case, certainly looks as if the assertion in Dan. 1: 1, 2, were true.

"But how could Jeremiah, then, in the *fourth* year of Jehoiakim (25: 1 seq.), threaten an invasion of the Chaldees, and seventy years of exile? The exile, according to this view, had already begun." But to this question one may reply, that Nebuchadnezzar's first work, viz. the subjection of Jehoiakim and the making of him a tributary, had indeed already been done; but all of the work which Nebuchadnezzar was to perform, was not yet completed. In his victorious march from Carchemish, where he had been successful, through all the countries of hither Asia and Lower Egypt, and of course through Palestine, he was still to collect more booty, and to carry away such and so many captives as he thought would effectually prevent insurrection after his departure. It is not probable that he sent away many captives to Babylon, immediately on his first capture of Jerusalem. He could not then spare the troops necessary for such an escort as was required to do this. In all probability, therefore, he contented himself with sending away a sufficient number of *hostages*, belonging to the princes and nobles, to secure the fidelity of Jehoiakim. The book of Daniel (1: 1—3) merely avers, that in the *third* year of Jehoiakim, a part of the vessels of the temple, and *some of the king's seed and of the princes*, were sent to Babylon. Nothing could be more natural or probable than this, under such circumstances. One has only to call to mind, that *hostages*, and those of princely descent, were usually demanded by conquerors, where want of fidelity in the subdued was suspected; and also, that the booty of gold and silver was one main object, in all such expeditions as that of Nebuchadnezzar's. Hence, in Jer. 52: 27—30, no mention is made of those first hostages as exiles; first, because they were few in number, and secondly, because their condition was different from that of ordinary exiles. When we find Jeremiah, therefore, in 25: 1—11, in the *fourth* year of Jehoiakim, threatening subjugation and exile to the Jews, it cannot reasonably be doubted that he did so, because Jehoiakim, the former ally of Egypt, and who moreover had been set on his throne by the Egyptian king, was meditating revolt. Nebuchadnezzar's success at Carchemish was probably as yet unknown in Judea. Jehoiakim, therefore, hoped for a different result, and was ready to join his former master, in case of his success. To prevent this catastrophe, Jeremiah uttered the comminations of chap. 25: 1—11. And that Jehoiakim's intentions were known to Nebuchadnezzar, seems quite probable from the treatment which, according to Berosus, the Jews experienced at the close of Nebuchadnezzar's expedition, viz. the deportation of Hebrew captives. Still, as this class of exiles is not particularized in Jer. 52: 27—30, they probably consisted mostly of such as might come under the denomination of hostages, i. e. they belonged to the more wealthy and influential families.

That all which has been said of the disposition of Jehoiakim to rebel, is true, seems to be confirmed by the fact, that not long after this period, as soon as Nebuchadnezzar had gone to Babylon and become stationary there, i. e. probably about the end of 604, Jehoiakim did actually rebel, and throw off his allegiance to Babylon. The king of Babylon, however, was so intent on beautifying his capital and his temples, and thus expending the immense wealth which he had collected in his predatory incursions

(Berosus in Jos. Cont. Ap. I. 19), that he did not immediately undertake to chastise the Jewish king. But at the close of 600 B. C., or early in 599, he again marched up to Jerusalem, and inflicted the penalty that was usual in cases of revolt.

Lengerke and others assert, that Nebuchadnezzar did not invade Judea again, during the life of Jehoiakim, and that this king died and was buried in peace, contrary to the threats of Jeremiah, 22: 19, and 36: 30, viz. that he should be destroyed by violence, and his dead body be cast out unburied. The appeal for proof of this is to 2 Kings 24: 6, which states, that "Jehoiakim *slept with his fathers*, and that Jehoiakim his son reigned in his stead." Lengerke (p. 7) avers, that the expression *slept* or *rested with his fathers* means, always and only, that "the person in question descended in quiet to the common grave of his fathers." Surely an entire mistake! That שָׁכַב of itself merely designates the *death* of an individual, without determining the fact whether it was *peaceful* or *violent*, is clear enough from Hebrew usage. In almost every narration respecting the death of a king, either in the book of Kings or Chronicles, it is said of him, that *he slept with his fathers*. But that this has no concern with indicating his *peaceful burial*, is quite certain from the fact, that in nearly every case of this nature, the burial of the king is the subject of a separate mention, showing of course that this is not involved or implied in the first expression. Nor does שָׁכַב (*slept*) even involve the idea of a *peaceful death;* for it is said of Ahab, who perished of wounds received in battle, that "he slept with his fathers," 1 Kings 24: 40. In v. 36 is the equivalent expression: *So the king died;* and it is then added: "They buried him in Samaria." In the same way שָׁכַב alone is used for death, and mostly for the designation of violent death, in Isa. 14: 8, 17. 43: 17. Job 3: 13. 20: 11. 21: 26. Not a word is said in 2 Kings 24: 6, of Jehoiakim's *burial;* and of course there is nothing there to show that Jeremiah, in declaring that he should perish *unburied*, had predicted what proved to be untrue. On the other hand; what are we to make of לְהַאֲבִידוֹ, *to destroy him* (i. e. Jehoiakim, as Lengerke himself (p. 6) concedes), in 2 Kings 24: 2? And what of 2 Chron. 36: 6, which says that the king of Babylon *bound Jehoiakim in fetters to carry him to Babylon*, but makes no mention at all of his being actually sent thither? That Jeremiah has not given an account of the fulfilment of his own prediction respecting Jehoiakim, is not strange, unless the principle is to be assumed, that prophets are obligated to write full and regular *history*, as well as prediction. I might even argue in favor of the fulfilment of the prediction, from the silence of the prophet. It was an event so well known, one might say with probability, that a special record of it was not needed on his part. Yet I think the books of Chronicles and of Kings, as cited above, have *impliedly* recorded the event in question. Still more express do I find, with Grotius, the recognition of it in Ezek. 19: 9. Here, the preceding context describes the reign and fate of Jehoahaz or Shallum; comp. 2 Kings 23: 31—33. Then the prophet comes, in his parable, to the *successor* of Shallum, viz. Jehoiakim (in case he means the *immediate* successor), and he says of him, that "the nations set against him . . . and he was taken in their pit, and they put him in ward *in chains*, and brought him to the king of Babylon: they brought him into holds, that his voice should no more be heard upon the mountains of Israel." To interpret all this of Jechoniah, as Rosenmüller, Lengerke, and others have done, seems to me very incongruous. The prophet says of this *lion*, that "he went up and down among the lions . . . learned to catch prey, and devoured men; and he knew their desolate places, and laid waste their cities, and the land was desolate, and the fulness thereof, by reason of his roaring." All this now, of a boy *eight* years old, according to 2 Chron. 36: 9, and according to 2 Kings 24: 8, only *eighteen;* and of a child, moreover, who, as both records aver, reigned only about *three months!* A most extravagant parable would Ezekiel seem to have written, if all this is to be predicated of such a child, whether aged eight or eighteen, and of only a three months' reign.

There is indeed a difficulty, arising from the extreme brevity of the sacred writers, in finding out the *particulars* in the history of the closing part of Jehoiakim's reign. But certain it is, that nothing against the supposition that he died a violent death, and was left unburied, can be made out from what is recorded. Would Jeremiah have left his predictions standing as they do in his prophecy, if they had not been fulfilled? Lengerke intimates, that the peaceful accession of Jehoiachin to his father's throne, shows that Nebuchadnezzar was not in Palestine, at the time of Jehoiakim's death. But if Nebuchadnezzar had already chastised Jehoiakim on account of his rebellion, and put him into fetters, in which he died through hard usage or violence, may he not have ceded to Jehoiachin the throne of Judea, in consequence of renewed and solemn stipulations to become his vassal? And specially as he was so young, that little was to be feared from him? I see nothing of the impossible, or even of the improbable, in all this. The fact that Nebuchadnezzar was very suspicious of Jehoiachin, is clear from the circumstance, that after only three months, he returned with his army, and carried off that king and many of his subjects, into exile at Babylon. The phrase לִתְשׁוּבַת הַשָּׁנָה, in 2 Chron. 36: 10, indicates something more, in my apprehension, than has been usually noticed by commentators. In all probability, this *return* or *turning of the year* means the Spring of the year, when kings were wont to go out on military expeditions. But still the word *year* here plainly stands related to some other period of time, from which it is reckoned. And what can this be, except the antecedent period when Jehoiakim was deposed and slain? If this were done in the autumn, and Jehoiachin made king either by Nebuchadnezzar himself, or by the people rebelling against Babylon after his departure, he might reign during the three winter months, and in the spring of the year be attacked and carried into exile by Nebuchadnezzar. No doubt this conqueror had large standing garrisons, in all the conquered countries, ready to act at short warning. Hence the shortness of the time, between the first and second invasion at this period, according to the statement made above.

That I have reasoned correctly in regard to the mere *summary* or generic accounts of Jehoiakim's reign, both in the sacred records and in Berosus, I must believe no one will deny who takes due pains minutely to examine them. It follows of course, unless the credibility of these historians can be reasonably impeached, that the omission of particulars by any one of them, is no argument against the verity of another who does state some particulars. This is notably illustrated by Jer. 52: 28, 29. In v. 28 it is stated, that Nebuchadnezzar carried away captive in his *seventh* year, 3023 persons. In 2 K. 24: 12, it is stated, that Jehoiachin and his court gave themselves up to Nebuchadnezzar in the *eighth* year of his reign, who carried him away to Babylon, with 10,000 captives and all the craftsmen and smiths, v. 14. In Jer., then, the statement refers to what was done one year (i. e. in 599) before that took place which is related in the book of Kings. Both the time and the number of exiles mentioned in the two passages, are discrepant; and consequently we may regard this circumstance as heightening the probability of two invasions, as stated above, which took place within a small period of time. Again, in Jer. 52: 29 it is stated, that Nebuchadnezzar, in his *eighteenth* year, carried away captive 832 persons. In 2 K. 25: 3—10, it is declared that Nebuchadnezzar, in his *nineteenth* year, took Jerusalem, burned the temple, and carried away captive all except the poor of the land (v. 12). How many were the captives, is not stated ; but there must have been a great many thousands. The same thing is repeated in Jer. 52: 12—16. Here then (in 52: 29) is a statement of deportation, in a different year and in very different numbers from what is stated or implied in the book of Kings. Jer. 52: 29 seems evidently to relate to captives sent away *one year before the siege was completed ;* for it lasted some twenty months. Then, again, there is a third deportation mentioned in Jer. 52: 30, in the twenty-third year of Nebuchadnezzar ; of which we have no other account. Who will venture now to say, that the books of Jer. and of Kings are at variance, or rather, that they are contradictory, in regard to the deportation of exiles ? Both may be regarded as true, without doing the least violence to probability.

"But both Daniel and Jeremiah call Nebuchadnezzar *king*, some two or more years before he was king. How can such a mistake be accounted for ?"

Easily, I would say ; or rather, I would deny that there is any real error in the Jewish historians or prophets, with regard to this matter. Of the father of Nebuchadnezzar, viz. Nabopolassar, the Hebrew Scriptures know nothing. Nebuchadnezzar was generalissimo of the Chaldean invading army. Before he left the country of Palestine, in order to return to Babylon, his father had died, and he had become actual and sole king. The books of Daniel and Jeremiah, written some years afterwards, and also the books of Kings and Chronicles, call him by the name which he had long and universally borne. In the narrations of Jeremiah and Daniel, and also of the other books named, the writers all give him the title of *king*, which was so familiar to them all. The same thing is every day practised, even at the present time. We speak of Alexander the Great, of the emperor Augustus, of the emperor Napoleon, etc., as having done or said this and that, even when we are relating, in a popular way, the things which took place before the sovereignty of these men actually existed. The object of the sacred historians is mainly to designate the leading individual who achieved this or that, not to show in particular how and when he entered on his highest office. The Hebrews, who knew Nebuchadnezzar as the *leader* of the Chaldean army and also as *king*, before he had actually ended the expedition against them in which he was first engaged, would very naturally of course speak of him as a *king*, when he first invaded Judea. We may easily concede, that he is *anticipatively* so called ; for the usage is too common to be either a matter of offence or of stumbling. It cannot fairly be put to the ccount of error or mistake.

I do not feel, therefore, that we need to resort, as many writers have done, to the expedient of showing that Nebuchadnezzar was constituted by his father a *joint partner* with him of the throne of Babylon, before he set out on the celebrated expedition against hither Asia, which established an extensive Babylonish empire. Yet this *partnership* is, after all, far from being improbable. Nabopolassar was so enfeebled as to be unable to lead the invading army. Berosus says of him : *συστήσας τῷ υἱῷ Ναβουχοδνοσόρῳ, ὄντι ἔτι ἐν ἡλικίᾳ, μέρη τινὰ τῆς δυνάμεως, ἐξέπεμψεν ἐπ᾽ αὐτόν, κ. τ. λ.* Jos. cont. Ap. I. 19. But *δυνάμεως* does not here mean *regal power*, (as has been maintained), but *military force*. This seems plain from a preceding declaration, in which Berosus states that " Nabopolassar sent his son (Nebuchadnezzar) *ἐπὶ τὴν ἡμετέραν γῆν* — (against Palestine) . . . *μετὰ πολλῆς δυνάμεως*, i. e. with a large military force." But there is another passage in Berosus, which seems more probably to favor the idea of *copartnership* in the throne, at the time of Nebuchadnezzar's expedition. After the war is finished, Nebuchadnezzar returns, and is formally installed by the Magi as sole and supreme king. Berosus says of him : " *Κυριεύσας ἐξ ὁλοκλήρου τῆς πατρικῆς ἀρχῆς*, i. e. becoming supreme over *the whole* of his father's domain." Is there not a natural implication here, that before this he was in part a *κύριος* ? So Hitzig concedes, (Begriff der Kritik, p. 186), and states expressly that Nebuchadnezzar's father made him *co-regent*, before the battle at Carchemish. Knobel (Prophetism. II. p. 226) also states this as probable. The like do many others ; but I deem it unnecessary to make this a point of any moment. The various sacred writers can be harmonized with each other, and with probable facts, independently of this circumstance. But still, it would be an additional reason for the Hebrew usage, in regard to the appellative *king* as applied to Nebuchadnezzar previously to his father's death, that he was *co-regent* with his father, from the time that he entered on his first Palestine expedition. The contrary of this cannot be shown. That *Berosus*, a Babylonian, should count dominion as belonging to Nabopolassar until his death, seems to be a matter of course, for such dominion was matter of fact. That Nebuchadnezzar, the appointed heir, then obtained his father's *domain* or *dominion* (*ἀρχῆς*), was also a matter of course ; but that he then obtained it *ἐξ ὁλοκλήρου*, would seem to imply what has been stated above. Be all this however as it may, it seems that all the Hebrew writers, in Kings, Chronicles, Jeremiah, and Daniel, are uniform in regard to the appellative in question. Whatever may have been the state of actual facts, it is a sufficient vindication of the Hebrew historians and prophets, that they have followed the usage of their country in regard to this matter. If they had been writing the particular history of Nebuchadnezzar's life and reign, the matter might then be viewed in a different light, in case a *co-regency* never actually took place.

But we are met, in regard to our views of the *time* of Nebuchadnezzar's *first* invasion, by the allegation of Lengerke, Winer, and others, that in that expedition Nebuchadnezzar did not overrun Judea, nor send away any captives from that country. To confirm this, they appeal to Josephus, Ant. X. 6. 1, who, after describing the capture of Carchemish, says, that " Nebuchadnezzar then passed over the Euphrates, and took all Syria even to Pelusium, *παρὲξ τῆς Ἰουδαίας*, i. e. *excepting Judea.*" One is led to wonder, at first view, how Josephus could make this exception ; and this wonder is much increased by comparing the declaration in question with what he says in Cont. Ap. I. 19. Beyond any reasonable doubt, the two passages are at variance. In the latter passage, he quotes Berosus as saying, that Nebuchadnezzar's father "sent him with an army against Egypt, and against τὴν ἡμετέραν γῆν, i. e. against Judea." And in the sequel he quotes Berosus as also saying, that, at the close of this expedition, Nebuchadnezzar 'sent to Babylon τοὺς αἰχμαλώτους Ἰουδαίων, *the captives of the Jews*, as well as of the Syrians, Phenicians, and Egyptians.' Yet Berosus and the Hebrew Scriptures were, beyond all reasonable question, the only authorities which Josephus had, or at least which he employed, in respect to the history of Nebuchadnezzar. But the source of Josephus's mistake in Antiq. X. 6. 1, is in all probability to be found in a passage from Berosus in Cont. Ap. I. 19, where, in making a summary in a single sentence of the achievements of Nebuchadnezzar, the Chaldee historian says: "The Babylonian [king] conquered Egypt, Syria, Phenicia, Arabia, and in his achievments far exceeded all the kings who had before reigned over the Chaldeans and Babylonians." In this mere summary sentence, Berosus omits *Judea*, i. e. the small country of the two tribes, (for this was Judea, at that period); as he also omits Moab, the country of the Ammonites, etc. — omits them evidently because of their comparative smallness. Josephus has unwittingly overlooked this, and so he has *excepted* Judea, in Antiq. X. 6. 1, because Berosus has not mentioned it in the passage just quoted. It does not, indeed, much commend his careful accuracy to us, when we find him so doing, because Berosus, as quoted by him, both before and after the sentence in question, has explicitly averred that Nebuchadnezzar came up, in that very first expedition, to attack *Judea*, and that he carried away captives from that country. But negligences of this kind are somewhat frequent, in this otherwise very valuable historian. E. g. in respect to this same portion of history, Josephus states (Antiq. X. 7. 1), that, when Nebuchadnezzar took Jehoiachin captive, he carried away with him 10832 others into exile. Now this statement is palpably made out from combining together 2 K. 24: 14 and Jer. 52: 29; Josephus having added together the numbers in both passages, without noticing that one deportation is in the *seventh*, and the other in the *eighth* year of Nebuchadnezzar. This discrepancy he does not even notice, much less pretend to reconcile. And so he has not unfrequently done elsewhere. He needs to be closely watched in such matters. Haste, and carelessness of such a kind, may not unfrequently be charged upon him. I cannot think, however, that he meant to make any wrong statements.

It is impossible for me, after having carefully examined all that Berosus or Josephus has to say on these matters, to attach any historical value to the παρὲξ τῆς Ἰουδαίας, which has been quoted above and examined. All things being duly compared and considered, I cannot but think that the evidence of a Babylonian invasion, commencing in the latter part of the third year of Jehoiakim, repeated in 599 at the close of his reign; renewed against Jehoiachin in 598; and then, lastly, at the close of Zedekiah's reign; are facts as well made out, and as probable, as most facts of such a nature in ancient history. Had there been no gain to be made out of this matter, by warmly enlisted partizans, I do not believe that it would have ever been seriously controverted.

I do not see, then, why Lengerke should be so liberal of his *exclamation points*, when speaking of the intimation of Hengstenberg and Hävernick, that the book of Daniel, by assigning the invasion of Palestine to the *third* year of Jehoiakim, has shown an unusually minute and accurate acquaintance with the history of the Hebrews. Is it not certain, that Nebuchadnezzar's father began his reign as independent king, in 625 B. C.? Is it not well established that he died near the end of 605 or at the beginning of 604? Is it not sufficiently established by historical testimony, that Nebuchadnezzar had reduced Carchemish and overrun all Syria, Phenicia, Moab, northern Arabia, Palestine, and Egypt, *before* the death of his father? Was it possible to accomplish all this in less than some *two* years? If not, then Dan. 1:1, 2, seems plainly to be in the right, which assigns Nebuchadnezzar's first invasion of Palestine to the *third* year of Jehoiakim. It could not have been later. Exclamation-points, it would be well for Lengerke, and sometimes for his opponents too, to remember, are not arguments, either ratiocinative or historical. The book of Daniel must, as it would seem, be in the right as to the main point in question. Nor does it contradict at all the other books.

The appeal made to Jer. 35: 11, in order to show that Nebuchadnezzar had not yet invaded Palestine, in the fourth year of Jehoiakim, is not valid, because there is no note of time in chap. xxxv, and because, as Nebuchadnezzar probably passed through Judea several times during his first invasion, there are no data in this chapter to decide which of his transitions occasioned the flight of the Rechabites to Jerusalem. The fact that Jehoiakim was the known ally and vassal of Pharaoh Necho, would of itself show, that the attitude of Nebuchadnezzar toward Palestine must have been one of hostility. The probability seems to be, (comparing this chapter with the following one), that the Rechabites fled from Nebuchadnezzar when he was on his return from Carchemish; for then he was accompanied by troops from the conquered nations mentioned in Jer. 35: 11.

I would merely observe, at the close of this difficult and perhaps too long protracted investigation, that no one who has experience in these matters will think of arguing against the actual occurrence of certain particular events, merely because they are not stated in this book of Scripture or in that, since nearly all of the Jewish history in later times is given to us in professed and acknowledged *summaries* only. One writer sometimes sees fit to insert some special particular, which the rest have passed by. E. g. Jer. 51: 59 seq. mentions a journey of Zedekiah, with some of his courtiers, to Babylon, in the fourth year of his reign. In 2 Chron. 33: 11 seq., we have an account of Manasseh as having been carried to Babylon, and of his penitence, and his return to Jerusalem. Nowhere else is either of these events even alluded to, so far as I can find. Yet after the recent investigations respecting the books of Chronicles by Movers, Keil, and others, I think no sober critic will be disposed to call in question the position, that neither of these accounts is improbable, and that neither can, on any grounds worthy of credit, be fairly controverted. And I would again suggest, that when leading events as to time and place are certain, an assumption of particular circumstances and events attending them, which is built upon the common course of things and supported by probability, is surely neither uncritical nor unsafe. When we suppose, for example, that Daniel and his associates were sent to Babylon as *hostages*, at the time when Jehoiakim first became a vassal to Nebuchadnezzar, and combine this supposition with the declaration in Dan. 1: 1 seq., we suppose what seems to be altogether probable, although we cannot establish this particular by any direct testimony, but merely by implication.

It may not be useless to add, that as the Jews evidently called Nebuchadnezzar *king*, from the time that he invaded Palestine, so by a comparison of Dan. 1: 1 seq. Jer. 25: 1. 2 K. 25: 27, we make out forty-five years (inclusively) as the period of Nebuchadnezzar's reign, according to the Hebrew method of reckoning. At the same time, Berosus and others make out only forty-three years. Still, there is no real disagreement in the case. The Jews began to reckon two years earlier than Berosus, who counts only upon the *sole* reign of Nebuchadnezzar after the death of his father.

CHAPTER II.

[Nebuchadnezzar is filled with anguish by reason of a dream, the particulars of which escaped from his memory after he had awaked. The astrologers and their associates are summoned to disclose both the dream and its interpretation; they are threatened with severe punishment in case of failure, and splendid rewards are promised in case of success; vs. 1—6. They request the king to disclose the dream, in order that they may interpret it; but he declines to make any disclosure, and accuses them of prevarication, and repeats his threats, vs. 7—9. On their part, they accuse him of making a demand unreasonable and without any precedent, and avow that none but the gods can accomplish such a task; vs. 10, 11. The king in a fury decrees the destruction of all the Magi; vs. 12, 13. Daniel and his associates, as being among this class, are sought for by the executioner, that they might be slain. Daniel repairs to the king and intercedes for delay, during which he and his companions betake themselves to prayer; vs. 13—18. The secret of the dream is revealed to Daniel in a night-vision, who praises God for his mercy; vs. 19—23. Daniel is at his own request brought to the king, and discloses the dream; vs. 24—35. Then follows the interpretation of the same; vs. 36—45. The king falls prostrate before Daniel and does him homage. He acknowledges the superiority of the true God, and promotes Daniel to the office of governor of Babylon, and chief governor of the Magi. His companions, at his request, are also promoted to office; vs. 46—49.]

(1) And in the second year of the reign of Nebuchadnezzar, Nebuchadnezzar dreamed dreams, and his mind was agitated, and his sleep failed him.

מַלְכוּת, a later Hebrew word for the earlier מַמְלֶכֶת, *reign, dominion*, not *kingdom* in such a connection as the present. For the omission of Daghesh lene in the כ, see § 21, 2. *e.*—חֲלֹמוֹת, in the *plural*, while in vs. 3, 4, 5, the *singular* is employed. As the king, in this case, does not require an explanation of more than *one* dream, the *plural* form before us would seem to indicate that the same dream was often repeated; a circumstance which would naturally give rise to the anxiety which he felt, and which was adapted to make a deep impression on his mind.— רוּחוֹ, *his spirit* or *mind*, i. e. the interior man.—וַתִּתְפָּעֶם § 63, 3. n. 1. *b.*—נִהְיְתָה Niph. of הָיָה. The very existence of this Conj. in such a verb, shows that some peculiarity of meaning is attached to it. In general, it seems to be virtually a passive of Hiphil, and so means *was made to be*, *was caused*, *brought about*, or *happened*. From this branches off a peculiar meaning, here and in Dan. 8: 27, a kind of *was was*, i. e. something which has completed its existing state and has ceased to be, =*fuimus Troes*. Ges. *confectus est*, *deficit*, rightly as to the real meaning; and so I have translated נִהְיְתָה עָלָיו, *failed him*. The idea is, that his sleep, which was once sound and refreshing, was now *past* or *gone* in respect to him. The seeming repetition of *his*, in the suff. of עָלָיו, is not incongruous in Hebrew, but rather common. עַל is = אֶל, in a multitude of cases; and so we may translate literally: *for him*, or (as above) *in respect to him*. The construction is not unlike to לֶךְ־לְךָ, Gen. 12: 1, and other idioms of this nature. In vulgar English we say: *He is gone for it;* which is like to the shape of the phrase before us; but the ־ָיו being *masc.*, it appears in this case to indicate the *person of the king*, and not the sleep. Schultens, Rosenm., Häv., and some others, however, refer עָלָיו to שְׁנָתוֹ after this tenor: *His sleep was against him*, *contra ipsum*, i. e. oppressive or burdensome to him, a meaning not unusual to עַל, Lex. A. 1. γ., comp. 4. *a*. But, to say the least, this is not a natural mode of expressing such an idea, although it may be a possible one. Surely, after saying that the very soul of the king was agitated by his dream, it would not seem to be making much progress, to add, that "his sleep was troublesome to him." Much more expressive and natural is the idea, that *he was sleepless*, which is the idea given by the first interpretation. Berth. and Winer: *His sleep went away from him;* and so Theodotion: ἐγένετο ἀπ᾽ αὐτοῦ; well enough as to the general meaning, but עָלָיו cannot mean *from him*, as if it were מֵעָלָיו. The (Chaldee) example in Dan. 6: 19, שִׁנְתֵּהּ נַדַּת עֲלוֹהִי, which most translate *his sleep fled from him*, although evidently of the same general meaning as the phrase before us, will not justify the rendering by ἀπ᾽ αὐτοῦ in the case before us. The examples of a Dative (*pleonastic* form) after a verb of *motion*, are indeed by no means uncommon, e. g. Gen. 27: 43, בְּרַח לְךָ, *flee*, lit. *flee for thyself;* Isa. 31: 8, נָס לוֹ, *he has fled*, Gen. 12: 1. Cant. 2: 11. Prov. 13: 13. But these all differ from the present case, because the suffix pronoun relates to the *subject* of the verb. To translate Dan. 6: 19, by *his sleep fled from him*, gives indeed the general idea in our language, but not the *shape* of the expression in the Hebrew. That the case before us is simply one, where the person is strongly marked to whom the assertion relates, cannot well be doubted. It is clear that עָלָיו does not refer to שְׁנָתוֹ.

EXC. II. A second charge of *chronological* error against the book of Daniel is, that it makes an evident mistake in respect to the period when Nebuchadnezzar's dream took place, and Daniel interpreted it. The dream was in the *second* year of Nebuchadnezzar's reign, Dan. 2: 1. Previously to this, Daniel and his fellows had been subjected to a *three* years' discipline, as preparatory to waiting upon the king, Dan. 1: 5. That period had passed, before Daniel was presented to the king, Dan. 1: 18. How, it is asked, could Nebuchadnezzar, as *king*, appoint to Daniel *three* years of discipline, and yet bring in the same Daniel, in the *second* year of his actual reign, to interpret his dream, when it is evident, from the author's own showing, that this Daniel had already completed his three years' course of discipline, and taken his place among the Magi before he was called to interpret the dream? Dan. 1: 20. 2: 2, 13.

If the result of the preceding investigation be admitted, then is the solution of this seemingly difficult problem rendered quite easy. Nebuchadnezzar is called king, in Dan. 1: 1, after the usual manner of the Hebrews (comp. 2 Kings 24: 1. 2 Chron. 36: 6), and in the way of anticipation. In fact he became sole king, before that expedition had ended. But when a Jewish writer in Babylon (Daniel) comes to the transactions of his actual reign as reckoned of course in Babylon, (for of course the date of his reign there would be from the period when he became *sole* king), the writer dates the events that happened under that reign, in accordance with the Babylonish reckoning. So it seems to be in Dan. 2: 1. According to the result of the preceding examination, Daniel was sent to Babylon in the latter part of 607 or the beginning of 606. Nebuchadnezzar became actual king, by the death of his father, near the end of 605 or at the beginning of 604. Nebuchadnezzar's *second* year of actual and sole reign would then be in 603. If we suppose the latter part of this year to be the time when the dream occurred, then we have a period of nearly four years between Daniel's exile and his call to interpret the king's dream. Any part of 603 saves the accuracy of the book of Daniel, in respect to this matter. In fact it lies on the very face of this statement in the book of Daniel, that it is scrupulously conformed to historical truth; for how could the writer, after having announced Daniel's deportation as belonging to the *third* year of Jehoiakim, and his discipline as having been completed in *three* years, then declare that Daniel was called upon as one of the Magi, to interpret dreams in the *second* year of Nebuchadnezzar? If Nebuchadnezzar was actual king in the third year of Jehoiakim he was so when Daniel was carried away to Babylon; and plain enough is it, that Daniel's course of discipline was not complete until the *fourth*, or at least the end of the *third*, year of Nebuchadnezzar. The error would, in such a case, be so palpable, that no writer of any intelligence or consistency could fail to notice and correct it. We are constrained to believe, then, that Nebuchadnezzar is named *king* merely in the way of *anticipation*, in Dan. 1: 1 (and so in 2 Kings xxiv., 2 Chron. xxxvi., Jer. xxv.); and that the date of his sole and actual reign is referred to in Dan. 2: 1, as the Babylonians reckoned it. Thus understood, all is consistent and probable. We need not resort as Rosenmüller and others have done, to a *long series* of dreams on the part of Nebuchadnezzar, in which the same thing was repeated; nor to the improbable subterfuge, that, although he dreamed in the *second* year of his reign, he did not concern himself to find out an interpreter of his nocturnal visions, until some considerable time afterwards. Both of these representations seem to me to be contrary to the plain and evident tenor of the whole narration. The agitation was immediate, and the stronger because it was immediate. Procrastination of the matter might, and probably would, have liberated him from his fears, and blunted the edge of his curiosity.

That Jeremiah reckons in the Palestine Jewish way, i. e. *anticipatively*, is certain from Jer. 25: 1. 46: 2. That he did not this by mistake, but only in compliance with the usage of the Jews in Palestine, seems altogether probable. On the other hand, the state of facts as to Nebuchadnezzar's conquests, as exhibited above, shows that his invasion of Judea must have begun as early as Dan. 1: 1 asserts. In truth, facts and events vouch for the writer's minute historical accuracy in this matter, in case it be conceded, that Nebuchadnezzar is called king, in Dan. 1: 1, in the way of *anticipation*, and in accordance with the common Hebrew usage.

(2) And the king commanded to summon the sacred scribes, and the enchanters, the sorcerers, and the astrologers, that they might show to the king his dreams; and they came, and stood before the king.

וַיֹּאמֶר, *commanded;* see 1: 3.—לִקְרֹא, *to summon* = *arcessivit;* for לְ, see Lex. B. 3. It may take the Dat. with לְ, or it may omit it; for the usage continually varies. In the present instance, however, the nature of the sense would seem rather to demand the *Acc.* after the verb; in which case the following nouns may be, in accordance with the later Hebrew idiom, which often puts לְ before the Acc., after the manner of the Aramaean; Lex. 3. 4. *c.* ad fin. Yet if we translate thus, *to make proclamation to the sacred scribes*, etc., the *Dative* is preferable. For the first two nouns, see 1: 20. The root אָשַׁף seems to mean *incantavit*, i. e. by chanting some formulas of imaginary potency, to influence in a mysterious but potent manner. The like to this has prevailed in most of the heathen forms of religion.—מְכַשְּׁפִים, participial noun (Piel), which probably designates a species of *enchanters*, who sing magic songs in a low and peculiar tone. In Syriac, the verb (in Ethp.) means *to supplicate;* in Heb., *to mutter* or *speak with a low voice.* The literal sense would seem to be nearly designated by that of the Latin *incantator*, i. e. *one who cantillates* supplications, execrations, and the like, in order to prevent or remove evil, or to obtain some disclosure of interest to the party concerned. But still, the Latin word is probably too generic to be strictly accurate. It is unquestionably near akin to אַשָּׁפִים; which, if we may trust to the shade of meaning disclosed in אַשְׁפָּה, *quiver* or *cover for arrows*, probably meant originally *to cover, conceal,* and the like. Hence אַשָּׁפִים may mean merely *those who practised hidden or concealed arts.* What these were in particular, no text informs us; but a comparison of the practices of the Greek and Latin soothsayers will easily show how many and various these might have been. מְכַשְּׁפִים, a kindred participial word which seems to designate the *suppresed cantillation* or *low muttering* of the formulas of conjurers, may of course imply a particular species of the Chaldean Magi. — כַּשְׂדִּים, *astrologers* here, but originally this was the name of the people inhabiting Babylonia. So far back as the time of Abraham, the *Mesopotamian* region was called *the land of the Chaldees,* Gen. 11: 28, 31. 15: 7. Comp. Ezek. 1: 3. 11: 24.

EXC. III. *On the Chaldees.*

Some Greek writers frequently apply the word *Chaldees* (*Χαλδαῖοι*) to a fierce people, in the mountainous country bordering on Armenia. Xenophon met with such on his retreat, and he has often made mention of them; e. g. Anab. IV. 3. 4. V. 5. 17. VII. 8: 25. Comp. Hab. 1: 6 seq. Job 1: 17. Strabo notices tribes of the same name, in the country of Pontus, XII. c. 3. p. 26, 27, 36, Tom. III. edit. Lip. From the Armenian [Assyrian] Chaldees many writers have of late supposed the Babylonian Chaldees to have come; which Isa. 23: 13, as interpreted by them, seems to favor: "See! the country of the Chaldeans, this people was not; Assyria assigned it [the country] to the dwellers of the desert; they [the Chaldees] erect their watch-towers, they set in commotion the palaces of it [Tyre], they make it a heap of ruins." As Assyria anciently extended her dominion over all middle Asia, and of course over the Armenian Chaldees, the latter might, under their permission, have emigrated to the plains, and being a courageous and warlike people, they might have obtained preëminence wherever they settled, over the feeble inhabitants of the plains. But if the Nomades of Chaldean Armenia were indeed the *predominant* portion of the Babylonish people, so that the country was early named from them, those Nomades must at least have emigrated at an early period of the Assyrian dynasty, i. e. during the one which preceded the invasion of Arbaces, and (according to Ctesias) ended with Sardanapalus, B. C. 747.

The deductions from Isa. 23: 13, by Gesenius, Hitzig, Knobel and others, viz. that the Chaldean power and even name in southern Mesopotamia and Babylon are of *recent* origin, must depend mainly on the correctness of their exegesis of the text in question. But this is far from being made out. On the other hand, substantially with Hupfeld (Exercitt.), and Leo (Allgem. Geschichte, s. 106), we may with much more probability translate thus: "Behold! the country of the Chaldeans — this people was not [a people]; Assyria — it has assigned it to the beasts of the desert; they erected their towers, they watched her palaces; [but] it has made her a heap of ruins."

In this way we have one main agent, viz. the Chaldean people. The "heap of ruins" is Nineveh, and the "desert" made by invasion, is the Assyrian domain. The prophet is threatening Tyre, and bids her look to what the Chaldeans, their invaders, have already achieved in Assyria. It were easy to vindicate the interpretation just given, but Hupfeld (Exercitt. Herod.) has sufficiently done it, and it would be out of place here. The reason why I have now introduced the subject is, because this text is the main dependence of many recent critics for establishing a favorite position of theirs, to which I have already adverted, viz. that the *Chaldean* power, and even name, in southern Mesopotamia and Babylon, is comparatively recent, and that Chaldea was unknown to the biblical writers before the time of Jehoiakim, at least as a national and independent country.

Facts, strong and (as it seems to me) irresistible, make against this. Schleyer, in his Würdigung der Einwürfe, s. 48 seq., 138 seq., has made objections to it which cannot well be met. *Shinar* was the older name of Babylonia, Gen. 11: 2. This had a king (Amraphel) in the days of Abraham, Gen. 14: 1, 9. That Babylon justly claims a very high antiquity, cannot be denied. Ctesias, Herodotus, Berosus, the Jewish SS., all agree in this. The latter make Nimrod its founder, who was a grandson of Noah (B. C. 2218), Gen. 10: 8. Its walls, towers, palaces, bridges, dykes, and architecture of every kind, most of which was on a gigantic scale that rivalled or exceeded that of Egypt, prove incontestably an advanced state of knowledge in Babylon at a very early period, and indicate a metropolis of the highest grandeur. Other facts of much importance are in accordance with this. Simplicius (Comm. ad Aristot. de Coelo, p. 123) tells us, that Calisthenes, who accompanied Alexander the Great to Babylon, found astronomical observations there which reached back to 1903 years before that period, and which he sent to Aristotle; and also that the Magi claimed to be in possession of much older ones still. Ptolemy, in his famous Canon, plainly allows their astronomical observations to be correct as far back as Nabonassar (about 747 B. C.), and there begins his era from which he dates events. Larcher, and above all Ideler (on the Astronomy of the Chaldees), have shown that the period of 1903 years is neither impossible nor improbable; as Gesenius himself appears to concede, Comm. in Es. III. p. 350. But be this as it may, Diodorus Sic. (II. 29) says expressly, that the Chaldean priests (whom, like Daniel, he calls *Chaldeans*), are of *the most ancient Babylonians*, Χαλδαῖοι τοίνυν τῶν ἀρχαιοτάτων ὄντες Βαβυλωνίων. All this seems to show, that the *Chaldees* (both nation and priests) are of the highest antiquity, and that an emigration from the northern mountains, if it ever took place so as to give a name to the country, must have been at a very remote period. Whenever it was, priests and people appear to have come to Babylonia together. There they amalgamated with the population; and the *Magi*, (the priests of the fire-worshippers, such as are described by Zoroaster in the Zend-Avesta), probably engaged in the studies, and united in some of the pursuits, of the native priests in Babylon; the conquerors thus assimilating to the conquered, their superiors in knowledge, like the Goths and Vandals assimilating to the Romans. Hence the mixture of Parsism and gross polytheism in the religion of Babylon; for plainly the latter contains both elements. In this way, moreover, can we account for that mixture of the Zend and Pehlvi languages with the Semitic, in the composition of many names and offices in Babylon, in the time of Daniel. *Mag* (מָג Jer. 39: 3) is the same as the Sanscrit *maha*, Pers. *mogh*, Zend *meh*, and is equivalent to the Hebrew רַב; and the חַכִּימִין in Daniel are the same as the מָגִים and רַבִּים. But although many, or perhaps even most, of the proper names of men and of *civil* offices among the Chaldeans are best explained from the Zend, or the old Persian, yet the names of their gods and of their *religious* offices are mostly of a *Semitic* origin; e. g. *Belus* = בַּעַל or בְּעֵל; Mylitta = מוֹלֶדֶת (genetrix); חַרְטֻמִּים from חֶרֶט, Dan. 1: 20. 2: 2, and also in Gen. 41: 8. Ex. 7: 11, 22. 8: 3, 14, 15. 9: 11; אַשָּׁף, Dan. 1: 20. 2: 2 (Chald.), 10, 27. 4: 4. 5: 7, 11, 15, = Syr. ܐܫܘܦܐ; מְכַשֵּׁף, Dan. 2: 2, also Ex. 7: 11. 22: 17. Deut. 18: 10. Mal. 3: 5; and so the generic Chaldee word חַכִּים (= *Magus*), Dan. 2: 12, 21. 4: 3. 5: 7, 8, is notoriously the same as the Hebrew חָכָם. But many of the names of kings, and of the higher civil officers, seem to be compounds of Semitic with the Parsi, Pehlvi, or Zend; such as Nebuchadnezzar, Belshazzar, etc. (see Lex.) The internal evidence, therefore, of a *mixture* of inhabitants in Chaldea, from some quarter or other, appears to be inscribed in high relief upon the language of the Chaldeans, in the time of Nebuchadnezzar. The religion of the Babylonians, (as exhibited best of all by Münter in his Essay on this subject, and by Gesenius in his Excursus at the end of his Comm. on Isaiah), affords striking evidence of Parsism and polytheism commingled by the union of different nations who retained some of their respective rites, and by the natural progress of the attractive sensual parts of those rites, as the metropolis progressed in riches and luxury and debauchery.

This general view of the subject seems necessary in order to place the reader of the book of Daniel in a position, in which he may rightly estimate the various phenomena of the book. There is a mixture throughout of the Assyro-Median and Semitic, both in the names of men and offices, and also in the rites, customs, and opinions of the inhabitants. That the *Assyro*-Chaldean at the time when Daniel lived, was the common spoken language of the court and king, seems to be plainly *negatived* by Dan. 2: 4 seq. The Magi address the king אֲרָמִית i. e. in the *Aramaean*, which is substantially the same that we now name *East Aramaean* or *Chaldee*. In this language, more than half of the book of Daniel is composed. Doubtless the Jews who lived in that quarter when Daniel wrote the book, could read and understand it; and indeed to the younger part of them, at that period, it must have been vernacular, or nearly so. It is even quite probable, that the history contained in the book of Daniel would thus be more easily read by the younger portion of the Hebrew community in that region, than if it had been in the Hebrew; and this, perhaps, might have been the inducement to write it in Aramaean.

But to return to the הַכַּשְׂדִּים of our text; I have only to add, that this name, employed to designate a *literary order of men* (equivalent to חֲכָמִים, Chald. חַכִּימִין, and *Magi*), passed into very common use among the Greeks and Romans. So Strabo XV. Tom. III. p. 326. ed. Lips. Diod. Sic. 2. 29 seq. Cic. Div. 1. 1, 2. Ammian. Marc. 23. 6. Arrian Alex. 3. 16. In still later times, fortune-tellers and magicians from the East were called *Chaldeans*, by European nations. The progress of meaning in regard to the appellation is obvious. First, the Chaldees are conquerors, and offices, or whatever else is eminent, are called Chaldean *par excellence*. Then, as Chaldea abounded in astrologers and soothsayers, it was natural for Greeks and Romans to call these classes of men by the name of *Chaldeans.* Last of all, among the western nations, soothsayers and magicians were called by the same name, without any special regard to the country from which they sprung. One meets, not unfrequently in the classics, with the appellation employed in this manner.

Several questions, of some importance in regard to the genuineness of the book of Daniel, have been recently made, first in regard to the *number* of classes specified in the verse before us, and then in respect to the employment of כַּשְׂדִּים, as designating only one portion of the Magi.

To begin with the latter; Gesenius (Comm. in Es. II. s. 355) seems to call in question the limited meaning of the word, and Bleek (on Dan. in Schleiermacher, etc., Zeitschrift, s. 225) even doubts whether there was any such thing as different classes. Both doubt against the evidence of usage widely extended. Daniel plainly uses the word to denote a *class* of the Magi, in 2: 2, 10. 4: 4 (Engl. Vers. 4: 7). 5: 7, 11. And when Gesenius and Hitzig suggest, that in Dan. 2: 4, 10, the name *Chaldeans* is generically employed, Lengerke himself, (sufficiently inclined to all which can make against the genuineness of the book), avers very justly that this is only in the way of breviloquence, where one class that is preëminent is named instead of recapitulating or particularizing all, (Comm. s. 50). Decisive, as to the usage of such a method of expression by the writer, is Dan. 3: 24, where only the הַדָּבְרִין (state-counsellors) are addressed, while v. 27 shows that they are only one class of the State-officers then and there assembled, to witness the spectacle which is described. Such methods of breviloquence are quite common; and besides all this, we have heathen usage of the same kind as that under discussion; e. g. Herod. 1. 181, οἱ *Χαλδαῖοι, ἐόντες ἱερέες τούτου τοῦ θεοῦ* [i. e. *Βήλου*], comp. I. 183, where *Χαλδαῖοι* occurs three times in the same sense; Diod. Sic. II. 24, *τῶν ἱερέων, οὓς Βαβυλώνιοι καλοῦσι Χαλδαίους*, and again in c. 29, *Χαλδαῖοι τοίνυν τῶν ἀρχαιοτάτων Βαβυλωνίων . . . παραπλησίαν ἔχουσι τάξιν τοῖς κατ' Αἴγυπτον ἱερεῦσι*; and so Hesychius, *Χαλδαῖοι, γένος Μάγων.* Ctesias (edit. Bähr, p. 68) seems, indeed, to use *Chaldeans* and *Magi* as synonymes; and so, as we have seen above, later usage among Greeks and Romans often employed the words. But even in Ctesias, the context shows that by *Chaldeans* is there meant the *higher order* of the Magi. So in Dan. 2: 4, 10.

Thus much for the *limited* use of the name *Chaldeans*, which is sufficiently clear and certain. As to the *number* of the classes, with respect to which Lengerke (s. 49 f.) thinks he detects the error of a *later* writer who was not intimately acquainted with Chaldean matters, the question seems not to be one of any great difficulty. He admits, as do nearly all others, that there were *divisions* or *classes* among the Magi. This was notoriously the case as to the priests in Egypt, Ex. 7: 11. Herod. II. 36. 58. Jablonsky, Panth. Egypt. Prol. c. 3. The division of priests in India, from the remotest period, is well known. The Medes and Persians admitted the like divisions among their Magi. The author of Daniel, in 2: 2. 4: 4. (Eng. 4: 7). 5: 7, 12, appears to name *five* classes of Magi, (if indeed the מְכַשְּׁפִים of 2: 2 be not merely another name for the גָּזְרִין of the other passages); on account of which Lengerke accuses him of mistake; and he declares (p. 47), that 'all other ancient writers everywhere acknowledge only *three* classes,' and concludes from this that the writer of the book was some person of a later age and of a remote country, where tradition gave an indistinct and uncertain report. His authorities as to the 'united report of all antiquity,' are Jerome (Contra Jovin. I. p. 55), and Porphyry (de Abstin. 4. 16). These are somewhat late writers as to the matter of testifying, 'for all antiquity,' to a particular usage in Babylon about a thousand years before their time. But in fact neither of these give their own testimony. They both appeal to Eubulus. If Eubulus the philosopher is meant, he lived about 200 B. C. If either the comedian or the orator of the same name be meant, (which seems not probable), they lived about 376 B. C. In his history of Mithra, Eubulus asserts, that 'the Magi were divided into *three* classes.' When ? In his time, or at an earlier period ? Among the Persians, or among the Babylonians of Nebuchadnezzar's time ? Unquestionably he refers to the *Persians*, inasmuch as the history of *Mithra* concerns them. But even admitting the correctness of the testimony at the time when it was given, it proves nothing in respect to the custom or usage at Babylonia, in the seventh century B. C. Magi indeed there were at Babylonia ; for among the military chieftains of Nebuchadnezzar, at the siege of Jerusalem in Zedekiah's time, was Nergal Sharezer רַב מָג, *chief Magian*. The priesthood, so far from excluding men from civil or military office in those times, was a leading recommendation of them to appointments of this nature, because it implied an unusual degree of knowledge. Thus Ctesias represents Belesys, the leader of the Chaldeans when Nineveh was destroyed, as "the most distinguished of the priests, οὓς Βαβυλώνιοι καλοῦσι Χαλδαίους," Diod. Sic. II. 24. So a Magian was elevated to the throne of Persia, after the death of Cambyses ; Ctes. Persica, c. 13 seq. So, after the death of Nebuchadnezzar's father, while the former was carrying on the war in Judea, the affairs of government, before the return of the prince to Babylon, were administered by priests [ὑπὸ Χαλδαίων], and the supremacy was vested in the *archimagus*, who gave it up, in due time, to Nebuchadnezzar, according to Berosus in Joseph. Antiq. X. 11. 1. In fact the oriental and Egyptian kings, as well as some of the Caesars, paid the homage to the priesthood of becoming members of their body, if they were not already so when they became kings. It may, I readily concede, have been the usual fact, that the leading divisions of the *Persian* Magi were *three* in number.* But this would be of little avail in showing that such was the custom of the Babylonians, among whom, although the priesthood retained, as it would seem, the honorary name of *Magi*, yet their religion differed in the most striking manner, in many re-

* But this is not established by the Zend-Avesta, as cited by Heeren, (Ideen I. s. 480, ed. 3d) ; for in Kleuker's edition, II. 261, only *two* classes are spoken of, viz. *Herbeds* and *Mobeds*. But in Yesht Sades, (LXXXIII. ad fin. II. p. 194), the Avesta speaks of the *three* orders of the *Athorne* = priests ; again (ib. p. 276), the same thing is mentioned ; once more (p. 156), " the *threefold*, like the Athorne." But in another passage *four* orders of priests seem to be designated. So in Zend Avesta, III. p. 225, we find *Herbed* (=candidate for the priesthood), *Mobed* (priest), *Destur-Mobed* (teacher-priest), and *Destur Desturan* (= archbishop), a provincial superior. Probably the case is the same in the Zend-Avesta as in Daniel ; i. e. sometimes the leading class only is noted, as in 2: 4, 10 ; then again we have four classes, in 2: 2 ; in 5: 7 are three classes, (one a new one) ; four classes in 4: 4 ; three in 5: 7 ; and four in 5: 11. To insist, now, that any one of these passages exhibits the full and exclusive designation of all the classes of the Magi, would be entirely nugatory.

spects, from that of the Parsis. In the rites of the latter, there was no temple, no altar, no sacrifice of human victims, no consumption by fire even of any victims, no images of gods, no prostitution-worship of Mylitta, in a word none of the impurity, cruelty, ridiculous prodigality of expenditure, and abominable rites of the Babylonians. All matters of religion had been changed, by the commingling of the (Assyro-) Chaldean conquerors with the grosser and more sensual heathen of Babylonia, if indeed we concede such an intermixture. How then can testimony about the Magi in a country where pure Parsism prevailed, be applicable to the case of the Babylonian priests and literati, as described by Daniel? But if we must resort, in the present case, to the testimony of Greek writers, the position of Lengerke is far enough from being confirmed. Diodorus Sic., in speaking *περὶ τῶν ἐν Βαβυλῶνι καλουμένων Χαλδαίων*, represents them as practising astrology, soothsaying, magic, incantations, augury from the flight of birds, and the interpretation of dreams and remarkable occurrences, II. 29; all of which plainly betokens different classes.* Strabo, most of all among the Greeks to be relied on in such matters, says (XVI. 1. § 6), "There are, among the Chaldean astronomers, *γένη πλείω many kinds* or *classes*, some are called *Orcheni*, and some *Borsippeni*, besides *many others* (*ἄλλοι πλείους*), who affirm different things in respect to their doctrines, according to their respective sects." Here then is abundance of room for the four or five classes of Daniel; and it is indeed quite probable that the subdivisions must have amounted to many more, although it was not to his purpose to name any more than the leading ones. At all events, the testimony of Daniel stands high above any fair exception, in regard to the classification of the Magi. Certainly he has named no improbable class. Nearly all of the classes named, indeed, appertain to the priesthood of the heathen, as elsewhere exhibited in the Scriptures; and if there be a class *sui generis* in Daniel, there can be no good reason to charge him with error; for how can we reasonably suppose, that there was not some one class or more of the priesthood that was peculiar to Babylon?

* Certainly this assertion seems very probable, if we turn our attention, for a moment, to the divisions of the priesthood among the Greeks, in relation to such matters. With them every god and goddess had a separate order of priests; and even the same orders differed from each other in different places. Again, each of these orders had a *high-priest*; in some places two; the Delphians five. Then there were *assistants* of the sacred order, viz. the *Parasiti* or those who provided materials for the celebration of religious rites, and then the *Κήρυκες* or *criers*, who also acted the part of cooks and butchers. Besides these classes, there were the *νεωκόροι*, who kept clean and adorned the temples; then the *ναοφύλακες* who guarded those temples; and lastly the *πρόπολοι* or general waiters; Potter's Gr. Antiq I. p. 222 seq. Beyond these general divisions, were subordinate ones almost without end; e g. as to diviners, *μάντεις, χρησμολόγοι, θεομάντεις*, of three kinds; interpreters of dreams, *ὀνειροκρίται, ὀνειροσκόποι, ὀνειροπόλοι*; divination by sacrifices employed at least six classes; by birds, at least as many more; by lots, at least three; by ominous words and things, many classes; by magic and incantation, at least nineteen; Potter ib.pp.327seq. We must add to all this, that the priesthood among the Romans was arranged in quite a similar way. I do not aver that the Chaldeans made all of these subdivisions, which are almost endless; but I may well say, that the offices which Diodorus ascribes to their Magi, involves, from the very nature of the case, something not unlike to this.

The suggestion of Gesenius (Comm. II. p. 355), that the writer in all probability merely brought together the various designations of such classes of persons as are mentioned elsewhere in the Heb. Scriptures; and the assertion of Lengerke (p. 47), that 'he undoubtedly did thus;' seem to have no other basis than an inclination to throw discredit upon the book, and industriously to collect and reckon up everything which may help to show, that the writer was lacking as to accurate knowledge. Something more than this, however, seems necessary in order to discredit the book in question.

Equally nugatory seems to be the assertion of Bleek, (Schleierm. etc. Zeits. s. 225), that 'it is altogether wonderful, that Nebuchadnezzar should summon all classes of the Magi to interpret his dream, instead of summoning the appropriate class, viz. the ὀνειροσκόποι.' It is enough to say in reply, that as Nebuchadnezzar had forgotten all the particulars of his dream, and these were required to be disclosed as well as the interpretation to be given; and moreover, since he knew, as the Magi assert (Dan. 2: 10), that 'no king or ruler was wont to make such a demand;' the very difficulty and extraordinary nature of the case would naturally induce him to summon all classes of his חַכִּימִין, so that what one class could not accomplish, another perhaps might be able to do. Nothing was more common among the Greeks and Romans, than, where one method of divination failed, to resort to another. Probability, therefore, and consistency are stamped upon the very face of the narrative, in regard to this matter.

One other objection against the probability of the narration in Dan. ii., has been strongly urged, viz. 'the improbability that a *foreigner* should be admitted among the Magi; and above all, that a most rigid Jew could at all be promoted to *supremacy* over the whole order, as it is related of Daniel (2: 48), that he became רַב־סִגְנִין עַל כָּל־חַכִּימֵי בָבֶל; or if he was promoted, that such a man as Daniel could accept the office, and discharge its duties.'

That the Magi had a *supreme head*, is plain from Jer. 39: 3, where Nergal Sharezer, a military chieftain of Nebuchadnezzar, is named רַב מָג, i. e. *arch-Magian*. So Sozomen (Hist. Ecc. II. 13) speaks of *μέγας ἀρχίμαγος*. Berosus, as cited by Athenaeus (Deipnos. XIV. 44), in speaking of the Sakea (i. e. Saturnalian feast) of the Babylonians, mentions the *overseer* as being arrayed in kinglike robes, and as called *Ζωγάνης* (=סְגָן), which means *praefect*. Diodorus Sic. says of the priest Belesys, who led the Babylonians in revolt against Sardanapalus, that he was *τῶν ἱερέων ἐπισημότατος*. Every large town, province, and kingdom, had an *ἀρχίμαγος*, Zend. Av. III. p. 226.

That a foreigner, by special favor of the king, could be introduced among the Magi, seems quite probable from the usage of the Persians, who, although they excluded foreigners in general from that order, did this, as Philostratus (in Protagora) asserts, *ἢν μὴ ὁ βασιλεὺς ἐφῇ*, i. e. only in cases where the king did not demand his admission. The Magi, and all others, were at the disposal of the absolute monarch, either in Persia or in Babylon. So Brissonius, de Regno Pers. II. § 67, 68. So, likewise, Moses is said to have been "learned in all the wisdom of the Egyptians," being the adopted child of Pharaoh's daughter, Acts 7: 22. Lengerke however says: "We know nothing of his being admitted into the order of the priests." But we do at least know, that the Egyptian kings and princes, as a matter of honor and respect, were admitted to this order; nor is there any probability of Moses' being thus instructed, unless he had been admitted into that order.

That Daniel was a *Jew*, would, so far as we know, be no more objection to his promotion, in the eyes of Nebuchadnezzar, than if he had been a foreigner of any other country. This king does not seem to have used the Jews more roughly, than he did all his conquered subjects. That Daniel, as one of the Magi, was made a civil ruler, i. e. Satrap of Babylonia (Dan. 2: 48), as well as Chief Magian, is perfectly in accordance with oriental usage in general, and with that of Babylon in particular, Jer. 39: 3.

'But it must awaken great doubt,' it is said, 'when Daniel is described as holding the office of chief overseer, over priests who worshipped Bel and Mylitta.' (Leng. p. 50). It might, I am ready to concede, if the acceptance of such an office obliged him to the personal performance of heathen rites. But it should be remembered, that *priests* were only a portion of the Magi. I do not say that Daniel's office was a *sinecure;* but I may say, that there was little or no probability, that as *chief* Magian he was subjected to perform the details of priestly rites. He decided cases of appeal; prescribed general rules of order; participated in the studies of the Literati; and, (which seems to have been the king's special object in promoting him), received the honors and emoluments attached to his high station. Was it not quite possible for an intelligent man, so situated, to avoid participating in the details of heathen worship? The whole book of Daniel shows him to be both conscientious and fearless. His station must have subjected him, indeed, to severe trials; but it also afforded him great opportunity to aid his exiled countrymen, and to mitigate the severity of their captive state. Reasonably may we suppose, that this was his motive for accepting the office.

Lengerke represents the author of the book of Daniel, (who in his view belonged to the period of the Maccabees), as 'evidently introducing Daniel among the Magi, that he might, by his interpretation of dreams, elevate the God of Israel above the vanities which the heathen worshipped,' (p. 51). That the narration has such a purpose in view, I would readily concede; but that the whole matter is a mere figment of a sagacious writer in the second century B. C., in order to accomplish such an end, is an assertion which needs some proof. The *ultima ratio*, in all such cases, of this writer, and of others who sympathize in feeling with him, is plain enough. It is simply the denial of all supernatural interposition and occurrences. Against such views, the present volume would not be an appropriate place for argument. The N. Test. has given its clear and decided testimony in favor of the truthfulness of this book. A consistent man who renounces the book of Daniel as a record of true history, must also renounce the N. Testament. My own belief is, that the God who made the world, *governs* it; and that he can interpose, and has interposed, in respect to the regular and established order of things, where special purposes were or are to be accomplished that cannot well be brought about in another way.

(3) Then said the king unto them: I have dreamed a dream, and my spirit is troubled to get knowledge of the dream.

The form תִּפָּעֶם (=תִּתְפָּעֶם) is made by assimilating the תְ; ־עֶם for ־עֵם because the tone is retracted. Not simple agitation, but *perturbation*, is designated by the verb. — לָדַעַת refers to both a knowledge of what the dream was, and of the interpretation of it.

(4) Then spake the Chaldeans to the king in Aramaean: O king, live forever! Tell the dream to thy servants, and we will then show the interpretation thereof.

וַיְדַבְּרוּ, in earlier Hebrew usage, stands mostly absolute, corresponding to our verb *speak;* while אֲמַר (*said*) is followed usually by the words spoken, making an Acc. of object. But in Kings, Ezek., and Daniel, it is often used in the same manner as אֲמַר. So here; but in such a way, however, that one may well suppose a לֵאמֹר to be supplied after אֲרָמִית. — כַּשְׂדִּים, which is the name of one class of Magi mentioned in v. 2, is here employed, in the way of breviloquence, as a designation for the whole, or it is used *par excellence.* Doubtless this class took the lead, among the Magi; for they were (of course as it would seem) the speakers on the present occasion. — מַלְכָּא, stat. emphat. of מֶלֶךְ, which Segholate form in Chaldee is rare except in the biblical Chaldee, where it conforms to the Heb. Segholates; the usual Chaldee Segholate form would be as מְלֵךְ, in most cases; Gramm. § 34. No. IV.* p. 94. — In עָלְמִין the learner will notice the Chaldee idiom, which often employs (ָ) instead of the Heb. (וֹ); so in the Part. Pres. of verbs, and in many other cases; which shows (as it seems to me), that the sound of *Qamets* was like our *a* in *all;* § 33. Par. III. — חֱיִי, Imper. of חֲיָא or חֲיָה, Gramm. p. 72. — חֶלְמָא, stat. emph. of חֵלֶם, which, in biblical Chaldee, thus conforms to the Heb. Segholates. — לְעַבְדָיךְ, the Hebrew note on the margin of the Bible says, that the (י) is here superfluous. As to *sound* it is so; but, although often omitted, it is often retained in writing the biblical Chaldee, apparently as an *index pluralitatis* of the noun. Here the root in the Sing. takes the genuine Chald. Seghol. form, viz. עֲבֵד, Gr. p. 91. IV. b. — פִּשְׁרָא, stat. emph. of פְּשַׁר, another genuine Chald. Segholate, Gr. ib. — נְחַוֵּא, Fut. Pael of חֲוָא, Gr. p. 73.

Xenophon (Cyrop. VII. 5. 31) describes the inhabitants of Babylon, when it was taken by Cyrus, as speaking *Συριστί,* (comp. Isa. 36: 11), by which the same language seems to be meant that is indicated by אֲרָמִית in our text. — The salutation *Live forever!* is truly oriental in its style. See the same salutation addressed to David, 1 K. 1: 31. So Aelian (Hist. Var. I. 32) represents a Persian as addressing Artaxerxes with *βασιλεῦ . . . δι' αἰῶνος βασιλεύοις!* So Q. Curtius (VI. 5) represents Alexander the Great as being addressed by Artabagus: "Tu quidem, Rex, perpetua felicitate floreas!" This harmonizes well with "king of kings," "lord of the world," "light of life," and other court-like names, by which the oriental sovereigns were, and still are, commonly

* The Grammar referred to throughout the Chaldee part of the book of Daniel, is that of WINER, translated by *Professor Hackett* of Newton Theol. Seminary, and published at Andover in 1845.

addressed. In the sober language of common life it would run thus: May your life be very long! — The ancient versions seem to have read פִּשְׁרֵהּ, (with suff.), i. e. *the interpretation of it*, viz. the dream; and some Codd. read פִּשְׁרָה, written *more Hebraico*, the like of which is frequent in biblical Chaldee.

The Chaldeans seem to have taken it as a thing of course, that the dream would be first told, as was usual, before they could be expected to interpret it; and some interpreters maintain, that Nebuchadnezzar told the Magi that it had escaped him, merely to put their skill to the test. But the context seems to afford no room for such a supposition. And when it is asked: Whether a *forgotten* dream could trouble the king? one may reply: Certainly the mind could be greatly agitated by seeing the dream, and this general impression might remain afterwards, although the particulars of the dream had escaped recollection. Experience of this nature is not unfrequent. In fact it is easy to suppose cases, where the agitation would be even increased by the very fact, that particulars were no longer remembered, and the relief that might be hoped for could not therefore be so readily sought in the way of obtaining an explanation.

(5) The king answered and said to the Chaldeans: The word is gone from me, if ye do not make known to me the dream and the interpretation thereof, ye shall be cut in pieces, and your houses shall be made a dunghill.

The words עָנֵה and אָמַר are *participles*, which the Chaldee employs for verbs far more frequently than the Hebrew; Gr. § 47. § 11. 4. — לְכַשְׂדָּיֵא is pointed for the regular marginal reading לְכַשְׂדָּאֵי, which is the regular emphat. pl. (abbreviated from כַּשְׂדָּאֵיָא) of the sing. כַּשְׂדַּי, a *forma gentilis*, Gr. § 30. *b*. The biblical Chaldee, instead of the regular form as given in the margin, retains the (י) of the *gentile* ending, and reads כַּשְׂדָּיֵא; see 2:10. 5:7, also the like endings in 3:2, 8. Ezra 4:9 (nine times), 12. This peculiar biblical form is simply a Syriasm, e. g. ܟܠܕܝܐ (*Kal-do-ye*); see Gr. p. 96, No. VIII. p. 91, Par. VIII. — מִלְּתָה, stat. emph. of מִלָּה (= מִלָּא), Gr. p. 96. 2. A. It may mean *word*, or *thing*, *matter*. In the latter sense many have taken it, and referred it to the *dream* of the king, in the sense of *forgetting*; a possible, but not a probable sense. — אַזְדָּא, part. fem. from the masc. form אָזֵד, Gr. § 12. 1. c; used only here and in v. 8. Most of the older interpreters, and many of the modern ones, refer מִלְּתָה to the dream, and make אַזְדָּא equivalent to אָזְלָא (from אֲזַל), *gone, escaped*. More recent interpreters, (Ges., De Wette, Häv., Leng.), compare with it the altogether similar phraseology in Est. 7:8. Dan. 9:23. Isa. 45:23. Dan. 2:13. 3:29. 4:

3. Ezra 6: 11. So Luke 2: 1, ἐξῆλθε δόγμα. The meaning is: 'The matter is decided.' The *l* and *r* sometimes are exchanged, (comp. δάκρυον, *lacryma*), see Ges. Lex. ד. The Rabbinic phrase quoted by Gesenius, viz. אזדא לטעמיה, means: *he has gone off* [from other Rabbies] *to his own opinion.* Buxtorf (Lex. Chald.) refers only to Dan. 2: 5. 8 for authority as to the meaning of אַזְדָּא; which is little more than assuming the sense of the word, without either illustrating or proving it. In case of such a word as the present, which is almost an ἅπαξ λεγόμενον, the example given by Gesenius seems to be sufficiently decisive. — הֵן, *if,* seems at first view, to be quite a departure from the Heb. meaning (*ecce*) of this particle. But the lexicon will show, that in the later Hebrew, *an, num,* interrog., and *si, if,* are not unfrequent meanings of it. — לָא, *not,* affords another example of the *Hholem* in Hebrew (לֹא) becoming *Qamets* in Chaldee. — תְּהוֹדְעוּנַּנִי, Fut. Aphel of יְדַע with suff.; for in the *biblical* Chaldee, א, the usual formative prefix of the Chaldee in Aphel, is commonly written ה, and this formative is often *retained* in the Fut.; Gr. § 12. 5, p. 49, and see in Lex. — For suff. see p. 58. Rem. 1. — וּפִשְׁרֵהּ, with *masc.* suff. relating to חֶלְמָא, see § 8. 3, in parad. of Suff. — הַדָּמִין תִּתְעַבְדוּן, lit. *ye shall be made pieces, frusta, fragments;* like the Greek μέλη ποιεῖν, 2 Macc. 1: 16. The ה before nouns in Chaldee is never an article, (the Chaldee has no article), so that it is always to be considered as a *radical* letter when not a formative. The verb is Fut. Ithpael, pass. of Pael, Gr. p. 53. 1. — בָּתֵּיכוֹן, plur. of בַּיִת with suff., being irreg. in the same way as the Hebrew. — נְוָלִי, fem. instead of נְוָלִית, the ת of the fem. forms in ־ִית, וּת — וֹת — being usually omitted, Gr. § 31. 1. — יִתְּשָׂמוּן, Fut. of שׂוּם, in Ithpeal, Gr. p. 68. Par. — Such a punishment as is here threatened, viz. the cutting of the body in pieces, the chopping off of the limbs, and the like, was, and still is, common in all the barbarous countries of hither Asia, in Egypt, and in ancient Greece and Rome. Lengerke has accumulated references to it. As to the threat, *Your houses shall be made a dunghill,* it is unnecessary to urge its literally exact sense. It is a strong expression employed to indicate, that their houses would be utterly destroyed, or converted into ruinous heaps which were employed as receptacles for all manner of filth.

(6) But if ye will show me the dream and the interpretation thereof, ye shall receive from me gifts and presents and much honor; therefore show me the dream and the interpretation thereof.

תְּהַחֲוֹן (tehā-hh"vōn) = תְּחַוּוֹן, Aph. of חֲוָא, the ה formative in Aph. being retained in the Fut. (Gr. p. 49. 5), and the quiescent ו of the suffix-formative being omitted in the writing. The ו in the verb is radical and movable, (*-vōn*). — מַתְּנָן, fem. plur. of sing. fem. מַתְּנָא. — נְבִזְבָּה, prob.

of Persian origin, *nuvaza* meaning *donation* in that language. The derivation from the Greek *νόμισμα* is improbable; for this means *coined money*, while we meet with no notice of such in Babylon. The derivation from בִּזְבַּז , by prefixing נ formative and omitting the second ז, is rather forbidding, as so little that is really analogous can be found. Maurer (Comm.) derives the word from נְבָא = נְבַע, *to gush forth*, and זְבָה = זוּב, *to flow*, the combination meaning *copious* or *large donations*. For the form יְקָר, see § 34. No. II. The word may mean *splendor*, *honor*, or (which entitles to honor) *elevated office*. Honor, in the sense which may comprehend the latter, seems to be here meant — שַׂגִּיא, see § 28. b. 10, for the form. — תְּקַבְּלוּן , Fut. Pael. — מִן־קֳדָמָי = the Hebrew מִפָּנַי , i. e. the suff. pronoun is joined with the plural form of the word, which throws out י (the *index pluralitatis*) when it takes the suff. ־ַי , which in pause (as here) is ־ָי . The mode of expression is of the intensive kind, meaning that all which is promised in the case is within the king's purview or in his possession, and therefore is ready to be bestowed. For the *form* of it, comp. Dan. 2: 15. 5: 19. 7: 8, 10. Ezra 7: 14. —לָהֵן , lit. *on account of this* = therefore. — הַחֲוֹנִי, Aph. Imper. plur., the ה = א; the ו (*vo*) = וֹ; and נִי is a verbal suffix; comp. Aph. p. 73. Gramm.

(7) They answered again and said: Let the king tell the dream to his servants, and we will show the interpretation thereof.

עֲנוֹ , 3 plur. Peal, Gr. p. 72. — תִּנְיָנוּת , adverbial fem. form, out of תִּנְיָן . — אָמְרִין , Part. plur. instead of the praeterite verb, § 47. 1. — יֵאמַר , Fut., see for vowels, § 21. a. — לְעַבְדוֹהִי , for suff. to the plur. noun, see Gr. p. 35. Par. 2. — נְהַחֲוֵה , Fut. Aph. with ה retained, p. 49. 5. — The demand made by the Magi seems to be one to which an answer in the way of compliance was of course expected, and which they had a right to expect according to common usage.

(8) The king answered and said: Of a certainty I know, that ye are seeking to gain time, because ye see that the word has gone from me.

Four participles as verbs, viz. עָנֵה , אָמַר , יָדַע , זָבְנִין (plur.), § 47. 1. The latter I have rendered *seeking to gain*, lit. *buying*, *purchasing*, which however can here have only the meaning that the version represents, and which is quite of a different tenor from either Cicero's *emere tempus* (cont. Verr. 1. 3), or the expression of Paul: *καιρὸν ἐξαγοράζεσθαι*, Eph. 5: 16. *To buy time*, in our text, means *to procure more time*, i. e. longer delay. — עִדָּנָא , stat. emphat. of עִדָּן , which comes from the root עדד and has a formative ־ָן , comp. § 28. c. 20. — For אַנְתּוּן זָבְנִין used as a verb, see § 47. 1. *b*. — The threat of the king, with the consciousness that they were unable to satisfy his demand on the spot, made the Magi desirous of obtaining a respite, during which they might perhaps hit upon some expedient to extricate themselves from their very unpleasant dilemma. — כָּל־קֳבֵל דִּי, lit. *all because that* = altogether for the reason that, an intensive of the simple קֳבֵל דִּי, *because that.* Such accumulated forms of particles are frequent in Chaldee. — חֲזֵיתוּן, Peal of חֲזָא. For the rest, see v. 5. In other words, 'You wish delay, because I demand, on penalty of death, that you should give the requisite information.

(9) But if ye will not make known to me the dream, one thing is your purpose, both a false and deceitful word have ye agreed to utter before me, until the time shall have changed; therefore tell me the dream, and then I shall know that you càn show me the interpretation thereof.

דִּי הֵן, apparently = *quod si,* for דִּי = אֲשֶׁר in Hebrew, which often stands for the conjunctive *that.* But this will make no sense here, unless we refer it back to יָדַע אֲנָא of v. 8, and regard it as coördinate with the clause דִּי עִדָּנָא וגו׳ of the same verse. The discourse will then proceed thus: 'I know that ye are seeking to gain time — [I know] that if ye do not make known the dream, ye have agreed upon one purpose, viz. to deceive me by 'false and deceitful words.' If we might render דִּי by *but,* or by *moreover,* it would apparently relieve the difficulty of the construction, yet not really. דִּי, however, will bear neither of these renderings. Rosenm. says of it, "redundat, ut apud Latinos *quod* in *quodsi.* So Leng., *quodsi.* In his German version he gives it no meaning, but merely translates הֵן; and so De Wette. This is *cutting* the knot, but not untying it. But the connection proposed above, preserves the usual meaning of דִּי. That the clause is *asyndic,* when so constructed, is no objection, in a book where this is a striking trait in the syntax. — תְּהוֹדְעוּנַּנִי, see in v. 5. — חֲדָה fem. of חַד, written in the Hebrew manner (as usual in biblical Chaldee) for חֲדָא, the fem. being used in relation to דַּת. And so with הִיא, used here as a copula = *it is,* § 40. 1. 4. חַד = the Heb. אֶחָד, and is formed by an aphaeresis of the א. — דַּת usually means *decree, placitum;* here, however, as in Syriac, = *voluntas, purpose.* To render it *decree, statute,* would make no tolerable sense. — וּמִלָּה וגו׳, an epexegetical clause more fully developing what immediately precedes; so that we may render וּ by *namely, even;* מִלָּה is fem. — כִּדְבָה = כִּדְבָא, (see חֲדָה above as to ה for א), fem. of כְּדַב, the ד being here used instead of the Hebrew ז in כָּזָב, see Ges. Lex. under ז. — שְׁחִיתָה, (ה for א), fem. of the Part. passive, used as an adjective, like כִּדְבָה. — הִזְמִנְתּוּן, the vowels belonging to the *Ithpael* form or Qeri in the margin, viz. הִזְדַּמִּנְתּוּן, in which the formative ת not only exchanges place with ז radical (in זְמַן) but becomes a ד, p. 29. b. But there is no need of the proposed emendation in the Qeri, for the Kethibh makes a good sense, inasmuch as it is in Aphel, and should be read accordingly, הַזְמִנְתּוּן. The two vowels under the מַ in the text, indicate of course, that they belong to another form of the word. — קֳדָמַי points out the person to whom the lying words are specifically directed; the form is that of plur. regimen or suffix, § 38. 2. *b.* — יִשְׁתַּנֵּא, Ithpael of שְׁנָא, the ת formative taking the place of the sibilant, p. 29. b. — אֱמַרוּ, Imper. of אֲמַר with Fut. (ַ); for retaining the מַ in an open syllable (instead of מָ), see p. 42. 6. a. Here the word is used in the sense of our verb *tell.* — וְאִנְדַּע = אֵידַע 1st pers. Fut. Peal, from יְדַע, the נ epenthetic being put instead of ־ֵי, p. 30. 2, comp. the like forms in 2: 30. 4: 14. The Fut. usually takes this epenthetic letter (נ). — תְּהַחֲוֻנַּנִי, with suff. here which has נ epenthetic before it; see the form in v. 6. For its *potential* meaning, see p. 115. 3. c. The ־נַּנִי at the end of the verb, is, in some copies, read ־נָּנִי, because of the Silluq.

(10) The Chaldeans answered before the king and said: There is no man on earth, who is able to show the matter of the king; because that no great and powerful king has required a thing like to this of any sacred scribe, enchanter, or Chaldean.

For כַּשְׂדָּיֵא see v. 5. — אִיתַי = the Heb. יֵשׁ, *there is*, a form *sui generis*, which, as in Hebrew, often marks its subject by making a *suffix* of it. — יַבֶּשְׁתָּא emph. of יַבֶּשֶׁת, an unfrequent form in Chaldee; Gr. p. 98. C. Rem. 1. — יוּכַל, *Hophal* of יְכֵל, which Conj. is constantly employed in biblical Chaldee instead of *Ittaphal*, p. 50. 6. — לְהַחֲוָיָה, Inf. Aph. with ה pref. instead of א, § 49. 5, and ending ־ָה for ־ָא, as is common in biblical Chaldee. — כָּל comes to mean *no*, *none*, here by virtue of the לָא before the verb that follows. For the epithets רַב וְשַׁלִּיט, comp. Isa. 36: 4, and Ezek. 26: 7 — *king of kings.* — מִלָּה, in the present case, means *matter*, *thing*; *matter of the king* means 'matter which concerns the king,' or 'matter which the king requires.' — כִּדְנָה, *like this* (־ָה for ־ָא), § 9. 1. c. p. 36. — שְׁאֵל Peal with final Tsere, § 10. 2. For the rest, see v. 2. Here one of the orders of the Magi, mentioned in v. 2, is omitted, viz. מְכַשְּׁפִים, showing that the usage of naming a part for the whole is continually varying. The Chaldee construction admits of לְ after the verb and before the person asked.

(11) And the thing which the king requires is difficult; for there is none other who can show it before the king, except the gods, whose dwelling is not with flesh.

דִּי *of*, i. e. *which is of* = אֲשֶׁר. It is a sign of the Gen. of the noun that follows, and allows the preceding word to have the meaning of the const. state, while it retains the abs. or emph. form; § 56. 1. — יַקִּירָה,

fem. of יַקִּיר, *gravis, weighty* — in the sense of *difficult to manage.* — אָחֳרָן, with ־ָן formative, I have translated *other, alius,* in conformity with general usage. Still, it might be doubted, whether it is not a noun = אַחֲרִית of the Hebrew, signifying the *future.* But as the fem. suffix in יְחַוִּנַּהּ does not relate to אָחֳרָן, but to מִלְּתָא, the word must mean *another.* The Magi did not mean to deny their power to disclose the future, in case the dream should be made known to them. — In יְחַוִּנַּהּ, Fut. Pael of חֲוָא, the suff. ־ָהּ is augmented by the epenthetic ־ִנ; p. 58. Rem. 1. — לָהֵן, *if not, except,* is different from the לָהֵן in vs. 6, 9, where it comes from לְ and הֵן; here it seems to be a compound of לָא הֵן = *if not.* — אֱלָהִין, in the mouth of the Chaldeans, must mean a plurality of gods; for in such they believed, inasmuch as they worshipped the sun, moon, and all the planets, besides subordinate deities almost without number. — *Whose dwelling is not in flesh,* I understand as designating the *dii majores,* and indicating their immortal nature, in opposition to the frail and decaying nature of flesh. The apparent sameness and perpetuity of the heavenly bodies seems to have inspired the idea here expressed; for it is not probable, that the Magi had correct philosophical notions of pure spirit, such as are now common with us. For דִּי מְדָרְהוֹן, *whose dwelling,* see § 41. 1. — אִיתוֹהִי with a suff. belonging to the plur. form of nouns; which is usual with אִיתַי, see Lex. The ־ַי of the root is of course dropped, when the suffix is attached. The suff. pron. repeats here the subject of the verb; a very common idiom in Chaldee; § 61. In English, the Chaldee form would run thus: Whose dwelling — with flesh it is not.

(12) Because of this, the king was angry and greatly enraged; and he gave commandment to destroy all the wise men of Babylon.

For כָּל וגו׳, see on v. 10. — לְהוֹבָדָה, Inf. Aph. (־ָה for ־ָא) of אֲבַד, § 21. — לְכֹל, Acc., which is often marked by לְ, § 56. 2. — בָּבֶל may mean the city or province of *Babylon;* but the former is most likely here. Strabo testifies that the Magi lived in various provincial towns; and those at a distance were not the immediate object of the king's indignation, on this occasion.

(13) And a decree went forth, that the wise men should be slain; and they sought Daniel and his companions to slay [them].

נֶפְקַת, 3 fem. Peal, with *Syriac* form instead of the proper Chaldee נִפְקַת. — מִתְקַטְּלִין, Part. of Ithpael, *interficiendi* [*sunt*]. — וְחַבְרוֹהִי, Pl. of חֲבַר with suff., p. 35. 2. — לְהִתְקְטָלָה, ה pref. and suff. for א, Inf. of Ithpael; which often has a sense like the Middle Voice in Greek; § 10.

5. The Acc. pronoun (־ֵנּוּן, *them*) is omitted, and must be mentally supplied; the Chaldee shape of the word, however, may be imitated in a translation thus: *For the being killed*, in which case the suffix pronoun is unnecessary.

(14) Then did Daniel prudently and wisely answer Arioch, the chief of the executioners of the king, who went forth to slay the wise men of Babylon.

הֲתִיב (ה for א), Aph. of תּוּב, p. 69. Par.— עֵטָא = Heb. עֵצָה, *counsel, prudence;* ט for the Heb. צ, see Lex. צ.— וּטְעֵם, *sagacity.* Both nouns are in the Acc. *adverbial*, qualifying the preceding verb. One might say, that בְּ is implied before them both; but there is no need of this; § 37. 3. b.—The Chaldee construction, הֲתִיב . . . לְאַרְיוֹךְ, may be exactly imitated in English, viz. *replied to Arioch.*— טַבָּחַיָּא, pl. emph. of טַבָּח, see form in § 28. b. 6. These *executioners* always constituted a part of the body-guard of the oriental kings, as they still do; and sentence pronounced by the king was often executed on the spot by them, in presence of the monarch, when the criminal was before him. Arioch was *chief-executioner;* and as such, he went forth to carry into execution the sentence of the king against the whole class of the Magi. For the same office in the Egyptian court, see Gen. 37: 36. 39: 1. 40: 3, 4, al.; for the same among the Babylonians, see Jer. 39: 9, al. It is not said, on the present occasion, that Nebuchadnezzar's decree against the Magi was made and executed on the spot. Indeed it could not be, for they were not all present. They were probably dismissed by him with contempt and indignation; and these feelings gave birth to the decree that speedily followed. Had those before the king been immediately killed, the writer would hardly have refrained from noting it.

It deserves consideration, moreover, that Daniel and his companions, although belonging to the order of the Magi (v. 13), probably were not present with them, when they had this interview with the king. The Hebrews in question were very young; and diffidence, as well as an abhorrence of all idolatrous magic, might have united their influence to keep them back; or their engagements might have detained them. They might, moreover, not wish to excite the jealousy of the native and older magicians, by thrusting themselves into the company of court-counsellors on a special occasion. Lengerke (p. 62) puts their absence to the account of the writer's sagacity of plan, who will not expose them to the disgrace of a failure to disclose and interpret the king's dream. But my impression is, that the writer is quite free from such a calculating sagacity as this. Whether Daniel is a real or an imaginary character, the writer of his life does not appear in the least to fear his being brought into difficulties or dangers, nor does he dexterously shun either.

(15) He answered and said to Arioch, the king's officer: Why this urgent decree from the king? Then Arioch explained the matter to Daniel.

דִּי־מַלְכָּא, Gen. § 56. 1. — מְהַחְצְפָה, Part. Aph. with ה formative retained, p. 49. 5, fem. in reference to דָּתָא. It may mean *severe, cruel;* but it is hardly probable that Daniel would speak so as designedly to communicate this idea, before Arioch the king's confidant, whose favor he wished to conciliate. *Hasty*, moreover, is a shade of meaning which is of the reproachful cast. I have therefore given what I deem to be the right sense, in the version. — אֱדַיִן, *then*, prop. the pl. form of אֱדֵא, which comes from אֲדָא, *to pass on* or *by, preteriit.* Particles are often formed in such a way. — הוֹדַע, Aph. of יְדַע, § 20. 2. c. It is plain from this verse, that Daniel, by communing with Arioch, could come to be cognizant of all that had passed in presence of the king, without having been personally present.

(16) Then Daniel went and requested of the king, that he would give him time to show the interpretation to the king.

עַל, Praet. Peal from עֲלַל = the Heb. בָּא, § 19. 1. 1. — יִנְתֶּן־ for יִנְתֵּן, because the Maqqeph shortens the final syllable. The full form of the Fut. is usual in biblical Chaldee; p. 59. bott. — פִּשְׁרָא is Acc. placed *before* the verb לְהַחֲוָיָה (Inf. Aph. with form. ה); and this Inf. stands connected with זְמָן, in the way of explanation. The reason for requesting this appears in the sequel. Whether Arioch went with Daniel to the king or not, does not appear from the text. Others in attendance on the king could introduce him, (which was necessary according to oriental custom), and it seems probable that Daniel relied on the favorable impression before made upon Nebuchadnezzar (1: 18—20), for a kind reception. Lengerke (p. 65) thinks it possible that the lapse of some little time had abated the king's violent anger; and, as Daniel was a favorite, he was inclined, on his account, to suspend the execution of the decree against the Magi. But inasmuch as the book, (according to him), is so full of contradictions, it becomes the duty of the interpreter, as he suggests, to assume that there is one here; for first, the suspension, as he thinks, would be very unlike Nebuchadnezzar; and secondly, the author of the book needed such a plan to bring about an opportunity to display the superiority of Daniel, and that of the God whom he worshipped. This, however, seems to be reversing the common laws of generous criticism upon authors, which prescribes, that where they can be reasonably conciliated, they should be. Besides, what is more mutable than the angry passions of oriental despots? Did not Nebuchadnezzar know, after a few moments of reflection, that he had demanded of the Magi what all the world would regard as unreasonable? And what, moreover, was to become of the stability of his throne, if a universal massacre of the Magi were attempted? No king could stand before them, in such an exigency. — It has also been regarded by some critics as very strange, that Daniel makes no mention here of showing the *dream itself*, but only of its *interpretation*. Does not the latter, however, necessarily involve the former? And why should simple breviloquence in a writer be put to the account of mistake, or of patching together two different authors who varied in their accounts (Bertholdt s. 62. f. 194., f.), or of negligent brevity? (Leng. p. 66). Was not the *interpretation* the main object and end of the whole? And as such, may it not easily and obviously, by a usage very common, stand as the representative of the whole?

(17) Then went Daniel to his house, and made known the matter to Hananiah, Mishael, and Azariah, his companions.

The position of the Dat., or Acc., or both, before the verb, the reader must already have remarked, is uncommonly frequent in this Chaldee portion of Daniel; much more so than in Hebrew. Here the verb comes last of all.

(18) That they might ask for compassion before the God of heaven, in regard to this secret matter, in order that they might not destroy Daniel and his companions with the rest of the wise men of Babylon.

רַחֲמִין, like the corresponding Heb. word, used only in the plural, in the sense which it here bears. — לְמִבְעֵא, Inf. Peal with לְ, lit. *for* [their] *seeking*. As the Heb. Inf. with לְ often stands for a verb of definite mood and tense, so here the Inf. appears to designate the same idea that the 3 pl. would express, the suff. pronoun 3 plur. being implied after it, as designating the subject of the verb. — *God of heaven* resembles the Heb. *God of hosts;* while this latter expression occurs not in the biblical Chaldee. *God of heaven* means either the God who dwells or reigns in heaven, (comp. Our Father who art in heaven), or the God who is exalted over all, = ὕψιστος. *God of hosts* = almighty, or more exactly, ὁ παντοκράτωρ. — רָזָא, stat. emph. of רָז. — דְּנָה *this* or *that*, refers to what the preceding context relates of the forgotten dream. — יְהוֹבְדוּן, Fut. Aph. with ה retained, p. 49. 5. — שְׁאָר retains the (ָ) in the const. state here; as some other nouns of this form occasionally do; § 34. No. II. a.

(19) Then to Daniel, in a vision of the night, was the secret revealed; then Daniel blessed the God of heaven.

חֶזְוָא, stat. emph. of חֱזוּ, which is of like form with some Heb. Seghol. derivates of verbs לה. The דִּי which follows before the Gen., renders the const. form unnecessary. — לֵילְיָא, makes one and the same abs. and emph. form; which is not unfrequent in other cases; § 32. 1. The old abs. form was probably לֵילַי; and the Hebrew nearly always employs לַיְלָה for לַיִל. — גְּלִי, in v. 30 גֱּלִי, Part. pass., with a comp. Sheva instead of a simple one; which is peculiar to this participle in verbs לא; p. 74. 5. — Revelation by visions of the night is no new thing. It is frequently spoken of in the O. Test. and in the New. — בָּרִךְ, Part. in Peal, § 12, 1. *c*, used as a verb, comp. v. 8 with four participles used in like way, and so *passim.* — לֶאֱלָהּ is Acc. § 56. 2.

(20) Daniel answered and said: Let the name of God be blessed forever and ever, for the wisdom and power which is his.

עָנֵה, Part. Peal used for the verb. One use of the root עֲנָא, as of the Heb. עָנָה, is to designate the *commencing of any discourse* or *address*, whether strictly in the way of answering or not. The German *anheben* corresponds to this; our nearest word is *address;* and where this will not suit well, we may translate *began discourse*, *commenced speaking*, in case we decline the old translation, *answered.* — לֶהֱוֵא, Inf. with ל apparently, but used repeatedly in this chapter and elsewhere for the 3 pers. sing., and so with (varying form) for 3 plur., (לֶהֱוֹן v. 43). For sing., see also Dan. 2: 28, 41, 45. 3: 18. 5: 29. 4: 22. 6: 3. Ezra 7: 23, 26, al.; for 3 plur., Dan. 6: 2, 3, 27. Ezra 6: 10. 7: 25; in the fem. Dan. 5: 17. Now as this prefixing of לְ happens never to the second and third persons of the verb הֲוָא, but only to the third sing. and plur., Beer (Inscriptt. pap. vet. Semit. p. 18 seq.), and after him Maurer and others, regard the ל in this case as a peculiarity of the Hebrew-Aramaean at the time when the book before us was written, and they compare it with the لَ added to the Fut. in Arabic = *ut*, and also with the נ which is the common formative prefix of the 3 pers. of the same tense in Syriac, and often in a portion of the Chaldee Targums. Maurer (Comm. in loc.) has given the whole passage from Beer. Winer seems to favor this view, Gramm. p. 75. Rem. 2); and I know of no better solution of the matter. That the examples above referred to are not in the *Inf.*, is plain enough, both from their meaning and their form. But whatever may be said of the *forms*, the meaning at least is plain. — In שְׁמֵהּ there is an *anticipative* pronoun-suffix, related to the noun that follows; lit. *the name of him — of God.* This idiom is very common in Chaldee, and sometimes occurs in Hebrew; § 40. 3. *a.* — מְבָרַךְ, pass. Part. of Pael. — חָכְמְתָא and גְּבוּרְתָא in stat. emph. — דִּי־לֵהּ הִיא = אֲשֶׁר־לוֹ, § 41. 1. Lit. *wisdom and power — it is* (הִיא § 40. 1) *to him,* i. e. are his. The pronoun sing. (הִיא) refers to the next preceding noun. *Wisdom* here has special reference to God's knowledge of רָזָא; *power* refers to a might or ability to overcome difficulties, however great they may apparently be. The idiom, so frequent in the O. and N. Test., exhibited by the phrase *name of God,* seems to have arisen from the consciousness of men that they could not fully and directly comprehend what God in himself is, and so his *name* (יהוה), designed to comprehend all that is known and unknown of him, is often put, in an expressive way, for all which it imports; see Cred. in Joel. p. 220. There seems to be a degree of designed intensity in this mode of expression.

(21) And he it is who changeth times and seasons, who removeth kings and setteth them up, who giveth wisdom to the wise and knowledge to the intelligent.

וְהוּא, *and he it is,* § 40. 1. — מְהַשְׁנֵא, Part. Aph. with ה formative retained, p. 49. 5. Every Part., if no subject is expressly designated, implies a relative pronoun (= ὁ, ὅς,) of itself for a subject. We might translate simply thus: *and he changeth,* etc.; but the version given is more exactly adapted to the form of the original. — *Times and seasons* (both plur. emph.) differ not essentially. Of the two עִדָּן is the more generic, answering to χρόνος, זְמָן to καιρός. The *change* here referred to, seems to be that from a season of great danger, to that of the hope and prosperity which were now apparently before the speaker. The *removal* of kings and the *setting of them up* I should refer, in the way of anticipation, to the mighty changes in monarchies which the dream already disclosed to Daniel indicated. *Wisdom to the wise and knowledge to the intelligent* refers specially to what had been imparted to the speaker, so as to give him a knowledge of the great secret in question. Daniel ascribes all his peculiar knowledge, on this occasion, to God as its author. — מַנְדְּעָא, emph. with formative נ instead of Dagh. forte in the ד, from the root יְדַע, p. 30. 2. The last phrase literally means: *et scientiam cognoscentibus intelligentiam,* i. e. intelligent knowledge, in any who possess it, is of his gift. — בִּינָה is fem., and not masc. emph.

(22) He revealeth deep and secret things; he knoweth what is in the darkness, and light dwelleth with him.

גָּלֵא and יָדַע (Part. for verb) mark, more strongly than the verbs themselves, what belongs to customary and continued action or state. —

עֲמִיקָתָא, emph. pl. of עֲמִיק, an adjective of the Part. Peil form. — מְסַתְּרָתָא, emph. pl. fem. of Part. pass. in Pael. — נהירא in Kethibh should be pointed נְהִירָא; the vowels now attached to it are appropriate to the Qeri, נְהוֹרָא. The reading of the Kethibh is equally good, and needs no change, as both forms are legitimate. — שְׁרֵא, verb with final (ֵ). The sentence, carried on before by two participles, now goes forward by a verb. This usage is also very frequent in Hebrew. — This verse is a repetition, in another form, of the leading idea of the preceding one. "He who gives wisdom to the wise," reveals secrets, and discloses what is dark; which he can easily do, because he dwells in light. This last clause exhibits a sentiment often repeated in both the O. and N. Test.

(23) Thee, O God of my fathers, do I thank and praise; for wisdom and ability hast thou given me, and now thou hast made known to me that which we sought for from thee, for the matter of the king hast thou made us to know.

לָךְ, Acc. § 56. 2. — In אֱלָהּ, the Chaldee usage of putting (ָ) for (וֹ) is very plain; for the Heb. is אֱלוֹהַּ. — אֲבָהָתִי, suff. plur. irreg. of אַב, § 35. — מְהוֹדֵא, Part. Aph. of יְדָא, with ה retained. It sometimes means *to praise, laud;* but when joined with another verb (as here) which expresses the idea of *praising*, it is equivalent to the Lat. *gratias agere.* — בְּעֵינָא, Peal 1st plur. of בְּעָא. The speaker uses this person, because he and his associates had in common (vs. 17, 18) sought for the disclosure that had been made. — דִּי, like אֲשֶׁר, *that which.* The next דִּי is *causal* in its sense, *because that, since.* — *Made us to know*, like the phrase above where *we sought* is the mode of expression. The modesty and humility of Daniel seems evident in all this. To his associates as well as himself he ascribes the successful supplications that had been made; and when he becomes the honored instrument of disclosure, he takes no special credit to himself for this, but considers it as equally pertaining to them.

(24) Because now of this, Daniel went to Arioch, whom the king had appointed to destroy the wise men of Babylon, he went and spake thus to him: Destroy not the wise men of Babylon; bring me into the presence of the king, and I will show the interpretation to the king.

For the composite conjunction at the beginning, see under v. 8. The intensity given by כָּל to the conjunction clause, I have aimed to express by *now.* — עַל, see v. 16. — מַנִּי, Pael of מְנָא. — לְחַכִּימֵי, Acc. const., § 56. 2. — אֲזַל = עַל, resumes by an equivalent word what had been interpreted by the preceding exegetical clause. — The second לְחַכִּימֵי is also in the Acc., governed by the verb that follows. — הַעֵלְנִי, Imper. Aph. of עֲלַל, *Qamets* under ה because of the Gutt. which follows, § 19. 1. 1. b.

— פִּשְׁרָא alone is here again named, as in v. 16 above; and for the same reason as there, viz. that of breviloquence, the disclosure of the dream itself is not named.

(25) Then did Arioch in haste bring Daniel before the king, and thus spake he to him: I have found a man, of the sons of the captivity of Judah, who will make known the interpretation to the king.

בְּהִתְבְּהָלָה, Inf. noun of the form Ithpeal, here used adverbially, or as a noun with an adverbial sense, like הַרְבֵּה in Hebrew. — הַנְעֵל for הַעֵל, Aph. of עֲלַל, the נ being inserted to compensate for the long vowel which is dropped; § 19. 1. 1 ad finem. — דִּי is here merely the sign of words quoted, as כִּי often is in Hebrew, and ὅτι in Greek; so in 5: 7. 6: 6, 14. It is translated sufficiently, by any sign which marks words as quoted. — הַשְׁכַּחַת, Aphel of שְׁכַח, the ending (ַ ַ) being occasioned by the final Guttural; p. 53, verbs 3 Gutt. Without a Gutt. ending, these vowels would be (ֶ ָ). — גָּלוּתָא, fem. emph. of גָּלוּת, *captivity, exile;* abstract for concrete. — דִּי יְהוּד, *of Judah,* is added to distinguish these exiles from others at Babylon, brought from foreign countries, or possibly to distinguish Daniel from the native Magi. Lengerke (p. 72) thinks the writer has here been guilty of a ὕστερον πρότερον, inasmuch as he makes Arioch *introduce* Daniel to the king, before he mentions who he is. Is it then certain, that such a special confidant of the king, as Arioch plainly was, might not venture to take Daniel with him, and tell the king whence he was, when standing with him in the royal presence? Lengerke has even cited a long passage from the Greek commentator, Polychronius, which descants on this "inversion of order;" whereas it is plain enough, that the whole thing might have depended on the familiarity of Arioch with the king, and also on the well known favorable regard of the king for Daniel. How much one may sometimes see, when he is on the watch for the halting of a writer whom he strongly suspects!

(26) The king answered and said to Daniel, whose name was Belteshazzar: Art thou able to make known to me the dream which I have seen, and the interpretation thereof?

דִּי שְׁמֵהּ, *whose name,* the דִּי showing the *relative* sense of the הּ־ that follows, like אֲשֶׁר in Hebrew; § 41. 1. — בֵּלְטְשַׁאצַּר, בֵּל = Belus; *tsha,* a sign of the Gen. in the Zend; צַר = *prince;* and so *prince of Belus,* which means either *noble* or *exalted prince,* or else *prince whom Belus favors* or *protects.* The first syllable is closed, and yet the vowel is long and without the tone; the laws of the Hebrew, in this respect, apply but partially to the Chaldee. The reason why this epithet is here added to the usual name of Daniel seems to be, to remind the reader that the king himself had imposed this name (1: 7), and that the favor of the king, on this occasion, might in part be owing to his acquaintance and familiarity with Daniel. — הַאִיתָיךְ, הַ interrog., the suff. ־ָיךְ has the form of a suff. to the plural, and here indicates the subject of אִיתַי; see Lex. — כָּהֵל Part. pres. = *potens.* — לְהוֹדָעֻתַנִי, Inf. Aph. of יְדַע, the Inf. with suff. assuming the termination ־וּת, while the suff. is ־ַנִי; p. 56. e. — חֲזֵית, Peal, 1st Sing. of חֲזָא, p. 72. Par. Nebuchadnezzar speaks of the dream *which he saw*, because the main object presented to his vision in it was the gigantic image or statue.

(27) Daniel answered before the king and said: The secret which the king asks for, no wise men, enchanters, sacred scribes, astrologers, are able to show to the king.

Four *participles* in this verse, all having the sense of verbs — for even יָכְלִין is pl. part. of יְכֵל; the pl. verb would read יְכֵלוּ. — For the first three nouns which are denominatives here, see on v. 2 above. — גָּזְרִין, particip. noun, probably from גְּזַר *to cut, divide;* for the astrologers divided the heavens into different sections, each having, as they viewed the matter, an appropriate significancy. Gesenius (Comm. Es. s. 353) has given a figure exhibiting this division, as before exhibited by Brücker, Hist. Philos. I. p.139. This illustration of the word can hardly fail to be satisfactory. — לְהַחֲוָיָה, Aph. Inf. with ה for א, as frequently before. In this declaration, Daniel shows a sympathy with the Magi, on account of the violence done to them by the king's making a demand on them of that which was beyond their power. He endeavors to convince the king of the unreasonable nature of the demand, by showing him the impossibility on their part of complying with it. At the same time, an excellent opportunity is afforded him to vindicate the superior claims of the God of Israel; which he manfully and nobly uses to the best advantage. He must surely have possessed great firmness and presence of mind. Lengerke intimates more than once, that the whole of this narration is made up, by preconceived design, in order to impress the moral truths which it inculcates; for he plainly discards all ideas of the *supernatural,* at any time, or on any occasion. My views of Revelation lead me to a very different conclusion.

(28) But there is a God in heaven, who revealeth secrets, and he hath made known to the king Nebuchadnezzar, what shall take place in the latter days. Thy dream, even the visions of thine head upon thy couch, was this.

שְׁמַיָּא, pl. emph. of שְׁמַיִן, destitute of a sing. form, and like the Heb. שָׁמַיִם. The idea of בִּשְׁמַיָּא seems here plainly to be, *who dwells in heaven,* in distinction from the visible and idol gods which Nebuchadnezzar worshipped. — רָזִין, here used in a generic sense, i. e. *secrets* of any kind, or of all kinds — a more expanded idea than that of רָזָא above, which there means the concealed dream of the king. — מָה fully expressed would mean *what is*, and דִּי *that which*. I have compressed them in the translation. — לֶהֱוֵא, see under v. 20. — בְּאַחֲרִית יוֹמַיָּא, not a generic expression for any subsequent or future time, as De Wette and Hävernick assume, but *latter portion of days* = the Messainic period, and not to be explained by אַחֲרֵי דְנָה in v. 29. The *like* to this, in Gen. 49: 1. Num. 24: 14. Deut. 4: 30; the *same* as our text, in Isa. 2: 2. Mic. 4: 1. prob. Jer. 48: 47; comp. ἐπ' ἐσχάτου τῶν ἡμερῶν in Heb. 1: 1, et al. in N. Test. Lengerke says, that only the *commencing part* of this last age of the world is meant. If merely the distinctive mark between the preceding age and the latter were the object in view, this would be correct; but the things predicted, in connection with this אַחֲרִית, cannot all be developed at its commencement. The דִּי לֶהֱוֵא shows the conviction of the speaker, that the God who foretells will surely accomplish what he foretells. — חֶזְוֵי pl. const. of חֵזוּ, *visions of thine head* means conceptions or notions which are formed in the brain, the seat of thinking. Here the phrase is merely exegetical, and designed to show that the dream was occasioned by the operations of the mind. The *sing.* דְּנָה הוּא shows of course that חֶלְמָךְ is treated as the real subject of the sentence. Comp. for the phraseology, Dan. 4: 2, 7, 10. 7: 1.

(29) Thou, O king, — thy thoughts upon thy bed came up, [as to] what will be hereafter; and he who revealeth secrets hath made known to thee what shall be.

רַעְיוֹנָךְ, pl. with suff., p. 35, 2d Par. These *thoughts* appear to refer to the meditations of Nebuchadnezzar before sleep came on him. If he had been dwelling in his mind, as is probable, on the subject of the future condition of his conquests, fame, and kingdom, it was a good preparation to make the dream impressive. The form סְלִקוּ I do not regard, with Gesenius (in Lex.), as a Part. pass. or Peil (see Gramm. p. 51), but as a verb 3 pl. Peal, from the root סְלִק or סְלֵק, (which also has סְלַק), like קְרֵב and קְרִב, p. 48, comp. § 12. 1. *Came up*, alluding to ascension to the brain. — לֶהֱוֵא twice here, see v. 20. — גָּלֵא, Part. used here as a noun in the construct state, the Qamets being immutable, see p. 91. Par. VII. *a.* — מָה דִי again as in v. 28.

(30) And I — not by wisdom which is in me above all the living, is this secret revealed to me, but that the interpretation may be made known to the king, and that thou mightest know the thoughts of thine heart.

וַאֲנָה *and I*, Nom. *abs.*, as often in Heb. and Chaldee. — מִן, here used as when marking the compar. degree, = *above, more than.* — חַיַּיָּא (hăy-yăy-yā), emph. pl. of חַיִּין, *living creatures* or *living men;* more probably the latter here. — גְּלִי, for the pointing, see on v. 19. — עַל דִּבְרַת דִּי, *because that,* lit. *on account of the matter that.* דִּבְרַת is of the const. form, and the whole clause that follows is virtually a Gen. after it. — יְהוֹדְעוּן, lit. *that might make known,* etc. The 3 plur. is often employed, as here, with an *indefinite* subject, (and so in Hebrew), and thus it comes to be equivalent to the *passive* voice; comp. § 49. 3. b. See the like in Dan. 3: 4, 21. 4: 13, 22, 23. 5: 21. 7: 9, 12, 13, 26, al. — *The thoughts of thine heart* here means the same as the *visions of the head* in v. 28. The Hebrews, like us, could refer both to the *head* and *heart* as local sources whence thoughts come. — תִּנְדַּע , p. 30. 2.

(31) Thou, O king, wast looking, and behold! a great image; this image was lofty, and the splendor of it excessive; it stood before thee, and the appearance of it was terrible.

אַנְתְּה , i. e. (as the Kethibh should read) אַנְתָּה, for which the Qeri has substituted the more usual form אַנְתְּ. The former is the Hebraizing Chaldee, and no valid objections can be made against it. — חָזֵה הֲוַיְתָ the Part. with the verb הֲוָא *(to be),* here appropriately designating the *continuance* of the action, § 47. 1. *a.* The Part. is specially adapted to such a purpose; as one may see in Dan. 5: 19. 7: 2, 2, 4, 6—9, 11, 13, 21. 8: 5, al. — אֲלוּ seems to be the same as אֲרוּ, the ל and ר being exchanged; which is not unfrequent. Possibly the latter comes from an inversion of רְאוּ , of the root רְאָה *to see.* Or perhaps אֲלוּ is simply an adverbial form from the demonst. pronoun אֵלֶּה , *those, these,* and so means *there* = see there; just as הִנֵּה *ecce,* comes from a demonstrative pronoun, in Hebrew. The later derivation seems to me more probable, on the ground of analogy. Coupled with the preceding, it reminds us of the εἶδον καὶ ἰδοὺ of John in the Apocalypse. — חַד corresponds, as in later Heb., to our indef. article *a, an;* so εἷς in the N. Test. — רַב I have translated *lofty,* because the word indicates *extensiveness* in any direction. In Heb. it is said of a *long* way, 1 K. 19: 7, and of long continued attention, Isa. 21: 7; and it is not probable that the simple idea of *magnitude,* marked before by שַׂגִּיא, would be repeated again so soon. The sense I have given to רַב is evidently appropriate. So Leng., *hoch.* — זִיו *(ziv)* from זְהָה *to shine,* the first ה of the root conforming to the vowel which precedes, the second ה is dropped, and the original י of the root (verb לֹה) resumed. — קָאֵם , Part. of קוּם, see Par. p. 68. — רֵוֵהּ, ־ֵהּ suff., רֵו *(rēv),* for רְאֵו, from רְאָה *to see.* The whole verse forms a simple but very graphic description.

(32) This was the image — its head was of pure gold; its breast and arms of silver; its belly and thighs of brass.

דִּי־דְהַב, the Gen. of material. Strictly considered, however, the noun רֵאשׁ is mentally supplied before this; and the like in respect to the following Genitives. — טָב *good*, applied to *gold*, of course means *pure*. — חֲדוֹהִי, pl. with suff., from חֲדִין, plural because the breast is biform. — וּדְרָעוֹהִי, in the same way as the preceding, the pl. being employed because the Chaldee has no dual. — מְעוֹהִי, pl. of מְעִין. — יַרְכָּתֵהּ, suff. pl. fem. of יַרְכָּה. As to the suff. הּ- instead of ־וֹהִי— as before, see Gramm. p. 36, top. The plur. fem. often takes suffixes which belong to the sing., because the form is too well marked to be mistaken. So in the Syriac.

(33) The legs were of iron, the feet partly of iron and partly of clay.

שָׁקוֹהִי, suff. pl. of שָׁק (= Heb. שׁוֹק) *leg*. — רַגְלוֹהִי, suff. pl. of רְגַל or רֶגֶל. — מִנְּהוֹן, so the Kethibh should be pointed; but the vowels in the text are designed for the Qeri, which reads מִנְּהֵן fem. plur. because רֶגֶל (the antecedent) is feminine. Yet many nouns (and perhaps this one) are of the *common* gender. מִן is the const. of מַן, *part* or *portion*. It is quite plain, that the different materials, which constituted the different parts of the gigantic image, are designed to symbolize different dynasties; and that the last, the extreme lower part of which is a mixture of iron and clay, (besides the divisions of the toes in the feet), is designed to symbolize a very heterogeneous and mixed domination.

(34) Thou didst continue looking, until a stone was cut out without hands, and it smote the image on its feet of iron and clay, and crushed them.

עַד דִּי, lit. *until that*, i. e. until the time when. This shows that the cutting out of the stone, and its action upon the image, were *subsequent* to the complete formation of all parts of the image. It is of importance to note this circumstance, as it has an important bearing on the explanation of this compound symbol. — הִתְגְּזֶרֶת, Hebraizing form of 3 fem. Ithpeal. A common form here would be הִתְגְּזֵרַת, (p. 49. 2); but the double Seghol-ending is very common in verbs which end in ר, and so here we have זֶרֶת — for זֵרַת —, p. 53. 3d Gutt. 3. — דִּי־לָא, lit. *which was not* = without. So in Syriac, ܕܠܳܐ (dᵉlō), *without*. — בִּידַיִן, Hebraizing *dual* form of יַד, with ב prefix prep. The proper Chaldee has no dual. Only a few forms of this kind find a place in the biblical Chaldee; § 31. 2. — מְחָת, 3 fem. Peal of מְחָא, p. 72. — חַסְפָּא emph. form of חֲסַף in v. 33. — הַדֶּקֶת, 3 fem. Aph. of דְּקַק, the reg. and proper Chaldee form would be אַדִּקַת (p. 63), but the ה prefix is Hebraistic (p. 49. 5), and the Segholate form דֶּקֶת - shows the tendency to Hebraize in the terminations of these fem. forms; comp. p. 49. 3. 4. — *Without hands* plainly means, without human power or aid, the *hand* being the common symbol of power;

comp. Dan. 8: 25. Job 34: 20, for the like expressions. — הַדֶּקֶת is a very strong expression; for it designates, more appropriately, the *crushing* of grain in a mill. That the force of expression is fully transferred here, is evident from the next verse, which represents the crushing to be so complete, that the wind takes away that which has been crushed, as it does the chaff of a threshing floor. The blow of the stone, although it directly fell upon the feet of iron and clay, was so vehement, that the *whole* image, by violent concussion and consequent fall was reduced to powder. Whatever the four kingdoms in reality were, which in this case are symbolized, one thing is clear, viz. that the stone, when it makes its appearance and falls upon them, utterly annihilates them all. So much, at all events, lies on the very face of the symbol in question.

(35) Then were crushed at once iron, clay, brass, silver, and gold, and they became like chaff of the summer threshing floor, and the wind took them away, and no place was found for them; and the stone which smote the image, became a great mountain, and filled all the earth.

בֵּאדַיִן, the first vowel being a contracted one, from the original בֶּאֱדַיִן, lit. *in the then*, i. q. then. — דָּקוּ, root דְּקַק, with long vowel under ד as a compensation for Dagh. f. omitted in ק; § 19. 1. b. — כַּחֲדָה, adv. compounded of כְּ and חֲדָה = חֲדָא, which is either fem. or emph. of חַד. In the four nouns that follow, the emph. form of all shows an implied *article*, (so in v. 24), since in v. 33 they take the simple absolute form. The *asyndic* construction here is also remarkable; but, as has already been noted, it is frequent in this book. Here it is in good taste, also, for all the parts named are closely connected in one whole. — הֲווֹ, 3 pl. Peal of הֲוָה, here (as often) meaning *became*. — עוּר, *chaff*, need not be derived from עִוֵּר *to blind*, nor from עָפָר *dust*, (whence עִוֵּר, Ges.), because chaff blinds one when blown in his eyes, or dust produces the same effect. This is too fanciful. It seems to be plainly allied to עוֹר *skin*, i. e. of men, while עוּר (distinguished merely by the mode of pointing) is the *cuticle* of grain; both words being from עוּר *nudus fuit*. — אִדְּרֵי, const. pl. of אִדַּר, which is probably from נדר, *excidit*, *to fall out*, as grain from the sheaf. — קַיִט = the Heb. קַיִץ, *summer*, irreg. Segholate, § 29. 5. b. — כָּל ... לָא, *no*, *none*. — הִשְׁתְּכַח, Ithpeal, with שׁ radical transposed, § 10. 5. b. — הֲוַת, 3 fem. Peal of הֲוָא, the usual form would be הֲוָת, p. 72, Peal. But sometimes the fem. here imitates the fem. in the other conjugations (which is ־ַת); see מְטַת, Dan. 4: 19.* — לְטוּר = Heb. צוּר, and הֲוָא לְ means *to become*, in Chaldee, in the same way as in the Hebrew. — מְלָאת, contracted for מְלַאַת (see p. 53. 3d Gutt. 3), א being here a

* This remark is omitted in Gramm. p. 74. 1.

Gutt. in the root, and not a mere Quiescent. — אַרְעָא, emph. of אֲרַע = Heb. אֶרֶץ. This word exhibits the transmutation of the Heb. צ into the Chald. ע; an occurrence not very unfrequent.

The reader must not suppose, that all the four monarchies are symbolized here as *coëxisting* and *contemporaneous*, when the final blow is given. The explanation in the sequel shows plainly, that they are *successive*. But inasmuch as one dynasty went over into another, in regular succession, the last became the *tout ensemble* and *representative* of the whole; and when it was smitten, in a certain sense all perished together. One thing should be specially noted here, viz. that an end of *all* is made, when the fifth kingdom *begins* to be set up. So the text: "They were crushed *at once* or *altogether*, the iron, clay," etc. Their utter destruction is most graphically described, by the subsequent image of chaff blown away by the wind. No place, therefore, is found for them.

(36) This is the dream; and the interpretation thereof will we now declare before the king.

נֵאמַר, § 21. Daniel again includes his companions with himself; for this seems to be the meaning of the 1st plur. here. The *pluralis majestaticus* he surely would not apply to himself, on such an occasion; and it would therefore seem that he speaks *communicativè*, comp. vs. 17, 18, 23, above.

(37) Thou, O king, art king of kings, on whom the God of heaven hath bestowed dominion, strength, and power and glory.

אַנְתְּה, see v. 31. — לָךְ . . . דִּי, lit. *to whom* of the 2d pers., which we cannot so express in English, but the sense of which I have given above. The דִּי of course belongs to the לָךְ, and gives to it a *relative* sense, although separated far from it. — אֱלָהּ, Nom. before the verb for the sake of emphasis. — The four nouns that follow are all of the emph. form, and from their specific meaning here, would claim an *article* in the Hebrew; § 32. 1. — תָּקְפָּא, with ŏ, comes from תְּקֹף, a Hebraizing Segholate. The two first nouns are *asyndic*, but the last two have each a (וְ). The writer probably designed to couple them as one compound — *splendid power*. The firmness of Daniel is conspicuous here. He does not merely ascribe splendor and power to the king, (which he might well do), but solemnly reminds him, that all this is due to the *God of heaven*, who is not only *King of kings*, but King of him who is every day saluted with this high title.

(38) And wherever dwell the sons of men, the beast of the field, or the fowl of the air, into thy hand hath he given [them], and made thee ruler over them all; thou art that head of gold.

וּבְכָל־דִּי = בַּאֲשֶׁר in its *local* sense, *wherever*. The כָּל is an intensive here, as in כָּל־קֳבֵל דִּי, v. 8 above. Our English word *wherever* expresses the idea with sufficient exactness. — דָּאֲרִין, Peal Part. of דּוּר, but the vowels belong to the Qeri, דָּיְרִין, with a movable Yodh. The Kethibh would be appropriately pointed דָּאֲרִין, and thus written, it is simply a Hebraizing form (like קָאמִים); and inasmuch as it stands here so written, and also in 4: 32. 6: 26, it appears that the Masorites have been too solicitous to conform the text to the proper Chaldee. I prefer the Kethibh, as being Hebraeo-Chaldaic. — *Sons of men*, common in Hebrew for *men, mankind*, but more frequent still in Chaldee and Syriac. — חֵיוַת, const. of חֵיוָה (hē-vā), from חֲיָא *to live*, final א here being put for ו of the root (§ 20. 1), the *Vav* is resumed where the fem. formative ה ָ is added. — בָּרָא, emph. form of בַּר, *field;* but the probable root (ברר *inanis fuit*) seems to indicate either *desert*, or (like ἔρημος) an *uncultivated place*, i. e. destitute of houses, hedges, etc. — *Fowl of the air*, generic like חֵיוַת. That שְׁמַיִן often designates the *air*, there can be no more doubt, than that the corresponding Heb. word does. — In יְהַב בִּידָךְ, the בְּ before the noun conveys the appropriate sense, *into*. The hand grasps and wields. To put anything *into it*, is to commit it to the disposal of the person to whom the hand belongs. — וְהַשְׁלְטָךְ, Aph. with suff., *hath made thee to rule*. The root of this word points out the meaning of *Sultan*, i. e. שלטן with ן– formative. — In בְּכָלְּהוֹן, כֹּל is a noun (root כלל) with a suff.; hence the Dagh. forte in ל, lit. *over the totality of them*. — הוּא = the verb *art*, § 40. 1. Still it carries a kind of demonstrative force with it, like that of the Greek οὗτος, and is equivalent to *thou art the very* or *that same*. — רֵאשָׁה emph. of רֵאשׁ for רְאֵשׁ. The description given in this verse of the extensive dominion of Nebuchadnezzar, is of course not to be literally urged; for in a court-compliment or address, (which must be such as not to give offence), who can exact *literal* exegesis? Is Paul to be taxed with uttering a fulsome compliment, when he addresses Festus with his usual title κράτιστε? Acts 26: 25. That this method of describing extensive dominion was common in the Semitic dialects, is evident from Gen. 1: 26. Ps. 8: 6—8, comp. Heb. 2: 7, 8, and Jer. 27: 6. 28: 14. The reader would err, as I apprehend the matter, if he should attempt to prove from this *golden head*, that the Babylonish empire under Nebuchadnezzar was actually larger and more powerful than any of the three that followed. Nebuchadnezzar is placed at the *head*, because the symbolic vision *begins* with him; and the natural mode of describing the image was to begin with its most striking part — *the head*. The assumption, that the whole is a mere artifice of the writer, by which he makes Daniel flatter the king, by giving him such a preference (for in this light some view it) over others, seems to be but ill-matched with the bold and faithful and fearless character of the man as elsewhere represented. *Diversity* of parts and of metals, in the present case, is requisite in order to designate *variety* of dynasties. No comparison of their respective extent or importance is to be made out of this; for, plainly, the writer has himself made the comparison in the sequel by express language — *inferior to thee — rule over all the earth — mighty as iron which crusheth everything.*

(39) And after thee shall arise another dominion, inferior to thine; and another third dominion of brass, which shall rule over all the earth.

וּבָתְרָךְ, suff. form of the prep., from בָּתַר. — מַלְכוּ = מַלְכוּת, § 31. 1. — אָחֳרִי, adj. for אָחֳרִית, ib. — אֲרַעא, the points belong to the Qeri, אֲרַע. The Masorites rejected the emph. form, because they regarded the word as *adverbial;* but the word may be fem., and the objection then virtually ceases. The Kethibh should be read אֲרְעָא. — מִנָּךְ, the מִן of comparison. The *silver* portion of the image, to which this second dominion corresponds, is not here named; but in respect to the *third* dominion, *brass* is specified as the corresponding symbol, which of course shows that the writer couples, in his own mind, the second dominion with the *silver,* see in v. 32. — תְּלִיתָאָה, fem. of תְּלִיתַי, formed like the stat. emph. in Dec. VIII. p. 91. In this case, it distinguishes the אָחֳרִי here from the same word above, and is in apposition with the latter אָחֳרִי. — *Reign over all the earth,* an expression not to be taken in a literal geographical sense, but as a popular phrase, indicating wide and uncontrolled domination; comp. Gen. 41: 54. Jer. 34: 1. 50: 23. Ezek. 22: 4. 2 Chron. 36: 23, where Cyrus, in his proclamation, says: "All the kingdoms of the earth hath the Lord God of heaven given unto me." So Luke 2: 1. To this third dynasty is ascribed a wider domain than to the preceding one. The second is described as inferior to the first, אֲרַעא מִנָּךְ; while the third is represented as a domain of the widest extent. What dynasty is represented by the respective portions of the compound Colossus, will be a subject of inquiry in the sequel.

(40) And a fourth dominion shall be strong as iron; altogether as iron crushes and grinds to pieces everything — even as iron which dashes in pieces — all these will it crush and dash in pieces.

מַלְכוּ apoc. of מַלְכוּת, § 31. 1. — רְבִיעָיָא, the vowels belong to the Qeri רְבִיעָאָה, which is the usual normal form of the fem. in nouns with the ending ־ִי, e. g. רְבִיעַי. Instead of the normal form, (which changes the last י into א when accession is made), the biblical Chaldee retains the *Yodh* final, and makes it movable. Our text, therefore, should be written רְבִיעָיָא; see p. 96, under No. VIII. — תַּקִּיפָה is an epithet primarily applicable to *physical hardness, compactness, strength,* like that of iron, as the text intimates. It does not designate, in respect to the fourth dynasty, its potency by reason of *numbers*, but its resistless energy in destroying. — כָּל־קֳבֵל דִּי is not *causal* here, but simply *just as, altogether as, quite like*, etc.; see on v. 8 above, for the form of expression. — מְהַדֵּק, Aph. Part. with ה retained; the idea of *crushing* as grain is crushed in a mill, which is the appropriate meaning of this word, is very graphic. — חָשֵׁל, Part., *comminuit* to reduce to small pieces, or *contudit* to bruise to pieces, answer well to the Chaldee word. Our vulgar *smash* comes very exactly to it. It serves to increase the intensity of the description. The corresponding word is מְרָעַע and תֵּרֹעַ, both of which (from רְעַע) are nearly synonymous with חָשַׁל. *Even as iron that dashes in pieces*, resumes or repeats the comparison already intimated, for the sake of impressing on the mind of the reader the iron-like power of the dynasty. — כָּל־אִלֵּין, according to the accents, belongs to מְרָעַע. But this mars the sense and the grammar. To what can אִלֵּין relate, if such a construction be adopted? As the apodosis must begin, therefore, with כָּל, we might expect another כְּ (*as*) = *so* before it. But this is often left *unexpressed;* which is frequent also in Hebrew. The subject of תַּדִּק וְתֵרֹעַ is מַלְכוּ. תַּדִּק is Aph. 3 fem. Fut. of דְּקַק, and תֵּרֹעַ is Fut. Peal of רְעַע, תֵּ because the ר excludes the Dagh. forte. In English, the three verbs are well represented by *crush, smash,* and *dash to pieces.*

(41) And since thou sawest the feet and the toes, a part of them the clay of the potter and a part of them iron, the dominion shall be divided, and there shall be of the firmness of iron in it, inasmuch as thou sawest iron mingled with the whitish clay.

דִּי = אֲשֶׁר, *quod, since that, because that.* חֲזַיְתָה, ה paragogic, 2 sing. Peal. — מִנְּהֵון twice, the vowels being for the Qeri מִנְּהֵן, see on v. 33; מִנְּהוֹן (so the Kethibh) being masc., the Punctators have changed it to the fem. form. so as to agree with the usual gender of the antecedents. But may not רְגַל have been of the common gender? If so, the change is unnecessary. — נִצְבְּתָא, emphatic fem. Part. of נְצַב, used here as an abstract noun, *that which is stable, firm*, i. e. stability, firmness. — טִינָא, *argilla, white clay*, such as potters use, and so (with חֲסַף) it is named above *clay of the potter.* The idea must be, that the clay in the image was hardened by fire, otherwise the feet and legs could hardly be imagined to support the body of the Colossus. But still it was, even in that condition, far inferior to the iron in point of hardness and firmness.

(42) And since the toes of the feet were partly of iron and partly of clay, in part the dominion shall be strong, and in part it shall be brittle.

מִנְּהֵון as above. — מִן קְצָת, see on 1: 2 above. — תְבִירָה fem. (ת for the Heb. שׁ), *brittle, friable*, i. e. that which can be easily broken or separated. There is a clear intimation, in these last two verses, that the fourth dynasty is of quite a different complexion from the other three. The *brittle* and the *strong* are commingled in it. But not merely this. In describing the second dynasty above, which includes the breast and arms, nothing is said or made of the *fingers* attached to the hands, because no special significancy is designed to be given to them. But here the *toes* are twice mentioned separately from the feet, (vs. 41, 42). Why? Let the reader turn to chap. vii, where is another vision of these four monarchies much more full and explicit than the present one, and he will there find *ten horns* of the fourth beast (vs. 7, 20), distinguished in the same way, which are explained by the angel-interpreter (7: 24) as meaning *ten kings*, — ten who are to *precede* the little horn (vs. 8, 20, 24), which, beyond all reasonable doubt, symbolizes Anthiochus Epiphanes. The *ten toes*, in the passage before us, partly of iron and partly of clay, appear, therefore to designate, in a special manner, the ten kings who precede the king symbolized by the little horn, whose reign and character correspond well with the symbol of the iron and the clay. But the ten kings, although enigmatically intimated, are not here brought to special view, nor is anything here said of the *little horn*. Diverse in the mode of representation, but not in substantial meaning, is Dan. 8: 8—12. But we shall find some further characteristics of this dynasty in the next verse; to which we now come.

(43) Since thou sawest iron mingled with the whitish clay, they shall intermingle with the seed of men, but they shall not cleave together this with that, see! even as iron cannot mingle with clay.

Since thou sawest, etc. It does not seem to have been duly noticed by interpreters here, that v. 43 is coördinate with vs. 41, 42, which commence with the same expression. That the וְ of connection is omitted, is quite usual in this book, as already remarked. The ground of such an arrangement may be easily explained. Vs. 41, 42 explain the mixture of the iron and clay, as symbolizing an empire which is both weak and strong, i. e. has some weak points and some strong ones. Evidently the mixture of iron and clay in the feet and toes, indicates that the colossal image has but a frail support. Accordingly when the stone from the mountain strikes the feet, the whole image falls and is crushed to powder. But here (v. 43) the *mixture* of the iron and clay is represented as symbolizing another remarkable characteristic of the dynasty in question, viz. the intermixture of the party-chiefs of the fourth dynasty by marriage, in order to promote their respective designs, and also the failure of these arrangements to accomplish the end proposed. This circumstance is so peculiar from its nature, that one at first wonders that such a matter should be introduced, in order to characterize a dynasty. It implies, of course, that there were several chiefs who negotiated intermarriages; for the marriage of a single reigning prince with some one, or any one, is such an ordinary circumstance, that there would be nothing distinctive or characteristic in a symbol of it. It also implies, that while the object of such alliances was union, or at least a design to bring about a peaceable state of things, that object was in a peculiar manner defeated. But the solution of such an enigmatical symbol it would be difficult to make out, had not the writer himself suggested it in another almost historically graphic prediction respecting the fourth dominion in chap. xi. 6, 7, and 17. Chap. vii. and viii, which bring before us the fourth dynasty, and particularly one of the most formidable among the chiefs of it, omit indeed all reference to the peculiarity now in question. But chap. xi, as just referred to above, gives us an ample view of what is meant. That both this and the passage before us belong to the same events, and to the same dynasty, no one, I think, can reasonably call in question for a moment. The nature of the case is so entirely *sui generis*, that the coincidence of symbol and events in both chapters is conclusive. But the *historical* facts connected with the illustration of this, must be reserved for a fuller account of this matter in remarks on ch. xi. 6, 7, 17.

מְעָרַב, Part. pass. of Pael, is here substituted instead of the מִפְּחוֹן in the preceding verses. It is probably adopted here, because it is needed in the next clause to designate *intermingling* by marriages. — מִתְעָרְבִין, Part. of Ithpael; the implied subject here is the *divided* kings. — לֶהֱוֹן for יֶהֱוֹן, see on v. 20 above. — *By* or *with the seed of men;* this last phrase, *seed of men*, in 1 Sam. 1: 11, means simply *a male*. But this would not make the requisite sense here. The word זְרַע also means *family, offspring, descendants;* which fits well here, viz. *they shall intermingle by* or *in the way of family alliances.* אֲנָשִׁים serves merely to show, that the literal sense of זְרַע is not to be thought of. — דָּבְקִין, Part. Peal; for the commentary, see Dan. 11: 6, 7, 17. The design of *junction* or *union*, in a political point of view, is wholly frustrated; דְּנָה עִם־דְּנָה — לָא דָבְקִין, *one with the other*, or lit. *this with that*, which is the only way in which the Chaldee can express the idea contained in the first version. — הֵא, *ecce, see now*, calling the special attention of the reader to the fact, that disappointed alliances by marriage are also symbolized by *the mixture of the iron and clay*, as well as a mixed condition of weakness and strength, which had already been described. Altogether of the like nature is the symbol of the beast (Apoc. 17: 3, 9, 10), which has *seven heads* (v. 3). These indicate, first, "seven mountains," [of Rome]; then, "seven kings," (vs. 9, 10). In other words, a significant symbol may be used for more than one purpose; but when it is so, the writer always takes care, for the sake of perspicuity, and in order to aid the reader, to declare that he employs it in this way. So in the case before us.

(44) And in the days of those kings, the God of heaven shall set up a kingdom, which shall never be destroyed, and a dominion that shall not be left to another people. It shall crush and bring to an end all those kingdoms; but itself shall stand for ever.

Those kings must of course mean the kings that belong to the fourth dynasty, although they have not thus far been expressly named, but only by implication. It is not to be limited, as I apprehend the matter, merely to the kings who contract alliances, but is designed to comprise the kings at large who reign during the dynasty. — The phrase בְּיוֹמֵיהוֹן is a general one, and not of specific limitation like the ταῖς ἡμέραις ἐκείναις of the N. Test. From the nature and order of all the preceding cases, this fifth kingdom is to be *successive*, not coetaneous. This indestructible and immutable kingdom is to be built on the ruins of all the others; and so it is described as *crushing* and *making an end of them*. The explanation agrees with the account of the symbol, vs. 34, 35. There the stone cut out of the mountain smites the feet of iron and clay, and the whole image falls and is dashed to pieces. The symbol is perfectly congruous. All the four empires are symbolized by one and the same image connected together. When the feet therefore that support this image are crushed, then falls the whole Colossus, as a matter of course. But as a matter of *historical fact*, the empires represented by the image are successive, and must be so considered; and indeed they are so represented by Daniel in his interpretation of the symbol. In the present verse, the writer has merely followed out the symbol, in his explanations; and what he says, if strictly urged without any reference to the nature of the symbol, would imply the *contemporaneous* existence of all the four monarchies, when the fifth commences its course. Yet as this would altogether disagree with the actual nature of the case, and with the author's own representation of the matter in other passages, we cannot for a moment hesitate to say, that when the fourth dynasty is crushed, which virtually comprised all the others, then the whole are represented as being crushed. It is not necessary, moreover, to suppose this crushing to take place, after the time when the fifth kingdom had actually begun. If it took place as being necessary to *prepare* for the coming or ushering in of the fifth kingdom, then it may well be said that this kingdom occasioned the crushing. It is enough, that before the fifth dynasty becomes actually established, the other preceding dynasties are no more. This last circumstance seems very plainly to oppose the idea that the *Roman* domination constitutes the fourth dynasty; for this had not reached its acme when Christianity was established. — תִּתְחַבַּל, Ithpael. — תִּשְׁתְּבִק, Fut. Ithpael of שְׁבַק, תְ transposed, p. 40. 5. 6; for Hireq in בִּ, see p. 49. 2. — וְתָסֵף, Fut. Aph. of סוּף, p. 67, top. — מַלְכְוָתָא, p. 92. Par. A. c.

(45) Inasmuch as thou sawest, that from the mountain a stone was cut out without hands, and crushed the iron, brass, clay, silver, and gold, the great God hath made known to the king what shall be hereafter; the dream moreover is certain, and the interpretation thereof faithful.

כָּל־קֳבֵל דִּי here = דִּי in vs. 41, 43; only more intensive in form. — הִתְגְּזֶרֶת, 3d Fem. Ithpeal, p. 53. 3d Gutt. 3. — דִּי לָא וגו׳, see on. v. 34. — *Iron, brass*, etc., again *asyndic;* see on v. 35. — לֶהֱוֵא, as in v. 20. — יַצִּיב is a *predicate* of חֶלְמָא, and therefore needs not to be in the stat. emph. — מְהֵימַן, Part. pass. Aph. from אֲמַן, with ה prefix retained, p. 49. 5. The object of Daniel's assertion in this case is plainly to assure the king that all which he had said was from such a source, (viz. from that "God in heaven who revealeth secrets," v. 28), that it might be confidently relied on. There is doubtless an implied reflection upon the divination and soothsaying of the Magi; but not in such a way that the king, or they, could justly take any exception to it. That Daniel stakes his future credit and condition upon the certainty of what he had disclosed, lies upon the very face of the matter. The sequel shows, that the consciousness of Nebuchadnezzar, awakened by the disclosure of Daniel, testified to him that the Hebrew seer had correctly related the dream; and therefore he might well conclude, as he seems for the time to have done, that all which was predicted would take place.

Inasmuch as this dream of Nebuchadnezzar contains only the *germ* of what is more fully unfolded in chap. vii, viii, xi, I shall defer the discussion respecting the *different empires*, to which it alludes by bringing to view the different substances and different parts of the colossal image, until the reader has further opportunity to become more acquainted with the nature and object of the present book.

(46) Then king Nebuchadnezzar fell on his face, and worshipped Daniel, and oblation and sweet odors he commanded to bestow abundantly upon him.

אַנְפּוֹהִי, pl. suff. of אֲנַף, which however is not used in the sing., = Heb. אַפַּיִם where the נ is asssimilated. — Comp. προσκυνέω, e. g. in Matt. 2:11. *To fall on one's face* means to prostrate one's self to the earth, until the face comes in contact with the ground, — comp. וַיִּשְׁתַּחוּ אָרְצָה, Gen. 18:2. This of itself would not determine the question, however, whether Nebuchadnezzar meant to pay *divine* or *civil* honors to Daniel; for such prostration was common before kings, princes, or indeed before any one intended to be specially honored, as well as before God, when in the attitude of adoration. Abraham paid such an honor to the children of Heth, who had given him a burying place for Sarah, Gen. 23: 7. Moreover, the word סְגִד (§ 12. 1. 1), *worshipped*, or *paid homage*, is not decisive of religious worship. Neither would the *sweet odors* presented to Daniel, indicate with certainty the design of the king; for these are as common in the East as prostration, and are in themselves merely a token of special honor. But the מִנְחָה is relied on, by Leng., as evidence of religious homage, for he speaks of it as distinct from מַתָּן, the latter meaning *present* or *gift* by one man to another, while the former, as he avers, designates *oblations* made to God. A glance at מִנְחָה in Ges. Lex. dissipates all this; for the word is often employed for common, and especially for liberal, gifts of men to each other, and also for *tribute* paid to the government, (which bears the soft and courteous name of מִנְחָה). From the state of Nebuchadnezzar's mind, who was overwhelmed with astonishment, we may reasonably conclude, that at least he meant, by his prostration, oblations, and odors, to acknowledge Daniel as the accredited interpreter of the God who had thus revealed secret things, and through him to present his homage and oblations to the God of the Jews, who could perform such wonders. Still, reasoning of this kind presupposes some illumination of mind on religious matters, and how much of this Nebuchadnezar possessed, it would be difficult to say. That any abiding conviction of the immeasurable superiority of the God of the Jews above the Babylonish divinities, was now fastened on the king's mind, is clearly negatived by the following chapters. But he was a man of vehement passions and strong impulses, and at such a moment as the one before us, it is no wonder that he went all lengths in testifying his astonishment and solemn awe. Daniel seems, if we consult the next verse, to have been rather the *medium* of worship (such as it was), than the direct object of it. — לְנַסָּכָה, Inf. Pael of נְסַךְ, lit. means *to pour out*, or (like the Greek *σπένδειν*) *to make a libation*, etc. In this sense it would apply only to נִיחֹחִין, *sweet* (liquid) *odorous substances*, and then we must assume a *zeugma* in respect to the preceding noun. To avoid the necessity of this, I have given to the verb a secondary or tropical sense, and rendered it *abundantly bestow;* which, at least, accords well with the nature of the occasion.

(47) The king answered Daniel and said: It is true that your God is the very God of gods, and Lord of kings, and the Revealer of secret things, inasmuch as thou hast been able to reveal this secret.

מִן קְשֹׁט, lit. *of a truth*, i. e. it belongs to truth, or is a part of it = *truly, verily*. I have rendered the phrase simply *true*, in order to conform the expression to our usual idiom. — אֱלָהֲכוֹן, sing. with 2 plur. pron. suff., where *your* relates to Daniel and his companions. הוּא = αὐτός ἐστι, = *the very, the self-same.* — מָרֵא, Part. noun, Dec. III. *b.* p. 91, א being radical not emph. — גָּלֵה, another Part. noun, or it may be taken in a verbal sense. — יְכֵלְתָּ, 2d pers. sing., for Daniel was the only one who revealed the mystery which the king had in view. The suffix above (*your*) points to the God of both Daniel and his friends, to whom these Hebrews held a common relation; but the interpretation of the dream was given only by Daniel. Lengerke insinuates, that all which is here ascribed to Nebuchadnezzar, is the result of design in the author of the book, who wrote it in the Maccabaean times, intending by it to make a show of the manner in which the heathen were constrained to acknowledge the superiority of the God of Israel; and he compares the narration of what was now said, to that which is ascribed to Antiochus Epiphanes on his death-bed, as related in 2 Macc. ix. It must be acknowledged, however, that nothing could be more natural than for such a person as Nebuchadnezzar to demean himself in the manner here described, in circumstances such as his. But to controvert such matters with Lengerke, would force me to quit the appropriate business of commentary, and go to arguing the question : Whether anything of a *miraculous* nature is possible? I deem it to be out of place to pursue such a discussion here. I have professed my belief in the *supernatural*, whenever and wherever an important object was to be accomplished by it, which could not well be accomplished in other ways. *Credible testimony* then becomes the main question, for those who admit such a position; and for myself, I feel disposed to regard the book before us as containing such testimony. Our Saviour calls Daniel a *prophet*, Matt. 24: 15.

(48) Then the king promoted Daniel, and gave him large and numerous presents, and made him ruler over all the province of Babylon, and chief overseer over all the wise men of Babylon.

רַבִּי Pael of רְבָא, lit. *made great*, i. e. great in office or station = promoted. — רַבְרְבָן, intens. form of רַב, with the fem. plur. ending. — מְדִינַת, const. form, *province;* which here probably means the *satrapy* of Babylonia. — רַב סִגְנִין, *principal* סְגַן = *overseer* or *praefect.* What the particular duties of this office were, we do not know. That Daniel so managed them as to keep clear of divination by sorcery or astrology, and of the performance of heathen rites, would seem to be implied by the account of his demeanor which is given in the book of Daniel. That every overseer of the kind here named should have *deputies* under him, (ὕπαρχοι, οἰκονόμοι), was the common custom of the East; which accounts for the circumstance mentioned in the next verse.

(49) And Daniel made request of the king, and he appointed over the business of the province of Babylon, Shadrach, Meshach, and Abednego. And Daniel was in the gate of the king.

עֲבִידְתָּא, prop. *service* of any kind, but here the *business* of the king, whether it concerned government or revenue. — בִּתְרַע, *in the gate.* This was of course at the entrance into the palace, and hence it seems indirectly to designate the palace itself, e. g. as *threshold* designates the whole building. Thus: "Lift up your heads, O ye gates!" seems to mean: 'Be thou loftily erected, O temple,' viz. as a fit dwelling place of God, Ps. 24: 7. When it is said that Daniel was at the door or gate of the king, I understand the idea expressed to be, that he was the leading courtier, or was he who introduced to the king those who visited the palace. To this place, as head of all the Magi, Daniel was probably now entitled by virtue of his office, as well as by the favor of the king.

CHAPTER III.

[This chapter might be entitled: The *martyrdom* of Shadrach, Meshach and Abednego. Nebuchadnezzar makes a colossal image, and erects it near to Babylon. He summons all his leading civil officers to the dedication of the new idol. When they had assembled, proclamation is made, that all shall fall down and worship it, whenever the music shall give the signal. All who refuse to do this are to be cast into a fiery furnace, vs. 1—6. The mass assembled at the dedication obey the king's command. But some of the Chaldeans (Magi), perceiving that the three friends of Daniel failed to do so, give information to the king, vs. 7—12. Nebuchadnezzar, in a rage, sends for the disobedient Hebrews, and inquires of them whether the information is true; threatening, at the same time, severe punishment in case of continued disobedience. The offenders do not deny the charge of transgressing the king's commandment, and moreover they openly declare their intention not to obey him in this matter, vs. 13—18. The enraged king instantly commands them to be thrown into the fiery furnace, which is heated to an unusual degree. The men who were the immediate instruments of executing this command, are destroyed by the vehement heat of the furnace, while the three Hebrews, being bound and cast into it with all their garments upon them, are not so much as scorched by the flames, vs. 19—23. Speedily the king, who seems to have been present to see the execution of his sentence, perceives that the three men are loosed from their bands, and that a fourth personage, who wore a supernatural aspect, was walking calmly and conversing with them, in the midst of the furnace, vs. 24, 25. Overawed by this spectacle, the king comes near the furnace, and commands the three Hebrews to come out from it. All the king's officers around him perceive, that the fire had made no injurious impression upon the accused. Nebuchadnezzar, filled with awe and consternation, declares his gratitude to the God of the Hebrews for having delivered them; proclaims a decree that none shall speak ill of him, and elevates to a still higher rank in the province of Babylon, Shadrach, Meshach, and Abednego, vs. 26—30.]

Objections almost without number have been made against this chapter. 'An image so huge and expensive,' it is alleged, 'is utterly an improbable thing. The proportions of it, 60 cubits (= 90 feet) high and only six cubits broad, are ridiculous, and make it impossible that it should keep an upright position. Daniel too — where was he? Not a word of him on this occasion. Who can believe that he was permitted to be absent? Besides, we have no credible account of any prophets or miracles among the Jews in their Babylonish exile. How comes it, too, that a heated furnace was already in waiting, before it was known whether it would be needed or not? There is, on the whole face of these matters, a manifest effort in the writer to represent everything as wonderful; the furnace is heated seven times more than usual; the men who cast the victims into it are destroyed, while not even the smell of fire comes upon the victims themselves (v. 27). Besides all this, the monstrous height and more monstrous proportions of the image, are preposterous, and its expense almost beyond conception. The assembling, moreover, of all the superior officers, from the most distant provinces, at the dedication of the idol, — this and all the other circumstances show, that we have romance rather than history before us. The Arabian Nights Entertainment presents us with many a striking parallel to this chapter — parallels that in themselves are equally credible.'

This is a specimen of what has of late often been alleged against the historical verity of Dan. III. Bertholdt is taken to task by Lengerke (p. 105), for even allowing that the story related in this chapter has any basis in fact, or any germ of truth in it. Bertholdt, who could go far enough on an exigency into the "neuere Kritik," was somehow a little cautious on this occasion; for he supposes that Nebuchadnezzar did actually set up a large statue, and summon his officers to the dedication of it. He also concedes, that Daniel's companions, true to their Hebrew feelings, refused the homage demanded, and were consequently condemned to a severe punishment; from which Daniel probably procured a reprieve. "*Abzuweisen ist*" (to be rejected), says Lengerke of all this. Differently, however, does he speak of Hitzig. The latter (in Heid. Jahrb. 1832. h. 2. s. 125) says: "Hengstenberg passes over the essence of the wonder [deliverance from the furnace] in silence. This is quite intelligible; for here he must yield the ground, and betake himself to an *a priori* faith. Forsooth! A miracle which changes the very nature of an element, must truly be a great one. It is indeed the greatest of any in the Old Testament; but not on this account the most credible." *Treffend!* (striking), says Lengerke of all this; and in a somewhat different sense we also might say: *Treffend!* He then cites a long passage from Redepenning (Stud. and Krit. 1833, s. 856), the amount of which is, that 'the miracles of the O. Test. are more *colossal* than those of the New, because they are addressed to the inferior senses, and are adapted to take hold of the imagination.' Finally, Lengerke asserts (p. 111), that the narration before us 'will find credit only among those, who believe in the veracity of a certain Benjamin [of Tudela], who asserts, that the oven into which the three Jews were cast, is still to be seen standing at Babylon.'

So much for *liberal criticism;* and so much, I might add, for *decorum* and real *liberality* of feeling, in those who glory in being called their defenders.

I shall not now examine *seriatim* the various allegations above recited, inasmuch as it would make the introduction to chap. III. too long; but specially because I deem it more satisfactory to the reader, and more feasible to the writer, to pay the requisite attention to objections, after we have duly considered the explanation of those assertions in the history, on which the allegations in question are founded. A safer and better judgment can then be formed of these matters.

(1) Nebuchadnezzar the king made an image of gold, sixty cubits in height and six cubits in breadth; he set it up in the plain of Dura, in the province of Babylon.

צְלֵם, properly = σκία, *shadow*, thence *image, likeness.* Like the Heb. סֶמֶל, Ezek. 8: 3, 5. Deut. 4: 16. 2 Chron. 33: 7, it is also used for *statue*, to which was attributed a *likeness.* In the case before us, no god is named whose likeness the statue bore; and so we are at liberty to conjecture what is most probable, among a people of such religious views as the Babylonians cherished. That *Belus* was the principal god, is admitted on all hands. Gesenius (Lex. בַּעַל) thinks that Belus is a symbol of the planet *Jupiter.* That at a later period this was so among several oriental nations, there is little room to doubt. But to my mind, Münter (Relig. der Bab. s. 16 f.) has given satisfactory proof, that the *sun* was the leading divinity of the East. *Baal* seems to be rather an appellative which might be applied to any leading god = *Dominus;* the article would of course make it significant of the chief god. That Münter is in the right, in these views, I should argue from the fact, that all of middle and hither Asia were worshippers of the heavenly bodies. Well might all be such, who had sprung from the regions where Zoroaster's religion once bore universal sway. The soul and centre of this was ORMUSD; and the home and symbol of Ormusd was the *sun.* When, in process of time, Parsism, i. e. the religion of Zoroaster, was modified by foreign intercourse, and by views growing more and more heathenish, then *statues* or visible *symbols* of the gods worshipped began to be made, (for Parsism had none); and as long as the worship of the heavenly bodies was the leading principle of any modification of Parsism, (and such it was over all hither Asia down to quite a late period), so long the *sun* would be regarded at least as *Primus inter pares.* But is it certain, what *shape* a צְלֵם of the *sun*, (for such probably was Nebuchadnezzar's image), would take among the Babylonians? That the statues of Belus at Babylon, mentioned by Ctesias and Herodotus, were of the *human* form, seems altogether probable, perhaps certain. But it is easy to see, there might be *two* forms of an image made to represent the sun; one of the *human* form, symbolizing the divinity who was supposed to dwell in the sun; another after the form of the natural sun itself; for this would equally well remind the worshipper of the god whom he worshipped.

7

If the latter may be supposed, in the case before us, then a *pillar-form*, i. e. an obelisk-body, with a head or top formed in the sun's likeness, not only may, but must, naturally be supposed. For a moment we will rest the matter here.

שִׁתִּין = 60, from שֵׁת or שִׁת = the Heb. שֵׁשׁ, *six*. — פְּתָיֵהּ, suff. form of פְּתַי.

EXCURSUS IV.

This enormous height of ninety feet or sixty cubits, and breadth of only nine feet, is that which has called forth, as we have seen above, the sarcasms and the sneers of so many recent critics. Yet a sober inquirer may be permitted to ask: If the statue exhibited a similitude of the *human* form, why did not the writer name the part of the body from which the breadth was taken? Was it head, neck, breast, shoulders, loins, or what? for surely the difference is not a little in the breadth of these parts. If it was of pyramidal shape, then we might expect the measure of *breadth* to be estimated of course from the base near to the earth. The form of the narration looks very much like this. Where, in all the accounts we have of the large size of the human form, is an account of its breadth given, without any reference to the part that was measured for it? The Egyptian obelisks are from fifty to one hundred and fifty feet in height. Might not one of ninety feet, if the base were sunk deep in the earth, stand erect without any difficulty, (just as well as the trunk of a lofty tree), if it were of the breadth here named? The huge disproportion (ninety feet high and only nine feet broad), which is so often spoken of with a contemptuous sneer, vanishes entirely when we suppose the form to have resembled an obelisk. Is it not a conceded fact, moreover, that between the ancient Egyptian and Babylonian religion, priesthood, objects of worship, and architecture, there were striking resemblances? Jablonski has shown, (Pant. Aegypt. p. LXXX. seq.), that the obelisks of Egypt were *idol-pillars*. The Chronicon Alex. (p. 89) says: "The Assyrians [i. e. those who lived beyond the Euphrates] first erected *columnam Marti*, and worshipped him among the gods." The Amyclaean Apollo, in Lacedemonia, was a *pillar*, to which were appended head and feet, (Münter Rel. der Bab. s. 59). Among the ruins of Rome have been dug out two images, formed by a pillar-basis, surmounted by a bust of the head and breast, (Bottari Sculture, etc. tab. 22 and 82). If difficulty be made, on the ground of erecting such a huge obelisk of gilded wood, what is to be said of the obelisks in Egypt which are of one stone, and are from fifty to one hundred and fifty feet high? And what of the brass Colossus at Rhodes, which, according to Pliny (Hist. Nat. XXXIV. 18), was seventy cubits high? And as to the alleged *grotesqueness* of the proportions or symmetry, who that is familiar with the monstrous and the gigantic which is everywhere apparent in the Babylonish structures — walls, temples, towers, dykes, and hanging gardens — will be disposed to make anything of this? Gesenius himself very justly says, (Art. *Babylon*, in Ersch and Grub. Encyc. Th. VII. p. 24), when speaking of the ruins of the tower of Belus: "They are imposing merely on the ground of their *colossal greatness*, not on the score of beauty. All the ornaments are *rude* and *barbarous*." In fact, the huge, the grotesque, the gigantesque, belongs to nearly all the Babylonish works of art, which have gained celebrity. Why was not Nebuchadnezzar's צְלֵם in good keeping with all this?

"But the astounding, the incalculable, the incredible expense of such an image of *gold!* It surpasses all faith, except an *a priori* one, like that of Hengstenberg!"

But what if the image in question were first carved from wood, or rather, constructed with wood, and then a strong gilding or thin gold plate were put upon it — could it not then be called *golden?* Was not this usually so? In Ex. 37: 25, the altar of incense is said to have been made of *acacia-wood;* yet in Ex. 39: 38 this is called the *altar of gold* (מִזְבַּח הַזָּהָב); and so in Ex. 40: 5, 26. Num. 4: 11. In like manner, Ex. 38: 1 tells us, that the altar of burnt-offerings was made of *acacia;* and yet in Ex. 39: 39 it is called מִזְבַּח הַנְּחֹשֶׁת, *the altar of brass.* In both cases, the appellations *gold, brass,* are of course to be understood as applied to the *plating* which consisted of those metals. Clearly it was so with the idol-statues; see Isa. 40: 19 seq., where the whole process is minutely described. So again in Isa. 46: 6 seq., where (in v. 7) the *carrying of the idol on the shoulder* is mentioned, which excludes the idea of a solid casting. Comp. also Isa. 44: 9—17. Again, the like is graphically described in Jer. 10: 3 seq., specially in vs. 4, 9. To make out the whole shape of a large idol, *wood* was necessary; for this the carver could easily fashion. But to cast a statue of thirty, forty, or more cubits in height, from molten metals, surpassed all the knowledge and power of antiquity. If indeed the whole statue was metal of any kind, it must have been hollow, and only a metalline surface (so to speak) was constructed. The probable cost of Nebuchadnezzar's image, made in either of the ways above described, (and these are the only feasible ones), need excite neither the astonishment nor the sarcastic smile of critics, provided they are more solicitous to inquire carefully after *facts,* than prone to ridicule what they do, not readily understand.

But on almost any ground, there is not much occasion for the contemptuous rejection of our narrative. Of all the cities of the ancient world, Babylon, the great medium and metropolis of communication between the commercial agents of the East and West, was the richest, most luxurious, and most magnificent. See the common views in regard to this capital, as developed in Rev. xviii. If we are astounded, moreover, at the *expense* of such an image as that of Nebuchadnezzar, what shall we say of the accounts of Herod. and Ctesias? The latter says (in Diod. Sic. II. 9), that the statue of Belus was forty feet high, and weighed 1000 Babylonian talents. Larcher estimates the 800 talents, which Herodotus (I. 183) says the statue weighed, at 56,160,000 *Francs* (= $11,240,000), which makes each talent to be worth about 14,000 dollars;* and reckoning with this the

---

* This estimate seems to be made on the ground that the talents in question were *Babylonian;* which is not improbable, although Herodotus does not expressly say this. But in III. 89 he specifies the Babylonish talent, as differing from the Attic or Euboean talent. The latter weighed sixty *minae,* and the former seventy; see Be-

other statues that Ctesias mentions, and the apparatus of tables, bowls, censers, etc., we have the sum of 5500 talents of gold = about 77,800,000 dollars. If the account of such expenditure be deemed in part fictitious, (it is at least of a somewhat suspicious character), then let us calculate what merely the single pyramid of Cheops at Ghiza cost, and see whether it will not far exceed this sum. Take into account, moreover, the walls of Babylon, said to be 250—300 or more feet high, and sixty miles in compass. Add to these the tower of Belus, the palaces, the hanging gardens, the dykes, the artificial lakes and canals, etc.; and then a glance at the statue of Nebuchadnezzar makes it dwindle down to quite a pigmy by the side of all these stupendous structures. If we disclaim the allowance of any credit to such accounts, how shall we dispose of the testimony of Herodotus and Ctesias, who both visited Babylon, and report from personal observation? Nothing can be more true or timely than the remark of the sober and judicious Heeren, (Ideen, etc. I. 2. s. 170): "The circle of our own experience cannot, as a matter of course, furnish us with the measure of that, which, in other countries, in a different climate, and in different circumstances, is possible. Do not the Egyptian pyramids, the Chinese wall, and the rock-temple at Elephante, mock as it were at our criticism, which arrogates to itself the power of defining the limits to which the united power of whole nations can go?" In accordance with the spirit of this, the most recent classical critics of name seem to be united in the opinion, that the more Herodotus and some other ancient historians are studied and understood, the higher will their credit stand. It is not seemly, then, for us to assume a lofty air of skepticism, in respect to such an obelisk-statue as that of Nebuchadnezzar. The like is still before our eyes, and is beyond denial. Look at Cleopatra's Needle; at Pompey's pillar; at the obelisk standing in Heliopolis, near Cairo, sixty feet in height, more than 2000 years old, of one solid mass of stone, cut out of the quarry at Syene, i. e. at the cataracts of the Nile, and floated down some 600 or 700 miles to its present locality, and there erected. Will Prof. Lengerke sarcastically suggest here, too, that we have another "story of a certain Benjamin?" This last obelisk, moreover, is only six feet and a half square at the base; and yet it stands, and has more than 2000 years stood, firm. The image of Nebuchadnezzar was nine feet at the base, and was one third higher than the one at Heliopolis. Are not the proportions then of the height and base of the Babylonian, altogether homogeneous with the Egyptian obelisks? These range from four and a half to twelve feet wide at the base, and from fifty to one hundred and fifty in height. There they are, too, at this very moment, palpable, visible, and of one solid mass — not a dream or phantasy of some wonder-loving Jew in the time of the Maccabees, as Lengerke would fain persuade us, in respect to the passage under examination. If the image erected by Nebuchadnezzar was so large as to exceed all credi-

loe's Herod. II. p. 229. But all this amount of gold in Belus's statue, (if indeed it were really all of gold), is only one item in the list which Ctesias gives. He states that the statue of Rhea weighed 1000 talents; that of Mylitta, i. e. Venus, 800; a table for the idols, 500; two drinking cups, 300; two censers, 60; one bowl for Jupiter, 1200; for the other two statues also one each, 1200 together; amount of the whole, 5,500 talents = 77,800,000 dollars.

bility, what must be said of one which Asseman mentions, in his Biblioth. Orient. II.? The passage runs thus: "In the year 866, the idol of the sun in Heliopolis, a city of Phenicia, was struck with lightning, and together with the temple was reduced to ashes. It is said that it was 150 cubits high, and 75 broad."

In truth, if the account before us is so monstrously incredible as some critics of a recent class assert; if the incongruities are so staring, and in such high relief; then what kind of a witling was he, who wrote the book of Daniel at so late a period? Did he hope to make the impression that the book was true, or that it was false? Doubtless the former. How then could he write such incongruities and monstrosities, that would wither away at the scornful rebuke of even common sense, not to speak of searching criticism? In short, in whatever light we look at the matter before us, we cannot well do otherwise, in respect to the difficulties alleged against it, than say to the latest advocate of *liberal criticism* on the book of Daniel, to whom I have just now referred, — *Non in rebus, sed in teipso.* A deeper acquaintance with antiquity, and more of generous candor, would help very much to cure the malady of such skepticism.

To take leave (for it is time) of this protracted discussion, I would merely remark, that as the great plain of Mesopotamia abounds not in any quarries of stone, it is scarcely probable that the mass of Nebuchadnezzar's image was of this material. All the ruins of Babylon, with very few exceptions, are of sun-baked and of burnt bricks. It is barely possible, that such an obelisk of stone might have been floated down the Euphrates, from the Armenian mountains. But in respect to making fast a wooden structure, so slender, and of such a height, no imaginable serious difficulty could exist, any more than our ship-wrights now experience, in making firm masts that are higher, and have all the pressure of the sails to bear, when urged by vehement winds. A single tree of fir, or cedar, or cypress, could easily have been found in the Armenian mountains, which might be set very deeply and fastened in the ground, and running up through the centre of the obelisk, keep it secure in its position. Had the idol been of *stone*, it would not probably have been either gilt or plated. All Egyptian analogy is against this. But if it were of wood, and was surmounted by either an image of the natural sun, or a supposed resemblance of Belus wrought as a bust, and if the whole was then gilded or plated with gold, the appearance would be striking, and at least in harmony with the pride and superstition of Nebuchadnezzar.

As to the *time* when the erection of this image took place, nothing definite is stated in the text, and we are cast upon conjecture. In all probability, the last time that Nebuchadnezzar invaded Judea (B. C. 588), destroyed the government, "rifled all the vessels of the house of God, great and small, and the treasures of the house of the Lord, and the treasures of the king and of his princes," might have afforded him the occasion and the means of erecting the idol in question, as the monument of his victories, and as a token of gratitude to Belus. Tyrant as he was, he was strongly tinctured with heathen superstition. Subsequent to the first siege and capture of Jerusalem, Nebuchadnezzar, after rifling the temple in part of its furniture, "brought the vessels into the treasure house of his god," Dan. 1: 2. When, at the last invasion, he had obtained possession of the treasures of the temple, king, and nobles, might he not have easily erected his new idol? And is not this a probable occurrence at the period in question? The return from the *first* invasion was too early for the transactions before us. As to wealth, it should be remembered, that the father of Nebuchadnezzar had helped to rifle and destroy Nineveh; and that Nebuchadnezzar himself had overrun and rifled most of hither Asia and Egypt, before he went to Babylon to assume the crown. Lengerke should look well to his own position, when he treats with a sneer the opinion, that the matter before us bears the impression of *history*, and not of *romance*. A romance, one would be apt to think, would have given a different view of a merely imaginary idol, and taken care to make it more analogous to those in the temple of Belus, as described by Herodotus and Ctesias.

Some have supposed the *statue of Belus*, mentioned by these authors, was the same which is brought to view in the text before us. But that was placed in the temple of Belus; this, on the plain of Dura, (some circular intervale, as the word דּוּרָא imports), near to Babylon. Another *Dura* there was, on the Tigris; and still another on the Euphrates, near the mouth of the Chaboras; see Lex. Neither of the two latter could be the one in question. The word בִּקְעַת, const., does not mean merely a *valley*, in our limited sense, but a *plain, extended flats*. So in Gen. 11: 2, where the same country is meant as that afterwards occupied by Babylon. *Province of Babylon* shows that the writer means to say, that the statue was not erected within the city.

---

(2) And Nebuchadnezzar the king sent to assemble the Satraps, deputy governors [or praefects], overseers, chief judges, treasurers, the learned in law, counsellors, and all officers of provinces, to come to the dedication of the image which king Nebuchadnezzar had set up.

After שְׁלַח *sent*, some word is of course implied which indicates *messengers*, i. e. agents employed to give publicity to the summons of the king. — מִכְנַשׁ, Peal Inf. — אֲחַשְׁדַּרְפְּנַיָּא, emph. form, *satraps;* this and most of the names of civil officers that follow, appear to be wholly or partly derived from the northern Zend or Parsee language. The most probable etymology of the words is inserted in the Lex., and it would be needless to repeat it here. One thing, in respect to these names in general, must be obvious, viz. that in European governments, and in ours, there are no officers which exactly correspond; so that an exact verbal translation in this case would be as impossible as it is literally to translate *tribunus, consul*, and the like. I have employed *Satrap*, because the word is now somewhat common among us, in treating of oriental history. The basis of this appellation is plainly discernible in the four letters (שדרף) of the word above. It designates the governor of a whole region, province, or country; and frequently the office amounted to a *Vice-regency* over the whole of a tributary nation. It may well be compared with the modern office of *Pasha* under the Turkish government. Officers of this class of course stood next to the king in dignity; and so they are here naturally named first. — סִגְנַיָּא doubtless designates here the civil officers next in rank to the Satraps. I have rendered it *deputy-governors*, intending to designate by this term those officers in different portions of country within a *Satrapy*, who acted in lieu of the chief governor or Satrap, *pro re nata*, and whose business it was to see that all went on in an orderly manner. Hävernick (p. 99) supposes it to designate an overseer of the State-council or Magi, because in Dan. 2: 48 it is applied in such a sense to Daniel. But I take the generic idea of the word סְגַן to be that of *praefect, vicarius* [sc. principis]; and so it is often applied to the Jewish nobles and overseers, in the time of Ezra. Ezr. 9: 2. Neh. 2: 16. 4: 8, 13. 5: 7. 7: 5. 12: 40. There is scarcely room for doubt, that the word designates the order of civil officers in the provinces next to that of Satraps. — פַּחֲוָתָא, emph. pl. of פֶּחָה = פַּחָה with Dagh. f. implied in the ח. The etymology is somewhat uncertain; see Lex. It designates an *overseer* or *praefect* of a small province, and is of nearly the same meaning, to all appearance, as the preceding word. Still, however, it probably designated a class of officers, who might not indeed be unlike to the סִגְנַיָּא as to rank, but whose duties at least were specifically different. — Of אֲדַרְגָּזְרַיָּא there can be little or no doubt. This word is apparently *Semitic;* for אֲדַר means *magnificence*, and גְּזַר signifies *to cut, cut off, decide, decree.* So we have, somewhat plainly, the *supreme Judges* of the king's court. — גְּדָבְרַיָּא, put for and = גִּזְבְרַיָּא, (ד for ז), compounded, as it would seem, of a Semitic root and a Persian termination, see Lex. That it means *treasurers*, there is no good room for doubt. Comp. גְּנַז in Lex. — דְּתָבְרַיָּא, emph. pl. from דְּתָבָר, compounded also of the Semitic דָּת, *law, statute*, and the Persian formative termination *-bar.* The meaning is plain, viz. *jurisconsulti, men learned in law.* — תִּפְתָּיֵא, emph. pl., of Semitic origin again, like the Arabic مُفْتِى *Mufti, counsellor*, one who responds to questions in law, or respecting right; comp. the illustration in the Lex. — שִׁלְטֹנֵי, pl. const., embraces all officers not specifically named, to whom any considerable power or sway was committed, i. e. public civil functionaries or magistrates; but in this connection it plainly does not comprise those of the lowest or of the lower classes, inasmuch as these would add no important honor to the dedication-feast; and their presence, moreover, in the provinces was necessary for the preservation of peace and good order, while the superior officers were absent. — לְמֵתֵא, Inf. of אֲתָא, with the initial quiescent א dropped in the writing. — *To the dedication of the image;* for by this ceremony of consecration or dedication, the image became a public and authenticated object of national worship. No new god is mentioned as introduced by Nebuchadnezzar on this occasion; nor is this probable. The new image, however, which may probably be regarded as a votive offering on the part of the king, was more imposing and conspicuous in appearance than any that had been made before. Pride, exultation, superstition, and love of display, all combined to produce this new colossal structure. — הֲקֵים = אֲקִים Aph. of קוּם, with a Hebraizing form as to the consonants; for vowels, see § 10. 4. 2.

In respect to the *great assemblage* of officers, on this occasion, comp. a similar transaction in Est. 1: 3 seq., (probably a general consultation by Xerxes, previous to his invasion of Greece). The objection made to both these accounts, viz. that such a desertion of their posts by so many officers, would occasion disorder and revolt in the provinces, can have but little weight. All the governments of the East were *military;* and everywhere the soldiers remained under their active officers, to quell any disturbance. Such a warrior as Nebuchadnezzar knew well how to manage matters of this kind. The efficient part of the military *regime* probably remained at their posts. One object of such an extensive assemblage doubtless was *display;* but the principal one seems to have been, a determination to make the worship of the new idol imposing and universal.

(3) Then were assembled the satraps, deputy-governors, overseers, chief judges, treasurers, the learned in law, counsellors, and all officers of provinces, for the dedication of the image which Nebuchadnezzar the king had set up; and they stood before the image which Nebuchadnezzar had set up.

קָאְמִין = קָיְמִין, § 22. 1 ad fin. — לָקֳבֵל, lit. *at the before,* used as a preposition, and translated *before.*

(4) And a herald proclaimed aloud: To you, ye people, nations, and tongues, is it commanded;

כָּרוֹזָא, emph.; the Nom. abs. כָּרוֹז = כַּרּוֹז, § 28. b. 6. — קָרֵא, Part., denoting continued or repeated action. — בְּחָיִל, in pause, lit. *with strength* or *might;* which, when applied to the *voice,* of course means *with loudness,* i. e. a herald loudly proclaimed. — אָמְרִין, lit. *do they command,* for אֲמַר in Chald. often means *command;* see on 1: 3. An indef. or impersonal verb is expressed by the 3d sing. or plur., § 49. 3. a. b; and more generally requires to be translated by the *passive* voice; see ib. — עַמְמַיָּא, emph. pl.; the Hebrew, instead of עַמִּים sometimes has עֲמָמִים; the Aramaean does not write the first מ by a Dagh. f., as is usual in most derivates of ע״ע, but presents the form in full; for the usual formation of nouns which double the middle radical, see § 28. b.

(5) At the time when ye shall hear the sound of the cornet, pipe, harp, sambuk, psaltery, bagpipe, and all kinds of music, ye shall fall down and worship the golden image, which Nebuchadnezzar the king hath set up.

קָל = Heb. קוֹל. — קַרְנָא, emph. of קֶרֶן, a Hebraizing Segholate, lit. *horn*, and so *cornet* (from *cornu*) well translates it. We might compare, for illustration, our *French horn*. — מַשְׁרוֹקִיתָא (from שרק *to whistle*) designates a *shrill piping instrument* like a fife. The Greeks have transferred the word to their language, e. g. σύριγξ, σύριγ, σύριγμα, συρίγγιον, and hence the verbs συρίζω and συρίσσω, the noun denoting the *reed-pipe* or *Pan-flute*. That it was a shrill, loud instrument, is clear, since שָׁרַק is employed to denote the giving of the signal sound for the assemblage of distant troops, Isa. 5: 26. *Fife* comes the nearest to it, perhaps, of any instrument in use among us. — קִיתָרֹס, the vowels here, and in vs. 7, 10 below, belong to the Qeri orthography, viz. קִתְרֹס. The Kethibh however is preferable, which would read קִיתָרֹס, seemingly the Greek κίθαρις, *harp* or *guitar*; for the word seems to be, of itself, rather generic than specific, and to designate stringed instruments beaten with the fingers. The allegation, that the word is a *Greek* one, in Daniel, appears to have little solid foundation. Strabo seems to have settled this question (x. 3): κιθάραν Ἀσιᾶτιν ῥάσσων, *beating the Asiatic harp*; and Lengerke himself confesses the probability, that both the Greek and Chald. word comes from the Persian *Sitareh*, which means *a six-stringed instrument*. — סַבְּכָא, in vs. 10, 15, written שַׂבְּכָא (*Sin* for *Samekh*), was a triangular instrument, furnished with strings, and beaten with the fingers or a plectrum. Athenaeus (Deip. iv. 23) says: Σύρων εὕρημά φησιν εἶναι, i. e. *one says it is a Syrian invention*. The variations of the Greek orthography show that it was probably a foreign word, about the manner of spelling which there was no fixed rule, e. g. σαμβίκη, σαμβύκη, ζαμβίκη, ζαμβύκη, ἰαμβύκη, and (abridged) σάμμα. Not having any instrument among us that specifically resembles it, I have felt obliged merely to *transfer* the word, as we do *shekel*, *epha*, *bath*, and many others of the Hebrew. It resembles the *khanoon* of Cairo, as described by Mr. Lane in his well known work, *Modern Egypt*, II. p. 71. — פְּסַנְתֵּרִין, *psaltery* or *dulcimer*, which translation, however, explains nothing, inasmuch as it merely designates an instrument, the music of which was accompanied by the voice of the player; and of these there were many kinds. In Egypt they have an instrument evidently of the same name, سَنْطِير, *santir*, (Mr. Lane, p. 77, writes it *sunteer*), which is a species of the dulcimer, is stringed, and is beaten with two small sticks. This also resembles the *khanoon*.

Those who advocate the *late* authorship of the book of Daniel, say with great confidence, that the writer must have lived where he became acquainted with Greek, since this word is plainly the Greek ψαλτήριον, the *l* being exchanged for *n* in the Chaldee — an exchange which was very common; see in Lex. under ל and נ. But although there can be little room to doubt, that both the Greek and Chaldee words are substantially the same, yet it is not quite so obvious from what language the *original* name was derived. In the Chaldee פְּסַנְתֵּר, (= the Egyptian *Santir*), one does not see why the נ should have been inserted instead of the ל which would correctly represent the Greek form; for ל is as congruous as נ after the ס; while in the Greek form, it is easy to see how the Chaldee נ might be changed to λ, because thus the word would bear a seeming relation to the verb ψάλλω. In other words, the Greeks had an evident motive to make the change in question: the Chaldee writer had none. I should not hesitate then to say, that the evidence preponderates in favor of an origin *not* Greek, were it not that the first syllable פְּסַנְ- looks like an attempt to translate the Greek ψ in ψαλτήριον, and such a syllable seems to be one which is not of the usual Semitic formation. But as the *P* in Egyptian words is a masc. preformative, (as in פַּרְעֹה), the Arabians in Egypt have dropped it, and now sound the word *santir*, while the Chaldeans retained it. We may account for the Chaldee form, without any reference to the Greek language, by supposing the name to have come from Egypt. But be all this as it may, Greek instruments of music, with their names, might easily have wandered to Babylon, the great metropolis of all the commerce between the East and the West.

Hävernick suggests for the word פְּסַנְתֵּרִין the etymology of פַּס, *extremity* (of the hand), and נתר *to strike, beat;* which name thus explained may seem at first view to fit the instrument in question well enough, for it might be stricken with the hand. To this suggestion Lengerke has replied by an argument very common in his book, viz. a conspicuous [!]. There can be no doubt, however, that פַּס means the *extremity of the hand* (Dan. 5: 5, 24); but נְתַר means something more than *to strike*, for it is applied to *striking off* leaves from a tree (Dan. 4: 11), *to setting loose* captives (Ps. 105: 20), to *loosening* the hand by putting it into action, etc., (Job 6: 9). To *beat* a stringed instrument seems to be quite another kind of action. There is ingenuity enough, however, in this etymology, to deserve something more than an *exclamation point* in the way of answer. From the Egyptian name *santir*, now in use among the Arabs in Cairo, we may well argue the probability that the instrument was *Egyptian* in its origin and name. If so, the ending ִ-ין is *plural*, and not an imitation, in the sing., of the Greek ending -ιον, as Lengerke and others have supposed. That the other nouns are of the *sing.*, is no conclusive argument for the sing. here; for if, among the Chaldeans, the name, from some particular cause (as in many other cases), assumed a plural form (as it surely might do), that would of course be here employed. So in Hebrew we have שָׁמַיִם, but the plur. is not necessary nor usual in Arabic.

סוּמְפֹּנְיָה, in v. 15 is written סוּמְפּוֹנְיָה, and in v. 10 סִיפֹּנְיָה. If the word be of *Greek* origin, the latter orthography (which the Syriac also exhibits, and which agrees with σίφων, *reed, tube*), would be sufficiently descriptive ; for the instrument was a *tube*. If however the Greek *συμφωνία* (*harmony*) is the etymon of the Chaldee name, this would be still more exactly descriptive ; for the instrument, (still used in Egypt, and called *summarah* or *zummarah*, Lane, ut sup. II. p. 81), is a *double* one, giving two symphonious sounds. Mr. Lane has given us a drawing of it, II. p. 82. It is very common in the concert songs of the boatmen on the Nile. Polybius (Frag. xxvi, xxxi, Tom. IV. Schweigh.) describes Antiochus Epiphanes as "going to feasts with horn and *symphony* (*συμφωνίας*) ;" and tells us that the same instrument gave the signal for that king, when he entered upon a contest in the games. The Hebrew interpreters translate the word into their language by עוּגָב, and explain it as meaning a *double flute* (as in Lane, sup.) or *shalm*. If it is derived from a Semitic root, the ending ־יָה may be of a fem. adjective nature, and thus may be as it were merely formative. In Asia Minor, the same instrument, as seems probable, is called *Sambonga ;* in Italy, *Zambogna*. That it was a *wind-instrument*, there can be no good room to doubt; but whether *bag-pipe* is the best translation of the word, may perhaps be doubted.

Fall down and worship, both combined, show the thorough homage or worship demanded for the new idol. *Prostration* is both a preparatory act for worship, and one which accompanies worship itself.

Mr. Lane, however, tells us that one species of the *zumarah* "is a rude kind of bag-pipe, . . . its bag being a small goat's skin." p. 83. I have, therefore kept the word *bag-pipe* in the translation. — The assumption that the word סִיפֹּנְיָא is the genuine form, and the derivation of it from סְפַן, *contignavit*, (so C. B. Michaelis), will hardly bear. *To plank* or *timber over* anything, corresponds not at all to the form of the instrument. If the orthography סִיפֹּנְיָא be adopted, *σίφον* seems to be the natural etymon. On the whole, the probability of a *Greek* origin here seems to be somewhat strong. But the reasoning from it, by Bleek, Lengerke, and others, that the writer borrowed the name from the Greek circle in which he lived, seems to manifest an eagerness to make much of a very small circumstance. How comes it, one may fairly ask, that the writer, among the names of all his civil and military officers, has not one of *Greek* origin ? How comes it, that in the present case, only one of all the instruments named has, on the whole, a probable Greek origin ? How did a writer in Palestine, so late as 140 or 150 B. C., become so familiar with all these names in our context, (Assyro-Medo-Persico-Semitic names too), which, as a mere Hebrew of such a late period, he would be little likely to know ? Then as to the *intercourse* of the East and the West — had not Sennacherib overrun a large portion of Asia Minor and Egypt, more than a century before Daniel lived ? Does not Berosus relate that he even built *Tarsus* in Cilicia ? Did not Nebuchadnezzar himself overrun most of those regions, before he took the crown ? And as to *commercial intercourse* — Babylon was, long before Nebuchadnezzar's time, the metropolis of the world. That a musical instrument, with its name, should have been transferred from Grecian countries to Babylon, in this state of affairs, before Daniel came upon the stage, is a thing so probable and so very feasible, that nothing can be made out on any such ground as this, against the ordinary date of the book of Daniel. The whole thing is insignificant, as an argument. It cannot amount to a grain of sand, in the balance by which the time of writing the book is to be adjusted; for nothing can be more probable, than that such a luxurious and pleasure-loving city as Babylon, should seek on all sides for every means of increasing gratification to the eye and ear. Foreign musical instruments would be sought after with the same, or with the like, avidity which is manifested in all great cities of the present day, in respect to objects of the same nature.

(6) And whosoever shall not fall down and worship, at that very moment shall be cast into the midst of the furnace of burning fire.

יִפֵּל, Fut. (ֵ) of נְפַל, § 18. ad fin. — שַׁעֲתָא, emph. of שָׁעָה, which has שַׁ (not the normal שִׁ with Dagh. f. after it) because of the Gutt., § 29. 6 *c*. Literally שָׁעָה, from שְׁעָא, *to look*, means *look, wink, twinkling of an eye*, (not *hour* in the English sense). So I have translated it *moment*, (ad sensum). The בַּהּ (*in it*) is the usual anticipative pronoun, which strengthens the *definiteness* of the whole expression = *in that very moment;* § 43. 6. *b*. This special idiom is much more frequent still in the Syriac. — יִתְרְמֵא, Ithpeal, p. 72. — לְגוֹא, const. of גַּו (*gav*), for in the const. state the ו becomes quiescent, and the word is written גוֹא or גוֹ; comp. מָוֶת, const. מוֹת in Heb. — אַתּוּן, root תְּנַן *to smoke;* for אַתְנוּן with א as a form. prefix, see § 28. c. 16. Comp. in verbs ע״ע, יִדֹּק for יִדְקֹק, Gramm. p. 63. — יָקִידְתָּא, fem. Part. of יְקַד, the second syllable being written with a superfluous (י), probably to denote, in the unpointed text, that it was to be pronounced with *Hhireq* (short) instead of Seghol. The masc. Part. is יָקֵד. In vs. 23 and 26, the word is written יָקִדְתָּא. That *burning* was not an unusual punishment in the East, is sufficiently known. As to the Persians, see Brissonius De Reg. Pers. II. cap. 216. So the Hebrews, 2 Sam. 12:31, comp. Matt. 5:22. Jer. 29:22 mentions a certain "Zedekiah and Ahab, whom the king of Babylon *roasted in the fire*." This then was a favorite method of punishment with Nebuchadnezzar; and Chardin (who was in Persia, 1671—77) relates, that in a time of scarcity, two furnaces of fire were kept burning a whole month, in order to consume such as exacted more than the lawful price for food; Voyages, VI, p.118. At all events, it agrees well with the character of Nebuchadnezzar, to threaten such a punishment; comp. 2: 5. 3: 29.

(7) Because of this, at the very time when all the nations heard the sound of the cornet, pipe, harp, sambuk, psaltery, and all kinds of music — all these nations, peo-

ple, and tongues, falling down, worshipped the golden image which Nebuchadnezzar the king had set up.

The Participles נָפְּלִין and סָגְדִין (instead of verbs) are well adapted to denote the continuance and repetition of religious prostration. The סוּמְפֹּנְיָה is omitted in this list of the music; like to what we have seen before, in respect to some of the classes of the Magi. Omissions of such a nature are a characteristic of the writer's style. For בֵּהּ זִמְנָא, see § 43. 6. *b*.

(8) On account of this, at the very same time, men who were Chaldeans drew near, and made accusation against the Jews.

קְרִבוּ, 3 plur. Peal, see in § 12. 2. 1. — גֻּבְרִין, pl. irreg. of גְּבַר, with form as if from גֻּבְרָא. — אֲכַלוּ קַרְצֵיהוֹן, lit. *devoured the pieces of them*, a figurative expression indicating *calumny, slander, malignant accusation*, etc.; the noun pl., with pl. suff., is from קְרַץ. For the pron. suff. anticipative, § 43. 6. *b*. — דִּי a mere sign of the Gen., § 56. 1. The form of expression here is not widely different from the figurative sense of *rodere, mordere, dente carpere*, etc., in Latin. The Arabians express the same idea by the phrase, *eating the flesh* of a brother, etc. The principal cause of the accusation was probably a malignant jealousy towards the young and aspiring Hebrews, who were already invested with desirable offices. Possibly superstition, or (last and least of all) loyalty, might have been the moving cause of their conduct.

(9) They addressed Nebuchadnezzar the king, and said: O king, live forever!

עֲנוֹ, Peal, p. 72. The sentence is continued by a participle, אָמְרִין, used in the same manner as a verb. This mixed construction is frequent in Heb. and Chaldee.

(10) Thou, O king, didst establish a decree, that every man, who should hear the sound of the cornet, pipe, harp, sambuk, psaltery, bag-pipe, and all kinds of music, should fall down and worship the golden image;

Here the vowels in סיפֹּנְיָה belong to the marginal Qeri, סוּמְפּוֹנְיָה; see on v. 5.

(11) And whosoever would not fall down and worship, he should be cast into the midst of the furnace of burning fire.

The repetition of the decree in v. 6 is, as usual, very close and exact; and we often find the like in Homer, and other ancient writers. Only the circumstance, בֵּהּ שַׁעֲתָא is omitted.

(12) There are men, Jews, whom thou hast appointed over the business of the province of Babylon, Shadrach, Meshach, and Abednego — those men pay no regard

to thee, O king; thy gods they do not serve, and the golden image which thou hast set up, they do not worship.

For (ָ) in גֻּבְרִין, see on v. 8. — דִּי ... יָתְהוֹן, *whom*, דִּי is like the Hebrew אֲשֶׁר followed by a pronoun, which gives to it a relative sense. יָת = אֶת of the Heb., and is a mere sign of the Acc. For the seq., see on 2: 48. — לָא שָׂמוּ ... טְעֵם *pay no respect* or *regard*, lit. *do not place* or *fix the mind.* — עֲלָיךְ is noted in the Qeri as having a superfluous *Yodh.* But עַל with a suff. often assumes, as here, the plur. form, and the Kethibh is the preferable reading. — לֵאלָהָיךְ, Acc. pl. with suff., for לְ see § 56. 2. Here again the Qeri repudiates the plural, and marks (י) as superfluous. But wrongly. The malignant courtiers doubtless mean to accuse the Hebrews of impiety toward the Babylonian gods in general, as well as towards the new idol. The first syllable (לֵא־) is a *contract* form of לֶאֱ, as usual.

(13) Then Nebuchadnezzar, in a furious rage, commanded to bring Shadrach, Meshach, and Abednego; then those men were brought before the king.

חֱמָא is like nouns in § 28. a. 2. Winer has neglected to mark it in its proper place, viz. § 29. 6. Both nouns lit. thus: *in rage and fury*, i. e. in a furious rage. — לְהַיְתָיָה, Aph. Inf. of אֲתָא, with ה for א prefix formative. — לְשַׁדְרַךְ, לְ before the *Acc.* again. — הֵיתָיוּ, a form *sui generis*, which seems to be a *passive* of the Aph. הַיְתִי from אֲתָא, and to correspond with the Heb. Hophal in meaning. See Lex.; and see also a fem. form of the verb which is of the same nature, in 6: 18. It would be difficult to find analogies for the pointing of these forms. If it is correct, they must belong to *dialect* in a narrow sense.

(14) Nebuchadnezzar addressed them and said: Is it of design, Shadrach, Meshach, and Abednego, that ye do not serve my gods, nor worship the golden image that I have set up?

אָמַר, Part. — In הַצְדָא, the הַ is interrogative. If the noun comes from the verb צְדָא, *insidiari*, it would seem to intimate *wily design;* which meaning is not improbable. See other conjectures in Leng. in loc. — אִיתֵיכוֹן, i. e. אִיתַי (*is*) with pl. form, and suff. constituting its subject; both are united with the participle that follows; § 47. 1. *b.* The king, seemingly with more than usual moderation, first inquires into the truth of the accusation. He probably suspected the accusers of envious motives, and was desirous of sparing these Hebrews on whom he had bestowed special favors. In הֲקֵימֶת, the final syllable would regularly have a Tseri (ֵ), but in a closed syllable, this is occasionally shortened into (ֶ), see p. 48, under *a*.

(15) Now if ye are ready, that, at the time when ye shall hear the sound of the cornet, pipe, harp, sambuk, psaltery, and bag-pipe, and all kinds of music, ye will fall down and worship the image which I have made — but if ye will not worship, in that very moment ye shall be cast into the midst of a furnace of burning fire; and who is that god which will deliver you out of my hand?

The like *σιώπησις* we have in Ex. 32: 32; but Zech. 6: 15. Jer. 12: 16, 17. 1 Sam. 12: 14, 15, referred to by Leng., are of another tenor. In Homer (Il. I. 135 seq.) is a case of the same nature. Comp. also Thucyd. III. 3. IV.13. A plain case of the same nature is in Luke13: 9. עֲתִידִין דִּי . . . תִפְּלוּן, the first is a plur. adj. from עֲתִיד. The דִּי that follows, belongs to the subsequent תִפְּלוּן 2 plur. Fut., in the office of the conjunctive *that.* It would be an equally correct version, as to the sense, to transfer עֲתִידִין and put it immediately before the verb, and then render it *adverbially* thus: *If ye will readily fall down*, etc. But I have endeavored to imitate, with some good degree of exactness here, the *form* of expression in the original. — After the words *which I have made*, there is a *σιώπησις*, the king suppressing the declaration of טָב, *it is well*, or something equivalent to this. So all the ancient versions; and so Junius, De Wette, and most others. Hävernick: "If ye will hear . . . then shall ye fall down," etc. Inadmissible, because עֲתִיד is not appropriate to such a conditional sentence, nor is such a sentence appropriate to the feelings of the king. But the *threat*, at the end of the next clause, comes out in full; and the *antithesis* to the preceding clause is made plain by the הֵן לָא at the beginning of the second clause. It is natural to suppose, that the king discerned a *refusal* in the looks of the accused, which, as it kindled his rage, led him to suppress the טָב he was about to utter, and hasten to the threat. — *Who is that god*, etc., is designed to give efficiency to the threat, by suggesting the impossibility of preventing its execution. Had the king reflected on the power of that God who had revealed secrets to Daniel, he might have hesitated to utter a challenge so audacious. "Furious rage" however rarely reflects, but is ever prone to threaten. Altogether like to this was Sennacherib's boasting and challenging; see Isa. 37: 10 seq. 2 K. 18: 30—35. 19: 10. This whole matter, with the words uttered, is very graphic, and presents us with some characteristics of oriental despots altogether genuine. In יְשֵׁיזְבִנְכוֹן we have a kind of pluriliteral form, or at least an *unusual* conjugation, § 14. Coming from שְׁזַב, it is formed like a *Poel*, or rather a *Päël*, where the Dagh. f. would be normally written in the ז, but here it goes into a Quiescent with a compensative long vowel (ֵי); hence שֵׁיזִב = שֵׁיזְיב instead of שַׁזֵּב. The penult syllable (בְנְ) is shortened because it loses the accent, which rests on the ultimate. — יְדָי, in pause for יְדַי.

(16) Shadrach, Meshach, and Abednego, answered king Nebuchadnezzar, and said: We are not under any necessity to answer thee a word in respect to this matter.

חַשְׁחִין, Part. of חֲשַׁח, חַ for the regular חָ because of the Gutt.; lit. *we are not necessitated.* — לַהֲתָבוּתָךְ, Aph. Inf. of תּוּב (p. 69), with the ending וּת–, because of the suff., p. 56. e. The *matter* about which they declined to give any answer, was Nebuchadnezzar's threat in the preceding declaration. There is a difference of opinion among critics, whether דְּנָה should be joined with פִּתְגָם, or be separated from it, as the *distinctive* accent upon it indicates that it should be. Grammar allows either method of construction. Out of deference to the accents, I have followed the latter method; which may be done, for פִּתְגָם = דָּבָר, and *to answer thee a word* or *by a word*, makes good sense. In case the first method of construction should be preferred, then one may regard דְּנָה as placed *before* its noun, in order to indicate that it is emphatic.

Lengerke, as usual, turns this account of the demeanor of the three Hebrews, into an argument for the *lateness* of the book. It savors, as he thinks, only of the superstition of the Maccabaean age, when the Jews thought it a glory to suffer martyrdom rather than sacrifice to idols at the bidding of Antiochus Epiphanes. "We find," says he (p. 132), "a like speech in 2 Macc. 7: 2, although somewhat less pert (kecke)." Vain, he asserts, is the defence of the young Jews by Hengstenberg and Hävernick. On the other hand, Lengerke accuses these martyrs of an uncivil silence, on this occasion, and of "precipitating themselves inconsiderately (leichtsinnig) into danger." Was it so, then, that a pious Jew could hold himself at liberty to equivocate on such an occasion, and renounce his obedience to the two commands which stand at the head of the Decalogue? Is he therefore a simpleton and a fanatic, who would cast himself on divine Providence in such a case, and leave the consequences to God, while he persevered in the plain path of duty? If so, what shall we say of the worthies named in Heb. xi.? What of those "who were beheaded for the testimony of Jesus and for the word of God, who refused to worship the beast and his image?" Rev. 20: 4. The writer of the Apocalypse counts such peculiarly "blessed and holy, inasmuch as they have part in the *first* resurrection," Rev. 20: 6. Are not the very Hebrews now in question placed among such worthies in Heb. 11: 34? But enough. All men have united in praising the constancy, the fidelity, and the fearlessness of martyrs in a good cause. Those now before us need no defence from the interpreter. Lengerke has very probably disclosed here his own feelings, and thus virtually told us what he would do on such an occasion. Without calling in question what he would do, we may well be content with the course which the noble Hebrews pursued. Lengerke would have us believe, that such superstition or fanaticism belonged only to the Maccabaean times. What then are we to think of the martyrdom which so many prophets underwent, and which is attributed to the ancient Jews, both in the Old Test. and the New? And is it in any measure to be credited, that the Maccabaean times were the only ones, which produced men who were ready to expose themselves to death, rather than deny or dishonor the living God?

(17) If our God whom we serve is able to deliver us, from the furnace of burning fire and from thy hand, O king, he may deliver.

הֵן is here rendered by the ancient Versions *for;* by most moderns, *ecce, lo!* No doubt the word has sometimes such a meaning. But here it seems plainly to be the antithesis of הֵן לָא, *if not,* in v. 18. The meaning, after all, is one which does not necessarily imply doubt or uncertainty. The sense which I take to be conveyed, might be expressed thus: "If it so be that there is a God able, etc." The amount of the matter then is, that instead of directly and positively asserting that God will deliver them, they modestly suggest to the angry tyrant, that this may be so, and that deliverance is possible, both from the furnace and from the power of the king himself. If we suppose, on the other hand, the announcement to be *positive,* i. e. in the shape of an absolute prediction, and regard the three Hebrews as divinely assured of escape at this time, much is taken from their constancy and courage. Assurance absolute of safety dispenses with courage in its higher sense. They might have *hoped* for such an issue; they probably did; but it seems not to be improbable, that they were not positively assured of it. Hence the alternative in the next verse, apparently founded on the possibility, or perhaps probability, that they might not escape. This places their courage and constancy in a true light. In the face of danger really apprehended, they remain quiet and firm. On the grounds alleged, we may render יְשֵׁיזִב, at the close of the verse by the *Subj.*, as the form of the Imperf. permits us to do, § 44. 3. c. I have followed the accents in beginning the *after clause* with מִן־אַתּוּן, and not (as Lengerke does) with וּמִן־יְדָךְ. On this ground, the first שֵׁיזָבוּת has no complement expressed, and it may well be translated as absolute, viz. *to accomplish deliverance.*

(18) And if not, be it known to thee, O king, that we shall not serve thy gods, nor worship the golden image which thou hast set up.

לֶהֱוֵא = יֶהֱוֵא, see on 2: 20. — יְדִיעַ, Part. Peil, § 47. 1. — לֵאלָהָיךְ, pl. with suff. p. 35. No. 2. — אִיתָנָא, i. e. אִיתַי with 1st pl. suff. which constitutes its subject, joined with the Part. פָּלְחִין, and used for the Fut., § 47. 1. *b.* The לְ before the noun here, and also before לְצֶלֶם, marks the Acc., § 56. 2. Firmly and plainly, without the least equivocation or apology, the young Hebrews here express their steadfast determination. But the uncontrolled despot of a great empire, as might be expected, could not endure any show even of reluctance to obey his commands, as the sequel will fully declare.

(19) Then Nebuchadnezzar was filled with indignation, and the form of his coun-

tenance was changed in respect to Shadrach, Meshach, and Abednego, and he gave command to heat the furnace seven times more than it was wont to be heated.

צְלֵם, usually *image*, σκία, as above, but here plainly it designates the *appearance* or *form*, *look*, of the countenance. — אַנְפּוֹהִי, suff. plur. of אֲנַף, *facies*. — אֶשְׁתַּנּוֹ, the Kethibh is 3 plur. Ithpaal from שְׁנָא, with שׁ and ת exchanged, p. 40. 5. b, and (ֶ) under the first letter, § 12. 1. 5, i. e. the first syllable has the Syriac punctuation, comp. § 25. 2. If we retain the pl. reading, (with the Kethibh, which written *plene* would be אֶשְׁתַּנִּיו), then the plur. verb agrees with the noun immediately before it, (as often in Hebrew, see Heb. Gramm. § 145. 1); the Qeri here, אֶשְׁתַּנִּי, substitutes the verb sing., so that it may accord with צְלֵם, i. e. the Masorites have conformed the text to what they deemed to be grammatical analogy. I prefer the Kethibh, deeming it to be more probably the original reading. What is meant in this clause clearly is, that the color of Nebuchadnezzar's face and the aspect of it were changed. Passion made him pale, or else highly flushed, (the text does not decide which), and the expression of his visage was ferocious. — עַל, either (as in the version above) *in respect to*, or *on account of*, viz. because of, what Shadrach, Meshach, and Abednego, had said and done. — עָנֵה וְאָמַר, both participles have their complement in לְמֵזֵא etc. It was usual, and still is so, in the East, oftentimes to execute judgment in a capital case upon the spot, and under the king's eye. Hence the command to make immediate preparation for the death that had been threatened. — לְמֵזֵא, contract form of לְמֵאזֵא, Inf. Peal of אֲזָא, first א omitted because it is *quiescent* in the contracted form. — חַד שִׁבְעָה, lit. *one seven*, or *seven-fold*, § 59. 5. *a*. I have translated the phrase by *seven times*, because our idiom requires us to express the idea in this manner. — עַל דִּי, *beyond that which*, or *above what*. — חֲזֵה, Part. Peil of חֲזָא, lit. (the whole phrase) *beyond what had been seen in respect to the heating of it*. The idea is expressed in the version above, in accordance with the idiom that we usually employ. — לְמֵזְיֵהּ, suff. Inf. in Peal, of אֲזָא, contracted as above. When the suff. is appended, the final א of the root becomes movable, and is converted into (י), in order to make the pronunciation more facile. — The command, given in such a style, is altogether in accordance with the passionate character of Nebuchadnezzar. Refined cruelty in putting the condemned to death, is an ordinary expression of savage vengeance. In reality, however, as to the present case, if the augmented fire could have exercised its usual power, the sufferings of the victims would have merely been shortened by the king's command. Boiling rage, however, does not stop to calculate. As to *seven*, it has the usual force of intensity here, for plainly the mere literal meaning is not to be urged.

(20) And he commanded the most powerful men of his army to bind Shadrach, Meshach, and Abednego, in order to cast them into the furnace of burning fire.

גִּבָּרֵי חַיִל, lit. *mighty of strength*, i. e. the strongest, § 58. 2. — בְּחַיְלֵהּ, חַיִל in a derived and secondary sense, *force*, *army*, with a suff. and a pref. prep. The soldiers of his body-guard, who doubtless were men of the character here described, are those to whom this command is directed. — לְכַפָּתָה, Inf. of Aph., with לְ pref. — לְמִרְמֵא, Inf. Peal of רְמָא, ל denoting the design or object in view, as τοῦ before the Inf. in Greek often does.

(21) Then those men were bound in their wide nether garments, their tunics, and their mantles, and their clothing, and were cast into the midst of the furnace of burning fire.

כְּפִתוּ, Part. Peil used as a verb pass., § 13. 2. — בְּסַרְבָּלֵיהוֹן, designates *wide and long pantaloons*, such as are still worn in the East, covering the lower limbs and the hips; see Lex. — פַּטְּישֵׁיהוֹן, the vowels belong to the Qeri, which takes פַּטִּשׁ as the ground form, and makes the pl. פַּטְשֵׁיהוֹן, (like the Syriac). The Kethibh, however, is well enough, and should be read פַּטִּישֵׁיהוֹן, pl. with suff. This means, the under garment of the upper part of the person, = a *tunic*, or *shirt* of full dimensions, but differing in form from ours, and made of various material, according to the condition of the wearer. — As to כַּרְבְּלָתְהוֹן, there can be no doubt. It means the *outer garment*, the *broad mantle*, girded around the body; see Lex. The last noun, לְבוּשֵׁיהוֹן, comprehends all the articles of clothing not before mentioned, and is in apposition with the preceding nouns. — רְמִיו, Part. Peil of רְמָא, § 13. 2. The object of mentioning these articles of clothing, is to indicate the haste with which the execution was urged on, not leaving time for the usual disrobing of the condemned.

(22) On this account, because the command of the king was urgent and the furnace was exceedingly hot, those men who led up Shadrach, Meshach, and Abednego — them did the flame of the fire destroy.

מַחְצְפָה, fem. Part. Aph., which conjugation here means *ursit, properavit*. *Urgent* is our appropriate word — אֵזֵה, Part. Peil, pointed under the א in the Syriac manner (with ֵ), and employed for אֵזֵה. — הַסִּקוּ, Aph. of נְסַק, lit. *caused to ascend*, which I have rendered *led up*. It designates here the leading of the men up to the opening in the top of the furnace, whence the flame and smoke issued. Into this they were to be precipitated. It seems that there could have been but little room, on the top of the furnace, for the executioners to stand outside of the prisoners; otherwise they could easily have kept back and avoided the flames. Thus the unwonted augmentation and fury of the fire occasioned the death of all who came near. This circumstance Lengerke, as usual, attributes to the *romancing* of the author of the book; for, as he regards the matter, by mentioning this, the writer designs to augment the wonder of the reader when he finds the Hebrews to be unharmed. On a like ground of course we must, if consistent, suppose that John relates the raising of Lazarus from the dead; and so of all the other miraculous phenomena related in the N. Test or the Old. As I cannot harmonize with such views, so I can find, at least thus far in the narration before us, no special evidence of any such preconcerted design, as is usually apparent in romance writing. I have imitated the original in the arrangement of the last part of the verse, viz. *those men . . . them,* etc. This is often the manner of expression in Chaldee and Hebrew, where the design is to make any object peculiarly prominent. Comp. § 40. 3. c, where the like usage is noted.

(23) And those three men, Shadrach, Meshach, and Abednego, fell bound into the midst of the furnace of burning fire.

תְּלָתֵּהוֹן, lit. *the threeness of them,* § 59. 1. *b.* — מְכַפְּתִין, *bound,* Part. pass. of Pael. Probably both the hands and feet were bound; for this was usual, in order to prevent either resistance or escape. This may account for it, that the executioners were obliged to approach so near the furnace, (in order to throw the prisoners into it), that they themselves became the victims of its fierceness. That the prisoners escaped death, was of course by miraculous interposition; for the matter cannot by any ingenuity be explained away. We have seen above what Lengerke and Hitzig think of the whole narrative, but specially of that part of it which declares that the fire had no power over the bodies of the young Hebrews. To all who reject entirely the idea of any miraculous or supernatural interposition, such views will of course appear plausible. For myself, I cannot see any satisfactory reason, even in philosophy, for embracing such views; and as to the Scriptures, both of the Old and New Testaments, it is beyond any fair question that they abound in such narrations. With that enlightened disciple of the primitive age of Christianity, whether he be Paul or Apollos, who wrote the Epistle to the Hebrews, I believe, that "the violence of the fire was quenched," Heb. 11: 34. Nothing therefore urges me to make any effort, in order to avoid the plain and simple meaning of the narration before us.

(24) Then Nebuchadnezzar the king was astonished, and rose up in haste; he answered and said to his State-councillors: Did we not cast three men bound into the midst of the fire? They answered and said: Certainly, O king!

בְּהִתְבְּהָלָה, Inf. Ithpeal, with pref. בּ, used as a noun; lit. (as a verb) *in hastening himself.* — לְהַדָּבְרוֹהִי, pl. with suff. That הַדָּבָר comes from

דַּבַּר, *to lead, guide*, etc., (a meaning which the Heb. also has in Kal), can scarcely be doubted, because the etymology gives a meaning so appropriate here. The persons addressed, on this occasion, were evidently those who attended the person of the king, i. e. the royal council. Gesenius thinks the word to be compounded of the Chaldee דַּבְרִין and the Heb. article הַ. But there is no other known case of the like nature in Chaldee. Is it not more probable, that the ה here is a formative prefix (= א), and thus distinguishes דַּבְרִין here from the usual meaning attached to it elsewhere without such formative? The Dagh. f. does not necessarily stand in the way; for we have גַּן, אַגַּן, *garden*, as Maurer remarks; although, since the root here is of the form ע״ע, the two cases are not quite parallel; comp. the Dagh. compensative in the first radical, in the Fut. of verbs ע״ע. Kindred words in Chaldee seem to be מְדַבֵּר *orator*, מְדַבְּרָא, *dux*. Von Bohlen's derivation from the Persian (Symb. p. 26), seems too remote. I prefer to take the ה here, as usual in this book, to be a Hebraizing equivalent for א; and that א prosthetic and formative is sometimes admitted by the Chaldee, see fully confirmed in Gramm. p. 30. e; although the present case is not exactly like to those there produced. A word was probably needed of a form *sui generis*, to distinguish the king's *privy council* from all others whom he might consult; and this seems to be such a word. — רְמֵינָא, the pl. Peal, from רְמֵא. — עָנַיִן, plur. Part. Peal; for this form of plurals (seemingly Dual) in verbs ל״א, see p. 91, Par. VII. a. In such forms the (ׅ) of the plur. ending is omitted in writing, because of the (ׅ) in the end of the root; so one must read *yīn*, not *yĭn*; comp. גּוֹיִם = גּוֹיִּים in Hebrew. — יַצִּיבָא, *an established* or *settled thing* [is it], the fem. adj. being employed as indicating neuter gender or abstract quality. We might translate: *certainty.*

(25) He answered and said: Lo! I see four men unbound, walking in the midst of the fire, and there is no harm to them; and as to the appearance of the fourth — he is like to a son of the gods.

שְׁרַיִן, pl. Part. pass. Peal, of שְׁרָא; for pl. form see v. 24 on עָנַיִן. — מַהְלְכִין, Part. Aph.— וְרֵוֵהּ וגו׳, lit. *and the appearance of him, of the fourth*, רֵו (*rēv*) for רְאֵו, root רְאָה. The suff. here *specificates*, and is pleonastic in our idiom, § 40. 3. *a.* — In רְבִיעָיָא, (–ā-yā), the vowels belong to the Qeri רְבִיעָאָה; the form of the Kethibh is a Hebraizing one, the fem. form being of the masc. gender, § 36. 2. — לְבַר־אֱלָהִין, *to a son of the gods*, in the mouth of Nebuchadnezzar must mean, either a descendant of the gods, or a being of a superior i. e. godlike nature. In other words, Nebuchadnezzar recognizes in the *fourth* the appearance of a supernatural being. Simply this, and nothing more, as I apprehend, can be drawn from the expression; which, in the mouth of an idolatrous polytheist, must convey merely *his* views of beings endowed with a superior nature. How far the expression before us will lead us to decide on the acquaintance of the writer with the sacred mythology of the Babylonians, it might be difficult to determine. Thus much is clear, viz., that all middle and hither Asia believed in gods superior and inferior; that a writer, living anywhere in that region, could hardly fail to be acquainted with this fact; and that the expression before us might easily arise from such knowledge. At all events it cannot well be denied, that Nebuchadnezzar here speaks altogether in accordance with what we know of the Babylonish mythology.

(26) Then Nebuchadnezzar drew near to the door of the furnace of burning fire; he answered and said: Shadrach, Meshach, and Abednego, servants of God most high, go forth and come out! Then Shadrach, Meshach, and Abednego went forth from the midst of the fire.

לִתְרַע, *the door* must have been, of course, a *side-aperture*, by which the furnace was fed, and into which the king could look without danger. — עַבְדוֹהִי, pl. suff., for the use of which see § 40. 3. *a.* — עִלָּיָא, where the Masorites, jealous for the purer Chaldee of the book, have given us a Qeri עִלָּאָה. But the other form is too common here to suppose it not to have been original. — פֻּוקוּ, Imper. of נְפַק. — אֱתוֹ Imper. of אֲתָא. This word is not repeated in the sequel, but נָפְקִין only is employed. It was very natural for Nebuchadnezzar, in his wonder and excitement, to employ *two* imperatives nearly synonymous; for this gives intensity to his command = come out forthwith! In giving the account of their *going out*, one verb of course suffices.

(27) Then were assembled the satraps, the deputy-governors, the overseers, and the privy-councillors of the king; they looked at those men on whose bodies the fire had no power, and not a hair of their heads was singed, and their wide nether garments were not changed, nor had the scent of fire come upon them.

וּמִתְכַּנְשִׁין, וּ *then*, as often in Hebrew. The Part. is in Ithpael, but the Dagh. f. in נ is omitted, as often when the Sheva would be movable. — For the names of officers here, see vs. 2, 24, above. — חָזַיִן asyndic, which, as we everywhere see, is a common characteristic of this book. — בְּגֶשְׁמְהוֹן, sing. with suff. from גְּשֵׁם, (ֶ) under the ג in the suff. form, where we might expect (ִ), indicating that the word belongs to the E class of Segholates. — הִתְחָרַךְ, Ithpael, חָ because the Dagh. is excluded from the ר. שְׁנוֹ, Peal 3 plur. of שְׁנָא. — עֲדָת, Peal 3 fem. of עֲדָא. Mark the gradation here: the body is not burned; the hair is not singed; the lower garments of light stuff are not changed in their appearance; and to crown all, not even the scent of fire has come upon them. Even

Lengerke, while he regards the whole account as romance, is constrained to acknowledge, that "there is a climactic gradation in the language which is almost poetic in its expressions," (p. 141).

(28) Nebuchadnezzar answered and said: Blessed be the God of Shadrach, Meshach, and Abednego, who hath sent his angel and delivered his servants, who trusted in him, and transgressed the commandment of the king, and gave up their bodies, that they might not serve nor worship any god except their God.

אֱלָהֲהוֹן, with suff. intensive and anticipative, § 40. 3. *a.* — מַלְאֲכֵהּ, ־ֵהּ suff. — שֵׁיזִב, see on v. 15. — הִתְרְחִצוּ, 3 plur. Ithpeal, with (־ְ) under the second radical ח, p. 49. 2. — עֲלוֹהִי, i. e. עַל with a plur. suff., as is usual, § 38. 2. *b.* — שַׁנִּיו, 3 pl. Pael, lit. *changed,* but this, when predicated of a subject and not of the lawgiver or sovereign, must of course mean *transgress.* So in Ezra 6: 11. — גֶּשְׁמֵיהוֹן, as it ought to be pointed, in accordance with the Kethibh and all the ancient Versions, all of them giving the *plural* here. As usual, in this book, the *Kethibh* is the better reading. The pointing in the printed copy belongs to the *Sing.* גֶּשְׁמְהוֹן, which here is inappropriate. — *Giving up their bodies* is breviloquence; *giving themselves up to expected destruction* is what the king means to intimate. Nebuchadnezzar, astounded by the miraculous preservation of the condemned, and awed by the appearance of "a son of the gods," yields to the impulse of the moment, and testifies his homage to the God of Israel. He was doubtless like the Herod, who "heard John the Baptist gladly;" and like the Jews, who glorified God when Christ performed surprising miracles, and sung hosannas when he was riding meekly in triumph, but immediately afterwards, with a change of circumstances, changed their minds, and joined the procession to the crucifixion. Convictions wrought by the display of miraculous power, seem better adapted to arrest the attention and check the daring course of the transgressor, than to work a permanent change in his mind. So Paul seems to have viewed the subject, 1 Cor. 14: 22 seq. On a ground like to this, perhaps, we may account for it, that since the primitive age miracles have ceased to be a constituent part of the so-named *means of grace.*

(29) By me then is a decree established, that every people, nation, and tongue, who shall utter any blasphemy against the God of Shadrach, Meshach, and Abednego, shall be cut in pieces, and his house be made a dunghill; because there is no other god who can deliver in such a manner.

שִׂים, Part. Peil of שׂוּם. — שָׁלָה is only an *orthographic* variation of the regular שָׁלוּ; which the Qeri, as usual, supplies. It means *error,* and (applied to language) *falsehood.* Falsehood uttered against God is *blasphemy;* and I have translated accordingly. — יִתְעֲבֵד, Fut. Ithpeal;

for the whole phrase, see Comm. on 2: 5. — בַּיְתֵהּ, lit. *his house*, individualizes, and is equivalent to *the house of each*, viz. of each blasphemer. — יִכֻּל, Fut. of assimilation, from יְכִל, § 20. 4. — לְהַצָּלָה, Aph. Inf. of נְצַל, Par. p. 60.

(30) Then the king promoted Shadrach, Meshach, and Abednego, in the province of Babylon.

הַצְלַח lit. signifies *made prosperous* or *happy*. But as it here stands connected with *in* or *over the province of Babylon*, it must of course mean, that the king placed them in office again over this province, comp. 2: 49; possibly, or rather (from the nature of the verb) probably, it means here, that they were *advanced* to a higher grade of office than before.

After perusing the account of Nebuchadnezzar's demeanor, which is contained in ch. ii, the reader cannot be much surprised at his conduct, which is related in ch. iii. He was a despot, and a man of violent passions and strong impulses. Like most men of this temperament, he went from one extreme to the opposite. Allowing what is here related to have been matter of fact, and a thing which took place under the king's own eyes, we surely cannot be surprised that he was overawed and brought to a kind and gentle state of mind.

[Here ends the narration, and here should end the chapter; as in all our Versions it does. To avoid mistake, I would notify the reader, that for Dan. 3: 31—33, he must look in the English Bible for 4: 1—3; and for all the references to our version through ch. iv, he must go forward of the reference as made here, and pass over three verses in order to find the corresponding English translation. My references are, for consistency's sake, to the *Heb. arrangement* of chapter and verse; although the division of chapters in this case is palpably wrong.]

CHAP. III. 31—33. — IV. 34.

[This purports to be a proclamation of Nebuchadnezzar to his subjects, after his recovery from a derangement of mind which he had suffered, and his restoration to his former dignity. This proclamation, therefore, must have been made near the close of his life and reign; and it closes the account of this king, which is contained in the book of Daniel. But the reader must not for a moment suppose, that because this book has related some occurrences at the beginning, near the middle, and at the close, of his reign, it has therefore undertaken to present the whole history of Nebuchadnezzar's reign. It touches those points, and those only, with which some extraordinary development that has a bearing upon religion is connected. It is not Nebuchadnezzar as head of a great empire, nor yet simply as the conqueror of Judea, who is presented, but Nebuchadnezzar as rebuked, punished, disciplined, and instructed, by an all-wise and overruling Providence.

The fact that such a proclamation as is before us was made, is a singular testimony to the susceptible and variable temper of mind possessed by Nebuchadnezzar. As this last document reaches a period so near to the close of his life, and inasmuch as in his own person he had been made to feel the terrible effects of haughtiness and ambition, may we not hope, that what he expresses in 4: 34 (37) continued to be his prevailing sentiment until his death? Many recent critics are fond of comparing him with Antiochus Epiphanes, and zealously maintain, that the author of the 'romance before us [book of Daniel], intended throughout to present in Nebuchadnezzar a likeness of the Syrian tyrant.' On this assumption, indeed, much of their criticism on the book is founded. But if all this be so, what an egregious failure in making out a characteristic *similitude!* Nebuchadnezzar was a man of impulses, of strong passions, and of a haughty spirit. But he exhibited when the storm of passion had blown over, many generous impulses; as we see in his treatment of Daniel and his companions. Antiochus was indeed possessed of a character nearly allied to the bad part of Nebuchadnezzar's, although on a much lower and more bestial scale; to this he superadded his own vulgar and swinish habits; and all this apparently with scarce a single virtue to redeem him from the lowest infamy. He was the unrelenting and insatiable persecutor of the Jews and of Judaism; while, excepting the conquest of Judea, to which Nebuchadnezzar had been provoked by the treachery of Jehoiakim and Zedekiah, and excepting the usual military executions always attendant upon the subjugation of revolters (Jer. 39: 5—7), there is no evidence of his having treated the Hebrew exiles with any more than the ordinary severity of bondage, in all cases of the like nature. The promotion of Daniel and his companions to important offices in the satrapy of the metropolis, shows that the king had no particular bitterness of feeling toward the Jewish nation as such. The declarations which he made, (including the proclamation before us), respecting the God of the Hebrews, shows that his mind was capable of estimating the weight of evidence, and that his conscience was in that state of susceptibility, that he could be deeply affected by the majesty of holiness and truth. In all these respects, how different was Antiochus Epiphanes, that נִבְזֶה (Dan. 11: 21), i. e. *despicable wretch,* who crept into power by flattery and by falsehood, and who, when living, was commonly surnamed ἐπιμάνης (*mad-man*) by his subjects, instead of ἐπιφάνης (*magnificent, illustrious*), a title by which he named himself! If the writer of the book of Daniel did indeed mean to hit off Ephiphanes in the sketch that he has given us of Nebuchadnezzar, he was one of the most unskilful of all the *likeness-painters,* with whom it has been my lot to form an acquaintance. But I shall have occasion elsewhere to touch upon this subject, and in order to avoid repetition, I shall close here this train of thought, and pass to the contents of the Proclamation.

The salutatory part of this communication is addressed to the whole empire, which, in the usual style of the oriental monarchs, is described as embracing the whole earth, 3: 31. (4: 1). The king states, that the wonderful dealings of God with him, and the greatness of his power and dominion thereby manifested, have led him to make the declaration that follows, to his subjects, vs. 32, 33. (4: 2, 3). Nebuchadnezzar then relates, that he had a dream which terrified him, and that all the Magi being summoned to interpret it, they were unable. At last Daniel came in, whom he recognized as endowed with a superior knowledge, and to whom he appealed for an interpretation; 4: 1—6 (4: 4—9). He gives an account of the dream to Daniel, vs. 7—15. (10—19).

Daniel, recovering from the deep impression which his foreboding thoughts made upon him, interprets the dream, vs. 16—24 (vs. 20—27). Having thus related the dream, and its interpretation, the king proceeds, in the usual style of historical narrative, to tell the story of his madness. A voice from heaven announced the beginning of it, and it forthwith followed. After wandering for some time in this state among the beasts of the field, and taking his sustenance with them, he at length recovered his reason, and also his kingly authority and splendor. In testimony of his humility and of his gratitude, he publishes this to all his subjects; apparently with the design, that they also should recognize the hand of the God of Israel in all these events, vs. 26—34. (vs. 29—37). Under the guidance of an overruling Providence, there can scarcely be room for doubt in a believing mind, that all this was designed to arrest the attention of the Babylonians to the religion of the Jews, and particularly to render them kind and respectful toward the Hebrew exiles now sojourning with them.

CHAP. III. 31.

(31) Nebuchadnezzar the king to all people, nations, and tongues, who dwell in all the earth: May your peace be multiplied!

דָּאֲרִין, Part. Peal of דּוּר, p. 68. Par. The *Qeri* gives the more usual Chaldee form, דָּיְרִין; but the difference is merely orthographic. — שְׁלָמְכוֹן, the suff. state of שְׁלָם = Heb. שָׁלוֹם. — יִשְׂגֵּא, Fut. Peal, here used *optatively*, § 44. 3. *a*.

(32) The signs and wonders which God most high has wrought in me, it seemed good in my view to declare.

אָתַיָּא, pl. emph. of אָת = Heb. אוֹת. — וְתִמְהַיָּא, pl. emph. of תְּמַהּ. In Hebrew, we have אֹתוֹת וּמוֹפְתִים; in the N. Test. σημεῖα καὶ τέρατα; both in the same way. *Signs* designates not the ordinary tokens or symbols of common events, but always, when employed as here, something *extraordinary* or of a miraculous nature. *Wonders* is another name for the same events, but this name is intended to designate that effect on the mind which *signs* produce. Both words together mean: 'miraculous events which call forth wonder.' — עִמִּי = *apud me*. The speaker refers to the changes that had taken place in regard to his own person. — עִלָּיָא, see on v. 26 above. — קֳדָמַי, prep. with plur. form and suff., = ἐνώπιον προσώπου μου, i. e. in my view. — לְהַחֲוָיָה, Inf. Aph. of חֲוָא, ־ָיה for ־ָיָא, as usual in this book. That the passionate and afterward insane king had now come to sober reflection, seems plain from the tenor of his thoughts and views.

(33) His signs — how great! His wonders — how mighty! His kingdom is an everlasting kingdom, and his dominion is unto generation and generation.

רַבְרְבִין, adj. of reduplicate intensive form = *very great*. — In עִם דָּר וְדָר, the עִם here marks the idea of *with* in respect to time, and so it is equivalent to our word *during*. See the like usage, in Dan. 7: 2. Ps. 72: 5. Neh. 5: 18. Ezra 1: 11. So in the Latin: " *Cumque* sole et luna, semper Aratus erit," Ovid, Ars Am. I. 15. 16. In ascribing an *eternal kingdom* to God, Nebuchadnezzar evidently means to contrast it with the mutable and perishing nature of a dominion like his own.

CHAP. IV.

(1) I Nebuchadnezzar was at ease in my own house, and flourishing in my palace.

שְׁלֵה, participle Peil, Par. p. 72, or participial adj. from שְׁלָה, designating the idea of freedom from all that could disturb or annoy. — הֲוֵית, 1st pers. sing. Peal, from הֲוָא. — רַעְנַן, applied to trees, designates their fulness of sap and vigor of growth; tropically applied to persons, it means *prosperous, flourishing, fortunate* (as we say). It is a Pilel form of רְעַן, used here as an adjective; comp. § 28. C. 11. This statement of his condition is designed to be contrasted with that of his subsequent afflictions; thus rendering his chastisement more conspicuous.

(2) I saw a dream, and it terrified me; and thoughts upon my couch and visions of my head agitated me.

I saw a dream, in 2: 1 *dreamed dreams*. The difference is in the manner of representation, not in point of fact. *To see*, in dreams or prophetic ecstasy, means a *mental*, not an *ocular*, seeing. *I saw a dream* = a dream was presented to my mind, i. e. to the intellectual or spiritual eye. — וִידַחֲלִנַּנִי, for ־נַּנִי suff., see p. 58. Rem. 1. — הַרְהֹרִין, of the Pilpel form, from הֲרַר, § 28. b. 11. — *Thoughts upon my couch* designates the reflections of his mind upon the dream after he had awaked. These, together with the dream itself (*visions of my head*) troubled him. In 2: 28. 7: 1, חֶזְוֵי רֵאשׁ, as here, only designates the thoughts that arise in a dream. — יְבַהֲלֻנַּנִי, Pael Fut. with suff., p. 58. Rem. 1. It is a stronger word than דְּחַל, which is confined to *terror* or *fear;* while בְּהַל expresses the agitation of the whole man.

(3) And by me a decree was made, to bring before me all the wise men of Babylon, that they might make known to me the interpretation of the dream.

שִׂים, Part. Peil of שׂוּם. — לְהַנְעָלָה, Aph. Inf. of עֲלַל, with נ epenthetic instead of Dagh. f.; p. 30–2; see also in Lex. — לְכֹל, לְ before the Acc., as oftentimes, everywhere. — דִּי, *that, in order that;* Lex. B. 2. — יְהוֹדְעֻנַּנִי, Aph. Fut. of יְדַע; with ה pref. retained, p. 49. 5, and suff. ־נַּנִי, p. 58 Rem. 1.

(4) Then came in the sacred scribes, the enchanters, the Chaldeans, and the astrologers, and I told the dream before them; but the interpretation thereof they did not make known to me.

עָלִּלִין, Part. pl. the points belong to the Qeri עָלִּין. Better to adopt the Kethibh, omitting Dagh. f., and read עָלְלִין, which is the usual form in this book. The present confusion in the word has arisen from mixing two modes of orthography together. — The *Chaldeans;* see on 2: 4; and for other accompanying words, on 2: 2. — אָמַר, Part. for verb, § 47. 1. *b*, here in the sense of *told, related.* — מְהוֹדְעִין, Part. Aph. of יְדַע, with ה retained.

(5) And at last came Daniel before me, whose name is Belteshazzar, according to the name of my god, and in whom is the spirit of the holy gods; and I told the dream before him.

אָחֳרֵין Gesenius (Lex.) regards as a mere adj. form, in the sing.; but others consider it as an abridged plur. used abstractly, and with an *adverbial* sense. Adjectives of such a form are rare; while the contracted plur. ֵ־ן (so Qeri which writes אָחֳרֵן) for ֵ־ין is not unfrequent; comp. אַתַּיִן, אַתֵּן; אִנֵּין, אִנֵּן, and the like. — עַל, Peal of עֲלַל. — *According to the name of my god*, see on the name in 1: 7. After giving the Hebrew name of *Daniel*, the king, in order to specificate, adds the name by which Daniel was ordinarily known to his subjects.—*In whom is the spirit of the holy gods*, comp. the words of Nebuchadnezzar in 2: 47. 3: 29. The speaker uses his accustomed dialect. He was a *polytheist;* and as such, he might consistently speak of *holy gods*, even where he ought to have said: *of God most holy.* But of such a God the mass of his subjects knew little or nothing; and so he adopts the usual manner of parlance in respect to the matter. — אַמְרֵת, 1 pers. sing. Peal.

(6) Belteshazzar, chief overseer of the sacred scribes, (for I know that the spirit of the holy gods is in thee, and that no secret is too difficult for thee), as to the visions of my dream which I have seen, even the interpretation of the same, tell me.

רַב חַרְטֻמַּיָּא, applied to Daniel here, shows the same usage, in this book, which is exhibited in 2: 4, where the *Chaldeans* are made the representatives of all the classes of the Magi; i. e. a leading or influential class is named as the representative of the whole. In 2: 48, Daniel is said to be רַב־סִגְנִין עַל כָּל־חַכִּימֵי בָבֶל, *chief overseer over all the wise men of Babylon;* where חַכִּימֵי is equivalent, in its generic meaning, to חַרְטֻמַּיָּא in our text. — אָנֵס, Part. of אֲנַס, which literally means *to force, impel, do violence to.* The meaning here is, that no secret thing *constrains* Daniel to relinquish its explanation, or makes such explanation troublesome to him or difficult. — *Tell me the visions of my dream*, etc., seems, at first view, to require of Daniel to do again what he had before done, viz. to tell both the dream and its interpretation. But this it can hardly mean in this connection, for the king himself proceeds forthwith to relate the particulars of the dream. We seem constrained, therefore, to translate thus: "*As to the visions of my dream* . . . even the interpretation of the same, tell [me"]. The ו before פִּשְׁרֵהּ is explicative; as e. g. in v. 10, וְקַדִּישׁ, *even a holy one*, and often so elsewhere. — אֱמַר, in pause, Imper.

(7) In respect then to the visions of my head upon my couch: I looked, and behold! there was a tree in the midst of the earth, and its height was very great.

וְחֶזְוֵי, Nom., or rather Acc. absolute, in which וְ *connects*, but is also a *transition-particle* that may well be represented by our word *then*. *The visions of my head* are the same here as *the visions of my dream* in the verse above, only that the diction is derived from another source, viz. from the *head* as the source of thought and intelligence. — חָזֵה הֲוֵית, Part. joined with the verb of existence, denoting continued action, § 47. 1. a. — אֲלוּ, prob. for אֲרוּ, by exchange of ל and ר, which is not uncommon; see Lex. — אִילָן, *tree*, generic in Chaldee, while in Hebrew אַלּוֹן means *oak*. *In the midst of the earth* is a phrase in accordance with the language of Nebuchadnezzar's address *to the nations in all the earth*, 3: 31. Not improbably the metropolis of Babylon was regarded as the *middle point* of the earth; like the Oracle at Delphos, and like Jerusalem in Palestine. As the dream took place in the palace at Babylon, the tree most probably appeared to be near there. בְּגוֹא, const. of גַּו with בּ, and it may be written גּוֹ or גּוֹא, without any variation of meaning. — רוּמֵהּ, with suff., *its height*. שַׂגִּיא, more intense than רַב, and so I have translated it *very great;* for the form, § 28. b. 10.

(8) And the tree became great and waxed mighty, so that its height reached to the heavens, and the sight of it to the end of all the earth.

רְבָה and תְקִף are both *verbs* intrans. I have given them as literal a translation as our idiom will allow. The reader must not make adjectives of them; see in § 12. 2. 1. — For יִמְטֵא (Fut.), see on v. 17. — וַחֲזוֹתֵהּ, *aspectus ejus, its aspect*, means that its *visibility* reached to the ends of the earth, or (in other words) *it was visible*, etc. The hyperbole, in this case, is altogether in keeping with the style of the country. Oriental usage employs it, beyond all example in the western languages. See striking instances of it, in Gen. 11: 4. Deut. 1: 28. 9: 1. Ps. 57: 10, 11. 107: 26. Job 20: 6. Comp. Matt. 11: 23. Even Herodotus (II. 138) has δένδρεα οὐρανομήκεα. It was the custom at the Assyrian, Babylonian, and Persian courts, to speak of the empire as universal; just as is now done in China, when "the lord of the world" is addressed. In the more chastened style of the west, Nebuchadnezzar would have said, that the tree was very high, and could be seen at a great distance.

(9) Its foliage was goodly, and its fruit abundant, and there was food for all upon it; under it the beast of the field sought shade; and among its branches did the birds of the air find lodging; and by it was all flesh supplied with food.

עָפְיֵהּ, suff. state of עֳפִי, *its foliage.* — אִנְבֵּהּ, for אִבֵּהּ from אֵב; the Dagh. f. omitted is compensated by נ epenth., p. 30. e. 2. — מָזוֹן, from זוּן, see form on p. 83. No. 5. *c.* 4. — לְכֹלָּא, emph. form, which of course develops the Dagh. implied in the לּ. — תְּחֹתוֹהִי, prep. תְּחוֹת with pl. suff.; p. 106. 2. 2. — תַּטְלֵל, Aph. fem. Fut., *caused,* i. e. *procured shade;* Fut. for the designation of what is *habitual,* (as in Hebrew). Winer has omitted to notice this, in his Grammar. — חֵיוַת, const. form. — עַנְפּוֹהִי, pl. of עֲנַף with suff. — יְדֻרוּן, the vowels belong to the Qeri יְדֻרָן, 3 pl. fem. of Peal. There is no need of the designed correction, for צִפְּרֵי is of the *common* gender. Read therefore יְדֻרוּן. — צִפְּרֵי is derived by Ges. (in Lex.) from צְפַר, like the forms in § 28. b. 7. Lengerke prefers the ground-form צִפַּר or צְפַר, and so makes Dagh. to be merely *euphonic* in the פ. I prefer the former etymology. — יִתְּזִין, Ittaphal (p. 69) of זוּן, *were provided with food.* For the use of three *Futures* here, see on v. 18. — בִּשְׂרָא, *flesh* is predicated collectively of animals (as here), as well as of men. In this case, the animals symbolize *men,* and so the verb is put in the masc. plural. The oriental dress, in respect to hyperbole, is quite manifest here. But the description is poetically and tastefully made out.

(10) I beheld, in the visions of my head upon my couch, and lo! a Watcher, even a holy one, came down from heaven.

The repetition, in the first clause, of what had been already said in v. 7, probably indicates that the sequel was in a second and continuous dream, which took place soon after having been waked by the first. — עִיר, a much contested word, which has given rise to a multitude of whimsies. Whoever wishes to see them, may consult Hävernick in loc. I prefer a resort to a more direct method of investigation. I will merely state the result here. That the appellation here is a mere exchange of names, seems plain from 3: 25, where *a son of the gods* designates the same personage that is called מַלְאֲכֵהּ *his angel* in v. 28. So Polychronius (Comm. in loc. in edit. Maii), a writer of the fourth century, when commenting on the Greek version of Theodotion: "Εἴρ is a Heb. word, and signifies *watchfulness, angel.*" Still further confirmation of the view given above is it, that in Dan. 8: 13, Gabriel is expressly named קָדוֹשׁ, just as עִיר is here said to be קַדִּישׁ. — נָחִת, Part. act.; for vowels, see § 12. 1. c.

First of all, it is plain that this expression, in the mouth of a *polytheistic* speaker, is to be explained, if possible, in accordance with his theosophy. In regard to this, one thing is certain, viz. that the worship of the sun, moon, planets, and stars, was originally spread over all middle and hither Asia. Rhode, in his learned and fundamental investigation of Parsism, (Die heilige Sage des Zendvolks), has shown beyond fair controversy, at least as it seems to me, that the religion of Zoroaster *preceded* the empires of Assyria, Babylon, and Persia; and that the worship just mentioned, pervaded, at an early period, the whole extent of the empire of Jemshid, i. e. the whole extent of the ancient Aria. Subsequently to this, each empire that followed, and each country of any considerable eminence and extent, engrafted more or less of idolatrous rites upon the original *nature-worship* of Zoroaster. So it clearly was in Babylon, at the time of Nebuchadnezzar. But still, we find here the *Magi*, an order of priests appropriate to the religion of Zoroaster. We may therefore reasonably expect to find other relics of the more ancient religion.

The Bun-Dehesh, a commentary on the Zend-Avesta, contains an extract from it which shows clearly the name and object of the *watchers*, in the ancient system of Zoroaster. It runs thus: "Ormuzd has set four *watchers* in the four quarters of the heavens, to keep their eye upon the host of stars. They are bound to *keep watch* over the hosts of celestial stars. One stands here, as the *watcher* of his circle; the other, there. He has placed them at such and such posts, as watchers over such and such a circle of the heavenly regions; and this by his own power and might. . . . Tashter guards the east, Satevis watches the west, Venant the south, and Haftorang the north." Rhode, p. 267. Zend-Avesta, Bun-Dehesh, II. pp. 60, 61. Now as it is certain, that the Babylonians retained the worship of "the host of heaven," it seems very rational to suppose, that Nebuchadnezzar here alludes to those secondary deities, who were commissioned by superior ones to *watch* and to *oversee*. The names of these, as given above, are the names respectively of four of the *planets*; each of which was under the guardianship of one of the *Amshaspands* or archangels of the Zoroastrian system. They ranked next to the sun and moon, and were undoubted objects of Babylonian worship. It would seem that Nebuchadnezzar adds the epithet קַדִּישׁ, in order to distinguish the *good* class of *watchers* from the bad ones; for Ahriman, the evil genius had his *Archdevs* and his *Devs*, who corresponded in rank with the Amshaspands and Izeds of the Zend-Avesta, and who *watched* to do evil as anxiously as the others did in order to do good. Nebuchadnezzar means then, by using עִיר, to designate one of the gods, i. e. a superior or spiritual being, and one who is employed as a *watcher* and *messenger* of the highest deities, which he calls the *holy gods*, whom, as supreme, he had just before mentioned. That the word עִיר in itself is of a *generic* meaning, seems quite probable from the explanatory וְקַדִּישׁ, which is in apposition and exegetical; and still further, from the fact that the Syriac Liturgies not unfrequently employ it to designate archangels, sometimes Gabriel, and at other times the evil angels; i. e. it designates rank or station, not character. So the book of Enoch employs it for *good* angels, (e. g. in ch. xx. it is said of the seven archangels, that "they watch"); and for *evil* ones, Enoch 1:5. 10:11, 13, 18, et al. saepe; see in Ges. Thes. p. 1006. The suggestion that עִיר = Heb. צִיר, *nuncius*, seems not to be entitled to much weight.

Lengerke has brought out a conclusion similar to the one just stated, but from somewhat different premises. He fixes upon a passage in Yesht Farvardin (Zend. Av. II. Carde 23. p. 257), which says, in respect to the Amshaspands: "O that they might watch over souls from on high!" This falls in with what is said above; but being merely a part of the *Zend-ritual* of prayers, it would not be so likely to be known to the Babylonians of Nebuchadnezzar's time, as the more general principles of the system to which I have made an appeal. It may serve, however, as a confirmation of them. Nor is the opinion, which I have ventured to give, anything new; although the reasons for it, in part, may not heretofore have been produced. Jerome (Comm. in loc.) says: "Theodotion has retained the word εἴρ (= עִיר), which signifies *angels*, because they always *watch*, and are in readiness for the divine commands." This would be sufficient ground among Hebrews, with their views of angelology, for employing such a word to designate angels; but still we find no example of it in actual Heb. usage. Nebuchadnezzar had reasons different from those of the Hebrews, for naming his secondary gods *watchers*, as we have seen above.

(11) He cried aloud and spake thus: Cut down the tree and lop off its branches; strip off its foliage, and scatter abroad its fruit; let the beasts fly from beneath it, and the birds from its branches.

בְּחַיִל, *with strength*, which, when applied to the voice, means of course *aloud*.— גֹּדּוּ, Imper. Peal of גְּדַד. This is applied to *felling*, or *cutting down* the tree. — קַצִּצוּ, Pael Imper. of קְצַץ; for (ִ) in the second syllable, see § 12. 1. *b*. The word means (as we express it) *clip off, lop off*.— אַתַּרוּ, Aph. of נְתַר, (אַתַּרוּ instead of the normal אַתִּרוּ, because of the final ר), *decussit, strike off*, or *strip off*, appropriate to removing the foliage. — בַּדַּרוּ = Heb. בָּזַר, Pael (ַ for ֵ because of the Resh), *scatter, disperse*. Applied to the *fruit*, it means that it is no more to be appropriated for food, as before. The *commands*, in all these cases, are addressed to the implied attendant retinue of the *watcher*. — תְּנֻד, Fut. Peal of נוּד. The beasts and birds are to flee, lest the fall of the tree should crush them. The ruinous state of the tree after felling, is clearly indicated; but the sequel shows that its utter destruction is not intended. The imagery employed designates, in a lively manner, the wealth, splendor, and extensive influence or power of Nebuchadnezzar, who was very conspicuous as the head of a great empire and had dependants almost without number. Of all these appendages he was to be deprived.

(12) But its root-trunk leave in the earth, and with a chain of iron and brass among the tender herbage of the field; and with the dew of heaven shall it be bathed, and with the beasts shall be its portion among the herbage of the earth.

שָׁרְשׁוֹהִי, *of its roots*, with pl. suff. from שֹׁרֶשׁ. The *root-trunk* means, the trunk that is left after the tree is felled, which is attached to the roots that bury themselves in the earth. This contains a *germ*, which will again sprout up; comp. מַצֶּבֶת in Isa. 6: 13, and גֶּזַע in Isa. 11: 1, which present the same idea. — *The chain of iron and brass*, to be put round the trunk, seems designed to preserve it from being opened or cracked by the heat of the sun, so as to admit moisture which would rot it. There could be no need of chaining the trunk to the earth in order to secure it, for the roots made it fast there. I do not understand this, moreover, as symbolizing the chaining of Nebuchadnezzar as a madman, but merely as a token of the care with which the *germ* of the tree would be preserved, notwithstanding the destruction of all besides. See the interpretation in vs. 20—23. — בְּדִתְאָא, emph. of דֶּתֶא; some editions Hebraize here, writing דִּתְאָה. — בָּרָא, emph. of בַּר. — טַל, see Lex. under Heb. טָלַל. — יִצְטַבַּע, Fut. Ithpael, with the ת in אִת transposed and changed to ט, § 10. 5. b. A copious bedewing, or (as we say) *bathing with dew*, is naturally meant here; for what would *plunging into the dew* mean? — חֵיוְתָא, emph. of חֵיוָא. — *Its portion shall be among the herbage*, etc.; here the writer forsakes his symbol, viz. the *root-trunk*, and speaks appropriately only of that which the symbol represents, viz. the person of Nebuchadnezzar, who, during his madness, was to feed upon the herbage of the field. — חֲלָקֵהּ, with suff., from the rather unusual ground-form חֲלָק, § 28. a. 2. The difference between עֲשַׂב and דִּתְאָא is, that the latter means *fresh, green, growing herbage*, while the former designates the generic idea.

(13) His heart shall be changed from [that of] men, and the heart of a beast shall be given to him, and seven times shall pass over him.

In other words, he shall lose his human sympathies, and acquire those of the brutes. But there is diversity among critics, in the explanation of the first clause of the verse. Gesenius, Rosenm., Winer, De Wette, and others, take מִן in מִן אֲנָשָׁא, in a *privative* sense, (which is frequent in Hebrew), and give the meaning thus: *His heart shall be changed from that which is human*, i. e. from being the heart of a man. Lengerke contends, that the only grammatical sense of which the phrase is properly susceptible, is this, viz. *his heart shall be changed while he is far from men*, i. e. when he is driven into exile among the beasts. But although he is very confident in this peculiar view of the passage, it seems to have something of the ὕστερον πρότερον in it; for the king's change of heart was the *occasion* of his fleeing from the abodes of man, not an event that followed after he had gone away. Besides, from the usage of this book, the verb שְׁנָא, associated with מִן, has appropriately the meaning *diversus fuit ab, aliud esse, mutari*. comp. Dan. 7: 3, 7, 19, 23, 24. We might therefore well translate thus: *Cor ejus diversum fiet ab humano*. In the version above, I have expressed the first clause thus: *His heart shall be changed from* [that of] *men;* and I can have no doubt, that the Chaldee phrase is elliptical, or rather brachylogical, in which (as oftentimes in the Hebrew) a repetition of the preceding noun is implied, although not expressed. I have substituted the *pronoun* for it. The second clause makes the sense thus given altogether clear. In אֲנָשָׁא, the vowels belong to the Qeri אֲנָשָׁא, but the Kethibh shows a not improbable Hebraizing form, and is to be read אֱנוֹשָׁא, as also in v. 14. Yet since vs. 22, 30, support the Qeri here, it is perhaps orthographically preferable. — יְשַׁנּוֹן, Fut. Pael of שְׁנָא, 3 plur. without a subject, and therefore to be translated *passively*, § 49. 3. *b.* — יִתְיְהִב, Fut. Ithpeal of יְהַב; for the end-syllable ־הִיב, see p. 49. 2. — עִדָּנִין, pl. of עִדָּן, which shows itself (by the Dagh.) to be a derivate of עֲדַד, *to compute, number*, etc. Etymologically, then, it would seem to mean a *computed* or *defined time* or *season.* C. B. Michaelis, Ges., Rosenm., Winer, Leng., and nearly all the critics agree, that *year* is the probable meaning; for in 7: 25, (and so מוֹעֵד, a kindred form in 12: 7), and in Apoc. 12: 14, this meaning is quite certain; comp. here vs. 20, 22, 29, where עִדָּן is connected with חֲלַף, *to pass on* or *over*. But Hävernick comments thus on Winer, who in his Heb.Lex. says: "Tempus prop. definitum, hinc *annus* [sic.!], deinde generatim [?] *tempus*." The comments are contained in the exclamation and interrogation points, which Häv. has inserted. After all, he is obliged to concede that some definable season or time is meant; only he says, that 'this must be some *astrological* period.' But as Nebuchadnezzar is not the original speaker here, but only relates the words of the watcher; moreover, since עִדָּן is elsewhere employed in this book plainly for the common *year;* and since there is nothing in the context here that points us to an *astrological* period, or enables us to determine what it is; I do not well see how we are to avoid the conclusion of C. B. Michaelis and so many other Hebraists. — עֲלוֹהִי, *over him* or *upon him*, the prep. עַל conveying the adjunct notion of something which is *burdensome* or *troublesome.* That the number *seven*, in this case, is to be *literally* and not figuratively understood, seems the more probable, because the nature of the case easily admits of a literal construction. Whatever difficulties our present lack of historical knowledge may throw in the way of explaining the matter, it cannot alter the plain and obvious exegesis of our text. (These difficulties will be canvassed, at the close of the present chapter). The attempt, made by many of the ancient Fathers, to lessen the period of seven years, by adopting the Persian mode of counting years by their half-yearly feasts, and so making six months equal to an עִדָּן, stands directly opposed to 7: 25 and 12: 7. The phrase יֹדְעֵי הָעִתִּים, in Est. 1: 13, casts no light on the expression before us, since it applies to *political times* and *State-occurrences*, (just as we employ the word *times* for a like purpose), and not to defined periods of time proper; so that we have no parallel for the sense here defended by Hävernick.

(14) By a decision of the Watchers is the decree, and a command of the holy Ones is the thing required, in order that the living may know that the most High is ruler over the kingdom of men, and giveth it to whomsoever he pleases, and setteth up over it the humblest of men.

Here again is much controversy. I shall not detail it, but simply state the grounds of my own exegesis. That גְּזֵרַת (const. st.) means *decision*, there can be no room to doubt, inasmuch as the root is גְּזַר, lit. *secare*, metaph. *decernere*. The word עִירִין, in this case means *the Council of the watchers*, as viewed by the king, i. e. this king relates the decree of Heaven in language accordant with his own views of theology. The Amshaspands were the associates and councillors of Ormuzd, who indeed was only *primus inter pares*, in an emphatic sense. To them the actual government of the world was committed. They are the *overseers*, the *watchers*. The messenger, although only one of them (v. 10), employs the united authority of all in the present case, in order to strengthen his declaration. — פִּתְגָם, *decree*, see Ezra 4: 17. This is one undoubted sense of the word; and one, moreover, which is altogether appropriate here. — מֵאמַר, *command*, from the well known sense of אֲמַר, *to command*, in the Chald. dialect. — קַדִּישִׁין, the same here as in v. 10, עִיר וְקַדִּישׁ, only that the pl. is here used, in conformity with the preceding עִירִין. *The holy Ones* are the Watchers, whose united council have determined on the humiliation of Nebuchadnezzar. — שְׁאֵלְתָא, emph. of שְׁאֵלָא, *requisition, demand*, referring, as I apprehend, to the preceding command given in v. 11, to *cut down the tree*, etc. The declaration here is, that the whole sentence of humiliation, which had been proclaimed by the עִיר, i. e. a single *watcher* (v. 10), is a matter decreed and fixed upon in the council of heaven. — עַד דִּבְרַת דִּי, lit. *until the circumstance* or *matter that*, stronger and more periphrastic than עַד דִּי in v. 22, but in substance the same = *until that, until*. In manner it resembles the כָּל־קֳבֵל דִּי, which we have already so often met with. — יִנְדְּעוּן, Fut. of יְדַע, § 6. e. 2. — חַיַּיָּא, pl. emph. of חַי, *the living*, means men in general, or all men. It is expressed generically here, although a special application to Nebuchadnezzar is intended; for so Daniel applies it in the sequel. — שַׁלִּיט, adj. form, *endowed with dominion*, i. e. ruler. — עִלָּיא, Qeri עִלָּאָה, emph. of עִלַּי, see on 3: 26. — אֲנָשָׁא, as in v. 13. — יִתְּנִנַּהּ, suff. Fut. Peal of נְתַן, for suff., p. 58. Rem. 1, the נַהּ being fem. and = נָהּ (see Par. on

p. 34), and referring to מַלְכוּת. The change of vowels here (ֶ for ָ) seems to depend on the Gutt. ה. — For שְׁפַל אֲנָשִׁים, as indicating *the lowest of men*, see § 58. 2. — עֲלַיהּ, the vowels belong to the Qeri עֲלַהּ, which gives a sing. form and suffix, contrary to usage in regard to this preposition, which with a suff. has a *plur.* form, § 38. 2. *b.* It should be written עֲלָיהּ which is a contraction of עֲלָיהָא, see Par. 2, p. 35. In this last clause also the sentiment is generic, not being applied individually, but intended to show that God can elevate to dominion the lowest of men as well as the highest, so that full and entire power and dominion belong to him, and not to perishing men.

(15) This is the dream which I king Nebuchadnezzar saw; and do thou, Belteshazzar, declare the interpretation, because that all the wise men of my kingdom are not able to make known to me the interpretation; but thou art able, for the spirit of the holy gods is in thee.

אַנְתָּה the Kethibh should be read, which the Qeri has changed to the more usual אַנְתְּ, without any necessity; comp. 2 pers. sing. masc. in the Praet. of Pael and Aphel, Par. p. 44, which have a like ending in this person. — אֱמַר, with Qamets in pause. — יָכְלִין, Part. pl. — לְהוֹדָעוּתַנִי, Inf. with suff. p. 56. e. *The spirit of the holy gods*, etc., shows that Nebuchadnezzar retains his customary diction in speaking of superior beings.

(16) Then Daniel, whose name is Belteshazzar, was stricken with astonishment, for a moment, and his thoughts agitated him; the king answered and said: Let not the dream and the interpretation agitate thee! Belteshazzar answered and said: Let the dream be to those who hate thee, and the interpretation of it to thine enemies.

The repetition of the name of Belteshazzar, which is here made by the king, accords with his description of Daniel in v. 5. above. — אֶשְׁתּוֹמַם, Ithpoal of שְׁמַם, § 14. 1. 1, corresponding with the Hithpoal of the Heb. from verbs ע"ע. For the exchange of שׁ and ת, see § 10. 5. *b.* For the first syllable with *Seghol*, see § 12. 1. 5, comp. § 25. 2. It is Syriasm. — שָׁעָה, prop. an intensive form, § 28. *b.* 6, the Dagh. f. being omitted in the ע, of course the preceding vowel is prolonged. The emph. form is שַׁעְתָּה. As שְׁעָא means *to look*, so this derivate means *a look, a glance of the eye, the twinkling of an eye*; and accordingly, I have rendered it *moment.* Our English version here (*hour*) mistakes the true sense of the word, and thus states what seems to be very improbable. — חֲדָא = our English indef. article *a*; and often so in Chald. and in the later Hebrew. — רַעְיֹנֹהִי (*rā-yō-nō-hī*), pl. suff. of רַעְיוֹן. The root רְעָה has for its leading sense, *to desire, will, wish, purpose*; but a secondary sense appears plainly to be that of *thinking, reflection, cogitation.* Evidently *desire* or *will* would be inappropriate in our text. — יְבַהֲלָךְ, Fut. Pael with suff. For suff., see p. 58. Rem. 1. — פִּשְׁרֵא, with vowels for the Qeri פִּשְׁרֵהּ,

i. e. the Qeri adopts the suffix form which occurs in the sequel of the verse; while the Kethibh retains the absolute emph. form, which is equally well. — מָרְאִי, contract for מָרְאִי, a participial from מְרָא, meaning *my lord.* A marginal reading bids us write מָרִי, and the vowels in the text belong to this latter form. But the emendation, although feasible, is unadvisable, since the dropping of the א obscures the etymology. — לְשָׂנְאָיךְ, pl. Part. pres. with pl. suff., from שְׂנֵא; for suff., p. 35. Par. 2.* — לְעָרָיךְ, pl. of עָר with suff.

The astonishment of Daniel, (not for an *hour*, which would have rendered Nebuchadnezzar very impatient, but for a *moment*), was evidently the result of his consciousness, as soon as the dream was fully related, of the interpretation which must be given to it. His complaisance, kind feeling, and fidelity to the truth, are equally conspicuous in his answer. Comity led him to say, (what at the moment he undoubtedly felt): *Let the dream be to those that hate thee*, etc.! Sympathy for the king who had bestowed so much honor and kindness upon him, was a very natural and commendable feeling. What he means to say, may be thus expressed: 'I would that what this dream indicates, might fall rather upon your enemies than on yourself!' The king on his part is kind and condescending. He encourages his pale and trembling minister to go on with the interpretation assigned to him, be it what it may. He summoned resolution to give such a command, even after he saw the agitation of Daniel, when the narration of the dream had been completed. Doubtless the former experience of Nebuchadnezzar, as to the prophetic power of Daniel, must have inspired him with respect for the man; and hence his lenient treatment of him.

(17) As to the tree which thou sawest, which became great, and waxed mighty, so that its height reached to the heavens, and the sight of it to all the earth;

I have made the English construction of the sentence to accord with the Chaldee. אִילָנָא is absolute, and דִּי רְבָה וגו׳ is mere specification of particulars belonging to it, i. e. exegetical apposition, which is continued through the remainder of the verse, and also through v. 18. — יִמְטֵא, *venit, advenit, came to, reached.* It has a *Fut.* form, which indicates that the וְ at the beginning of the clause is conditional, viz. *that, so that*, § 44. 4. — חֲזוֹתֵהּ, see on v. 8.

(18) And its foliage was goodly, its fruit abundant, and food for all was upon it; under it dwelt the beast of the field, and among its boughs the birds of the air found lodging;

---

* In the copy of the Gramm. which is before me, the ־יךְ suff. is without its vowel (ָ); which should be supplied.

See v. 9 above. — תְּדוּר, in the Fut. and יִשְׁכְּנָן Fut. fem. pl. (צִפֲּרֵי being of the common gender) seem to be used like the Hebrew Future, to designate action habitual, i. e. they are real *Imperfects.*

(19) Thou art he, O king, who hast become great and waxed mighty, and thy greatness hath increased and reached to the heavens, and thy dominion to the end of the earth.

The apodosis of the sentence, which begins with v. 17 and comprises v. 18, begins with this verse. — רְבַית, Qeri רְבַת, a possible but not usual orthography. The true form is the Kethibh, which should be written רְבַיְתְ. — תְּקֵפְתְּ, 2 pers. of תְּקֵף. — רְבַת, 3 fem. of רְבָא. — מְטַת, 3 fem. Peal, for מְטָת, i. e. Peal 3d fem. is pointed so as to correspond with the ending of the same person in all the *derived conjugations ;* see in Par. p. 72. The Oriental court-style is sufficiently evident in this verse, as often elsewhere. Faithfulness to the truth in Daniel did not require him to break through all the usual forms of courtesy, as to the manner of communicating it.

(20) And that the king saw a Watcher, even a Holy One, descending from heaven, who said: Cut down the tree and destroy it; yet leave the root-trunk in the earth, and with a chain of iron and brass, among the tender herbage of the field; and with the dew of heaven shall it be bathed, and with the beast of the field shall be his portion, until seven times shall pass over him.

See on vs. 12, 13 above. — נָחֵת, Part. § 12. 1. c. — חַבְּלוּהִי, Pael Imper. with suff. p. 34. Par. 2. The last clause forsakes the symbol, and introduces the person signified by it; see on v. 12.

(21) This is the interpretation, O king; and it is a decree of the most High, which comes upon my lord the king.

Comp. in v. 14, for the language. — מְטַת, see in v. 19. — מָרְאִי, as in v. 16. — In Daniel's mouth the decree is no longer called a decree of the *watchers,* but of the *most high God.* Each party represents the matter, in a manner which accords with his own theology.

(22) Thou shalt be driven from men, and with the beast of the field shall be thy dwelling, and herbage shall they give thee for food as the oxen, and with the dew of heaven shall they bathe thee; and seven times shall pass over thee, until thou shalt know that the most High is ruler over the kingdom of men, and giveth it to whomsoever he may please.

לָךְ, Acc. — טָרְדִין without any Nom., and therefore to be rendered *passively,* as in the version. Lit. *They shall drive thee away,* § 49. 3. *b.* — לֶהֱוֵא, see on 2: 20. — מְדֹרָךְ, deriv. of דּוּר, with suff. — כְּתוֹרִין, i. e. *like* [the herbage] *of the oxen ;* see v. 13, where is a like ellipsis after מִן. — יְטַעֲמוּן, Pael Fut.; מְצַבְּעִין, pl. Part. both without a subject, and therefore they might be rendered *passively* as in the first part of the verse. But in these last cases, our idiom does not forbid a literal version with an indefinite Nominative. — יִתְּנִנַּהּ, see on v. 14.

(23) And that they commanded to let alone the root-trunk of the tree, thy kingdom is established for thee, from the time when thou shalt know that the Heavens bear rule.

קַיָּמָא, adj. fem. of קַיָּם. — דִּי, like אֲשֶׁר, is often used in respect to a point of *time=when.*— שַׁלִּיטִן, written *defectivè* in the final syllable, טִן — for טִין —. *Heavens do rule* expresses the dominion of the Godhead, and is a phrase nowhere used in the O. Test., except in this book; but in the N. Test., and among the Rabbins, it is very common. So in the heathen writers. It seems to be employed partly in accommodation to the Chaldee diction, e. g. *the watchers, the holy Ones*, etc. It must be regarded as brachylogy here, and as being equivalent to *the heavenly Powers.* In the mouth of Daniel, we cannot regard it as designed to signify what it might do in the mouth of a *Parsi*, who would employ it in a kind of literal way.

(24) Wherefore, O king, let my counsel seem good to thee, and so break off thy sin by righteousness, and thine iniquities by compassion to the afflicted, if perhaps there may be a prolongation of thy prosperity.

מִלְכִּי, suff. st. of מְלַךְ *counsel.* — עֲלָיךְ, which the Qeri wrongly changes to עֲלָךְ. It is stronger than לְ simply would be here, i. e. it conveys the idea of a stronger impression upon the king's mind than לָךְ would designate. — חֲטָיָךְ, sing. with suff. of חֲטָי, a derivate of חֲטָא *to sin.*— עֲוָיָתָךְ pl. suff. emph., for the more normal עֲוָיָתָךְ; in the former, ַ with a Dagh. f. after it stands in lieu of the ָ in the latter; but this diversity is merely orthographic. The sing. is עֲוָיָא, fem. (sometimes written עִוְיָא); the pl. abs. would be עֲוָיָן, lit. *perversities.* — מִחַן Inf. nominascens of חֲנַן. — עֲנָיִן, in pause, pl. Part. Peil of עֲנָה, p. 91. Par. VII. — הֵן, *if, if perhaps;* comp. *εἰ ἄρα* in Acts 8: 22. — — שְׁלֵוְתָךְ the suff. state of שְׁלֵוָה, lit. *tranquillity, safety*, and so *prosperity*, as translated above. Many critics render בְּצִדְקָה by *alms* or *kindness;* which sense indeed the word has among the Talmudists and the Rabbins, and also in the Samaritan. Ges. (in Lex.) so translates it, in the present case. In Heb. it sometimes means *liberality, kindness;* but in the instance before us, it stands as the opposite of חֲטָיָךְ, which does not mean *avarice* or *rapine*, but is more generic. I have given it, therefore, an appropriate meaning in the version above.

The sum of what Daniel says in this verse, is, that although the sentence of chastisement has gone forth, still a speedy and thorough repentance and change of conduct may perhaps avert it. With the Hebrews in general he might well believe in this. The threatening of Jonah to the Ninevites was averted, Jonah 3: 10. Hezekiah's predicted death was averted by prayer, 2 K. 20: 1—5. See a full declaration of such a principle in the divine government, in Jer. 18: 7, 8; and the like elsewhere, in a variety of ways. Daniel, with his deep sympathy for the king, opens before him a probable way of escape from the threatenings, of which he had been the medium of communication. It seems to me more than probable, that by עֲוָיָתָךְ he means to designate the capricious and tyrannical behaviour of Nebuchadnezzar on some occasions, when he fell into a rage; perhaps also to remind him of the heavy hand that pressed on all the captives whom he had led into exile. Daniel however does not name the Jews in particular; for he might apprehend that the king would deem him selfish or partial, if he should openly plead their cause. Still, that עֲנָיִן *afflicted*, *oppressed*, had reference in his own mind to the case of his unhappy countrymen, seems quite probable. It was a deed both of benevolence and of patriotism, to attempt to soften the king's mind in respect to all who were hardly dealt by.

(25) The whole came upon Nebuchadnezzar the king.

כֹּלָּא, emph. = Heb. הַכֹּל, *the whole.*

Vs. 25—30 narrate in the *third* person; seemingly as if the writer himself had broken in upon the course of the king's proclamation by his own narrative. Lengerke and others accuse the writer here of forgetting himself; and, after a period of alleged absence of mind, they describe him as coming to his recollection again in v. 31, and then employing, as at the outset, the *first* person. Lengerke has a very long note to enforce this view, adorned with his usual (!?). Hävern. and Hengstenb., in different ways, had sedulously endeavored to clear the passage in question from the alleged difficulty; and against them his remarks are directed. A simple solution, indeed, they do not seem to have fallen upon. It lies, as I apprehend the matter, in two things, viz. (1) In the frequency with which the Orientals are wont to change persons, where the same individual is spoken of; e. g. from the *first* person to the *third*, Prov. 8: 17 (Kethibh), "*I* love them who love *her*" [me]; Judg. 16: 18 (Kethibh), "Delilah . . . said: Come hither now, for he [Samson] has told his whole heart to her" [to me]; 1 K. 1: 33, "The king said to them: Take with you the servants of your master" [i. e. of me]; Est. 8: 8, "And the king said . . . Write ye . . . in the name of the king" [i. e. in my name]. So also in Isa. 44: 24 seq. 42: 24; comp. Job 12: 4. 13: 27, 28. The like exchange between the 2d and 3d persons is still more frequent. But,

(2) The tenor of narration looks as if the king, in his proclamation, did not intend to present himself as retaining the same rank and standing, during his mania, that he assumes everywhere else. He narrates occurrences which befel him, as he would those which respected a third person. So Maurer; and so, (for the reason first given above), Rosenmüller. In short, this whole matter, which Lengerke molds into a shape that will favor the *late* composition of the book, may well be concluded in the words of Maurer: " *Citra necessitatem*, Lengerke non regem, sed scriptorem sui oblitum, hic loqui existimat." We cannot, indeed, compare this case with that of Moses in the Pentateuch, or of Cesar in his Commentaries, (who employ the *third* person), because each of them employs this person *constantly*. It is the *change*, in this case, from the *first* person to the *third*, in the same discourse, which creates embarrassment. But as this change or use of the third person is strictly limited to the history of the king's actual madness, it would seem to be the effect of *design*, and not of mere forgetfulness.

(26) At the end of twelve months, he was walking upon the royal palace of Babylon.

לִקְצַת, in some Codd. לִקְצָת, rightly, if we may judge from this latter form in 1: 2, 15. 2: 42; for the (ָ) is immutable. The form in the Kethibh must, if correct, come from קְצָה. — תְּרֵי עֲשַׂר, *twelve*, see Par. masc. on p. 102. — עַל הֵיכַל מַלְכוּתָא, lit. *upon the palace of the kingdom.* The meaning is given in the version above. So it is said of David, 2 Sam. 11: 2, that " he arose from off his bed, and walked upon the roof of the house of the king." Both expressions are easily explained. The roofs of the houses in the East are *flat*, and during the warm weather they are the favorite resort of the inhabitants, during the night-season. But Bertholdt and Lengerke find here again the marks of composition by a foreigner; for no one, writing at Babylon, as they aver, would think of saying what every body knew, viz. that the king's palace *was in Babylon*. Of course the usual (!) is appended to a recital of Hengstenberg's defence of the phrase. But I may beg leave to ask: Had Nebuchadnezzar only *one* palace? Had he not, like all oriental kings of that time, palaces in different places of his dominions? And if so, is there anything suspicious in the fact, that the writer of this book, or rather, that Nebuchadnezzar in his proclamation, should name specifically to the people of his empire the exact place where his misfortune came upon him?

(27) The king spake and said: Is not this the same great Babylon, which I have built for a habitation of royalty, by my mighty power, and for the honor of my glory?

עָנֵה, Part., *to commence* a discourse or address; *spake* is the nearest word we have in English for such a case. The king is speaking within himself, so that we cannot translate by *addressed.* — הִיא = αὐτή, *the same, the very,* § 43. 6. *b.* — רַבְּתָא, emph. fem. of רַב. — ־ֵהּ . . . דִּי, *which.* — בְּנַיְתַהּ, first pers. sing. with suff. ־ָהּ, from בְּנָא. — The normal form would seem to be בְּנֵיתָה, see Peal, p. 72; but in this case the analogy of the 2d pers. sing. is followed, a case which Winer fails to notice. — מַלְכוּ = מַלְכוּת, § 31. 1. — בִּתְקָף, in some Codd. בִּתְקֹף (the usual form), in others בִּתְקַף; all of which are conformable to the Chaldee idiom. If the Kethibh is correct, the (ָ) is immutable, and so it remains in the const. state. This word, joined with חַסְנִי (lit. *might of my strength*), conveys the idea given in the version. — לִיקַר, (Codd. al. לִיקָר, with Qamets immutable), in its literal meaning, designates *what is precious; honor* is a secondary and derivate meaning, but not an unfrequent one. — הַדְרִי, *my glory,* I understand as pertaining to the *splendor* of his own condition, and of all things about him. In other words, the magnitude and splendor of the Babylonish structures would redound to the honor of Nebuchadnezzar who erected them.

That the language here ascribed to Nebuchadnezzar is in good keeping with the spirit of Oriental despots like him, there can be no question; comp. Isa. 10: 13. 14: 13, 14. 36: 18—20. It has indeed been suggested, that 'the writer of the book here betrays a want of knowledge as to *facts,* inasmuch as Babylon was built long before the time of Nebuchadnezzar.' It was so, in truth, if we mean by *built* merely the *founding* of a city; for its first origin goes back to the *mighty hunter,* Nimrod, Gen. 10: 9, 10. Ctesias, (in Diod. Sic. II. 7 seq.), has given us a very protracted account of its magnificent structures, and ascribes them, with only one exception, (the hanging gardens, ib. § 10), to the famous and fabled Assyrian Semiramis. Whoever or whatever she was, the probability that she did all which Ctesias ascribes to her, nay even the possibility, is out of all question; as every intelligent reader may easily see for himself by reading the narration in Diodorus. That Babylon, however, was a large city before the time of Nebuchadnezzar, there can be no doubt. But as Babylonia had become an *independent* province or kingdom only a few years before the reign of Nebuchadnezzar, beyond a question the city of Babylon itself, before this last period, was much inferior both in size and splendor to what it became under the fostering care of its mightiest king. When Nebuchadnezzar returned from his predatory expedition into Asia Minor and Egypt, richly laden with spoils, Berosus says, that "he built the temple of Belus, and adorned other structures with great profusion; moreover, that which was from ancient times a city, he made *another city* by his munificence, *building it anew;*" Berosus, as quoted by Josephus, Antiq. X. 11. 1. With this account we may easily reconcile what Herodotus says of this city. The judgment of E.O. Müller (Handb. der Archaeol. etc. s. 265) seems worthy of confidence here, for he was no ordinary critic: "We decidedly prefer the history of Berosus, drawn from the archives [of the temple of Belus], respecting the origin of these structures, to the fables in Ctesias and Diodorus, which rest in part on the popular appellation (*Semirămis-works*) for all the great works of the East." When our text applies the verb בְּנָה to what was done by Nebuchadnezzar, this word is to be taken in a sense that is by no means unfrequent, viz. that of *restoring, renewing,* quasi *rebuilding;* see Ges. Lex. בָּנָה, No. 2. It is even extended to the mere *fortifying* of a city, 1 K. 15: 17. It was not a mere empty boast, then, on the part of Nebuchadnezzar that he had made Babylon great and splendid. But the haughty spirit with which he uttered his self-gratulations, was the signal for the divine displeasure to light upon him. As to Babylon itself, the Heb. Scriptures frequently mention it in such a way, as to show that the statement of Nebuchadnezzar, in regard to its magnificence, is not overstrained; comp. Isa. 13: 19. 14: 4. 47: 5, 7; to which add Rev. 16: 19. 14: 8. Pausanias calls it "the greatest city on which the sun looks down;" and Strabo (Lib. XVI.) says, that "one might apply to it the verse: *The great city is a great desert,*" probably in reference to its vast extent (not its desolation), in which one might lose himself. The *mighty power* which Nebuchadnezzar ascribes to himself in building the city, doubtless refers to the vast numbers of men at his disposal, who must have been employed in the accomplishment of his work.

(28) While the word was yet in the mouth of the king, a voice came down from heaven: To thee is it said, O King Nebuchadnezzar, the kingdom departeth from thee.

נְפַל, *fell, came down;* so of the *word of the Lord* in Isa. 9: 7. The design of employing this verb is to indicate the source from which the message came, i. e. from *above* or from *heaven.* So Mohammed employs the like verb, when speaking of his pretended revelations in the Koran. — אָמְרִין, lit. *they say,* but as no *subject* of the Part is indicated, I have rendered it *passively,* as in general it should be rendered in such cases, § 49. 3. *b.* — עֲדָת, 3 fem. of עֲדָה. — מִנָּךְ, מִן, when it takes a suffix, inserts a Dagh. f. before it, § 38. 2. note. Lengerke suggests, that before אָמְרִין (Part. pl. indef. and so *passive*) the usual לֵאמֹר should be supplied by the mind of the reader. This is erroneous as to the *Chaldee* grammar and usage, for this word is no Chaldee Inf. (which is מֵאמַר). If the full construction were expressed, it would be so by another participle; comp. in v. 27. But this is quite unnecessary. Doubtless Nebuchadnezzar means to refer the voice to the *Watcher* (v. 10), whom he had before seen to descend from heaven.

(29) And from men shalt thou be driven out, and with the beast of the field shall be thy dwelling; herbage shall be given thee to eat, like the oxen; and seven times shall pass over thee, until thou shalt know that the Most High is ruler over the kingdom of men, and that he giveth it to whomsoever he pleaseth.

טָרְדִין, lit. *they shall drive out* or *expel,* and so the Part. governs the Acc. לָךְ. In rendering the Part. (impersonal) *passively,* I have been obliged to forsake the Heb. mode of constructing the clause. For the rest of the verse, see on vs. 12—14.

(30) At that very moment, the declaration respecting Nebuchadnezzar was accomplished, and from among men was he driven out, and herbage did he eat like the oxen, and by the dew of heaven was he bathed, until his hair grew like [that of] the eagles, and his nails like [those of] birds.

Comp. v. 22. In the three cases where כְּ is here employed before nouns, it is plain that the preceding noun is to be mentally supplied, i. e. repeated, after it, or (as twice in the version) a pronoun which is the representative of it, is to be inserted. — שַׂעְרֵהּ designates the rough coat of hair which an exposed human body naturally forms, in order to defend itself against the elements. In the implied phrase, *the hair of the eagles*, שְׂעַר will not bear the same sense, strictly speaking, but the meaning is, *like to the natural covering given to the eagles*. The comparison touches only the point of a natural growth of covering for the body. The roughness of the covering may seem, perhaps, to be an adsignification here, inasmuch as it is compared to feathers. — טִפְרוֹהִי, pl. with suff., *his nails*, viz. of the fingers and toes, which, being neglected, grew to an extraordinary length, like the claws of birds. Neither of these circumstances indicates anything very unusual, in the case of such a maniac. Not unfrequent have been cases, where madmen have shunned all human society, and betaken themselves to the haunts and to the food of wild beasts. The *wild men* that have been caught, at one time and another, show what our bodily nature is capable of bearing, and how it may be supported. In a climate so excessively warm as that of Babylonia, there was no great danger to life from mere exposure to the air. And as to *nutriment*, there can be no question but wild fruits and herbage would supply it. To the many objections made against this whole account, some reply will be made at the close of the chapter.

(31) And at the end of the days, I Nebuchadnezzar lifted up mine eyes to heaven, and my understanding returned to me, and I blessed the most High, and Him who liveth forever I praised and glorified; for his dominion is an everlasting dominion, and his kingdom to generation and generation:

End of the days, viz. of the times named by the decree of the Watchers. — *Lifting up the eyes to heaven* designates the gesture and posture of prayer. — *My understanding returned to me;* not to be regarded, however, as *subsequent* in point of time to the prayer, for how could he pray without any understanding? It is merely a *sequency in the narration* explaining and expanding the preceding clause; and such a sequency cannot be avoided in a narration, which can communicate only one thing at a time. — *I blessed the most High*, recounts part of the address to Heaven; לְעִלָּיָא Acc. governed by בָּרְכֵת, which is in Pael, בָּ because of the following ר. — לְחַי, the Acc. governed by שַׁבְּחֵת; the latter is in Pael, as also חֲדְרַת. — שָׁלְטָן עָלַם, lit. *dominion of eternity.* — עִם דָּר, lit. *with generation;* but as עִם marks *with* in the sense of *contemporaneous,* (see on 3: 33), I have given the meaning of the phrase in a manner that accords with our English idiom.

(32) And all the inhabitants of the earth are counted as nothing; and he doeth according to his own pleasure in the army of the heavens, and [among] the inhabitants of the earth; and there is none that can stay his hand, or say to him: What doest thou?

דָּאָרֵי, see on 2: 38. — כְּלָה = כְּלָא, which stands in the margin, and means *as nothing,* lit. *as not.* — חֲשִׁיבִין, *reckoned, counted,* in Heb. and Chaldee usage often equivalent to *are.* — מִצְבְּיֵהּ, Inf. Peal. of צְבָא, with a suff. after the manner of a noun, § 16. 2. c. — עָבֵד Part., which is specially adapted to express continued or repeated action. — *Army of the heavens,* in the mouth of Nebuchadnezzar, was probably meant to comprise both the *heavenly bodies* and the *spiritual beings* supposed to preside over and govern them. The *star-worship* of the East generally retained this feature of Parsism. — *Stay his hand,* lit. *smite his hand,* i. e. by a blow to avert the direction of the hand, and prevent its hitting the mark intended. This expression, borrowed from literal action in the first place, passed over afterwards into the figurative sense given in the translation. — The whole verse stands connected with what was uttered in Nebuchadnezzar's prayer (as given above), and is a description of the power and irresistible dominion of the Most High, which is here continued, but which has its commencement in v. 31.

Lengerke, in order to show that the proclamation of Nebuchadnezzar is only a figment of some late author, and not a matter of fact, asserts that the verse before us is evidently copied from Isa. 40: 17. 24: 19. I can only say, that if the reader can find anything more than a similarity of ideas as to two or three particulars, he must be more sharp-sighted than I can claim to be. That either of the passages is a *copy* of the other, or a designed imitation of it, does not seem to my mind at all probable; for the minuter characteristic shades of expression are clearly diverse. What can be more easy and natural, than that the same clear conviction and deep impression of certain great and plain truths, should be uttered by different persons, in language that discloses some general points of similarity?

(33) At the same time, my understanding returned to me; and, for the honor of my royal dignity, my glory and my splendor returned to me, and me did my privy-councillors and my nobles seek, and over my kingdom was I placed, and much power was added to me.

בֵּהּ זִמְנָא, § 43. 6. *b.* — יְתוּב, simple Fut. Peal, and yet necessarily translated as a simple *Preterite*. Of this I find no notice, either in the Chaldee Grammar of Winer, or in any of the commentators. In § 44. 3, seq. Winer assigns five different shades of meaning to the Fut., but the one before us belongs to neither of these. Yet this same Future form is repeated again, in this same verse, and often elsewhere, as has before been noticed. We cannot rank it here under a like category with the Heb. Fut., which is used to designate things *habituallg done*, or *often repeated;* for the *return* of Nebuchadnezzar's understanding cannot well be placed on this footing, unless indeed it be maintained that, in his case a gradual restoration of intellect and honor took place. This is very possible in itself, but the connection here makes against it. It is more probable, that *at the end of the days* Nebuchadnezzar was completely restored to his reason and his office. The secret of such a usage of the Fut., in this case, lies perhaps in בֵּהּ זִמְנָא; for in *Heb.*, after particles of *time*, the Fut. designates the *past*, comp. Roed. Heb. Gramm. § 125. 4. *a*, comp. *c* ib. Our text seems, in regard to this, to Hebraize. — עֲלַי, *to me*, עַל in Chald. very often is the same as אֶל, see Lex. — In arranging and translating the next clause, there is much division of opinion among critics. C. B. Michaelis, Lengerke, Maurer, thus: *To the honor of my kingdom, of my glory, and of my splendor it* [my reason] *returned to me.* Hävernick divides the clause at the end of the word *glory*, and then throws the sequel into another clause, thus: *And my splendor returned to me.* This last method is against the *accents*, which connect together הַדְרִי וְזִיוִי. Leng. asserts (p. 200), that the *accents* favor his method of arrangement; in which he doubtless refers to the Pashta on זִיוִי; but this is a mere attendant upon the *Zāquēph Qātōn* that follows (עֲלַי), and will not at all prove that *my glory and my splendor* are to be regarded as Genitives in apposition with מַלְכוּתִי. In fact the contrary of this is true; for when a clause with *four* words terminates with a Zāqēph Qātōn (◌ֽ), the accents are arranged just as here in עֲלַי . . . הַדְרִי, see Nordheim. Heb. Gramm. p. 388. *d.* I have therefore translated as above, in the same way as Rosenmüller. To make *mine understanding* an implied Nom. to the second יְתוּב, not only exhibits a useless repetition of this verb (for the same thing has already been twice said, vs. 31, 33), but mars the sense, at least in part. Nebuchadnezzar means simply to say, that first of all his reason returned, and then returned with it all his former regal splendor. The second יְתוּב has for its Nom. the proximate preceding noun; a construction common to most languages, and especially to the Semitic. — וְלִי, *and me*, Acc., differing from עֲלַי which twice precedes; placed first in the clause for the sake of peculiar emphasis. — יְבַעוֹן, Fut. Pael of בְּעָא, בָ because the Daghesh is excluded from the ע. There is no need of the marginal יְבַעוֹן, which substitutes Peal for Pael. As for the accent on the *ultimate* here, see p. 25 in the Note. — הָתְקְנַת, Hoph. of תְּקַן, instead of the Chald. Ithpael, § 12. 6, p. 50; the final נַת —, instead of the normal נֵת —, is common in Guttural verbs; p. 53. n. 3 (at bottom) gives an analogy, and so on p. 49. 2 (ad fin.). Gutturals and Liquids not unfrequently take Pattah final, in the 3d fem., and in the first person; although the Grammar has not distinctly recognized this. — רְבוּ for רְבוּת, I have translated power, because one meaning of רבה is, *potens fuit*. *Amplitude* would be more literal; but it fails to designate the respect in which there was an augmentation. — הוּסְפַת, Hoph. again of יְסַף, p. 50. 6. Here the third pers. sing. has its regular ending in Pattah. The reading סַ instead of the regular סְ, is only for the sake of distinctness. The difficulties which recent criticism has found in the declarations or assertions of this verse, will be noticed in the sequel.

(34) Now I Nebuchadnezzar highly praise and exalt and glorify the king of the heavens, all of whose doings are truth, and whose ways are justice; and those who walk haughtily, he is able to humble.

The three Part. are in Pael, Polel (§ 14. 2), and again in Pael, all intensive, and so translated. — לְמֶלֶךְ, Acc. — מַעֲבָדוֹהִי, plur. with suff. — קְשׁוֹט, *truth*, i. e. without deceit or falsehood; and so דִּין, *justice*, i. e. just, or in accordance with justice; both phrases are like *God is love*, i. e. abstract for concrete. — אֹרְחָתֵהּ, pl. fem. form, having a suffix; *ways* means *proceedings*, *doings*, *actions*, which use of the word is very common in Heb. and Chaldee. — יָכִל, Part., for form see § 12. 1. 1. *c*.

[EXCURSUS. — *Objections* to a chapter like the preceding, we might naturally expect, from the fashionable criticism of the day. A considerable host of them have been mustered into the service, by many agents. I shall notice only such as seem to deserve serious consideration.

(1) It is alleged, that 'the publication of such a decree by Nebuchadnezzar, a decree which holds him up to the contempt of his subjects and to disgrace, is an utter improbability.' Lengerke (p. 151) is so confident of this, that he expresses disapprobation of Bertholdt, Bleek, and Kirms, for conceding that Abydenus, who relates a story of Nebuchadnezzar's madness, had any even fleeting rumors of this kind to build upon. The whole, he thinks, is nothing more nor less than pure fiction.

What particular inducement there was for Abydenus to invent such a fiction *de novo*, he does not tell us. It is easy to see, that tradition, when it reached Abydenus, (who not improbably lived in the second century B. C.), might have added some circumstances to the story, in order to make it the more wonderful, and that Abydenus himself, (no very skilful or critical writer), may have helped to adorn it. But the simple categorical assertion that he had *no basis* to build upon, in writing his account of Nebuchadnezzar's madness — may pass for what it is worth, with all candid judges.

In the mean time, conceding for the present that Nebuchadnezzar was seized with *mania*, and recovered from it, how is it to be made certain, that he was not, on his recovery, in a state of mind that would lead him to publish the whole matter to his subjects, in order that they also might be led to praise "the king of heaven" as well as he? If anything could humble a haughty tyrant, like him, what he had suffered was well adapted to do so. And if all that had come upon him, had come in accordance with the predictions of Daniel, the impression made on a highly susceptible mind, like his, must needs be very strong. The first thing to which all strong emotions of penitence lead, is ample confession of sin. Who can show us that Nebuchadnezzar did not now become truly penitent? But be that as it may, he may well be supposed to have felt deep regret for his pride and haughtiness, and a strong sense of humiliation. In this state, I know of no way in which a man of powerful emotions, like him, can be shown to be incapable of acknowledging his offences and deploring his folly. Taking the statement of his whole demeanor together, the writer of the book may be well acquitted of any *incongruity* in his account of these matters. He presents Nebuchadnezzar as so humbled, and so affected by the discipline that he had received, as to seek the opportunity of publishing to the world his bitter experience, and his acknowledgments of gratitude for restoration. A state of mind like this leaves no room for selfish and honor-saving devices, which, as many critics allege, must have prevented his making such a proclamation as is contained in chapter iv. But do not these critics draw conclusions rather from what they themselves would do or be likely to do in such circumstances, or from what Nebuchadnezzar would have done in the height of his prosperity and his haughtiness, than from what Nebuchadnezzar as a disciplined, sobered, humbled, and penitent man would do? In a word, if Nebuchadnezzar was humbled, (and it would seem that he had suffered enough to humble him), he was, judging from all the characteristics of him that we can collect, and especially from the ardor and intensity of his emotions, very likely to do such a thing as the one in question. Nothing is more common than for such men to go from one extreme to the other.

I crave the liberty of making one more remark. The reader of the book before us, who acknowledges an overruling and a merciful Providence, will not fail to see, that such a proclamation as that of Nebuchadnezzar, coming from the renowned hero and conqueror who had advanced his country to the highest pinnacle of dominion and fame, would have a very important influence on the minds of the Babylonians, and lead them to treat the Hebrew exiles among them with more than usual respect and lenity. The writer of the book of Daniel may have had higher ends and nobler objects in view, than some of the critics have attributed to him.

Thus much as to the *fact* of publishing such an *Exposé*. The next step, on the part of objectors is, to deny the historical probability of the circumstances stated. 'His madness,' they say, 'for so long a period, although possible, is utterly improbable, because no writer mentions anything of it, except the author of Daniel. Who can believe that so extraordinary a thing, and one which must have put at peril all the great interests of the kingdom, would have been passed by, in giving the history of this king? The whole affair, therefore, wears the air of fiction and not of fact.'

Taking these assertions as founded in truth, in regard to the absence elsewhere of any account of Nebuchadnezzar's *mania*, and comparing this with our modern method of writing history and biography, there seems to be at least an appearance of something formidable in it, with respect to the credit of the book before us. But he who is familiar with the fragments of early oriental history that remain, will be slow to set up such a standard of judging. The *argumentum a silentio* is one of the most treacherous of all that encumber the logic of history. For example; it is very easy for us to ask: How, in writing Solomon's life, could his excessive polygamy and sensuality, his idolatry, and finally his danger arising from the aggressions of numerous and powerful enemies, near the close of his life, be passed over? And yet the writer of the Chronicles has not even mentioned one of these circumstances. In a life of David, how could his adultery and murder be passed by? Yet the same author has not even adverted to them. And if we go to the N. Test., it is easy to raise like questions there. How could such miracles as that at the pool of Bethesda, or the raising of Lazarus from the dead, be passed over in silence by three of the Evangelists? And because they are so, is that enough to convict John of writing mere *romance?*

Who, moreover, are they that have undertaken to write the history of Nebuchadnezzar's later life? The scriptural histories give us only the former part of his long reign, and cease with that. The prophets Jeremiah and Ezekiel ceased to write, and in fact were dead, before the close of Nebuchadnezzar's reign, and of course have left us nothing concerning it. The Grecian writers, even Herodotus himself who speaks so much of Babylon, say nothing of Nebuchadnezzar; and indeed, how little dependence can be placed on any history of the remote East by the Grecian writers of a late age, seems now to be generally understood and acknowledged. Josephus (Antiqq.) and Eusebius (Chron.), who have industriously brought together all they could find respecting Nebuchadnezzar, have mentioned only *six* writings which recognize him. (1) The Phenician Annals; which merely mention his attack on Phenicia. (2) The Phenician History of Philostrates, which merely mentions his besieging Tyre. (3) Megasthenes (flor. c. 280 B. C.), who in his History of India, mentions the overrunning of Libya and Iberia by Nebuchadnezzar, (which is probably an error). (4) Diocles, in his Persian History, makes a merely casual mention of him, (Jos. Antiq. X. 11. Cont. Ap. I. 21.). We are reduced then to *two* historians, Berosus and Abydenus, who both drew from Chaldee annals or tradition. Of these we have, indeed, only a few remnants; but we seem to have all which they wrote respecting Nebuchadnezzar. In Berosus, the whole account does not amount to two pages 12mo; and about half of this is occupied with an account of the structures which Nebuchadnezzar reared at Babylon; see Richter's Berosus, p. 65 seq. In such a mere table of contents, or skeleton-sketch, of a reign of more than forty years, and of the conquest of all hither Asia, how could it be expected that a writer would give a detail of private personal infirmities? Suppose, for example, some three centuries hence, a writer should undertake to give the history of George the third, and of his doings in England during a long and most eventful reign. If confined to a page and a half, would he be likely to tell the story of this king's mania, and the particulars of the interim Regency?

And if he omitted these, would it be any proof that there was neither *mania* nor *regency?* Besides, Berosus not improbably had other feelings toward the Babylonish heroes, than such as would lead him to dwell on particulars like the one in question. How comes it, that Manetho, and the Greek writers who have followed him, while they celebrate the victory of Pharaoh Necho over the Syrians, in the time of Josiah, say not a word of his defeat at Carchemish? It is plain, that Manetho did not wish to wither the laurels of his conqueror; and so he has refrained from the latter part of the story. And do the Persian histories recognize the defeats of Xerxes by the Grecians, and that of Darius by Alexander in Asia? Such things are too common among ancient historians, to excite any surprise on the part of him who is conversant with them.

As to *Abydenus*, what we have of him is still less than the remains of Berosus. And yet, as we shall soon see, there is something in what little he does say, that deserves our particular examination. In Euseb. Praep. Evang. IX. 41, is a quotation from him, the amount of which is, that just before his death, Nebuchadnezzar, ascending his palace, was seized with a *divine afflatus*, uttered certain gloomy predictions concerning Babylon, in respect to the future, and then suddenly disappeared.* The last part of this passage has a singular air, and seems to be a kind of popular version of the story of Nebuchadnezzar's madness, as told in his proclamation. But along with this, there is seemingly an evident attempt to cover the disgrace of that *mania*, by converting it into a *furor propheticus*. Daniel has predicted (7: 5) the rise and progress of the Medo-Persian dominion, and its all-devouring nature; and Nebuchadnezzar himself, in his dream of the colossal image, had a view of the same, 2: 39. By mixing this with what is said of his madness, and giving to Nebuchadnezzar himself a *prophetic afflatus*, (which not unnaturally connected itself with his foreboding dreams), the whole paragraph of Abydenus seems to be made up. I should not suspect him of having seen the book of Daniel; but that the traditions from which he drew, had been formed among the populace, and partly modified by that book, or at least by popular rumor according in some good measure with it, among the Hebrews in exile, one can hardly see good reason to

* The passage is so singular, that I deem it expedient to present a translation of it to the reader, that he may judge for himself. Abydenus first quotes Megasthenes as an authority, in regard to Nebuchadnezzar's conquest of Lybia and Iberia. He then proceeds to relate the further tradition of the Chaldeans respecting him: "After these things [the conquests above named], *as it is said by the Chaldeans*, having ascended his palace, he was seized by some god, and speaking aloud he said: 'I Nebuchadnezzar, O Babylonians, foretel your future calamity, which neither Belus my ancestor, nor queen Belis, can persuade the Destinies to avert. A *Persian mule* will come, employing your own divinities as his auxiliaries; and he will impose servitude [upon you]. His coadjutor will be the *Mede*, who is the boast of the Assyrians. Would that, before he places my citizens in such a condition, some Charybdis or gulf might swallow him up with utter destruction! Or that, turned in a different direction, he might roam in the desert, (where are neither cities, nor footsteps of man, but wild beasts find pasturage, and the birds wander), being there hemmed in by rocks and ravines! May it be my lot to attain to a better end, before such things come into his mind!' Having uttered this prediction, he forthwith disappeared."

doubt. How came tradition to assign such a prediction, concerning the *Persian mule*, to Nebuchadnezzar? In his life time, the Persians were not known as anything more than a mere clan of a province. There must have been something to originate such a *unique* prediction, in the minds of the Chaldees. I can think of nothing more likely to do so, than a cursory and hasty reading of the book of Daniel among them, or at least a Hebrew tradition such as has been before named. Nebuchadnezzar was the main subject, for he was the object of the national boasting and glory; the things, which are described in Dan. iv. as about to come on him, he is made to shift from himself, and to desire that they may be put upon the *Persian mule.* Finally he vanishes from the sight of men, in a manner like to that in which he disappears, when struck with madness. Abydenus may be quite honest in relating all this, (and I see not why we should doubt of it), and yet the popular rumor which he copied, may have been, and evidently was, a confused and heterogeneous mixture. It was difficult to reconcile the account of Daniel with the glorification of the renowned hero. Hence such an amalgamation of rumors, as would save the credit of Nebuchadnezzar; for a divine *afflatus* and a sudden disappearance were considered by most heathen, as marked tokens of the good pleasure of the godhead. The least that we can now make of all this is, that in Abydenus' time there was still, among the Chaldees, a tradition about something extraordinary and peculiar in the closing part of Nebuchadnezzar's life. At all events, the account in Daniel is by far the most rational, sober, and credible. Indeed the other is little short of a mere monstrosity; and no one will for a moment deem it credible, in the shape in which it is presented to us by Abydenus. There are, however, with all the incongruities, some striking *coincidences* between Abydenus and Daniel. Both represent the extraordinary event, whatever it was, as occurring after the close of Nebuchadnezzar's conquests, and near the close of life. Both present the thing as happening, while Nebuchadnezzar was on the top of his palace. According to the Greek text as amended by Scaliger, (and now confirmed by the Armenian Version of Eusebius' Chronicon), Nebuchadnezzar is said to be seized ϑεῷ ὅτεω δή, *by some divinity;* which, in the mouth of Chaldees, can scarcely mean anything else than *some foreign god.* What then can be the import of this, unless there is mingled with it some of the elements contained in Dan. iv.? Disfigured these elements are, by the inaccuracy of traditionary report, and by the spirit of hero-worship which pervaded the Babylonians. But after all, the impression is inevitably made by Abydenus, that according to Chaldee tradition, Nebuchadnezzar ended his life in some unusual or extraordinary manner.

But what says Berosus in respect to this? He says (in his *third* book, cont. Apion. I. 20), that "Nebuchadnezzar, after beginning the aforementioned wall, ἐμπεσὼν εἰς τὴν ἀῤῥωστίαν, *falling into a sickness*, departed this life, after reigning forty-three years." 'But is there anything *uncommon* in this?' is the question which we are called upon at once to answer. 'Do not men usually sicken before they die? Why should we consider this as anything special?' For the very reason, I answer, that sickness is so common before death as not to need being mentioned; and therefore the particular mention of it is adapted to awaken a suspicion, that something special is meant by a specification of this nature. Of Neriglossar and Nabonned, both successors of Nebuchadnezzar, who, according to Berosus, both died a natural death, nothing is said in respect to their falling sick.

'But does not Berosus say the same thing (in regard to *sickness*), of Nebuchadnezzar's father Nabopolassar?' 'And as nothing special is to be made out of the latter case, why should we attempt to make out anything special in the case of Nebuchadnezzar himself?'

This statement, however, as it seems to my mind, is not altogether correct. There is a special reason why the sickness of Nabopolassar is mentioned. Berosus first states, that the king had intelligence that his Satrap in Western Asia had revolted, and *οὐ δυνάμενος αὐτὸς ἔτι κακοπαθεῖν*, *being unable himself any longer to undergo hardships*, he sent his son to subdue the revolters. While Nebuchadnezzar was engaged in this mission, "it happened to Nabopolassar his father, *who was sick at this time* (*κατὰ τοῦτον τὸν καιρὸν ἀῤῥωστήσαντι*), to die at Babylon." Now the obvious reason of mentioning his infirm state here, is to show why he sent his son with his army, instead of heading it himself. His death is afterwards connected with this sickness, in order to show, that he continued infirm during the expedition led by his son, until the time of his death. Of course, the mere ordinary idea of a sickness which precedes death, is not the one which the writer aims to communicate; and if something special in this case is denoted, by the mention of the sickness, we may well suppose that something special in the second case is meant. But what is it? It is that Nebuchadnezzar had begun a wall of some kind, the completion of which was interrupted by his *falling sick*, *ἐμπεσῶν εἰς ἀῤῥωστίαν*. Lengerke makes light of this mode of expression, and thinks that Hengstenberg mistakes the nature of the Greek idiom, when he attributes more to it, than to the simple *ἀῤῥωστήσαντι* employed to describe the condition of Nabopolassar. Most clearly Hengstenberg is substantially in the right; for at least it carries with it the accessory idea of being *suddenly invaded by sickness*, which the other (the latter) does not. What this sickness was, Berosus does not say; nor could we expect him to do so. But independently of this, his mode of expression conveys at least the idea of a sudden and unexpected sickness. Our text affords an ample explanation of the matter.

'But the two cases are not alike; nay they are directly opposed to each other. Daniel says that Nebuchadnezzar was stricken with mania; and that he *recovered* both his health and station; Berosus, that he died of his sickness; and even Abydenus, that he suddenly disappeared in his ecstasy. Here then is contradiction, not *confirmation*.'

So Lengerke, p. 146 seq. But as to Abydenus, this part of his account is too plainly fabulous to support an objection. The single clause of Berosus, in which he tells the story, seems indeed to connect the sickness with the death of Nebuchadnezzar. But no limitation of time is made, in respect to the duration of the sickness. No particulars whatever are given. In the absence of everything of this nature, we cannot well make out from Berosus a *contradiction* of Daniel. Do the books of the Chronicles contradict those of the kings, because they *omit* any account of the failings and sins of David and Solomon? A spirit of liberal criticism will hardly venture upon such a position. If now, as seems quite probable, Nebuchadnezzar died very soon after his restoration, then there were no special political achievements of his to be recorded by the Chaldee historian. At all events there appears to be no *contradiction* between him and Daniel, when the nature of the case is fully considered. The one gives a mere general statement, in the briefest manner practicable; the other goes into particulars.

'But *seven years* of madness! And during all this time no revolution of government, and no other king placed on the throne! How is all this to be rendered probable?'

As to the *length of time*, commentators seem to have been somewhat perplexed by it. Calvin thinks that *seven* is here an indefinite number, employed to denote *a considerable period*. So Hengstenberg (Authentie, s. 113); who also intimates, that it is not necessary to consider *times* as denoting *years*. Hävernick has gone further, and maintains that these times were *astrological periods*. But the idiom of the book (see 7: 25. 12: 7), seems to forbid this. I do not think that we can fairly shun the conclusion that *years* are meant. But then a *seven years'* madness is no uncommon occurrence, and therefore presents no difficulty. But we are called upon to show how the kingdom was managed, without another king. And this question we may answer by saying, that it was probably managed just as it was after the death of Nabopolassar, during the expedition of Nebuchadnezzar to western Asia, i. e. by the Magi, and in particular by the head of this order, who seems to have been officially a kind of *viceroy*, in case of an exigency. So Berosus expressly represents the matter, when he speaks of Nebuchadnezzar's return to his capital. On this occasion he says, that "he took upon himself the affairs which had been managed by the Chaldees [Magi], and the royal authority *which had been preserved for him by their chief*," (Jos. Antiq. X. 11. 1). So when the Medes and Babylonians combine to destroy Nineveh, the *chief priest* of the Magi, Belesis, is presented as the leader and prince of the Chaldeans; Diod. Sic. II. Moreover as Hengstenberg remarks, the nobles may have had many reasons for continuing a regency in this way, as it put great power into their hands without subjecting them to danger from the exercise of it. That Nebuchadnezzar was a thorough disciplinarian, and well understood order and subordination, the extent of his conquests and the durability of his power would seem to show. His affairs, therefore, might have gone on as usual, with but little trouble. The case before us, then, in respect to the *interregnum*, presents no very serious difficulty.

'But if Nebuchadnezzar ran wild at large, with the beasts, how could his nobles *seek after him*, and where would they go to find him? How, moreover, should they know *when* to go; or *when* his reason returned; or indeed that it did at all return?'

Questions, as it seems to me, of much less significancy and difficulty, than have been attached to them by many of the recent critics on the book of Daniel. Some of them, too, depend for what little importance they have, on a wrongly assumed exegesis of the text. When it is said that "Nebuchadnezzar's nobles *sought for him*" (יְבַעוֹן), this phrase is not to be understood in the sense of looking for something which is *lost;* like our phrase *to hunt up* or *hunt out*; for when Arioch and his guard *sought after* (בְּעוֹ) Daniel to kill him (2: 13), he had neither absconded nor concealed himself. *To seek after* is, in the style of the book before us, to *make inquiry for* or *of.*

This the nobles of Babylon did, so soon as they heard of the king's restoration.

As to wandering away from the abodes of men, and lodging and feeding with the wild beasts, all the questions that are raised as to the probability or possibility of this amount to little or nothing. A fierce madman of this disposition would easily elude the most thorough vigilance, and make his escape; comp. Mark 5: 1—5. Hengstenberg, indeed, represents Nebuchadnezzar as chained the whole time (see v. 20), and attended by a watch-guard, to see where he might go, and to secure him from injury. But our text conveys to my own mind quite a different impression. The *chain* of v. 20 seems to be applied to keeping in security the *root-trunk* of the tree, and so to preserve it that a germ would in due time shoot up. That Nebuchadnezzar roamed at large, seems to lie on the face of the representation in chap. iv. That his haunts were known, and that some kind of watch-guard was placed over him whose business it was to look to any exigency that might occur, seems highly probable when we consider the rank and popularity of Nebuchadnezzar. When he became rational, he would of course return to his home and his friends. He needed not to be *hunted out*. It often happens, that persons fall into a mania which lasts many years, and on coming out of it suddenly, their consciousness is connected with the state in which they were immediately before their malady, and the intervening period is entirely lost. In case of the king's return, it would at once be known, not only where he was, but also what was his then present condition.

As to the various fantastic representations that have been made of the description of Nebuchadnezzar during his madness, transmuting him into some compound of an animal with claws and feathers, and the like, it is unnecessary to canvass them. Origen, not knowing, as it would seem, what to do with the representation, makes it (*more suo*) an allegorical representation of the fall of Satan; and Jerome (Comm. on 4: 7) uses the *argumentum ad hominem* against heathen objectors, and asks, whether the story is not as probable, as their reports about Chimaeras, Hydras, Centaurs, and the like. It would be unreasonable to ask assent to such views as these; but we may boldly say, that due allowance being made for oriental costume in the description of Nebuchadnezzar's person and demeanor, there is nothing in either beyond the common bounds of probability. To draw from the expression " his hair became like that of eagles," the conclusion that he became *feathered*, would be following up the literal meaning beyond all reason. The covered hirsute condition of his body is the point of comparison, and the object is not to assert that he became a feathered animal. Besides, the word which we translate *eagles* (נִשְׁרִין) is more generic in the original, and comprises the various species of the *vulture*. The *bald eagle*, however, (for which the word also stands), seems to be the particular object pointed at in the comparison. If so, no further defence of the language is needed. Madmen have so often acted over scenes like those here described, that wonder at such a condition would seem to betoken ignorance of facts.

Finally it is urged, that the whole chapter has a mere *paraenetic* or *hortatory* tendency; and that in order to impress the *moral* ideas designed to be communicated in this way, the whole romance is introduced; not for the purposes of fraud, as even Lengerke seems willing to concede, but for a purpose like that which produces so many moral romances at the present day. The object is, as critics of this class affirm, to present the character and the doom of Antiochus Epiphanes, and to encourage the Jews to persevere in their opposition to that tyrant.

But of such romances, written in such a way among the Hebrews, we have no certain examples. We have parables and fables; but they are always explained by the context. Such as we have, moreover, are very short, and of a very different tenor from the present narration. As to *Antiochus* — what is there in his life to correspond with the chapter before us? If he deserved the name of *madman*, it was by his vile conduct, and not because his intellect was really supposed to be deranged. Besides, Nebuchadnezzar did not persecute the Jews for their religion; Antiochus did, even to the last extremity. Nebuchadnezzar repented after his madness, and proclaimed his penitence to the world; Antiochus did neither. Both indeed were *heathen* kings, and both were zealots for idolatry; but so were hundreds of other kings, and there is no speciality in this. But if this be excepted, then what is left in ch. iv. to remind any one of Antiochus, either as to his life or his death?

That the whole book of Daniel has a moral and religious *substratum*, which is ever kept in view, I would fully and most readily acknowledge. It would not be what we should expect from such a man as Daniel, if this were not the case. But as to a *prototype* in the present case of Antiochus, it needs a magnifying-glass of peculiar power to discover it.

CHAP. V. CONTENTS.

[The reader of this book would make a great mistake, if he should regard it as designed to give anything like a regular history of the Babylonish kings, or of the Jewish nation, during the Babylonish exile. Only such occurrences are noted as have a high religious interest, and in combination with this, occasionally, a high national interest for the Jews. Such is the narrative before us. The Babylonish king, heated with wine, shows contempt to the sacred utensils of the Jewish temple, or at least a haughty exultation in his possession of them. He is admonished, in the midst of his excess, of his impending and awful doom; and speedily it comes upon him. An important lesson to blasphemous kings is taught by this, and cheering encouragement is given to those who were bowed down under the yoke of slavery, and were insulted and treated with scorn in respect to their most sacred feelings. The sum of the narration is as follows:

Belshazzar makes a great feast, and invites to it a multitude of his princes and potentates. In the midst of it, he commands the vessels of the Jerusalem-temple to be brought from the temple of Belus, that he and his companions might quaff wine from them. While doing this, they break out into praises of their idol-gods, vs. 1—4. Then came forth the appearance of a man's hand, and inscribed mysterious characters on the wall over against the king. Greatly terrified, he summoned all the Magi to decipher them; but they could not, vs. 5—9. Then came in the queen-mother, who reminded him of Daniel, as having formerly performed the office of interpreter, vs. 10—12. The king sends for him, relates to him what he had already done, together with his disappointment, and appeals to him for a disclosure of the mysterious characters, vs. 13—16. Daniel relates the demeanor and punishment of Nebuchadnezzar; sets before the king the true nature of his offence; and then reads and explains the writing on the wall, which predicts the speedy destruction of Belshazzar, and the dissolution of his kingdom, vs. 17—28. Daniel is promoted; and the same night Belshazzar is slain by the invading Medo-Persian army, vs. 30, 31.]

---

(1) Belshazzar the king made a great feast for his thousand nobles, and before the thousand he drank wine.

The name here written בֵּלְשַׁאצַּר, in 7: 7 is written בֵּלְאשַׁצַּר; and in 1: 7 al. we have still another equivalent form, viz. בֵּלְטְשַׁאצַּר. They are all one name, with merely a different orthography. The last has the Zend sign of the Gen. in full, טשׁא (*tsha*), which in the others is softened down by omitting the ט. Meaning: *Belus prince.* — לְחֶם, *feast*, an unusual Segholate form; omitted by Winer, § 28. 1, where it should be inserted. Usually the final vowel is not (ֶ), unless preceded by Holem, as in קְטֶל. The word properly means *food, bread*, and so a meal, for which this is of course provided. — A *thousand nobles* is but a moderate number for such an empire as that of Babylon. It is probable that at the feast of Ahasuerus (Xerxes), Est. 1: 3—5, more were present; see in v. 3, "all his princes and servants;" and this feast was kept 180 days, v. 4. Ctesias says, that the king of Persia furnished provisions daily for 25,000 men; see Heeren, Ideen, etc. I. s. 493, 3d edit. Quintus Curtius says that 10,000 men were present at a festival of Alexander the Great; and Statius says of Domitian, that he ordered, on a certain occasion, his guests to "sit down at a thousand tables. — וְלָקֳבֵל, *and before;* but in what sense? The meaning does not seem to be simply, that he drank wine in their presence, while they looked on; for this would be jejune. The probable meaning would seem to imply, that the king's seat was a separate one, at the head of the table, so that all his guests were before him, and could have a full view of him. The assertion of the text then would seem to be, that he sat down to the feast with them, although separated in some way from them and opposite to them. When it is said, that "he drank wine before the thousand," the predominant element at such a feast is named as the representative of the whole. Accordingly, in v. 10, the place where the guests assembled is named בֵּית מִשְׁתְּיָא, *banqueting-house.* The Babylonians were famous above all men for intemperance, specially in *drinking.* The *feast* in question some have thought to be the *Sacae (Saturnalia)* of the Babylonians; others, that of a *coronation day;* others, a *birth-day* festival. Either of the two latter is more probable than the former. But whatever feast it was, it seems to have been attended with religious rites and services, comp. vs. 4, 23. To *drink deep* appears in fact to have been a part of their polluted and degrading services. The sequel is not to be wondered at.

(2) Belshazzar, while tasting the wine, gave command to bring in the vessels of gold and silver, which Nebuchadnezzar his father had carried away from the temple in Jerusalem, that out of them the king, his nobles, his wives, and his concubines, might drink.

בִּטְעֵם, *in tasting*, which however does not mean merely *sipping* in order to determine the flavor, or as a prelude to drinking more freely, but *drinking with relish*, and therefore plentifully. — הַיְתָיָה, Inf. Aph. of אֲתָא, § 24. 2. Aph. — לְמָאנֵי, Acc. with לְ, plur. const. of מָאן = מַאֲנֶה, from אֲנָה. — הַנְפֵּק, Aph. — אֲבוּהִי, § 35. — בִּירוּשְׁלֶם, also written with final לֵם—, see Lex. — וְיִשְׁתּוֹן, Fut. Peal of שְׁתָא, here connected with יְ, and employed in like manner as the Heb. Fut. with this particle often is. — בְּהוֹן, lit. *in them*. So the Greeks: *πίνειν ἐν ποτηρίοις*; Lat. *in auro bibitur, in ossibus capitum bibere, to drink in skulls*; French, *boire dans une tasse*, etc. Our idiom demands *out of* instead of *in*. To render בְּ in this case *by* = *by means of*, might bring the Chald. idiom and ours together; but I doubt whether the particle has that meaning in the original here. — שֵׁגְלָתֵהּ, pl. of שֵׁגַל with suff., which latter is in the Sing., p. 36, top. The form of this noun is omitted in Winer. It should have been inserted in § 28. 1, after No. 3. — לְחֵנָתֵהּ, plur. with sing. suff. attached in the same way. The circumstance here mentioned, viz. that the king's wives and concubines were admitted to the feast, shows how different the manners of the Babylonians were from those of the Persians, Greeks, and other nations of the East. Vashti, the Persian queen, would not appear at the feast-table, even when commanded by the king, Est. i.; and among the Greeks, none but women of a degraded character sat down at a feast with men. Herodotus tells us, I. 109, that 'it was a detestable religious law among the Babylonians, that every woman should once prostitute herself, in the temple of Mylitta, to the first comer.' Curtius says, that 'women were not only present at the feasts, but as the guests became warmed with wine, they divested themselves gradually of their clothing.' "Nor was this," adds he, "merely a disgraceful affair of prostitutes, but it was deemed an act of comity by matrons and virgins." What sort of a banquet Belshazzar was engaged in, seems to be sufficiently evident from such testimonies. Hence the aggravation of the insult to the God of heaven.

(3) Then they brought the vessels of gold which had been carried away from the

temple of the house of God, which is in Jerusalem, and out of them drank the king and his nobles, his wives and his concubines.

הַיְתִיו, Aph. of אֲתָא. — הַנְפִּקוּ, for Hhireq under פ, see § 12. 1. *b*. — וְאִשְׁתִּיו, Peal of שְׁתָא with an א *prosthetic* — a peculiar idiomatic form, see Lex.

(4) They drank wine, and praised the gods of gold and silver, of brass, iron, wood, and stone.

אָעָא, emph. = Heb. עֵץ, see Lex. ע, צ. The word *wood* doubtless designates the frame-work of the image, which was first carved and then gilded. Probably the *brass* and *iron gods* were cast images, plated with gold or silver. The *stone* was an unfrequent material for images in Babylon; but some marble images are found among its ruins at the present time.

(5) At that very moment, there came forth fingers of a man's hand, and they wrote over against the chandelier, on the plaster of the palace-wall of the king; and the king saw the extremity of the hand which wrote.

בֵּהּ, § 43. 6. *b*. — נְפַקוּ, so the Kethibh would read; but the vowels here belong to the Qeri נְפַקָה = נְפַקָא 3 pl. fem. The Kethibh assumes the masc. gender of אֶצְבַּע; which is not improbable, although not elsewhere so employed. — כָּתְבָן, Part. fem. plur., following the usual construction. — The writing being *over against* (לָקֳבֵל) the chandelier, would be very conspicuous. To deduce from גִּירָא, *plaster*, the conclusion that the feast-hall must have been in the *court* of the palace, and not in the building, seems to be going quite too far. The *outside* of buildings in the East is alleged to have been *plastered*, and not the *inside*. But I see nothing here to render it probable that the guests were in the outer court. — פַּס יְדָא, the *extremity of the hand*, i. e. the fingers, was all that was visible. — כָּתְבָה, Part. fem. used for the verb. The *accents* bid us render the last clause thus: *The king looked, an extremity of the hand* (there was) *which wrote*. I prefer the translation given above.

(6) Then the king changed his color and his thoughts agitated him, and the joints of his loins were loosed, and his knees smote one against the other.

Lit. the first clause: *Then as to the king — his splendors changed for him*. In שְׁנוֹהִי, the suff. הִי is sing. masc. (p. 34, 2nd Par.), while זִיוֹ has a suffix of the same form which is plur. (p. 35, Par. 2), and which of course indicates that the noun itself is plural. On this account it seems necessary to render the suff. to the verb intransitive (שְׁנוֹ), as being in the Dative — *changed for him*, or in the Acc. *in respect to him*, § 57. 2. *b*, comp. Heb. Gram. §

116. 3. If not, then we must interpret שְׁנוֹ as transitive, and translate thus, *changed him*, which will hardly make any good sense, unless we interpret it as meaning *changed his appearance*. Perhaps the true solution is to be found in the *assonance* of the two words as to their ending; for in making out this, an irregularity (here and at times elsewhere) as to normal construction is occasioned. That the suff. הִי– after the verb שְׁנוֹ is to be rendered by an *oblique* case, seems to be confirmed by v. 9 below, where that which is here a simple verbal suffix, is exchanged for the separate pronoun with a preposition, viz. עֲלוֹהִי; and another example of this latter construction may be seen also in 7: 28, and the like in 10: 8. Lengerke takes the suff. to the verb as virtually a *reflexive* pronoun, and renders: *veränderte sich, changed itself;* in which case he also changes זִיוֹהִי to the *sing.* number. But as the verb is plural, and the Nom. to it is plural, how comes the verbal suff. to be singular? Besides, inasmuch as the verb is in its very nature *intransitive* in Peal, examples are wanting to justify the position, that such verbs may take and properly govern a reflexive pronoun-object. With Rosenm., Gesenius, Winer, and Maurer, therefore, I prefer the other construction. *Analogy* in the other examples quoted, seems indeed fairly to decide the matter. — יְבַהֲלוּנֵּהּ, Fut. Peal pl. with suff. and parag. נ, p. 58. Rem. 1. — חַרְצֵהּ, sing. of חֲרַץ with suff. = Heb. dual חֲלָצַיִם, ל and ר (as often) being exchanged. The Chald. and Syr. use the *sing.* here, instead of the dual; see Lex. *The joints of his loins* probably means his hip-joints or the joints in the lower part of the spine. The meaning seems to be, that he was unable to keep his standing, by reason of these natural supports being rendered tremulous. Let the reader compare Ezek. 21: 7. Ps. 69: 24 (23). Deut. 33: 11. Isa. 13: 8, and specially 21: 3. Nah. 2: 10, and he will see how commonly violent emotions, especially of fear and of suffering, were ascribed to the loins by the Hebrews. — מִשְׁתָּרַיִן, Part. Ithpaal of שְׁרָא, exchange of שׁ and ת. § 10. 5. *b*; (ַ) under ת because the ר excludes the Dagh. forte, p. 32, 3d line. — אַרְכֻבָּתֵהּ, fem. pl. (with suff.) of אַרְכֻּבָּה. Ges. has given no account of the formation or etymology of the word in his Lex. I take it to be a derivate of בְּרַךְ, *to fall on one's knees*, by a transposition of letters, and also by the addition of a prosthetic א. — דָּא לְדָא, § 43. 5. *a*. — נָקְשָׁן, Part. pl. fem. Supposing the fact to have been as here related, in respect to the mysterious hand and its conspicuous hieroglyphs, none can wonder at the terror of the king, who was in a state where excited feeling was of course to be expected. A fear of some dreadful evil, if not a consciousness of great guilt, must have pervaded his very soul. Even if the account be a *romance*, as many recent critics affirm, it must at least be conceded that the writer has put a skilful hand to the completion of his picture.

(7) The king cried aloud to bring in the enchanters, the Chaldeans, and the astrologers. He answered and said to the wise men of Babylon : Any man who will read this writing, and will show me the interpretation thereof, shall be clothed in purple, and a collar of gold [be put] on his neck, and he shall rule as the third in the kingdom.

לְהֶעָלָה, Aph. Inf. of עֲלַל. The Dagh. f. in Aph. of these verbs (see p. 63) is excluded by the ע, and would naturally go into a long vowel (ָ) under the preceding ה. But as this letter precedes a Guttural with *Qamets*, its proper vowel must be exchanged for (ֶ) ; see Roed. Heb. Gramm. p. 66. Note 2. *b.* — The לְ that follows marks the Acc. — דִּי, *that*, but here (as ὅτι often in Greek) a mere sign of quotation, and needs not to be translated. — כְּתָבָא, not fem., but masc. and emph. form of כְּתָב. יְהַחֲוִנַּנִי, Fut. Aph. of חֲוָא, with suff., p 68. Rem. 1. — אַרְגְּוָנָא, emph., and in the Acc. after יִלְבַּשׁ, § 50. 2. *b.* — הַמְנוּכָא, so the Kethibh should be pointed ; to the Qeri, הַמְנִיכָא, belong the vowels in the text. While this word may mean any kind of metal ornament attached to one's person, it has here a specific meaning, as the context shows, viz. *collet* or *collar.* — וְתַלְתִּי, a form *sui generis;* in v. 16 is an emph. from תַּלְתָּא; which seems to come from תְּלַת. The Chald. has a regular form, תְּלִיתַי, *third;* and תַּלְתִּי seems to be a word that has been shortened from it, probably in order to make a kind of proper name for the officer *third* in rank. The Grand Vizier (as we say in reference to Turkey) was the *second* officer, i. e. was prime minister of the king who was *first ;* the תַּלְתִּי stands next to Vizier.

(8) Then entered all the wise men of the king, and they were not able to read the writing, and make known the interpretation thereof to the king.

עָלְלִין the Kethibh should read ; the vowels now appended belong to the Qeri , עָלִּין. The Kethibh is preferable. — כָּהֲלִין, Part. again, the verse having no proper definite verb in it. — מִקְרֵא, Inf. Peal of קְרָא. — From the circumstance here related of their inability to read the inscription, it seems c lear, hat the characters were neither the usual demotic nor the hieratic. That the Babylonians used both, seems to be rendered nearly certain, by Grotefend, whose Essay on the subject is printed by Heeren, at the end of Vol. II. of his *Ideen.* But the Magi must of course have been able to read both characters ; as was the case with the priests of Egypt. Much speculation there has been on the *form* of the characters in question, and many things have been said, which it would serve but little purpose to relate. Enough that the characters were such as frustrated all the efforts of the Magi to read them.

(9) Then Belshazzar the king was greatly agitated, and his color was changed upon him, and his nobles were perplexed.

מִתְבָּהַל, Part. in Ithpael, בָּ because Dagh. f. is omitted in the ה. — As to זִיוֹהִי etc., see on v. 6 above. Here עֲלוֹהִי *upon him*, seems to indicate the diffusion of the color *over him*, i. e. over the surface of the skin. — שָׁנַיִן, Part. pl. see in Par. VII. p. 92. — מִשְׁתַּבְּשִׁין, Part. Ithpaal of שְׁבַשׁ, with the usual exchange of ת and שׁ.

(10) The queen — because of the affairs of the king and his nobles, she had come to the banqueting-house — the queen answered and said: O king, live forever! Let not thy thoughts disturb thee, nor thy color be changed!

But who is the *queen?* Not Belshazzar's *wife;* for his wives and concubines were already at the table; see vs. 2, 23. It seems, then, to be his *mother* or *grandmother*, who had once enjoyed the title of *queen*, which by courtesy (as usual) was continued after her husband's death. Either of these, but specially the latter, would well know all that is said in the sequel of Nebuchadnezzar and what befel him. — מִלֵּי, pl. const., seems to mean *affairs* here. We might render it *words*, and refer it to the command of the king to bring in the Magi, of which the queen had heard, were it not that it stands related to the *nobles* as well as to the king. — עַלַּת, for so reads the Qeri, is probably the right reading here, and is 3 sing. fem. Peal of עֲלַל. But עֲלַלַת (the Kethibh) is no bad or improbable reading; for the Part. may have such a fem. form, so common in the verb. The Part. construction is about as frequent as that with the verb. — עֲנָת, 3 fem. Peal. — וַאֲמֶרֶת, 3 fem. Peal, p. 53. 3 Gutt. Note 3. — זִיוָיךְ, plur. with suff., ־ָיךְ retaining (י) as the index of the plural. — יִשְׁתַּנּוֹ, Fut. Ithpaal of שְׁנָא, ת and שׁ exchanging places as usual. In this case there is neither suff. nor separate pronoun, but the verb is reflexive, and equivalent to *Let* (them) *not change themselves.* — The repetition of the מַלְכְּתָא in the first clause, by the second clause, is a mere resumption of the sentence after a *parenthetic* clause had been thrown in.

(11) There is a man in thy kingdom, in whom is the spirit of the holy gods, and in the days of thy father, intelligence, discretion, and wisdom like the wisdom of the gods, was found in him; and king Nebuchadnezzar, thy father, appointed him the chief of the sacred scribes, the Chaldees, the astrologers, [even] thy father, O king!

Spirit of the holy gods is the same language which Nebuchadnezzar employs in speaking of Daniel, 4: 8, 9, 18, (Eng. Version). — נַהִירוּ (וּ for וּת־ § 31. 1), form in § 28. *a.* 4. *Light* intellectually or tropically understood, is the meaning, i. e. intelligence. — שָׂכְלְתָנוּ, (וּ־ for וּת־). Here are two sufformatives, first the syllable ־ָן, and then the וּת or וּ; see § 30. — הִשְׁתְּכַחַת, Ithpael 3 fem. of שְׁכַח; for ending, p. 53, 3 Gutt., Note 3. — *King Nebuchadnezzar thy father*, Leng. with Rosenm. takes as Nom. abs.; with Maurer, I prefer the arrangement in the version, which makes it the *subject* of the verb that follows. Then at the close; the repetition, *thy father, O king*, has an intensive, emphatic meaning, as much as to say: 'Even a man of such sagacity and distinction as thy father, made this appointment.'

(12) Inasmuch as an excellent spirit, and the knowledge, and discretion of one who interpreteth dreams, and explaineth dark sayings, and solveth knotty points, was found in this same Daniel, whom the king named Belteshazzar, let Daniel now be called, and let him give the interpretation.

The construction is somewhat difficult, and interpreters are not agreed respecting it. C. B. Michaelis supplies רוּחַ before the nouns that follow, e. g. spirit of knowledge, etc. I prefer to carry forward שָׂכְלְתָנוּ, and mentally to repeat it before the two latter clauses thus: "[the discretion, i. e. power to distinguish nicely] belonging to the explanation of dark sayings, [discretion] of one who solves knotty points, etc. — אַחֲוָיַת is the const. form of the *noun;* I have rendered it as if it were a *participle*, like מְפַשַּׁר and מְשָׁרֵא, because this better suits our idiom. — אֲחִידָן, fem. pl., formed from חוּד by א prosthetic, *enigmas*, or *dark sayings.* — The word קִטְרִין is rendered *joints* in v. 6; which is its literal sense. Here it means *knots* or *joints* in a tropical sense, i. e. matters that are hard or difficult to be solved. — בֵּהּ בְּדָנִיֵּאל, *in this same Daniel*, § 43. 6. *b.* — יִתְקְרֵי, Fut. Ithpeal of קְרָא; here it means *called* in the sense of *summoned.* — יְהַחֲוֵה Fut. Aph. of חֲוָא, with ה praeform. retained, p. 49. 5. The tone in which this last clause is spoken, betokens that the speaker herself is conscious of an elevated rank and a kind of authority, or at least a right to give advice; a tone which only such a woman as stood in the relation of a *mother* (not of a wife) could assume in the East, before a king.

(13) Then Daniel was brought before the king. The king answered and said to Daniel: Art thou the same Daniel that belongeth to the captives of Judea, whom the king, my father, brought away from Judea?

הֻעַל = הוּעַל, the *Hophal* of the biblical Chaldee, which is always employed in the Chald. of the O. Test., in the room of Ittaphal, the pass. of Aphel, § 12. 6, root עֲלַל. — *The same Daniel*, § 43. 6. *b.* — גָּלוּתָא is abstract, *captivity;* but here it is plainly a case of the abstract for the *concrete*, and so I have translated it *captives.* — יְהוּד is the Chald. name of the *Jewish country.* — In דִּי הַיְתִי, the דִּי may relate to Daniel, or to the captives at large. I prefer the latter sense, as being the fuller, and in this case the more probable; הַיְתִי 3 pers. sing. Aph. of אֲתָא. — אַבִי is anomalous as to accent; since there is no apparent reason for placing the tone on the penult, and if placed there, we should of course expect a (ָ) and not a (ֶ) in the tone-syllable. What guided the Punctators in this case, it would be difficult to say. This suffix is nowhere else appended to אַב, either in Chaldee or in Hebrew. Maurer thinks that the word should be read אֲבִי (*ăbh*), after the Syriac manner of pronouncing it. It may be that the Punctators, having no other exemplar to guide them, designed to follow that analogy as to the stress of the voice.

(14) And I have heard respecting thee, that the spirit of the gods is in thee, and that intelligence, and discretion, and much wisdom is found in thee.

עֲלָיךְ, with the usual Qeri עֲלָךְ, which is needless. — נַהִירוּ, in some Codd. נָהִירוּ; but Qamets before ה in such a case is not very frequent. The Pattah is long here, if the form has a *Dagh. implicitum.* But this is hardly probable. For the rest, see v. 11.

(15) Then were brought before me the wise men, the enchanters, that they might read this writing, and to show me the interpretation thereof; and they were not able to show the interpretation of the thing.

הֻעַלּוּ, Hoph. 3 plur. (instead of Ittaphal), from עֲלַל, § 12. 6. — יִקְרוֹן . . . דִּי, *that . . . they might read,* just as in Heb., אֲשֶׁר followed by the Fut. designates the same shade of meaning; Ges. Lex. אֲשֶׁר. B. 2. Instead of such a construction, we have an Inf. with לְ in the next clause, viz. לְהוֹדָעֻתַנִי, ־נִי suff.; הוֹדָעוּת (written *plené*), Aph. Inf., for ending, p. 56. *e.* For change of construction, comp. 1: 5. — מִלְּתָא, *matter, thing,* meaning the whole of the extraordinary transaction that had taken place. The place of the noun here, (being *twice* put *before the Inf.* which governs it), deserves to be noted. It is frequent in the Chaldee; see v. 16. 2: 16, 18. 4: 15, al.

(16) And I have heard concerning thee, that thou canst skilfully interpret, and solve knotty points; now if thou canst read the writing, and show me the interpretation thereof, thou shalt be clothed in purple, and a collar of gold shall [be put] on thy neck, and thou shalt rule as the third in the kingdom.

תוּכַל, (so the Kethibh should be read) agrees with the form in 2: 10, and shows that it is the Hebraizing Hophal. The Qeri has put in its place the regular Fut. Peal form, viz. תִּכּוּל, without any necessity; root יְכֵל. — פִּשְׁרִין לְמִפְשַׁר, lit. *to interpret interpretations,* a Chald. and Heb. idiom, which means *to practise making interpretations,* or *to interpret skilfully.* Our idiom excludes a literal version; see the whole clause in v. 12. — Read תוּכַל as before; the case is the same. For the rest, see on v. 7 above.

(17) Then answered Daniel before the king and said: May thy gifts be for thyself, and bestow thy rich presents on another! The writing, however, I will read for the king, and I will show him the interpretation.

מַתְּנָתָךְ, plur. const. form, with suff.; which (in the fem. pl.) is always appended to the *const.* form, p. 88. 4. *d.* — לֶהֶוְיָן, see on 2: 20. — נְבְזְבְּיָתָךְ, see on 2: 6. — אָחֳרָן, adj. with a sufformative ָן, not unfrequent in this class of words. — הַב, Imper. of יְהַב. — Daniel must not be regarded as saying this contemptuously. Plainly it is merely designed to express his willingness to interpret without any fee or reward; and it is as much as to say: 'At the king's disposal may all the blessings remain, that he would bestow upon me! If he insists on *giving*, I would rather he should do this to some other person than to myself.' — אֲהוֹדְעִנֵּהּ, Aph. Fut. with suff., for which see p. 58. Rem. 1.

(18) As to thee, O king, the most high God gave to Nebuchadnezzar, thy father, dominion, and greatness, and honor, and glory.

The Nom. independent, (such are the two first words), is no unusual construction; it is even much more frequent in Chaldee than in Heb. prose. — עִלָּיָא, so it should be read, is the emphatic form, from the abs. form עִלַּי. — See and compare 2: 37, for the verse in general.

(19) And because of the greatness which he gave to him, all nations, people, and tongues trembled and feared before him, whomsoever he would he killed, and whomsoever he would he kept alive; whomsoever he would he exalted, and whomsoever he would he humbled.

יְהַב has for its Nom. אֱלָהָא implied, as in the preceding verse it is expressed. — זָאֲעִין has another orthography given to it by the Qeri, but needs it not, for זוּעַ may be thus declined in the Part.; see in Par. p. 68. The verb of existence, joined with it, strongly marks what is continued or customary. — דִּי *whoever, whomsoever* = אֲשֶׁר, is in the Acc., and is directly the object of קָטֵל. The so frequent repetition of the helping verb here with the respective participles, is rather unusual. The whole array of the diction is adapted strongly to mark what was continued and customary. — מָחֵא, for מַחְיֵא or מַחְיֵי, Aphel Part. apoc. of חֲיָא; some Codd. read מַחֵא, which is well enough, (comp. the Hebrew מְחַיֶּה), for Pattah will answer well before the ח. But מָחֵא is not a bad reading, inasmuch as the closed syllable מַח (in the full form) becomes an *open* one in the apoc. form, and may therefore take *Qamets.* — מָרִים is Part. Aph. of רוּם; for (ָ) under the מ, see § 22. 1. — מַשְׁפִּל, Aph. Part.; for the final *Hhireq*, see § 12. 1. 1. The arbitrary and despotic power of an Oriental sovereign is very briefly and graphically expressed in the two parallel *στίχοι* contained in the latter part of this verse. Some critics have rendered מָחֵא as if it were a Part. of מְחָא *to strike, beat:* but this breaks up the *antithesis* between this word and קָטֵל, and disturbs the easy and obvious course of thought.

(20) And when his heart was lifted up, and his spirit was emboldened to behave with insolence, he was thrust down from the throne of his kingdom, and honor did they take from him.

רִם might be taken as 3d Praet., for in part this verb is ע״ו; but more probably it is the Part. Peil here; comp. שִׂים in 3: 29. 6: 27. The particle כְּדִי, *when*, is naturally joined with a participle; see in 3: 7. — תִּקְפַת, 3 fem., for its Nom. רוּחַ is comm. gender; lit. *grew strong* or *firm, firmavit*, but figuratively, in relation to the mind, *was* or *became emboldened.* — לַהֲזָדָה, Inf. Aph. of זוּד, *to be proud, to act haughtily* or *insolently*, the ה in both cases is for א of the regular Chaldee. — הָנְחַת, a plain case of the *Hophal*, in the place of Ittaphal. — כָּרְסֵא, in Heb. כִּסֵּא (forma Dagh.), and the double *s* in Hebrew is in Aramaean usually exchanged for *rs*, which softens the hissing; see Ges. Lex. ר. The word originally means a covered or protected place, in reference to the tapestry hung around the regal seat or throne. — וִיקָרָה, *honor*, means his *honorable office* or *royal dignity.* — הֶעְדִּיו, 3 plur. Aph. of עֲדָא, without any subject, and so it might be rendered *passively*, § 49. 3. b.

(21) And from men was he thrust out, and his heart was like the beasts, and with the wild asses was his dwelling; with herbage like the oxen was he fed, and by the dew of heaven was his body bathed, until he acknowledged that God most high is ruler over the kingdom of men, and whomsoever he pleaseth he setteth up over it.

For this verse in general, comp. 4: 29. — שַׁוִּי, as it is now pointed, can be made only in Pael, 3 pers. Perf. But then, who is the *subject* of the verb? If the reply is: *God*, then the context gives no support to this. If *Nebuchadnezzar* be the subject, and the meaning be: *he made his own heart like the beasts*, the history in chap. iv. seems to make against this, for according to that, the malady fell on him as a divine judgment. The present punctuation seems to me as designed for the 3 plur. impers., i. e. שַׁוִּיו; for the ו now standing apparently as a conjunction before the next word, seems originally to have belonged here, and has been transferred to the next word by the mere oversight of transcribers. It is on this basis, that the version given above rests; see § 49. 3. *b*. But a more simple and easy way, perhaps, is to point שוי thus: שְׁוִי, in which case it is a Part. Peil, § 23. p. 74. 5. Verbs of comparison may take after them עִם, as here, or כְּ might be employed. Whichever of these particles is employed, the mental repetition of לְבַב after it, is of course to be supposed. — *With the wild asses shall be his abode*, is a circumstance added by the speaker, and not found in 4: 29. It is added for the sake of stronger impression. — יְטַעֲמוּנֵהּ, Pael, 3 plur. impers. of טְעַם, and so, *passive* in its meaning, § 49. 3. *b.* — יְדַע does not mean merely *mental perception* of the truth in question, but also what we call *acknowledgment*, i. e. acting in conformity with what cognition demands. — יְהָקִים, Aph. Fut. of קוּם, with ה retained (p. 49. 5); and as to the *Qamets* under it, see § 22. 1. — עֲלַיהּ suff. fem. sing., but not inserted in Par. of suffixes, p. 35. See p. 36, end of 2d paragraph, and comp. in Dan. 7: 19.

(22) And thou, his son Belshazzar, hast not humbled thine heart, notwithstanding thou hast known all this.

בְּרֵהּ, suff. state of בַּר. — הַשְׁפֵּלְתְּ, Aph. 2 pers. — יְדַעְתָּ, where the ending (תָּ–) is full; see § 12. 2. This verse plainly exhibits the charge against the impious king, and contains the reason for his speedy excision. The next verse enlarges and confirms the charge.

(23) But against the Lord of the heavens hast thou lifted up thyself, and the vessels of his house have been brought before thee, and thou, and thy nobles, wives, and concubines, have drunk wine out of them; and the gods of silver, gold, brass, iron, wood, and stone, which neither hear, nor see, nor know, hast thou praised; but the God in whose hand thy breath is, and whose are all thy ways, thou hast not glorified.

הִתְרוֹמַמְתָּ, Ithpolel of רוּם, § 14. 1. 2; for תָּ–, § 12. 2. — וּלְמָאנַיָּא, Acc. according to the Chald. construction, after הַיְתִיו, 3 pl. Aph. of אֲתָא. But as this verb has no subject, I have, as usual, translated it *passively*. For the sequel of the verse, see v. 3 above. — שָׁתַיִן, Part. pl. for verb, Par. VII. *a.* p. 91. — לֵאלָהֵי, Acc. after שַׁבַּחְתָּ, which is in Pael. This is an unusual removal of the verb to a great distance from its object, but it is occasioned by the copious explanatory matter thrown in. I have given the words the like order in English, inasmuch as it does not obscure the sentence. With peculiar emphasis are the participles, חָזַיִן, etc., employed, i. e. they exhibit what is customary and continued. — *In whose hand*, i. e. in whose power, at whose disposal, is *thy breath*, i. e. thy life. — *And whose are all thy ways*, lit. *and all thy ways are his*, i. e. at his disposal. The first version is easier in English, and equally perspicuous. *Ways* are *courses of conduct*, *design*, *purposes*, and the like. All these belong entirely to the control of the God of heaven. The king can achieve nothing, nor accomplish any of his purposes, unless the Godhead give permission. This is surely plain and faithful admonition; and probably the king's conscience was smitten by it.

(24) Then from him was sent the extreme part of a hand, and this inscription was written.

For the use of two participles Peil here for the passive verb, see p. 51. — קֳדָמוֹהִי, pl. form of the particle with suff., lit. *from before him*, which has the force of denoting a special and immediate interference on the part of the God of heaven.

(25) And this is the inscription which was written: *Menē, menē, tekēl, ū-pharsīn.*

I have repeated the original words as nearly as our alphabet will permit; and so we have them in our common English Version. The explanation of these words immediately follows.

(26) This is the interpretation of the language. *Menē*, God hath numbered thy reign, and brought it to completion.

מִלְּתָה, *word*, and here *language.* — מְנֵא, Part. Peil or passive, lit. *numbered, numeratum, computatum.* The word מְנֵא is not repeated in this case, as in the verse above, because it is followed by the verb מְנָה. *God hath numbered* means, that God has fixed the number of his days, i. e. the days of his reign, beyond which they cannot be extended. So the next clause declares: *And brought it* [thy reign] *to completion.* — הַשְׁלְמַהּ, Aph. with fem. suff.

(27) *Tekēl*, thou are weighed in the balance, and art found lacking.

תְּקֵל, Part. Peil of תְּקַל, § 12. 1. 1. c. exhibits this form, which is somewhat unusual when the verb is regular. — תְּקִילְתָּא, as to *form*, may be 2d sing. Peal, for (ִ־), see § 12. 1. 1; for תָּא, § 12. 1. 2; but as the sense is *passive* here it is more probably the pass. Part.; see p. 51. — הִשְׁתְּכַחַתְּ, as the vowels and diacritical points are, has a *furtive* Pattah under the ת; if it were a proper vowel, the final ת would omit the Dagh. lene. The second Pattah, therefore, is a mere euphonic contrivance, in order to ease the pronunciation. — חַסִּיר, *lacking, deficient.* The meaning of the figurative language is easily made out from the usual *rejection* of that which is *deficient* in weight.

(28) *Perēs*, thy dominion is broken, and is given to the Medes and Persians.

פְּרֵס, Part. Peil here; see תְּקֵל in v. 27. In v. 25, the word takes the form of a noun plural, i. e. *divisions, breaches;* here the Part. *divided* or *broken, fractum*, is employed. Both פָּרַס and פָּרַשׂ in Heb. mean *frangere. Broken* is the better meaning here, for *divided* between the Medes and Persians, would convey the idea that each of these was a separate and independent power; which was not the fact when Babylon was captured. They were combined under one head. — פְּרִיסַת, Part. fem. Peil, § 14. 2. — וִיהִיבַת, Part. Peil also, in the same way; both for verbs of the passive voice. — Lit. *To the Mede and Persian*, singular and *generic*, as often everywhere. I have accordingly translated by the plural. The coincidence of פָּרָס with פְּרֵס is evident. *Assonance* reigns throughout the whole; as is often the case in short sententious sayings. It is this which gives an unusual form to תְּקֵל and פְּרֵס, so that they may sound like מְנֵא. Nothing can be argued, as it seems to me, from the use of פְּרֵס in order to indicate *the breaking in pieces* of the Babylonish dominion, to show that the Persians were then the principal power. There is no verb that would chime with מָדַי, and give the meaning here required. But for פָּרָס, it was easy to find one that corresponded well. This seems to be all that is mysterious in the case; and this mystery is easily understood.

(29) Then Belshazzar commanded, and they clothed Daniel with purple, and a collar of gold [was put] on his neck, and proclamation was made respecting him, that he should be third ruler in the kingdom.

הַלְבִּישׁוּ, Aph., the subject of the verb, if we make it a personal verb, must of course be those *attendants* to whom the king gave command. I have translated in accordance with this view. We may, however, take the verb as 3 plur. impers., and then render it passively: *Daniel was clothed*, etc. — וְהַכְרִזוּ, Aph., for vowels, see § 12. 1. 1. I have rendered this *passively*, for otherwise it might seem, that the same persons who decorated Daniel with his *insignia*, were the ones who made proclamation; which, although quite possible, is not very probable. In a great court, every department has its appropriate officers and servants. — לֶהֱוֵא, see 2. 20. For the rest, see on v. 16.

(30) In that very night, was Belshazzar king of the Chaldees slain.

קְטִיל, Part. Peil used as a passive verb, § 13. 2. According to the account here given, the occurrences related in the preceding part of the chapter must have taken place sometime during the first part of the night; for the assault upon the city was probably made not far from midnight, when the Babylonians were in the deepest part of their revelry, and the king and his nobles had not yet withdrawn from the banquet. It would be an important object, as viewed by the invader, to come upon them when thus assembled; for by a single assault all the leaders of the city might be taken off at once, and all resistance prevented.

That the first verse of the following chapter should be attached to the present chapter, seems plain, both from the וְ with which it commences, and from the nature of the information which it contains. Daniel had interpreted the inscription on the wall as meaning two things, viz. first that the king's days were at an end; and secondly, that his kingdom should be given over to foreign nations. The fulfilment of the first of these predictions is related in 5: 30; that of the second, in 6: 1. In the remarks which follow, I shall regard these two verses, therefore, as comprising a part of one and the same narration.

REMARKS ON CHAP. V.

[The objections raised against the narrative in chap. v. are somewhat numerous. Some of them, in particular, are urged with great zeal, even by critics to whom is generally attributed a good degree of acquaintance with the historical records of antiquity. Whether this knowledge is accompanied by a candid and discriminating judgment, in respect to those records, so far as they concern the matters before us, is a question which may be answered to better advantage, after the subject has been canvassed.

First of all, I shall briefly advert to some of the minor objections against the probability of some of the narrations in chap. v.; and then pass on to examine those, where appeal is made for confirmation to the earliest historians of Babylon and Persia. Lengerke has industriously collected everything which is worth notice; and it is for this particular reason, that I bring him so often into view, rather than previous writers.

(1) 'Why does not Daniel appear before the king, with the Magi who are summoned, and of whom he was chief? It is very strange, nay, altogether improbable, that he should be absent on such an occasion;' Leng. p. 238.

That Daniel had been the *chief* of the Magi (2: 48), is true. But it seems also to be a fact, that both the *astrologers* and *physicians* of an oriental king were usually removed from office by his successor; the first, because they had not foretold his death, the second because they had not prevented it; see Bähr ad Ctes. p. 16. Chardin, in Harmar's Observations on Scripture, Part. II. It is not decisive, therefore, that Daniel was then *chief* Magian, because we find him, in the *third* year of Belshazzar (8: 1), employed in "the business of the king," 8: 27; for this may have been a subordinate business, and most probably was. Conspirator against the regular and legitimate monarch as Belshazzar was, (according to Berosus and Abydenus), it is not likely that one who had stood so high as Daniel did under Nebuchadnezzar, would be retained in an important office, and near the person of the usurper. His able services to the State the king might indeed require, in another and lower capacity, at least for a while. But even if we concede that Daniel was high in office, in the *third* year of Belshazzar's reign, that reign lasted seventeen years, and the king might well be supposed, long before the end of it, to have dismissed from important and active service near his person, a man who was at least on the verge of four-score years when he began to reign. That a *Jew*, and one so very aged, should not be summoned by the Babylonish king (5: 7 seq.), in an exigency of fearful import, is far enough from presenting anything strange.

(2) 'But how can we imagine Belshazzar to have been so entirely ignorant of Daniel, and of his peculiar sagacity, as the narration in 5: 10 seq. supposes ?'

The force of this objection I do not perceive. Was not the usurper, (although he might be a descendant of Nebuchadnezzar ; perhaps in a female line, as vs. 11, 13, 18, 22, seem plainly to intimate), a person who did not belong to the regular line of heirs apparent, i. e. who was not in the regular line of succession ? And is there anything specially remarkable in the narration, which seems to represent Belshazzar as unacquainted with the merits and claims of Daniel, after some half a century had passed away since Daniel's first achievements and promotion ? Lengerke affirms, that 'the account in ch. V. contradicts itself; for v. 11, he says, shows the king to be ignorant of Daniel, and v. 13, that he recollected him.' But v. 13 seq. merely repeats what Belshazzar had just heard from the queen, and affords no semblance of a contradiction. How can it be regarded as improbable, that an ambitious and reckless adventurer and usurper, like Belshazzar, should have neither known nor cared anything about Daniel individually and personally, although he had once been in his service ? 8: 27. Or if he had heard something of his story, who can give us any assurance that he believed it, or treasured it up in his mind ?

(3) 'But the *hand* and the *writing !* Here is miracle upon miracle, and altogether without an object. There is no historical basis whatever, on which such an account can rest. The whole must be pure fiction ;' Leng. p. 239 seq.

So far does the objector go, moreover, in this case, that he even taxes Bertholdt with incongruity, because he admits that some sleight-of-hand trick, as to the writing, had been played off by some of the nobles upon the king, and that the story is founded on this. For rejecting such a conceit, I should not indeed be disposed to find fault with Lengerke ; for the idea of such an imposition goes altogether beyond the bounds of probability. The king's *friends* could have no motive for such an exhibition ; and if some of the nobles then present were his enemies, and wished for his fall, how could they think of putting him on the alert, in order that he might guard against an attack ? Or why should the writing be in mystical characters ? Lengerke, therefore, regards the whole story as a mere *fiction.* In his view, anything miraculous is out of question for that very reason. It must be either mere pretence or a matter of superstition, or some ingenious imposition, and the like. Of course the whole narrative here is got up, as he intimates, merely to exalt Daniel, and to show the doom of the tyrant, i. e. Antiochus Epiphanes. But if a writer, at or near the time when this last named tyrant was raging against the Jews, invented such a fiction, he did this either *before* his death, or *after* it. If *before,* how could he tell whether the death of Antiochus would verify his representation ? If *after,* what was the use of *predicting* what had already come to pass ? Still more ; Antiochus died a *natural* death from disease, not by the hand of conspirators or enemies ; what resemblance was there, then, between the two cases ? And lastly, the dynasty of Antiochus went over immediately to his *son* and *successor,* and not into the hands of the Medes and Persians.

(4) 'But a man like Belshazzar would never have received such an ominous prediction from the mouth of Daniel, and have rewarded him for

it. The whole thing is a palpable forgery, got up merely to magnify Daniel.'

But if what is stated about the writing was matter of *fact*, is there anything incredible in the assertion, that the king was stricken with awful terror? It would be little short of miraculous, if he were not. As to the *reward*, the king had publicly and solemnly pledged it, 5: 7; how could he retreat from his pledge? The writer evidently supposes the whole to have been *matter of fact;* and on this ground there is nothing incongruous or improbable, in his account of Belshazzar's conduct. In order to make out incongruity, then, we must assume a position directly opposite to that which the writer has assumed.

(5) 'But how could the writing be explained, Daniel be promoted and proclaimed as third in the government, and the city be taken besides, all in one night? Improbable altogether, if not impossible.'

Yet, on such an occasion, when the Magi beyond reasonable doubt were assembled to keep the feast, and in the vicinity of the palace, (for so every one must readily imagine, since they were so often to be consulted), what difficulty is there in supposing, that within some eight or ten hours all this happened? The time is amply sufficient for the whole that was transacted or took place. Officers ready for every kind of duty, and in great numbers, must have been present at the court, on such an occasion as the great feast.

(6) 'But the shocking profanation of Belshazzar! All antiquity fails to supply us with any such example.'

Has Lengerke, then, never read the history of what Cambyses did to the gods in Egypt, and Darius and Xerxes to those in Babylon? Besides, as Belshazzar was haughty and impious, it was very natural, when heated with wine, that he should send for the splendid temple-vessels, as evidences of his magnificence, and in order to place the God of the Jews in a light inferior to that of his own. While his conduct was indeed impiety toward the God of Israel, it was probably deemed by himself and his nobles to be an act of commendable devotion, or at least to be a testimony of gratitude to the Babylonish gods, who had made the Chaldeans to be a victorious nation.

(7) 'Daniel *contradicts* himself. In v. 17, he declines all reward and honor; in v. 27, he willingly receives both.'

I read both passages with different feelings. In the first, Daniel modestly and humbly disclaims any title to reward, on the ground of any service which he may render to the king; in v. 29, the king's command to honor him is obeyed by his servants, as we might well expect. Whether Daniel received his promised rewards *willingly* or *unwillingly*, is not said; nor is anything said in the context, which implies any desire on his part to receive them.

Thus much for the lighter weapons by which the narration before us has been assailed. Let us now come to those which appear to be of a somewhat more formidable description. Lengerke avows, at the outset of his attack, that the narration in ch. V. has indeed some historical basis as to certain facts, but that "the whole story is disfigured and falsified by the author, who was neither an eye-witness of the occurrences, nor accurately acquainted with the history of them," p. 204. The *falsification* consists of several particulars; viz., 1. The last king of Babylon was not a *son* of Nebuchadnezzar. (2) His name was not Belshazzar. (3) He was not slain when Babylon was taken by Cyrus. (4) There was never any such person as *Darius the Mede*, who was concerned with the taking of Babylon, or who reigned as king over that region. These allegations I shall now examine in the order stated.

If it be a fact, that 'the last king of Babylon was not a *son* of Nebuchadnezzar,' then, indeed, there is a discrepancy between real history and the narration before us; for vs. 11, 13, 18, 22, plainly assert this, and even with emphasis. But it is unnecessary, in order to vindicate the assertion of our text, to show that he was an *immediate* descendant of Nebuchadnezzar, in the first degree. The Semitic use of the word in question goes far beyond the first degree of descent, and extends the appellation *son* to the designation of *grandson*, and even of the most remote *posterity*. Examples of this there are in abundance. In Ezra 5: 1. 6: 14, the prophet Zechariah is called *the son of Iddo;* in Zech. 1: 1, 7, the same person is called *the son of Barachiah the son of Iddo.* So Isaiah threatens Hezekiah (39: 7), that *the sons whom he shall beget* shall be conducted as exiles to Babylon; in which case, however, four generations intervened before this happened. In Matt. 1: 8, three kings are omitted between Joram and Uzziah (see 2 Chron. xxii. seq.); yet Uzziah (Ozias) is called by the evangelist the *son of Joram*, (the language is: "Joram begat Ozias"). So in Matt. 1: 1, "Jesus Christ, the son of David, the son of Abraham." And so we speak, every day, e. g. "The sons of Adam; the sons of Abraham; the sons of Israel; the sons of the Pilgrims," and the like. So Ges. Lex. "בֵּן, *filius, nepos, posteri.*" If then Belshazzar was a *descendant* of Nebuchadnezzar, it is enough fully to vindicate the language. Nor is it of importance to its vindication, whether he was a son in the male or female line of descent. The appellation could be applied in either case with entire propriety, according to Hebrew usage.

To disprove the *sonship* now in question, an appeal is made to Berosus (in Joseph. cont. Apion. I. 20), who says of the last king, whom he calls *Nabonnidos*, that the conspirators who had destroyed the young king Laborosoarchod, "invested Nabonnidos with the sovereignty, τινὶ τῶν ἐκ βαβυλῶνος, ὄντι ἐκ τῆς αὐτῆς ἐπισυστάσεως, i. e. a certain personage who was a Babylonian, and of the same faction." This passage shows that Nabonnidos did not belong to the regular line of the heirs apparent; for the king that had just been destroyed was a mere child (παῖς), and had no progeny; but at the same time, it does not inform us what was the real rank or previous condition of the new usurper. Something peculiar must have recommended him to the choice of his fellow-conspirators. In case now that he was a descendant of Nebuchadnezzar in a *female* line, he had no legal right to the throne, which could be claimed only by *sons* and their progeny. But his origin of course would procure for him a place of distinction, and if he was ambitious, (which seems highly probable from his course of conduct), such a distinction would be likely to gain for him a precedence. At all events, what Berosus says, extends only to a denial of *regal right*, but not to a denial that Nabonnidos was in any way related to Nebuchadnezzar.

But the main reliance is placed on the testimony of *Abydenus*, (preserved in Euseb. Praep. Evangel. IX. 40, 41, and also in Euseb. Chron. Armen. I. c. 10). Abydenus appeals to and quotes *Megasthenes* as his authority, who says, that "Labassoracus (Laborosoarchod) being destroyed by violence, they made Nabonnidochus βασιλέα, προσήκοντά οἱ οὐδέν, i. e. *king, having no claim to this rank*," or they bestowed on him "*a kingly office not belonging at all to him*." I can find now in this assertion, no more than I find in that of Berosus, viz. a denial of right to the throne according to the usual law of descent. So much I would readily concede; but this surely does not amount to a contradiction of the statement, that Belshazzar was a descendant of Nebuchadnezzar.

Is there then any evidence that he was such a descendant, besides the declarations of our text? There is. Herodotus, after describing the famous queen Nitocris, says: "Cyrus conducted his army against the *son* of this woman, whose name was Labynetus,(the same with that of his father), and who ruled over the Assyrians" [Babylonians]; I. 188. In another passage (I. 77), Herodotus says, that "Labynetus ruled over the Babylonians," when Croesus sent to them for aid against Cyrus. In I. 74, the same author represents *Labynetus* of Babylon as one of the party, who helped to conciliate Cyaxares I. of Media and the Lydians. Here *Nebuchadnezzar* is undoubtedly meant; as Prideaux, Wesseling, Beloe, and Bähr, all agree. This last passage explains the first quotation, where "Labynetus is said to have the *same name* with his father" [Nebuchadnezzar]; and it shows in all probability, as Bähr remarks (Comm. in Herod. I. 188), that the name is a *title of honor* or *office*, rather than a proper name. The same remark may well be made of various other names which were common in Persia, Media, and Babylon. Different names of the kings of these countries, as we shall soon see, is one of the weakest of all arguments to prove a difference of persons.

Herodotus was born about 60 years after Babylon was taken by Cyrus. He travelled thither in the height of his strength, and had an opportunity to know respecting a matter so recent as this. The testimony of Berosus and Abydenus, (or rather of Megasthenes), is later than his, by a century and a half or two centuries. Berosus was probably a native of Babylon; but Megasthenes was a Greek, and of far inferior authority, compared with Herodotus, in such circumstances.*

I am aware that Hoffman, (Weissag. and Erfüll. I. s. 296), and Hävernick (Neue krit. Untersuch. s. 72 seq.), in accordance with the suggestions of some earlier writers, suppose the Belshazzar of ch. V. to have been *Evil*

* BEROSUS was a Chaldean priest of Belus, at Babylon, in the time of Alexander the Great and his successors, who wrote the *History of the Chaldeans*, from which the extracts in Josephus, Eusebius, and other writers, are taken. The rest of his works have perished. Richter's edition of his *Remains* (1825) has put on a good footing the credit of the Chaldee writer, his history of the fabulous ages alone excepted. It is said that he drew from the records in the temple of Belus. ABYDENUS wrote a history of Assyria; but his age has not been ascertained. It is certain that he lived *after* MEGASTHENES, whose age we know to have been that of Seleucus Nicator, i. e. 312—280 B. C.; for Abydenus often appeals to Megasthenes, as in the passage above quoted. But both he and Megasthenes are of secondary authority, for both are Greeks, who wrote long after the events in question. The authority of Berosus, as to Chaldean affairs, is deservedly in higher repute. See Richter, Beros. p. 35, seq.

Merodach, the immediate successor and son of Nebuchadnezzar, and that a considerable interval of time took place between the death of Belshazzar and the occupation of the throne by *Darius the Mede*. But of this I cannot feel persuaded. Such is the connection of 5: 29 with 6: 1, and of both these with the fulfilment of the prophetic inscription on the wall, that they cannot be separated without violence. If dissevered, in accordance with the views of those critics, how can it be accounted for that 6: 1 begins with a ו conjunctive, וְדָרְיָוֶשׁ? Or how, that no time is either named or alluded to, when Darius took the kingdom? We should confidently expect a designation of time, if the writer did not suppose it to be designated by what he had already said. If such an exegesis, therefore, be not impossible, it seems on every ground of philology to be improbable. See Vitringa, Observatt. Sac. V. 19, where he has fully refuted Stanley (in Eschyl. Pers. p. 776), who has broached the same opinion that I have stated above. Whatever difficulties may result from the natural exegesis of the text, it is better to meet them fairly, than to get rid of them by a forced interpretation.

At all events, (and I make the remark both for present and future use), the testimony of the Hebrews respecting matters of such a nature as that before us, is entitled to much higher regard than that of the Greeks. The Hebrews were at and near Babylon, in their exile; they were there when the city was taken; large numbers of them continued to live there until Babylon was in ruins. Even if the book of Daniel was written in Maccabaean times, its being of a Jewish source would, *caeteris paribus*, give it higher authority than one from a Grecian source. The Greeks in general knew little indeed of Middle Asia, until after the conquests of Alexander the Great.

2. 'The name *Belshazzar* is a mistaken one. The name of the last king was *Nabonned*. The writer has given us a mere figment instead of a real name.'

The *internal* evidence, however, seems to be against this; for the composition of the name is of the true Chaldee stamp; see on 5: 1. But to argue from any one name of an oriental prince, that he has no other names, ought to be the last thing that any one well informed in these matters should undertake. Let us examine a few cases. The father of Nebuchadnezzar is usually called *Nabopolassar*; but Josephus has Nabolassar; and in Chron. Euseb. Arm. the Latin has Nabopalsarus. *Nebuchadnezzar* is also *Nebuchadrezzar*, and in Ptolemy (Can.), Nabocolassar. *Belshazzar* is called by Berosus, Nabonnidos; by Herodotus, Labynetus; by Abydenus, Nabannidochus; by Ptolemy, Nabonadios; by Syncellus (in ἐκκλησ. στοιχ. p. 393 ed. Dind.), Nabonadios, Astyages, Darius of Ahasuerus, and Artaxerxes; (in p. 431) Nabonnedus, Darius, Astyages of Ahasuerus; (p. 436) Neriglesaros, the Baltasar (Belshazzar) of Daniel. The younger son of Cyrus, *Tanyoxarces* or *Tanaoxanes*, is called Smerdis by Herodotus; by Justin (after Trogus), Merdis; by Aeschylus, Mardos; by Ctesias, Sphendadates; in Scripture, Artashashta (Heb.). It would be easy to extend this list much further, but I deem it superfluous. I would merely add, that *Belshazzar* bears marks of being a mere appellation or title of honor. And the same may be said of *Darius*, in 6: 1. The Lex. will show, that the corresponding Persian noun, from which this Heb. or Chaldee-formed name comes, means *king*; see Ges. Lex. s. v. דָּרְיָוֶשׁ. In this way we perceive, that there is no difficulty in harmonizing the *Cyaxares* of Xenophon with the *Darius* of Daniel. The latter is distinguished by the appellation מָדָיָא, *the Mede*, both words signifying *the Median king*, 6: 1; and also by בֶּן־אֲחַשְׁוֵרוֹשׁ in 9: 1, i. e. *the son of Ahasuerus*. Of course these adjunct names answer the purpose of making the common appellative *Darius* (king) specific.

3. 'Belshazzar was *not slain* at the capture of Babylon, as Daniel asserts, but escaped and was treated with great lenity by the conqueror.'

Here Herodotus deserts us, not having said a word about the king or his fate, at the capture of the city. Ctesias also deserts us, since, in his *Persica*, he says nothing even of the invasion and subjugation of Babylon by Cyrus; which is passing strange. But Berosus represents Nabonnedos, 'after a defeat before the walls of Babylon, as flying to Borsippus, and there giving himself up to Cyrus, who treated him humanely, and sent him to Carmania, where he spent the remainder of his life;' Richter, Beros. p. 69. Jos. cont. Ap. I. 19, 20. Euseb. Praep. Evang. IX. 40. In Euseb. Chron. Arm. I. 10 and Praep. Ev. IX. 41, we have also the narration of Abydenus, who says: "Cyrus, after taking Babylon, sent him [Nabonned] to be governor of Car mania, Καρμανίης ἡγεμονίαν δωρέεται. In narrating the fact that the las king was spared, there is an agreement, then, between these two writers but in regard to the condition of the king, banished from his capital, they disagree, although one does not contradict the other. Berosus says nothing of the new office of Nabonned, which Abydenus expressly mentions. That Abydenus often borrows from Berosus, is, I believe, generally conceded. We are therefore at a loss, whether it comes only from one witness, or is derived from two independent sources.

On the other hand, we have Xenophon, in his circumstantial history of the capture of Babylon, in full agreement with Daniel; and besides this, there are various passages in the O. Test. prophets, which accord entirely with the same view. One might indeed almost argue *a priori* for the probability of the scriptural account, when he had once made himself acquainted with the thirst of vengeance that was in the minds of Gobryas and Gadatas, who led on the storming-party of Cyrus; Cyrop. VII. 5. 24, 30 seq. The probability that Cyrus (according to Abydenus) would make such an enemy as Belshazzar the satrap or subordinate king of Carmania, a powerful province and not far distant, seems quite small, to say the least. But passing by all this, we have to adjust the balance between Berosus and Abydenus on the one side, and Xenophon and Daniel and the Heb. prophets on the other. The histories of the first two are merely skeletons; but Xenophon is full and circumstantial; Daniel is brief but unequivocally direct; and the Prophets seem to agree fully with his view. In respect to these last witnesses, I must refer the reader to Isa. 21: 2—9. Isa. 14: 9—21, specially vs. 18—20. Comp. Jer. 50: 29—35. 51: 57. I am fully aware, that poetical descriptions of this nature are not to be urged to the letter; but the position that *the king and nobles of Babylon will fall*, in the attack of the storming-party who capture the city, seems to me deeply imbedded in the language of the prophets. If the Literalists insist on the *lateness* of these compositions, so much the worse for their cause; for how could late writers take such a position, i. e. assume the death of the king to be true, in case notorious facts contradicted it?

This is all the testimony we have respecting the matter before us, which is worth canvassing. All that is later, is merely a repetition of what had already been said. In regard to the point before us, then, we are left in a predicament, like to that in which we find ourselves with respect to many others that are concerned with early Oriental history. Herodotus and Ctesias, on whom we principally depend for a knowledge of these matters, with the exception of some scriptural notices, leave us here entirely destitute of aid; and even if they afforded any information, in all probability it might be, as most of their other history of these times (specially that of Cyrus) undoubtedly is, of such a nature as to present us with real contradictions and irreconcilable and inexplicable difficulties. Xenophon and the Bible, which last includes Isaiah and Jeremiah and Daniel, are witnesses of a different character. Whatever may be said of Xenophon's writing *romance*, it is at least plain and clear, that he is free from the superstition and credulity of many heathen writers, and that in all his works, no attempt can be met with to confound the mythic, the fabulous, and the absurd, with the plain and sober history of facts.

The reasonable decision of the question, then, which respects the death of Belshazzar when Babylon was taken by assault, lies within a narrow compass: Which of these classes of witnesses is entitled to the most credit? Berosus and Abydenus, the latter of whom is clearly an inferior and secondary witness, or Xenophon, Isaiah, Jeremiah, and Daniel? The great portion of critics have said and still say, that the latter must have the preference; and with them I heartily concur. The allegations made against the credit of Xenophon, as to his Cyropedia, in order to avoid this conclusion, I shall touch upon, at the close of this discussion. In the mean time, in a matter of this kind, where the great mass of critics, (the *liberal* ones included), have adopted the conclusion to which, after much investigation, I have felt compelled to come, it is matter both of surprise and regret to see the confident air and hear the sarcastic tone of Lengerke, who adopts the conclusion, that both Daniel and Xenophon have either falsified the whole matter, or wrote in utter ignorance of the true state of things. Quite different is the course which Gesenius, Winer, Knobel, and other Liberalits, have pursued.

4. 'No such person as *Darius the Mede* coöperated in the taking of Babylon, nor did any such person reign there, after the deposition of Belshazzar.'

Here Lengerke is most confident of all. The appeal is made to Herodotus and Ctesias, both of whom conclude the *Median* empire with Astyages, the grandfather of Cyrus, according to Xenophon (Cyrop. I. 3) and Herodotus (I. 107, 108), but according to Ctesias (Persica § 2) not at all related to him. The account of Herodotus is, that Cyrus with the Persians threw off the yoke of the Medes, attacked and deposed Astyages his father-in-law, and kept him prisoner until his death, when Cyrus succeeded him in his authority; Herod. I. 127—130. Ctesias represents the matter differently in some respects: 'Cyrus was not related to Astyages; he gave him his personal liberty; married his daughter; and finally, that Astyages, being sent for by Cyrus and his wife, was left to perish in a desert by the servant by whom the invitation was sent! (Ctes. Pers. § 2. § 5); and with him ended the Median empire. Berosus says nothing of any other king except Cyrus, when he mentions the capture of Babylon (Jos. c. Apion. I. 20. Richter, p. 69); and Abydenus fails us here also, as reported in Euseb. Chron. Armen. I. 10. 3, unless we understand the *Darius* mentioned in the same passage of Eusebius as meaning the same person as Darius the Mede — "a Dario autem rege eâdem provinciâ pulsus est" [viz. Nabonedochus]. This clause is wanting in the extract from Abydenus, in Euseb. Praep. IX. 41, and appears to be merely the opinion of Eusebius, or perhaps it was added by the Armenian translator. But however this may be, I am disposed to believe (with Leng. p. 217), that the Darius here named was Darius Hystaspis; although I perceive that Gesenius (in Thes. Heb. s. v. דָּרְיָוֶשׁ) applies the name to the Darius of Daniel.

We have then the declarations of Herodotus and Ctesias that Cyrus made war upon *Astyages*, took him captive, and then reigned over Media; and our other witnesses, Berosus and Abydenus are wholly silent as to the termination of the Median empire. The appeal to later writers, such as Dionysius Hal., Justin, Strabo, Diodorus Sic., and the History of Bel, which Lengerke makes, is out of place, because it is the mere echo of the earlier writers just named. What have we then to oppose to this? We have the whole Cyropedia throughout; for from the outset (I. 5. 2), the formal history is begun of Astyages' death and of Cyaxares as his son and successor; and the history of this last personage is not dropped, until we come almost to the very close of the Cyropedia. Cyaxares is presented as giving his daughter in marriage to Cyrus, and making his kingdom her dowry. Of these particulars the Scriptures say nothing, inasmuch as it was not their object, and they make no attempt to give the history of Persia. But that Cyrus was the successor of *Darius the Mede*, is plainly developed in 5: 30. 6: 1. 9: 1. 11: 1, comp. 10: 1. 1: 21. That *Astyages* cannot be meant by the Darius in question, seems evident from the fact, that he died long before the taking of Babylon.

Here then we have to adjust our balance as before. That the testimony is *apparently contradictory*, no one can hesitate to say. Is it in reality so? This question deserves a moment's consideration.

The first thing, then, to be inquired after is: Whether either Herodotus or Ctesias designed, or even pretended, to give a *complete* history of Media, Persia, or Babylon? It is easy to answer this question. The works of both are compilations of historical anecdotes and interesting stories; they are really that and nothing more. To use the words of Gesenius, a critic in such matters of very high rank: "Passing by men of moderate talents, Herodotus is wont merely to mention one and another in a long series of kings, who has rendered himself more eminent. His history of Babylon, as well as other matters, shows this; in which he mentions merely the queen Nitocris, and her son Labynetus [Belshazzar], passing in silence all other kings, not excepting even Nebuchadnezzar himself;" Thes. Heb. s. v. דָּרְיָוֶשׁ. Nothing is plainer to the critical reader, than the correctness of this judgment. If it is not equally applicable to Ctesias, it is in a great measure so; witness his total omission in the life of Cyrus, of his conquest of Babylon, which was the most signal act of his whole life. The *argumentum ex silentio*, rarely of much value, would, in respect to these historians, be little short of an absurdity. That they have omitted *Cyaxares* or *Darius the Mede*, is most probably owing to his insignificance either as a king or as a general. In all his long wars in Asia Minor, Cyrus, his ally, was the actual commander in chief—the real Executive of the army. In the attack upon Babylon, Cyaxares was not even present; for he preferred the enervating pleasures of his palace, to an active and military life. Cyrus did all in taking the city; he made all the arrangements after the capture; but the *supremacy* was still theoretically retained by Darius, and conceded to him by Cyrus. In the very last book of the Cyropedia, we have the account of Cyrus' visit to Cyaxares, after the splendid conquest of Babylon; on which occasion the Median king gave him his daughter to wife, and his kingdom for her dowry. Lengerke, in order to show that Cyaxares is a mere phantom, alleges that all the arrangements were made by *Cyrus*, at Babylon, "in a kingly manner." True enough; but it so happens, that these, with the exception of such as pertained to military occupation and safety, were made *after* Cyrus had received his *dowry*, and not before. I know of no ancient composition that affords an analogy which will warrant the supposition, that the Cyropedia is a book of pure romance, like many of our modern novels. Fabulous legends of gods, and demigods, and heroes, are indeed abundant, but the whole scope, character, and design of these, are entirely different from those of a regular *didactic romance*. Nor can it well be shown, that the plan of a romance, in which the model of a wise and brave prince should be exhibited, demanded at all the introduction of such a character as that of Cyaxares. Something indeed might be gained on the score of *contrast* between him and Cyrus; but if this was the main object of the writer, he has failed to give much efficacy to his production, since Cyaxares is of too mixed a character to make the contrast very striking. If it was true, that Cyrus was at that time king of the Medes, and this by succeeding Astyages directly, would it not have made the picture of the former more striking and magnificent, had Xenophon presented him in that light, and still as exercising great moderation and humanity?

On the whole, the direct evidence of the Scriptures and of Xenophon to the reality of a Median king between Astyages and Cyrus, seems to me very decidedly to outweigh the accounts given by Herodotus and Ctesias in respect to the time and manner in which Cyrus became king of Media and Persia. Herodotus himself states, that there were three other different accounts of Cyrus' life and actions besides that which he gives, and that he merely adopts the one which seemed to him the more probable; I. 95. At any rate the story of Ctesias, which not improbably is one of those three, is very different from his; Xenophon differs widely from both; and Aeschylus, in his Persae, appears to follow another account differing from all these. As the narration of Xenophon presents us with no mythical legends, and no absurdities or impossibilities, it has, in this respect, greatly the advantage over those of his rivals, specially over that of Herodotus.

I venture another remark here, respecting a circumstance which I have not seen fully illustrated. If well founded, it serves to confirm the conclusion to which we have arrived. It is this, viz., that the biblical writers seem to accord well with that view of the subject before us, to which we have given the preference. In Daniel throughout we have the phraseology, *Medes and Persians*, showing, by this *order* of the words, that the Medes take the lead; Dan. 5: 28. 6: 9 (8). 8: 20. In Est. 10: 2 is the same order, because ancient *Chronicles* are there referred to, in which the *Medes* have the precedence. So great indeed was the preëminence of the Medes, in earlier times, that the prophets who foretold the destruction of Babylon, sometimes make use of only the name of the *Medes*, in order to designate the invaders, Isa. 13: 17. Jer. 51: 11. In Jer. 25: 25, "the kings of Elam (Persia), and the kings of the Medes" are mentioned as about to be invaded by Nebuchadnezzar; the expression here being merely descriptive of the two countries with their rulers, and in the order of their local proximity. In like way is *Elam* (Persia) mentioned alone in Jer. 49: 34, where threatening against her is uttered; and so "province of the Medes" means the *country of Media*, in Ezra 6: 2 and 2 K. 17: 6. In Isa. 21: 2, the prophet calls upon both *Persia* and *Media* to march forth to the destruction of Babylon. Beyond a doubt he regarded them as associated for the purpose of attack. But this is the only passage, in the older writings, where Persia (Elam) is put *before* Media. We cannot lay much stress on the position of the words in this case, however, because in a poetical composition such as Isa. xxi, *assonance* with the עֲלִי which precedes, seems to be the obvious reason for placing עֵילָם immediately after it. On the contrary, when Ahasuerus (Xerxes) is on the throne of Persia, we have (and very naturally) the order of names thus: "Persia and Media;" see Est. 1: 1, 14, 18, 19. The like to this indeed is to be found in the book of Daniel itself; for we have *Darius the Mede* 6: 1 (5: 31). 9: 1. 11: 1; while Cyrus, his successor, is not called *king of the Medes*, but *Cyrus king of Persia*. Throughout the Scriptures, then, usage as to *names* is conformed to the state of facts. This, on the whole, seems to be one of those accidental circumstances, which casts strong light on the truthfulness of the narration before us. If, at the taking of Babylon, the Medes were not the leading and paramount power, how comes it that Isa. 13: 17 and Jer. 51: 11, speak of them only? But all is plain and obvious, when the accounts of Daniel and Xenophon are admitted.

That such an admission has been general, even Lengerke himself concedes, p. 219. Thus, in ancient times, Josephus, Jerome, Polychronius (in his Comm.); in modern, Venema, Vitringa, Grotius, C. B. Michaelis, Bertholdt, Jahn, Heeren, Hengstenberg, Hävernick, and the leading men among the Liberalists themselves, viz. Rosenmueller, Gesenius, Winer (often and most pointedly in his Bib. Lex.), and Knobel. Few, indeed, have ventured upon the experiment of denying the conclusion which has been stated above. But Lengerke is more in earnest than most of his compeers, to destroy the credit of the book of Daniel. *Delenda est Carthago* seems to be the motto on his standard; and what cannot be accomplished in one way, must needs be accomplished in another.

So much has recently been said and written on the *romantic character* of Xenophon's Cyropedia, and on the superior credit due to Herodotus, Ctesias, and Berosus, that it seems to be necessary here to subjoin a few considerations which may help to cast a stronger light on the results of the preceding discussion.

That the Cyropedia is a *mere and simple historical narrative* in all its parts and specifications, no intelligent critical reader can for a moment believe. That Xenophon had a *politico-didactic object* in view, when he wrote the book in question, cannot be reasonably denied. To this end, very much, nay even most, of what he says is directed. He meant to teach *rulers* how to be good, wise, and brave. But how came he, at a period when Greece was still filled with the most bitter reminiscences of Persia and oriental invasions, to choose the *hero* of his work from that feared and hated country? This can be reasonably accounted for on no other ground, than that Cyrus was an eminent character, and indeed a very different man from him whose portrait is sketched by Herodotus and Ctesias. Xenophon had his account, doubtless, from Cyrus the younger, with whom he was united, or from others in his army; and he has given us the *Persian* story respecting the first Cyrus. Herodotus, (who appears never to have been in Persia, see Blum, Herod. and Ctes. p. 63 seq.), has given us the Median story; and Ctesias took his account, as he tells us, from the *βασιλικαὶ διφθέραι . . . κατά τινα νόμον συντεταγμέναι* (Diod. Sic. II. 32), i. e. *the regal histories composed in a kind of measure*, or, in other words, the *Book of Kings* poetically written; like the *Shah Nameh* of Firdusi in the modern Persian, which is professedly taken from the public records; see Blum, Herod. und Ctesias. s. 120 seq., and Malcolm's Sketches of Persia, chap. XII. Whether this *King-book* of Ctesias was Persian or Median, might be doubted. But be that as it may, Xenophon, with his nice discernment and taste, cannot be supposed to have chosen a hero whose character was in bad odor among the Greeks; and such must have been the case, provided the Greeks generally gave credence to the accounts of Herodotus and Ctesias. The very fact of his making such a selection, shows that different views were current among his countrymen; and at all events we know that the credit of Ctesias was very low among them.

That Xenophon, in pursuit of his special object, has thrown around the main figures of his picture a great variety of drapery, which is merely accidental, or rather, which is the production merely of his own inventive and luxuriant imagination, there cannot be a shadow of doubt. The book is filled with conversations, harangues, communications by letter or mandate, and the like. Indeed these make a large part of it, and constitute by far the most interesting and instructive portions of the work. Who would think, for a moment, of giving *historical reality* to all these? Some apothegms, witty or wise sayings, striking repartees, and the like, tradition may in fact have preserved; for this is usual in respect to distinguished men after their death. All that calls for remark in respect to matter of this sort is, that Xenophon has maintained a wonderful consistency and appropriateness in all these, with respect to the persons to whom they belong. Such narratives, moreover, as that of Abradatas, Panthea, and Araspes (Lib. VI.), have unquestionably received much of their costume from the Grecian artist. Such incidents, also, as those in respect to Gobryas and Gadatas, have been moulded by his skilful hand. But how all this can prove or even render it probable, that the *substantial* part of such narrations is not matter of fact, I am not able to see. One single question would seem to place these and the like matters on their proper basis; and this is: Have not Herodotus, Thucydides, Livy, nay all ancient historians, introduced speeches and conversations everywhere, and in like manner? Have they not adorned, more or less according to their ability, the accounts they give of interesting occurrences? And are all these writers nothing more than romancers, whose historical credit has no good foundation? This question, considered in all its bearings, would seem to settle the general account of this matter, on a basis that cannot well be shaken.

In modern times, we regard it as a capital defect in a romance, professing to be *historical*, if it departs widely from the truth, and indeed even if it does not keep somewhat closely to historical verity. We allow all possible scope for the writer to indulge his descriptive powers, in the development of character, as to minor circumstances. But we do not not allow him to represent to us the peaceful end of a man, at his own home, who died on the battle field in consequence of aggressions upon his neighbors. In ancient times, a plan of romance which is throughout a mere offspring of fiction, is not to be found. If Xenophon wrote such a book, he anticipated the natural course of things, by more than a thousand years. "The ancient Greek historians," says a recent and very sagacious critic (Blum), "even where they choose, like Xenophon in his Cyropedia, to indulge their inventive fancy, attach themselves, if possible, to some historical narration;" (Herod. und Ctes. s. 176). This writer adverts to a signal instance of this in Xenophon himself. In Cyrop. Lib. III., the author introduces a notable story of Tigranes, the prince of Armenia, a character unknown to all other Greek writers; of course one at the mention of whose name some recent critics exclaim: *Romance!* Yet Moses of Chorene (I. 23), says "that this same Tigranes excelled all the kings of Armenia in bravery and in intelligence;" to which he adds a copious recitation of his virtues and his deeds. Must we not conclude, then, that Xenophon, on his march through Armenia at the head of the Ten Thousand, collected the facts respecting Tigranes from old songs, ballads, and tales; the very sources from which Moses of Chorene drew his information? And may we not — or rather, must we not — reasonably conclude, that Xenophon obtained his views of Cyrus in like manner among the Persians?

That this author has held the reins of his historical Muse loosely, and purposely omitted some of the usual accompaniments of history, at least of such history as he writes in his Anabasis and Hellenics, is plain to every observing reader. For example; *time* and *place* receive comparatively very little attention from him. It must be remembered, however, that when he wrote, there was, as yet, no fixed era. So again, in the closing part of his work (VIII. 6), a single paragraph is all that Xenophon bestows on Cyrus' conquest of Egypt and all the neighboring countries. His work was done, when he had seated his hero on the throne of all hither and middle Asia, which he had acquired by the display of his skill, his bravery, and his power.

But to draw the conclusion from all this, that *Cyaxares*, who mingles with the whole work from beginning to end, is a mere figment of Xenophon's imagination, seems very strange, and, if I may say it, very uncritical. What purposes of fiction which the writer had in view, does Cyaxares answer to? He serves no good purpose, either of *contrast* or of *example;* or if subservient to either purpose it is only in a slight degree to that of contrast. He is an insignificant character at the most. Would Xenophon's genius have created such a fancy-actor as this is? In fact, if he is really anything, he is a kind of *mar-plot* of the work — a puppet gaudily dressed, but saying nothing, and doing nothing, to the main purpose of the writer. The advocates of pure romance here seem to be nonplus'd by the principles of *aesthetics.* Xenophon was one of the last men to offend in this particular; and Cyaxares must either have been better or worse, if he was a creation of Xenophon's fancy. *Cui bono?* is a question, which the advocates of entire *fiction* in Xenophon have never yet answered, in respect to Cyaxares.

I have a deep and abiding impression from the reading of Xenophon, that the character in question was forced upon him by historical fact, preserved in songs, records, and traditions; and that otherwise such a character would never have made its appearance in the Cyropedia. At the very outset of his work (I. 1. 6) he states, after drawing some general outlines of his hero, that he had *made inquiry* respecting his birth, disposition, education, and art of governing. He then adds: "*Whatever I have learned, or think I know, concerning him, I shall endeavor to relate.*" In VIII. 5. 28, he refutes those λογοποιοί, who assert that Cyaxares gave his *sister* to Cyrus as a wife, strenuously maintaining that it was his *daughter*. Such passages show, that, as to *historical occurrences*, he meant to keep within the bounds of a *narrator*, and not to roam at large with a mere romancer. Add to all this, the entire freedom of the whole work from all that is mythic, and extravagant, and incredible; a circumstance which speaks loudly as to its historical character. Could a pure work of romance, or one composed from fables, have well assumed such a character?

This last suggestion obliges me, for a moment, to allude to the characteristics of those, who are appealed to as proper *historians* of the reign of Cyrus, and whose account is received by critics like Lengerke, as altogether worthy of more credit than that of Xenophon. A candid man, well versed in matters of antiquity, cannot possibly read the narration of Herodotus, without an instinctive conviction of its mythic nature. The whole tenor of the story about his birth and marvellous escape from death; of Harpagus, and the shepherd, and the *Thyestean* feast prepared for the former by Astyages; and after all this, the conducting of the army against Cyrus committed to this same Harpagus; are (to speak with Vitringa, in Es. I. p. 543) not only *paradoxa*, but παραδοξότατα *omnia*. So the whole view which Herodotus takes of the Persian poverty and destitution of all that belongs to wealth and luxury and civilization, before they subdued Croesus and the Lydians, is entirely inconsistent with his other representation, viz., that they were already masters of Media when they engaged in this expedition, in which country was great affluence and splendor. Last of all, the final attack of Cyrus on the Scythian Massagetae, the manner in which it was conducted, and particularly the violent death of Cyrus, and the barbarous manner in which his corpse was treated by the Scythian queen Tomyris, are not only in themselves altogether improbable, but they are contradicted by the fact, that Cyrus' remains were deposited in his well known tomb at Pasargadae, and found there by Aristobulus, an officer of Alexander the Great, deputized to examine into the alleged robbery of that tomb. Thither Alexander himself repaired and ordered everything to be restored as far as possible. This story is told by Strabo (XIV.), by Arrian (Exped. Alex. VI. 29), and by Q. Curtius in his Life of Alexander; and in all, it is circumstantially related, and is utterly at variance with the account of Herodotus as to the death of Cyrus. An explicit statement is made, that a guard and lamps and sacrifices had been regularly established there ever since the time of Cambyses, the son and successor of Cyrus. This circumstance, moreover, teaches us how to dispose of the narration of Diodorus Siculus (II. 44), that Cyrus was taken prisoner in a battle against the *Amazons*, and by their queen condemned to crucifixion, by which he actually perished. Ctesias assigns to him a still different death. Cyrus gives battle to the Derbici; is wounded by an Indian, (the Indians were allies of the Derbici); and he dies the third day afterwards, Persica, § 8. Ctesias adds, that his body was sent to Persia and buried there by Cambyses his son, ib. § 9. Lucian (de Longaevis) makes him live more than a hundred years. Of all these accounts, only that of Ctesias is reconcilable with the place of his tomb, and with the fact that not only his relics were found there by Alexander, but also a definite inscription upon the monument which related to him. We have then to choose between him and Xenophon. I see not how we can hesitate to give the preference to the latter. If we are met again with the salutation of *romance*, why is it any more to Xenophon's purpose, we may reply, to let him die in peace, than to represent him as falling gloriously on the field of battle, in defence of his country — the place of all others, where heroes of the Grecian stamp wished to die? Nelson died just where, if not when, he wished of all things to die, i. e. in the arms of victory; and victory, according to Ctesias, was connected with the wound and death of Cyrus, for the Derbici met with a signal defeat.

Plutarch, Aristotle, Lucian, Arrian, Strabo, and others among the ancients, accuse Ctesias loudly of narrating fabulous and incredible stories. Partially Herodotus also has a share in their censure. Bähr has examined the subject at length in the Preface to his *Ctesias*. It would be out of place to pursue it here. But I may add the deliberate judgment of the best editor both of Herodotus and Ctesias who has yet appeared. He is speaking of the difference between the narrations of Ctesias and Herodotus, respecting the death of Cyrus; and he says: "That I may begin with the narration of Herodotus, I will speak openly what I think. It is not wanting in *tragical ornament;* and in this way Herodotus has *adorned* other things respecting Cyrus, beautifully imagined according to the lofty conceptions of the Greeks;" (Bähr in Ctes. p. 11.) In this judgment, he says, Osiander accords; and he then appeals to the tomb of Cyrus at Pasargadae as contradicting Herodotus' account of Cyrus' death.

Let not the reader suppose, that it is my design to discredit either Herodotus or Ctesias, where they give facts within their knowledge, or which are derived from authentic sources. But when Herodotus relates the *mythic* and the *marvellous*, (which is not very unfrequent), he nearly always tells us his sources, (as he does in the case of Cyrus), and contents himself with the office of merely reporting what is told him. This is honest and upright; nor should I scruple to assign to him a character corresponding to these qualities. Ctesias, however, has less scruples, and often tells stories which he expects will surprise the reader, excite his wonder, and serve to entertain him. The monstrosity of many of his statements respecting the Assyrian Semiramis, and concerning many things that he saw in India, no one can fail to notice who reads him critically.

No Grecian fable of the origin of Minerva or of Venus surpasses his genetic account of Semiramis, as related in Diod. Sic. II. 4. When Ninus dies, Semiramis, as he tells us, erected a monument to his memory nine stadia in height [$= 1\frac{1}{8}$ mile]; which, he asserts, was still standing, (viz. when he wrote), so long after the destruction of Nineveh. This same Semiramis, moreover, builds Babylon, with sixty miles of wall around it 300 feet high, in one year. When she makes war on India, inasmuch as Mesopotamia had no elephants, she makes 300,000 *mock-elephants* out of the stuffed skins of so many black oxen ; she collects 3,000,000 footmen, 500,000 horsemen, and 100,000 chariots of war. To finish her story, she flies away at last in the shape of a dove, and never reappears. — All this without any caution to the reader ! And then, the gross errors in topography ! Ascalon (in Palestine) has a *large lake* near it, into which the mother of Semiramis casts and drowns herself, Diod. II. 4. *Nineveh* is often and always placed on the *Euphrates*, § 7 seq. These are only mere specimens. Whatever now Ctesias, or his supporters, may say of his drawing his accounts from the διφθέραι βασιλικαί, we cannot well suppose, that a man born and brought up at no great distance from Ascalon could be a very accurate observer, who could believe that there was a *great lake* near that town ; and what can be said to apologize for the gross ignorance of geography manifested in placing *Nineveh* on the *Euphrates ?* Bähr labors somewhat to soften this matter ; but this is done by appealing to other writers who assert the like, but who were themselves in all probability led by Ctesias, Ctes. p. 391. Not so Wesseling ; " Ctesias," says he, " places this city on the Euphrates, *turpi errore ;*" Notae in Diod. II. 7. Yet a direct design to mislead cannot justly be attributed, I apprehend, to Ctesias. He may be trusted, where there is probable evidence of his acquaintance with the subject-matter, and no inherent improbability ; but his love of the marvellous, his apparent desire to produce astonishment and wonder in his readers, and his evident lack of geographical knowledge, render it necessary to read him with caution, and not unfrequently with distrust. Blum (ut sup. p. 120 seq.) has shown, at last, the probable ground of Ctesias' fabulous aspect, viz. that the διφθέραι βασιλικαί from which he drew, were, like the *Shah-Nameh*, poetical ballads in commemoration of kings. The Persians and other Orientals had their *poets laureate ;* and Ctesias has given us some of the fruits of their poetic imaginations, in respect to their ancient kings and heroes.

It is but just and proper, that all these things should be taken into the estimation, when we make a comparison between Herodotus and Ctesias on the one hand, and the Bible and Xenophon on the other. Xenophon is perfectly sober. He had good opportunity to study the Persians and their affairs. He brought to this study a mind of the first order. The Hebrews, of all the western Asiatic nations, had most occasion to know, and must have best known, Babylon at the time of its fall, and those concerned with bringing about its fall. There is therefore a strong presumption, that they have given us a narration in regard to those subjects which is worthy of credit.

An accidental passage, in Aeschylus, which I have not yet adduced, serves strongly to confirm the account as given by Xenophon and the book of Daniel. In his *Persae*, the ghost of Darius is introduced, and among other things he gives an account of the gradual conquest of hither and middle Asia by the Medo-Persian arms. The passage runs thus :

Μῆδος γαρ ἦν ὁ πρῶτος ἡγεμὼν στράτου,
Ἄλλος δ' ἐκείνου παῖς τόδ' ἔργον ἤνυσε,
Φρένες γὰρ αὐτοῦ θυμὸν ῳακοστρόφουν.
Τρίτος δ' ἀπ' αὐτοῦ Κῦρος, εὐδαίμων ἀνήρ. κ. τ. λ.

That is: "A Mede [Astyages] was the first leader of the army; the second, his son [Cyaxares], carried on the work; for understanding guided his purpose. The third, after him, was Cyrus, a fortunate man," etc.; Pers. 765 seq. Lengerke dispenses with this passage, by asking how the eulogy of Cyaxares, in the third line, would fit the Cyaxares of Xenophon; and by remarking, that Aeschylus was probably in the same plight with those oriental writers, who, since the establishment of the dynasty of the Kayanidae, know of only two (generic) royal names, Kaicobad and Kaikawus. But is this a satisfactory answer, in respect to such a man as Aeschylus? Born within some three or four years after the death of Cyrus (B. C. 525), in an elevated station of society and probably of royal descent, he mingled in the fiercest contests of the Greeks against the Persian invaders, and fought in person at the battles of Marathon and Plataea, as also in the sea-fights of Artemisium and Salamis. Of the latter he has given a picture, in immortal verse, in his Persae. Could a man like him, not inferior in talent to any Greek poet that ever wielded the pen, and personally connected with all the great battles of his country with the Persians, be ignorant of what had passed in their country the very generation before he was born? It is allowed by all competent judges, that he has in his Persae, the only Greek play that makes a foreign ground its basis, given a truly oriental picture, which shows his intimate acquaintance with oriental matters. Yet this same Aeschylus has given the succession of kings as Xenophon gives it, and in entire accordance with what the book of Daniel declares. Well did Bertholdt (Comm. on Dan.), and Gesenius in his Thesaurus (art. דָּרְיָוֶשׁ), appeal to this evidence as conclusive against the silence of Herodotus and Ctesias, in respect to a Median successor of Astyages.

As to *Berosus*, there is nothing to decide the question. It is true, that he names Cyrus merely as the conqueror of Babylon. But this he was *de facto*; and Darius never seems to have been an agent in the matter, in any such way as to draw him into special notice. Besides, he was far advanced in years, and held even nominal dominion but for a short period; and this he committed to the active management of Cyrus. Nothing of any importance, then, against our position, can be brought from this quarter.

'But Xenophon,' says Lengerke, 'is not to be credited in his Cyropedia, because in his Anabasis, which is all sober history, he contradicts the idea, that Cyrus took in a peaceful manner the dominion of the Medes; for he says (Anab. III. 4. 8), that when the Persian king took the dominion of the Medes, he attacked the city of Larissa [belonging to Media], but could not take it. Again, in Anab. III. 4. 11, it is said of Mespila [another Median city], that 'a Median queen fled thither when the Medes lost their dominion by reason of the Persians.' But since Media, like Persia, was made up of many different tribes and clans, who all had their chiefs, what is there improbable in the supposition, that when the government passed to Cyrus, some of these chiefs, having very strongly fortified cities, set up for themselves, and refused allegiance to the new king Cyrus? That some queen of Cyaxares, disliking his dowry to Cyrus, should have fled to one of these cities, would be no strange occurrence.

If any results of *chronology* can be depended on, it would be difficult to suppose that Astyages was an important actor, during the period of Cyrus' active services, which continued for some thirty years. Astyages died about

560. Cyrus took Babylon about 538—539 B. C., i. e. twenty-two years after the death of Astyages. The probability of an *intermediate* king is therefore very great. Lengerke says, that 'to make room for this shadowy king, Xenophon has cut off twenty-two years from Cyrus' reign, which was twenty-nine according to Herodotus, and thirty according to Ctėsias.' But this difficulty is easily solved. The two latter reckon from the time when Cyrus took the chief command of the Persian forces, at the beginning of the war in Asia Minor, while Xenophon counts only upon his universal empire, after the death of Cyaxares.

Some stress has been laid on the testimony of Suidas (s. v. δαρεικός), of the Scholiast to Aristoph. Eccles., and of Harpocration, that the coin אֲדַרְכּוֹן (mentioned in Ezra and Nehemiah) is older than Darius Hystaspis. If so, it not improbably belongs to the age of the Darius mentioned in Dan. 6: 1. But as this Persian name means *king*; and as Herodotus (IV. 166) denies that the Persians had any coined money before the time of Darius Hystaspis, some doubt may be felt in regard to reliance upon this argument.

Finally, (for this Note already too much protracted must come to a close), I do not pretend to assert that there are no difficulties in the matter before us. It would argue a very incompetent view of the whole subject, if any one should assert this. But I am persuaded that our difficulties are no greater here, than they are in respect to many a question pertaining to Assyrian, Median, Babylonian, and Persian history. For the first three, we are dependent on Herodotus and Ctesias; for of other authors we have only mere fragments, mainly preserved in Josephus, Diodorus Siculus, and the Chronicon of Eusebius. Nothing can be more diverse, than some of the most important narratives in Herodotus and Ctesias. All attempts to reconcile them are beyond question fruitless; e. g. Herodotus represents the Assyrian empire as lasting 520 years; Ctesias, as continuing 1305; the former makes the Median empire to have six kings and to continue 150 years, the latter gives to it nine kings and more than 282 years. And so of many other matters. It is manifest, therefore, that the writers must have drawn from very different sources, and that these were used with little, or at least without any effectual, critical discrimination.

But one of the most important things to be kept in view is, that *silence* or an *omission* in respect to this fact or that, is a most slippery and feeble foundation to build upon. All accounts of those ancient times are mere *historical anecdotes*, selected mostly with a view to *effect* upon the mind of the reader. In a modified sense, this remark applies to the O. Test. history. It is a series of historical narrations respecting interesting events or persons, but it is not a full and minute history, and it makes no pretensions to being a complete historical record. I cannot argue, therefore, from the *silence* of the book of Chronicles about certain facts related in the book of Kings, that these facts are not true. In like manner, I cannot argue from the silence of the Bible, or of Xenophon, about a battle before the walls of Babylon between Cyrus and the last Babylonian king, that there was no battle. Berosus and Herodotus both assert that such a battle was fought; but Abydenus (Chron. Euseb. I. 10) says not a word of it, in his account of the capture of Babylon. If Herodotus and Berosus *contradict* Daniel and Xenophon, as Lengerke declares, then do they contradict Abydenus also. And what shall be said of Ctesias, who does not even advert to the conquest of Babylon at all? It is indeed no contradiction of one author, when another has omitted to record what he has recorded. The Bible has nothing to do with the life of Cyrus, excepting in his relation to the Jews; much less does it give the whole history of Babylon. The omission of Cyrus' battle, as mentioned above, was of course to be expected, and is no incongruity. As to Xenophon, we might well suppose, that the Cyropedia would have described the contest in question, because it makes for the glory of the hero. But this historian has given a mere sketch of the march of Cyrus from Sardis to Babylon (VII. 4), and he mentions only, that on that march he overthrew the Phrygians, the Cappadocians, and the Arabians. As these were in league with Babylon, or at any rate coöperating with it, it may be that the battle in question is included in this brief notice. All the conquests of Cyrus, moreover, subsequent to that of Babylon, are merely touched upon by Xenophon, in a single paragraph, (VIII. 6). We can no more give the reason, perhaps, why such an omission exists in Xenophon, than we can why Ctesias omitted all mention of Cyrus' conquest of Babylon. Everywhere in Herodotus and Ctesias, such *omissions* abound. But to represent Berosus and Herodotus who mention the battle in question, as *contradicting* Xenophon and Daniel who mention it not, (as Lengerke does), seems to be hardly consistent with either critical candor or proper discrimination. To appeal to Isa. 43: 14, 17, as testifying to the battle in question (p. 217), when it is a mere general and poetic picture of subjugation, and also to Isa. 42: 13 as confirming this, only adds new proof that this writer is animated by the spirit of *Delenda est Carthago.*

In fine, one must be cautious, as to great confidence in any particular statement of Herodotus or Ctesias, in respect to very remote times and oriental countries. That Herodotus acknowledges three different accounts of Cyrus, besides his own, and that with him it is a mere choice between traditions, is replete with instruction. That Ctesias drew from heroic and regal songs, i. e. old ballads, is not to be forgotten. Hence it comes to pass, as one of the most acute critics on the sources of the histories in question has said, "that should any one attempt to force an agreement between Herodotus and Ctesias, forthwith the result of all his laborious efforts is found impinging against other stories respecting the same object, which make no less claim to tell the truth than those on which he has relied; Blum, Herod. and Ctes. s. 230. So Wesseling has often acknowledged the impossibility of reconciling Ctesias and Herodotus in his Notes on Diod. Sic. II. Bähr, by far the most able of all the editors of the works of both those ancient historians, has said, again and again, that all efforts to reconcile them seem to be nothing more in amount than *oleum et operam perdere;* a judgment, in my view, unquestionably just.

Shall we then, where such authors are contradicted by Xenophon and the Scriptures, credit them, or either of them, in preference to consistent, sober, consentaneous authorities? This is at last the simple question. Lengerke decides for the former; my reason and judgment give preference to the latter.

CHAPTER VI.

[Darius, being possessed of the whole empire of hither Asia, sets over it 120 Satraps to regulate its affairs. These were superintended by three Praefects; and of these Daniel was chief. The king, because of his qualities and services, was desirous to make him a leading officer over the whole realm, i. e. Satrap of the Satraps or chief Satrap; vs. 1—3. Daniel's under officers of both grades were envious toward him, and desirous of degrading and ruining him, but they could find nothing in his official conduct on which they could lay hold for this purpose. They therefore devised a scheme to entrap him, on the ground of his religious duties, vs. 4, 5. They persuaded Darius to make a decree, that no request should be made of God or man, for thirty days, except of the king alone; vs. 6—9. Daniel, with full knowledge of this, worshipped, as usual, in his chamber, where he could be seen by others through the window of his apartment; v. 10. His accusers who were on the watch, inform the king, and urge the execution of the statute that had been made, the penalty of which was to be cast into a den of lions; vs. 10—13 The king is greatly distressed by the information respecting Daniel, and seeks for some expedient to justify him in his release, but he finds none. The accusers return, and urge the execution of the penalty; to which the king feels himself obliged to assent; 14—16. The den of the lions is closed upon Daniel and sealed; and the king goes mourning to his abode; vs. 17, 18. The king after a night of agitation, goes early in the morning to the den; calls aloud to Daniel; and is answered by him with an account of his safety; vs. 19—22. The king orders Daniel to be taken from the den, and his accusers and their families to be thrown into it; vs. 23, 24. Darius issues a proclamation, that the God of Daniel should be feared and reverenced, because of the wonders which he had done; vs. 26, 27. Daniel remains in favor with the king, and afterwards with Cyrus; v. 28.]

(1) And Darius the Mede took the kingdom, when he was about sixty-two years of age

That this belongs to the preceding narration, seems to me quite clear; and in this light most of the commentators have regarded it. It serves to complete the historic view of the fulfilment of the third clause contained in the writing on the wall, viz. "Thy kingdom shall be taken from thee, and given to the Mede and the Persian." — כְּבַר, כְּ = the Lat. *circiter, about.* The idiom, *son of so many years*, is too familiar to need remark. — קַבֵּל, *took, received;* from whom? The implication seems very clear, that he took the government of which the Babylonish king had been deprived; or, in other words, that he took that kingdom which Belshazzar had left. — תַּרְתֵּין, fem. form of תְּרֵין, which is a contracted dual for תְּרַיִן, and being of a fem. form, it agrees with the masc. noun שְׁנִין, § 36. 2. This is the only *dual* form in Chaldee.

(2) It seemed good to Darius, and he appointed one hundred and twenty satraps over the kingdom, who should be over all the empire.

קֳדָם, *before* = בְּעֵינֵי or לִפְנֵי, *in the sight of, in the view of,* comp. in 4: 24, where עַל follows the same verb, in a like sense. — לַאֲחַשְׁדַּרְפְּנַיָּא, Acc. with לְ, § 56. 2. — לֶהֱוֺן, see on 2: 20. The last clause here serves to explain and expand the meaning of the preceding one, so that the reader may know that the arrangement in question is extended to the *whole* of the empire, to that newly acquired as well as to the rest.

(3) And over them three directors, of whom Daniel was one, in order that those satraps might render an account to them, so that the king might suffer no loss.

עֵלָּא, emph. form = Heb. עַל, *over.* — מִנְּהוֹן, מִן with Dagh. f. before a suffix, § 38. note, lit. *of them.* The whole phrase, in its literal form, runs thus: *In the above of them* or *from them,* i. e. in the superiority of them = over them. The idiom is Chaldaic purely. So in Targ. Onk., Gen. 22: 9, עֵיל מִן אָעַיָּא, lit. *above from the wood* = above the wood; Deut. 28: 43, עֵיל מִנָּךְ, *above from thee* = above thee. — סָרְכִין is plain enough as to its necessary meaning here; but its etymology is uncertain; see in Lex. — דִּי . . . מִנְּהוֹן, *of whom,* § 41. 1. — יָהֲבִין, Part. in Peal, joined with the following verb of existence, and denoting continued or customary action, § 47. 1. — טַעְמָא, emph. of טְעֵם, *ratio, account.* — נָזִק has a *passive* sense, because the verb is intrans.; the form is that of an act. Part. in Peal, § 12. 1. *c.* The *loss* referred to here, seems to be that of revenue.

(4) Then the same Daniel was made chief over the directors and the satraps, because an excellent spirit was in him; and the king intended to set him over the whole empire.

מִתְנַצַּח, Part. Ithpaal, final Pattah before a Guttural. — יַתִּירָא *preeminent,* or *that which exceeds* or *goes beyond* others. — עֲשִׁית, Peal form, § 12. 2. 1. *a.* — לַהֲקָמוּתֵהּ, Inf. Aph. with suff., p. 56. *e.*

(5) Then the directors and satraps sought to find some pretence against Daniel, in regard to the government; but no pretence nor corrupt dealing were they able to find, because that he was faithful, and fault or corrupt dealing was not found against him.

בָּעַיִן, Part. pl. of בְּעָא, for form, p. 91. Dec. VII. *a.* — לְדָנִיֵּאל, lit. *in respect to Daniel;* I have translated above *ad sensum,* in conformity with our idiom. — מִצַּד, lit. *on the side of, on the part of* = in regard to. The word וּשְׁחִיתָה I have rendered as a noun, for the fem. of adjectives or participles easily goes over into a noun. — מְהֵימַן, Part. pass. Aph. of אֲמַן, see p. 66, אמן in note. — שָׁלוּ apoc. form of שָׁלוּת, § 31. 1. — עֲלוֹהִי, lit. *upon him,* i. e. resting on him as a burden; in this way עַל comes to mean *against,* as I have rendered it above.

(6) Then said those men: We shall not find any pretence against this Daniel, unless we find [it] against him with respect to the law of his God.

דִּי is here the mere sign of words quoted. A double comma would sufficiently translate it. — נְהַשְׁכַּח, 1st plur. Aph. Fut. with ה retained, p. 49. 5. — הַשְׁכַּחְנָא, Aph. Praet. 1st. plur. The noun עִלָּה, or rather the pronoun in its place, is here omitted. The translation above supplies the latter. — דָּת has special reference to a *law* or *statute* in regard to matters of religion. The word seems to be Persian in its origin; see Lex. This is high testimony in favor of Daniel's integrity and piety. It would seem, that even his rivals apprehended that he would remain firm and unwavering in his religious duties.

(7) Then those directors and satraps rushed tumultuously to the king, and spake thus to him: O king Darius, live forever!

הַרְגִּשׁוּ, the Heb. form of Aph. p. 50, near the top; it means *to assemble and move along with tumult*, like a mob. — For the rest of the verse, see on 2: 4. Lengerke thinks 'the writer has here forgotten himself, and wonders how all these satraps could be there in Babylon, when they were bound to be in their respective provinces, for the sake of discharging their duties! But inasmuch as they had just been appointed, and had not yet fully prepared to go to their respective stations, may it not be easily supposed, that during the delay necessary for preparation, all happened which is here related? However, his principal objection is, that satraps were not yet in fact appointed. Of this, more anon.

(8) All the directors of the kingdom, the deputy-governors, satraps, state-councillors, and overseers, have given counsel to establish a decree of the king and confirm a prohibition, that whoever shall make request of any god or man for thirty days, except of thee, O king, he shall be cast into the den of lions.

אִתְיָעַטוּ, Ithpaal 3 pl. Perf., from יְעַט = Heb. יָעַץ, see Lex. under letters ט and צ; ִ instead of ַ with Dagh. f. after it, because of the Guttural that follows. *Reciprocal* action, i. e. *mutual counsel*, is denoted by Ithpaal here — like Niphal in Hebrew, § 10. 7. — For the officers' names, see on 3: 2, 24. — קַיָּמָה, Inf. Pael of קוּם. — קְיָם, lit. *something confirmed* or *established;* for the form, see § 28. a. 1. 2. — תַקָּפָה, Inf. Pael. — אֱסָר, *prohibition* from אֲסַר *to bind, constrain;* the form is like קְיָם above. — בָּעוּ = בָּעוּת, § 29. 6. *a*. The two following nouns have the same form with the first two in this verse, as noted above. — תְּלָתִין, 30, from תְּלָת, with pl. form added which makes it into so many *tens*, p. 101. — יִתְרְמֵא, Fut. Ithpeal. — אַרְיָוָתָא, pl. of אַרְיֵה fem. form, with ה ֵ apparently paragogic, so that the word = אֲרִי; in declining, however, this letter is treated as if it were of the root, and a substitute (as usual elsewhere) for a final ו; comp. p. 92. Par. A. b.

(9) Now, O king, do thou establish a prohibition, and inscribe a writing which cannot be changed, according to the law of the Medes and Persians which cannot be repealed.

תְּקִים, 2 sing. Fut. used as the Imper. of entreaty. — לָא לְהַשְׁנָיָה, the verb is Inf. Aph. of שְׁנָא with praeform. retained; the verb of existence being understood after לָא, the phrase lit. means: *it is not for change*, or *for being changed;* see § 46. 3. note, and comp. Heb. Gramm. § 129. 3. — תֶּעְדֵּא, lit. *pass away.* As to the *immutability* of laws written and sealed with the king's signet, comp. Esth. 1: 19. 8: 8. Observe that here the *order* of the two nations is: *Medes and Persians;* which agrees with the fact asserted, viz. that the king now on the throne was a *Median.* But in Est. 1: 3, 14, 18, 19, when a *Persian* is on the throne, the order is: *Persians and Medes.* The use to be made of this fact, has already been pointed out in the remarks at the close of the preceding chapter.

(10) Because of this, king Darius wrote down a writing even a prohibition.

I have taken וֶאֱסָרָא here as merely exegetical; and nothing is more common than to connect an exegetical clause or word to that which precedes, by placing וְ before it.

(11) Now Daniel, when he knew that the writing was completed, went to his house, and his windows were open in his upper chamber, toward Jerusalem, and, three times each day did he kneel upon his knees, and make supplication, and utter praise before God, entirely as he had done before this.

Writing was completed, lit. the writing was written. But our idiom hardly admits such a form of expression, at least it would not be allowed as *good usage.* — כַּוִּין, pl. of כַּו, as if from a root כּוּ, treated as *fem.* here, by the Part. which follows in the fem. plur. — עִלִּית with suff.; comp. § 29. 2. *b*.10, but here the noun has the fem. ending as in § 31. — וְזִמְנִין, we might translate the וְ here by *even, etiam*, and it would then serve to render emphatic the number of times that Daniel went to perform his devotions. But the probable sense of it is merely as translated above.—*In his upper chamber*, an apartment probably built on the top of the house, with a roof of its own, and designed for retirement; comp. 2 Sam. 19: 1. (18: 33 Eng.) 1 K. 17: 19. It was the usual place for prayer: see Acts 1: 13. 10: 9. — *Toward Jerusalem*, because that was the place where the special presence of God was supposed to be, by every Hebrew; comp. for the like, Ps. 5: 8 (7). 28: 2. See the ground of this practice adverted to, in Ps. 20: 3 (2). So Solomon, in his prayer, 2 Chron. 6: 34, and repeatedly in 1 K. 8: 33, 35, 38, 44, 48. In like manner the Mohammedans turn their face toward Mecca, in their devotions; and the worshippers of Ormusd, as presented in Ezek. 8: 16, looked to the rising sun, the symbol of Ormusd.

In like manner, the ancient Christians used to pray with their faces toward the east; Orig. Hom. V. in Num. Bertholdt accuses the writer of mistake here, on the ground, (as he avers), that the Jews had as yet no such custom, and because the temple was now in ruins. The first objection is clearly erroneous, as the quotations above show; and the second, of no importance. Was not the ground where the temple stood still *sacred* in their eyes? And did they not expect, according to the prediction of Jeremiah, that they should return, and rebuild the temple? — *The three times* of prayer are adverted to in Acts 2: 15. 10: 9. Dan. 9: 21, i. e. at 9 o'clock, A. M., at 12 M., and at 3 P. M. — בָּרֵךְ, Part. Peal with pronoun הוּא, § 47. 1. *b.*, strongly expresses habit or continued action. — בִּרְכּוֹהִי, pl. suff. of בֶּרֶךְ. — מְצַלֵּא, Part. Pael. — מוֹדֵא, Part. Aph. of יְדָא, § 20. 2. c. — הֲוָא עָבֵד, § 47, *a.* — דְּנָה has the const. state here before it, lit. *a priori tempore hujus* (rei).

(12) Then those men came tumultuously, and found Daniel praying and making supplication before his God.

הַרְגִּשׁוּ, Aph. like the Heb. Hiphil, p. 50 near the top. The לְ that follows, marks the Acc. — מִתְחַנַּן, Ithpaal Part., like the Greek Mid. voice, *making supplication for himself.*

(13) Then they drew near, and spake before the king respecting the royal prohibition: Didst thou not write a prohibition, that every one who shall make request of any god or man, during thirty days, except of thee, O king, shall be cast into the den of lions? The king answered and said: The thing is established, according to the law of the Medes and Persians which cannot be repealed.

קְרִבוּ, § 12. 1. 1. For the sequel, see v. 8 above. — מִלְּתָא may be rendered *word,* viz. what they had just said, or *thing,* viz. the whole affair as represented. I have preferred the latter.

(14) Then they answered and said before the king: Daniel, who is of the sons of captive Jews, pays no regard to thee, O king, nor to the prohibition which thou hast written, for three times in a day does he make his request.

The first דִּי here is a mere sign of words to be quoted.— לָא שָׂם עֲלָיךְ... טְעֵם, see on 3: 12. — וְעַל, *nor to,* the וְ following a negative clause, and standing before another in the like predicament, should be translated *nor.* — זִמְנִין, pl. of זְמַן, and used just as we use the word *time* with a numeral, denoting repetition. — שָׂם, Praet. Peal, is followed in construction by the Part. בָּעֵא, instead of a *verb* which our own idiom demands. Often so in Chaldee.

(15) Then the king, when he heard the report, was much grieved on account of it,

and he set his heart upon Daniel to rescue him, and to the going down of the sun he was contriving to deliver him.

שָׂם בָּל, *to set one's heart* or *mind on* anything, i. e. to revolve in one's mind what can be done with it. Both the Syriac and Arabic employ בָּל in the like sense. — שֵׁיזָבוּתֵהּ, root שֵׁזַב, Pēel (instead of Pael with Dagh. f.), p. 52, note under No. 1. For the Inf. ending, p. 56. e. — מֵעָלֵי, *occasus*, const. pl. of מֵעָל, root עֲלַל. — מִשְׁתַּדַּר, Ithpaal of שְׁדַר with tranfer of שׁ. — הַצָּלוּתֵהּ, Inf. Aph. of נְצַל, with suff. form as above. Beyond the setting of the sun, the execution of the penalty could not be delayed. In Persia, this usually follows the sentence without delay.

(16) Then those men came tumultuously to the king, and said to the king: Know, O king, that to the Medes and Persians there is a law, that every prohibition and decree which the king shall establish, is unchangeable.

דַּע Imper. of יְדַע. — יְהָקֵים from קוּם, Aph. Fut. with ה retained, and final vowel *Tsere* instead of the usual long Hhireq; these vowels being often interchanged in Chaldee. — לְהַשְׁנָיָה, see in v. 9. Inf. Aph., lit. *is not for changing.*

(17) Then the king commanded, and they brought Daniel, and cast [him] into the lion's den. The king answered and said to Daniel: Thy God whom thou servest continually, he will deliver thee.

הַיְתִיו Aph. of אֲתָא, see in § 24. 2. Aph. — רְמוֹ, 3 pl. Peal, omits the suff. pronoun; which omission is frequent in Chaldee, in the like cases. — פָּלַח, Part. with final Pattah, because of the final Guttural. — יְשֵׁיזְבִנָּךְ p. 58. Rem. 1.

(18) And a stone was brought, and placed on the mouth of the den, and the king sealed it with his signet and with the signet of his nobles, that the design respecting Daniel might not be changed.

הֵיתָיִת, a pass. fem. form of הַיְתִי Aph. of אֲתָא. See a plur. of the same kind in 3: 13, and the remarks there. Both forms are anomalous, and evidently stand for the *Hophal* of the Hebrews in regard to meaning. If the forms are legitimate, they were probably made thus anomalous, (like many words in all languages), by vulgar usage. One is at a loss to know whence such vowel-points come, as analogies are wanting. — שָׂמַת most probably a Part. pass. in the room of the usual fem. שִׂימַת, as declined on p. 51. These two forms are sometimes connected in Hebrew, e. g. 2 Sam. 23: 32, text שִׂימָה, Qeri שׂוּמָה. There is, at any rate, no other form of the verb שׂוּם to which it is so near a resemblance; and thus taken, it gives the requisite meaning. — גֻּבָּא, lit. *pit;* and such was doubtless the den of the lions. The mouth of this pit seems to have been covered, and a door or passage way inserted, through which the lions were fed. This door was now closed and sealed, so that neither Daniel's friends might interfere, (for it was the intention of the nobles to exclude them, when they put their seal on the door), nor his enemies be permitted to annoy him, in case the lions did not destroy him, (which seems to have been the king's design in putting his own seal upon it). The sentence of law was thus strictly executed, and an arrangement so made, that there should be no interference with it, by the different parties who were actuated by different motives. — וְחַתְמַהּ, Perf. Peal of חֲתַם with suff. fem., which relates to אֶבֶן a fem. noun. — עִזְקְתֵהּ, *his signet*, i. e. a ring on which was fastened an engraving of the king's name. It would seem that wax, or some impressible substance, was placed on the edge of the stone door and of the covering around it, so that if it were opened, the seal would be broken, and of course this would be proof of unlawful interference. As before suggested, the nobles doubtless designed that the king should not interfere, when they put their seals upon the stone door. See the like process in Matt. 27: 66. — צְבוּ = צְבוּת, *purpose, design*, which is more significant than the rendering of Ges., De Wette, and others, viz., *matter, affair*. — תִשְׁנֵא has an intransitive or passive sense, and so I have rendered it in the version above.

(19) Then went the king to his palace, and spent the night in fasting, and his concubines were not brought before him, and his sleep fled from him.

בָּת Praet. of בּוּת. — טְוָת, a noun from טְוָא, like קְצָת, מְנָת, etc., here used in an adverbial way, or we may regard it as the Acc. of manner. — דַּחֲוָן, plur. fem. of דַּחֲוָה, from דְּחָא, the corresponding Arabic verb meaning *feminam subegit*. — הַנְעֵל, *one did not bring*, the verb having no subject expressed; of course it is equivalent to the *passive* voice, and so I have translated it; it is the Aph. of עֲלַל, for the נ see § 6. 2. — נַדַּת Peal of נְדַד, *fled*, comp. Esth. 6: 1. — עֲלוֹהִי, עַל = אֶל here, as often elsewhere; lit. *his sleep fled for him*, like לֶךְ־לְךָ in Gen. 12: 1, *go for thyself*. This construction is not unfrequent after verbs of motion; comp. the like expression in 2: 1, and the remarks upon it. All this is related to show the sincere concern and regret of the king for what had taken place.

(20) Then the king arose at early dawn, when it was light, and went in haste to the lion's den.

שְׁפַרְפָּרָא, a reduplicate form, § 28. b.11. The Syr. has the simple ܫܦܪܐ, and employs it in the same sense, viz. that of *early dawn*. — נָגְהָא seems to be equivalent to the preceding word, but is in fact exegetical of it;

just as we say: "Very early, as soon as it was light." — *In haste*, so the Inf. noun בְּהִתְבְּהָלָה (Inf. of Ithpaal) means.

(21) And when he drew near to the den, he cried out to Daniel with a loud voice; the king answered and said to Daniel: Daniel, thou servant of the living God, has thy God, whom thou servest continually, been able to deliver thee from the lions?

כְּמִקְרְבֵהּ, Inf. with suff. in the same way as a noun, § 16. 2. c. In such cases כְּ means *when;* lit. it would run thus: *in accordance with the drawing near of him.* — זְעִק, § 12. 1. 1, also *ib.* 2. 1. *The crying out,* here designated, was doubtless a shout of some kind, to see whether Daniel was alive and would respond. In like way we may suppose Daniel to have responded. Then follows the address to him, on the part of the king. — חַיָּא, *living,* in the mouth of a Persian or Median king, is not strange; for idolatry was proscribed by the *Parsis,* and they had neither temples nor images. Ormusd, in their view, was the author of all desirable life. But here Darius seems to conform to the usual Heb. method of naming their God. — הֲיִכִל, interrogative הֲ, and the verb יְכִל = יְכֵל, §12.2.1.

(22) Then Daniel spake with the king: O king, live forever!

מַלִּל, Pael, *entered into conversation, spoke colloquially;* for Hhireq, see 12. 1. 1. — אֲמַר is omitted before מַלְכָּא, and is unnecessary.

(23) My God hath sent his angel, and stopped the mouth of the lions, and they have done me no harm, because that before him innocence was found in me, and also before thee, O king, have I done no harm.

מַלְאֲכֵהּ, *his angel.* Angelic interposition is very common in the remainder of this book. Comp. John 5: 4. Acts 12: 11. Heb. 1: 14, and the Apoc. throughout. — פֻּם, § 29. 5. a. — חַבְּלוּנִי Pael with suff. — זָכוּת = זָכוּ, § 29. 6. a. § 31. 1. — לִי, lit. *for me, Dat. commodi.* Our idiom requires a different mode of expression, viz. *in me.* — אַף is put before a clause where the sense is climactic, or at least where a special stress is laid upon it. *Offence against the king* was, in this case, the main thing to be disclaimed, in order to accomplish his exculpation. He was not accused on any other ground.

(24) Then the king was very glad within himself, and he commanded to raise up Daniel from the den; and Daniel was raised up from the den, and no injury was found on him, because he trusted in his God.

עֲלוֹהִי might be applied to Daniel, and then we must translate: *on his account;* but in v. 15 above we have בְּאֵשׁ עֲלוֹהִי, where the pronoun refers to the same *subject* as the verb. In the version above, I have followed the analogy of the last phrase, in the present case; and so Ges.,

Maurer, Lengerke, al. — לְהַנְסָקָה, Aph. Inf. reg. as to נ, § 18. Note. — הֻסַּק, a purely Hophal form from the same stem as the preceding verb, p. 50. 6. — הֵימִן, Aph. of אֲמַן, p. 66, in note.

(25) And the king commanded, and they brought those men, who were the accusers of Daniel, and cast [them] into the den of lions, them, their children, and their wives; and they had not come to the bottom of the den, until the lions had the mastery of them, and crushed all their bones.

הַיְתִיו, Aph. of אֲתָה. For the next clause see 3: 8. — דִּי דָנִיֵּאל, in the Gen.; for suff. pronoun anticipative before this Gen., see § 40. 3. a. — רְמוֹ has its Acc. pronoun implied; the אִנּוּן that follows belongs to the next clause. The version above exhibits this. — שְׁלִטוּ § 12. 1. 1. — הַדִּקוּ, Aph. of דְּקַק, for Hhireq under the second radical, p. 49. 5; or it may be a Hebraizing form, see p. 62, last par. The representation designed to be made is, that when the accusers were cast into the den, the voracious lions seized them ere they struck the bottom of the pit, and crushed them into pieces. As to the *frequency* of the like punishment in all barbarous countries, there can be no manner of doubt.

(26) Then Darius the king wrote to all people, nations, and tongues, who dwelt in all the earth: May your peace be multiplied!

דָּאֲרִין, Par. of דּוּר, the vowels are adapted to the form דָּיְרִין in the margin. Appropriately *vocalized* it would stand thus: דָּאֲרִין. — The pregnant meaning of the word *peace*, in the Semitic languages, is well known to all who understand them. Neither *εἰρήνη* nor *salus*, nor our word *peace*, fully reaches a translation.

(27) By me is a decree established, that in every principality of my kingdom [men] shall tremble and fear before the God of Daniel; for he is the living God, and endureth forever, and his kingdom shall not be destroyed, and his dominion [shall be] unto the end.

For the first clause, see 3: 29. — שָׁלְטָן probably denotes the *satrapies* into which the empire was divided, see v. 2 above — לֶהֱוֺן, see 2: 20. — זָאֲעִין from זוּעַ, vowels as above in דָּאֲרִין. The *continued* action expressed by these participles with the verb of existence, is very apparent here. — מִן קֳדָם, the same as מִן or מֵ, but the fashion of the Chaldee is to multiply such particles. We may translate: *Fear before his God*, or *Be afraid of his God.* The pronoun suff. after אֱלָהֵהּ is superfluous with us, but gives a specific hue to the Chaldee representation; § 40. 3. *a.* — הוּא, *he is*, § 40. 1. קַיָּם, *enduring*, is a participial adjective, § 28. b. 6. I have translated it as a verb, in order to conform to our idiom. — מַלְכוּתֵהּ וגו׳, lit. *his kingdom is what* (or *that which*) *shall not be destroyed.*

Exact conformity to this, in our idiom, would be incongruous. — *Unto the end* seems, at first view, to be the same as קֵץ in 12: 13; and so it is understood by Lengerke, and Ges. (in Lex.) seems to regard it in the same light. Hävernick says it is equivalent to לְעוֹלָם; C. B. Mich., that it means *the end of the world.* But a due consideration of the person who speaks, will, as it seems to me, give the phrase a different turn. The *Hebrew* ideas of the end of the world, or of the end of the ante-Messianic period, the Median king probably did not entertain; and *end* of life, (an idea that might be expressed both by Hebrews and Persians by the use of such a word), is inappropriate here. The *Parsis* expected the world would end in 12,000 years. But even these years did not make an end to the reign of Ormusd, and so it is not probable that Darius assigned such limits, in the present case. Having just said (of the God of Daniel), that *he endures forever,* it is obvious that he means to make his *dominion* as enduring as God himself is; so that we come to the necessary conclusion, that עַד סוֹפָא is but another, although less accurate, form of expressing the idea contained in the preceding לְעָלְמִין above. Obviously the same idea is expressed by עַד־סוֹפָא, on the supposition that the speaker did not suppose a real *end* would ever actually come. But if he did believe this, even then the expression designates at least an *undefined period,* to which no one can set limits.

(28) It is he, that rescues, and delivers, and does signs and wonders in heaven and on earth, who hath delivered Daniel from the power of the lions.

מְשֵׁיזִב, Part. Aph. of שׁוּב. — מַצִּל, Part. Aph. from נְצַל, retaining the Heb. form of Hiphil, p. 50, near the top. — *Signs,* as usual, means remarkable or miraculous exhibitions. — תִּמְהִין, pl. of תְּמַהּ, means those things which excite *wonder* in the beholders. — *In heaven and on earth* = everywhere, or in all places. — לְדָנִיֵּאל, Acc. after שֵׁזִיב. In this last word, the first syllable is written *defectively,* the last *fully.* The reverse is usually the case, e. g. שֵׁיזִב.

(29) And this same Daniel was promoted during the reign of Darius, and during the reign of Cyrus the Persian.

הַצְלַח, lit. *was prosperous,* Aph. with an intrans. sense, § 10. 4. 2. The idea connected with this is, promotion to a place of honor and profit.

Thus ends the *historical* part of the book of Daniel. It is easy to see that the object of the writer has not been, to give a regular and complete history, either of the Babylonish kings, of their successor, or of Daniel himself. Those, and only those, events are noticed, which make for the purpose of the writer; and this is, to exhibit a God working wonders among those who held the Hebrews in bondage, in order to fill them with respect for this people, and to prepare the way for their final liberation. Most plainly, moreover, is it a part of the design of the writer, to commend a steadfast adherence to the principles and practice of piety and virtue amidst the trials and temptations to which this people was subjected. The religious and ethical design of the narrations presented in the book before us, lies upon the very face of it, and no one should hesitate to avow this. But to prove that all this was calculated and designed merely for the times of the Maccabees, is quite another matter, and seems to me to have very little probability in its favor.

[As everywhere, in the book of Daniel, critics of the New School have here been on the watch for the supposed haltings of the writer. In the present case, indeed, we find a full proportion of them alleged. I shall briefly touch only upon those which seem to be worthy of any grave notice.

(1) 'The very outset of the story in ch. vi. contains a palpable misstatement, or at least an error which betrays the author's ignorance of Medo-Persian history. He represents Darius as having appointed 120 satraps over his kingdom; which far exceeds all bounds of truth, and even of probability.'

But why so? The answer is, that 'Cyrus appointed only *six*, (Cyrop. VIII. 6. 1, comp. VIII. 5. 19), when the empire was still larger than in the time of Darius; and that even under Darius Hystaspis, when Thrace and hither India had been conquered, there were only *twenty*,' Herod. III. 89 seq. — What then were these *satraps?* The *name* is Zend (see Lex. אֲחַשְׁדַּרְפְּנִים), and the origin, therefore, either Median or Persian. The office was at first that of a mere superintendent of tribute or revenue; to which a general inspection of the king's affairs and interests was appended. The military of each province was under its own appropriate officers. In the sequel, however, the satraps won to themselves both offices. It is perfectly clear, from Herod. III. 89, that mere *geographical* limits were not regarded in the arrangement of the Satrapies, but only the convenience of the revenue and of the government-affairs. Of course, officers of this cast must always have existed, under every form of the despotic governments of the East, whether the *name* in question is of earlier or later origin. At all events we find the name in the time of Cyrus, and therefore it is quite probable that it existed under that of Darius. The *extent of jurisdiction* was a matter that lay entirely with the sovereign to prescribe; and the *number* of satraps, therefore, depended on his will. How then can it be shown, that Darius could not have appointed 120 satraps, because Cyrus had 6, and Darius Hystaspis 20? Certain we are, that the successor of this last king "reigned over 127 provinces," Est. 1: 1. That each of these had governors or satraps, needs not to be proved. Every one acquainted with ancient Medo-Persian history knows, that to the satraps belonged ὕπαρχοι, i. e. *sub-satraps;* and it would be of course at the pleasure of a writer, whether he would include or exclude these, when he employed the word *satraps.* It is impossible, then, to convict the author of the book before us of incorrectness, when he states the fact that Darius appointed 120 satraps; for if Xerxes had 127, he may have appointed 120.

Besides this, it would seem very probable, that the six satraps of Cyrus, and the twenty of Darius Hyst., were of the same grade as the three סָרְכִין mentioned in 6: 3. The extensive conquests of Cyrus, after he became sole monarch, would naturally demand an increase of these; and so six were appointed. Darius Hyst. made extensive conquests in Thrace and in India, which may naturally have given rise to an increase of that number. As a *satrapy* depends not on national limits, nor on that of tribes, but only on the conveniences of government, so it is impossible to convince our author of either ignorance or falsification. On the contrary, the minuteness of statement respecting the three general officers, and the leading member or head of this little *corps*, and the care of the revenue which was committed to them, indicates a familiarity of the writer with the matters in question. Such an objection, therefore, owes its existence, as it would seem, more to the zeal than to the enlarged and accurate views of those who oppose the genuineness of the book before us.

(2) 'But the decree of Darius, that no request, for thirty days, should be made of God or man, except of himself — this decree which could proceed only from the inmate of a madhouse — is a thing utterly incredible.' Leng. p. 271 seq.

He might indeed well deserve a *madhouse*, rather than a palace, who could make such a decree. But as to the *improbability* of the matter, it is not quite so easy to make that out. *Parsism* taught its votaries to reverence the king as the symbol or personification of Ormusd. When Themistocles fled from Athens to Persia, and wished to be presented to the king, the courtier Artabanus said to him: "It is our custom . . . to honor the king, and worship the image of God who preserves all things," Plutarch, in Themistoc. c. 27. Xenophon (Agesil.) blames the Persians, because "they thought themselves worthy of enjoying the honors of the gods." Isocrates (Panegyr., in Brisson. De Reg. Pers.) censures them, "because they worship a mortal man, and call him a divinity (δαίμονα), and had rather treat the gods with neglect than their fellow men." Arrian (VI. 29) and Q. Curtius (Vit. Alex.) both give an account of sacrifices and divine honors paid to Cyrus, at his tomb in Pasargadae. Q. Curtius (VIII. 5) says: *Persas reges suos inter deos colere.* Alexander, in imitation of the Persian kings, required divine honors to be paid him, on his entrance into Babylon. De Sacy (Mem. de l'Inst. II. p. 184, 188) observes, that the Persian kings call themselves "the celestial germ of the race of the gods." On the ruins of Persepolis, kings are evidently presented as objects of adoration. Grotefend has found on one inscription: *Stirps mundi rectoris.* In fact, the matter is beyond all doubt. *Parsism* did not indeed require men to regard the king as a god in his own proper nature, but to pay him supreme homage as the *representative* of Ormusd. Such being the state of the case, it is easy to see that the account of Darius' behavior, when he was importuned by his courtiers and nobles, wears no special marks of improbability. That the Cyaxares of Xenophon was a weak, vain, and ambitious man, is abundantly evident, if the picture which the Greek historian has drawn of him be acknowledged as a likeness. The plan of Daniel's enemies was dexterously formed. Daniel, the courtiers had good reason to believe, would not swerve from his religion. Darius could be easily persuaded, as they believed, to admit not merely the ordinary homage that was paid to him as monarch, but an extraordinary one, which exalted him above all other kings. Doubtless the whole thing was managed by the utterance of many and flattering professions of reverence and honor toward the king. As he was addicted to an excessive use of wine, it is not improbable that the affair was transacted near the close of a banquet. "Worthy of a madhouse" it surely was; but as to its wearing the stamp of utter improbability, or even of any, I am at a loss to discover where or what that stamp is. Many a decree from drunken despots, has been more outrageous than this, and even equally absurd. Has not Lengerke read the history of a Nero, a Caligula, a Genghis Khan, or Aga Mohammed Khan? The intention of the king was, to gratify his own vanity. He did not dream of the consequences; as is evident from the whole of his subsequent demeanor.

Lengerke has summoned up *eight* objections against the verity of ch. vi. The first is, that there was never any such king as Darius the Mede. The second, that the country was not, at that period, divided into satrapies. (These have already been considered above). The third is the one just canvassed. The fourth is, that 'the phrases *living God*, and *unto the end* (עַד סוֹפָא), in v. 27, savor of *Jewish* conceptions, and not of Persian or Median ones; and of course Darius cannot be supposed to have employed them in his proclamation.' But if we consider the intercourse he had with Daniel, and the state of mind in which he was, after witnessing his preservation, there would seem to be little in this objection. Besides, that a *Parsi* should speak of the *living God* and his *endless rule*, would be nothing strange. (5) 'Daniel must have been a sheer fanatic, to suppose he could be safe in the lion's den.' And so, in Lengerke's view, are all men who believe in miracles. (6) 'The description of the lion's den, shows that it came not from an eye-witness.' But how, or why, we are not informed; and since we are not able of ourselves to discover the incongruity alleged, we must wait for its development. (7) 'The decree, at the close of the chapter, bears the stamp of most incredible intolerance.' But how? It calls on the subjects of the king *to do reverence* to the God of Daniel; but it does not bid them to forsake their own religion, nor compel them to become Jews, nor even annex a penalty for disobedience to the mandate. Where is the *persecution* or the *intolerance?* And even if we should find both in the decree, how is it to be proved, that a man so freakish and ever-changing as Darius, could not, or did not, commit such a deed? His indignation against the accusers of Daniel was very strong; and, abating the usual barbarity of the East in destroying whole families for an offence of the head, was just. In that state of mind, it is easy to see, that he might have taken the part of Daniel very strongly. (8) 'The lions could not live in a pit, where there was no air; and a second miracle was needed to keep them alive, as well as Daniel.' So! And was then the covering over the pit so compact that no air was admitted; and no light? This would at least be a singular way of managing the royal *menagerie* — unknown, I apprehend, to all the later managers of like establishments.

To complete the whole, Lengerke avers, that "any miracle here, in a general view of the subject, would not be less destitute of all good purpose, nor less against the divine economy, than the signs and wonders of ch. iii—v." So we also may believe; but then we may likewise believe, that the wonders related there, and in ch. vi, had a highly important end in view, and were neither destitute of special design, nor against the divine economy. If there be any force in the objection, it rests entirely upon assuming the position, that miracles are impossible and absurd. But such an assumption can hardly be called a legitimate *argument.*

I merely add, in view of such objections as these, that one must needs feel himself hard pressed, in order to resort to them. It is a confession which imports, that he who makes it is conscious of weakness in his cause. One thing, however, such objections do show, which is, a determination at all adventures to destroy the credit of the book. Simple candor, and consciousness of a good cause, are not apt to lead men to employ argumentation so captious.]

CHAPTER VII. INTRODUCTION.

[IN the remarks made upon the symbol of the colossal statue seen in the dream of Nebuchadnezzar (ch. ii.), no particular discussion was entered upon respecting the *four great empires.* Mere hints were thrown out, and it was assumed, that in all probability the Babylonish and the Medo-Persian empires were symbolized by the head and breast of the image; that the abdomen and loins represented the dominion of Alexander the Great; and finally that the legs and feet were symbols of that intermingled and confused empire, which sprung up under the Grecian chiefs who finally succeeded him. To this conclusion I have been forced to come, after an attentive consideration of the various schemes of interpretation that have been proposed and urged. As this must have an important influence on my views respecting the prophecies that follow, I feel bound to lay before the reader, the reasons which have led me to adopt such a conclusion. This I shall do as briefly as the nature of such a controverted case admits. And in order to do it briefly, I feel compelled to depend on reasons drawn almost wholly from the book itself. *A priori* reasoning, in this case, the basis of which is an assumption of what we *ought* to expect from the pen of Daniel; or reasoning borrowed merely from the Christian fathers, who assumed as a part of their basis, that the *Romish Antichrist* was before the mind of the prophet; we cannot assume without examination, if we would keep our exegetical conscience quiet. There is no expositor of an author, so legitimate and authoritative as himself. And it is by an appeal to Daniel himself, that I hope and I shall endeavor to explain Daniel. If this may be done, it is not worth while to occupy our time with either relating or refuting the almost numberless schemes of interpretation which have been applied to the book before us. Long ago was it said, (and with sound common sense), that *The best way to refute error, is to teach the truth.* If a subject can be made plain, and withal be so presented as to convince and satisfy the mind, it becomes unnecessary to dwell upon all the discrepant views that have been taken of it, or to describe the causes which operated to produce them, or to refute one by one in detail the errors that have been committed. It would occupy a volume by itself to do this, on the present occasion.

15*

In order to throw upon the subject now before us the light which the book of Daniel itself affords, it becomes necessary to compare with each other the various representations which are made of the same things or persons. What is obscure to us in one passage, may thus perhaps be fully illustrated by another; what in one case is expressed only in a generic way, may be found sufficiently specific in another to remove all uncertainty. It is in this way, that we proceed, or at least should proceed, with difficult passages in any book whatever, either sacred or profane; and in like manner, and for a like purpose, do we compare the different Evangelists with each other.

Before I engage in this process of comparison, I would premise a few general remarks, to which I would hope a general assent will not be denied. (1) The book of Daniel is not to be regarded either in the light of a general *syllabus* of civil history, nor even in that of a particular history of the four empires named. The Assyrian empire is not touched upon at all in it, nor that of India, or China, or Tartary; not to speak of European and African kingdoms in general. And with regard to Babylon, Persia, Greece (in the personal conquests of Alexander), and the mixed dominion which is fourth in order, nothing more than mere out-line sketches are given, which may suffice to identify the empires in view. To this there is but one exception, which is the Syrian part of the fourth dominion. The sketch of this is more particular; but that which occupies more room here than all the rest, is the description of Antiochus Epiphanes and his deeds. Such being the state of *facts*, the reason or ground of such a course in the writer of the book, becomes quite apparent. It is *the people of God*, *the Hebrew nation*, which is everywhere the highest and ultimate object of the writer. Those dynasties only which have, or will have, a special concern with the Hebrews, are touched upon; and these are brought successively into view, down to the time when deliverance from disasters, little short of those occasioned by the Babylonish exile, shall have been completed. Subsequent and temporary invasions of Palestine, which wrought no essential and permanent change in the state or affairs of the Jews, are not in any degree noticed. The writer's plan or design evidently does not, in any degree, resemble a regular chronological history, or annals that both preserve the order of time and record all particular events which are worthy of notice. Daniel gives mere outlines, rapid, striking, brief, generic. It is evident that his design is mainly a *religious* one. The people of God; the *foreign* sway to which they are, and are to be, subjected; the period in which a second Nebuchadnezzar shall lay waste Jerusalem and profane the sanctuary; the leading trials through which the Hebrews must pass before the Messianic period commences — these are the topics concerned with the prophetic part of the book of Daniel. Above all, the second great catastrophe to the Jewish nation, under Antiochus Epiphanes, which in some respects was more grievous than that of the Babylonish exile, is that which is most particularly and graphically set forth; and with this the writer concludes his development of Jewish history, excepting that the introduction of the subsequent Messianic period is here and there set forth, and placed in a very striking light. In a word, ch. vii—xii. might be justly characterized by giving them the title: SKETCHES OF THE LEADING EVENTS PREPARATORY TO THE MESSIANIC PERIOD. The *nucleus* lies in Nebuchadnezzar's dream (ch. ii.); the development in ch. vii—xii. Great errors in the exegesis of this book may be committed, by either ascribing *too much* to its design, (which is the common error), or else *too little*.

(2) The reader must not look here for the common traits of regular annals, which are found in a book merely historical. Here (in vii.—xi.) all is *prophetical*. It has the costume of prophecy, and is replete with figurative language and with symbol. It gives leading characteristics of an empire by a single sentence, without minute specification ; sets up no chronological boundaries to the respective kingdoms ; presents simply changes and transitions of empire without any detail of the means by which they are brought about ; and introduces those empires, and only those, which are concerned with the Jewish people. As a whole, these productions are merely generic and prophetic pictures of the mutable and perishable empires that have concern with the Hebrews, until the Messianic period, so as materially to affect them for good or for ill. The Persian dominion affects them mostly for good, (see Ezra and Nehemiah) ; that of Alexander indeed scarcely touches them, but it prepares the way for an empire (the Syrian), which most of all persecuted and injured them. The prophetic part of Daniel, I readily concede, is not regular Hebrew *poetry* as to its form ; but it is poetic in its spirit and imagery, like Ezekiel, and Zechariah, and the Apocalypse, and demands the application of poetical exegesis in order to interpret it. A part of the 11th chapter is the only exception to be made to these remarks ; where the representation is so historically graphic, that Porphyry and others, specially many of the recent critics, have even brought against it the charge of being written *post eventum*. The particularity of the description here fully shows, how prominent in the writer's mind were the cruelty and persecutions of the נִבְזֶה, i. e. Antiochus Epiphanes.

(3) The reader, who wishes to discover with certainty the real empires that are the subject of prediction in the book before us, should carefully investigate *the particular period, when they will individually and severally have all passed away*. The Messiah's empire, as is clearly and repeatedly asserted, is to be *built on their ruins*. It *succeeds* them all, in order of time and of events. So chap. ii. vii. xii. plainly represent the matter. And if so, this will be one decisive test, as to the empires brought into view by the prophet. That they are *Asiatic* empires, although some of them are swayed by men of Grecian origin, seems to lie upon the face of the book, and accords with the nature of the case. In the time of Daniel, Rome was a petty State of Italy, and was scarcely known, still less feared, in Palestine or in Babylon. It is not the manner of the Hebrew prophets, to concern themselves with the history of nations or empires sustaining no relation to the Hebrews. It is true, indeed, that some sixty years before the birth of Christ, Palestine was overrun by Pompey ; and in the sequel it was made an allied province. But it was not until *after* the Christian era had begun, that it was deprived of its kings, and subjected to a Romish governor. Nor did the Romans undertake to crush it, until about A. D. 67. The book of Daniel "prepares the way of the Lord." The coming of the Messiah is its main design ; and the state and circumstances of the Jews, until that period, are passed in brief and rapid review.

With the considerations in view that have now been suggested, we may next proceed with the development of THE FOUR GREAT EMPIRES.

The FIRST is thus described:

I. 37, "Thou, O king, art king of kings, to whom the God of heaven hath given dominion, strength, and power and glory; (38) And wherever dwell the sons of men, the beast of the field, or the fowl of the air, into thy hand hath he given [them], and made thee ruler over all; *thou art that head of gold*."	VII. 4, "The first was like a lion, and it had the wings of an eagle; I looked attentively until its wings were plucked, and it was lifted up from the earth, and stood upon its feet as a man, and the heart of a man was given to it."

That the four empires in chap. vii. are the same as in chap. ii., has scarcely been denied by any. The last clause in 2: 38 makes it certain that *Babylon* with its head is the metropolis of the first empire. The *past*, i. e. the time of Hebrew subjection to the *Assyrian* empire, is entirely omitted. *Prophecy* occupies itself with the present and the future. Daniel therefore begins with *Babylon*. It is not so much the *person* of Nebuchadnezzar, as his dynasty — his empire — with which 2: 37, 38, are concerned. The *head of gold* refers to the colossal image described in 2: 31, 32. The *splendor* of the Babylonish monarchy is plainly indicated by the *gold*; for Babylon exceeded all other ancient cities in its wealth and splendor. It is put at the *head* of the four monarchies principally because it *begins* the prophetic series, and not in order to denote its superiority over them as to extent or power. In 7: 4, the imagery is quite diverse, and the *lion*, the leader or chief among the beasts, is the symbol. Great power and majesty are doubtless indicated by this, as well as destructive conquests by means of which they are obtained. The wings of an eagle indicate velocity and strength; which were peculiarly characteristic of Nebuchadnezzar's movements and conquests. The plucking of the wings, the assumption of the upright position of a man, and the acquiring of the heart of a man, are all indications of the humbling of the Babylonish pride and power, and of reducing her rulers to moderation and reason in their measures. The language employed to indicate this, seems plainly borrowed from the humbling process through which the haughty Nebuchadnezzar passed, during his mania, until he was restored to reason and humanity. In other words, the empire is portrayed in colors borrowed from the individual who mainly established it.

This is all we have in the prophetic part of Daniel concerning the *first* empire. Chap. viii. xi. entirely omit this empire, while they enlarge much upon the third and fourth. About this first empire, however, there is no controversy, or none worth notice.

THE SECOND EMPIRE. Different is the case in respect to this. Some regard it as the *Median* empire; some as the *Medo-Persian*, and others as that of Nebuchadnezzar's successors in Babylon. If the reader will have patience, he may, as I think, be satisfied in respect to this matter. In chap. ii. vii. the description is quite brief.

II. 39, "And after thee shall arise another kingdom inferior to thee."	VII. 5, "And behold another beast, like to a bear, and it stood up on one side, and three ribs were between its teeth, and to it they said thus: Arise, devour much flesh."

Chap. ii. gives no other clue to the meaning than that of mere *succession*.

At first view, it seems as if it were intended to designate the Babylonish successors to the throne of Nebuchadnezzar; for the language is: *after thee*. But then comes the expression: *another kingdom* (not king), by which of course must be meant a *different empire* from the Babylonish; and the whole taken together shows, that Nebuchadnezzar is only considered and spoken of as the representative of the Babylonish empire. Hence *inferior to thee*, must mean, inferior to thee as to dominion. If now we fix upon mere *extent* of territory as the point of comparison, whether we take into view the *Median* or *Medo-Persian* empire, it would be difficult to make out the correctness of the description. We must conclude, therefore, that the inferiority in question has respect to *energy* and *executive efficiency*, in bearing down all opposition and crushing all who resist. And in regard to this, we can easily credit the assertion of the text. Nebuchadnezzar overran all hither Asia and Egypt between 607 and 604 B. C., while Cyrus and Cyaxares were more than ten years in subduing Croesus and his allies. Cyrus was indeed a brave and skilful warrior; but resistless impetuosity and energy, like those of the Babylonian conqueror, could not well be ascribed to him. As to his successors, it is true that Darius Hystaspis enlarged the boundaries of the empire in Thrace and India; but he lost ground in Greece and Scythia; and Xerxes was wholly defeated by only a part of the little States of Greece. Thenceforth the Persian empire was on the decline. The *inferiority* in question seems then to have a special relation to energy and efficiency.

As to the symbol in 7: 5, the *bear* is a fierce and rabid animal, and may well symbolize rapacity for dominion and conquest, such as characterized Cyrus and his next three followers. The *devouring of much flesh* refers to the great destruction of life occasioned by frequent invasions and conquests. The *three ribs in the mouth* seem to be indicative of a rapacity to devour; and the particular ground of the number *three* here, (unless indeed it be used in a tropical way), seems to be the *three divisions of the empire* made by Darius the Mede, after the conquest of Babylon, 6: 3 (2). These the bear has within his grasp, and they are of course at his disposal. The call to *devour* more, seems to allude to the subsequent extensive conquests of Cyrus. — As to the position of the bear, kneeling with one foot and standing up with the other, it graphically denotes that the beast is on the alert, ready to observe and speedily to spring upon its prey. What illustrates and confirms this heretofore dark passage is, that on the ruins of Persian monuments a symbolic animal is found sculptured in this very position; thus showing that it was in all probability one of the symbols on the insignia of the Median and Persian dominion; see Münter, Relig. der Bab. p. 112. and Tab. iii.; also Fundgruben des Orients, III. Tab. 2, fig. 3, and specially Layard's Ruins of Nineveh. Indeed, a little consideration of this matter will serve to show, that there is much significancy in the symbol. The position of the animal indicates watchfulness and a degree of repose combined. By it the Persian monarch could signify, that while his enemies were not deemed important or powerful enough to call forth all his energies and keep him in a state of excitement, yet they might be assured that he was not unobservant of them, or unprepared for them.

But thus far we have obtained nothing which determines with any certainty, whether the *Median* or the *Medo-Persian* dynasty is intended. It remains, therefore, to compare other passages in chap. viii. xi.

VIII. 3, "Behold! a ram standing before the river, and it had two horns; and the horns were high, but the one was higher than the other, and the higher one sprang up after [the other]. (4) I saw the ram pushing westward, and northward, and southward, and none of the beasts could stand before him, nor could any one deliver out of his hand; and he did as he pleased, and waxed great. (5) And while I was considering, behold, a he-goat came from the west, on the face of all the earth, and he touched not the ground; and the he-goat had a notable horn between his eyes. (6) And he came to the ram which had the two horns, which I had seen standing before the river, and ran to him in his strong indignation. (7) And I saw him approaching near the ram, and he became enraged at him, and he smote the ram, and brake his two horns; nor was there strength in the ram to stand before him, but he cast him down to the earth, and trod upon him; nor was there any to deliver the ram out of his hands."

[Explanation by the angel interpreter.] VIII. 20, "The ram which thou sawest, having two horns, is the kings of Media and Persia. (21) And the he-goat is the king of Greece; and the great horn between his eyes is the first king."

[Further development in chapter xi.] XI. 2, "And now will I show thee the truth: Behold, there are yet three kings c Persia who will stand up; and the fourtl will acquire great riches, and when he becomes powerful by his wealth, he will stir up all the dominion of Greece, (3) And a mighty king shall stand up, and he shall rule an extensive dominion, and do according to his pleasure. (4) And when he shall stand up, his kingdom shall be broken in pieces, and it shall be separated to the four winds of heaven."

It is not within my present design to descend to minuteness in the explanation of words and phrases; for this belongs to the commentary. I shall confine myself to general and obvious remarks. (1) The composite nature of the dominion of the ram is evident, for it lies upon the very face of the symbol. *Two* horns are given him; and the one of these which was highest, grew up *last;* i. e. the Persian domination, which became altogether predominant under Cyrus, followed that of the Medes, which had then lasted some 200 or more years, Persia being at that time only a province. The rapid march of Alexander, and his resistless impetuosity and fierceness, are most graphically and undeniably set forth in 8: 4—7. (2) If any doubt could remain, it is removed entirely by vs. 20, 21. (3) More firmly still is it established, that the Persian or Medo-Persian dominion next precedes Alexander's empire, by 11: 2—4. In this last case, a historical notice, connected with the rise of Alexander's invasion, is inserted. Xerxes, the *fourth* from Cyrus, (the prophecy is dated in the third year of Cyrus' reign, 10: 1, and the three kings, therefore, yet to rise up, must be Cambyses, Smerdis, and Darius), rouses up all Greece by his invasion. The spirit thus excited never slept, but afterwards broke out in the invasion of the Persian dominion by Alexander. In 11: 2 the kings are naturally named *kings of Persia*, because the writer designed, in the case before him, to name only the predominating part of the kings of the second empire, and because the *later* horn is the higher one. But in 8: 20, the same kings, whose dynasty is overthrown by the king of Greece, are named *kings of Media and Persia.* All this is plain, when we follow Xenophon and the Bible. The troops who took Babylon were Medes and Persians. They were led by Cyrus, while Cyaxares or Darius the Mede retained the nominal and theoretical sovereignty of the new empire. In the person of Cyrus both governments and both nations found their king. Hence the expression: *laws of the Persians and Medes*, in the book of Esther, during the reign of the *fourth* king, mentioned in Dan. 11: 2. From the nature of the case, it is evident, that *Media and Persia* may be combined, and spoken of as one kingdom; as they clearly are in 8: 20. 5: 28. 6: 9, 13, 16, (Eng. 8, 12, 15). And this, as appears from the books of Daniel and Esther, was the common usage at court. For particular purposes, however, it is equally plain, that *Darius the Mede* (6: 1, Eng. 5: 31), and *Cyrus the Persian* (6: 29, Eng. 28), might be spoken of, when reference was had to the sources whence they respectively sprung. Moreover, since the *later horn* was higher than the other (Dan. 8: 3), *the king of Persia* was also a common appellation among the Hebrews who returned from exile. So in 2 Chron. 36: 22, 23. Ezra 1: 1, 2, 8. 3: 7. 4: 3, 5 al.; and so, Darius, *king of Persia*, Ezra 4: 5, and Artaxerxes, 4: 7. In Ezra 5: 13, Cyrus, *king of Babylon*.

It would seem, then, from a comparison of all these passages, that no reasonable doubt can remain, that the *second* dominion, (the silver breast and arms of the colossal statue in chap. ii.), is the Medo-Persian. The insignificancy of Darius the Mede; the fact that he in person took no active part in the conquest of Babylon, and reigned there only some two years, all conspired to throw Cyrus into prominent notice, and to make him the principal subject of remark, whenever the change of dominion is spoken of. Still more certain will this become, provided it can be shown, that Alexander's dominion is the *third* in the series of the four monarchies; for the *third* of course succeeds the second; and if the third *destroyed* the second, and Alexander is the representative of the third, and it was he who destroyed not the Median, but the *Medo-Persian* empire, then our conclusion seems inevitable. Our next inquiry then will be directed to the

THIRD DOMINION. This is exhibited in chap. ii. vii. as follows:

II. 39, "And another kingdom of brass [shall arise], which shall rule over all the earth."	VII. 6, "And after this I looked steadfastly, and behold another [beast] like to a panther, and it had four wings of a bird on its back, and there were four heads to the beast, and dominion was given to it."

In 2: 39, the *wide extent* of dominion is the only thing which is designated. Nothing more is to be deduced from the *brass*, than that it differs as to material from the symbols of the two preceding kingdoms, in order to show that it is symbolic of a kingdom *diverse* from them. As to 7: 6, a *panther* stands next to the lion in agility and strength, has even more swiftness, and is not less fierce or blood-thirsty. If the *wings* on the lion (7: 4) indicate *velocity* of movement, as they plainly appear to do, then *two pair* of wings on the panther indicate an intense degree of velocity. This and nothing more seems to be the import of double pairs of wings. How characteristic this is of Alexander the Great, during his conquests, needs not to be shown. *The four heads*, however, present a symbol of more difficulty. We cannot resort to Apoc. 17: 3, 9, 10, for explanation; for there the *seven heads* are symbols of *Roma septicollis*, and also of its first seven emperors. Alexander had no proper successors (Dan. 11: 4), and he was himself, strictly

speaking, the beginning and end of his empire; so that the *four heads* of the panther cannot denote four *successive* kings of the third dynasty. Many refer these heads to the four monarchies which eventually sprang up among the successors of Alexander. But if the third dynasty *ceased* with Alexander, such an application would be quite incongruous. The *third beast* must symbolize the *third empire*, and not the fourth. The sequel moreover will show, that the dynasty of Alexander is plainly separated from that of his generals. If we resort once more to the Apocalypse, (which is intimately connected by its style and symbolic imagery with the books of Daniel), we shall there find a case of a like nature, which cannot be applied to any *succession* of kings. In Rev. 12: 3, the great dragon (who is the devil, v. 9), is said to have seven heads, and seven crowns, with ten horns. Plain it must be, in this case, that the heads and crowns and horns, (the numbers seven and ten being taken in their tropical sense), denote *great power and dominion*. Accordingly Jesus himself calls Satan *the prince of this world* (John 12: 31. 14: 30); and so does Paul speak in Eph. 6: 11, 12; he also names Satan *the god of this world*, in 2 Cor. 4: 4. The *four heads*, therefore, must be regarded as designating *dominion in the four quarters of the world;* just as, when the third dynasty is broken, it is said to be "scattered to the *four winds* of heaven," 11: 4. I speak of the *four quarters* of the world, on the assumption that the number *four*, applied to heads in our text, is intended to have a special significancy. But I doubt, in reality, whether anything more than mere *intensity* of meaning was designed by the writer. As *four wings* are indications of great rapidity, so *four heads* seem to be the corresponding indications of great or extensive power. But it may mean somewhat more; and if so, it must indicate, so far as I can see, *dominion in all quarters;* for among the Hebrews, the four cardinal points are all that have a name, and they embrace all the rest. What objection can well be made to this view, when 2: 38 represents Nebuchadnezzar, or the first dynasty, by the symbol of the *head* of the colossal image? As in the Apocalypse *seven* is a predominating number, so in Daniel *four* seems to be employed in a like manner. Thus there are four dynasties; a fourth king of Persia invades Greece, 11: 2; the panther has four wings, and the like. Each book, as to the use of numbers in a tropical way, conforms to its own particular custom.

But we have not done with this matter. We have yet to compare chap. viii. xi., in order to complete our view. In both these cases, the dynasty of Babylon is omitted, and the writer begins with the Medo-Persian; see 8: 3—7. 11: 2. Of course the dynasty which is *third* here next follows the Medo-Persian; and this next following one is that of Alexander. This is thus represented:

VIII. 5, "Lo! a he-goat came from the West, on the face of all the earth, and he touched not the ground; and the he-goat had a notable horn between his eyes. (6) And he came to the ram which had the two horns, which I had seen standing before the river, and ran to him in his strong indignation. (7) And I saw him

XI. 3, "And there shall stand up a mighty king, and he shall bear rule over a great dominion, and he will do according to his pleasure. (4) And when he shall stand up, his kingdom shall be broken in pieces, and it shall be divided toward the four winds of heaven; but not to his posterity, nor according to the dominion approaching near the ram, and he became enraged against him, and he smote the ram, and broke his two horns, and there was no strength in the ram to stand before him; but he cast him down to the earth and trode upon him, nor was there any one to deliver the ram out of his hand. (8) And the he-goat waxed exceedingly great: and when he became strong, the great horn was broken in pieces, and there came up to view four horns in its room, toward the four winds of heaven."

of his rule, but his kingdom shall be plucked up, and given to others besides these."

The coming from the *West*, the rapidity of the movement, and the notable horn, are all characteristic of Alexander. Moreover we are not left here to any doubt. The angel-interpreter leads the way:

VIII. 20, "The ram which thou sawest, having two horns, are the kings of Media and Persia. (21) And the he-goat is the king of Greece; and the great horn between his eyes is the first king. (22) Now as to that which was broken, and four stood up in its room — four kingdoms shall stand up out of the nation, but not in his power."

In 8: 8 above, the third empire is represented as broken to pieces when at the height of its power. Such was notoriously the case with Alexander's dominion. His death caused the empire to fall in pieces. In vain was his son nominated as successor. The aspiring chiefs of the conquering army sought for kingly power, rather than to be provincial governors or satraps. But it is in 8: 22, 23, and in 11: 4, that we learn the relation of the succeeding kingdom to this. In 8: 22, the *third* dynasty is represented as broken to pieces; and in 11: 4, as scattered to the four winds of heaven. Chap. 8: 8 says of the new kings that arise, that they are toward the four winds of heaven; and in 8: 22, they are declared to be of Grecian origin. In 8: 22, these kings are said not to possess his (Alexander's) power; and 11: 4 asserts, 'that *his kingdom shall not be given to his posterity*, and that the fourth dominion shall *not* be like the other.' Again, it confirms all this by a reassertion: "His kingdom shall be plucked up, and given to others besides these," viz. to others different from his posterity. How language can more strongly declare, that Alexander's dominion *differs* from that which follows, and that it *ends* with his destruction, I do not see. The fact that Antiochus Epiphanes springs from the dynasty that *next follows* (7: 8. 8: 8—12, 22—25. 11: 4, 21 seq.); that this dynasty is so complex that no specific beast is named which can symbolize it (7: 7, 19); and that it arises *out of the ruins* of Alexander's dynasty (8: 8, 9, 22); seem to settle the question where the fourth dynasty is to be sought for. We shall see how all this is confirmed by a view of the

FOURTH DYNASTY. The materials for comparison are somewhat copious; but the matter is too important to omit anything that may cast light upon it.

II. 40, "And a fourth dominion shall be strong as iron, altogether as iron that crushes and grinds to pieces everything — even as iron that dashes to pieces, all these will it crush and dash to pieces.

VII. 7, "Behold! a fourth beast, terrible and mighty and very powerful, it had large teeth of iron, it devoured and crushed, and trampled the remnant under foot; and it differed from all the other beasts

(41) And since thou sawest the feet and toes, a part of them the clay of the potter, and a part of them iron, the dominion shall be divided, and there shall be of the firmness of iron in it, inasmuch as thou sawest iron mingled with the whitish clay. (42) And since the toes of the feet were partly of iron and partly of clay, in part the dominion shall be strong, and in part it shall be brittle. (43) Since thou sawest the iron mingled with the whitish clay, they shall intermingle the seed of men, but they shall not cleave together, this with that, see! even as iron cannot mingle with clay."

that were before it, and it had ten horns. (8) I considered attentively those horns, and lo! another little horn rose up among them, and three of the former horns did it root out from before it; and behold! there were eyes like the eyes of a man in that horn, and a mouth speaking great things. (9) I continued looking, until the tribunals were set, and the Ancient of Days was seated. . . . (11) I continued looking, on account of the voice of the great words which the horn uttered, I looked until the beast was slain, and its body destroyed, and it was given to the flaming fire."

In connection with the passage from 7: 7—11, is an account of the perplexity of spirit into which Daniel was thrown, by the vision there related, and of his application to the angel-interpreter in order that he might explain to him the vision of the *fourth* beast; for this seems specially to have troubled his mind, and filled him with apprehension. Then follows the angel's answer:

VII. 23, " Thus, he said, shall be the fourth beast; a fourth kingdom shall arise in the land, which shall differ from all other kingdoms, and shall consume the whole land, and beat it, and crush it in pieces. (24) And as to the ten horns of that dominion, ten kings shall arise, and another shall arise after them, and he shall be different from the former, and three kings shall he humble. (25) And words against the most High shall he utter, and he shall destroy the saints of the most High, and he shall think to change times and law; and they shall be given into his hand, for a time and times and a division of time. (26) And the tribunal shall be seated, and his power shall be taken away, even to lay waste and destroy [it] unto the end."

To this, as in chap. ii., succeeds the fifth or Messianic kingdom. Omitting this for the present, let us now recapitulate the main points in these representations of the fourth dynasty. In 2: 40—42, we have three leading ideas; (1) The oppressive and crushing power of the dynasty. (2) An incongruous mixture of the various sovereignties which constitute, collectively considered, the fourth dynasty. That on which it stands (the feet and toes, v. 41), in other words, its basis, consists of materials that will not combine. (3) The vain attempts by intermarriage-alliances, to cement any permanent union. The special significancy of this is not developed, until we come to the eleventh chapter. In 7: 7—11, the symbol of the fourth dynasty is changed. *A beast terrible and powerful* is the image. But this beast has no name like the three preceding ones. The reason is obvious. This dynasty has not one monarch, but many. These were so far from harmonizing together, that, like iron and clay, they could not possibly be combined in a symmetrical whole. Of course, only some *monster beast*, of which the natural world furnished no example, must be supposed in this case — a beast possessing parts or qualities at variance with each other. Ten horns are given to it, and these are symbols of ten kings. (The monuments in Middle Asia now present an abundance of the like monsters, quite significant in their way, but having no prototypes in nature). After these springs up a little horn, which roots out three of the others. Sagacity of management and blasphemous insolence are ascribed to it. After being tolerated for a while, divine justice and indignation destroy it. In the explanation (7: 23—26), the same ideas are for substance repeated, and some particulars are added, in order to enlarge and illustrate. It speaks also in still stronger language of the *destructive* power of this monster. The ten horns, the subsequent appearance of the eleventh, and the subjugation of three out of the ten, are nearly the same in both passages; while the boasting and blasphemous character of the new king is portrayed in a stronger light in vs. 23 — 26. He not merely speaks *great things*, but he utters them against the *most High*. Here too comes in a further elucidation of his *destructive* power, when we are told against whom it is to be exercised, viz. he will destroy *the saints of the most High*. In connection with this, also, another addition is made to the original picture: "He shall think to change times and law; and they shall be given into his hand, for a time, and times, and a division of time," i. e. for three years and a half. All this, it must be admitted, is a striking and faithful portrait of Antiochus Epiphanes, too striking to admit of any doubt. Finally, as in 7: 7—11, it is declared that he shall be destroyed by divine justice and indignation. The tribunal before which the tyrant is summoned, condemns him to utter excision; and the sentence is carried into execution.

With this ends the sketch of the fourth dynasty, in this vision. The Messianic reign then follows. With regard to this, both the vision in chap. ii. and the one in chap. vii. agree; and with both these agrees the explanation by the angel; 7: 23—26.

We must not fail to mark here the *gradation* of the prophetic development. In 2: 40—42, the fourth dynasty is rapidly and generically sketched by mere general outlines, which are, however, of a diagnostic nature. The turbulence of this fourth dominion, the irreconcilable feuds of its leading chiefs, and a declaration of their vain efforts to bring about peaceable alliances by intermarriages, are the distinctive marks of it. But there is a specialty in what is said of the *iron*, which "grinds and crushes in pieces" all which it assails. Surely the writer does not mean, that this fourth dominion, comparatively considered, so far exceeds in its *destructive* power all which had preceded it, that the ravages in general committed by them may be passed over in silence, when brought into comparison with those of the fourth dynasty. Facts speak against such an assumption. Of the ravages and slaughter perpetrated by Nebuchadnezzar, we have indeed no minute historical account. But they must have been very great, considering the extent of country which he overran. Those committed by Cyrus and his successors, no doubt, far exceeded his, as they were more often repeated and of longer duration. As to Alexander, we know well the devastation and ruin, that attended his long continued, rapid, and victorious aggressions. But of all these, neither chap. ii. nor vii. make any special mention. Why? Because they do not respect *the people of God*, on whom the prophet ever has his eye. What they suffered under the Babylonish domain, had in great part already passed. They appear to have lived at Babylon, without any special molestation or persecution, other than what naturally befel all exiles. Under the Persian monarchy, with some little annoyance by Cambyses or Smerdis, they were the subjects of remarkable favor throughout. Alexander, on his march to the East, paid them a visit; but he did them no harm. At first, and for sometime, they experienced no very hostile treatment from the chiefs of the fourth dynasty, i. e. from those two chiefs, which, being almost perpetually at variance with each other, lived on the north and south of Palestine. But this country was unfortunately the arena of contest between them, and the Jews experienced of course a great variety of trials, in their efforts to keep a neutral position. As these efforts were not always successful, the aggrieved party would make incursions upon Judea. Finally that reckless tyrant, Antiochus *Ἐπιφανής*, (whom his subjects very significantly named, *Ἐπιμανής*, i. e. *the mad-man*), invaded them with the spirit of rankling vengeance and of blasphemy, and he maltreated and destroyed them not only beyond all former example, but even beyond any example, until the final destruction of the Hebrew Commonwealth. Here then is the plain and palpable reason, why the fourth dynasty (which includes Antiochus) is described as being *powerfully destructive*, in a manner not asserted of any of the preceding dynasties. This view makes it quite obvious, that the description of the destructive power of the fourth dynasty is not to be regarded as absolute, nor as designed to be compared with the other dynasties, but only as having a relation to the people of God, and to the country where they dwelt. The Roman power did not, until long after the time of Antiochus, attain to an amplitude of dominion that could be compared with that of either of the four dynasties. Much less did it occasion the Jews any very serious trouble, until the time of Vespasian, some thirty years after the Messianic reign had begun its development.

The representation now made in general of the subject before us, I cannot help regarding as fundamentally authorized by the whole tenor of the book of Daniel. *General history* it clearly is not; the particular history of either of the dynasties it as clearly is not, with the single exception, that the fourth dynasty, one half of whose chiefs lived in the neighborhood of Palestine, and which alone gave the Jews (after the time when the book of Daniel has been usually supposed to be written) comparatively all their trouble, is in part brought upon the scene, and identified by quite a series of *historical particulars*, in chap. xi., such as appear nowhere else on the pages of prophetic writing. It is scarcely possible to mistake the little horn of 7: 8, 24. The context is so entirely decisive with regard to the *Syrian* tyrant and blasphemer, that there seems to be no room for critical doubt.

But we have not completed our view. Daniel resumes the subject again in chap. viii., and chap. xi. We must follow his steps, and see what additional evidence can be brought to light.

VIII. 8, "And the he-goat [Alexander] waxed exceedingly great; and when he was strong the great horn was broken, and there came up the appearance of four horns in its place, toward the four winds of heaven. (9) And from one of them came forth a little horn, and it waxed very large toward the south, and toward the east, and toward the goodly land. (10) And it waxed great even to the host of heaven, and it cast down to the earth some of the host and some of the stars, and trod upon them. (11) And even to the Prince of the host did it magnify itself, and from him

[Explanation by the angel-interpreter]. VIII. 20, "And the ram which thou sawest with two horns, are the kings of Media and Persia. (21) And the he-goat is the king of Grecia, and the great horn between his eyes is its chief king. (22) And as to its being broken, and four standing up in the place of it — there shall stand up four kingdoms from the nation, but not in his strength. (23) And in the latter part of their reign, when transgressors are come to the full, a king of cruel aspect shall stand up, and one who understands dark things. (24) And his power shall did it take away the daily sacrifice, and the dwelling of his sanctuary was cast down. (12) And a host was set over the daily sacrifice by impiety, and it cast down truth upon the earth, and did [its will] and prospered."

be strong, yet not by his own strength; and he shall destroy wonderfully, and prosper, and do [his will]; and he shall destroy the mighty, even the holy people. (25) And on account of his cunning he will make deceit to prosper in his hand, and in his heart will he wax great, and in a time of quiet he will destroy many, and against the Prince of princes will he stand up; but — he shall be broken without a [human] hand."

Such is the additional description of the fourth dynasty, in chap. viii. Several particulars here added, deserve a special notice. In 8: 8—12, we have, (1) The scattered condition of the fourth dynasty; "toward the four winds of heaven is it separated." (2) The *little horn* that rises up afterwards, becomes very great in the south (Egypt), in the east (on and beyond the Euphrates), and in the goodly land (of Palestine). (3) It magnified itself in an impious manner, invaded the temple-services, and the priests ministering there, and some of this host of God it cast down, even the stars (comp. Rev. 1: 20. 2: 28), and trode upon them. It assailed the Prince of the host himself, and took away the daily offering made to him, and profaned his sanctuary. (4) It offered up impious sacrifices in the room of the lawful ones, and set over them a heathen priesthood. (5) It opposed and rendered inefficient the truth of God's word, and for sometime had undisputed control and prospered. Some of these particulars are indeed adverted to in chap. 7: 23—25; but they are more expanded here, and new ones are added. These are all graphically characteristic of Antiochus.

In 8: 20—25, (the words of the angel-interpreter), the time in which Antiochus shall make his appearance is designated, viz. the latter part of the dominion of the horns, that sprang up after the great horn (Alexander) was broken, v. 23. The cunning and sagacity of Antiochus, in perpetrating the work of destruction, are more fully developed than before, and specially his massacre of the quiet and unoffending. Finally, the divine judgment which destroys him is rendered more conspicuous and prominent. At the close, Daniel is told to seal up his account of the vision, because it has respect to a future that comes not until after *many days*, v. 26. The time of this vision was the third year of Belshazzar, v. 1; and thus it was near to the period, when the Persian dominion (that of the ram) would commence.

In the third year of Cyrus, the fourth and last vision respecting the empires was disclosed, 10: 1. The first part of it takes a brief and rapid survey of the two empires which precede the fourth, viz. the Persian and Alexandro-Grecian. It runs thus:

XI. 2, "Behold three kings of Persia are yet to stand up; and the fourth shall obtain riches greater than all, and when he waxes strong by his riches, he will rouse up all the dominion of Greece. (3) And a mighty king shall stand up, and he shall rule with wide dominion, and do according to his pleasure. (4) And when he standeth up, his kingdom shall be broken, and it shall be divided to the four winds of heaven, but not to his posterity nor according to the dominion with which he ruled, but his kingdom shall be plucked up, and given to others besides these.

Here is a special limitation, in regard to Persia, of a time when it shall make war with Greece, viz. in the time of the *fourth* king after Cyrus. From this the prophet passes, (without stopping to describe the issue of the Persian invasion, except that it will rouse up all Greece), to the third dominion under Alexander, which in fact took its rise from the union of Greece under him, in order to avenge the Persian aggression. He makes no special note of time, i. e. as to the distance of it from the fourth king of Persia, but indicates it merely by the *sequency* of the events under the "mighty king." Finally, the ruin of this king's dominion; its being scattered to the four winds; the rejection of his posterity from all regal claims; the absolute plucking up of Alexander's government, and the giving of it to other persons than his children; and the comparative inferiority of the subsequent dynasty; are all set forth in terms as strong as language can well employ.

Thus far respecting the *second* and *third* dynasty in chap. xi. The rest of a long chapter is occupied entirely with a historic sketch, as it were, of those chiefs of the fourth dynasty, who came in particular contact with Palestine, for good or for evil, but mostly it notices such events as characterize the reign of particular princes, who most concerned themselves with the country of the Hebrews for selfish or sinister purposes. The historic sketch begins with Ptolemy Lagus, "the king of the south," v. 5. It proceeds with sketching a succession of events under the kings of the south and the north (Egypt and Syria). In vs. 13—19 Antiochus the Great of Syria is introduced; in v. 20, Seleucus Philopater his son; in vs. 21—45, the history of Antiochus Epiphanes is sketched at a length, which, as has already been said, has no parallel in the prophetic compositions of the Scriptures. Indeed this history is so minute and circumstantial, that, as has been noticed, ancient and modern doubters of the genuineness of the book have accused it strongly of being written *post eventum*. This matter seems to have suggested a hint to many recent interpreters, which they have expanded into numerous objections against the older date commonly asssigned to the book of Daniel, and arguments for its being composed in the later time of the Maccabees, or at least near the period of Antiochus' death. I shall not extract the whole of this ample account of Antiochus, as it is unnecessary for my present purpose. I shall merely bring into comparison those parts of it which serve to identify the individual here described, about whom no one can doubt, with the one who is made the object of special reference and notice, in chapters vii. and viii.

We have already seen (p. 182 above), that in chap. ii. there is merely a *generic* description of the fourth dynasty. But into this, as has already been remarked, a singular circumstance is introduced, viz. "they shall intermingle with the seed of men, but they shall not cleave one to another, even as iron mixes not with clay." In chap. xi. we are explicitly taught what the meaning of this is. In v. 6, the marriage of Antiochus Theos with Berenice, the daughter of Ptolemy Philadelphus king of Egypt, is described; a marriage of mere policy and kingly chicanery, which, as there declared, turned out badly for those concerned in the matter. So in v. 17, we have an account of Antiochus the Great, and of his giving his daughter Cleopatra, to Ptolemy Epiphanes the young king of Egypt; which was done entirely for crafty purposes, in order that Antiochus, who was annoyed by the Romans, might break up the alliance between Rome and Egypt, by winning the king of the latter country to his side. These circumstances not only confirm the passage in 2: 43, but identify the dynasty in 11: 5—45, as being the same with that described in 2: 40—43.

In 11: 21 comes in the נִבְזֶה, (nothing could more graphically characterize him than this appellative), not as having any *right* to the kingdom of Syria, but as obtaining it by his wily flatteries; and in the like manner is he presented to us, in 8: 23, 25. In 11: 22, not only many others, but even the prince of the covenant (the high priest) is destroyed. With this must be compared 7: 7, specially 7: 25; then 8: 10, 11, 24, 25. In 11: 30—33, is an account of Antiochus as polluting the sanctuary at Jerusalem, and taking away the daily sacrifices; and this is to be compared with 7: 8, 25, and 8: 11, 12, 24, 25. In 11: 36, the impious and blasphemous conduct of Antiochus is described, and also the successful prosecution of his profane designs for a time; and this is to be compared with 7: 8, 11, 25, and 8: 11, 12, 24, 25. In 11: 45, the fearful doom of Antiochus is presented to our view; and with this must be compared 7: 11, 26. 8: 25. I am not able to see how a shadow of doubt can remain, as to the identity of the same personage in these passages. That personage, moreover, is clearly Antiochus Epiphanes.

I have refrained hitherto from introducing Dan. 9: 25—27, into the comparison of similar passages respecting Antiochus Epiphanes, because that portion of Scripture is very brief and compressed, and withal a very difficult one, as the almost endless variety of criticisms upon it shows. But since my own mind is now fully satisfied respecting the general meaning of the passage, I deem it expedient here to introduce it, and I ask the reader to compare it carefully with the passages referred to in the preceding paragraph. A literal translation runs thus:

Dan. ix. 25, " Mark well and understand; from the going forth of a command to rebuild Jerusalem, unto an Anointed one, a Prince, shall be 7 weeks; and 62 weeks shall it be rebuilt, with broad spaces and narrow limits, and in troublous times. (V. 26) And after 62 weeks, an Anointed One shall be cut off, and there shall be none for it [the people], and the city and sanctuary shall the people of a prince that will come destroy; but his end shall be with an overwhelming flood, and unto the end shall be war, a decreed measure of desolations. (V. 27) And he shall firmly covenant with many for one week; and during half of the week shall he cause the sacrifice and oblation to cease; and a waster shall be over a winged-fowl of abominations; but unto destruction, even that which is decreed, shall there be an outpouring upon him who is to be destroyed."

Here now are all the leading particulars of Antiochus' doings. Here is his assault on Jerusalem and the temple; his profanation of the sanctuary; his causing the oblation and sacrifices to cease for three and a half years; and finally his fearful end near the close of this period. Compare now this passage with ch. 7: 8, 20, 25, 26. 8: 9—12, 23—25. 11: 21, 30—32, 36, 41—45. 12: 7. Nothing seems to be more plain, than that the same personage is described in all. Specially does the particular notation of the three and a half years during which Antiochus will cause the temple-service to cease, and of the speedy and terrible death of the tyrant that will ensue, definitively mark sameness of personage and description in all the passages to which I have just referred. If the reader will carefully note these facts, it will aid him much in deciding the question, whether the *Roman* power is at all concerned with any of these prophecies, excepting the mere casual allusion to it in 11: 30, which speaks of "the ships of Chittim" as coming to Egypt, and arresting the progress of Antiochus in that country; and also the implied interference of the Romans with Antiochus Magnus, as stated in 11: 28. But of this, more in the sequel.

Having given such a detailed and comparative view of the different prophecies of Daniel respecting the fourth dynasty, it remains only to make a few remarks of a more general bearing, which may help us to make out a satisfactory general conclusion.

(1) It is evident from even a cursory reading of these predictions, that the dynasties follow each other in *succession*, and occupy in the main the same countries. One grows up when another becomes extinguished, or (in other words) by destroying the former. Thus the Medo-Persian succeeds the Babylonian; and Alexander's dominion overthrows the Medo-Persian, and stands up in its place. And in like manner, it is by the destruction of Alexander's dominion, that the fourth dynasty comes into being. In the last case, the separation between Alexander's dynasty and that which follows, is as strongly marked as the separation of any of the three former from each other; see 7: 7, 23. 8: 8, 22, and particularly 11: 4, which seems fairly to admit of no other explanation.

(2) To interpret the fourth beast (7: 7, 23), and the legs and feet of the colossal image (2: 40 seq.), as symbolic of the *Roman* empire, seems to be an exegetical impossibility. That the fourth beast was *diverse* from the three others, is explicitly said in 7: 7, 23. The fact that the fourth beast was a monster without a name, i. e. had no parallel in the animal world, indicates the mixed and incongruous condition of the fourth dynasty. The symbol of it in 2: 40 seq. in the mixture of the iron and the clay, is an indication of the same nature. Then it is explicitly declared in 8: 8, that the four notable horns, which came up in the room of the great horn (Alexander), symbolize the four kingdoms "towards the four winds of heaven," which kingdoms sprang up as *a succession of the third dynasty*. In 8: 22 it is explicitly stated, that these four horns denote four kingdoms, *which stand up out of the nation* or *people* who governed the preceding dynasty, i. e. from the *Grecian* nation. These *four horns*, denoting the partition of the fourth dynasty, are quite different in their signification from the *ten horns* in 7: 7, 20, 24. In the latter case, a succession of kings is denoted in that branch of the fourth dynasty, which "devours the whole land [of Judea], and treads down, and breaks in pieces." In what sense, now, can the *Roman* dominion be said to *succeed* that of Alexander? Many years after his death, Rome was neither known nor feared in the East; and certainly it had no concern with breaking in pieces the Hebrew people. And if the difficulty in respect to immediate *succession* could be disposed of, in what sense can it be said, that the *Roman* dominion sprung from the nation that ruled the third dynasty, 8: 22?

But besides this, the Roman empire, until some time after the *fifth* kingdom was introduced, never covered even any portion of the ground included in the domain of the three preceding dynasties. It lies on the face of the whole representation, that the successive monarchies occupy in the main the same countries, as I have already had occasion to state. But if the *Roman* empire be the fourth, this point must be given up; for Rome, at the height of her growth, never stretched beyond the Euphrates, so as to have anything more than a merely temporary and military occupation of some provinces; and from these they were soon driven by the Parthians. Much less was Rome concerned with crushing the Jews, at the early period in question.

The *immediate succession* of the *fourth* empire which arose out of the ruins of Alexander's; the *four* great divisions of the fourth dynasty; the ten kings that sprang up in one of the four divisions; and the *different countries* occupied by the Romans; are unequivocal and unanswerable arguments against applying the fourth dynasty to *Rome*.

But there is another proof, if possible still more decisive. This is, that all the prophecies of Daniel agree in asserting, that Antiochus Epiphanes, the נִבְזֶה, sprang from the bosom of the *fourth* dynasty. Thus in 7: 7, 8, from among the ten horns of the fourth dynasty springs up the *little horn*, which plucks up three of the others. This is reasserted in 7: 24. Again, in 8: 8, 9, out of one of the four horns of the fourth dynasty, springs up the *little horn*, which waxes great, and assails the temple and people of God. In 11: 21, Antiochus is represented as the successor of Seleucus Philopator, and of course as belonging to the *Syrian* part of the fourth dynasty. These facts seem too plain to admit of any doubt. But if Antiochus springs from a portion of the *fourth* dynasty, (which is plain), then how could the fourth dynasty be *Roman?* Antiochus was no Roman.

(3) Although the things already stated seem to decide the question against *Rome*, beyond all reasonable doubt, yet there is another circumstance, which is, if possible, still more decisive. This is, that the commencement of the *fifth* or *Messianic kingdom* takes place only when those four dynasties are broken up and subverted. This is explicit in 2: 44, 45; in 7: 11—14, 26, 27; and it seems to be implied in 12: 1—3. "All those kingdoms" (2: 44) are to be consumed, and broken in pieces," when the new kingdom shall arise. "Their dominion is taken away" (7: 11, 12), *before* the Son of Man enters upon his dominion, (7: 13, 14); and the same is said in vs. 26, 27. This is a circumstance too decisive to admit of any appeal. Unless then the Roman dynasty was destroyed before the coming of Christ, the fourth dynasty was not Roman.

I can see no good reason here, to appeal to *Antichrist*, and to the *Pope*, as being symbolized by the *fourth* beast. All the other beasts are symbols of *civil* powers, of actual monarchical governments. It is out of question, then, for us, with propriety to regard the fourth beast as a representative or symbol of a mere *religious apostasy* from Christianity, and then make, as we must, Antiochus to spring out of that. The *diversity* of the fourth beast, (spoken of in 7: 7, 19, 24), is not of such a nature, but it consists in its peculiar character, in its destructive influence upon the Jewish nation, in its unusual cruelties, and in its blasphemies. And since the little horn which waxed great, the blasphemer, the profaner of the temple and the altar, the persecutor of the holy people, must be destroyed *before* the Son of Man commences his reign, it would seem to be clear, that neither *Antichrist* nor the *Pope* is represented by the little horn. At all events, neither of those last named springs from the succession of the ten Syrian kings; and yet Antiochus must and did proceed from them.

Let me not be understood as denying that the N. Test. writers have, in a variety of cases, applied the language of Daniel (for substance) to the description of persons, or things, or events, which belong to the Christian era. When our Saviour (Matt. 24: 15. Mark 13: 14) describes the invading Roman power, by the use of language borrowed from Daniel's description of the desolations occasioned by *the abomination of desolation*, (probably Dan. 9: 26, 27, possibly 11: 31. 12:11), it is plain that he compares the consequences of the Roman invasion, with those which followed the invasion of Judea by Antiochus. I can hardly refrain from expressing my surprise, however, to find that Hengstenberg and Hävernick, who make the *Roman* power to be the *fourth* dynasty, should appeal with such entire confidence to Matt. 21: 15. Mark 13: 14 (essentially one and the same), as proof that the destructive *Roman* power was plainly *predicted* by Daniel. They argue the point with great earnestness; but so far as I can see, upon very insufficient and unsatisfactory grounds. Hengstenberg himself confesses (Authent. 265), that "excepting Dan. 9: 25—27, no other part of the book does even apparently relate to the destruction of the Jewish State by the Romans." But to fortify his position, that Dan. 9: 25—27 applies to the Romans, he appeals to Josephus, who (Antiq. X. 11. 7) says: "Daniel also wrote respecting the government of the Romans, and that desolations should be made by them." Josephus does indeed say this; but he says it after fully detailing the prophecies of Daniel in ch. viii, specially that concerning "the little horn," which he alleges was fulfilled in Antiochus. Now that he believed Daniel to have predicted, in his book, the invasion of Judea by the Romans, is quite a possible thing; perhaps a probable one; but to my own mind, his single short sentence respecting the Romans wears the aspect of something complimentary to them, and apologetic for them. "What they had done was a notable thing; and as they had only fulfilled what had long before been predicted, they could not therefore be blamed." Be this however as it may, it depends merely on the exegesis of Josephus. Nor do we know that the Jews in general were of the same opinion. But whether they were or not, does not settle the question before us. Hengstenberg, Hävernick, and some others, insist that the Saviour's words in Matt. 24: 15, viz. "spoken of by Daniel the prophet," (in Mark 13: 14 this clause is now rejected by recent criticism, and marked as probably spurious by Hahn), necessarily imply an express and direct prediction, on the part of Daniel, of the destruction of Jerusalem by the Romans. I cannot feel the force of this appeal; at least I am by no means persuaded that it is convincing. Many are the appeals in the N. Test. to passages in the Old, with an ἐπληρώϑη attached to them (which makes them look like appeal to *prophecy*), that are not by any means to be placed on the list of direct and proper predictions. For example; the flight of Joseph with Mary and the infant Jesus to Egypt, and their return from that country, is said (Matt. 2: 15) to have taken place, that "what was spoken of the Lord by the mouth of his prophet *might be fulfilled*." What then did the prophet say, which is *fulfilled?* He merely made a declaration—a simple categorical declaration—of a historical *fact*, as follows: "When Israel was a child I loved him, and called my son out of Egypt," Hos. 11: 1. Here is no *prediction*, but merely a simple averment of certain facts in former times. What is the *fulfilment* then? It is, that what happened in ancient times, in respect to a nation who were reckoned as the children of

God, had now been repeated in a higher and more significant sense. The *Son of God*, in the most eminent sense, was called from exile in Egypt back to the promised land. This is a πλήρωσις *par excellence*. The like to this occurs again, after a single intervening verse. The Evangelist (Matt. 2: 16) relates the slaughter of the infants by Herod at Bethlehem. He then subjoins a remark, viz. "Then was fulfilled what was spoken by the prophet Jeremiah, saying: In Rama a voice was heard, lamentation and weeping and great sorrow; Rachel weeping for her children, and refusing to be comforted, because they are not." This is quoted from Jer. 31: 15, where the prophet employs the expression as descriptive of the mourning of Rachel over her children (Benjamites) slain, and going from Rama into exile. It is simply a poetic description of a mournful fact, sketched out indeed with vivid coloring. What now happened at Bethlehem (Rachel's burying-place) to *fulfil* this? The slaughter of the infants, Rachel's later progeny. What took place of old, then, is here substantially renewed by repetition. But there is no trace of a *prediction proper*, in Jer. 31: 15.

It were easy to go on in this way, and to show that at least one half of such πληρώσεις in the N. Test. are of the same character. An appeal then to Matt. 24: 15 and Mark 13: 14, in order to show that the passage of Daniel referred to is proper prediction, is very far from being satisfactory. Christ does not even say that there is a *fulfilment* of Daniel's words. His declaration is: "When ye shall see the abomination of desolation, spoken of by Daniel the prophet, standing in the holy place, (in Mark — *standing where it ought not*), then let those flee, etc." But there is another remarkable circumstance. After the clause *standing in the holy place*, the Saviour adds, in a parenthetic clause, (ὁ ἀναγινώσκων νοείτω); which parenthetic addition, moreover, both evangelists exhibit. Now what is the meaning of this unexpected suggestion or innuendo? It amounts simply to this: 'Let the reader of Daniel well consider the essential meaning of the prophet.' But in case of a plain and direct prediction of Daniel, such a caution would hardly have been added. At all events it is very unusual in such cases. To what then does the caution amount? To this, viz. 'Consider well, that when a foreign, heathen, and hostile army has surrounded the holy ground, the sacred city, it is time to flee, for destruction is near. Daniel has described such an occurrence; therefore take warning by it.' Luke has given us, indeed, the exact gist of the passage, in his account of the same matter in 21: 20. His words are these: "When ye shall see *Jerusalem surrounded by armies*, then flee, etc." Here we have the πλήρωσις of the passage in Daniel, viz. the presence of a hostile heathen power (a desolating abomination) on holy ground. The Saviour would say: 'When this takes place, consider that what Daniel has described as happening in ancient times is about to happen now. Take warning and deliver yourselves.' Thus much, but plainly nothing more when all the passages are compared, can be made out from the texts to which appeal is made, as containing *predictions* of the *Roman* invasion.

That I am well grounded in this position, appears from a cursory glance at Dan. 9: 25—27. There, a prince and his people are spoken of, who shall come and lay waste the sanctuary; this they will do for one *week* = seven years (the Roman war lasted but little more than *three*); then in the midst of that week, the destroyer will cause the daily sacrifice and the oblation to cease, i. e. during the latter half of the seven years this will be done; and soon after, the destroyer shall himself be destroyed with consummate decreed destruction. Now in what part of the Roman invasion did all this happen? When did they suspend the temple services? And where shall we find the three and a half years of suspension? And above all, where, after the suspension, are we to find the *restoration* of the temple-services? for this is implied in Daniel. The Roman suspension remains from that day to this. Last, but not least, the *desolator* in this case is given over to a decreed destruction, to take place soon after the three and a half years were ended. Was this true, now, of either Vespasian or Titus? Not at all. Both died a natural death, and in peaceful circumstances, Vespasian A. D. 79 and Titus in 82. Both were greatly beloved and honored as princes. What resemblance did either of them bear to the abhorred tyrant in Dan. 9: 26, 27?

The answer then to that exegesis which makes the *Roman* power to be the fourth dynasty in Daniel, is, that history contradicts such an application of his predictions. That fourth power is of *Greek* origin; its sphere of action is *oriental* ground; its acts are consummated in Epiphanes, (so far as prophecy has any concern with it); and the leading tyrant of that dynasty is the enemy and blasphemer of God, and is cut down in the midst of his career by divine vengeance, shortly after the temple desolations were completed. Which of all these things now is applicable either to Vespasian or to Titus? And above all, what are we to do with the suspension of temple-services for three and a half years, and for this period only?

But enough. It is impossible to carry through the views of Hengstenberg and Hävernick, in relation to Dan. 9: 25—27, and make them comport either with history or with the design of the prophet. Events that *precede* the Messianic kingdom are the objects of Daniel's vision. Through and through he tells us, that the new and perpetual kingdom, i. e. the fifth dynasty, is built upon the complete destruction of the other four dynasties. Was the Roman power destroyed then, when the Messiah's kingdom began? This simple question brings the whole matter to a conclusion.

I see no way of making out a prophecy of *Roman* invasion in Daniel, unless we force a *double* sense upon the passage in question; a thing which neither Hengstenberg nor Hävernick admitted to be done, when their books were written. And indeed it cannot be done without great violence. A *double* sense I must deem inadmissible, moreover, for reasons already often given to the public. To what the German critics call an *apotelesmatic* accomplishment of predictions in the O.Test., I should not strenuously object, provided it be kept within due limits. The epithet means a final or concluding, or complete accomplishment, in distinction from a prior literal or obvious accomplishment. If the matter be plainly stated, as it lies in my own mind, it might stand thus: 'A prophecy may contain a *generic principle* of God's government, or of development in regard to occurrences; and then there may be a primary and obvious accomplishment of the prediction, and afterwards a development of the same generic principle in other events. To such an *apotelesmatic* accomplishment I should make no objection; I would even freely admit it.

The matter as to Dan. 9: 25—27 and Matt. 24: 15, would then stand thus: 'For the sins of the ancient Jews, Daniel foretold chastisement by a foreign heathen enemy, which happened; for the sins of the Jews of our Saviour's time, Jerusalem must be again surrounded by hostile heathen armies. The like to what Daniel foretells and what took place, was again presented in the time of Christ's ministry, and was going on to completion.' To such an apotelesmatic view, I see no reasonable objection. Daniel predicts peculiar punishment for special sins; when those special sins again occur, the punishment may be again expected.

When Paul describes the *Man of Sin* (1 Thess. 2: 3, 4), we cannot well doubt that he had in his mind that *son of perdition* in former days, who is described in Dan. 7: 25 and 11: 36. In other words, the like of what happened in Antiochus' time, is again to happen under the new dispensation. Of the same tenor with these and other like cases, are such passages as we have produced above, viz. Matt. 2: 15, compared with Hos. 11: 1; Matt. 2: 17, 18, compared with Jer. 31: 15. It requires, indeed, a good degree of familiarity with the usage of the N. Test. writers, in regard to passages of the O. Test. which they quote or refer to, in order to be well satisfied respecting the wide extent in which they make the application of such passages to the Christian era. But I feel no hesitation in saying, that, in my apprehension, no passage in the N. Test. can be pointed out, which makes it necessary to regard any portion of the predictions in Daniel *that respect only the four great dynasties*, as a direct prediction of events or persons under the fifth monarchy. The *fifth* monarchy has an abundance of prediction which respects only that monarchy. The reason for this opinion is obvious, and it seems to me to be conclusive. All which pertains to the four monarchies has *passed away*, when the fifth monarchy commences. I say *commences*, for the interpretation which makes the fifth monarchy begin only with the Millennium, or the end of the world, is evidently at variance with all the declarations of the Saviour, that his kingdom was at hand, and that it had indeed *already begun*. For this kingdom *fully to come*, if interpreted in the most ample sense that the phrase admits, would place the whole matter in quite another attitude than that which here belongs to it.

Finally, I do not see any possible way of harmonizing the development of the Roman empire, with the description of the fourth dynasty in 2: 41, 42. Clearly the *iron* and the *clay*, as symbols, both belong to the same dynasty. The prophet says: "The kingdom shall be *divided*," and that "it shall be partly strong and partly broken." Of all the great empires that are within our cognizance, we know of none to which this is so little applicable as to the Roman. Parties under this dominion, I readily concede, were formed from time to time, and civil broils and wars ensued for a while. But they were of short continuance. Rome had a firm, steady, compact, powerful, solid growth, amid all the partial troubles that she experienced within herself. Civil and party hostility subsided, when foreign enemies called on the Romans to show their love of country and their pride of conquest. "Partly strong and partly broken!" No; never until the conquest by Goths and Vandals, and the subsequent division of the empire, was Rome *broken*. A more compact, undivided, powerful dynasty never arose on earth. Such characteristics then as *divided* and *broken*, are utterly at variance with the whole history of Rome, until near the fifth century after the birth of Christ. I must confess myself unable to see, how any one, who is familiar with history, could ever think of applying Dan. 2: 41, 42, to the empire of Rome. The *contrary* of what these verses declare, is true of that dominion in a most remarkable degree.

[After the introductory remarks already made, the contents of ch. vii. may be sketched in a few words. The prophetic vision of Daniel was by night, and in a dream, v, 1. After great commotion of the sea by stormy winds, four great beasts come up from it, strong and ravenous, yet diverse in kind, vs. 2, 3. The first is a *lion*, furnished with wings, to which, after severe castigation, a more gentle and humane spirit is given, v. 4. The second is a *bear*, whose position, and grasp of prey, as well as the language addressed to it, indicate a watchful rapacity for conquest, v. 5 The third is a *panther*, with four wings and four heads, bearing extensive sway, v. 6. The fourth is a monster without a name, strong and terrible, with teeth of iron and ten horns; out of which comes up a little horn, which roots out three of the others, and becomes insolent and blasphemous, vs. 7, 8. When the destruction occasioned by it reaches its height, the Ancient of Days prepares his tribunal, and ascends it surrounded by flaming fire and myriads of ministering servants. The trial proceeds, the charges are made, and the beast is condemned to excision; which sentence is executed, vs. 9—11. The like had been already done to the other three beasts, v. 12. The Son of Man now makes his appearance before the Ancient of Days, and dominion universal and permanent is given to him, vs. 13, 14. Daniel, overpowered by the vision, is troubled in his mind, v. 15. He approaches an angel-interpreter, and seeks to know more particularly the meaning of the vision. He is told, in a few words, the sum of its meaning: There are and will be four dynasties; to be followed by a fifth which belongs to the saints, and is to be perpetual, vs. 16—18. But his curiosity is not satisfied, in regard to the *fourth* beast, the characteristics of which he recapitulates, vs. 19, —22. The interpreter informs him, that the fourth kingdom will be diverse from the other three, and very destructive; that the ten horns signify ten kings; that another (the little horn) shall arise, who will humble three of the ten, utter boasting and blasphemy, and undertake to change times and abrogate the law; that these latter transactions of the little horn are limited to three and a half years, vs. 23—25; and finally that the destroyer shall himself be condemned and destroyed, v. 26. After this, "the people of the most high God" shall receive a dominion that shall never end, v. 27. Here ends the vision; but Daniel was filled with agitation and concern respecting the things predicted, although he kept the whole matter to himself, v. 28.]

CHAPTER VII.

(1) In the first year of Belteshazzar king of Babylon, Daniel saw a dream, and [there were] visions of his head, upon his couch; then he wrote down the dream, and related the sum of the matters.

This chapter begins the second and peculiarly *prophetic* part of the book of Daniel, in which the writer forsakes the *chronology* of the preceding historical part that he had brought down to the Median dominion, and goes back some seventeen years to the first year of Belshazzar. The date of the time, when a prophecy was received, is commonly affixed by the Hebrew prophets to the oracle itself. It is not unusual for prophets to receive a special command, to *commit to writing* their disclosures; comp. Isa. 30: 8. 8: 1, 16. Hab. 2: 2. Apoc. 1: 19. 21: 5. 14: 13. Daniel does not inform us, whether he in this case received a special command to write down his vision, nor of the time when he did write it; but the importance of the subject-matter of the vision, and the trouble that it gave to his mind, would be very likely to lead him to a speedy record of what he had seen. — חֵלֶם חֲזָה, lit. *saw a dream ;* but חזה, in Heb. and Chaldee both, is employed to designate the *mental perception* of any kind of prophetic communication, whether by symbol or by message. Thus in Isa. 2: 1, we have חָזָה דָּבָר, i. e. *saw a message* or *communication.* "To see a dream," is to have a mental perception of one, to be impressed with what is seemingly presented to vision. — *And the visions of his head,* i. e. of his brain, which was regarded as the organ of the mind, *head* being taken for that which it contains ; as often with us. Accordingly we might translate רֵאשׁ by *mind.* One might also employ the word *brain ;* but in such a connection, our idiom would give to this word the meaning of something which is merely imaginary. Daniel means more than this. *On his couch* seems to be added as an accompaniment to the word *dream,* in order to indicate, that it was not a waking prophetic ecstasy, but a vision seen when he was sleeping on his bed; comp. 4: 2, 10. — כְּתַב, *wrote out, wrote down,* see Lex. on the Heb. כָּתַב, — רֵאשׁ, *sum, summary, amount ;* see Lex. Heb. under רֹאשׁ, and comp. Ps. 119: 160, where the Heb. ראשׁ means *sum, substance ;* so Ps. 137: 6. — מִלִּין, pl. of מִלָּה fem., 31. 3. — אֲמַר, *related, communicated,* whether by speaking or writing. The writer means to say, that he communicates the *substance* of the visions, omitting particulars not specially important.

(2) Daniel answered and said: I looked steadfastly during my vision in the night, and behold! the four winds of the heavens burst forth upon the great ocean.

חָזֵה הֲוֵית, Part. with helping verb (§ 47. 1. *a*), denoting continued action. — עִם לֵילְיָא, lit. *with night,* but עִם is employed for the purpose of designating something *contemporaneous ;* e. g. Dan. 3: 33. Ps. 72: 5. So Ovid: *Cum* sole et luna semper Aratus erit, Ars Amor. I. 15, 16. — רוּחֵי, const. pl. in its primitive sense, *wind.* — מְגִיחָן, Aph. Part. pl. fem. of גִּיחַ, agreeing with רוּחֵי which is here treated as fem. — לְיַמָּא, לְ showing the direction in which the winds burst forth. — *Great ocean,* the world-sea of the ancients; not an *abstract* noun, of course, but still it is here used in a generic way. I take it to be here the symbol of the heathen world, the mass of the world's people ; and in the same way is the phrase *many waters* employed in Rev. 17: 1, 15. The imagery is allied to the tropical use of *overflowing rivers* and *mighty waves,* for the designation of invading armies which overrun a country without control. The image is so frequent, that it needs no further illustration or confirmation.

(3) And four huge beasts came up out of the sea, differing one from another.

שָׁנְיָן, Part. Peal, pl. fem. (from שְׁנָא), like סָלְקָן. As all these beasts are of the *ferocious* and *powerful* kind, it is evident that they are intended to be symbols of powerful and warlike dynasties. The differences between them is designed to indicate rather the *successive changes* of empire, than any discrepancies in regard to their respective power or cruelty. Similar imagery the reader may find in Ps. 68: 31 (30), "beast of the reeds;" Ezek. 29: 3, "dragon in the midst of the river" [Nile]; 32: 2, "young lion of the nations;" Ps. 74: 13, "thou brakest the heads of the dragons in the waters; Isa. 27: 1, "leviathan, the crooked serpent . . . the dragon that is in the sea." On all the ancient monuments of the East are found *formae monstrosae*, the symbols of dominion and of conquerors. The whole picture is in perfect keeping with ancient Mesopotamian symbols. In Apoc. 13: 1, one monster-beast is represented as possessing the united qualities of all the four beasts here; and well; for there the mighty *Roman* power is symbolized, which united the characteristics of former empires, in respect to everything which inspires dread and forces submission. That the *sea* is here represented as the element from which the monsters come, is nothing strange; comp. Isa. 27: 1. Apoc. 13: 1. The sea is the natural element of the largest monsters; the sea with its tempestuous waves has an overwhelming and destructive power; and therefore the representation here is congruous and well chosen.

(4) The first was like to a lion, and it had the wings of an eagle; I looked steadfastly until its wings were plucked, and it was lifted up from the earth, and was raised up on its feet like a man, and the heart of a man was given to it.

אַרְיֵה = אֲרִי, but having (it seems to be for the sake of euphony) a paragogic ה־ formative at the end. It is generic, and includes of course both sexes. Two pronouns in the verse may seem to relate to it, which are of the *fem.* gender; and probably also the suffix in גַּפַּיהּ, (p. 36, par. 2) is fem. On account of this, some translate אַרְיֵה *lioness*, and endeavor to vindicate this by remarking, that the *lioness* is fiercer and more ravenous than the lion. Still I have translated the Heb. word by *lion*, because it seems clear to me, that all these pronouns, as well as קַדְמָיְתָא, refer to חֵיוָה implied, and because our own usage rarely, if ever, makes the *lioness* an object of comparison. It seems plain here, as in respect to the *golden head* of the colossal image (2: 37, 38), that the *lion* is not designed to represent the strength or extent of the first kingdom as comparatively greater than that of the others; for surely Alexander's empire exceeded that of Babylon in both these respects. It is mainly a *precedence of rank*, then, which is symbolized. As in respect to the *image*, one naturally begins with the *head* in order to reckon up in order its various elements and parts, so we should begin with Babylon in reckoning up the empires symbolized by the four beasts. The lion is indeed called *the king of beasts;* but the *mountain-bear* is very fierce and strong, and the *panther* even more fierce and ravenous than the lion. Babylon is the oldest of the kingdoms here designated; and the lion, which is commonly regarded as the superior of other beasts in respect to dignity of nature (if I may so speak), is a fit emblem of the splendid and more ancient kingdom of Babylon. Further than this, I think the differences between the beasts are not to be carried. To assume that the differences in *extent* or *power* are symbolized by the differences between the beasts, and that the later empire in each case is to be considered as the weaker, or the inferior with regard to extent or power, would lead us to conclusions which unquestionably disagree with facts. Still, all the beasts which are named in ch. vii. are characterized by strength and rapacity. In Hebrew, nothing can be more frequent than the use of the particular symbol now in question, to designate destructive power. *Lion of God* makes an accession to the idea of *lion*, as it forms a kind of superlative; e. g. Isa. 29: 2. 2 Sam. 23: 20. This is the name which Mohammed gave his heroic uncle, Hamza. — גַּפִּין, masc. here, plur. where the Heb. would employ the dual. The Chaldee has no *dual*, excepting a few cases that are retained in the biblical Chaldee. — *Wings of an eagle*, is an additional image of swiftness and strength; comp. Jer. 4: 13. 48: 40. 49: 22. Lam. 4: 19. Ezek. 17: 3, 7. Ob. v. 4. Hab. 1: 8; not the image simply of haughtiness or of the spirit of domination, as some have explained it. — לַהּ, pron. *fem.* as has already been noted. — מְרִיטוּ, Peil Part. 3 pl. for pass. verb, § 13. 2. — גַּפַּיהּ, plur. masc., with a suffix fem. relating to חֵיוָה, for both יהּ- and ַיהּ- are sometimes used as fem. sing. forms of the suffix instead of ָהּ-, see p. 36, 2nd par. — נְטִילַת, Part. pass. fem.; used for the passive verb, § 13. 2. *It was raised up from the earth as a man*, does not mean that the whole beast was lifted up into the air, but that it stood up on its hinder legs, taking the upright position of a man. The purpose of this is explained more fully, by the clause that follows. — — רַגְלַיִן, a Hebraizing *dual* form, found only in biblical Chaldee. — הֳקִימַת, Hebraizing Hophal of קוּם = Ittaphal, § 12. 6. — *The heart of a man was given to it*, i. e. (in connection with the preceding verse) not only did it take the outward position of a man, but also partake of his internal mind and feelings. I understand the design here to be, to characterize the greater moderation and humanity which the Babylonish dominion exhibited after Nebuchadnezzar's malady and restoration, or, to use the language of the prophet, after *its wings were plucked.* The language seems plainly to be borrowed from the case of Nebuchadnezzar, who, driven from men by his madness, associated with the beasts of the field, and ate grass like the oxen, 4: 29. As he imitated the beasts in this, it is not at all improbable that he may also have imitated them in his position and movements. From this state he rose, by the restoration of his reason (4: 33), i. e. *the heart of a man was given him.** As the Babylonish empire is designated or represented by him (2: 38), so here, the humbling of the Babylonish dynasty, and the rendering of it more humane and less assuming, is set forth by a likeness taken from Nebuchadnezzar and his condition. The particular object of this seems after all to be, the distinctive designation or specification of the first dynasty. To suppose, as Bertholdt does, that the last two clauses of v. 4 serve merely to show, that dynasties of *men* and not of beasts are in reality meant, is, to say the least, quite needless. What reader ever supposed, that Daniel is here describing the literal dominion of beasts?

(5) And behold! another second beast, like to a bear, and it was lifted up on one side, and three ribs were in its mouth between its teeth, and thus said they to it: Arise, devour much flesh!

תִּנְיָנָה, *second*, marks the order, while אָחֳרִי merely designates the idea of *difference, distinctness.* — דָּמְיָה, Part. fem. of דְּמָא. — לְשְׂטַר חַד, as rendered above, is in the Acc., governed by the Hiphil-formed verb הֳקִימַת. Many (26) Codices and editions read שְׂטַר (with *Sin*); and many critics prefer this reading, because the Targumic word סְטַר, appears to be the same word with merely a different orthography, and סְטַר means *side.* However, the form שְׂטַר has no appropriate root. But what is *lifting* or *raising up one side?* Not *stood aside, stetit seorsim,* i. e. stood aloof from harming the Hebrews, as the ancient Rabbins, Jerome, Grotius, al., supposed; nor, (as some others suppose), *stood aside* in the sense of retiring from a part of the former wide domain of Babylon, for the Medo-Persian kings did not relinquish any of that domain; nor, (as C. B. Mich. and Rosenm.), *stood by the side,* viz. of the lion, i. e. Media and Persia were on the boundaries or sides of Babylon; much less does it mean, as Bertholdt and Hävernick assert: *stood on its hinder feet,* viz. in the attitude of attack, for *side* is not *hinder feet,* and as yet the bear is not roused up entirely, but is subsequently called upon to *arise.* It is in itself, indeed, a somewhat difficult phrase; but the difficulty seems to have arisen from the fact, that until lately, we have been ignorant of a like symbol sculptured on the ancient monuments of Persia.

* Since this was written, I have met with Hoffman's *Weissagung und Erfüllung,* and find this able writer has presented a similar view of Daniel's imagery.

Münter (Rel. der Bab. s. 112) has given us a description (with an engraving) of an animal of the symbolic kind, in a group near the star of Belus, which, kneeling or lying on the right foot, has its left one erect. A sense of security combined with watchfulness, seems to be the indication. Probably this symbol now on the monuments of Persia and Babylon, was a part of what belonged to the *insignia* of the royal and national standards; (see p. 177 above). Its significance, when viewed in such a light, is certainly striking. — הָקִימַת, as some editions have it, (to which many versions have conformed), is the pass. or Hophal; but it may be read as in Hiphil (הֲקִימַת), and applied *actively*, (which is grammatical in respect to this Conj.), to the beast as *raising up one side*, viz. by putting one of its fore legs into an erect posture — עִלְעִין, from עֲלַע = the Heb. צֵלָע (comp. in Lex. ע and צ); *ribs*, not *tusks* (Berth.); not *three classes of teeth*, viz. side, cheek, and incisor teeth (Häv.); for how can these be said to be *between the teeth*? But *three ribs* constitute a large portion of prey or ravin already in the animal's power, or (in words borrowed from the nature of the symbol) a large mouthful. It seems to me quite incongruous, to consider these *ribs* as teeth, in as much as they are *between the teeth;* or to regard them (with Jerome, Ephrem Syrus, and Rosenm.) as indicative of Media, Persia, and Babylon. The Medo-Persian empire is itself the *bear*. What it grasps, or devours, must be something else. It may be, that Babylonia, Assyria, and Lydia, are symbolized by the ribs; or, with some modification of the design of the symbol, the three ribs may indicate the great divisions of the empire, 6: 2. But if the latter be true, then the symbol does not relate to *devouring*, but to the *complete grasp* of power. — בֵּין שִׁנַּהּ, *between its teeth* clearly indicates, of course, that the עִלְעִין in his mouth is *prey*, and not the teeth themselves; the fem. suff. has relation to חֵיוָה. The word as Chaldee I do not find in Ges. Lex.; but it follows the analogy of the Heb. שֵׁן, § 29. 2. *a.* — אָמְרִין, lit. *they said*, Part. 3 plur.; it might be rendered passively, § 49. 3. *b.* — קוּמִי, Imper. *fem.* in relation to חֵיוָה again; see Hoffman ut sup. I. s. 283. — *Eat much flesh*, exhibits the imagery carried consistently through. *Flesh* is the appropriate food of bears. Of course, when a dynasty set up and supported by conquest and rapine is characterized in this way, the meaning is: Rise up, and make extensive conquests, i. e. seize upon much prey. Such was the case with Cyrus, according to Xenophon, Cyrop. VIII. 7. He extended his dominion to Syria, and Egypt, even unto Ethiopia, and reigned over the countries from the Mediterranean Sea to India, and from the Euxine to the Red Sea. Afterwards Darius Hystaspis extended the boundaries of empire still further, even into Thrace and India. But how any one could satisfy himself that dominion thus characterized designates that of *Media* under Darius the Mede, as Lengerke appears to have done, I do not see. That king was more conspicuous for intemperance and debauchery, than for ambition and love of conquest; and to gratify his disgraceful appetites, he retired from all personal participation in the conquest of Babylon, and ever afterwards staid at his palace and houses of pleasure. Nothing more, worthy of note, was undertaken until after his death; which happened in about two years subsequent to the capture of Babylon. Lengerke indeed holds the account of such a prince as Darius the Mede, both in Xenophon and the Bible, to be a mere fiction. But even if this were conceded to him, why should we suspect the writer of representing the dynasty in question as doing things, which are wholly incongruous with the inefficiency and the slothful timidity of Darius the Mede? If the book before us be a fiction, it does not show any want of talent, or any lack of knowledge as to Oriental history or customs. At least it seems to me, that just and generous criticism will not venture to affirm that it does. As to the idea conveyed by the phrase, *the devouring of flesh*, comp. Mic. 3: 2, 3. Rev. 17: 6. As to the *rapacity* of the bear, it is a well known characteristic. Aristotle calls it *σαρκοφαγῶν* and *ζῶον πάμφαγον*, (Hist. Nat. VIII. 5). Not unfrequently it attacks men, as well as the larger animals. The overruling hand of Providence, moreover, is not lost sight of by the writer in the whole matter respecting this dynasty. — *It was said* or *they said*, means, that God or Heaven gave command or permission to *devour much prey*, i. e. the concerns and conquests of this dynasty were under the government of a superintending Providence.

(6) After this I looked attentively, and lo! another [beast] like to a panther, and it had four wings of a bird upon its back, and four heads belonged to the beast, and dominion was given to it.

כִּנְמַר, *like a panther*, which seems to be the true sense, rather than *leopard* as in our Eng. version. This beast is swifter than the lion or bear, and equally powerful. — *Four wings of a bird* is quite intelligible. If, in v. 4, the wings of an eagle assigned to the lion indicate *power* and *velocity*, the two pairs of wings given to the panther must indicate *great velocity*. As the writer does not here repeat the word *eagle* in connection with *wings*, but merely says *wings of a bird*, the natural conclusion is, that he means to represent the first beast as the stronger of the two, but not so swift. Facts correspond. Nebuchadnezzar had a mighty force, a great sway; Alexander, with a handful of troops subdued the oriental world: Nebuchadnezzar founded an empire which lasted almost a century; Alexander one which ended with his life. The point of comparative *strength*, therefore, is not here taken into view, but that of *rapid movement.* In this Nebuchadnezzar excelled much, but Alexander outstripped all other conquerors in the East or West. Hence *two pairs of wings* to symbolize his movements. But how are we to find any adequate meaning of the imagery, if we apply these wings (with Lengerke and some others) to the Medo-Persian dynasty? Neither Cyrus, nor Darius, nor Xerxes, were remarkable for *rapidity* of conquest, beyond other conquerors. Cyrus was as long in subduing Asia Minor, as Alexander was in subduing all the East. — גַּבַּיהּ, plur. with fem. suff., in reference to חֵיוְתָא. — *Four heads*, not indicative here of *four kings*, as Leng. supposes. To establish this, he appeals to Dan. 11: 2 and Rev. 13: 1. But the first passage makes no mention of *heads*; and the last mentions *seven heads*, which symbolize seven kings (Rev. 17: 10), but they also symbolize *seven hills* (Rev. 17: 9). This symbol, then, is not limited to signifying *kings*. This is still more clearly decided in Rev. 12: 3, where *seven heads* are ascribed to the dragon. The four heads, then, may be regarded as the symbol of dominion in the four different quarters of the world, i. e. of universal dominion; for Satan's seven *heads* are clearly emblems of his great power. The ram (Medo-Persia) in 8: 4 is described as pushing his attacks northward, southward, and westward, but not *eastward*; while in the case before us, the four heads indicate all four directions, if I am right in my views of the meaning of the symbol. Well does 2: 39 ("he shall rule over *all the earth*") correspond with the passage before us; and also with 8: 21—23, and 11: 3, 4. Leng. plainly intimates, that the writer of the book of Daniel supposed, that there were only *four* kings of the Persian dynasty (11: 2), and that he has confounded Darius Codomanus with Darius Hystaspis, and so ranged Alexander next after him. He adds, that "the ignorance of the Maccabaean period respecting the history of the East, makes the whole matter a thing that ought not to strike us with any surprise," (s. 308). Yet I must be permitted to say, it would be somewhat surprising to me, that such a man as wrote the book of Daniel, and belonged to a nation that had been, from Cyrus down to Alexander, under the Persian domain, should have thought and said that Persia had only *four* kings, when it actually had *thirteen.* The knowledge of empires displayed in the book of Daniel, forbids such a supposition. Could events like those which took place in respect to the Jewish people under the Persian domain, be so little known, or so entirely forgotten, after a lapse of time so small? And although Lengerke assures us that there is *nichts auffällig* in all this, my own convictions are quite to the contrary. Finally, the superintendence of a higher power is again intimated: *And dominion was given to it.* "The powers that be are ordained of God."

So even the mischievous beast, in Apoc. 13: 3, is said to have "power given to it."

(7) After this, I looked attentively during the visions of the night, and behold! a fourth beast, terrible, strong, even exceedingly powerful, and it had great teeth of iron; it devoured, and crushed, and trode the remnant under its feet, and it differed from all the other beasts which were before it; and it had ten horns.

אֶמְתָּנִי, adj. (root מתן, which in Arabic means *to be strong, robust*), formed by א praefix, and י the adj. ending for fem. ־ִית. The second clause, תַּקִּיפָא יַתִּירָה, is merely an intensive of the preceding word. — שִׁנַּיִן, Hebraizing dual, lit. *two rows of teeth;* found only in biblical Chaldee, § 31. 2. — *Great iron teeth*, means a very destructive power. Hence, in the sequel, *devour, crush.* — מַדֲּקָה, Aph. fem. Part. of דְּקַק. — רָפְסָה, Part. fem. Peal — מְשַׁנְיָה, fem. Part. Aph., for the beast is here regarded as fem. — קֳדָמַיהּ, with fem. suff. p. 36, par. second. — קַרְנַיִן, dual form of קֶרֶן, Hebraizing like שִׁנַּיִן above. The writer gives to this fourth beast no particular name. Plainly it was a peculiar monster. The reason why he omits a name, seems to be, that in the world of nature no similitude could be found, for in no case of really existing beasts, are four of them united in one, so as to constitute an appropriate symbol for the four kingdoms of Alexander's successors. He classes these under the dynasty, comprehensively considered, which grew up out of the predominance or victories of the Greeks in the East. But when enough is introduced to designate the general nature of the dynasty, both here and in ch. viii. and xi, he goes over into a notice of only such kings as were in the neighborhood of Palestine, and had more or less to do with annoying it. As Antiochus Epiphanes was incomparably the most annoying and mischievous of them all, so a peculiar share of the prophecy respecting the fourth dynasty, is allotted to him in each of the chapters named. It is evident from a comparison of historical facts as well as from the nature of the case, that a dynasty is spoken of by Daniel as more or less dreadful and destructive, according to the measure in which Palestine was actually affected by it in this way. See the fuller discussion of this subject in the introduction to this chapter, p. 183 seq. above. A right view of this matter is of the highest importance to the proper interpretation of the book.

(8) I considered attentively the horns, and behold! another little horn came up between them, and three of the former horns were rooted out from before it, and lo! there were eyes like the eyes of a man in that horn, and a mouth speaking great things.

The introduction which the writer here makes to his account of the *little horn*, shows, by its specialty of manner and its solemnity, that he is going to bring forward something which is peculiarly worthy of the reader's attention — at least, something in which he himself felt the deepest interest. It is similar to that which is prefixed to the accounts respectively of each of the four beasts. That *horns* are the well known symbols of power, specially of power as directed against opposing forces, is too familiar to need proof; the reader may compare Deut. 33: 17. 1 Sam. 2: 10. 1 K. 22: 11. Ps. 18: 3 (2). 112: 9. 132: 17. 148: 14. The like is often found in the Apoc., and in the book of Enoch. — זְעֵירָה, *fem.* adj. for קֶרֶן is here treated as feminine. This is to be understood as the symbol of Antiochus Epiphanes, on his first accession to the throne, when the parties against him were numerous and strong, being the friends of the kings whom he had deposed. The progress of the little horn's growth is not here specified; but in 8: 9—11 there is a special allusion to the gradual increase of the same *little* horn, until it becomes a *great* one. In 11: 21, the origin of Antiochus' dominion is described in conformity with the זְעֵירָה of the verse before us. And when this same horn is said in 7: 20 to "look more stout than its fellows," this is no contradiction of the preceding passage. Antiochus began his reign with feeble means of supporting himself, but by flattery, craft, and dexterous management, he rose to formidable power, which he wielded so as to annoy the Jews beyond all former example. The seer keeps his eye upon him, during the whole course through which he passes; and it is in the latter part of his course, that he 'becomes more stout than his fellows. — סִלְקָת = סִלְקַת in v. 20, fem. 3 pers. sing. in Peal, with a final (ָ) instead of the normal (ַ), being pointed like the 3 fem. in verbs ל״א. In general, the Chaldee *vowel-points* vary, according to the Rabbinic usage, far more than the Hebrew, and the varieties of pronunciation are numerous and some of them perplexing. In בֵּינֵיהֵון the vowels are adapted to the corrected reading בֵּינֵיהֵן i. e. to a *fem.* suffix. But this is needless. The masc. בֵּינֵיהוֹן is equally good; for the gender of the horns is shifted in vs. 19, 20. 8: 9, al., i. e. the gender of those whom the horns symbolize, is applied to the horns themselves; which is often done in the Apocalypse. — אֶתְעֲקָרוּ (for so the Kethibh should be read) = אִתְעֲקַרוּ the normal form, the Pattah under the ק being prolonged, (as it is sometimes, particularly when in an open syllable), as in סִלְקָת above. The syllable אֶתְ- (for אִתְ) *Syraizes*, § 25. 1. The grammarians and critics have mostly overlooked these forms. Besides this, אֶת (for the normal אִת) is a liberty not unfrequent in the later Hebrew, specially when א is the first letter; for then it naturally inclines to take a *Seghol* in a closed syllable. The form of the verb in the Kethibh is masc., for קַרְנַיָּא is treated as masc., in accordance with what has just been said. The corrected reading changes the form so as to accommodate the *fem.* gender, viz. אֶתְעֲקַרָה. I have translated the word by *rooted out* (*evellit, eradicavit*) ; which however means, in our language, somewhat more than is here intended, unless we limit the idea to the kingly power or office. In v. 20, three horns are said *to fall* before the little horn ; and in v. 24, the same occurrence is thus described by the angel-interpreter: "three kings *shall be humbled.*" I understand the passages, when thus compared, as designating the *dethronization* of three kings, but not of their actual destruction as individuals. As *kings*, three of them are described by different modes of expression, viz., it is said that they are *rooted out, fall*, and that they are *humbled.* The least which these expressions are susceptible of meaning, is, that Antiochus will dethrone three kings, and humble them in respect to their claims of right to regal power. — וַאֲלוּ calls particular attention to a notable circumstance: *Eyes like to the eyes of a man were in this horn.* עַיְנִין, for form, see p. 94. No. IV. *c.* That *eyes* symbolize *sagacity, dexterity, watchfulness*, is plain. The eye speaks the meaning of the soul. One reason why this is said here, seems to be, in order to make the reader aware that the horn symbolizes a human being; for *eyes* belong not to the proper horn. Says Jerome: [He speaks thus] "that we may not, according to the notion of some, think it to be a devil, or a demon, but one of those men in whom the whole of Satan is to dwell bodily." Exactly what Jerome meant by the last clause here, it might be difficult to determine. However, that the watchfulness and sagacity of the little horn are here indicated, and that the word *horn* is entirely exempted from being understood in a literal sense, seems clear; comp. 11: 21—25. 8: 23—25. Coming to the throne under circumstances such as existed at that time in Syria, it was wonderful that Antiochus should succeed so well as he did; and it fully justifies what is said in the passages to which I have referred, respecting his cunning and his dexterity. Appian says of him: "He ruled Syria and the nations around her ἐγκρατῶς," De Reb. Syr. c. 45. — ופם וגו׳, *a mouth speaking*, etc., of course betokens that a *man* is designated by the symbol; for since he had ascribed to the horn the *eyes of a man*, he now proceeds (in accordance with this) to assign to it also *a mouth.* — *Speaking great things*, i. e. uttering words of boasting, haughtiness, and contumacy. This was a striking characteristic of Antiochus, when he had arrived at the height of his power; comp. v. 11, 20, 25. 23—25. 11: 36, and see 1 Macc. 1: 24. Comparing the whole of these passages, it would seem that the writer means particularly to characterize the *impious boastings* and *reproaches* of Antiochus against God, his temple, the holy city, and the Jewish people.

Next (vs. 9—11) follows the condemnation and excision of the blasphemer and persecutor of the Jews. Then, inasmuch as all the four beasts are now destroyed (v. 12), the kingdom of the Messiah supervenes — a kingdom that is to have no end.

EXCURSUS ON THE FOURTH BEAST. To facilitate our future progress, it may be well to satisfy ourselves of the position, which, as interpreters, we ought to take; for much is dependent on it. Having already discussed this subject at large, in the introduction to this chapter, I shall give here only brief and summary views of points already illustrated, touching occasionally on other points necessary to complete a view of the whole subject.

To me it seems a philological impossibility, provided we first make a thorough comparison of the third and fourth dynasties, (as presented in chaps. ii. vii. viii. xi., and fully spread before the eye of the reader in the preceding pages), to maintain that the third dynasty is not that of Alexander, or that the fourth is not that of his successors, the Grecian chiefs. But for the sake of obtaining still further satisfaction, let us for a moment reverse the method of considering the subject, and begin with the *fourth* dynasty. What are the discriminating features, the true and satisfactory diagnostics of this dynasty? I shall mention only such as I deem to be decisive and satisfactory.

(1) The *ten horns* belong to the *fourth* beast (7: 7, 19, 20, 24), and the *little horn* springs up *among them* (7: 8, 20, 24). The ten horns are *ten kings* (7: 24), and the *little horn* is the eleventh (7: 24). Now it is quite plain, from a comparison of 7: 7, 8, 23—25, with 8: 8—12, 22—25, and 11: 21—45, that the same individual is characterized in all these passages. His gradual growth, his cunning, his destructive aggressions, his persecutions, his pride, his boasting, his blasphemies, his profanation of sacred things, and his sudden and violent death, are all depicted in colors so nearly alike, and in outlines so exactly alike, (excepting that in some of the cases, e. g. in chap. xi., the sketch is much more amply filled out), that I cannot perceive any reasonable ground of doubt that they respect the same personage. But if this be a correct position, then is the fourth dynasty plainly designated beyond a reasonable question. "The little horn" did not spring from a *Roman*, but from the *Syrian* dynasty. It came up amidst ten horns, and rooted out *three of them* (7: 8, 20, 24); and if the *little horn* be Antiochus Epiphanes, then is it certain that the *ten horns*, i. e. the ten kings (7: 24), are *Syrian* and not Roman.

It is no objection to this argument, that the imagery employed in chap. viii. *varies* from that of chap. vii. What is a *bear* in 7: 5, is a *ram* in 8: 3 seq. What is a *panther* with four wings and heads in 7: 6, is a "*he-goat* that touched not the ground," with a notable horn, in 8: 5 seq. In chap. vii., the destruction of the beasts is not described severally, but collectively, (7: 11, 12); while in chap. viii., the destruction of each preceding dynasty is *severally* related (vs. 7, 8), before a new one is announced. The *diversity* of the fourth beast from all the others, is specifically declared by direct assertion in 7: 7, 19, 23, while in chap. viii. it is described by symbolic imagery, viz. "the great horn [Alexander] is broken, and in its room came up four notable ones, toward the four winds of heaven," (8: 8).

Now these four horns have no direct concern with the *ten horns* of 7: 7, 20, 24. The latter are *kings* (7, 24); the former are *kingdoms* (8: 8, 22); not kingdoms in the sense that they make what the writer, for his particular purpose, regards as *separate* dynasties, but minor kingdoms under one comprehensive view, viz. that of *Grecian sway*, or sway by Alexander's successors. So 8: 8, 22, and 11: 4, clearly show. The last or fourth is the *divided* kingdom; for it has no symbol among beasts that can be named (7: 7); it consists of *iron* and *clay* (2: 40—43); it is divided to the four winds of heaven (8: 8. 11: 4). Of course there is no incongruity between the *four horns* in 8: 8, 22, and the *ten horns* in 7: 7, 20, 24. The former merely symbolize the four great divisions of Alexander's empire (8: 21, 22. 11: 4); the latter signify *ten kings* (7: 24), which will precede "the little horn" (ib.), and *among which* this horn springs up (7: 8). The ten horns, moreover, all belong to *one* of the four great divisions; for out of *one of these four*, the little horn springs up (8: 9), which shoots forth in the midst of the ten (7: 8). Here then is no *incongruity*. It is merely a diversity in the mode of representation, grateful to the reader, and meeting the reasonable demand of aesthetics in regard to variety, in the modes of description. On the other hand, the *parallels* in the descriptions of the fourth beast, and above all in those of the *little horn*, ii. vii. viii. xi., are so striking, that *identity* of person or object in all of them seems to be a thing so evident, that fair denial is out of question.

Hengstenberg, who strenuously contends for the *Roman* dynasty as the fourth, acknowledges that the resemblances between the *little horn* in chap. vii., and the descriptions in 8: 9 seq. 11: 21 seq. are such as to constitute the most weighty argument in favor of *identity* of person in all, (Authentie des Daniel, s. 213). How then is this argument to be answered? In his view very easily, viz. 'Antiochus is the *prototype*, Antichrist the *antitype*; what had a partial fulfilment in the former, will have a complete one in the latter.' In other words, a ὑπόνοια is here to be supposed, i. e. a double sense must be given to the words. And why? "Because *Typik* is grounded in the very essence of the O. Test.," (s. 213). I deny not at all the *typical* nature of much that was Mosaic and Levitical, as to rites and ordinances. I fully assent to all which the writer of the Epistle to the Hebrews has said on this subject. But all the *types* relate to *Christ*, his offices, his sufferings, his atonement, and in a word to his whole work of redemption. Where are the types of Satan, and of his coadjutors, the *Antichrists* of the Christian period, to be found in the Jewish ritual? Hengstenberg appeals to 2 Thess. 2: 3, and avers that this is built upon Daniel. I accede; but only so far as to recognize a *similarity of description* in a case where there is *similarity of character and of action*. What does one need more to satisfy himself of such a usage among the N. Test. writers, than to turn to Matt. 2: 15, 18, 23, and compare these passages with the original Hebrew? The πλήρωσις of the N. Test. is far enough from being always a fulfilment of what is strictly *prediction*. From its very nature, a ὑπόνοια must always be merely a matter of *guessing*; for what language does not of itself speak, can only be *guessed at*. But how can we accede to a principle of interpretation so hazardous as this, and specially so indefinite and in fact undefinable?

(2) The four dynasties, whatever they are, *perish before the Messianic*

kingdom is introduced. Thus is it represented in 2: 44, 45. 7: 11, 12, 22, 26, 27. 8: 20—25. 11: 45. This is of itself so plain, and so conclusive, that it would alone be sufficient to decide that the fourth kingdom cannot be *Roman.*

(3) It lies upon the face of all the prophecies in this book, that the Messianic kingdom is their *ultimatum.* What will befall the Hebrews *before* this is introduced, is evidently the object which the prophet has in view to declare. But here, however, let it be remembered, that it is not at all his object, to give a minute civil history of all the Jewish affairs, but only to touch summarily on the most distressing of their trials. Under Antiochus they were to suffer even worse things, in some respects, than they had done under Nebuchadnezzar. Thus much disclosed, he passes over the interim, and touches upon the introduction of the *new kingdom.* Summarily does he describe even this, but he strongly asserts its *perpetuity.* To suppose Daniel to supply the place which John has filled in the Apocalypse, and to go beyond the simple generic views that I have suggested, would be to appropriate to an O. Test. writer all the views and feelings and knowledge of a Christian writer. The same spirit Daniel doubtless had. But he did not move in the same circle of action, nor did he address the same classes of readers.

(4) The difficulties that lie in the way of acknowledging the fourth dynasty to be *Roman*, not only appear great, but to me they seem insuperable. Applied to the *Roman* dynasty, what mean the *four kingdoms* in 8: 22, 8. What mean the *ten horns* in 7: 7, 20, 24 ? And the ten toes in 2: 42 ? And more than all, what means it, that Antiochus comes *from the midst of the ten horns ?* Hävernick confesses (Comm. s. 570), that "as yet the Roman history gives us no diagnostics by which we can ascertain the *ten* horns." What then is to be done ? "We must wait," says he, "with a believing confidence, that we shall yet see a time, when faith will be turned into vision, and thus will take the veil from our eyes, and make plain the secrets of the Lord." *Secrets* they are truly, and must remain so, on the ground which he takes. All hope of any intelligible meaning is out of question. But for myself, I must always doubt the soundness of a position, which forces us to conclusions like this, in regard to any matter of prediction.

But the advocates of that exegesis which assigns the *Roman dynasty* to the fourth beast turn the tables upon us, and object to the application of this symbol to the dynasty of Alexander's successors, on the ground that in this way no satisfactory account can be given, either of the *ten kings*, or of the *three* who were rooted out by the little horn, 7: 7, 8, 20, 24. Candor requires us to say, that this may be reasonably demanded of those who reject the application of what is said concerning the fourth dynasty to Rome, because they explain the prediction as applicable to a dynasty which existed and came to an end before the birth of Christ. Now as such a dynasty belongs to the history of the *past*, some probable application of the prophecy to it should be pointed out by those who decline the interpretation of Hengstenberg, if they expect to make good their position. This, as I apprehend the matter, is what may be done.

I must, first of all, ask the particular attention of the reader to what has already been intimated and explained, viz. that Daniel does not undertake to write universal history, nor even the particular history of the empires which he actually brings into view, but only describes such occurrences or personages as come in contact and conflict with the Jews, mostly to their harm and danger. The rapid outline in 7: 4—8 is proof of this; and like to this are the passages in chap. ii. viii., and also xi., with the exception of the Syrian kingdom, (the king of the north), and particularly that of Antiochus Epiphanes, 11: 21 seq. The *ten kings* belong to the *fourth beast*, as all the passages in chap. vii. show, and the little horn comes from the midst of the ten, vs. 8, 20, 24. But in 8: 8, 9, the *little horn* is expressly said to come *out of one of the four great divisions* of Alexander's kingdom. This then shows, that the generality of the dynasty as a whole is dismissed by the writer after merely touching upon it, and that he turns his attention only to that part of it which is annoying and terrible to the Jews. That the little horn means Antiochus may, after all that has been said, be taken for granted; and as he was a *Syrian*, so were the ten kings *Syrians*, whom he succeeded, inasmuch as he came from the midst of them. We have then simply to inquire, whether there were ten kings who actually preceded him in this dynasty. This inquiry seems not to be difficult.

1. Seleucus I. Nicator.
2. Antiochus I. Soter.
3. Antiochus II. Theos.
4. Seleucus II. Callinicus.
5. Seleucus III. Ceraunus.
6. Antiochus III. the Great.
7. Seleucus IV. Philopator.
8. Heliodorus.
9. Ptolemy IV. Philometor.
10. Demetrius I.
11. Antiochus Epiphanes.

All of these are unquestionable, excepting 8, 9, and 10. 'These,' says Hengstenberg (s. 208), 'were mere *pretenders* to the throne, and nothing more; whereas the text requires that they should be actual kings, and be dethroned.' I doubt whether his demand is not somewhat too strenuous here; at least a comparison with Rev. 17: 12 would not favor a construction so rigid. But be it so; we will not decline to answer even the rigid demand which he makes. Appian testifies (De Reb. Syr. c. 45), that Seleucus Philopator, when king, was destroyed by the conspiracy of Heliodorus. In the same passage he says, that Eumenes and Attalus, kings of Pergamus, in conjunction with Antiochus, and at his solicitation, deposed Heliodorus, ἐς τὴν ἀρχὴν βιαζόμενον, *who had seized by violence upon the government*. The simple history is this: Antiochus Epiphanes, son of Antiochus the Great, and brother of king Seleucus Philopator (who was destroyed by Heliodorus), had, for some years, been sent as a hostage by his father to Rome, and on his return, (being recalled by Seleucus his brother, who sent his own son Demetrius to supply his place), while at Athens, he heard of all that Heliodorus had done, and then visiting Attalus and Eumenes, on his way home, he persuaded them to assist him. Such was their interposition, that all other claims to the throne were silenced, and the parties awed into submission, without any bloodshed in the way of contest. In respect to Heliodorus, he was doubtless punished as a rebel. But still he had occupied the throne; he was "rooted out" from it by Antiochus, or (to use the language of 7: 20) "he fell before him."

The second of the three kings, "who were humbled" (7: 24), appears to be Ptolemy IV. king of Egypt. His mother, named Cleopatra, being guardian of this young child who was heir to the throne of Egypt, on the death of Seleucus Philopator, claimed the throne of Syria in behalf of her son. She was the sister of Philopator, as also of Antiochus Epiphanes, all three being children of Antiochus the Great. She claimed Palestine and Phenicia as the dower pledged to her by her father, when she was married to Ptolemy Epiphanes the king of Egypt. When her brother Seleucus was assassinated by Heliodorus, she, as already intimated, ambitious of her son's promotion, laid claim to the throne of Syria for him. We have no history of what was done to carry through her designs; for, unhappily, all the particular histories of that period which are now extant, are only a few fragments. But that she succeeded in forming a party in favor of her young son, Ptolemy IV. Philometor, seems to be a matter of fact; and also, that he had an actual investiture of the kingly office over Syria. Thus in 1 Macc. 11: 13, it is said of the prince in question: "And Ptolemy entered into Antioch, and put *two* crowns upon his head, that of Asia and of Egypt." The *Asia* named here undoubtedly means *the Syrian empire*, inasmuch as Ptolemy was now in its capital (Antioch). In Polybius' Reliquiae, XL. 12, this same prince is named "Ptolemy, *ὁ τῆς Συρίας* [*καὶ Αἰγύπτου*] *βασιλεύς*, i. e. king of Syria" [and Egypt], the latter words included in brackets being of somewhat doubtful authority. There is no good ground of doubt, however, that the Ptolemy in question is the one here named. It would seem, then, since it is certain that Antiochus got the better of all his antagonists, that Ptolemy was "*humbled* as to his claim upon the throne of Syria.

But who is the *third* king, that Antiochus *rooted out?* I cannot hesitate to say, that, so far as I can see, reference is made to *Demetrius I. Soter*, as he was afterwards named. He was the son of Seleucus Philopator, and of course the nephew of Antiochus Epiphanes. By right, i. e. by the established custom of regal succession in the monarchies of the East in general, the *inheritance* of the throne belonged to Demetrius, as soon as his father was dead. He was its rightful occupant. But Antiochus did not recall him from Rome, whither he had gone as a hostage, in order to redeem Antiochus himself from that condition. The Roman Senate could have no inducement to send him back. They kept him as a security of Antiochus' good behaviour; for in case the latter gave umbrage to the Roman power, they could set up Demetrius and urge his lawful claims against Antiochus; which would be very likely to defeat and overthrow him. Thus, by the collusion of Antiochus on the one hand, and the crafty policy of the Romans on the other, Demetrius was obliged to forego his rights as a prince, until after the death of Antiochus and his son. In this way did Antiochus defeat the claims of *three* kings, and "humble them," 7: 24. The two former of them he actually dethroned, the latter he excluded from the rightful occupation of the throne, at least so long as he and his son lived. He did indeed not actually *dethrone* Demetrius, but *he kept him out* of his throne. All this agrees well with 7: 8, 20, 24, and is sufficient to answer the demands of interpretation. He who has a *right* to a throne, and is kept from it either by the craft or violence of another, is *humbled* as to his pretensions, and *fallen* as to his purpose. All three were *rooted out* (7: 8), as to their *kingly office*, and Antiochus remained the sole and triumphant king of Syria. That all this should be done by craft, and flattery, and dexterous management, without any open war or contention, is indeed somewhat strange; but by no means impossible. See how graphically Antiochus is characterized in 8: 23, 24, but specially in 11: 21, 23, 24, 25, 27, 30, 32. "He shall come in peaceably, and obtain the kingdom by flatteries," says Daniel, 11: 21. One can hardly wonder that Porphyry was so struck with this and other like passages, as to affirm that it must have been written *post eventum*. But when Porphyry, and others since his time, suggest that Ptolemy VI. and Ptolemy VII. kings of Egypt, and Artaxias king of Armenia, are the three kings that were humbled, it seems to be a mistake. It is true that Antiochus gained victories over them in contest; but this was after some years, when he had become established in power. I understand 7: 8, 20, 24, as relating to what Antiochus did, in order to secure the throne to himself; for this is the natural implication of the passage.

What now can be done with these *ten kings*, and the *three kings* humbled by Antiochus, if the whole be referred to the *Roman* dynasty, no one can tell us. Hengstenberg and Hävernick give up the attempt, and resolve the whole into a prediction of an Antichrist yet future, and of ten future Roman kings or kingdoms, three of which are to be humbled by Antichrist; and they bid us to wait with patience, in expectation that *dies indicabit*, i. e. future events will make plain what is now dark and unintelligible. But I cannot think that a prophetic *revelation* is constructed of such material. A *prophecy* addressed to any class of men, must needs have at least some respect to the information of those for whom it is uttered, and to whom it is addressed. But for what valuable purpose a prediction altogether unintelligible can be uttered or written, it would be difficult to form any satisfactory conception.

Finally, whatever may be the difference of opinion about the *fourth beast*, and the dynasty symbolized by it, all must concede, that the facts respecting the *ten kings* and the *three kings*, as related above, are at least very singular and striking. Could there be such a coincidence between them and Daniel's prediction, unless they in reality are connected together? We may indeed concede the *possibility* of it; but can any one well defend the *probability* of it? After all that can be said on this subject, the simple but conspicuous truth, that *the Messiah's kingdom* FOLLOWS *the ruin of the four dynasties*, renders the application of the symbol of the fourth beast to the *Roman* dynasty altogether improbable, nay exegetically impossible.

Let those who are deeply versed in the prophecies of the O. Test., ask the question: Do any O. Test. predictions, in any other case whatever, describe the apostasies and the heresies that will spring up in the bosom of the *Christian church?* Unless the prediction in Dan. vii. is of this nature, no example, so far as I know, can be found. It is not impossible, I concede, that Dan. vii. may be *unique* in its kind; but unless some very good reason for a prophecy of such a character can be given, and some important object to be accomplished by it pointed out, I must regard it as altogether improbable.

On the ground that the views above given are reasonable and well supported by the laws of interpretation, our future progress in the exposition of the book before us, will be greatly facilitated. As these views appear to me just and well grounded, I must of course avail myself of them, and I shall often recur to them as matters no longer in need of a new defence, or to be regarded as mere conjectures.

In reviewing this whole subject, it seems plain to my mind, that Jerome, and others of later times, who refer the *little horn* in chap. vii. to *Antichrist*, were led to do so by the language of the N. Test., which in several instances is borrowed from Daniel, and applied to objects belonging to the period of the Christian dispensation. That like events, and like characters of this period, should be described in language borrowed as it were from ancient prototypes, is very natural, and is indeed what is often done in all parts of the New Testament. But it requires great care not to confound *prediction* with mere cases of *resemblance;* and it is a work not yet fully done, to separate the one from the other, and satisfy the intelligent inquirer where the metes and bounds actually are between the two things. This is a work, moreover, which, if well done, would dispense with any further necessity of resort to ὑπόνοια, in order to elicit the true meaning of the Old Testament. Those (and they are not a few) who find the *Pope* in the little horn, go still further than Jerome, who, although the Roman bishop in his day began sensibly to elevate himself, appears never to have thought of such an application.

(9) I continued looking, until thrones were placed, and the Ancient of Days was seated, whose garment was white as snow, and the hair of his head like pure wool, flames of fire were his throne, his wheels a burning flame.

I continued looking implies, of course, some interval of time, during which the scenes of the vision are shifted. — כָּרְסָוָן, is irreg. plur. form of כָּרְסֵא, the final א going into ו movable; the form in the text is suff.; for a fem plur., see § 31. 3. The root כסא means *to cover*, and the noun therefore designates a *seat covered* or *decked* with cloth, or other material, and so a seat for a king or chief judge, etc. The ר here is a mere euphonic substitute for the Dagh. f. in the original form כִּסֵּא, see Lex. But why the *plural?* Plainly it attaches itself to the idea of a *heavenly court* or *consessus*, where the supreme Lord and Judge is contemplated as being attended by his subordinate ministers. As to *attendants*, in such a case, of the highest rank, comp. Rev. 1: 4. 8: 2. Isa. 6: 2. 1 Tim. 5: 21. In regard to the *enthronization* of them, see Rev. 4: 4. The most distinguished ministers of the Supreme Tribunal are *seated*, as well as the Supreme Judge. In the N. Test., Christians are represented as sharing in the like solemnities, 1 Cor. 6: 2. Matt. 19: 28. Luke 22: 30. Rev. 3: 21. Not improbably such expressions as "Let *us* make man in our image;" "Let *us* go down and see;" "Who will go for *us?*" take their *plural* form from such views of the heavenly *Consessus.* The sum of the matter is, that the prophet presents the Supreme Lord and Judge to our view by imagery borrowed from earthly sovereigns, i. e. as having all the insignia of preëminence and supremacy around him. —

רְמִיו, either Part. pass. for verb, p. 51. 2, or more probably it may be 3 pl. Perf. Peal used impersonally, § 49. 3. *b*, which comes to the same sense. It refers to the action of depositing and putting in place a seat (throne), which is contemplated as being brought in and adjusted by appropriate attendants on the divine Majesty. — *The Ancient of Days* is an expression of a superlative cast, § 58. 2, meaning *He who is most ancient as to days*, the Gen. noun designating the *kind of quality* belonging to the adjective which precedes. The expression is equivalent to the French *L' Eternel*, Eng. *the Eternal.* — יְתִב, Part. pass., *was seated*, or Peal Praet. (§ 12. 2. 1) = *sat.* God is not specifically named here, but there can be no doubt that he is meant. The suppression of his proper name seems to be an indication of reverence toward the ὄνομα ἀφωνητόν, which was so customary among the Jews; see the like suppression in Gen. 32: 29. Job 24: 23 (*his eyes* for God). Isa. 17. 13. Ecc. 9: 9. Apoc. 1: 4, but an exact likeness of the case before us is in Rev. 4: 2. The attitude of *sitting* is appropriate to the dignity of the Judge, Isa. 6: 1. Ps. 9: 5 (4), 8 (7). 122: 5. The Latins say: *Judices sedent*, in order to designate the act of deciding on the part of the judges; and in like manner the Greeks. — *Whiter than snow*, in accordance with the usual custom of the Orientals, white garments being indicative of high station; e. g. in Heb., חוֹרִים, *the clothed in white*, means nobles. In case of a judge, the white garment is an indication both of dignity and purity. Comp. in the Apoc. 3: 5. 4: 4. 6: 11. 7: 9. 19: 8. — חִוָּר is an adj., § 28. *b*. 7. — *The hair of his head was like pure wool*, i. e. very white. As the *Ancient* of Days is here described, the idea of locks entirely white would not be inapposite; but in Rev. 1: 14 we find the same description of the risen Saviour, where this view of the matter would be inapposite. On the whole, therefore, I must incline to that view, which attributes the *whiteness* to exceeding splendor, like the *white heat* of a metal in the fire. The sequel shows that the divine Majesty is surrounded by fire. — *The thrones were flames*, i. e. they were exceedingly radiant and splendid. — גַּלְגִּלּוֹהִי, pl. of גַּלְגַּל, *his wheels*, implies that the throne on which the Ancient of Days is seated, is placed upon *wheels*, all which indicates rapid movement and universal presence, so to speak. See the image at full length, in Ezek. 1: 15 seq. 10: 13 seq. For the imagery of fire as accompanying the presence of the Deity, see Ex. 19: 18. 20: 18. 3: 2. Deut. 4: 24. 9: 3. Ps. 18: 9 (8). 50: 3. Ezek. 1: 4, 13, 27. Heb. 12: 29. Rev. 4: 5. *Fire* may be the symbol of *splendor*, or it may indicate a *destroying power*, or it may designate both. In the present case I should incline to the last view; for the excision of the beast follows.

(10) A stream of fire issued forth and went out from his presence; thousand thousands ministered to him, and ten thousand times ten thousand stood before him; the tribunal was seated, and the books were opened.

אַלְפִּים, a Hebraizing form, instead of the normal אַלְפִין; see the like in Ezra 4: 13, מַלְכִים. — רִבּוֹ = רִבּוֹת, sing. in form, although indicating *ten thousand*, = myriad. — רִבְבָן, fem. plur. of the same. — יְקוּמוּן, *stood, were standing*, denoting *continued* action, like the Heb. Imperf. — דִּינָא is abstract for concrete, i. e. *tribunal* or *judgment* for *judges.* — יְתִב is repeated here, in order to resume the sentence, begun with a design to indicate the process of trial. — *Books were opened*, i. e. the archives of heaven, where all of men's actions are recorded; comp. Rev. 20: 12. Dan. 12: 1. The scene here presented to view is very magnificent. The resplendence of the objects, the numbers present, and the solemnity that rests on the whole, are circumstances well adapted to strike the mind with force.

(11) I continued looking, then, because of the sound of the great words which the horn spake. — I continued looking, until the beast was slain, and its body destroyed, and it was committed to the flaming fire.

The repetition of חָזֵה הֲוֵית is here rather embarrassing to the clear run of the sentence. But I regard this repetition as a mere resumption of the sentence begun, and momentarily suspended for the introduction of other matter. The meaning seems to be, that he continued looking, until he saw the consequences of the haughty words which the beast had spoken. — קְטִילַת and יְהִיבַת, fem. Parts., having חֵיוְתָא for their subject respectively, p. 51. 2. The destruction of the beast, or little horn (Antiochus), seems to be regarded as an effectual breaking down of the fourth dynasty in the sense which is here attached to it, viz. that of an annoying power. Certain it is, that Daniel does not pursue the history of the Syrian kings beyond Antiochus. But the son of that king, and also other subsequent kings of Syria, annoyed the Jews not unfrequently, and at times very seriously. It is plain, therefore, that Daniel's *ultimatum* in his predictions, so far as the four great dynasties are concerned, is the capture and desolation of Jerusalem and of the temple — an event like to that which preceded the Babylonish exile. As such an event took place under Antiochus, the prophet's design is completed when he has described it. The minutiae of subsequent history are out of his circle of vision, and aside from his design.

An inquiry may here arise, whether the writer merely expresses in strong language the temporal destruction of the fourth beast, or whether he designs more than this, by saying that *it was committed to the flaming fire*. The likeness is very exact between the assertion here, and that in Rev. 19: 20. 20: 10, in respect to the beast, the false prophet, and Satan. Both again are closely allied with Isa. 66: 24. Lengerke contends strenuously, that the Hebrews indicated *future punishment in Sheol* by such passages. It would seem that they attached a certain degree of *sensitiveness* to a dead body, and supposed that the perpetual burning of it was adapted to torment it in a high degree. The book of Enoch, (probably written near the commencement of the Christian era), often repeats such views; e. g. 10: 16, 17. 21: 3—6. 89: 33—37. 99: 5, 7. 103: 5. 105: 21 seq., etc. Like Isa. 66: 24, the N. Test. seems to hold fast the imagery both of the *fire* and of the *worm* which devours dead bodies; see Matt. 5: 22. 18: 9. Mark 9: 43—48. See also Sirach 7: 17, and comp. Judith, 16: 17. The original image of *fire*, in such cases, or of *fire and brimstone* (as in some others), seems to have its basis in the overthrow of Sodom and Gomorrah. *Sheol* was placed by the Hebrews in the *world beneath*, see Isa. xiv.; as was Tartarus by the Greeks. The smoke, flames, and sulphuric odor of volcanic eruptions, not improbably furnished the occasion among the Greeks of the particular imagery in question. No images more dreadful could be found or imagined. Lengerke even strenuously urges, that the Jews regarded future penalties as *eternal;* which seems, in fact, to be much strengthened by the views of the book of Enoch in relation to the subject, and by those of Josephus and Philo. It is an acknowledged point, that the Greeks regarded a part of Tartarus as the *perpetual* prison of a portion of peculiar offenders. The idea of a *purgatory* they also had, which seems to have passed from the Roman to the Christian priesthood at Rome, during the fifth and sixth centuries. Daniel speaks of the beast as committed to the flame after its death; which looks as if he meant to designate a *punishment* which ensued upon the death of the body. The honorable *burning* (instead of *burying*) of the body, it would not be compatible with his design here to mention.

(12) And as to the rest of the beasts their power was taken away; but continuance in life was assigned to them, for a season and time.

As to the rest of the beasts, a clause in the Nom. absolute; as often elsewhere, e. g. 1: 17. 2: 29, 30, 32. 3: 22. 5: 18, etc. — C. B. Michaelis and Rosenmüller interpret this of *other* beasts in general, existing at the time when the fourth beast was destroyed. The sense is well enough; but the philology may be called in question. The writer brings *four* beasts into view. Of the last one only he has just related the destruction. When he now says the *rest*, what can be meant except the other *three?* The solution of the difficulty which this parenthetic verse occasions, must be looked for in another way. If the reader will cast his eye upon the preceding context, he will see that nothing is there said of the *destruction* either of the first, second, or third beast. Having now given in strong colors a sketch of the destruction of the *fourth* beast, this seems naturally to suggest, that something should be said in regard to the disappearance of the others. 'Others,' he goes on then to say, 'shared the like destiny, but not so speedily as did the little horn. They continued during the period allotted by Heaven to each.' — הֶעְדִּיו, Aph. 3 plur. of עֲדָא, impers. for pass. § 49. 3. 2. — שָׁלְטָנְהוֹן, the *dominion of them*, having a pron. pl. masc. for the suffix ; and this relates plainly to *kings*, i. e. kingdoms symbolized by the beasts; in other words, the pronoun accords with what the beasts symbolize. — אַרְכָה, lit. *prolongation*, and בְּחַיִּין designates the periods in which the three empires flourished. The *prolongation* in this case seems evidently in the way of contrast to the speedy destruction of the little horn, which comes, as the writer views the matter, to be the principal representative of the fourth dynasty. The reign of Antiochus was, in fact, only about 11 years. The *prolongation* was *for a season and time.* — זְמַן seems to come near to the meaning of our word *season*, i. e. opportune time ; while עִדָּן is a *defined* or *appointed period.* That the phrase is not intended to be minutely definite here, must be evident from the nature of the case. The three different dynasties were of very unequal duration, and of course a definite limitation of time, and the same limitation, could not be assigned to all alike. The meaning plainly is: 'For a period such as Heaven decreed. Some remained for *one time*, and some for *another time.* All was directed by the power and will of God.' The power or dominion of the beasts is here explicitly shown, by v. 12, to have been destroyed, at the time when the fourth beast was condemned and destroyed. How all this can consist with the *Roman history*, it would be difficult to show. But the endless variations of opinion concerning the passage, indicate that the application of the whole to Antichrist or to the Pope, has been the occasion of the difficulty about it. Daniel's four dynasties are not exactly dynasties of civil history, but *dynasties of prophecy.* The minute circumstances that attended them, when beginning or ending, are not detailed, with the exception of Antiochus Epiphanes in ch. xi.

Having thus disposed of the four dynasties, the writer next gives us a view of the glorious kingdom, which is the ultimate object of his prophetic contemplation.

(13) I continued to look during the visions of the night, and behold! with the clouds of heaven one like a Son of Man came, and he approached the Ancient of Days, and they brought him near before him.

בְּחֶזְוֵי לֵילְיָא, repeated from v. 2 above. The plural is used in reference to a series or succession of visions. — עִם, lit. *with*, it designates the idea of *accompanying*, i. e. the Son of Man came *accompanied* or *surrounded by clouds.* The idea doubtless is that of being enthroned on a moving cloud, and advancing with it; so in Rev. 1: 7. 14: 14. So Jehovah, in

Isa. 19: 1. Ps. 104: 3. Nah. 1: 3. The Sibylline Oracles have paraphrased this passage not unaptly:

> ἥξει ἐν νεφέλῃ ἄφθιτον ἄφθιτος αὐτός
> ἐν δόξῃ Χριστὸς σὺν ἀμύμοσι ἀγγελτῆρσι
> καὶ καθίζει κ. τ. λ.

On this account the Rabbins name the Messiah עֲנָנִי = *nubivagus*, or בַּר נִבְלִי *son of the cloud*. *Son of Man* means *a human being*, i. e. a being in human form, apparently a man. In Ezekiel, it is the usual appellation of the prophet himself. The phrase is used in this way, however, only in poetic and prophetic language. The symbols of all the four dynasties that precede, are ravenous beasts; as they might appropriately be. But here is a new kingdom, and one of an entirely different character. It is fitly symbolized, therefore, by an intelligent rational being. The symbol here is not of a *people* or *nation*, as some of the ancients interpreted it, who applied it to Jews in the time of the Maccabees. Nor is it the *holy part* of the Jewish nation, as Paulus, Jahn, Wegscheider, and Baumgarten Crusius have interpreted it. Rev. 12: 5 will not support this view, for there the *man-child* does not mean Christians, but the Messiah. Porphyry applied it to Judas Maccabaeus; upon which Jerome asks, how Judas came with the clouds, and whether his kingdom was perpetual. The sequel plainly points to the king Messiah. Here is no succession and no change of dynasty. So, moreover, the leading Rabbies, Jarchi, Saadias, Jos. Jachiades. Even the book of Enoch calls him *Son of Man*. Lengerke himself admits, that a *superhuman* nature is here assigned to him, because elsewhere God only comes in the clouds; also because angels conduct him to the throne of God, and because a universal and perpetual kingdom is assigned to him. Various reasons have been given, why the writer employs such an appellation to designate the new king. The matter, however, seems after all to be quite simple. Prophecy had declared that the Messiah would be *a son of David*, Isa. 11: 1. Mic. 5: 1, et al. The new kingdom is on earth; Christ is to appear, and act as the head of it; and to do this, he must assume a human form. Such a form angels were wont to assume, when they conversed with men. If we suppose, moreover, that Daniel in vision had a still more definite idea of the person and work of the Messiah, the name *Son of Man* might be employed by him in reference to a nature which was adapted to suffer and die; comp. Heb. 2: 14—18. 4: 15, 16. At all events, this is the *locus classicus* to explain the appellation *Son of Man*, which is given to Christ in the N. Test., and which he very often applies to himself, but which his disciples rarely indeed employed to designate him, as we find only one example, Acts 7: 56. It designates very significantly the frail and suffering condition of Jesus in his state of humiliation; while *Son of God* has reference to his higher and more exalted nature. Both appellations designate one and the same person; but one has reference to one aspect of that person, and the other to another. It is easy to see, moreover, that while *Son of Man*, in the Gospels, designates Christ in his state of humiliation it is quite remote from designating anything which is degrading. A reference of it to the passage before us, will always cast appropriate light upon it. — In הַקְרְבוּהִי, *they brought him near*, we have again the 3d plur. without any subject expressed, in the room of the pass. voice. The idea still is, that he was conducted to the throne by the attendant angels or ministering spirits.

(14) And to him was given dominion, and honor, and a kingdom, that all people, nations, and tongues should serve him; his dominion is an everlasting dominion, which shall not pass away, and his kingdom one which shall not be destroyed.

שָׁלְטָן is the *ruling power* which any one possesses, the right to rule; מַלְכוּ is the *domain* over which one rules. — יְקָר refers here rather to the *honor*, τιμή, which belongs to a king, than the mere splendor of his condition. — *The everlasting kingdom* is in contrast with other perishable dynasties, see in vs. 11, 12. Comp. also 2: 44. 4: 34. 7: 27, and the language of Gabriel to Mary, Luke 1: 32, 33. — יֶעְדֵּה, Fut. Peal, with the rough enunciation — תִתְחַבַּל, Ithpaal, fem. The דִּי, which is the subject, is fem. here, and = *one which*, or *that which*.

(15) As for me Daniel, my spirit was sorely troubled within me, and the visions of the night terrified me.

אֶתְכְּרִיַּת, 3 fem. Ithpeal, רוּחִי being of the common gender. The אֶתְ (instead of the normal אִת) in the first syllable, is Syriasm, § 25. 2. The word may mean *was sick;* but the meaning given to it above seems here to be the more probable. — רוּחִי, *my spirit*, is a periphrasis for *I*, but it is somewhat more intensive, § 43. 1. — The two following words I have translated as in the Nom. abs.; which indeed best suits our idiom. But in the Hebrew, they are in apposition with רוּחִי, and are designed not so much to be explicative of this word, as to designate the same personage intensively. — בְּגוֹ = בְּגוֹא, lit. *in the midst*, an intensive form of בְּ *in*, somewhat like our *within* instead of *in*. — נִדְנֶה, with ה ֶ paragogic, like לִבְנֶה, אַרְיֵה, etc., lit. *sheath* = body. That is, the body is to the soul, what the sheath is to the sword. Pliny (Hist. Nat. VII. 52) calls it the *sheath* (vagina) of the soul; and so spake a philosopher to Alexander the Great, who looked with contempt upon his corporeal deformity, (d'Herbelot, Bib. Orient. p. 642). Job 27: 8 seems to allude to the same figurative expression: "When God shall draw out *(extraxerit)* his soul," viz. as one draws out a sword from its sheath. Elsewhere the body is the *dwelling* of the soul; the *temple* of God's Spirit, etc. The Nasiraeans call it *robe* or *shirt;* the Rabbies, a *garment.* One idea only lies at the basis of all these figurative expressions, viz. something that covers or conceals the soul which dwells within. נִדְנֶה occurs nowhere else in the Scriptures; but with all the analogies adduced above to help us, it does not seem difficult to explain the word satisfactorily. It appears to be the object of the writer, to express the idea of *internal troubles,* while his bodily soundness was unimpaired. — It should be noted, moreover, that all this is presented as happening to him in vision, or while the vision continued; as the next verse clearly shows. The trouble that he had, seems to have arisen in part from the mournful aspect which some of the visions wore, betokening sorrow to his people and kindred, and in part from being as yet unable distinctly to understand the entire meaning of the visions. This last circumstance is fully confirmed by the inquiries that follow.

(16) I drew near to one of those who were standing by, that I might ask of him the certainty respecting all this; and he told me, that he would explain to me the meaning of the things.

קָאֲמַיָּא, Part. plur. emph. It means those who were *standing* in the attitude of ministering servants before the throne of the Ancient of Days; see in v. 10. — מִנֵּהּ, *of* or *from him,* implies asking him importunately. — וּפְשַׁר, *that the interpretation,* etc. If the verb in the Future (now at the end of the clause (stood immediately connected with the וּ, there would be no difficulty in rendering the וּ *that,* or *so that;* for nothing is more common than such a meaning of וְ at the beginning of an apodosis. But it is equally true, in Hebrew and in Chaldee, that when nouns intervene (as here) between the וְ and the verb Fut., the same meaning belongs to the whole clause as if the verb stood at the beginning. Winer has given but an imperfect account of such an idiom, in § 44. 4. — מִלַּיָּא, *matters, things,* viz. those which he had seen in his vision. — יְהוֹדְעִנַּנִי, Aph. Fut. p. 58, Rem. 1. The suff. here may be translated as in the Acc., *make me know,* or it may be regarded as virtually a Dat. with *to* or *for* to mark the relation in English, § 50. 2. *a.*

(17) As to those great beasts, which are four — four kings shall arise from the earth.

אִנִּין, fem. plur. = אִנּוּן, (omitted by Winer, p. 34), used here merely instead of the copula verb, (which usage Winer has also omitted, § 40. 1). — אַרְבְּעָה, masc. with fem. form, as the preceding אַרְבַּע is fem. with the masc. form, § 36. 2. מַלְכִין, *kings*, concrete for abstract, i. e. kings for *kingdoms*, as the sequel shows, see v. 23. The angel-interpreter speaks summarily in regard to these, and merely places them in a general point of view. The fourth kingdom, (which is afterwards resumed), is the special object he has in view, as to detail; and to this the subsequent inquiries of Daniel direct his attention. When it is said: *shall arise*, the Babylonish monarchy (one of the four) cannot be supposed to be yet *future*, inasmuch as the vision was in the first year of the last king's reign, 7:1. But—*a potiori nomen fit;* three of the kingdoms were yet future, and so they are spoken of *en masse*, and in the same way.

(18) And the saints of the Most High shall receive the kingdom, and they shall possess the kingdom for ever, yea forever and ever.

וְקַדִּישֵׁי = ἅγιοι, those consecrated to God, the pious. Jehovah says of the Hebrews, that they must be גּוֹי קָדוֹשׁ, Ex. 19: 5, 6. So those also must be, who will belong to the fifth or Messianic kingdom. This kingdom plainly supervenes, *after* the end of the four monarchies. These belonged not to the *saints*. The *pluralis excellentiae* here, עֶלְיוֹנִין, is found in no other case in Chaldee; for in this dialect, such a plural is rare, § 55. 2.

(19) Then I asked for certainty in respect to the fourth beast, which differed from all of them, was very terrible, his teeth were of iron, and his claws of brass; it devoured, crushed, and the remainder it trode down with its feet;

צְבִית, 1st pers. sing. Peal = צְבֵית, but not specially noted by Winer. — לְיַצָּבָא in the Acc., or it may be made in the Dat., and so we might translate: *wished for certainty*. — כָּלְהוֹן would be the proper pointing of the Kethibh, which is masc., agreeing with *kings* implied; the present pointing belongs to the reading כָּלְהֵן, as indicated in the margin. For the rest of the verse, see above in v. 7. One circumstance is here added, viz. *its claws were of brass*. This gives intensity to the image. It is evident, at once, that Daniel's principal solicitude has respect to the *fourth* beast. This he describes minutely, as he had first seen and described it, in order that he might place it distinctly before the interpreter's mind.

(20) And concerning the ten horns which were on his head, and another one that came up, and three fell before it, and the same horn had eyes, and a mouth speaking great things, and the look of it was stouter than that of its fellows.

This verse is the second clause of a sentence begun in v. 19, and before it, by implication, we must supply צְבִית לְיַצָּבָה. For the *ten horns*, see v. 7. For the אִתְעֲקַרוּ (so Kethibh) there, we have נְפַלוּ here, which the Qeri has changed into the fem. נְפַלָה, without any necessity, for *kings* are the implied subject; see in v. 7 on אִתְעֲקַרוּ. The next clause runs literally thus: *And as to that horn, eyes were to it.* For this and the next clause, see v. 8 above. — חֶזְוַהּ, suff. form of חֵזוּ, like a Heb. Segholate, lit. *the look* or *appearance of it.* — רַב *great* literally, but when applied to a *look*, it may mean what is expressed by our word *stout*, i. e. haughty, swaggering. But the clause may also mean nothing more, than that the appearance of the horn which sprang up, was greater as to magnitude than the appearance of the others, — חַבְרָתַהּ, fem. pl. with suff. fem. sing. relating to the horn; for suff. see p. 36 top. How the *little* horn could appear greater than the others, is easily explained. While the seer was looking at it, it became larger and larger, until it came to exceed the rest. We should not apply this to the mere extent of Antiochus' sway, but to the gradual strengthening of his own personal influence, by overcoming the parties in favor of other claimants of the crown, and specially does it apply to his becoming altogether more formidable to the Jews, than any other of the Syrian princes.

(21) I continued looking, and that horn made war with the saints, and prevailed against them.

What is here expressed in Daniel's relation of his vision to the angel, is omitted in his statement of it above; see v. 8 above, which compares with v. 20 here, but after the 8th verse, the matter of v. 21 is omitted. Daniel's agitation, in regard to what will be done by the little horn, and his desire of an explanation respecting it, lead him to be more minute concerning it, in his relation to the angel. — עָבְדָא, Part. fem.; in Chald. עֲבַד usually means *to make, do, practise;* while in Hebrew this is the less usual meaning — *to serve* being the common one. — קְרָב, § 28. *a.* 2. — יָכְלָה, Part. fem. Both the participles here plainly designate *continued action.* — לְהֹן I have translated *against them*, because the Eng. idiom demands this. We might render literally thus: *It was superior to them*, or *it prevailed in respect to them.* The writer of the Apocalypse has employed the same language in describing the contest of the beast with the two witnesses, Rev. 11: 7; with the saints, Rev. 13: 7; and with the Messiah, Rev. 19: 19. But to argue from this, that the Apocalyptist has the same personage in view as Daniel, because he applies Daniel's language to his own purposes of description, would betray very little acquaintance with the usages of the N. Test. writers.

(22) Until the Ancient of Days came, and the tribunal was seated for the saints of the Most High, and the appointed time came, and the saints possessed the kingdom.

Comparing this with vs. 9 seq. above, it will be seen that the substance of vs. 9—14 is here presented in a single verse. The reason of this is plain. Daniel already understood the *Messianic* part of the vision. His inquiries respected the fourth beast, and specially the little horn. He therefore enlarges on that part of the description, and compresses all besides. — דִּינָא וגו׳, see v. 9, abstract for concrete, *judgment* for *judge*. — עֶלְיוֹנִין, plur. see v. 18. — הֶחֱסִנוּ, instead of the normal הַחְסִנוּ in Aphel; it is simply a Heb. Hiphil form, p. 50, top. In vs. 9—14 above, the *leader* or *head* of the new and final kingdom is made altogether conspicuous; but here the same dominion is characterized, by describing the character of those who belong to it — *the saints of the Most High.*

(23) He replied thus: As to the fourth beast, there shall be a fourth kingdom in the earth, which shall differ from all the other kingdoms, and it shall devour all the earth, and tread upon it, and crush it.

Comp. v. 7 above, where the same summary account of the fourth dynasty is given. — מַלְכְוָתָא, emph. plur. fem. of מַלְכוּ. — וְתֵאכֻל, § 21. *a*, *it shall devour* = it shall destroy. — תְּדוּשִׁנַּהּ, Fut. Peal of דּוּשׁ, with augmented suff., p. 58. Rem. 1. — תַּדְּקִנַּהּ, Aph. Fut. of דְּקַק, with suff. as before. Both of the suffixes here are written, in some Codices, נַּהּ—; which merely shows how unsettled a part of the Chaldee vocalization is. — *Tread upon it*, דּוּשׁ, means trampling upon anything so as to crush it. But here the *crushing* is designated more graphically by a stronger verb, תַּדְּקִנַּהּ, which means *to crush into minute pieces.* The whole is vivid imagery of the great ravages made by the fourth beast. But as this was a *compound* beast (8: 8), consisting of four kingdoms, it was doubtless a matter of desire to Daniel, to know which of these must be expected to perform the work of destruction. The sequel tells us the particulars of the matter in question. — *All the earth* of course has reference here to "the glory of all lands," i. e. to Palestine; for the history of the whole world is not intended to be given, but only of that part of it which had to do with the people of God. The devastations committed in Palestine by Antiochus, are well described in the first book of the Maccabees, and tolerably in Josephus. It is clear, that the Jews were treated with severity and even reckless cruelty, such as Antiochus scarcely indulged with respect to any other nation. That the phrase in question — *all the earth* — often designates some particular country, and not literally the whole world, needs not any proof for the critical reader.

(24) And as to the ten horns — out of that kingdom ten kings shall arise; and another shall arise after them, and he shall differ from those who preceded, and three kings shall he humble.

מִנַּהּ *from the same*, the demonstrative meaning being designated by the position of the pronoun before the noun, § 43. 6. *b.* — *Ten kings shall arise*, not ten kingdoms, although *horn* might designate *kingdom*, as it does in 8: 8. But here the sequel shows that *kings* must be meant. — *Another shall arise after them*, comp. v. 8 above. There, instead of אַחֲרֵיהוֹן *after them*, we have בֵּינֵיהוֹן *among them*. The basis of the idea is the same in both. The writer means, that the little horn was from the same source as the others which preceded it. It sprang up *among them*, and came *after them* in succession. Antiochus Epiphanes was a son of Antiochus the Great, and a brother of Seleucus IV. Philopator, who was assassinated by Heliodorus. — *He was different from those who preceded him*, which was most fully true, specially as it respected his treatment of the Jews, (which doubtless is what this phrase alludes to), as well as actually in point of personal character.—*And three kings shall he humble*, viz. Heliodorus, Ptolemy IV. Philometor, and Demetrius the lawful heir to the throne; see on v. 8 above. Here the angel-interpreter mollifies the stronger verbs that had been used by Daniel, in v. 8 אֶתְעֲקַרָו, in v. 20 נְפַלוּ; which shows that the *rooting out* and the *falling* have respect to the *regal office*, not to the life of the kings. יְהַשְׁפִּל, Hebraizing Aph. with 'prefix ה retained, p. 49. 5; also p. 50 top, for the final Hhireq. *To humble* means to disappoint of their aspiring lofty claims to kingly authority. Heliodorus was doubtless treated as a rebel; but the life of the others was not molested. Such an interpretation has good authority for its voucher, viz. that of the angel-interpreter in using the verb יְהַשְׁפִּל. The passage being understood as he explains it, the death of three kings is not at all necessary to the fulfilment of the prophetic vision.

(25) And words shall he utter against the Most High, and the saints of the Most High shall he vex, and he shall think to change times and law, and they shall be given into his hand for a time, times, and the dividing of time.

לְצַד, lit. *to the side*, i. e. against, like the Latin *adversus*. — עִלָּיָא (so the Kethibh), *the exalted One*, of course means the Most High. — לְקַדִּישֵׁי, Acc. after יְבַלֵּא, the last being Pael Fut., and meaning *consume away, vex, harass*. — יִסְבַּר, *think, hope, expect*. — לְהַשְׁנָיָה, Inf. Aph. — זִמְנִין, *appointed times*, such as feasts, etc., in reference to the laws of Moses which set apart many of these. — דָּת means *law* in general; but here, as the reference is made to religious matters, it must mean the religious laws of Moses. In 6: 6, the word is plainly employed in such a sense. — עִדָּנִין pl. because the dual is wanting in the Chaldee. The nature of the case shows that *two times* is the probable sense here. The *singular* noun most naturally means a *year*, which is a *defined* period of time. So in 4: 13, *seven times* = seven years. The *half* of this period is designated by the phrase *time, times and dividing of time,* which last expression means *half year*. The like in Hebrew, in Dan. 12 : 7 and in 9: 27, we find *half of a week* or *heptade* [viz. of years]. See also the same in the Apoc. 12: 14, comp. 13: 5. 11: 2, 3. 12: 6. A comparison of all these passages seems to settle the matter conclusively, that the prophetic year consists of 360 days = 12 months at 30 days each. It is of importance to note this ; for accuracy of calculation must depend on it.

Is this expression of time poetical merely and figurative, consisting of round numbers (as they say), and comprising just half of the mystical number *seven*, which is so often employed in a kind of tropical way ? *Historical facts* seem to speak for the *literal* interpretation, in the book before us. Yet, considering the nature of the case and of the number usually concerned with such reckonings, (i. e. the number *seven*), we surely need not be solicitous about a day, a week, or even a month, more or less. The convenience of the reckoning, when it is near enough to exactness for all the purposes of prophecy, is very obvious, and will account for adopting it.

In exhibiting the historical facts, we will begin with an era which is certain, viz. the time when Judas Macc. expurgated the temple, and began the service of God anew. This was on the 25th of Dec. 148 ann. Sel. = 165 B. C., see 1 Macc. 4: 52. Counting back three and a half years, we come to June in 145 A. S. = 168 B. C. Livy has described the retreat of Antiochus from Egypt, in the *early spring* (primo vere, Liv. xlv. 11.) of that year. While on that retreat, Antiochus detached Apollonius, one of his military chieftains, to lay waste Jerusalem, (comp. 2 Macc. 5: 11, which makes the time clear), for he had heard that the Jews exulted at his misfortune, in being obliged by the Romans to retreat from Egypt, and he was determined to wreak his vengeance on them. He did so effectually, as 1 Macc. 1: 29 seq. fully shows ; and vs. 29, 20, of the same chapter, compared together, show that the year was 145 A. S. as above stated. From June, when Jerusalem was probably taken, to December, is six months ; and from December in 168 to December, 165, is three years. In the same way, as to time, does Josephus reckon, Proem. ad Bell. Jud. § 7. But to avoid perplexity, it should be noted that a different mode of reckoning, viz. *three years*, is sometimes employed. E. g. in 1 Macc. 4: 54, and 2 Macc. 10: 5, such a method appears to be implied ; and so in Jos. Ant. Jud. XII. 7. 6. An examination of the context in these cases shows, however, that this period designates only the time that intervened between the profanation of the temple by heathen sacrifices, 1 Macc. 1: 54, and the consecration of it by Judas Maccabaeus, 1 Macc. 4: 54. Some six months after capture of the city, during which all manner of cruelties and excesses were committed, appear to have elapsed before Antiochus began his *swinish* offerings in the temple. The consecration of the temple by Judas introduced regular Hebrew worship there; and the death of Antiochus happening shortly afterward, the period of his oppression was of course at its end. Thus did events correspond very exactly with the time designated in our text. We cannot indeed specify the exact *day*, because history has not done this ; but it is enough, that we come so near to the time designated, as to remove all serious difficulty respecting it.

Other passages corresponding, as to time, with the verse before us, may be found in Dan. 9: 27. 12: 7, and, with some modifications, the periods marked in 12: 11, 12, harmonize with these. The discussion respecting them, however, may be deferred until we come in course to consider them.

---

(26) And the tribunal shall be seated, and his power shall be taken away, to abolish and to destroy it for ever.

The tribunal, etc. comp. v. 9. *His dominion*, viz. that of the fourth beast, or rather of that *other king* mentioned in v. 24. — יְהַעְדּוֹן, Fut. Aph. with ה retained, from עֲדָא, 3 pl. without any subject, and so used in a *passive* sense, § 49. 3. *b*. The two verbs that follow are in Inf. Aphel, and I have so translated them; but as such an Infinitive often stands in a parallel construction with clauses having *definite* verbs, we might here translate: *it shall be abolished and destroyed*, etc. Winer has failed to illustrate this idiom; but see in my Roed. Heb. Gram. § 129. 3. Note 2. — עַד סוֹפָא, *in perpetuum*, as Jerome well translates it; or, if one insists on retaining the shade of idea, we may translate: *to the end*, i. e. of all things, the *final end*. It may have another shade of meaning, viz. *utterly*, *finally*.

(27) And the kingdom, and dominion, and power of the kingdoms under the whole heaven, shall be given to the people of the saints of the Most High; their kingdom shall be an everlasting kingdom, and all dominions shall serve and obey them.

רְבוּתָא hardly means *greatness*, i. e. extent, in this passage. It is rather the equivalent of δύναμις. The meaning of the whole clause is, that the dominion and power of all kingdoms shall be united and concentrated in the new or Messianic kingdom. — יְהִיבַת, Part. pass. fem. p. 51. — לְעַם, *to the people*, etc. In vs. 13, 14 above, the Head of this new kingdom is presented as taking the dominion. Here the subjects of that kingdom *en masse* are described as possessing it. The N. Test. often presents Christians as *reigning with Christ*. — מַלְכוּתֵהּ, not *his*, as referring to the Most High, but *its* (or as we must express it *their*) referring to the *people* possessing the dominion. So לֵהּ *it* (Acc. or Dat.) has reference to the *people* who possess the supremacy, and so I have translated it *them*. — יִשְׁתַּמְּעוּן, Ithpaal, § 10. 5. *b*.

(28) Here is the end of the matter. As for me Daniel, my thoughts greatly disquieted me, and my color was changed upon me, but I kept the matter in my own mind.

עַד־כָּה *unto here*, i. e. at this point, was the termination both of the vision and the explanation. The death of the fourth beast, or of the *other king*, and the subsequent new kingdom, was the end or completion of all that was disclosed. Some refer עַד־כָּה merely to the end of the angel's disclosure; with less probability. — זִיוַי, lit. *my splendors*, describes vividly the shining appearance of the skin in full health and strength. Paleness supervened in this case, and this is what the writer means to say. — יִשְׁתַּנּוֹן, Fut. Ithpaal of שְׁנָא, § 10. 5. *b.* — עֲלַי, *over me* or *upon me*, i. e. over the surface of the whole body. The last clause in the verse may denote either that Daniel revolved the whole matter carefully in his own mind, or that he kept it to himself, without communicating it to others; which, on the whole, I deem the more probable meaning. Light he could not well expect from others; and by keeping the thing to himself, he would avoid many importunate if not impertinent questions.

CHAPTER VIII. INTRODUCTION.

[In the third year of Belshazzar's reign, Daniel saw another vision, subsequent to that related in ch. vii. In this vision he was transferred to Shushan on the river Ulai, in the province of Elam, (the capital of the future Persian empire), vs. 1, 2. Here he saw a ram, with two elevated horns, the one being higher however than the other, but more recent as to its origin. In various directions did the ram push, and nothing could stand before him, vs. 3, 4. Upon this, a he-goat made his appearance, bounding over the earth without seeming to touch it; and this goat had a notable horn between his eyes, v. 5. He came to the ram with fury, smote him, broke his horns, and trode him down, while there was none to rescue, vs. 6, 7. The he-goat now became very great, and at the height of his power, his great horn was broken in pieces, and there came up four other notable horns in its room, v. 8. From one of these sprang up a little horn, which waxed great toward the south, and east, and the goodly land of the Hebrews, v. 9. It waxed so great that it assailed the host of heaven [the sacred officiators in the temple], and some of these it cast down and trode upon, v. 10. Even the prince of that host [the God of the temple] was deprived by him of his daily sacrifice, and laws and ordinances were prostrated, and success attended the undertakings of the tyrannical oppressor, v. 12. While contemplating this scene of desolation, the prophet hears one of the holy angels asking another, how long this state of things is to continue, v. 13. The answer is 2300 days, at the close of which the sanctuary will be vindicated, v. 14. Daniel makes for himself still further inquiry respecting the meaning of the vision; an angel, on the river's bank, requires Gabriel (the angel-interpreter, to make the requisite explanation, vs. 15, 16. This angel approaches Daniel, who swoons, and is lifted up and revived by his kind interpreter, vs. 17, 18. Gabriel informs him, that he shall make particular disclosures respecting what is to happen at the last part of the season of affliction, v. 19. He says, that the ram symbolizes the kings of Media and Persia; the he-goat, the king of Grecia; the great horn is its first king, and the breaking of it is the ruin of his empire; out of this ruin shall arise four dynasties, with inferior power, vs. 20—22. In after-times shall arise from one of them a king, cruel, cunning, a fearful destroyer, specially of the holy people, vs. 23, 24. By his craft and sagacity, he will destroy many without waging war; on account of his success, he will become haughty and set himself against the Prince of princes; by whom he shall be dashed in pieces, v. 25. Daniel is assured, that the vision is true, and he is directed to seal it up, because it pertains to a distant future, v. 26. Daniel again swoons, and is afterwards sick for some days. He after this returns to his ordinary official business, v. 27.]

It is plain, at first view, that the Babylonish monarchy is here omitted. Twice (ch. ii. vii.) had it already been described, and it was now near its close, and nothing specially worthy of particular note, in respect to the Jews, was to take place before that close. To Daniel, therefore, a further disclosure is made, in regard to those empires which would be particularly concerned, in future, either with favoring his countrymen or with annoying them. These were mainly the second and fourth dynasties, (so named in reference to ch. vii.) The third seems to be here introduced mainly because it stands between the Medo-Persian dominion and that of the fourth beast.

As might naturally be expected, Daniel, as he approaches nearer to the events predicted, becomes more specific in his statements respecting them. For example, in ch. vii. no account is given of the manner in which the second or Medo-Persian empire is overthrown ; but here, in vs. 5—7, we have a graphic account of its fall. In ch. vii, no account is given of the manner in which the third beast perishes and the fourth beast arises ; but in v. 8 here we have one specifically given. In ch. vii, the little horn is merely said to arise among the other ten horns of the fourth beast ; here it is stated, that it arose out of one of the four dominions of the last empire. In ch. vii, the blasphemous, boasting, persecuting character of the little horn is merely glanced at, (vs. 8, 24, 25) ; but here we have a full detail, as it were, of cruelties and abominations, vs. 9—12, 23—25. In ch. vii, we have a designation of the time, during which the desolations of Jerusalem and the temple shall take place beyond all former example (v. 25) ; while in ch. viii, we have a different designation of time, in respect to matters which are of wider extent. Finally, the whole circle of beasts in ch. vii, are different from those introduced in ch. viii. The beasts here are not chosen so much with reference to their rabid and destructive nature, as with reference to their active and rapid movements.

If any reader should be tempted to think it strange, that the same subjects should be repeated, even with additional specifications, (as is particularly the case with the fourth dynasty in this book, in chaps. ii. vii. viii. xi., and above all with the description of the little horn or Antiochus Epiphanes), he needs only to turn to Isaiah, and ask how often the Assyrian invasion is there depicted ; or to the prophets in general and ask : How many are the prophecies respecting the destruction of Babylon, Egypt, Moab, Tyre, Philistia, etc. The answer to these questions will remove any difficulty which the book before us seems to present, in regard to repetition.

In fact, how can we be competent to decide, how often peculiar circumstances among the Hebrews demanded a renewal of the same subject?

But in the present case, the later predictions are seldom, if ever, mere repetitions of the preceding ones. New circumstances are developed; or the subject is placed in a new attitude; or it is connected with some promise or threatening. In a word, there is always something in the later prediction, to adapt it to the time when it was uttered.

In the case before us, the time drew near when the Medo-Persian dynasty would commence. Before that period, the Jews were to change their outward circumstances in no important respect. The writer, therefore, now begins with the dynasty which would make a change. And in order to obtain an appropriate place of vision, he is transferred in his ecstasy to the capital of the Medo-Persian empire, and from its tower or citadel he looks out over the ground of empires yet future. And inasmuch as, from the nature of the case, the later vision is more specific than the earlier ones, it affords us very important aid in the explanation of what might otherwise be dubious from its brevity or generality, in the preceding oracles.

(1) In the third year of the reign of Belshazzar the king, a vision appeared to me, to me Daniel, after that which appeared to me in the beginning.

The reader will note, that the *Hebrew* language is now employed, and so through the remainder of the book. The Grammar to which reference is made, is the one quoted under chap. i. v. 1.—נִרְאָה, Niph. reflexive, *shewed itself*, i. e. appeared. — אֲנִי in the Dat. because the pronoun is repeated; see in Roed. Heb. Gramm. § 119. 3.—הַנִּרְאָה, הַ with Dagh. f. has the form of the article, but it is here a pronoun, *which* or *that which*, § 107. 1.—בַּתְּחִלָּה, lit. *in the beginning*, which however is equivalent in usage to our word *formerly, at first*. The reference plainly is to the vision in the first year of Belshazzar, recorded in chap. vii. This is a sufficient answer to Bertholdt's affirmation, that different persons were the authors of chap. vii. and viii. The necessary inference here is, that the same individual was the seer in both cases.

(2) And I saw in vision, and it was so, that while I saw, I was in Shushan the citadel, which is in the province of Elam, yea I saw in vision when I was by the river Ulai.

I saw in vision designates the prophetic ecstasy in which he was. The *place* of the vision is designated in two different ways. First, it is said to be *in Shushan the citadel* or *palace*, which was a portion of the city of Shushan, and doubtless was the germ from which the city sprang. The fortified part of the city, i. e. the citadel, would be of course the most probable place of the king's abode. In the book of Esther, the word בִּירָה denotes both *citadel* and *city;* in 3: 15, it has both meanings in the same verse. There can be no reasonable doubt, that this city was the leading capital of the new Medo-Persian dynasty. It lay on the river Choaspes, about some 250 miles east of Babylon. — *Elam the province* (so the Hebrew runs) shows, that *Elam*, at the time of writing, either did not mean the whole of Persia, (as however it often does), or else that Persia itself was then only a *province* of the Median, or of the Babylonian, empire. No satisfactory evidence seems to have been produced, that Babylon, at this period, held dominion over any part of the Median territory. Still, from the proximity of Elam to Babylonia, and from the fact that the Median kings had frequent difficulties with the Babylonish ones, it may, at that period, have been made a tributary province of Babylon. Our accounts of the minor political changes, in ancient times, in different countries beyond the Tigris, are so very imperfect, that no reliance can be placed on any *argumentum a silentio* made out from a lack in these sources, against the position just mentioned. But be this as it may, it is certain that in Daniel's time Persia was not independent, until near the close of his life, and that if it was not under the supervision of Babylon, it was at least a *province of Media*. — *I was by the river Ulai*, gives the *specific* locality, for purposes apparent in the sequel. The whole clause is parallel to the preceding one, and differs only in marking the locality with more minuteness. Both Pliny (Hist. Nat. VI. 31), and Arrian (Exp. Alex. VII. 7), make mention of the river *Eulaeus* at Susa or Shushan; but Herodotus and Strabo appear to call the same river *Choaspes*. The confusion of names among the Greek and Latin writers, with respect to the East, is not unfrequently great and quite perplexing. For example; Ctesias puts Nineveh on the *Euphrates;* Pliny, on the *west* of the Tigris; the Syriac Version puts Euphrates for *Tigris*, in Dan. 10: 4; and Lucian places Seleucia on the *Euphrates*, (Dea Syr. § 18). Enough for our purpose, that Ulai was at least one of the names by which the river that flows around Shushan was known. — But why *such a locality?* Because the prophet's present vision begins with the Medo-Persian empire, and Shushan was to be its capital. And why on the *river's bank?* Not because the Jews were wont to build *prayer-houses* in such places, Acts 16: 13; nor because Ezekiel had visions on the Chaboras, 1: 1, 3. 3: 15, 23 al., (Leng.); nor because of the solitude of the place (Maur.); but simply, as I understand it, because the castle (בִּירָה) stood on the banks of the river. The mention of the river, however, would still be in a measure superfluous, were not this mention a preparation for what is said in v. 16.

As to all the difficulties that have been raised, by asserting that Shushan did not belong to Babylon, in Daniel's time, and that he could not be there on the king's business (v. 27), and the like, it would be easy to reply, that the first cannot be proved, and that the second presents no real difficulty. The Babylonian king might surely have some business with the province of Elam, although it did not belong to his domain; and he might have sent Daniel to do it. But we have a readier answer, viz. that Daniel is on the Ulai *merely in vision*, not physically. So Pharaoh was on the banks of the Nile, Gen. 41: 1; Ezekiel (at the river Chebar) was in Jerusalem, 8: 3, and in the land of Israel, 40: 2. So John (while at Patmos) was taken to the wilderness, Rev. 17: 3, comp. 21: 10. This settles all difficulties at once, and comparing vs. 2: 27, one can see no room to doubt the correctness of this view.

(3) And I lifted up my eyes, and looked, and lo! a ram standing before the river, and he had two horns, and the two horns were high, but one was higher than the other, and the higher one sprang up last.

אֶשָּׂא, Kal. Imperf. of נָשָׂא. — הָאוּבָל, with art. referring to the same word in v. 2. — קְרָנַיִם, a dual which must come from קָרָן instead of the usual קֶרֶן. — הַשֵּׁנִית, lit. *the second*, which of course here means *the other*. — עֹלָה, Part. Pres. fem. denoting *continued* action, so that, during the vision, the prophet saw the last horn in an increasing state; comp. 7: 20. In 8: 20, the interpreter declares that the *ram* symbolizes *the kings of the Medes and Persians*. The imagery, then, which is here employed, corresponds very exactly with historical facts. The two horns are Media and Persia. The first of these, Media, was an independent kingdom long before Persia was anything but a province. But ever after Cyrus came to the throne, Persia was the *leading* kingdom. So the higher horn came up last.

(4) I saw the ram thrusting westward, and northward, and southward, and none of the beasts stood before it, nor did any deliver out of his hand, and he did according to his pleasure, and became haughty.

מְנַגֵּחַ, *to thrust at, to strike with violence*, in vulgar language *to butt*, in Latin *arietare*. This characterizes the impetuous assaults of Cyrus and Darius on foreign countries. — *Westward*, viz. Babylonia, Mesopotamia, Syria, Asia Minor; *northward*, Colchis, Iberia, Armenia, the Caspian regions; *southward*, Palestine, Egypt, Lybia, Ethiopia, etc. *Eastward* is not mentioned, for the Persians made no considerable conquests there until Darius' time, and then not of a permanent nature. After the Part. מְנַגֵּחַ the noun *beast* is implied, as the next clause shows. — חַיּוֹת is a symbol of *kingdoms*. — לֹא יַעַמְדוּ, *could not stand up*, i. e. could not maintain an erect and firm position, or (in other words) they were prostrated.

— מִיָּדוֹ, lit. *from his hand*, i. e. from his power; *constructio ad sensum.* — וְהִגְדִּיל, Hiph. but without any Acc. after it, i. e. Hiph. absolute. In such a case, this verb means: *behaved haughtily, acted proudly*, see Lam. 1: 9. Zeph. 2: 8. Flushed with success, we know from all quarters that the Persian kings assumed a haughty position. So Croesus, (in Herod. I. 89): *Πέρσαι . . . ὑβρισταί*: and so Aeschylus (Pers. v. 795), *ὑπέρκομποι ἄγαν.*

(5) And I was considering, and lo! a he-goat came from the west, on the face of all the earth, and he touched not the face of the ground; and as to the goat, a conspicuous horn was between his eyes.

הָיִיתִי מֵבִין denotes very prominently the *continued* action of a reflecting mind. — צְפִיר, lit. *the leaper*, i. e. *hircus.* — הָעִזִּים, from עֵז, which designates the genus *capra.* The addition of this word to צְפִיר, seems to indicate that this latter word of itself was not definite enough for the purpose of the writer. — *Came over* or *upon all the earth*, and *touched not its surface*, conveys a very vivid impression of the rapidity and irresistible force of Alexander's army in its marches and battles. So in 1 Macc. 1: 3: *διῆλθεν ἕως ἄκρων τῆς γῆς.* The first expression in our text denotes the extent of the conquests; the last, the rapidity with which they were achieved. In 7: 6, the panther has *four wings;* which conveys the like idea. Virgil (VII. 806 seq.) presents an expanded but beautiful image of Camilla, as skimming over the fields, and then over the ocean without tinging her feet; but it lacks the energy of the clause before us. — קֶרֶן חָזוּת, lit. *cornu adspectûs, a horn of visibility* or *conspicuity* (sit venia!). The meaning seems to be, that from its magnitude it was particularly conspicuous. Theodotion, very exactly: *κέρας θεωρετόν.* The pointing of De Wette, חַזּוּת (from حَزَّ), and the rendering by *sharp-pointed horn*, is ingenious, but unnecessary, and indeed less significant than the form above. The word *horn* is employed as the emblem of *power.* Rev. 5: 6. 13: 1. Zech. 1: 18, 19, al.; of *kingdoms* as Dan. 8: 8, 3; and also of *kings*, 7: 20, 24. In the text before us, the one *notable horn* symbolizes the one or sole dominion of Alexander in a very expressive way. — *Between his eyes* evidently is intended to designate its peculiar annoying power, in thrusting at those who opposed it, the position rendering it formidable.

(6) And he came to the ram which had two horns, which I had seen standing before the river, and ran to him in his strong indignation.

בַּעַל הַקְּרָנַיִם, lit. *master* or *possessor of two horns*, see בַּעַל in Lex. The Koran and the Orientals generally give to Alexander, the title *two-*

horned, in order to indicate his power and vehemence. — *He ran to him*, indicates the velocity of his movements. — *In the indignation of his power* (lit.) means *with strong* or *vehement impetuosity*, or *ardor*. כֹּחוֹ is the Gen. of quality.

(7) And I saw him as he approached near the ram, and he became enraged at him, and he smote the ram, and brake in pieces his two horns; and there was no strength in the ram to stand before him, for he cast him down to the earth and trode upon him, and there was none to afford deliverance to the ram out of his hand.

מַגִּיעַ, Hiph. Part. of נָגַע, lit. *an approacher*, or (like a Greek participle with its adsignifications) *as* or *when approaching*. — הִתְמַרְמַר, Hithpalpel of מָרַר, is intransitive, and so it is followed by אֶל to indicate the direction of the rage. — וַיַּךְ, Imperf. Apoc. of נָכָה, in Hiph., the Kal form not being in use. — אַרְצָה, with ה ָ *local*, § 88. 2. *a*. — לָאַיִל, לְ p. 190. *c*; it may be in the Acc. governed by the Part. before it, or we may make it Dat. by translating as above.

(8) And the he-goat waxed exceedingly great, and when he became powerful, the great horn was broken, and there sprang up the appearance of four in its room, toward the four winds of heaven.

Alexander, at the very height of his power, died suddenly at Babylon, B. C. 323. — *Sprang up the appearance of four*, i. e. of four horns, the symbol of four kingdoms. But this construction is somewhat doubtful, for חָזוּת may here mean, as before, *aspectabile*, i. e. something prominent and visible. If so, then קְרָנוֹת should be mentally supplied before it, as v. 5 teaches us. So Leng., *four large horns*. I still have doubts, whether חָזוּת here is not to be taken adverbially, as marking the distinctness of the appearance = *visibly, palpably*; or possibly it may mark simply the *appearance* in the sense of *apparently, seemingly*. But of this last meaning, I cannot find parallels elsewhere; yet it is so evidently within the compass of the word, that they are not much needed. As to *historical facts*, the Grecian empire was at first nominally left to Alexander's son, but in reality never came to him. The military chieftains of the different countries subdued by Alexander, fought continually with each other; and it was some twenty years after the death of Alexander, before the famous division into *four* monarchies came to be fully made and established. But of these subordinate events, it is not to the writer's purpose to take any particular notice. Chap. 11: 4 shows, quite plainly, that a complete end of Alexander's dominion, as such, was made by his death. Porphyry names the four kingdoms, in a generic way, Macedonia, Syria, Asia, Egypt. But these names must not be strictly taken. They are so named by him, merely on the principle that *a potiori nomen fit*.

(9) And from one of them sprang up a little horn, and it waxed great abundantly toward the south, and toward the east, and toward the goodly land.

מֵהֶם *of them*, masc., while *horns*, קְרָנוֹת, is fem. But the concord here is *ad sensum*, *kings* being symbolized by the horns. The same of יָצָא the masc. verb, § 143. 2. — מִצְּעִירָה, lit. *of smallness*, the fem. adj. being used as an abstract noun, § 105. 3. *b*. This meaning is made clear by זְעֵירָה in 7: 8. The meaning *more than small*, i. e. large, made by taking the מִ in a *comparative* sense, seems to have no good foundation here. Indeed the next clause refutes this; for, from a state of smallness, the horn *waxed exceedingly great*. — יֶתֶר is used adverbially. — *The south* means Egypt, into which Antiochus Epiphanes made four military incursions, for the most part successfully. — *Toward the East*, viz. Persia or Elymais, whither Antiochus made a predatory excursion, but at last met with a repulse there, when robbing a temple; and soon after this he died; comp. 11: 41—44. — הַצֶּבִי, lit. *the glory, the ornament* = אֶרֶץ הַצְּבִי in 11: 41, i. e. *the land of glory*, or *the glorious land*, an honorary name of Palestine. In the mind of a Hebrew, this appellation was fraught with meaning; let the reader compare Ezek. 20: 6, 15. Jer. 3: 19. The frequent incursions of Antiochus into Palestine, are of course well known to all who have any knowledge of ancient history.

(10) And it magnified itself even to the host of heaven, and it cast down to the earth some of the host and of the stars, and trampled upon them.

עַד, *to, unto, usque ad*, stronger than אֶל. The elevation is, in this way, made even more than superlative. But what is *host of heaven?* Everything depends on a right view of this word, as to the exegesis here. I have examined all the cases in which the sacred writings employ צָבָא, both sing. and plural. They are easily reduced to order. I rank first the generic idea, in the verbal stem, of *going forth in a company* or *band*. Hence the usual meaning of the noun צָבָא, *host, army*, and so *warfare*, trop. *hard service, trouble*. The great mass of examples is of this nature. But there are off-shoots from this stem. The generic idea of *band* or *company*, simply, may be found in Ps. 68: 12 (11). This is applied often to the multitude of stars, i. e. *host of heaven;* see Lex. In a few cases, also, where the sing. is employed, to the *angels*, e. g. 1 K. 22: 19. 2 Chron. 18: 18. Isa. 24: 21; but with the plur., e. g. *Jehovah of hosts, God of hosts*, etc., in an overwhelming mass of examples; see Fürst, Conc. Heb. It is remarkable, that all of these, except *four*, omit the article; which shows that the word צְבָאוֹת acquired something of the quality of a proper name. These last expressions also, for the most part, refer to the *angelic hosts;* some of them may apply to both stars and angels, in a generic sense. The

Sept. gives a great variety of versions; but the leading ones are στρατία, πόλεμος, παράταξις (a fine generic word), δύναμις, μάχη, λειτουργία. This last, which means *service* of any kind that is performed *catervatim*, i. e. in *bands* or *companies*, throws light on Num. 4:23. 8:24, 25, where, beyond a doubt, the *temple-service*, as performed by the *chosen band* of the priests, is designated. In connection with the *temple*, such a meaning of the word in question seems unavoidable. In Dan. 8: 11 it stands connected with *the sanctuary* (מְכוֹן מִקְדָּשׁוֹ); and in v. 13, again with the sanctuary (קֹדֶשׁ). I can therefore assign to it here no other meaning than that given in Num. 4: 23. 8: 24, 25, because its connection is the same. In my apprehension, the whole context, and the comparison of this passage with others of like tenor in ch. vii. xi., oblige us to assign this and no other meaning. *Host of heaven* cannot mean *stars* here, in a literal sense; nor *angels* in a literal sense; for this would make the passage absurd. It cannot mean *army*, *host*, in the military sense; for the *host* in question here is merely one connected with the *sanctuary*; comp. also Rev. 12: 4. Nor does it probably mean *people of God*, *saints*, *corps d'elites* i. e. the Jewish nation (Leng.); for in such a sense we find it nowhere else employed. That the word *stars* should be employed to designate distinguished leaders, teachers, etc., is easy and natural. But the *collective* nature of the idea comprised in צָבָא here forbids such an application to a mere individual. There remains, then, only the meaning in Num. 4: 23 etc., as above stated.

The application is easy. Other nations and kings were wont, in their wars, to respect temples and their priests; but Antiochus made war on both at Jerusalem. He first took away all the apparatus employed in the ordinary service of the temple; then finally he erected an altar there to his patron-god, and sacrificed swine upon it. The priests he killed, or drove into exile. So it is said in the sequel: *And it* [the horn] *cast down to the earth some of the host.* — מִן as before in a *partitive* sense, *some*, *some of*, *a part of*, see Lex. — וּמִן־הַכּוֹכָבִים appears designed (by prefixing וּמִן) not to be merely exegetical of the preceding word, but by itself to designate the like idea more intensively. *Some of the stars*, *the constellations* (the art. is prefixed), are of course *the leaders* among the priesthood, i. e. persons who from their influence deserve such a name preeminently or peculiarly. — *And trode them under foot*, a strong expression, (none too strong), to designate the cruel and contemptuous treatment that the priesthood met with from Antiochus.

(11) Even to the Prince of the host did he magnify himself, and from him did he take away the daily sacrifice, and the dwelling-place of his sanctuary was cast down.

The Prince of the host is doubtless *God himself*, as the sequel clearly shows;

comp. 7: 20, 21, 25. 8: 25. 11: 28, 30—36. — הֻרַים, the vowels belonging to the Qeri הוּרַם. But I prefer the Kethibh, הֵרִים, and have so translated. The meaning is more efficient than the simple passive. As to the *masc.* form of the two verbs here, it is necessary only to remark, that the concord is *ad sensum*, for the horn designates *a king*. — *The dwelling place of his sanctuary* means his *sacred dwelling place*, i. e. the temple. The whole temple was not indeed demolished by Antiochus; but the sanctuary was rifled, and shockingly profaned. In respect to the word הַתָּמִיד, it is plainly a breviloquent expression. The full form would require עֹלַת before it, which הַתָּמִיד would then qualify. A *breviloquent* method of expression is prevalent in Daniel, and is somewhat characteristic: see 8: 12, 13. 11: 31. 12: 11. For the actual doings of Antiochus, see 1 Macc. 1: 22. 3: 45—51.

(12) And a host was placed over the daily sacrifice by wickedness, and it cast down faithfulness to the ground, and it accomplished [its desire], and was prosperous.

The subject, or Nom. of the verb *was placed*, is צָבָא, *a host*. For the occasional *fem.* gender of this word, see Isa. 40: 2. *Put* or *place* is a very common meaning of נָתַן, as also the kindred signification *to appoint*, *constitute*; see Lex. — עַל *over*, in a hostile sense, implying that the *daily sacrifice* was subjected to oppressive and impious supervision. — בְּפָשַׁע *by wickedness* or *rebellion*, the abstract for the concrete = *by the wicked one*, or *by the rebel*. Hence, in the N. Test., 2 Thess. 2: 3, ἀποστασία (an exact version of פֶּשַׁע), also ὁ ἄνθρωπος τῆς ἁμαρτίας; and in v. 8 (ib.), ὁ ἄνομος; expressions having their basis, as I apprehend, in the verse before us, and applied by Paul to some personage of a character similar to that of Antiochus. No defence of this exegesis is needed, in regard to the principle on which it rests; for nothing is more frequent than a usage of this kind in the Bible, e. g. *God is love*. The article is indeed omitted in בְּפָשַׁע; but this circumstance is of little or no force, as it regards an *abstract* noun. The instances of the omission of the article in abstract nouns, are nearly three to one of its insertion, according to the result which I have before me, of a somewhat extensive register of examples of each kind. There is more of the arbitrary or *ad libitum scriptoris* here, than in almost any other usage of the Heb. language. Nothing *for* or *against* the meaning above given to פֶּשַׁע, can be made out then from this source. But when the article is omitted (as in fact it is) before וְצָבָא at the beginning of the verse, we may well deem it probable and even certain, that in this case the writer does not mean to use צָבָא in the same sense in which it is used in vs. 10, 11; for if he did, we might then well expect הַצָּבָא, i. e. *the host* already named, for so he writes the word repeated in v. 10. The simple meaning seems to be, that Antiochus would not only maltreat the lawful priesthood of the temple, and rob God of the *daily offering*, but also that he would put a priestly corps, i. e. a צָבָא of his own in the temple, or, in other words, a *band* or *host* who should offer a תָּמִיד in accordance with the demands of *wickedness*, i. e. of an impious person. The *similar* use of צָבָא, in vs. 10, 11, and 12, in such a construction, is very obvious. Hence too the sequel. This new *host*, appointed by the blasphemous king to offer swine's flesh on the altar of the temple, would *cast down to the earth faithfulness*, i. e. (abstract for concrete) the faithful servants of God, or (as it may mean) *true religion*. It is plain that אֱמֶת and פֶּשַׁע stand in contrast. The heathen servitors of the temple, while performing their own תָּמִיד, would of course interrupt and cause to cease the daily offerings required by *true religion*, אֱמֶת. — עָשְׂתָה is breviloquence. The noun to be supplied, and which sometimes is expressed, is עֵצָה or רָצוֹן. — וְהִצְלִיחָה, *and it was prosperous* or *successful*. There is no need of another subject (קֶרֶן) for the three *fem.* verbs; for צָבָא at the beginning of the verse is treated as being fem., and it comports well with the meaning of the passage to continue the same subject through the verse. It is in substance the same, however, if any one prefers קֶרֶן for the Nom. to these verbs, for this designates Antiochus.

(13) And I heard a holy one speaking; and one holy one said to a certain one who was speaking: Until when is the vision — the daily sacrifice, and the wicked one to be destroyed, the giving up of both sanctuary and host to be trampled upon?

The prophet represents the sight of what is done at Jerusalem, as making its guardian angel strongly desirous of knowing when such abominations shall cease. Some angel, (in the train of the angel-interpreter, as it would seem), puts the question to him. — וָאֶשְׁמְעָה, מֶ for מְ, § 10. 2. Note 2. *a.* — פַּלְמוֹנִי designates individuality, but it is that of a person whose name is not known; like our English phrase, *a certain person.* The apparent article before the Part. is here a rel. pronoun, as oftentimes elsewhere. — עַד־מָתַי, lit. *until when*, i. e. unto what time, how long? — הֶחָזוֹן, *the vision*, viz. that seen by the prophet, in a general sense. The inquiry is, to what limits of time this vision extends. — הַתָּמִיד and הַפֶּשַׁע refer to the same words in v. 12, and are here coordinate with הֶחָזוֹן and epexegetical of it, being designed to render prominent the most interesting objects of the vision. — The meaning of שֹׁמֵם has been much controverted. Gesenius has given it an *active* sense, viz. *waster*, *destroyer*. I must doubt the propriety of this. In all other cases besides some three in the book of Daniel, it is clearly of a *passive* tenor; and the stem is intrans., and therefore kindred to a *passive* verb in its meaning. In 11: 31 the like usage occurs as here, viz. of a noun with the article, and the Part. or participial adjective without it, namely הַשִּׁקּוּץ מְשׁוֹמֵם. This is no strange phenomenon; see Heb. Gram. § 109. 2. *b*. The form מְשֹׁמֵם in 9: 27 and 11: 31, I take to be *active;* but שֹׁמֵם means *desolandus, vastandus,* like נוֹלָד in Ps. 22: 32, and מֵת (Part.) in Gen. 20: 3. The sentiment then, expressed here and in 9: 27. 12: 11, by שֹׁמֵם, is one of condemnation, equivalent to *which ought to be laid waste* or *destroyed*, or *which deserves excision* or *desolation, vastandus.* The *article* would hardly be appropriate to the communication of this meaning, and so it is omitted. If one chooses, he may supply אֲשֶׁר before שֹׁמֵם, (Ewald's Gram. p. 538, 1st edit.), which it is common everywhere and often to omit. In such a case, the article would be manifestly out of place, as the Part. would be a predicate. But without resorting to this construction, it is not difficult to produce other cases where the Part. is associated with a *definite* noun, and yet has not the article; e. g. in Deut. 28: 31, 32, are five cases of participles *anarthrous*, joined with definite nouns (made definite by having suff. pronouns), and used in a *future* sense like שֹׁמֵם, *vastandus*. That *passive* participles have very commonly the meaning of the Latin participials in *-dus*, (like נוֹרָא, *metuendus*), is a well established and familiar principle, § 131. 1. But the active participles of *intransitive* verbs may have the same meaning, inasmuch as these verbs rarely have but one participial form, and the nature of the signification does not permit that to be active *transitive*.

The last clause of the verse, תֵּת וגו׳, is plainly in the same predicament as the preceding clause, viz. *the daily sacrifice, the wicked one to be destroyed*, i. e. it is *coördinate* with this clause, and also epexegetical of הֶחָזוֹן. In other words, both of these clauses present in particular the prominent subject-matter of the vision, or the objects of special interest which it discloses. The first of the two clauses brings to view the תָּמִיד and the פֶּשַׁע of v. 12; the second, the צָבָא and מִקְדָּשׁ of vs. 10, 11. — תֵּת is the well known Inf. of נָתַן, and is here an *Inf. nominascens*, retaining the Acc. after it; for I take the sequel to be the double Acc. after a verb which implies the making of one kingdom into another, § 136. 2. e. g. So far as תֵּת is considered a *noun*, it (with its associates) is the *subject* of a sentence, which would run literally thus: 'How long will be the giving up sanctuary and host as a trampling?' For the double Acc. here, see Ewald's Gram. 1st edit. p. 587. 1. 3. a. Only one difficulty remains; which is, that neither קֹדֶשׁ nor צָבָא has the article; which we should naturally expect in a case like this, viz. one of *repeated mention*. Undoubtedly they might have it; but that it must of necessity be added, can hardly be made out with much probability. Or rather, as the case when more closely examined appears, the article may well be omitted. As to קֹדֶשׁ, it should be observed that the *abstract* word is here employed, which more commonly *omits* the article, while in v. 11 we have מְכוֹן מִקְדָּשׁוֹ. That קֹדֶשׁ is used in preference to the phrase in v. 11, seems to be a matter of design, rather than of accident; for מְכוֹן מִקְדָּשׁ plainly designates the *temple-building* or material temple, while קֹדֶשׁ designates *all that is holy* or *sacred*, in a more comprehensive sense, not excluding but including the temple and its appurtenances, with all that is purified and consecrated to God; it is therefore abstract and generic. This enlarged sense is of course intensive and more significant. As to צָבָא, had the writer employed the *article* here, it would of course have made the word an echo of the צָבָא nearest to it, i. e. of צָבָא in v. 12. But *this temple-host* was the one which was placed there by פֶּשַׁע, i. e. Antiochus. The writer therefore omits the article, and throws the reader back, by means of the preceding context (קֹדֶשׁ), upon vs. 10, 11, viz. וַתַּפֵּל אַרְצָה מִן־הַצָּבָא וגו׳, as making clear the meaning which he attaches to צָבָא here. As to the first word then (קֹדֶשׁ), the article would narrow its designed meaning; and as to the second (צָבָא), it would be likely to mislead the reader. This may account for the seeming violation here of ordinary usage, in respect to the article. But beyond all this, as Ewald, Gesenius, and others have remarked, the later Hebrew is more various and inconstant with respect to the article, than the earlier. In Heb. poetry, also, the omission of the article in cases where prose employs it, has long been remarked by critics. And although the book before us does not exhibit rhythm, nor the usual Hebrew poetic parallelisms, it is still instinct with poetic thought and diction.—*Shall be made a* מִרְמָס, i. e. lit. *an object on which one treads* or *tramples;* expressive of contemptuous and abusive treatment. Sentiment: 'How long will be the trampling of Antiochus upon all the objects which are sacred, and upon those who perform the holy offices of the temple?'

(14) And he said to me: Until two thousand and three hundred evening-mornings, and then shall that which is holy be vindicated.

Interpreters are divided about the meaning עֶרֶב בֹּקֶר. Some maintain that it designates merely *the sacrifice* respectively *of evening and morning*, (evening is put first, because the Hebrew day began with evening, Gen. i.). This would make only 1150 days of time, there being two sacrifices each day. But this construction seems inadmissible. עֶרֶב בֹּקֶר have no copula or conjunction between them; it would seem, therefore, to be a popular mode of compound expression, like to that of the Greek νυχθήμερον (2 Cor. 11: 25), in order to designate *the whole of the day*. Compare Gen. i., where the evening and morning constitute respectively *day the first, day the second,* etc.; for it seems plain that the phraseology before us is derived from this source. In other words, עֶרֶב בֹּקֶר, as here employed, may be admitted to contain an allusion to the morning and evening sacrifices, and thus the phrase virtually becomes a kind of substitute for תָּמִיד, which is generic and includes both the morning and evening sacrifice. To the question then : *How long shall the* תָּמִיד *be taken away?* (see in v. 11), the answer is in effect: During 2300 repetitions of the תָּמִיד, i. e. 2300 *evening-morning offerings.* The time thus designated is, as usual, in the sing. number; while the larger numerals are in the plural. — *And then shall that which is holy be vindicated,* וְנִצְדַּק *shall have justice done,* i. e. the rights of the sanctuary shall be effectually restored, its claims shall be vindicated. This was done when Judas Maccabaeus, after the three and a half years in which all temple-rites had been suspended, and heathen sacrifices had been offered there, made a thorough expurgation of everything pertaining to the temple, and restored its entire services. This was on the 25th of Dec. 165 B. C., just three years from the time when swine's flesh was first offered there by Antiochus. We have then the *terminus ad quem* of the 2300 days; and it is not difficult, therefore, to find the *terminus a quo.* These days, at 30 in a month (which is clearly the prophetic mode of reckoning), make 6 years, 4 months, and twenty days. Dec. 25 of 171 makes six years, and the four months and twenty days will bring the time to the latter half of July in the same year, i. e. 171 B. C. During this year, Menelaus, the high-priest appointed by Antiochus on the ground of a proffered bribe, rifled the temple of many of its treasures in order to pay that bribe, and in this transaction he was assisted by his brother Lysimachus. The regular and lawful high-priest, Onias III, who had been removed, severely reproved this sacrilege committed by his brethren; and afterward, through fear of them, fled for refuge to Daphne, an asylum near Antioch in Syria. Thence he was allured by the false promises of Menelaus, and perfidiously murdered by the king's lieutenant, Andronicus. See the whole story in 2 Macc. 4: 27 seq. The Jews at Jerusalem, incensed by the violent death of their lawful high-priest, and by the sacrilegious robberies of Menelaus and Lysimachus, became tumultuous, and a severe contest took place between them and the adherents of those who committed the robbery, in which the patriotic Jews at last gained the victory, and Lysimachus was slain at the treasury. This was the first contest that took place, between the friends of Antiochus and the adherents to the Hebrew laws and usages. The whole of it was occasioned by the baseness of Antiochus, in accepting bribes for bestowing the office of high priest on those who had no just claim to it. The payment of the bribes occasioned the robbing of the temple and the sacrilege committed there; and this was the commencement of that long series of oppression, persecution, and bloodshed, which took place in the sequel under Antiochus.

We have, indeed, no data in ancient history by which the very day, or even month, connected with the transactions above related can be exactly ascertained. But the *year* is certain; and as the time seems to be *definite* in our text, the fair presumption is, that the outbreak of the populace, and the battle that followed, constitutes the *terminus a quo* of the 2300 days. See Froelich, Annales Reg. Syr. p. 46; and also Usher's Chronol. The first of these two solid and excellent writers, has taken the most pains to enucleate the Syrian history, and is the most to be relied upon. Both depend mainly on 2 Macc. 4: 39—42 as their source; where the *time* is not specifically noted. But Froelich seems most thoroughly and accurately to have developed the course of events.

As to the difference between the time here, viz. 2300 days, and the three and a half years in 7: 25, if the reader narrowly inspects the latter, he will perceive, that the time there specified has relation to the period during which Antiochus entirely prohibited the Jewish religion in every shape. This period, as is well known, corresponds with historical facts. In the passage before us, a more extensive series of events is comprised, as vs. 10—12 indicate. They begin with assaults on the priesthood, (which we have seen to be matter of fact, as stated above), and end with the desecration and prostration of all that is sacred and holy. It is unnecessary to show that each of the things described belongs to each and every part of the 2300 days. Enough that the events are *successive*, and spread over the time specified in our text. The *trampling down* or degradation of the priesthood and the sanctuary commenced the whole series of oppression and persecution; and this with most aggravated acts of sacrilege and blasphemy, was also the consummation of the tyrant's outrages.

(15) And it came to pass, that while I was beholding, I Daniel, the vision, that I sought for the meaning; and lo! there was one standing before me like the appearance of a man.

Above (v. 13) an *angel* asks a question of another. Here by subjoining *I Daniel*, the contrast is made more striking between the present and the former inquirer. — בִּרְאוֹתִי, Inf. of רָאָה with suff. prononn. — *I Daniel* is virtually the repetition of that pronoun, in another form which makes the expression more intensive. — *I sought the meaning* or *a meaning* as the Heb. runs. The הָ here appended to the verb, denotes an effort or inclination to seek, § 126. 1. *a*. Our idiom would employ *the meaning* in such a relation as that in which the noun בִּינָה stands. —

לְנֶגְדִּי, *before me*, i. e. within his view; for that the angel was as yet at some distance from Daniel appears from v. 17. This angel is the פַּלְמוֹנִי הַמְדַבֵּר of v. 13, and the *Gabriel* of v. 16. — *Like the appearance of a man* is designedly so expressed, in order to indicate that the angel assumed a human form only for the time being, or in appearance only, and not in reality. This is common throughout the Bible, when angels make their appearance; e. g. Gen. 18: 2, 16. Josh. 5: 13. Judg. 13: 10, 11. Luke 24: 4, etc. — גָּבֶר, used rarely out of the poetic and prophetic books, but very common in Aramaean. The stem of this word denotes *being strong, powerful;* and probably in the passage before us, the idea of a strong and powerful man, in accordance with the etymology of the word, is intended to be retained.

(16) And I heard the voice of a man between the Ulai, and he cried aloud and said: Gabriel, explain to this person the vision.

The voice of a man here means a voice like that of a man, i. e. the angel spake *more humano*. Who this angel was, is not said; and the conjectures that he was the Messiah (Theod.), or Michael (the Rabbins), are useless and inapposite. *Between the Ulai* can mean, as the word בֵּין naturally indicates, only *between the two sides* or *banks of the Ulai.* — וַיִּקְרָא denotes the loudness or distinctness with which the words were spoken. — לְהַלָּז, § 34. Note 1. — הַמַּרְאֶה is the equivalent of חָזוֹן. Lengerke says, that the name *Gabriel*, or rather the idea of seven *presence-angels*, is borrowed from Parsism. But "the angel of his presence" is no late idea among the Hebrews; the Pent. often discloses it. Out of the book of Daniel, it is not usual in the O. Test. to give proper names to angels. But *Gabriel* occurs also in Dan. 9: 21, and in Luke 1: 19, 26; and so in the book of Enoch, 9: 1. 20: 1. The angel must have been high in station, in order that he should give *commands*, as here, to Gabriel.

(17) And he came near to where I stood, and when he came I was terrified, and I fell upon my face; and he said to me: Son of man, mark well that the vision is for the time of the end.

Almost everywhere in the Scriptures, the vision of God or of angels is represented as producing agitation, consternation, or even swooning; Gen. 15: 12, comp. Job 4: 13 seq. Gen. 16: 13. 32: 30. Deut. 18: 16. Judg. 6: 22. 13: 22. Isa. 6: 5. Luke 1: 12, 29. 2: 9. Acts 9: 3, 8, etc. — נִבְעַתִּי, Niph. of בָּעַת, the ת with Dagh. forte comprising ת of the stem and ת of the formative suffix, § 20. 1. a. — *The time of the end* presents more difficulty than one might at first suspect. *End* of what? Of Antiochus? Or of a troublous state of things? Or *end* of the world? Not merely of Antiochus; for his importance, as exhibited in the book of Daniel, arises principally from his power to annoy the people of God. Not the end of the world; for in chap. viii. no Messianic period is developed at the close of its predictions, and yet the Messianic reign is itself the end or last time of the world. V. 19 gives us perhaps some light; בְּאַחֲרִית הַזָּעַם, *in the latter time of the indignation*, i. e. in the latter time of afflictions permitted to be brought upon Israel, because of the divine indignation against their sins. The vision itself in fact reaches only *to the end* of those special afflictions, that are to come on the people of the Jews *before* the Messianic period, and which are made the subject of prophecy because of their importance. The warning to *mark well* or *consider* the vision, because it discloses these afflictions, connects itself of course with a supposed importance attached to the knowledge of the final special troubles of the Jews before the coming of the Messiah. The Rabbins call those troubles חֶבְלֵי מָשִׁיחַ.

(18) And while he was speaking with me, I was in a deep sleep upon my face, on the earth, and he touched me, and made me to stand up in my place.

נִרְדַּמְתִּי I have expressed by circumlocution, for we cannot imitate the Niph. Conj. here. רָדַם means *to snore*, and then *to be in a deep sleep* or *stupor*. Daniel, however, does not mean to assert that he was literally asleep in the common way, but that he was in so deep a swoon as to lose all sensation and perception of outward objects, and to be stretched out helpless upon the ground. But the power of the angel's touch revived him, and enabled him to stand up.

(19) And he said: Behold! I will make thee to know what shall take place in the latter period of the indignation; for at an appointed time is the end.

הִנְנִי, Dagh. f. omitted in the first נ, § 20. 3. Remarks.—מוֹדִיעֲךָ, Part. Hiph. of יָדַע, here, as often elsewhere, used like the Latin Fut. in—*rus*.—*The latter period of the indignation* implies, that the whole period is to continue for sometime, for אַחֲרִית denotes only *the latter part of it*. The meaning of זַעַם here must be made out from the context. Vs. 10—14 show that God will give up his people, city, and even sanctuary, for a time, to a wicked oppressor and invader—designated by פֶּשַׁע in v. 12. The coming or happening of special evil is everywhere, in the Jewish Scriptures, spoken of as the effect of divine displeasure, and not unnaturally, therefore, is often named *the wrath of God*, in the O. Test. and in the New; e. g. Isa. 10: 5, 25. 26: 20. 30: 27. Matt. 3: 7. Rom. 1: 18. 2: 5. Eph. 2: 3. 5: 6. Col. 3: 6. Rev. 11: 18. From this familiar idiom it comes, that the writer has put the *article* before זַעַם, i. e. he takes it for granted, that the reader will refer *the* or *that indignation* to the same which has already been described in the context. It plainly means here *the season of indignation* on the part of God, who gives up his people to punishment, because they have sinned against him. Above, in v. 14, a *set time* (= מוֹעֵד) is named, (viz. 2300 days), when deliverance from the scourge will be granted. That which is to take place near the close of the indignation-period, (בְּאַחֲרִית), is the most prominent thing in the prophetic vision, and that which Daniel and the Jewish people were most interested to know. That קֵץ is the subject of the clause, and that the verb of existence is implied after it, seems to be clear, because, if we translate the clause thus, *for an appointed time of an end*, and ask the question: *What* is for an appointed time? the context gives us no answer. I take קֵץ to be equivalent to our phrase *final issue*, and usually involving the idea of such an issue in the way of judgment or punishment. In like manner is it employed in Dan. 9: 26, where it appears to be twice applied to the death of Antiochus Epiphanes. The like also in 8: 17, i. e. in our immediate context. That the angel calls the special attention of Daniel to this topic, (both in vs. 17 and 19), and mentions only this, shows, beyond any good reason for doubt, that the times and punishment of Antiochus — the *man of sin* פֶּשַׁע, the נִבְזֶה — constitute the burden of the vision just related. That other matters respecting the Medo-Persian dynasty, that of Alexander, and of his successors, are touched upon, seems to be mainly because they stand historically connected with the dynasty of Antiochus.

(20) The ram which thou sawest having two horns, is the kings of Media and Persia.

הַקְּרָנָיִם in pause, see for the form v. 3. above. — *Is* the kings, etc., the verb *is*, as usual, being implied. I have employed the verb *singular*, because אַיִל is its more immediate subject. Here also, as in cases almost without number, the verb *is* plainly conveys the same sense as *represents, symbolizes, means*, etc. — *The kings of Media and Persia*, i. e. the continued dynasty of Medo-Persian kings; and this of course is as much as to say, *the Medo-Persian empire*, for kings are the representatives of empire, or efficient agents in establishing and preserving it.

(21) And the he-goat is a king of Greece; and as to the large horn between its eyes — this is the first king.

הוּא masc., because קֶרֶן, although regularly fem., designates in this place a *king*. It should be noted, also, that here is only *one* horn, which represents Alexander as sole king of the empire here in question. When this is broken, another empire of a different kind arises out of its ruins;

comp. 11: 4, where this view of the matter is fully expressed. *First king* does not necessarily imply that there were other kings of the same stamp or condition after him, any more than *first born* necessarily implies that there are other children of the same parents. In Macc. 1: 1 it is said of Alexander: Ἐβασίλευσε πρότερος ἐπὶ τὴν Ἑλλάδα.

(22) And as to the [horn] that was broken, and there stood up four in the room thereof — four kingdoms from the nation shall arise, but not with his power.

הַנִּשְׁבֶּרֶת, fem. Part. Niph. agreeing with קֶרֶן implied, and so of the same number and gender. — On the other hand, תַּעֲמֹדְנָה is 3 plur. fem. Imperf., and agrees with קְרָנַיִם implied.—*In the room of it*, i. e. in the room of the great horn, which has now become broken. — מַלְכֻיוֹת, plur. of מַלְכוּת, see § 86. 2. — מִגּוֹי, without the article, lit. *from a nation.* Had the article been employed in Hebrew, it must refer either to a previous mention of גּוֹי, (which does not exist here), or else to the *Gentiles* (τὰ ἔθνη) collectively, in distinction from the Jews. This last meaning is not that which the writer intends to convey. He means *a* [heathen] *nation*, but not the whole mass of the heathen. Still, in English we cannot follow exactly in his steps; for *a nation* would with us be too indefinite, and would seem to indicate that the writer was uncertain from what quarter the four kingdoms would spring up. I have therefore rendered מִגּוֹי *from the nation;* and the meaning is, *from the heathen nation* once ruled by *the great horn.* — יַעֲמֹדְנָה, Imperf. 3 pl. fem., with fem. suffix formative, and (י) praefix as if masc. Two cases of the same kind we find elsewhere, viz. יֵחַמְנָה in Gen. 30: 38, and יִשַּׁרְנָה in 1 Sam. 6: 12, both having *fem.* subjects; see Ges. Lehrgeb. § 81. 2. In Syr., Chald., and Arab., the 3d fem. plur. is formed in the same way. Is our text then an oversight of transcribers, who unconsciously followed some of the kindred languages with which they were familiar? Or is it merely *Chaldaizing* Hebrew, which the original writer may have employed? With certainty we cannot decide; but I should, on the whole, rather incline to the latter supposition. — *But not in his strength*, i. e. not with the power or might of the great horn; for none of the four kingdoms were equal in power to that of Alexander. The suffix וֹ— is *masc.*, but still there is concord *ad sensum*, for *horn* symbolizes a *king*. If the reader has any doubt whether the *breaking* of the great horn here, and the standing up of four others in its room, indicates a transition from a third dynasty to a fourth, a comparison of this verse with 11: 4 may help to solve that doubt. In fact, I know not how language could more plainly and definitely express the idea of a transition from one dynasty to another, than the language of Dan. 11: 4

has done. That in both passages the same succession is under consideration, there can be no doubt.

(23) And in the latter part of their reign, when transgressors shall have come to the full, there shall stand up a king of stern aspect and skilled in fraudulent devices.

בְּאַחֲרִית cannot be properly rendered (with Hävernick) *toward the end.* It must mean *during the latter part* or *portion.* — In מַלְכוּתָם, the suffix must be referred to the kingdoms that rise up after the great horn is broken. Does the writer mean to convey the idea, that all four of the dynasties which followed that of Alexander, are to be brought into account here, or only the leading portion of them, viz. Syria and Egypt? If we may bring ch. xi. to bear upon this question, the answer will of course be: The two dynasties just named; for of them almost exclusively does the author speak in the eleventh chapter. Besides, these were the firmest and most lasting of all. In particular, with respect to Syria, the era of Seleucus Nicator (its first king in the Grecian line) begins with B. C. 312, and Antiochus commenced his reign in 175 B. C. The decline of the Syrian empire was hastened by his defeat and death; and although it had a nominal existence, down to the time when Pompey overran that region, yet it was in the hands of incompetent persons or foreigners, so that it was but little accounted of. It was then a matter of historical fact, that the dominion of Antiochus Epiphanes, commenced during the *latter part* of the Syrian dynasty, whether we have respect to time or to the declining state of the government, in computing such a period. Lengerke asserts, without any qualification, that the writer supposed Antiochus to be the last of the Syrian kings, or that with him the Syrian dominion would fall, and the times of the Messiah immediately succeed. I cannot regard אַחֲרִית as being so narrowly restricted. The אַחֲרִית הַיָּמִים so often employed to designate *the latter period of the world* in which the Messiah would make his appearance, is surely not confined to narrow limits. Enough, that in the declining part of the Syrian empire, the tyrant and persecutor, described in the sequel, came to the throne. The blow had already been struck by the Romans, in their defeat of Antiochus the Great, which inflicted a wound on the Syrian dominion that was never to be cured. Antiochus Epiphanes, by his wiles and stratagems, sustained himself for a while. But before his death, the virtual dissolution of his empire seemed to be at hand. I do not feel, therefore, any necessity of interpreting the passage, in respect to אַחֲרִית, as Lengerke would have us. — As to the *immediate coming* of the Messiah, after the defeat and death of Antiochus, is it not strange, if the author of the book of Daniel wrote after that period, (which Lengerke maintains), that he should have suggested such a sentiment, when his own observation would itself have contradicted it? In reality, however, the developments of this nature, in the book of Daniel, stand on common ground with those of Isaiah and other prophets, as we shall see more fully in the sequel. If what is said in relation to this subject by the book of Daniel, will serve as an argument to show that the book was not written by that prophet, then what Isaiah and other prophets have said in the like way will serve to show that their works are not genuine. What proves *too much*, does not go current among logicians as sound argument.

In regard to כְּהָתֵם הַפֹּשְׁעִים, *when the transgressors shall have come to the full*, i. e. completed the full measure of their iniquity, I understand this as having respect to *apostatizing Jews*, who, in the time of Antiochus Epiphanes, forsook their laws and usages, and after obtaining the approbation of Antiochus, introduced *heathen* rites and usages among the Hebrews, and even built a heathen gymnasium for their games in Jerusalem. See a full account in 1 Macc. 1: 11 seq., where the writer doubtless with his eye upon הַפֹּשְׁעִים here, calls them παράνομοι. The same occurrence is in view in v. 19 above, where the *time of the indignation* is spoken of. God gave up the Jews to chastisement by the hands of the 'stern-visaged and wily king.' It would seem that the inclination to apostatize already existed among many of the Jews, before Antiochus intermeddled with their concerns. His *rising up* (יַעֲמֹד) does not here so much designate his mere accession to the throne, as his becoming the active enemy and oppressor of the Jews. This he began to be, as soon as the pious Jews began to oppose the heathenish innovations which his partisans introduced among them. — עַז פָּנִים might mean *of an impudent look*, but here his *sternness* and *cruelty* are more probably intended to be characterized, as in Deut. 28: 50, and so I have translated it *stern of aspect*; comp. 7: 19, 23, 25. 11: 33. That Antiochus, with all his extravagance and follies, had much craftiness and subtlety, and often brought about his designs by means of flattery and cunning — מֵבִין חִידוֹת — appears abundantly from 11: 21—23, 25, 32. The same character is given him in Polyb. Reliq. XXXI, 5. Appian, de Reb. Syr. XLV. See also 1 Macc. 1: 30 seq. 2 Macc. 5: 24—26. To the Roman ambassadors he professed great regard and friendship for the Romans, while he acted in a manner directly the contrary. Eumenes and Attalus, kings of Pergamos, he won over to his cause by flattery and fair promises, so that they aided in dethroning Heliodorus, and in opposing the claims of the Egyptian Ptolemy to the throne of Syria. The same Ptolemy, his nephew, he inveigled and deceived by pretences of interposing in the affairs of Egypt for his benefit, while his real object was plunder; see Dan. 11: 25. Finally, he took possession of Jerusalem by stratagem and fraud, (ἐλάλησεν αὐτοῖς λόγους εἰρηνικοὺς ἐν δόλῳ, 1 Macc. 1: 30, comp. 2 Macc. 5: 24—26); so that the most conspicuous parts of his character, cruelty and fraud, are developed in our text.

(24) And his strength will wax mighty, and yet not by his own strength; and wonderfully will he destroy, and prosper in his undertaking, yea, he will destroy many, even the people of the saints.

Yet not by his own strength, [but by the might which God gives him], is the antithesis which Hävernick finds here; and so Theodoret, Ephrem Syrus, and some others. This sense, when the expression is taken in a modified way, is not in itself objectionable; but it seems more probable that the speaker means to say, that Antiochus will not be potent on the ground of real and proper strength of dominion, but on the ground of the artifice and cunning so conspicuously exhibited in the preceding verse, and in the other passages there alluded to. In what respects the accomplishment of his designs by power was manifested, the sequel informs us. — נִפְלָאוֹת, Part. plur. used adverbially, § 98. 2. *c.* — יַשְׁחִית is here employed *absolutely*, i. e. without any following Acc. case. — וְהִצְלִיחַ וְעָשָׂה, two verbs in one idea, either of which may be rendered adverbially; see § 139. 3, and 4. Note 1. We might, therefore, here translate: *And he shall execute* [his designs] *prosperously*. I prefer, however, the translation exhibited above; which is equally correct, and renders the supplement of a noun unnecessary. A literal translation our idiom will not well bear. I take עָשָׂה to be oftentimes a *constructio praegnans* in this book, the full form of which is given in 11: 36, וְעָשָׂה כִרְצֹנוֹ, *he shall do according to his pleasure.* — עֲצוּמִים, more usually means *mighty* or *great;* here it refers to *greatness of numbers*, and means *many*. If *the mighty* were meant, the article would of course be inserted. — וְעַם קְדֹשִׁים is epexegetical, particularizing the pious Jews. The Jewish nation, as consecrated to God, are called קֹדֶשׁ and קְדֹשִׁים, not unfrequently in the sacred books. It is not particularly to the speaker's purpose here, to describe the slaughter which Antiochus perpetrated among the heathen nations abroad. Of course the *people of the saints* must here mean the *pious* Jews, because the speaker has already spoken of the פֹּשְׁעִים among them, v. 23.

(25) And because of his cunning, he will render deceit prosperous in his hand, and in his own heart will he magnify himself, and unexpectedly will he destroy many; moreover against the Prince of princes will he stand up, and without hand [of man] shall he be utterly destroyed.

None of the ancient translations appear to have understood this verse, at least the first clause of it, and they have therefore rendered it in a variety of ways. The difficulty seems to have been with שִׂכְלוֹ, which is commonly used in a good sense, e. g. *wisdom, discretion*, etc.; but it is also capable of a different meaning, viz. *cunning, sagacity*, in doing evil as well as good; like Luke 16: 8, "The children of this world are *wiser* (φρονιμώτεροι) in their generation than the children of light," i. e. *more sagacious, dexterous*. In fact שֵׂכֶל is *dexterity* or *sagacity* simply; and thus being generic, it may be used in a sense either good or bad. In respect to *historical facts* which illustrate this, they have already been adverted to in the preceding verse. — יַגְדִּיל, *magnify*, and as no other object is here supplied, the verb itself supplies one, viz. *magnify himself*. How characteristic this is of Antiochus, all who have read his history must know. — בְּשַׁלְוָה, lit. *in peace;* but the Hebrew employs this expression to designate the idea of *suddenly, unexpectedly*, i. e. in a way which such as were in quietude were not aware of. In the same manner is the word employed in 11: 21, 24; and so בַּשָּׁלוֹם in Job 15: 21. In Syriac and Chaldee is the same usage. Still the idea of *peaceful pretences* seems to be included. A full exegesis of this is found in the narration in 1 Macc. 1: 30 seq.: "He [the military tribute-collector of Antiochus] spoke to them [of Jerusalem] *peaceful words* . . . and he fell upon the city *suddenly*, and smote it with great slaughter, and destroyed much people of Israel." — *And against the Prince of princes shall he stand up*, is designed to render the narration climactic. Not only does the impious tyrant destroy the people of God, but sets himself in array against God himself. So in vs. 10, 11, above. — בְּאֶפֶס יָד, lit. *without hand*, which plainly means, without the interposition of human power. — יִשָּׁבֵר, lit. *shall be broken in pieces*. The language is adapted to the symbol, viz. the *little horn*. The meaning is, *totally destroyed*. Facts correspond. According to history, Antiochus, after marching into Persia, and robbing the temple at Elymais, was driven away by popular tumult; and on his return back towards Syria, he was met with the news of the total defeat of his army in Judea, and of the restoration of the temple services there. Polybius (XXXI. 11) says of him, that "*he fell mad* (δαιμονήσας) and died;" 1 Macc. 6: 8 relates, that he fell sick of grief for his losses; Appian (De Reb. Syr. LXVI) says simply: φθίνων ἐτελεύτησε. Various shades are given to the picture by the different writers; e. g. in 1 Macc. 6: 8 seq., which narrates his penitent confessions. But these have a strong tinge of *Jewish* coloring. So much is undoubtedly true, viz. that he perished suddenly by a violent sickness, during which he probably fell into a state of mania. He died, therefore, without violence by the hand of man, and so as to make a deep impression of perishing by a peculiar visitation of God.

(26) And as to the vision of the morning and the evening, which was declared, it is truth; do thou then seal up the vision, since it appertaineth to many days.

The vision respecting the evening and the morning, (for this is the meaning of the expression), is exhibited in v. 14 above. As it there *follows* all the symbols which the prophet had seen, so the same order is here observed. The symbols are first explained or applied, and then the speaker touches upon the period of 2300 *evening-mornings*, i. e. days, which had been fixed as the limits of Antiochus' persecution and oppression, the cleansing of the sanctuary (v. 14) being constituted the *terminus ad quem* of that tyrant's domination in Judea. By declaring with emphasis, that the vision respecting time is *true* (אֱמֶת *truth*), the speaker means to call attention to the determined and unalterable purpose of God, that the פֶּשַׁע — נִבְזֶה — עַז פָּנִים — in question should not go beyond his defined limits. — *Seal up the vision* presupposes that Daniel is to commit it to writing. *To seal up* would be to guard it against change or interpolation, and so to preserve its integrity. The idea of *safe keeping* by sealing up, is plain in Deut. 32: 34. Jer. 32: 14. Of course, access to a writing is prevented by sealing it, as in Isa. 29:11; consequently all intermeddling with it is prevented. A case parallel with our text is Isa. 8: 16, where the prophet seals his prediction in the presence of witnesses, and casts himself on the future for its certain fulfilment. The *sealing* would render it secure against any change, either through his own interference, or that of others, and so put to a fair test his claim to the office of a prophet. But in that case the fulfilment was near at hand; whereas, in the present case, one reason given for the sealing is, that *it is for many days*, i. e. a long time. From the third year of Belshazzar (v. 1) to the death of Antiochus, 388 years intervened. The idea of *preservation*, then, (which is the predominant one here conveyed by the word *sealing*), has a leading place. The *forbidding of access* is secondary, and belongs merely to that of *securing against alterations*. The same may be said of Dan. 12: 4, 9. On the contrary, the writer of the Apocalypse is required "*not to seal up* his prophecy, because the time (of its inceptive fulfilment) is near" (Rev. 22: 10), and therefore little danger of alteration could be apprehended. I do not see, how Hengstenberg (Auth. d. Daniel, s. 215 seq.) and Hävernick (Comm.) deduce from this passage the sentiment, that the sealing up of the vision means, that it was to be unintelligible until the fulfilment of it. What purpose then could the vision subserve, if neither Daniel, nor any of his readers could understand it? And when the supposed events came, which were to constitute a fulfilment, if no one could understand the vision, with what were the events to be compared, in order to determine that there was a fulfilment? A fulfilment of what?

'Of something that no one understood,' must of course be the answer, on the ground taken by the writers in question. — Besides; Daniel is here required *to do something* himself, viz. *to seal up*. Did Daniel himself, then, make his own vision unintelligible? This would be a singular process in making out a new *revelation*. — For the meaning of לְיָמִים רַבִּים, comp. the same phrase in Ezek. 12: 27.

(27) And I Daniel fainted, and was sick some days; then I rose up, and did the business of the king, and was astonished by reason of the vision, and understood it not.

As to נִהְיֵיתִי, see under 2: 1. The translation gives substantially the *sense* here, but the *form* of the original the English language cannot imitate. — יָמִים, without any limitation or qualification, corresponds well to *some days*. It is employed only in cases where the expression is designed to be indefinite. — *Did the business of the king*, i. e. returned to his ordinary employment. *The astonishment* which the prophet felt, is not a new circumstance, when disclosures are made of a terrific nature, as here; comp. 4: 19. 7: 15, 28. 10: 8, 9, 15. — *I understood not*, (the same in 12: 8), should not be interpreted, as some have done, as meaning to say, that the words or symbols of the vision were in themselves unintelligible, specially after the angel had been commanded to explain the vision to Daniel, vs. 16, 19. But the explanation, like the symbols and the words, is *generic* and not specific. Events are merely sketched; and with the exception of the *terminus ad quem*, time, place, and persons, are not particularized. Daniel was astonished at the destiny which hung over his people. He did not understand how "the little horn" could achieve so great things. Jerome has hit the point here with great skill. His paraphrase of אֵין מֵבִין runs thus: "Reges audierat, et eorum nomina nesciebat; futura cognoverat, et quo tempore futura essent, dubius fluctuabat." "If," says Jerome moreover, "if no one could interpret the vision, how came it that the angel interpreted it?" The difficulty in Daniel's mind seems plainly to have been, that his astonishment and his intense interest in the things disclosed, urged him on, very naturally, to further and minute inquiries and particulars; but these were not revealed by the vision, and were not designed to be.

In several particulars the prophetic vision in this chapter differs from those in chap. ii. and vii. First of all, no notice is taken of the Babylonish monarchy, such as we find in 2: 37, 38 and 7: 4. Then, secondly, there is a somewhat extended view of the second or Medo-Persian dynasty and its fall, vs. 3—7. Very brief and summary is the account of this dynasty in 2: 39 and 7: 5; and its fall in consequence of being invaded by the head of the third dynasty, is not at all noticed, as it is in 8: 5—7. So likewise, in the third place, with respect to the third dynasty. It is summarily touched upon in 2: 39 and 7: 6 ; but a somewhat dilated account is given in 8: 5—8. Fourthly, the manner in which the fourth dynasty arises, is given neither in 2: 40, nor in 7: 7 seq. But in 8: 8, the manner of its rise is given. Fifthly, while the fourth dynasty is characterized in 2: 40—43, merely in a general way, no particular notice is taken of Antiochus Epiphanes. But in 7: 7, 8, 19—21, 23—26, this tyrant and persecutor is particularly described, and his end foretold. In 8: 8—14, 22—25, there is still greater particularity in the description of Antiochus, and a new limitation of the whole period, during which he will carry on his persecutions and vexations. In fact, with the exception of the Medo-Persian dynasty and the rise of Alexander's, it is evident that almost the exclusive subject of the prophecy before us is Antiochus.

It appears, then, that this third vision differs from the others in the *amplitude* of its descriptions of the Syrian tyrant, and in making him altogether the prominent figure in the picture.

Lastly, it is a striking circumstance, that the visions in chap. ii. vii. both close with an extended view of the *Messianic* kingdom, which follows the downfall of all the others, while in chap. viii. it is wholly omitted. This is the more worthy of note, because the circumstantial history of Antiochus, in chap. xi., is also followed by a development of a Messianic character. Such a departure from analogy, in the vision before us, would seem to have been occasioned by some circumstances of which we are ignorant. The character of Antiochus as exhibited in chap. ii. vii. xi. (and probably in ix.), is remarkably congruous; so much so, indeed, as to leave no good room for doubt, that the same individual is meant in all. If any one is disposed to object against the interpretation which admits the *repetition* of predictions respecting Antiochus, and ask: 'Of what use could so many repetitions of the same thing be?' The answer is easy. Of what use is the repetition of predictions, in Isaiah, respecting Assyria, Babylon, Tyre, and the like? Of what use is the frequent repetition of *Messianic* predictions? And the same questions may be put respecting the representations of other prophets. The general answer I should give would be, that different exigencies of the times demanded new and repeated developments. The same things are never simply repeated. The subject is placed in new attitudes, and new light is cast upon it. Events of deep interest to the civil and social, or to the religious community, will sometimes bear repetition to serious advantage. We must confide something, moreover, to the judgment of the prophets in regard to the importance of this, in cases where we have, and can now have, no knowledge of minute circumstances.

CHAPTER IX.

[Some fifteen years after the preceding vision, subsequent to the dethronement of Belshazzar and the fall of the Babylonish dynasty, and during the *first* year of the reign of Darius the Mede, into whose hands the fallen Babylonish empire came, Daniel, in hope that the time of the exile of his countrymen was near its end, betook himself after long continued prayer and fasting, to the diligent perusal of the prophecies of Jeremiah respecting the *continuance* of the captivity. There, in 25: 11, 12, and specially in 29: 10. he found seventy years definitely named as the period, during which the exile should continue, and at the end of which a return to their native land would be allowed to the Hebrews; Dan. 9: 1—3. Most fervently did he pour forth his supplications for the fulfilment of these predictions. But even this he ventured not to do, until he had first made most ample and humble and hearty confession of his own sins, and of the sins of the kings, the princes, and the people of the Jews who had disobeyed the prophets, and transgressed the laws of Moses, and rebelled against the Lord; vs. 4—15. The sequel, vs. 16—19, exhibits in a most striking manner, the fervency with which he wrestled with God in prayer, for his people, the holy city, and the temple.

Such prayers as this holy man uttered, are always heard before the throne of God. Forthwith Gabriel, one of the presence-angels, is sent to communicate with Daniel, and to make further disclosures to him respecting the Jewish nation. With such haste did the angel come, that before Daniel had done speaking, he drew near and addressed him, and told him the object of his mission; vs. 20—22. Even at the beginning of Daniel's supplication a message went forth, and the angel declares that he had come to communicate it, because Daniel is greatly beloved. He exhorts the prophet, therefore, to give attention to his message, and to consider well the import of he prophetic vision; v. 23.

Seventy weeks [of years] are distinguished or abscinded from the general course of time, as a peculiar period which must be passed through, before the new and glorious dispensation of the Messiah will introduce the expiation of sin, and reconciliation for iniquity; bring in everlasting righteousness, and confirm what the prophets have foretold; and consecrate a Holy of Holies belonging to the new and better dispensation; v. 24. These *seventy weeks* are divided into three different periods, each distinctly marked by specific events at the commencement or close, or else by what takes place during their continuance. *Seven weeks* [of years] begin with a mandate to restore and build up Jerusalem, and end with the appearance of an Anointed One who is a Prince. During three score and two weeks [of years], the city of Jerusalem shall be rebuilt and prosper, although in troublous times; v. 25. After this period, *an Anointed One* shall be cut off; in consequence of which the Jewish nation shall be destitute of a lawful and proper officer of this class. Moreover the people of a [foreign] prince shall come, and lay waste the city and the sanctuary; but he shall come to his end with overwhelming destruction. The invasion of the city and sanctuary will occasion resistance on the part of the Jews, and war will ensue; but unto the end of that war the desolations which it will occasion, are limited by Heaven's decree, and cannot exceed the appointed measure; v. 26. The invading foreign prince will form close alliances with many Jews, for *one week* [of years]; during half of that week he will cause sacrifice and oblation at Jerusalem to cease, an idol worthy of destruction shall be erected over an abominable bird [Jupiter's eagle], and unto consummation, even that which is decreed shall then be poured upon him who is doomed to destruction.]

The first thing that strikes the attentive reader of this chapter as an object of inquiry is, *how the predictive or prophetic part of it compares with the other prophecies of Daniel.* Those who find in it *simply and only a Messi-*

anic prediction, give it an interpretation which makes it entirely discrepant from all the other prophecies of this book. In all other cases where the fifth or Messianic kingdom is foretold, there are preceding dynasties and events also predicted. Only one vision (that in chap. viii.) is destitute of a Messianic part; and only one (in chap. ii.) is destitute of a more or less specific description of the Syrian tyrant and persecutor. As this last oppression of the people of God, whose influences and whose relentless fury threatened far worse consequences to the Jews and to their religion, than did the Babylonish exile, is made so conspicuous in all the proper visions of Daniel himself, it would be at least singular, if the prophecy in Dan. ix. should pass him by in entire silence. Indeed the very outset of this vision (v. 24) seems explicitly to declare, that its design is to describe events which will happen *before* the introduction of that peaceful kingdom, which is to reconcile man to God, propitiate their sins, fulfil the most important part of all prophecy, and consecrate a perpetual holy of holies. That *seventy weeks are appointed* or *limited* to pass away *before* this will take place, seems to be the necessary implication of v. 24. These weeks are then distributed into three different periods, and have a relation to things somewhat diverse and distinct from each other. How can we suppose, now, that what will take place during these respective periods, is passed by in silence? Yet the exegesis which makes the whole paragraph exclusively *Messianic*, makes a part of these periods to *precede* and a part to *follow* the commencement of the Messianic kingdom. This seems to be evidently against the tenor of the prediction before us, and certainly against the tenor of the book in general. A mixture of sorrow and joy, of trouble and deliverance, is everywhere else to be found; why should they be excluded here? To me it seems very clear that they are not, but that the prediction before us follows the analogy of the others, in regard to the matter in question.

The circumstance, that in the present case the Messianic part of the prophecy *precedes*, makes no important difference as to the nature of the case. The usual order in the prophets is, that the Messianic part of a prophecy comes at the *close*. But this is not always the case. Isa. ii. is a notable example of a contrary usage. So in the present case. The angel announces, that the expected era of spiritual deliverance will surely come; or, in other words, that what Daniel had already predicted more than once, would not fail of accomplishment. But these 'glad tidings of great joy' are mingled with information that fills the prophet with deep solicitude.

One very important inquiry, which has not always been made, presents itself at the outset. What was the object of Daniel's fasting and prayer? Was it to obtain information, whether the seventy years predicted by Jeremiah were now at an end? There is nothing to prove this. He tells us (v. 2), that he *understood* by the writings of Jeremiah, that seventy years, and only so many, were to be accomplished or completed, in order to fill out the measure of Babylonish exile. He was in no doubt, then, concerning this point. He surely could be in none as to the *terminus a quo* of the exile; for he was himself one of its first victims. Now as Babylon was taken by the Medo-Persian army in 538 B. C., the first year of Darius the king would be either the latter part of that year, or the former part of 537, or it might comprise both; and of course this would be the sixty-ninth year of the exile. Probably the vision was near the close of this year; for Daniel appears to believe that deliverance is near at hand, and therefore prays the more earnestly for it. Vs. 16—19 fully develop his wishes and designs. The angel is not sent then to solve his *doubts* as to what Jeremiah meant, or to show when the seventy weeks would end. He comes to comfort and enlighten the solicitous worshipper of God, and to inform him what further troubles await the Hèbrew nation, before their great and final deliverer will come. Wieseler (Die 70 Wochen, s. 13), lays it down as certain, that 'every explanation of vs. 24—27 is erroneous, which does not assign to them a disclosure of deliverance from the then present misery of the Jewish nation.' But whoever will carefully peruse vs. 16—19 must see, that Daniel has more solicitude about the worship of God and the desolations of Zion and the sanctuary, than in respect to the mere outward civil and social condition of the captive Jews. The probability surely is, that under such men as Daniel and his compeers, who bore an active part in the government of Babylonia, they had been treated with more than ordinary lenity. At any rate, no persecuting fury had increased the miseries of their condition, and their bondage seems to have been quite tolerable in respect to their outward condition. It is the honor of God and the promotion of true piety and religion, for which Daniel is most anxious; and v. 24 contains an assurance, that in due time these will be amply provided for. The remark of Wieseler is too broad and indefinite, unless, like him, we limit v. 24 to a mere promise of return from exile and renewal of religious rites, services, and privileges, after seventy weeks of days, i. e. literal weeks, from the time of Daniel's vision. For many reasons I cannot accede to this view. The leading ones are, first, that on such a ground v. 24 would be entirely at variance with vs. 25—27 in the mode of reckoning time, since the triplex division of time in the latter evidently appears to amount to the seventy weeks of v. 24. Secondly, the language of v. 24 is too general and too significant to be applied to the mere literal return from exile. Well has Hoffman (Weissag. und Erfüllung, s. 298) said: 'One can interpret the contents [of this verse] only in an arbitrary way, who applies it merely to the liberty of returning which Cyrus gave to the Jews, which liberty was so sparingly used, and so little satisfied anticipations.' Unquestionably there is a sense, an elevated one too, in which the angel's communication allayed the burdensome part of Daniel's solicitude about the honor of God and the interests of religion. But I find no specific limitation of the end of Jeremiah's seventy years. None surely was needed for Daniel. The *terminus a quo* was fully within his knowledge; the *terminus ad quem* of course could not be a matter of doubt to him.

This leads me to say, that the mode of interpreting the seventy years of Jeremiah adopted by some, who tell us that "the angel was sent to inform him, that so many *literal years* were not meant, but only a period of seventy mystic year-weeks," agrees very ill with the tenor of the book throughout. How any one can be brought to believe, that the *seventy weeks* of Daniel are merely a new exegesis of Jeremiah's seventy years, and not the designation of a new period comprising new events, I am not able to see. Not a word about the Babylonish exile is contained in vs. 24—27. How could this be, if the new designation of the seventy weeks comprised in part that exile, and merely extended the period beyond the limits which Daniel had attached to it?

It would seem that the angel must, in such a case, have been as uncertain about the distance of the *terminus ad quem*, as those interpreters suppose Daniel to have been.

That Daniel should feel solicitude about the posture of affairs, at the time of the vision now under consideration, was quite natural. The time for the exile to come to an end was very near. The Babylonish monarchy, which held the Hebrews in bondage, had been destroyed. A new dynasty had arisen, viz. that of Darius the Mede. Although not disposed to persecute and oppress the Jews, he appeared at least to be indifferent to their sufferings and wrongs. No movement was made to relieve them. They were doubtless, in view of Jeremiah's prophecy, expecting relief. What could be more natural, than for Daniel to ask with earnest importunity that this relief might come, for the honor of God and of religion? This was a strong plea; and in the mouth of such a man we might expect it would be regarded (as it was) with great favor.

The predictions in vs. 24—27 cannot be considered, in any sense, as an exegesis of Jeremiah. Nor is the communication made entirely a *new* disclosure. That the Messianic kingdom was to commence, after the four great empires had ceased, was not new. Chap. ii. vii. fully exhibit this. That Antiochus would oppress and persecute, was not new. That he would cause the sacrifices and oblation to cease for three and a half years, was not new, for 7: 25 discloses this. That his course of oppression in respect to the Jews, should continue about *one week* (of years), was not new; for 8: 14 substantially discloses this. That the tyrant should at last suddenly and fearfully perish was not new; for 8: 25 fully reveals this. But that the peculiarly oppressive trials and troubles of the Jews, before the coming of the Messiah, should be ended after a period of seventy weeks of years from the beginning or end of the Babylonish exile, was a fact not before revealed. That the existence and prosperity of the new Jewish Commonwealth, and the rebuilding of its metropolis, should be all along attended with "troublous times," and yet go forward — was a fact not before disclosed. That the Lord's *anointed* — the lawful high priest — should be cut off by violence, and have no proper successor, was a new fact. All this was deeply interesting to Daniel and to the Jews. Forewarned, forearmed. Return from the exile was speedy and certain; but the hopes of continued peace and prosperity immediately after this must not be indulged. The Lord had many trials other than the present in store for his people, before the great Deliverer would come. But it is not *all* of them, that the prophet is now commissioned to disclose and to dwell upon. Only such times as might be compared with past events, the laying waste of the temple and holy city, the destruction of large numbers of the people, cessation of religious rites and civil privileges, the profanation of the sanctuary by heathen rites, — such events, and such only, are prophetically disclosed. The communication of the angel to Daniel, apparently amounts to the following declarations: 'Thy people have suffered one exile and all its mournful consequences. Other like events, differing indeed as to manner and time, but even more trying, more dangerous to the good, and more disgraceful and fatal to the wicked, are still before the Jews. A portion of the *seventy weeks* will bring them through this fiery ordeal; and after this, until the great Deliverer shall come, they shall only experience the ordinary trials of a nation in circumstances like to theirs.'

It is on some such ground, I apprehend, that we are to account for the fact, that all the prophecies of Daniel, developing what is to *precede* the Messianic kingdom, end with the life and actions of Antiochus Epiphanes. Other subsequent enemies did indeed maltreat the Jews; but none of them attained to that consummation of wickedness and cruelty which were exhibited by him. They are not, therefore, made conspicuous in prophecy.

Should any one feel disposed to object, here, that there is somewhat of the *arbitrary* in these suggestions, I would appeal at once to the books of other prophets, yea to the whole body of Hebrew prophecy, and ask: Whether they have not respect to particular events of interest and importance, or, in other words, whether they are merely a regular series of *historic annals?* If not, then events, such as I have just mentioned, are the appropriate subjects of prophecy. What more can be said of the book of Daniel, or what more need we say, in order to vindicate the view just taken?

To those who know the course which a portion of recent criticism has taken, in order to show that the book of Daniel was written *after* the death of Antiochus Epiphanès, no apology need be made for these remarks. It is a common allegation among critics of the so-called *liberal class*, that the book of Daniel was written *post eventum*; and that the writer was not confident enough in his own *prophetic* powers, to venture anything beyond what history already gave him, excepting that, in common with all the Jews, he was full of ardent expectations in regard to the Messianic kingdom. Hence, as they conclude, he stops short with Antiochus, and expresses his confident belief, that immediately after his death the Messianic kingdom would be established.

On the full discussion of this topic I shall not now enter, but, leaving it for another occasion, merely remark at present, that the writer must have been a man of great peculiarities, to declare himself so confidently about the Messianic reign as *immediately* following the death of Antiochus, if he himself lived at that very period, and saw no certain tokens that such a reign had commenced, or was indeed about to commence. He appeals to no such tokens; he gives no hint respecting them. What moreover was to become of the credit of his book, in case of a failure? Then as to all his prophecies ending with Antiochus, (the Messianic kingdom only excepted), I would hope that the remarks already made above, suggest some other more satisfactory reason for the prophet's course, than that of his ignorance of the future. Revelation of events is made for *special* purposes, and to answer *specific* ends. It is not *annals*; it consists not of year-books and historical registers. The most hazardous period of the Jewish nation, down to its ruin by Titus, was that of Antiochus. It was the most trying to the good, and seemingly the most auspicious to the bad. It was the only period in which the sanctuary of God was daily polluted, for some years, by heathen rites and sacrifices. Should not such a period be designated, and the people of God forewarned? Daniel and the angel-interpreter seem to have so thought and decided. Might not prediction respecting the outward condition of the Jews before the coming of the Messiah, stop with events belonging to such a period, and omit the ordinary events that followed? So have other prophets done, in respect to other countries than that of Judea; and so, respecting the Hebrews; why should Daniel only be excepted from ordinary usage?

---

(1) In the first year of Darius, the son of Ahasuerus, of the seed of the Medes, who was made king over the kingdom of the Chaldees.

In respect to *Darius*, see under 6: 1.—אֲחַשְׁוֵרוֹשׁ has been the subject of much speculation and remark; see Lengerke Comm. s. 219 f. 231 f. The cuneiform inscriptions of Persia, lately deciphered, seem to have put the matter nearly at rest. The name is found in them, written *Khshhershe* or *Khshvershe*, the root of which seems to be the Persian شیرشاه (*shersha*), *lion.* The word therefore is a mere *appellative*, and might be common to many distinguished persons. Probably Astyages, the Median king, is here designated.—הָמְלַךְ, *was made king;* Schleyer (Würdigung der Einwürfe, etc., s. 185 seq.) alleges, that this word favors the idea which he defends, viz. that Darius was merely *viceroy* of Babylon. He further seeks to confirm this by 6: 1, קַבֵּל מַלְכוּתָא, *received the kingdom;* which shows, as he alleges, the *dependence* of Darius on a superior. So also we may say; but who is that superior? Had it been merely another and higher king, would he not have been named? But there is One who sets kings upon their thrones, and casts them down, at his pleasure, whom Daniel doubtless regarded, in this case, as the dispenser of office and of kingdoms. Even Lengerke concedes this, in the present case. If any one insists on it, however, I should not object to the exposition, which supposes Daniel to have the doings of Cyrus in view, who was the real conqueror of Babylon, and who, as Xenophon relates, took great care to provide for the regal claims of Darius.

(2) In the first year of his reign, I Daniel understood by the Scriptures the number of years; that the word of the Lord was to Jeremiah the prophet, to complete seventy years in respect to the desolations of Jerusalem.

The first year, etc., corresponds to 538—7 B. C.—בַּסְּפָרִים is said, by Lengerke and others, necessarily to mean a *corpus Scripturarum*, i. e. a public collection of the sacred books as already made and completed; and of course completed before the book of Daniel was written. But would a pseudo-Daniel thus betray himself, by a statement that savored of so late a period, as that after the canon was closed? Others represent the word as meaning a private collection of sacred books; others, as designating a *corpus propheticum.* None of these conjectures are necessary; and none of them are well-grounded. In Jer. 25: 13, the prophet names his written prophecy respecting the seventy years, הַסֵּפֶר הַזֶּה. A second prediction, sent to the exiles in Babylon, respecting the seventy years, he also names הַסֵּפֶר, 29: 1. Two *Sephers*, I suppose, may be called הַסְּפָרִים; and this is just what Daniel has called them, in view of their contents respecting the seventy years. To draw an argument from such a passage, and spread it out over more than a page, as Lengerke has done, in order to show that the book of Daniel was written *after* the canon was closed, is something quite aside from either good logic or fair criticism. I take the בּ in בַּסְּפָרִים to designate, as often elsewhere, instrumentality. By perusing these prophecies of Jeremiah, Daniel attained to a definite knowledge respecting the period of the exile. A perusal for the first time, on the part of Daniel at this period, it is not necessary to suppose; but only an attentive reperusal. It is unnecessary to make בַּסְּפָרִים *object* after the verb בִּינֹתִי; and of course unnecessary to translate this last word by *sought understanding* in the writings, etc., as Lengerke does, and then take the following words as being mere explanatory apposition. The more simple method of exegesis, seems to be that which I have adopted above. — אֲשֶׁר הָיָה וגו׳ I regard as coördinate with מִסְפַּר וגו׳, and designed to explain it: 'I understood the number . . . [I understood] that the word of Jehovah came to Jeremiah the prophet to complete seventy years, etc.' This last clause shows the amount of the *number*. — *Seventy years* is object to the verb לְמַלֹּאות. The form of this verb is like those of לה״; as is often the case with verbs לא״, § 74. Notes, VI. *c*. — לְחָרְבוֹת *for* or *in respect to the desolations*. These need not be limited to the final destruction only of Jerusalem, under Zedekiah, in 588 B. C., but to all the spoiling, plunder, and carrying into exile, which had taken place since the city was first captured by Nebuchadnezzar. Nothing can be plainer, than that Daniel himself reckons in this way; otherwise he could not make out a completion, or very nearly a completion, of the seventy years in question.

(3) And I set my face toward the Lord God, to seek prayer and supplications, with fasting, and sackcloth, and ashes.

Because Daniel saw, as yet, no approaching signs of liberty for his people to return from their exile to Judea, he betook himself to earnest supplication, that God would speed this event. — *I set my face to* or *toward the Lord God*, viz. toward Jerusalem where God was supposed peculiarly to dwell; see 6: 10, where the same posture in prayer is more explicitly stated. This was probably the common posture of the Jews when abroad, and not improbably of those at home. — הָאֱלֹהִים, *the God*, i. e. the only living and true God. — לְבַקֵּשׁ, *to seek earnestly* or *carefully* must signify here not to *look after*, *to seek up*, (which would make no tolerable sense), but *to betake one's self to*, *to engage in*. — תְּפִלָּה means *prayer* in its generic sense; תַּחֲנוּנִים signifies *supplication for mercy* or *favor.* This was done with the usual accompaniments during such special seasons of devotional exercises, viz. *with fasting*, while the person was clothed *with sackcloth*, and his head besprinkled *with ashes;* Job 2: 12. All these were the outward signs of internal humiliation and penitence.

(4) And I poured out supplication to Jehovah my God, and made confession, and said: Ah! Lord, the great and dreadful God, who keepeth covenant and mercy to those that love him and keep his commandments!

The frequent repetition here of the prolonged form (with ה ָ appended), seems to depend on the *Vav* prefixed (§ 126. 1. *e*), which often admits it in cases where the meaning is neither *hortative*, nor expressive of will or determination (§ 126. 1. *c*). Here is simply *narration.* — בְּאֶתְוַדֶּה, Hithp. of יָדָה, § 68. 2. e. g. — In וָאֹמְרָה, 1st pers. Imperf., the א of the stem is dropped, § 67. 2. — אָנָּא (read ăń-nā), compounded of אָהּ *ah, alas*, and נָא = *I beseech thee.* It is a common exclamation of a suppliant deeply affected. — אֲדֹנָי = יְהוָֹה, and pointed ָי in distinction from the common plur. with suff. אֲדֹנַי. — הָאֵל, emphatic. — *Great and dreadful*, great in the displays of his power, and dreadful in punishing impenitent offenders, e. g. such as the Jewish nation had been. While this thought naturally occurs first to Daniel's mind, because of the then existing state of the Hebrews, yet, as he is pleading for mercy, he does not forget another conspicuous part of the divine character, *who keepeth the covenant and the mercy.* The word *mercy* I take to be here exegetical of *covenant*, for it points out what particular part of the divine בְּרִית (*ordinance*) the speaker means, viz. that part which contains promises of *kindness* or *mercy* to the penitent and obedient. — The commencing address of the prayer is in the *Vocative* and *second* person, and so is הָאֵל, but שֹׁמֵר is in the *third* person, as are also the suffixes which follow; see § 134. 3. Note 3, as to change of persons.

(5) We have sinned, we have done perversely, we have acted impiously, and have rebelled, and have turned back from thy commandments and thine ordinances.

וְסוֹר, Inf. abs. used for the definite verb סַרְנוּ, stem סוּר. For this use of the Inf. abs., see § 128. 4. *b*. More literally the Inf. here might be translated: *there has been a turning back.* The *climactic* construction of the sentence is palpable. To turn back from obedience to the divine statutes, in the frame of mind which belongs to *rebels*, is the consummation of wickedness, and so Daniel rightly considers it. The variety of verbs employed here, indicates the design of the speaker to confess all sin of every kind in its full extent.

(6) And we have not hearkened to thy servants, the prophets, who spake in thy name to our kings, our princes, and our fathers, and to all the people of the land.

Prophets, speaking in the name, i. e. by the authority, of God are often and familiarly called his *servants,* as here. — The preposition אֶל is omitted before the second and third of the nouns which it virtually governs, § 151. 4. This is a frequent usage. The *we* of the first clause (comprised in שָׁמַעְנוּ) is explained both by the second and third clauses. The second particularizes various distinguished classes of the people; the third comprises all the remainder. הָאָרֶץ, with the article here, means of course *our land,* viz. Palestine.

(7) To thee, O Lord, belongeth righteousness, but to us shame of face, as at the present time, to each man of Judah and to the inhabitants of Jerusalem, and to all Israel, who are near and who are afar off, in all the countries whither thou hast driven them, on account of their offences which they have committed against thee.

בֹּשֶׁת הַפָּנִים means such a sense of shame as makes the countenance to *blush.* — כַּיּוֹם הַזֶּה designates *the then present time.* The whole phrase, Lengerke says, is *borrowed* from Ezra 9: 7. But suppose I should insist on reversing the order? There are many reasons for so doing; but to suspect *borrowing* or *lending,* in a case so simple and obvious as this, looks like grasping at trifles to accomplish some favorite end. — לְאִישׁ, being generic, might be translated *to the men.* Here, the לְ prefix is thrice repeated; which is done for the sake of emphasis. — *Who are near* etc., participles with the article used as a relative pronoun, § 109. 2. *a.* — שָׁם . . . אֲשֶׁר, *where, whither.* This whole clause is added so as to comprise all the Jews afar off and near, as well as those in Babylonia. — בְּמַעֲלָם וגו״, lit. *on account of the perfidy which they have perfidiously committed in respect to thee.* I have virtually retained the sense, in the translation above, but have conformed the mode of expression to our usual English idiom.

(8) O Lord, to us belongeth shame of face — to our kings, to our princes, and to our fathers, because we have sinned against thee.

A virtual repetition of vs. 5, 6. But here the prefix לְ, for the sake of emphasis, stands before the words designating each of the classes; which differs from the usage in v. 6. For אֲשֶׁר *because,* see § 152. II. *c.*

(9) To the Lord our God belongeth compassion and pardon; for we have sinned against him.

The article stands before הָרַחֲמִים וְהַסְּלִחוֹת as *abstracts,* § 107. 3. Note 1. *c.* The plur. form of these nouns denotes intensity in the manifestation, or the continued and extended exercise of these qualities or attributes; p. 201, Rem. at the bottom. The *article* before the nouns may also be accounted for, if one prefers this solution, on the ground of designating the things signified as belonging to God in a peculiar manner, i. e. on the ground of emphasis.

(10) And we have not hearkened to the voice of Jehovah our God, to walk according to his laws, which he has placed before us by his servants the prophets.

To walk, according to the usual idiom of the Hebrew means, *to demean one's self* or *to act* thus and so. — *Laws* has here its generic meaning, viz. *instructions* of every kind. — *Placed before us*, here includes the idea of being *reduced to writing*, so that the laws may be possessed and read.

(11) And all Israel have transgressed thy law, and turned back so as not to hearken to thy voice; and thou hast poured upon us the curse, even the oath, which is written in the law of Moses the servant of God, because we have sinned against him.

In respect to וְסוֹר, see on v. 5. — For the *curse* and the *oath*, see Lev. 26: 14—43. Deut. 28: 15—19. 29: 19. — וַתִּתַּךְ, 2 pers. Imperf. of נָתַךְ, with Vav continuative. § 486. 2. — לוֹ, suff. of the 3d pers., although the preceding address is in the 2d pers.; see on v. 4.

(12) And he has established his words which he spake concerning us, and concerning our judges who judged us, that he would bring great evil upon us, so that there hath not happened under the whole heaven, the like to what hath taken place in Jerusalem.

וַיָּקֶם, Hiph. with retracted accent, § 71. 3, and Note 7. — The שֹׁפֵט of the Hebrews designates every kind of magistrate. — נֶעֶשְׂתָה, Niph., *been done, happened, took place*. The meaning is: 'been brought about by thy providence.'

(13) According to what is written in the law of Moses, all this evil has come upon us; and yet we have not besought Jehovah our God to turn [us] from our iniquities, and to make [us] wise by thy truth.

אֵת before the Nom. case, (see § 116, Note at the bottom of the page), unusual, but not without precedent. The וְ in וְלֹא = *and yet*, for this particle often connects clauses which in some respects are contrasted, § 152. B. *b*. — חִלָּה lit. means, to address any one smoothly, gently, or persuasively, and so *to supplicate* in the way of softening displeasure. — *To turn us*, etc., means here not so much the pardon of sin, as grace to repent and reform. *To make us wise by thy truth*, i. e. wise in the moral sense, wise to avoid evil and to do good. In both cases *us* is omitted in the original, but is readily supplied by the reader. — בַּאֲמִתֶּךָ, suff. in the second person, referring to יְהוָה in the third; see the reverse of this in v. 4 above; § 134. 3. Note 3.

(14) And so Jehovah hath watched over the evil, and brought it upon us; for righteous is Jehovah our God in respect to all his doings which he hath done, for we have not hearkened to his voice.

וַיִּשְׁקֹד, the ו consecutive, in such cases as this, connects with itself the usual sense of the conjunction; and frequently this conjunction has the meaning *and yet, and so, therefore.* — *Watched over the evil,* i. e. kept it watchfully in store, that he might employ it in punishing, when we had deserved it. In all this God is צַדִּיק *just;* for to punish ill-desert is *justice.* — *Which he hath done* is purely a Hebrew mode of expression, and the like is very common in Hebrew. In our own language it is here a superfluity after the word *doings.* — The last clause might be rendered: *and we did not hearken,* etc. I have translated ו, however, as marking a kind of *causal* clause, see § 152. B. *c.*

(15) And now, O Lord our God, who hast brought thy people from the land of Egypt by a mighty hand, and hast made for thyself a name, as at the present time, we have sinned, we have done wickedly.

Here commences the *supplication* of the speaker; at least, this address is preparatory to it. The argument stands thus: 'O God, who in times past hast wrought wonderful deliverances for thy people, and thereby acquired a glorious name — repeat thy wondrous doings, and add to the glory which thou hast already acquired! As thou didst bring us out of exile in Egypt, so also bring us out of exile in Babylon.' — *A name, as at the present time,* i. e. such a name, glory, honor, as is attributed to thee even now. — *We have sinned* etc., the deep sensation of penitence forces from the speaker the repetition of confession.

(16) O Lord, according to all thy kindness let thine anger and thine indignation be turned away now from thy city Jerusalem, thy holy mountain, for, on account of our sins and the iniquities of our fathers, Jerusalem and thy people have become a reproach to all around us.

צִדְקֹתֶיךָ is here used in the sense of *favor, kindness, benignity,* as it often is when the plur. is employed (as here), which designates *repeated acts of benignity,* and is intensive. — נָא, a sign of the optative, § 125. 3. *b.* — הַר קָדְשֶׁךָ, lit. *mountain of thy holiness* = thy holy mountain, § 104. 1. — Daniel confesses the sins of the fathers which occasioned their exile, and the sins of the generation then living which continued that exile. The central point of his solicitude is *Jerusalem and the holy mountain,* i. e. the honor of God and religion. — *Reproach to those around us,* the preposition in the last word takes the form of a const. plur. noun, § 99. 1. § 101. 1.

(17) And now, O our God, hearken to the prayer of thy servant and to his supplications, and let thy face shine upon thy sanctuary which is desolate, for the Lord's sake.

Of thy servant, i. e. of the speaker, who mentions himself in the usual humble manner of the Hebrews, when one addressed a superior. — הָאֵר, *cause to shine*, i. e. to be bright, cheerful, to appear pleased, the reverse of frowning or looking dark. — הַשָּׁמֵם, Part. intrans. and *passive*, (as usual with this form), the הַ being a relative demonstrative, § 109. 2. *a*. — לְמַעַן אֲדֹנָי, third person instead of the second; and so oftentimes, when God is spoken of.

(18) Incline thine ear, O my God, and hear; open thine eyes and see our desolations and the city on which thy name is called; for not on account of our righteousnesses do we lay our supplications before thee, but on account of thy great mercy.

פְּקָחָה, (so the Kethibh should be pointed), is better than the marginal פְּקַח, because it is an intensive form, § 48. 5. — אֲשֶׁר . . . עָלֶיהָ, *upon which*, § 121. 1. — מַפִּילִים, lit. *let fall*, corresponding well with our word *lay*, which means *to put down* or *place before*, stem נָפַל. — Daniel has no hope, when he looks to the just deserts of his people, but only in the mercy of God.

(19) O Lord hear; O Lord forgive; O Lord listen and do, delay not for thine own sake, O my God, for thy name is called upon thy city and upon thy people.

עֲשֵׂה, *do*, viz. that which I request. The like often in this book, as to עָשָׂה. — אַל תְּאַחַר, opt., see p. 268. par. 3. — *For thine own sake* is explained by what follows. As common parlance made use of the phrases *city of God*, and *people of God*, so the honor of God is urged by Daniel as a reason why God should regard the Hebrew nation with special kindness.

(20) And while I was speaking, and interceding, and confessing my sin and the sin of my people Israel, and laying my supplication before Jehovah my God, in behalf of the holy mountain of my God; (21) even while I was speaking in prayer, then the man Gabriel, whom I had before seen in the vision, having been hastened in a swift course, approached me about the time of the evening oblation.

הָאִישׁ, *the man*, viz. the one whom I had before seen in vision, as the sequel declares. The reference is to what has been related in 8: 15. — בַּתְּחִלָּה, lit. *in the beginning;* but often the phrase means simply *before*, *aforetime*. I have here translated it simply by *before*. The reference is to 8: 15. — מֻעָף בִּיעָף is rendered by Michaelis, Dathe, Döderlein, Ges.,

Rosenm., al., *wearied by swift flight;* a strange idea to be associated with *Gabriel,* i. e. powerful man of God. We read of angels "swift to do the will" of God, but not of their being *wearied* by their swiftness. It is incongruous. Both words are evidently of the same root, and of kindred meaning, i. e. both come from יָעַף. מֻעָף = מוּעָף, Part. Hoph., means *hastened, caused to make haste.* בִּיעָף is the noun with a prep., and means *swift course,* or *haste.* We might well translate: *being hastened swiftly.* Our English translators derived the word מֻעָף from עוּף *to fly,* and have rendered the phrase accordingly. But יָעַף means simply *to hasten,* in its primary sense, and indicates nothing of the manner in which swiftness is effected. How long Daniel was making supplication, and of course how long Gabriel was in actually coming to him, we know not. Daniel's recorded prayer is, in all probability, only a specimen or summary of what he uttered on the occasion which called it forth. — נֹגֵעַ, Part. with a *praeterite* meaning, § 131. 1. and 2. *c.*

(22) And he made explanation, and talked with me, and said: O Daniel, I have come forth to teach thee understanding.

The first וַיָּבֶן is a summary of what the angel did, on this occasion. — *He talked with me* indicates a continued colloquy. — וַיֹּאמַר prefaces a quotation of words spoken. — בִּינָה *meaning* of anything, *understanding, intelligence.* Of what? Of the prophecies in Jer., say Lengerke and others. But then הַבִּינָה would be almost of necessity employed in such a case. We should therefore give to בִּינָה a more generic sense, and then the phrase = *to impart to thee understanding,* viz. respecting thy people. This confines the sequel neither to the predictions of Jeremiah, nor to the vision in ch. viii. These limits would be too narrow for vs. 24—27.

(23) At the beginning of thy supplications, a word went forth, and I am come to tell thee, for thou art greatly beloved; mark well then the word, and understand the vision.

חֲמוּדוֹת, plur. of intensity, lit. *loves* = Lat. *deliciae.* — יָצָא דָבָר, *a word, sentence,* or *communication went forth.* From whom? The text does not say explicitly from what quarter it proceeded. But the implication scarcely admits of a doubt. The *word* or *communication* must have come from some one *superior* to the angel; for his errand is to convey and declare it: *I am come* לְהַגִּיד, *to declare* [it]. Some supply לְךָ (*to thee*) after the verb in the Inf. To this there is no urgent objection; but even in case this view of the ellipsis is admitted, it is necessary to supply *it* (viz. *the word*) after לְהַגִּיד, for this verb surely falls back upon

דָּבָר, and must have a direct object. — The last two clauses of the verse make all this plain: *Mark well then*, or *consider well, the word* (בַּדָּבָר), where the article points of course to the preceding דָּבָר. — *Vision* has not exactly the same sense as דָּבָר *message*, but means both the *appearance* of Gabriel and the developments which he makes. In other words; the prophecy itself and the manner in which it is communicated, are required to be objects of special attention on the part of Daniel, for they are deserving of his most serious consideration. I do not see any way of fairly avoiding the interpretation, which regards the angel as having received from God the communication that follows, and as specially deputed to make this communication to Daniel. This is a plain and simple view of the matter; and this turn of the sentiment is altogether apposite to the exigencies of the case before us. The first דָּבָר in v. 23, not having the article, can point to no previous or well known communication, antecedent to the period then passing. *A* (not *the*) *communication*, therefore, must be its meaning. What this communication is, remains yet to be explained. The second הַדָּבָר, having the article, of course points to the preceding one. But this second one has a clear relation to the communication which follows. The exegesis which makes both of these refer to דְּבַר יְהוָה in v. 2, is clearly ungrammatical. Were this the case, both *must* have the article. We cannot admit, with Lengerke, that the angel only undertakes a new and mystical interpretation of Jeremiah's predictions concerning the seventy weeks.

(24) Seventy weeks are decided respecting thy people and thy holy city, to restrain transgression, and to seal up sin, and to expiate iniquity; and to bring in everlasting righteousness, and to seal vision and prophecy, and to anoint a holy of holies.

שָׁבֻעִים, from שָׁבוּעַ, and of an irregular masc. plur. form, retaining (ָ) under the first radical, (normally it would read שְׁבֻעִים). The *masc.* plur. occurs only in the paragraph before us, and in Dan. 10: 2, 3. The fem. form שָׁבֻעוֹת also retains the (ָ) of the first radical. Why? none of the lexicons or grammars tell us. Fuerst (Concord.) says: "retento Qamets *sibili*," in respect to the plural forms; by which I suppose him to mean, that *sibilant* letters have a propensity to a *Qamets* vowel-sound. If this be his assertion, it needs illustration and confirmation. It is disputed whether the masc. singular occurs; but as the Masoretic text of Gen. 29: 27, 28 stands (מַלֵּא שְׁבֻעַ זֹאת), there is a clear instance of a masc. form in a *const.* state, from שָׁבוּעַ, showing that the Qamets in the sing. is mutable. Wieseler however, (Die 70 Wochen, s. 14), says that "the Masorites have certainly erred," and that we should read שְׁבַע זֹאת, i. e. *these seven* (years), lit. *this heptade* (of years). As the form of the numeral is sing. and *fem.* (§ 96. 1), it may be united with זאת; and שָׁנִים seems to be fairly implied, as any one may see by comparing Gen. 29: 18, 20, 27 together. If this criticism be just, (it seems to me plainly to be so), then we have no instance of a *masc.* form of the word in question, out of the book of Daniel. This however will prove nothing against the existence of one, since it is altogether a feasible form. The simple truth is, that both שָׁבֻעִים and שָׁבֻעוֹת are *participial* forms, meaning *besevened,* (sit venia!), i. e. computed by sevens. Lit. then we might translate thus: *Heptades seventy are decided upon*, etc. This leaves the question entirely open, whether the meaning is heptades of days, or of ordinary years, or of sabbatical years; and this question must be decided of course by the context. The Jews had three kinds of *Heptades* in respect to *time;* first, that of *days*, seven of which make a *week;* secondly, that of *years*, seven of which make a *sabbatical year*, Lev. 25: 1—7; thirdly, that of the seven periods of years before the *jubilee-year*, for this last comprises seven times seven years = forty-nine years, after which comes the jubilee-year, Lev. 25: 8. Which of these three is meant in the present case? for the clause before us may be interpreted in either way. Not the first, for this would make but about a year and a half for the fulfilment of all that is predicted in the sequel, and would fill the passage with contradictions. Wieseler, indeed, in his work quoted above, has labored to show, that the first mentioned *seventy weeks* are merely literal and common weeks; for he holds that the sequel in v. 24 refers merely to the return from the Babylonish exile, and a restoration to all the rites and privileges of worship as prescribed by Moses, with an accompanying reformation of moral demeanor. But the subsequent *weeks* he counts as *year-weeks*, i. e. periods of seven years each. Ingenious and acute as this writer surely is, I cannot accord with this view of the case; for, (1) It makes a violent disruption in the meaning of שָׁבֻעִים, to translate it *weeks of days* in v. 24, and then *weeks of years* in the following verses of the same paragraph. (2) Nothing seems plainer, than that the tripartite, 7, 62, 1, are designed to make up the number seventy stated in v. 24; and of course, the seventy at the outset must have the same relation to שָׁבֻעִים, that the subsequent numbers (the component parts of it) have; and Wieseler himself concedes, that in vs. 25—27 שָׁבֻעִים means *week-years*, i. e. heptades of years. (3) The application of the magnificent promises, in v. 24, merely to a partial return from exile, and to the broken and troubled state (בְּצוֹק הָעִתִּים, v. 25) of the Jews for a long period (62 weeks), is something that savors too much of *deducere aliquid ex aliquo*, to commend itself to the simple interpreter. There is too much of what the Germans name a *hinein-exegesiren*, to meet with cordial reception. Hoffman (Weiss. und Erfüll. s. 298) rightly says respecting it: "The universality with which the consummation of all the hopes of Israel is here spoken of, renders it impossible for any one to interpret it, except in an *arbitrary way*, as merely applying to the scanty return from the Babylonish exile by permission of Cyrus — a return which hardly satisfied the anticipations respecting it." — We may therefore abide by uniform *consistency* through the whole paragraph, in the use of שָׁבֻעִים. Then, of course, we must regard the meaning as = $7 \times 70 = 490$ years.

So long a time, or thus much ground, is comprised in the prediction; not because this, (reckoned in any feasible way), reaches down to the Messianic period, but because so much of the time intervening, before the Messiah would appear, is for the most part 'troublous time,' and resembles in this respect, that of the seventy years' Babylonish exile. The speaker means to say: 'The Messiah will surely come, and Jerusalem will be restored in a high and spiritual sense; but before all this takes place, there must be, not seventy *years* of literal exile again, but seventy *times* seven *years* of trouble and of trial. How soon after this is over, the king of the new and last dominion will make his appearance, the speaker does not say, nor does the context inform us. Enough that the days of peculiar trial and trouble like those of the Babylonian exile, will pass away within the period named; for that period נֶחְתַּךְ, i. e. is *definitely limited* or *decided*.

As to the masc. form שָׁבֻעִים being employed here, in all probability the speaker meant to attract special attention to the word so important in the sequel, and therefore he has put it first, as well as given to it a peculiar form. He may also have been influenced in his choice of the form, by the שָׁבֻעִים which follows; or it may have been the prevailing dialect of the day. That he designs to designate *heptades of years* by it, would seem quite probable, if we merely compare 10: 2, 3, where יָמִים is added after it in order to explain it, and to tell the reader that he does not mean a שָׁבוּעַ of the same length or of the same kind as before. No explanation is needed, however, in the present case, except what the context gives. Daniel's meditation had been upon the seventy *simple years* predicted by Jeremiah. The angel tells him, that a *new-seventy*, i. e. seventy week-years or seven times seventy years, await his people, before their final deliverer will come. The reader almost spontaneously adopts this view of the meaning, who is familiar with the *week-years* of the Hebrews. As to the *third* way in which the Hebrews used the word שָׁבוּעַ, it designated the jubilee-year = forty-nine years or seven times seven. If now we choose this last period as the meaning of שבוּעִים,

then we should have $49 \times 70 = 3430$ years — a period incredible, on every ground, in respect to the events which follow. In other words, the first and last of the heptades lead to inconsistency or absurdity; neither of them, therefore, is meant by the text. 'In medio tutissimus,' one may safely say, in the present case. Nor is Daniel alone in such a mode of expression. Gellius (Noct. Att. III. 10) makes M. Varro say, that he had written *septuaginta hebdomadas librorum.* The like in Aristotle, Pol. VII. 16; and in Censorinus. De Die natali, c. 16.

נֶחְתַּךְ is found only here, in the Hebrew Scriptures, but is more common in Chaldee and Rabbinic. The literal meaning is *to cut*, but it does not necessarily involve the adjunct idea *to cut off.* The Vulgate, however, has rendered it *abbreviatae sunt*, probably in reference to the idea that *lunar* months are here to be counted for the years, rather than *solar* ones. Wieseler (s. 95 seq.) defends the translation *abbreviated* or *abridged*, and represents the angel as designing to say, that the period of seventy years' exile, as foretold by Jeremiah, is, through divine mercy, and in answer to the prayer of Daniel, *abridged.* As he makes the exile to begin with 599 B. C., (led, as he says, by Matt. 1: 12, who seems to assign its beginning to the deportation of Jechoniah), so, at the time when Daniel fasted and prayed, only sixty-three years of it had passed away, and seven years were therefore to be abridged. But I cannot admit the probability of such an explanation. The idea of *abbreviation* would have assumed quite another form. Nor is it easy to see, how Daniel, in case he began the exile with the year 599 B. C. when Jehoiakim was carried into exile, could have supposed that seventy years had already come very near to the close, when seven years were yet lacking; for the three first verses of our chapter evidently present him as supposing this. The conclusion is inevitable, if chap. 1: 1 be compared, that Daniel dates the exile in the third year of Jehoiakim's reign, or at least the attack of Nebuchadnezzar upon Jerusalem; and such being the case, there is no room for *abridging* the seventy years. They are already on the point of expiring, when Daniel betakes himself to prayer and fasting. We must admit, then, the figurative sense of נֶחְתַּךְ, viz. *decided, defined, determined, decreed;* for so the Latin *decido* means in its figurative sense, while lit. it means *cut off;* and so the Heb. גָּזַר and חָרַץ, and the Greek τέμνω. I would not aver, that simply *decreed* or *determined* would adequately translate the word, for it evidently means a *definitive separation* of the weeks in question from the mass of time, in order, that what is included in this separated and thus defined part, may present the extent of the ground which the predictions that follow are to occupy. In other words: 'Seventy weeks are *definitely selected and decided upon,'* as a period in which various things are to happen, before the final consummation of the hopes of the Jewish nation, viz. the appearance of the Messiah. As to the *sing.* number of the verb, I see no need of so much difficulty as has been made. The seventy weeks are a definite period here *generically* presented; and as such they are *one.* The *sing.* number of the verb, therefore, is a mere case of *constructio ad sensum.* We need not resort (with Hitzig) to the passive form impersonal, as retaining the Acc., nor suppose (with Hengstenberg) עֵת to be implied. Comp. the like in Gen. 46: 22, as to a plur. subject and sing. verb, although in other respects the case will not afford an exact parallel with the present one.

עַל עַמְּךָ וְעַל־עִיר קָדְשֶׁךָ, *upon thy people and upon thy holy city.* Here I have rendered עַל *upon,* (in the version above, *respecting*), in order to approach nearer to the true idea of the Hebrew; for עַל often designates the idea of *on* or *upon* in the sense of what is burdensome, or it is used in what the lexicons style a *hostile sense;* Ges. Lex. עַל, 4. *a.* Plainly it is so here. The seventy weeks comprise the special burden, the trials, the troubles, through which Israel must pass, before the Great Deliverer will make his appearance, or, in the language of the remainder of the verse, before sin will be thoroughly subdued and expiated, and righteousness introduced in the full measure often predicted. — *Thy people . . . thy holy city,* Wieseler (p. 16) says, 'indicate two things; (1) That the blessings promised pertain only to the Jews. (2) That they should share in them merely on *Daniel's* account, and not on their own.' I can find neither of these intimations in those expressions. Daniel was a native of Jerusalem, and probably of royal origin (1: 3); and so we have *thy city. Thy people* means simply the people to which he belonged, and *thy city* is merely the city of his birth where his affections centered. There is doubtless, however, an emphasis beyond this in the word *thy.* Daniel had just been most earnestly and anxiously pleading in behalf of the city and people to which he belonged; and *thy,* applied to both of them, conveys the idea of a people and city for which he was most anxiously concerned, and for which he had just made such fervent intercession. The sequel of the verse does not indeed 'preach the gospel to the Gentiles;' but neither does it confine the promised good to any one nation. It simply assures Daniel that his people are to participate in it. The idea that 'the Jews are to be blessed merely on Daniel's account,' I am unable to find in the passage.

לְכַלֵּא הַפֶּשַׁע, *to restrain transgression;* which version, however, takes for granted that the Kethibh, כַּלֵּא is a Piel form of כָּלָא. Most of the ancient versions, and the mass of recent critics, have preferred to derive the verb from כָּלָה; and they aver, that here is merely an exchange of form in the ה״ל verb, for a form of א״ל, which, as all concede, is a frequent occurrence; § 74. Note VI. and Note 22. *c.* ib. Hence they translate thus: *to consummate transgression* or *to fill up the measure of rebellion;* meaning, that during the seventy weeks, rebellion will reach its acme, and will not go beyond. Expressions similar to this there are, here and there in the Scriptures; e. g. in Gen. 15: 16, "The iniquity of the Amorites *is not yet full,*" (לֹא שָׁלֵם). In the like way 1 Thess. 2: 16, ἀναπληρῶσαι τὰς ἁμαρτίας; and so in Dan. 8: 23, כְּהָתֵם הַפֹּשְׁעִים. But objections not easily met, may be made against this view. (1) It comes not within the common usages of grammar, or of the book before us, to make such an exchange of כַּלֵּה for כַּלֵּא here. The verb כָּלָה elsewhere retains its ה throughout, e. g. Dan. 9: 27. 11: 36, and in Dan. 12: 7 we have the Inf. Piel כַּלּוֹת. This is of course the true Inf. of the Piel of כָּלָה; and where Gesenius and others find a כַּלֵּה Inf. form, (for which they say כַּלֵּא is substituted), I know not. It is an *Unding* in grammar or in the Heb. *usus loquendi.* (2) The whole sentiment which is thus assigned to the passage, has an erroneous basis. They understand the speaker as now describing what will take place *during* the seventy weeks, i. e. rebellion will then be consummated, etc.; whereas it seems to lie on the very face of the remainder of this verse, that *blessings* which are to *follow* the seventy weeks are foretold. I would not deny, that there may be a point of view, from which one may regard a consummation of iniquity as desirable, all things considered, (for then comes of course the hope of better times); but nowhere in the Bible, as I believe, can it be found, that the perfecting of rebellion is represented as a *blessing,* either present or in promise. If this view is correct, it is decisive of the whole question, and lays entirely aside the word כַּלֵּה, unless it be taken in another and very different sense, viz. that of *completing* in the sense of *bringing to an end, destroying.* But to change the text for the sake of this meaning, when כַּלֵּא comes virtually to the same point, and indicates an effectual check or restraint upon sin, is both unnecessary and uncritical. However, against retaining כַּלֵּא as a regular form from כָּלָא it is objected, that the word has no *Piel.* All that this can properly mean is, that Piel is not elsewhere found. But how many verbs are there in the Hebrew, in the same predicament, i. e. where only one example of this conjugation, or of that, can be found? כָּלָא has a *transitive* as well as intransitive sense (Num. 11: 28. Ecc. 8: 8, al.); and it may have a Piel of *intensity* or of *habitual action;* which is the very meaning appropriate to the passage before us. Then what objection can be made to the idea of *restraining,* or rather of *habitually and powerfully restraining* פֶּשַׁע? This last word is the most intense designation of wickedness, as it combines the idea of *apostasy* and *rebellion.* Both of these the prophet had confessed, in his prayer (vs. 5—11), to be chargeable upon Israel. These had taken the lead in bringing down divine judgments upon the nation. Hence the הַפֶּשַׁע (*the transgression*) as it is named in our text; viz. the apostasy and rebellion already described. When the Great Deliverer shall come, he will effectually restrain such transgressions as bring down divine judgments upon the nation and send it into exile. The allegation of Lengerke and some others, that כָּלָא, which means to *shut up, enclose,* as well as to *restrain,* should have the first of these meanings assigned to it here, because *to shut up transgression* means to *hide* it or *conceal* it, and so to *forgive* it, has no foundation in the *usus loquendi* of the word. When a Hebrew spoke of *covering* sin in such a sense, he employed כִּסָּה or כָּפַר. The text of the Kethibh may stand therefore untouched; and the meaning of it as it is, seems to be altogether apposite to the purpose of the speaker.

וּלְחָתֵם חַטָּאוֹת, *and to seal up sins,* where the vowel-points of the verb belong to the marginal Qeri, וּלְהָתֵם, Hiph. Inf. of תָּמַם. The text should be pointed and read וְלַחְתֹּם, as in the sequel. The imagery of the language is evidently progressive. First we have the *restraining,* lit. *shutting up;* then this work is completed by putting a *seal* upon it; comp. Matt. 27: 66. Where we use *bars* and *bolts* only, in many cases the ancients also employed *seals,* in order to make sure the object thus enclosed and guarded. See Lex. The *literal* meaning would be plain; the prisoner is first *shut up,* then the *seal* is put upon his prison door. Thus Job 9: 7, God *seals up* the stars, i. e. prevents them from shining; Job 37: 7, he *seals up* the hand of all men, i. e. hinders them from any development of activity. So here; to *seal up* sins, is to render them inert, inefficient, powerless. They are not only *restrained,* but rendered unable to break out, and bring men into danger of punishment. The other reading in the Qeri, viz. וּלְהָתֵם arose, in all probability, from a comparison with 8: 23, where we have בְּהָתֵם הַפֹּשְׁעִים, *when transgressors have come to the full* [measure of their sin]. But this meaning does not fit in 9: 24. It is what *follows* the 70 weeks, which is predicted; and after their expiration, there is no time for the consummating of wickedness; the time has come to *seal it up,* as God does the stars and the hand of all men, i. e. to render it inefficient, incapable of acting at liberty. With Wieseler, then, we may justly prefer the text as it stands, to any of the changes proposed. The objection of Ewald, that in such a case we must suppose a repetition of the same word too speedily, amounts to but little; for in the next three verses, חָרַץ and שֹׁמֵם are *thrice* repeated. Besides, the second case of חָתַם differs in the shade of its meaning from the first case.

וּלְכַפֵּר עָוֹן, lit. *to cover sin;* but this would not answer well here, inasmuch as sin is already *shut up* and *sealed upon.* It must then have one of the two tropical meanings which the word bears, viz. either that of *forgiving* sin, or that of *expiating* it. Either meaning would suit the tenor of the passage, the amount of which is, that sin is either to be put under entire restraint, as in the case of obstinate offenders; or to be *forgiven* or *atoned for*, as in the case of the penitent. In one way or another the power of sin to do mischief, or to occasion condemnation, is to be crippled. How well the idea of *atonement* accords with the epistle to the Hebrews, as the prominent feature in the development of the Messianic period, none need to be informed. Why not admit it here, where the angel is dwelling upon the distinguished blessings which will follow the 70 weeks of troublous times? Its *appropriateness* can hardly be doubted.

וּלְהָבִיא צֶדֶק עֹלָמִים, *to introduce everlasting righteousness*, i. e. the δικαιοσύνη θεοῦ of Paul, in his epistles to the Romans and Galatians. It is *everlasting*, because the Messiah's kingdom is so, Dan. 1: 44. 7: 14, 27. It is *introduced*, because it is of God's giving, and is procured by the Messiah. The people are to be transgressors no more, so as to need punishment and exile. The first three στίχοι disclose the *negative* portion of what is to be effected. Sin is to be checked, and removed. Now comes the *positive* part; righteousness, viz. that of the heart and life which God bestows, (not צֶדֶק in the sense of *prosperity*), that righteousness which is the opposite of a sinful state, is to be the characteristic of the new kingdom.

וְלַחְתֹּם חָזוֹן וְנָבִיא, lit. *to seal vision and prophet,* where *seal* has the sense of *confirming, authenticating.* A seal was put at the end of a writing, to show that it was completed and was authentic. Prophecy is *open* so long as it remains unfulfilled. When it is fulfilled, it is *completed,* which is one of the tropical meanings of the verb חָתַם. The old dispensation was one of "types and shadows of good things to come," and in its very nature *prophetic.* Under it many predictions concerning the Messianic period were uttered; when that comes, these are *sealed, completed, authenticated.* Of course the *good* which those prophecies foretold is here in the speaker's mind. — נָבִיא, *prophet,* has reference to the person who foretels, and חָזוֹן is his prophetic vision. Both are included here, because not only the vision is completed or fulfilled, but the character and claims of the prophet are authenticated. If this view be correct, then לַחְתֹּם, in this last case, has plainly a different shade of meaning from that in which it is first employed. Surely no one critically conversant with the Scriptures needs to be told, that cases of this nature are by no means of unfrequent occurrence. The idea of *sealing up vision and prophet* by the death of Christ, or by his coming and repealing the old dispensation, is quite foreign from the passage before us. Besides, were there no *visions* and no *prophets* under the new dispensation? So Peter did not view the matter, Acts 2: 17: 21. To maintain, as Wieseler does (s. 17), that the *vision* to be sealed or confirmed is only that of Jeremiah (25: 11), is palpably aside from the scope of the passage, which is of an extent much wider. Besides, this view of the matter would involve a *ὕστερον πρότερον*. All here related is to *follow* the 70 weeks; but the return from the captivity did not follow them. It occurred while they were *in transitu*, and during the early part of them. Wieseler escapes from this, only by making the 70 weeks, in the verse before us, to mean merely 70 *weeks of days*, which passed away before the proclamation of Cyrus in Ezra i.; a *new* exegesis, I admit, but hardly a *true* one.

וְלִמְשֹׁחַ קֹדֶשׁ קָדָשִׁים, *and to anoint a Holy of Holies.* Is it the Jewish sanctuary which is to be rebuilt and *anointed*, i. e. consecrated to the service of God again? Or is it a *new sanctuary*, such as becomes the new spiritual dispensation? Not the former; for then the article could not fail before קָדָשִׁים. Never is it omitted in any case, where *holy of holies* means *the most holy place* in the temple. The insertion of the article here would have misled the reader, and naturally obliged him to interpret the passage as designating the sanctuary of the temple at Jerusalem when rebuilt. In the present case, *a sanctuary*, i. e. such an one as is appropriate to the new state of things, is designated. Of such an one the writer of the epistle to the Hebrews speaks: "Christ, the high-priest of good things to come, when he presented himself through a greater and more perfect tabernacle . . . not with the blood of bulls and goats, but by his own blood, once for all entered *εἰς τὰ ἅγια, into the sanctuary*, procuring eternal redemption." Heb. 9: 11, 12. (*Τὰ ἅγια*, and *τὰ ἅγια τῶν ἁγίων* are N. Test. names for קֹדֶשׁ הַקֳּדָשִׁים). This is the *sanctuary* belonging to that temple, under whose altar the Apocalyptist saw the supplicating souls of the martyrs, Rev. 6: 9, comp. also 8: 3. 9: 13. 14: 18. Rev. 11: 19 speaks of "the temple of God . . . in heaven, where was seen, in his temple, the ark of his testament or covenant." And although in the New Jerusalem there will be no temple (Rev. 21: 22), yet before the final consummation of all things, the spiritual temple in heaven, the archetype of the earthly one (Heb. 8: 5), is always spoken of by the Hebrew sacred writers, in the New Test. and in the Old, as having an existence. It is that into which Christ as high priest enters, and presents his own propitiatory blood, Heb. 9: 11—14. To *anoint the sanctuary* there, of course means to prepare it for this new offering; just as the tabernacle and all its furniture was anointed, it order to prepare it for sacrifices and oblations, Ex. 40: 9. Indeed the phrase קֹדֶשׁ קָדָשִׁים might be regarded as meaning *temple* instead of *sanctuary* merely; for in Num. 18: 10 it is so employed, with the article before the second noun, and in Ezek. 45: 3 without the article. Yet I feel no need of resorting to this, as Hoffman does, (Die siebenzig Jahre, s. 65). The expression is more vivid, if we take the thing as presented in Heb. 9: 11—14. If Paul "knew nothing else among the Corinthians but Jesus Christ and him *crucified*," and "gloried in nothing save the *cross* of Christ," then the presentation of atoning blood in the eternal sanctuary, is the cause and consummation of all the blessings promised under the new dispensation. To *anoint that sanctuary* stands connected with this service in the temple above. Not that we are to suppose a material literal sense should be given to any of these descriptions, but that they are significant as symbolical or figurative. As God is a *spirit*, his sanctuary, and the heaven which he has prepared, are *spiritual*. Very significant surely must the language of our text have been, to a Hebrew under the ancient dispensation. Wieseler (s. 18) applies the passage under discussion to the *altar* mentioned in Ezra 3: 2, and remarks, (which is true), that the altar is sometimes designated קֹדֶשׁ קָדָשִׁים, as in Ex. 29: 37. 30: 29. I have no objections to *altar* as the meaning; but that any altar built by Jeshua or Zerubbabel corresponded to the one mentioned here, (if the passage indeed is to be so interpreted), I cannot admit. Well has Hoffman said, (I repeat it), that 'an interpretation which assigns to v. 24 only a description of the literal return from Babylon and its immediate consequences, is *arbitrary*.' In fact, such an exegesis would at once show, that the language of the speaker on the present occasion is extravagant and bombastic.

The interpretation which assigns to *holy of holies* a *concrete* sense, and makes it apply to Christ himself, (C. B. Michaelis, Häv.), or which makes it mean the *church* (Hengst.) is inadmissible. The phrase never designates *persons*. Besides, to apply it to the Messiah, would represent him as performing his whole work, before he is *consecrated* to it; whereas the offering which he presents in the eternal sanctuary is the consummation of his mediatorial work.

(25) Mark well and understand; from the going forth of a command to rebuild Jerusalem unto an anointed one, a prince, shall be seven weeks; and sixty and two weeks shall it be rebuilt, with broad spaces and narrow limits, and in troublous times.

The preceding verse in a generic way announces seventy weeks, which must pass away before a new and glorious period is ushered in, the characteristics of which are, the restraining and forgiving of sin, and the introduction of holiness and righteousness under a new dispensation. This is indeed the consummation, to which the whole passage in vs. 24—27 has relation. But vs. 25—27 are designed to answer the question that would naturally arise in the mind of Daniel: 'What then is to take place during this long interval of waiting for the accomplishment of our highest hope?' The angel informs him that the so-named *seventy weeks* may be subdivided into three portions, viz. into seven, sixty-two, and one. Each of these portions has peculiarities of its own, which mark and distinguish it. The period of *seven weeks* has a definitive beginning and end, by which it is distinguished, viz. "from the going forth of a command to rebuild Jerusalem unto an anointed one, a prince," thus making the *terminus a quo* and *ad quem*. The second has no *expressed terminus a quo*, but from the nature of the case it has apparently an *implied* one, viz. the end of the first period, or the appearance of an "anointed one, a prince." This takes for granted, that the periods named here are *successive*, and not parallel or contemporaneous. Such, it seems to me, is the first and spontaneous impression of every unbiassed reader; for how else can the period of seventy weeks be made out? The *end* of the second period is of course the end of the sixty-two weeks, i. e. sixty-two weeks from the appearance of the anointed one, the prince. But the end seems also to be marked by another circumstance, viz. *the cutting off of an anointed one.* So v. 26: "*After* (אַחֲרֵי) sixty-two weeks, an anointed one shall be cut off." Naturally this does not mean some indefinite time afterwards, but a time in near proximity with the end of the second period. The *third* period (one week) of course begins with the same excision of an anointed one, and continues seven years, during which a foreign prince shall come, and lay waste the city and sanctuary of Jerusalem, and cause the offerings to cease for three and a half years, after which utter destruction shall come upon him, vs. 26, 27.

Thus much for the definite beginning and end of the respective periods, considered as *successive*. We have further to say, respecting them, that each has its own appropriate occurrences. The *first* period (seven weeks) has indeed no specific and express description of events, which are to take place, attached to it. But the command *to restore and rebuild* seems to imply that the work was to be entered upon and advanced. The *second* period is characterized by the *continued rebuilding*, but in a stinted or scanty measure, because of "troublous times." Nothing of this kind is said of the first period. The *third* period is characterized by the occurrence of events, which have been stated in the preceding paragraph. Thus each is distinguished from the other, not merely by limitation of time, but by the events which were to take place respectively in each.

After taking this brief survey of the three component parts of the seventy weeks, and having seen how they are separated and distinguished from each other, let us now return to the seventy weeks, i. e. the generic period, and inquire where we are to begin in counting them.

Daniel regards the period assigned by Jeremiah as very near its close, 9: 2. He prays earnestly for the restoration of his people. The angel appears, and tells him, not that the seventy years are near their end (which Daniel already well knew), but that in the councils of Heaven another and larger period is assigned, viz. seven times seventy years, for still further trials of his people, before the great consummation of their highest hopes will be realized. *When* then does this new period of 490 years commence? The most obvious answer *a priori* would seem to be: From the time when Daniel is addressed. But the *events* assigned to the second and third portions of the general period forbid this answer. Daniel saw this vision in B. C. 538. If 7 times 70 years = 490 be subtracted from this, it would bring the *terminus ad quem* of the whole seventy weeks (counting them successively and continuously), down to B. C. 48, a year in which nothing special took place to distinguish it from the time that followed after it, or went before it. All correspondence of prediction with event, must in such a case, be given up, of course, if such a *terminus a quo* be adopted.

Let us go back then to B. C. 606, the time from which Daniel plainly dates "the desolations of Jerusalem" (v. 2), and assume this as the *terminus a quo;* in this case the seventy weeks would end, (counted as before), with B. C. 116; a period, again, which offers nothing in history to distinguish it, and therefore it cannot be the subject of the following prophecy. On either of the preceding grounds, then, we find ourselves at a complete stand.

If we go on now, for the sake of trial, and endeavor to ascertain the *terminus a quo* of the first part of the seventy weeks, viz. the 7 weeks = 49 years, and begin the count from B. C. 606, i. e. the commencement of the desolations, then we must end the first period with B. C. 557, a period when there was as yet no *command to rebuild.* Nor was there any *anointed one and prince* to mark the end of the seven weeks at that time. To make another trial, let us suppose the seven weeks to be counted from the exile of Jehoiachim, 599 B. C., then we must end them with B. C. 550, another period of the like description as that of B. C. 557. If we begin these weeks with the captivity of Zedekiah and the actual and final destruction of Jerusalem B. C. 588, then we obtain 539 B. C. as the *end* of the period. At this time no command had been given to rebuild Jerusalem, and Darius the Mede was, or was about to be, possessed of the Babylonish throne, who surely cannot be reckoned a מָשִׁיחַ נָגִיד on any tolerable ground. At all events, any of these modes of counting would be utterly at variance with the first clause in the verse before us; for the command to rebuild *precedes* the forty-nine years, and the anointed prince marks the *close*, while, in case Darius be made the *terminus ad quem*, no such command had been given seven weeks (i. e. forty-nine years) *before* he was king.

The same difficulty lies in the way, if we substitute *Cyrus* instead of Darius. According to Is. 45: 1, we might apply מָשִׁיחַ to him, for Jehovah speaks of him as his *anointed one;* and a נָגִיד, i. e. *preëminent civil ruler*, he certainly was. But history represents Cyrus as himself issuing a decree to rebuild (2 Chron. 36: 23. Ezra 1: 1 seq.); and Cyrus could not have been at the beginning and at the end of the forty-nine years, either at one and the same time or at any time, for he reigned only seven years after his appearance in sacred history. If we take, now, the *terminus a quo* of the forty-nine years which commence with the command to rebuild, and count from the proclamation of Cyrus, (which in itself would agree well with the command in question), then who is the anointed one and prince at the *end* of those forty-nine years? Xerxes was then on the throne, whose expedition into Greece does not favor his right to the magnificent title in question; and whose intended treatment of the Jews, at the instigation of Haman, as related in the book of Esther, favors it still less. Where then shall we look for the *command to rebuild*, and for an *anointed one, a prince*, forty-nine years afterwards? We have had no success thus far, and history down to the time of Cyrus, as it now lies before us, presents us with no *data* from which we can make out a period of forty-nine years so defined by events at the beginning and the end of them, as the first clause in v. 25 seems plainly to import or demand.

If we go lower down than Cyrus, we find under Darius Hystaspis the decree of Cyrus for rebuilding the temple renewed, in B. C. 519, (Ezra vi.); but forty-nine years after this would bring us again into the reign of Xerxes (B. C. 470), who, as has already been remarked, was no מָשִׁיחַ נָגִיד. If we descend still lower, down to Artaxerxes Longimanus (B. C. 445), who gave unto Nehemiah full liberty to rebuild (Neh. ii.), then the seventy weeks would reach forty-five years beyond the birth of Christ, which of course renders null this calculation. Besides, we can find no appropriate *anointed one and prince*, forty-nine years after the decree of Artaxerxes. We must abandon the hope then of satisfying ourselves in this way, as to the limits of the first period, i. e. the seven weeks. Nor is this all of the difficulty. The *seven weeks*, (and these only), are destitute of any express intimation of what was accomplished or happened, during their continuance. What then, it is natural to inquire, can be the object in view in designating them? Not events, as it would seem, *during* the forty-nine years, but events mentioned as the *terminus a quo* and *ad quem* of those years. Of course these must have their importance. But here again we are met with difficulties. The *command to rebuild Jerusalem* — when? By whom? After what destruction of it? for this command imports of course an antecedent destruction. Was this by Nebuchadnezzar? Or was it the more partial destruction by Antiochus Epiphanes? These are all the considerable destructions of which history gives us any account, before the final wasting by Titus. But this last is out of question; for the whole period of seventy weeks, (of which seven are a part), *precedes* the Messianic period. As to the destruction by Nebuchadnezzar, we have already put that to the test. There remains, as history now stands, only that by Antiochus. If Judas Maccabaeus gave command to rebuild what had been destroyed, when his victories were consummated, (as he probably did), then who is the מָשִׁיחַ נָגִיד that makes his appearance forty-nine years after this? Judas reinstated the temple worship B. C. 165, so that forty-nine years would bring us to B. C. 116. There was indeed on the throne of Judea, at that time, the most eminent prince that ever sat upon it after the return from the Babylonish exile, viz. John Hyrcanus, in whose praise Josephus is uncommonly lavish. However, he did not commence his reign then, but in B. C. 135, i. e. nineteen years earlier. Nor is there anything in the occurrences of B. C. 116, which distinguishes that year from any other of the thirty years of his reign. A *terminus ad quem*, therefore, of the seven weeks seems to be looked for here in vain. If we admit that the seven weeks must *precede* the sixty-two weeks, (and any other order seems to be unnatural, and apparently against the tenor of the whole passage), then we cannot go down to a period so late as that of Judas Maccabaeus and Antiochus, for the commencement of the seven weeks, or the issuing of the command to rebuild.

What can we do then, or where shall we go, to find the appropriate limits of the forty-nine years? Perplexed by questions like these, Vitringa, Hengstenberg, and many others, have adopted a peculiar course, in order to find an issue from these straits. First they have united the seven weeks into one mass with the sixty-two weeks, thus making in effect but two subdivisions of the seventy weeks, viz. one of sixty-nine, and the other of one. This is built on the assumption, that the command to rebuild, spoken of in v. 25, is that which was given by

Artaxerxes in the twentieth year of his reign, as recorded in Neh. ii. They then count sixty-nine weeks (62+7) forward, i. e. 483 years. But as the twentieth year of Artaxerxes is usually reckoned at B. C. 445, their reckoning makes thirty-eight years too much on this ground. To avoid this, they reckon some thirty years of it to the private life of Jesus, and make his public ministry (not his birth) the *terminus ad quem.* Still there remain some eight or nine years too much. This excess is disposed of, by adding some eight or nine years more to the reign of Artaxerxes than chronology usually reckons, (which would make his decree so much earlier), and thus making the time to adjust itself to the events. In the usual chronology, (vouched for by Ctesias and Ptolemy in his Canon), Artaxerxes is represented as reigning forty or forty-one years, and Xerxes as twenty or twenty-one. Hengstenberg insists upon fifty-one for Artaxerxes, and eleven for Xerxes. In this way the twentieth year of Artaxerxes falls back some ten years, just about enough to save the excess above mentioned, made by carrying forward the sixty-nine weeks = 483 years. The *terminus a quo,* then, of the sixty-nine weeks, is the decree of Artaxerxes to rebuild, Neh. ii.; the *terminus ad quem* is the מָשִׁיחַ נָגִיד in the emphatic sense, i. e. the *Lord's Anointed*, the *King of Israel*, when he enters upon his public office.

Certainly this is ingenious; and the result is rather striking, at first view. But further examination throws in our way insuperable obstacles; at which, however, I can but merely hint. (1) The main assumption, that Artaxerxes was the first who issued a *decree to rebuild Jerusalem*, (the terminus a quo), contradicts fact and Scripture both. FACT — inasmuch as Haggai, (in the second year of Darius = B. C. 520), more than seventy years before the twentieth of Artaxerxes, speaks of the people as "dwelling at Jerusalem in ceiled houses," while the house of the Lord lies waste, Hagg. 1: 2—4; SCRIPTURE — inasmuch as God says expressly of Cyrus, that he shall rebuild the city, Isa. 45: 1, 13 and 44: 28, comp. 2 Chron. 36: 23. Ezra 1: 1—3. In these two last cases, indeed, the temple only is specified; which, being the central and union-point of the whole enterprise of the returning immigrants, is very natural. But the implication of city-building at the same time, is unavoidable and plain. The history of the restored Israelites in Ezra shows beyond a question, that so early as the reign of Darius Hystaspis, (about 519 B. C.), there was a very considerable population in Jerusalem — not, I trust, without *houses* to live in. (2) There is no authority, and no good reason for amalgamating the seven weeks and the sixty-two weeks. The writer has separated them, or at any rate the Masorites have separated them, by putting an Athnahh on שִׁבְעָ֑ה. I say not that this is decisive authority; but I may say, that departure from the accents is generally undesirable, and mostly hazardous. A really good reason for it must be one which is of an imperious nature. (3) The nature of the case separates the two periods in question. In making the simple sum of sixty-nine, (for simple it is, as made out by Hengstenberg), who would ever think of dividing this period into two parts, one of which has no special significance, and has nothing assigned to it which can be a reason for its being reckoned by itself? According to this method of interpretation, the *terminus a quo* and *ad quem* of the first period both belong to the period of sixty-nine weeks, and not to that of the seven weeks. But where else, in all the Scriptures, is there such a method of making out a simple number by dividing it into arbitrary parts, and adding these together? (4) V. 26 disproves the assertion, that the speaker meant to reckon in the manner of Hengstenberg. What says he concerning the close of the great period in question? "*After sixty-two weeks* an anointed one shall be cut off," etc. But why does he not say: "After *sixty-nine* weeks?" If all is to be thrown into one period, this would be inevitable, in case he meant to be rightly understood. That he does not say sixty-nine, shows that he reckons the second period of sixty-two weeks as one in and by itself. Besides, if Hengstenberg reckons rightly as to the sixty-nine weeks, even they do not reach, by his own concession, to the *cutting off of the Messiah.* This was three and a half years after the close of that period. (5) I add, in order to complete the view of objections to his interpretation, that having reached the middle of the third period, (viz. the one week = seven years), the other remaining three and a half years are wholly unmanageable. With him, "the people of a prince that will come," and who will destroy the city and sanctuary, are the *Romans* under Titus. Did these invaders then come against the Jews, within three and a half years after the death of Christ? No; they did not come within a third of a century. Moreover, the tyrant or desolator who comes, is himself *to be wasted,* (be a שֹׁמֵם, v. 27). The implication is, that this will take place at the end of the latter half of the seven years. But Titus did not die within that period, nor until A. D. 81. If Vespasian be selected as the prince in question, the difference will be only about three years. Neither of them died a violent death. The "outpouring of what is decreed upon the son of perdition" (v. 27), may be looked for in vain, after the death of Christ, and within the limits assigned by the angel.

We must add to all this, that the *first* period has of itself neither a definite beginning nor end, according to Hengtenberg's interpretation. The *third* is also destitute (as to its latter half) of a *terminus ad quem.* He also assigns to the first period, what belongs to the second, viz. the slow and interrupted rebuilding of the city, (which can be done only by offering violence to the grammatical structure of the language), and consequently he leaves the second long period of 62 weeks, without cognizing anything that is accomplished during that period which would definitely mark it. Finally, to ground all this theory of interpretation, as the advocates of it do, on a disputed point of chronology, (the ten years to be added to Artaxerxes and taken from Xerxes), and one in respect to which, after the remarks by Hoffman (Die 70 Jahre, s. 90 seq.), we may venture to say the probability is strongly against them, can hardly meet the just demands of criticism in a case of such a nature, or satisfy the inquirer who has no favorite scheme to defend.

After all this, then, we are compelled again to ask, with still more emphasis: "When do the 7 weeks (and of course the 70) begin? And when do they end?

Wieseler has dropped the 7 weeks, by virtue of his views concerning נֶחְתַּךְ, which he makes to mean *abbreviated, abridged.* First the original 70 years of Jeremiah are abridged 7 years, in the execution of the threatening. Then, to correspond with this, the seven weeks of years are abridged or omitted from the new period of 70 year-weeks. Why? is a question that is hardly answered. The mere *exegete* might feel himself greatly relieved, if he could dispose of this difficulty so easily. But for myself, I am more inclined to confess my ignorance than to get rid of the matter in this way. Hoffman (Weissag. und Erfüll. s. 301 seq.), in his latest view of this subject, says, that the seven weeks can be applied to no period preceding the vision of Daniel, and to none during the 62 weeks, or during the one week. He thinks that the seven weeks, in which Jerusalem is to be splendidly rebuilt, and the מָשִׁיחַ נָגִיד to make his appearance, must come *after* both these periods. But when? How? He does not answer these questions, but cautiously abstains from giving any express opinion. I consider this, in both Wieseler and himself, as only a kind of ingenious way of confessing that they do not understand the matter. And if *they* do not, it is somewhat discouraging; for writers of more acuteness in philology do not often make their appearance; and these respective discussions of theirs, moreover, are the latest, and therefore are carried on under peculiar advantages.

Only one case more occurs, which calls for examination, viz. such an one as Hoffman supposes: Can we reverse the *order* of the periods, and find the 7 weeks in the period immediately *preceding* the advent of Christ? They would then close by the appearance of a *Messiah, a Prince;* and so far all is well as to the *end* of the period. But where is the *terminus a quo?* The 49th year before Christ, or any year proximate to it, is distinguished by no *command to rebuild Jerusalem;* nor indeed was there occasion for any, since the city had not of late been laid waste.

I do not see, then, but that we must suspend our investigations here, as connected with *history;* because we seem to have exhausted all the probable materials which history presents. We must betake ourselves at last, then, to simple *philology.* Can anything, and if anything, then how much can be gathered from it? Possibly a strict and thorough investigation of the words may throw some light on these dark sentences.

At the beginning of v. 25, וְתֵדַע וְתַשְׂכֵּל denotes that something specially worthy of attention, is about to be said. I have rendered וְתֵדַע by *mark well,* lit. it may be translated: *and thou must know;* but the Kal Imperf. here is used in a kind of Imper. sense, § 125. 3. *c.* וְתַשְׂכֵּל might well be rendered: *Pay particular attention.* It also means *to understand,* as connected with such an act of the mind. The sense of both verbs might be thus expressed: *Be thou well assured,* or *know thou for certainty.* Why is such an intimation here given? Plainly because there is a transition from a preceding generic to a specific statement; and not merely this, but the general declaration of Messianic blessings that had just been made, is now to be followed by the prediction of troublous times which are to *precede* those blessings. The change is so great, the things about to be said are of a tenor so different from those which had been said, that the speaker, in order to guard against surprise, or to fortify against doubt, calls the earnest and particular attention of Daniel to what he is going to disclose.

מִן מֹצָא דָבָר, as to the form of expression, reminds us of יָצָא דָבָר in v. 23. But in vain do critics seek to identify the first with the second, as to meaning. The דָּבָר in v. 23, plainly refers to the communication in. vs. 24—27. That in the verse before us as plainly means a *command* or *message* to rebuild Jerusalem. The fact that the דָּבָר now before us has *no article,* shows conclusively, that it does not renew the mention of דָּבָר in v. 23; for in v. 23 itself, when דָּבָר is there repeated, it has the article (בַּדָּבָר), because this last refers to the previous דָּבָר. So it would have the article here, in case a like reference were here intended. For the same reason, דָּבָר in v. 25 cannot refer to the דְּבַר יְהוָה of v. 2; whither so many critics refer it. That it has no article, is a proof that it has no antecedent to which it refers. It is a *new message;* and of course the article would give a wrong direction to the mind of the reader. The allegation made by several critics, that the negligence of the later Hebrew in respect to the article stands in the way here of any argument drawn from the presence or absence of it, may be credited by those who have some favorite views to be supported by such a position, or by those who are not conversant with the later Hebrew writings. Those who are in neither of these predicaments, will be slow to believe such allegations until they are proved, and especially in a case so plain as the present.

But *from whom* is the *command* or *message* to proceed? No one is designated in the context. From a *superior* a *command* (for plainly דָּבָר is of such a nature here) must proceed. Is it some *king?* If so, we should be at a loss to say *what king* is meant. He is not the מָשִׁיחַ נָגִיד for certainty; because the latter comes into view only at the *close* of the seven weeks. In such a case, then, we naturally turn to *God* as the author of the command; and in this we are amply confirmed by Isa. 44: 26, 28, לֵאמֹר לִירוּשָׁלַיִם תִּבָּנֶה וְהֵיכָל תִּוָּסֵד, *saying to Jerusalem, Thou shalt be built up, and to the temple, Thou shalt be founded.* — In simply designating *the going forth of a command*, the speaker has left unexplained what the nature of that command is. The sequel is designed to explain its object. It is *to rebuild Jerusalem.* The דָּבָר or *command* then is, that something should be done. By whom? Of course by those who have an interest in Jerusalem, i. e. by the Jews; certainly by the Jews, provided the rebuilding is to precede the Christian era.

לְהָשִׁיב וְלִבְנוֹת, *to rebuild*, or *to restore and to build*, which amounts here to the same thing. The verb שׁוּב, followed by another verb either with or without a וְ before it, may everywhere be found marking simply the idea of *repetition, again.* Commonly a *definite* mood and tense is employed; but I can see no reason why *Infinitives* (as in the present case) may not be employed in the same manner. The obvious idea, at all events, is that of *rebuilding.* Whether, however, we so translate, or render the phrase *to restore and build up*, the idea is for substance the same. To attach to הָשִׁיב an intensive idea, viz. that of *completely restoring*, belongs neither to the verb, the Conj. in which it is, or the nature of the case. To *rebuild* a city, does not of course mean to build it as largely or as well as it was before built. These are accidental circumstances, not essential ones. The implication in either way of translating is, that, previous to the command in question, Jerusalem has been laid waste. Whether utterly or partially, is not necessarily implied. This is left undetermined.

עַד מָשִׁיחַ נָגִיד, *to an anointed one, a prince;* not *to an anointed prince*, for then מָשִׁיחַ must take its place behind נָגִיד, according to the laws of the language. In its present position, moreover, standing after עַד, it cannot be a *predicate*, for this it could be only in case עַד were omitted, and then the assertion might be: *Anointed* [is] *a prince*. We must therefore put the word in *apposition* with נָגִיד. But what *Messiah* is it? If it be the expected and predicted Messiah, the great Deliverer, then, of course, מָשִׁיחַ being an appellative must have the article. Hengstenberg says, the article is omitted because the word is used as a proper name here. But if it be a proper name, then of course נָגִיד would be an appellative, and must have the article; just as in the case of דָּוִד הַמֶּלֶךְ. Besides, although so common as a proper name with us, and also in the N. Test., where is the proof from the O. Test. that it was *anciently* employed in this way? The word is used to designate the *high priest*, Lev. 4: 3, 5, 16; often for a *lawfully anointed king*, 1 Sam. 2: 10. 12: 3, 5. 16: 6, al. saepe; it is used to designate Cyrus as a specially chosen and consecrated instrument of liberating the Jews, Isa. 45: 1; and sometimes (in the plural) to designate patriarchs or nobles, Ps. 105: 15. 1 Chron. 16: 22. Only once in all the Heb. Scriptures is it applied to the Lord Jesus Christ, viz. in Ps. 2: 2, if we except the present case. This surely does not look like a *proper name* in ancient times; and most plainly it was not commonly so employed. The license then which is alleged, respecting the *omission* of the article, cannot be explained or vindicated on this ground. If *the Messiah* had been meant in the case before us, the article would seem to be natural, and one might almost say, absolutely indispensable. — Can it mean, then, a *heathen* prince? It might, because it is applied to Cyrus in Isa. 45:1. Yet evidently it is so applied there, only because he was a chosen instrument of the Lord, to accomplish his designs in respect to the Hebrews. The probability, in the present case, is strong against the idea of a *heathen* king, since there is nothing in the context which would explain the application of מְשִׁיחַ to such an one, while such an explanation is palpable in the case of Cyrus. Naturally it would of itself be understood as implying some lawful priest or prince of the Jews anointed to priestly or to regal office, or to both.

נָגִיד means one who is *prominent*, *preëminent*, *conspicuous*. Hence it becomes an appellative for *prince*. The office implied is a *civil* one. This I suppose to be the reason why it is added to the preceding word. מָשִׁיחַ might of itself mean either king or priest. To remove all doubt, נָגִיד is added to the preceding word, and put in apposition as explanatory, — an idiom by no means uncommon. Of course the article should not be employed, since it is omitted in the principal or leading word. The true idea then seems to be: *an anointed one who is a prince* or *civil ruler*. That some distinguished personage is meant, can hardly be questioned. *Who* it is, or *when* he was to appear, are questions, as we have seen, which cannot easily be solved by any history known to us.

As to שָׁבֻעִים שִׁבְעָה, enough has already been said. The *Athnahh* on the last word seems to be rightly placed there. If the following sixty-two weeks are to be combined in one period with these seven, then v. 26 could not say: *After those sixty-two weeks*, etc., but must say: *After those sixty-nine weeks* etc. Besides, there is no example in the Scriptures, as has already been remarked, of such a way of announcing or making up numbers. Moreover, the תָּשׁוּב that follows must have a וְ before it, in case the building of the city is to be referred back to the seven weeks, as some maintain, or even in case they are to be included in the sum of the building-period as announced in the second clause. It seems quite clear, moreover, that the seven weeks, which commence with a command to *rebuild* and end with a *distinguished and lawful king*, imply of course a *prosperous* rebuilding, which is consummated by the coming of a distinguished lawful sovereign. In contrast with this, the building of the city during the sixty-two weeks is to be scanty, and the declaration is made that it will be carried on *in troublous times*. Whether the seven weeks are to be arranged *before* or *after* the sixty-two, alters not the nature of the present case. A *contrast* between the two periods is, as it seems to me, plainly designed to be made. The seven weeks are *fausti temporis*, the sixty-two are *infausti temporis*. The seven weeks are to be followed by the reign of a מָשִׁיחַ נָגִיד; the sixty-two weeks are to be followed by the cutting off of a מָשִׁיחַ, and by the wasting of the temple and city during the *week* that follows. Presented in this light, the contrast between the seven and the sixty-two weeks becomes quite striking and palpable.

What then do we gather, at last, from our *philological* inquiries? We gather at least some things, with a good degree of conviction; (1) That the periods of seven and sixty-two are not only diverse and separate from each other, but are actually in *contrast* with each other, in regard to events respectively belonging to them. (2) That the period of seven weeks will follow some waste and desolate state of Jerusalem, which Heaven will, at the beginning of those weeks, give commandment to repair; and this reparation will be followed by the reign of a lawful and distinguished sovereign, i. e. this period will end in prosperity, under an anointed one, a prince. (3) The *terminus a quo* of this period is specified not by the designation of *time* but *event*, and this event (a command *to rebuild*) is different from anything that happened before the return from exile, and different from anything predicted by Jeremiah respecting the end of the exile. Consequently the seven-weeks period does not commence, at the same time with the desolations of Jerusalem by Nebuchadnezzar. (4) Of course, I do not see how the conclusion can be well avoided, that the seven weeks are to be regarded as a part of the seventy weeks which *precede* the Messianic times. I cannot accede therefore to the remark, that seven is here merely a mystical number, as often in the Apocalypse, and that it may, when thus understood, be regarded as designating a *completion* or *fulness* of time, unlimited by specific bounds; moreover, that we are of course at liberty to place it wherever and whenever events will correspond, without being restrained by the number of *years*. Why should this be the case with only one of the three periods before us? The other two are clearly specific and definite; and so are the numbers of this book in general. What authorizes us, then, to make the present case an exception to all the rest?

"But we can find nothing in history that accords with the period of seven weeks; certainly not in the history of the Jews before the Christian era."

This may be true. Hoffman (s. 301) thinks so much to be clear, viz. that 'the seven weeks come *after* the sixty-two weeks; and that the *terminus a quo* of the seven is not the same with that of the sixty-two, and that it cannot be found in any period antecedent to the time of Daniel's vision,' (s. 299). It is the *history* of the times, as he thinks, which forces us to such a conclusion. Unless such an appeal to history can be made with much force and propriety, it must certainly be natural to regard the three periods both as *successive* and *continuous*. But if now we appeal to actual history, as it lies before us, this seems to favor the view of Hoffman; for the proclamation of Cyrus, as we have seen, if taken as the beginning of the seven weeks, leads to no מָשִׁיחַ נָגִיד at the end, except either to Darius the Persian king, in the last part of his reign, or to Xerxes in the beginning of his. Neither of these corresponds to such an appellation. *Messiah Prince* cannot be Ezra, for he went up to Jerusalem some seventy-nine years after Cyrus' proclamation, instead of forty-nine years; it cannot be Nehemiah, for he went up ninety-one years after the same. Before Cyrus' time, no *command* or *liberty to rebuild* was given. Must we not then consider ourselves as forced, with Hoffman, to the conclusion that the seven weeks must come *after* the other periods? But if so, then we must ask: *How? When?* These are questions, however, that we seem not to have the means of answering satisfactorily. The most promising period disclosed by history, seems to be that between the time when Judas began to repair the desolations made by Antiochus Epiphanes, and the reign of that powerful and popular king, *John Hyrcanus*, the nephew of Judas. The forty-nine years, if begun with the repairs by Judas, would fall about the middle of Hyrcanus' reign; and under him, the Jews were an independent and respected nation. He too was both *high-priest* and *king*, a מָשִׁיחַ נָגִיד. But, as has been already said, the year

B. C. 116, (the middle of his reign), has nothing particular in itself to distinguish it; and this seems to make the application of the seven weeks to this period somewhat doubtful, or wholly so. Still perhaps it is not absolutely decisive against it, because there is nothing in the prediction, which obliges us to *commence* the reign of the Anointed one and Prince with the very last year of the seven weeks. Would it not be sufficient, if such a prince were already on the throne when they end?

If I have not given satisfaction to the reader, as to the resolution of the difficulty in question, (and doubtless I have not), I have at least shown him why I have not done it. I do not despair, after all, of a solution, at some future period, on the part of some one, who has better vantage ground than we now have. But I confess myself unable to answer all the questions that may be here raised. This, however, only proves my want of adequate knowledge, and not that the subject is necessarily inexplicable. But of this matter something more will be said in the sequel.

And sixty and two weeks תָּשׁוּב וְנִבְנְתָה, *shall it be rebuilt.* The subject is *the city.* The idiomatic תָּשׁוּב with the verb that follows, is the same as in לְהָשִׁיב וְלִבְנוֹת of the first clause. The *terminus a quo* of the sixty-two weeks, (since it is not specifically named), has been supposed by some to be the same with that of the seventy years of Jeremiah. The angel tells Daniel, that, instead of seventy years simply, 70 *weeks of years* are *determined on* or *decided* (נֶחְתַּךְ). As nothing definite is expressly said of the time when this last period of seventy *weeks* commences, it might seem to be, as some have maintained, the same time as that with which the seventy *years* of Jeremiah began. The Acc. of time here (sixty-two weeks) is the usual Acc. of *when* or *how long,* § 116. 2. It does not strictly imply, perhaps, that during all this period the city was in the regular process of building. It may be sufficient, that during the period named the building in question took place. Naturally, however, it must be understood as designating a protracted season of building up. But if we begin to reckon with B. C. 606, (according to the assumption above), there must be a considerable period (seventy years) during which the city was still in a state of entire desolation, viz., down to the time of Cyrus, B. C. 536. From the time of Cyrus, however, down to Antiochus Epiphanes, it was in a state of gradual although sometimes interrupted, advance. It was built *in troublous times.* Can we then, in view of all this, and after the preceding discussions, go back to B. C. 606 for the beginning of the second period, i. e. the sixty-two weeks?

רְחוֹב וְחָרוּץ, *with broad spaces and narrow limits.* I take these much-contested words as the *Acc. adverbial,* designating the manner in which the city will be built in the times of trouble. רְחוֹב *with breadth,* i. e. *with wide spaces*, LXX. εἰς πλάτος. *Street* the word often means, because street is *a wide space.* Also it designates larger openings in cities, like our technical word *place*, and the Latin *forum*. To reverse the order of the words, and to make רְחוֹב the Nom. to the verbs would be a degradation of the sense. Besides, where in the Scriptures do we find the expression *build* applied to streets? It seems quite probable, if not altogether certain, that רְחוֹב and חָרוּץ are opposites, and make a contrast; yet one which is very descriptive. The first shows that *large spaces* are left within the city, which are not built upon. Then, on the other hand, חָרוּץ designates that which is *limited, narrowed, clipped, narrowly defined.* Such were the houses to be; at least, if this does not pertain to the form of the houses themselves, (as probably it does not), it at least applies to the narrow and defined limits within which they are built. In a city full of inhabitants, small spaces are left and ample expansion is given to the mass of buildings. But here, because of the "troublous times," the reverse takes place. When the angel wishes to tell Zechariah that Jerusalem shall yet be *overflowing* with inhabitants, he says: "Because of the abounding of man and beast, Jerusalem shall be inhabited פְּרָזוֹת *with* [sub-urban] *villages.* The opposite to such an idea is implied by חָרוּץ. To translate this word *ditch, water-sluice, conduit*, or else *judgment, decision*, makes no tolerable sense, and indeed such a version is incapable of philological defence. To render וְחָרוּץ *it is decided* (Häv., Hengst., Wies.) presents two difficulties; first it makes a divulsion from the preceding word, with which the accents connect it; and secondly such an idea would demand חָרוּץ הוּא or חֲרוּצָה הִיא instead of וְחָרוּץ. It is evident, on the whole, that the word is one part of an antithetic couplet, of which רְחוֹב is the other. Of the translation: *it is decided*, Hoffman justly says: "It is opposed to all sound advance of expression or description." It certainly is an unlooked-for declaration, in case we interpret it in the manner now in question, i. e. such as to break the thread of the description. A signal good, or a signal evil, might readily be spoken of as *decreed;* but to affirm this of a mere subordinate circumstance in the building of the city, and interrupt the discourse in order to affirm it, seems at least not to be very probable.

וּבְצוֹק הָעִתִּים, lit. *and in straitness of the times*, in our English version, *even in troublous times.* The וּ prefix, however, need not be rendered intensive by translating it *even.* The idea is somewhat more generic than this last version would make it, inasmuch as the latter clause means, that the times in general of the rebuilding will be times of hardship and suffering. That they were so, is fully evident from the records of Nehemiah and Ezra, and from the history of the Maccabees; not to speak of Josephus, who depends almost wholly on these records. That the city made progress slowly, and with not a few interruptions, from the proclamation of Cyrus until the reign of Antiochus, is sufficiently apparent from the history of the Jews during that interval of time. The language of prophecy rarely dwells on minute particulars of history. It is enough, in the present case, that we can make a generic application of it.

(26) And after sixty and two weeks, an anointed One shall be cut off, and there shall be none for it [the people], and the city and the sanctuary shall the people of a prince that will come destroy; but his end shall be with an overwhelming flood, and unto the end shall be war, a decreed measure of desolations.

Two things are made very plain by the first part of this verse, viz. first, that the period of sixty-two weeks stands by itself, separated, in the view of the writer, from the preceding period of seven weeks. Otherwise it would be unavoidable that he should either say: *After sixty-nine weeks*, or else: *After seven weeks and sixty-two weeks.* This circumstance seems to be too decisive to allow us to amalgamate, as many have done, the first and second periods into one, as to the *terminus a quo* and *ad quem.* Secondly, the destruction of the city and temple by the people of a prince that would come, i. e. invade the holy land, shows that the issue of "troublous times" is into those far more troublous, and which are the consummation of all that is threatened against the Jews. In 8: 23 we have the like representation; (1) It is בְּאַחֲרִית, *in the latter part* of the fourth dominion, (= the latter part of the sixty-two weeks), and כְּהָתֵם הַפֹּשְׁעִים, *when transgressors have come to the full*, i. e. filled up the measure of their sins, that the destroyer and revenger comes in. (2) There, as here, the destroyer, when he has finished his work of desolation in the holy land, comes to a fearful and sudden end. In 8: 25, this is expressed by בְּאֶפֶס יָד יִשָּׁבֵר, here by בַּשֶּׁטֶף. The contrast between this and the end of the seven weeks, can hardly fail to strike the mind of an impartial interpreter. The seven weeks end in an *anointed one* who is also a *Prince*, i. e. a legitimate high priest and king, uniting in himself a double office, and reigning over a city rebuilt or repaired by the command of heaven, and made prosperous; the sixty-two weeks end in the destruction of a city and sanctuary, which had been but scantily built, and in seasons of pressure and calamity. A seven years of wasting and persecution is their immediate sequel. Whoever looks on the representation in this light, must of necessity concede, that the periods of seven and sixty-two are set in real contrast to each other, as has been intimated, and are by no means to be amalgamated, or either of them virtually removed out of sight. Both periods are equally real, at least they are so in the view of the writer; and we cannot properly dispose of either without making it significant.

יִכָּרֵת מָשִׁיחַ, *an anointed one shall be cut off.* Not THE *Messiah* or THE *anointed one*, for there is no article here, as there must be if such were the meaning. As we have seen, מָשִׁיחַ was not a *proper* name in ancient times; and as an *appellative*, it should of course take the article. But this being omitted, we are admonished to look in another direction for the meaning of the word מָשִׁיחַ. *Priest* or *king* we have seen that it may mean, (see on v. 25, מָשִׁיחַ נָגִיד), because both of these, when duly appointed, were *anointed* with oil in the name of the Lord. *An anointed one*, therefore, is the appellation of all who are thus consecrated to high office. Nor can the term be applied to any mere king solely because he is king; and specially is it inapplicable to any *heathen* king, unless indeed, like Cyrus, such an one be chosen on the part of heaven for specific and important purposes. But as the Scriptures apply it to an anointed *priest* or *king* under the Jewish dispensation, so we may here apply it to either, just as the context demands. It is not the same personage as the מָשִׁיחַ נָגִיד of v. 25, for if it were, the article would be demanded. Besides the omission of this, it is quite evident that the condition and circumstances of the two, are very diverse; the מָשִׁיחַ נָגִיד apparently reigns in prosperity, while the מָשִׁיחַ of our text is to be cut off and destroyed. Not that the word יִכָּרֵת always and necessarily designates a *violent death*, or the *death of a criminal*, as some allege; for sometimes the word means to *fail* or *lack;* e. g. Josh. 9: 23, לֹא יִכָּרֵת עֶבֶד, *a servant shall never fail* or *be lacking.* But in the passage before us it seems most probable, that the usual sense of the word is retained. We shall see, in the historical illustration, that such is the case. The מָשִׁיחַ I must therefore regard as the Lord's *anointed* high-priest, Onias III., conspicuous for his piety and his steadfastness, who was displaced from office by Antiochus, and his heathenish brother put in possession of his place. Soon after Onias was obliged to flee to Daphnae, near Antioch, for a refuge from the malice of his Jewish enemies; thence he was drawn by false promises, and murdered by the governor of Antioch, vicegerent of Antiochus. His son, instead of succeeding his father Onias, was obliged to fly to foreign lands, and finally built up Leontopolis in Egypt. But during the rest of Antiochus' reign, no lawful high priest had possession of the appropriate office. The people were forced to accept of heathenish Jews as their high priests; so that what is said in the sequel, although dark at first, and not a little embarrassed with the glosses put upon it both in ancient and in modern times, becomes intelligible when rightly interpreted.

וְאֵין לוֹ, our Eng. version renders *but not for himself*, evidently building on the assumption, that the *Messiah* here means *Jesus Christ*, and so expressing the idea that he died for the sins of the people, and not upon his own account, i. e. not because of anything which he had done. So also Vitringa, Hävernick, Rosenmüller. But the Heb. idiom forbids this interpretation. Were the idea conveyed by the passage that which our version gives, it must run thus: וְלֹא לוֹ. The word אַיִן is by no means a simple particle, expressing merely *negation* like לֹא, but a verb meaning *is not*. Like all verbs it demands a *subject*, expressed or implied. When expressed, it takes the subject, if a *pronoun*, as a suffix, and adapts its form accordingly; if other words are subjects, they are put in the Gen. after the *negative verb*, which then assumes, as in our text, the *construct* form. אֵין then must have a subject. Its very form (const.) is designed to show that one is implied. What then is it? Whence are we to supply it? From the context, all must concede. If this be admitted, then those interpretations, which take אֵין in the same sense as if it were לֹא, of course will not abide the test. So C. B. Michaelis: *And not to be will be his lot;* Sept. in Cod. Chis., καὶ οὐκ ἔσται. But this in Hebrew would be אֵינֶנּוּ. Others again translate thus: *And nothing will belong to him.* But אֵין does not mean *nothing*, but it means *is not*, i. e. something either expressed or implied *is not*. Others again thus: *And no one remained to him*, (Sack, Hitzig); which has to meet the same difficulty, for אֵין is not *no one*, but simply *is not*. Rosch (Stud. und Krit. 1834) gives the phrase this turn: *And no one was present for him.* In this way he applies it to designate the death of Seleucus IV. Philopator, at a time when neither his son Demetrius, nor his brother Antiochus, was near him. But אֵין does not mean *is not present*, but *is not*. Besides, if it did, it does not follow that the *one not present* is limited to son or brother, but *one* extends to any or all that belong in any way to the מָשִׁיחַ. Beyond all this, a mere *heathen* king, like Seleucus, would not be called by such a name as *Messiah*. — More improbable still is the turn given by the Vulgate, Jahn, and Scholl: *Non erit ejus populus*, sc. *qui eum negatarus est.* But whence comes *people* in this case? And if we might supply עַמּוֹ, אֵין cannot well mean, that the Jewish nation *should be cut off;* it merely denies their existence. — Hengstenberg, who has finely illustrated אֵין (Christol. II. s. 474—478), and shown the necessity of an *implied* subject, has not succeeded equally well in making out that subject. He says, the denial in אֵין must refer to what belonged to the מָשִׁיחַ; and this he thinks appropriately to be *Herrschaft*, i. e. dominion. Of course he regards the מָשִׁיחַ here as the suffering Saviour. But how was his *dominion* lost, by his being cut off? *Temporal domin-*

ion he never sought or claimed; but *spiritual* he *acquired* by the very act of enduring readily his sufferings, Phil. 2: 8, 9.

Passing by, then, all these various methods of interpretation, let us still further urge the question: What is to be supplied as a subject for the verb, from the context? I know of no other answer that can be made to this, on a ground strictly grammatical, but that מָשִׁיחַ must be regarded as the proper word. Altogether of a tenor like to the passage before us, is Ex. 22: 2, שַׁלֵּם יְשַׁלֵּם אִם אֵין לוֹ וְנִמְכַּר בִּגְנֵבָתוֹ, i. e. *he shall surely replace it; if he has not, then he shall be sold on account of his theft."* Here שַׁלֵּם, or its kindred noun שִׁלּוּם, is plainly to be supplied after אֵין. The same as to מָשִׁיחַ, in the case before us. It is forced upon us by the grammar of the language. But if this be admitted, (and I see no way to avoid it), then of course we must give to לוֹ a different meaning from that commonly given, and refer it to the עַם of v. 24. For to say that an *anointed one* shall be cut off, and then to say that *there is no anointed one to him* after such an event, would be unmeaning if not frivolous. To say, that when Onias the anointed high priest shall be cut off, there will be no authorized and proper מָשִׁיחַ to the *people* of the Jews, is pregnant with meaning, and accords with historical fact. If any one takes exception to the distance of the antecedent from לוֹ, it would be easy to point him to similar and even stronger cases of such a nature; e. g. Isa. 8: 21, בָּהּ; and the same in Ps. 68: 11, 15. So יְסוּדָתוֹ in Ps. 87: 1, and not a few other cases of a like nature. I concede that we are not to refer a pronoun very far either backwards or forwards, except when necessity calls. But here seems to be such a necessity; for no consistent grammatical sense can be made out in any other way, and this makes one quite apposite and facile. Steudel (Pfingst-programm. 1833, s. 36 seq.) was the first, so far as I know, who advanced the position that לוֹ refers to עַמְּךָ in v. 24. Hoffman (in his *Die* 70 *Jahre*, s. 72) pronounces against it, but after all he virtually adopts it, in his later work, Weissag. und Erfüll. s. 303. Nothing can be plainer, than that the difficulties of the passage are greatly diminished by this interpretation. I must add, in order to prevent misunderstanding, that I regard מָשִׁיחַ as more indicative of the high priest's *official dignity* and *circle of duty*, than merely of his person. When he is *cut off*, the people fail of having one lawfully to fill his place. But that the passage cannot well apply to Jesus the Messiah, seems plain from the fact, that his death *introduced* him to an eternal high priesthood, instead of cutting him off from such an office.

And the city and the sanctuary will the people of *the prince who is to come destroy.* — יַשְׁחִית does not necessarily mean a *total destruction*, but such a wasting as mars the object concerned, and renders it comparatively useless or worthless. The article before *city* and *sanctuary*, points to these words in v. 24. עַם נָגִיד omits the article before the second noun, because this נָגִיד is different from that in v. 25, and the article would give a wrong sense; or at least the insertion of it would make it dubious to the reader, inasmuch as it would naturally refer him to the נָגִיד in v. 25. The נָגִיד here is merely a heathen prince acting in a civil capacity, in distinction from a מָשִׁיחַ who belongs to the people of God. — הַבָּא is not a verb but a participle. The article makes it distinctive, lit. *of the comer*, or *of him who cometh* or *will come;* or the word may be understood of *coming* in a hostile sense, i. e. invading, as in Dan. 1: 2. Jer. 36: 29. It seems to point to a well known personage, who is to be the leader of the destroyers, viz. of the עַם before mentioned. In 8: 25 the same personage is fully and plainly described, and in a way much like to that in vs. 26, 27, of the present passage. הַבָּא, then, virtually appeals to the knowledge of the reader, who has perused the prophecy in chap. viii.

וְקִצּוֹ, *and his end;* whose? The obvious grammatical answer is, the end of the נָגִיד הַבָּא. One need but compare 8: 25, respecting Antiochus: *He shall be broken in pieces without* [human] *hand*, and to join with this 11: 45, *And he shall come to his end* (עַד קִצּוֹ), *and none shall help him* (וְאֵין עוֹזֵר לוֹ), in order to see how exactly all three of the passages agree. In all, the *end* in question follows the injuries done to the holy city and temple. Manifestly the same personage is concerned. We cannot, therefore, refer קִצּוֹ to *city* and *sanctuary* (Häv.), for the suff. should then be plural; nor to יַשְׁחִית, i. e. the action of destroying which ends in an overwhelming, (Hengst.). Indeed such an application would probably never have been thought of, had not that interpretation needed its aid, which makes Titus the Roman chief to be the נָגִיד in this case, who is to destroy city and sanctuary בַּשֶּׁטֶף. But such a construction is incompatible with grammar, and equally so with the parallel passages to which reference has been made above.

בַּשֶּׁטֶף, lit. *with an inundation* or *overwhelming flood.* But the literal sense is here out of question; and the figurative one of course is, that of being swept away by a resistless torrent of evils or calamities. The simple image of merely a vast or numerous army of men cannot be vindicated as an appropriate significancy of this word, which in its tropical meaning must indicate *overwhelming evil.* One needs but to compare 8: 25 and 11: 45, in order to see how entirely in accordance with each other these three passages are, respecting the sudden death of the tyrant and persecutor. The article in בַּשֶּׁטֶף may be explained in two ways; first as standing before a noun used here in an abstract sense, § 107. 3.

Note 1. *c;* or secondly, on the ground of a destruction already predicted, and regarded as known or understood, comp. 7: 26 and 8: 25. In brief thus: 'The city and sanctuary shall be marred by the subjects of a prince whose coming you know, and of whose fearful end you are also cognizant.'

וְעַד קֵץ מִלְחָמָה וגו׳, *and unto the end shall be war, a decreed measure of desolation.* A much contested passage, about which a great variety of opinions exist. Hoffman (Weissag. etc. s. 305) thinks, that קֵץ מִלְחָמָה here means *the end of a war,* viz. of a war that will arise against Antiochus in consequence of his persecution and oppression. But against this lies the objection, that the idea of another war, different from that which is implied in the preceding context that speaks of the *marring of the city and sanctuary,* can hardly be supposed to be distinctly in the mind of the reader here. In fact, if the idea was designed to be so *specific* as that which the context would naturally suggest, the article would be necessary before מִלְחָמָה. The fact that this word has no article, shows that it is not intended merely to reproduce the idea that lies concealed in the preceding clause, viz. that of a state of mutual hostility and contest. *War* in its more general sense, viz. a continued state of contest and desolation, following on after *the marring of city and sanctuary,* is plainly the idea conveyed by the text. Had the author written הַמִּלְחָמָה, the reader would spontaneously refer it to what is *implied* in the preceding clause. To prevent this, as well as to give the idea a more generic shape, the article is omitted. — As to קֵץ, is it in the const. state before מִלְחָמָה (as the conjunctive accent [֣] would seem to imply), or is there a pause here that would naturally require a lesser distinctive accent? The translation above is founded on the latter assumption; which, of late, is the more general one. The train of accents which ends in *Zakeph Qaton* (as here), has a great variety of changes, dependent on the fact whether the clause consists of two, three, or four words, and more dependent on this than on the sense or real connection of the words; as any one may see in Nordheimer's Heb. Gramm. II. p. 337. In fact, it is palpably before him in the present case; for קֵץ has a *Munahh,* while the particle before it (עַד) has a distinctive accent (named *a prince*), viz. a *Pashta.* Will it be pretended that קֵץ has a nearer relation to מִלְחָמָה, than עַד has to קֵץ? I grant that the consecution of accents shows that the Accentuators probably regarded קֵץ as being in the const. state. But *an end of a war* is too loose an expression, in this connection, to admit of any good defence. If, however, we translate *unto the end* or *an end shall be war,* and thus separate קֵץ from a const. state, then why has it not the article? We should perhaps expect הַקֵּץ, *the end,* viz. one which the reader had already been taught to anticipate, see 8: 17. But if the writer had inserted the article here, he would have cast the mind of the reader back upon the precedihg קִצּוֹ as the antecedent. The fact that he has omitted both article and pronoun suff. in קֵץ, makes it plain that he means another קֵץ, viz. one of *time*, and not merely of calamity or catastrophe. There is another ground, also, of the omission in this case, one founded in the peculiar usage of the author, which I have not seen noticed. This is, that he elsewhere speaks of the same period in the same same way, viz. by *omitting* the article. So in 8: 19, where it is said: *An end* (קֵץ) *will be at an appointed time* (לְמוֹעֵד). Observe that the writer does not say לַמּוֹעֵד, *at* THE *appointed time*, which would presuppose a knowledge of this period on the part of the reader, but AN *appointed time*, viz. a time which Heaven has fixed. Nor does he say הַקֵּץ in 8: 19, because he does not take it for granted that the reader has a limitation of the period in his mind. So in 8: 17, where לְעֶת־קֵץ has plainly the generic idea of *a period which has its limits*, i. e. which is fixed by an overruling Providence. Exactly so in 11: 35, עַד עֵת קֵץ, where it is again said, that this *end* will be לַמּוֹעֵד. Here observe the article in the latter word, in reference to 8: 19. Again in 12: 4, עַד עֵת קֵץ, as much as to say: *a period of consummation*. The same in 12: 9. Now in some of these cases, (indeed in all excepting the first mention of קֵץ), we might expect to find the *article;* but plainly it is the writer's design to communicate, by this phraseology, only the generic idea of *a period of consummation*. For this the article would be inappropriate, in any of the cases here presented. The sum of all is, that the idea here intended to be communicated is this, viz. that unto *an appointed time* or *limited period*, (limited by heaven), *there will be war*, viz. between the tyrant and the Jews. The next clause makes this general idea more specific, viz. that the desolations which this will occasion have their *fixed* boundaries beyond which they cannot pass.

נֶחֱרֶצֶת שֹׁמֵמוֹת, *a decreed limit of desolations*. The part. נֶחֱרֶצֶת is of the fem. and usual const. form, Niph. of חָרַץ. It is here used substantively, the fem. making as usual the abstract noun. In this way it parallelizes in some measure with קֵץ, which means *limit* in respect to time, while נֶחֱרֶצֶת designates an *abridged* or *strictly limited measure* as to *quantity* or *degree*. In other words, the evils of the contest have an *appointed end* and a *decreed* or *limited measure*. The ideas stand so closely connected together here, that a וְ between the clauses would injure the strength of the expression. שֹׁמֵמוֹת is itself a fem. part. noun, taken in the abstract sense. The sense is not *a desolating decree*, for

שְׁמֵמוֹת has a *passive* sense, but a *determined measure of desolations* to be suffered; or, to render literally, *a determined thing is desolations.*

The next verse is neither more nor less than the more explicit unfolding of the character and doings of the *desolator*, i. e. of the נָגִיד הַבָּא and of his קֵץ. He will form a close alliance with many Jews; he will make sacrifice and oblation to cease; he will plant the ensigns of heathen abominations in the temple, and render it desolate in respect to its appropriate rites employed in the worship of the true God; and unto his extinction shall an overwhelming flood be poured upon him who deserves to be destroyed. In other words, the *waster* shall himself be a שׁוֹמֵם, i. e. *something wasted* or *a waste.*

(27) And he shall firmly covenant with many, for one week; and during half of the week, shall he cause the sacrifice and oblation to cease; and a waster shall be over a winged-fowl of abominations; but unto destruction, even that which is decreed, shall there be an outpouring upon him who is to be destroyed.

וְהִגְבִּיר בְּרִית, *he shall firmly covenant*, or lit. *he shall make firm* or *strong a covenant.* The phrase can fairly mean nothing but this. The Nom. to the verb is the נָגִיד הַבָּא or desolating invader. The context supplies no other; and the sense fairly admits of no other. The explanation is found in 1 Macc. 1: 11 seq., "In those days there went forth from Israel transgressors [υἱοὶ παράνομοι, הַפֹּשְׁעִים 8: 23], and persuaded many [Jews], saying: *Let us go and make a covenant with the Gentiles round about us*... And their speech was pleasing in their eyes, and certain persons from the people *went unto the king, and he gave them power to carry into execution the ordinances of the Gentiles*, etc." The sequel shows how the Gentile customs were introduced by them into Jerusalem. In 1 Macc. 1: 41 seq. is a full account of the abominations practised by Antiochus in Jerusalem. Further explanation is unnecessary. — לָרַבִּים has the article, because it designates a whole class here; just as we have, in 8: 23, הַפֹּשְׁעִים in the same way, and to designate the same class. The additional idea here communicated is, that *many* took such a course. The לְ in this case, resembles the usual construction of כָּרַת בְּרִית, which puts לְ after it and before the persons with whom the covenant is made, when they are the inferior party; e. g. 2 K. 11: 4. 2 Sam. 5: 3. 2 Chron. 21: 7. Isa. 55: 3. 61: 8. Jer. 32: 40, al. When *equals* make a covenant עִם *with* or אֶת־ *with* is employed. In the present case, Antiochus *dictated* the firm league between himself and the Jewish apostates; so we have לָרַבִּים. The Hebrew, by the way, here exhibits a nicety of meaning and construction which our language cannot reach.

שָׁבוּעַ אֶחָד *one week*, i. e. seven years, is the Acc. of time, *during which* this matter is to continue. Antiochus began to meddle with the affairs of the Jews, in B. C. 171, and during that year deposed Onias, and covenanted with his heathenized and apostate brother, Jesus or Jason, to make him high priest, with the condition that he should introduce heathen usages into Jerusalem. In the latter end of B.C.165, or at the commencement of B. C. 164, Antiochus died. The persecution and oppression went on, in some form or other, during all that period of seven years, i. e. from 171 to 164. Hengst., Häv., and some others, make שָׁבוּעַ the Nom. to הִגְבִּיר, viz. *one week shall confirm a covenant*, etc. But why *seven* years? They admit that the ministry of Christ lasted only some three or three and a half years; what then constitutes the limits of the *seven?* Besides, the violence done to the language in this case is forbidding. Not to *time*, but to *events* that occurred during it, is the strengthening or nullifying of a covenant to be attributed. Comp. 8: 14, for a period nearly the same as the seven years, and designed to be somewhat more specific.

וַחֲצִי הַשָּׁבוּעַ, *and during half of the week*, Acc. of time how long, again. חֲצִי does not mean, as many have interpreted it, a *precise point* of time, just where half of the length of the whole would reach, but *one half* or *one division* of the whole duration. So is it clearly to be taken in 12: 7; and so here, because it can never be made to mean the same as בַּחֲצִי or לַחֲצִי, which would designate merely the half-way point of time. Then again, the הַשָּׁבוּעַ, with its article, points to the preceding *week* or *seven years*, and shows us, that as this marks length of time, so the *half* or *division* of it must also mark the same. Lastly, *facts* correspond. Antiochus, as is well known, suspended all the temple rites for three and a half years, during three of which he offered up his abominable heathen sacrifices (הַשִּׁקּוּץ שֹׁמֵם) to Jupiter Olympius in the temple. Surely it is the same personage *who lays waste city and sanctuary* (v. 26), that suspends the temple offerings in the present case. Ch. 8: 11 settles this question. To suppose, with Hengst. and Häv., that the death of the Messiah (v. 26) suspends the temple-rites, and that this is done merely in theory and by way of anticipation, and does not take place as a fact during the half of the seven years in question, is quite contrary to the tenor of the book before us. If then it be *fact* (the desolations of city and sanctuary surely are *facts*), that the sacrifices and oblations did not cease until more than thirty years after the death of Christ, how can all this be assigned here to the limits of three and a half years? Besides, the person who makes the *covenant with many*, is the same who causes the sacrifice and oblation to cease; and this covenant continues through the whole *seven years*. Of course Antiochus, or whoever makes it, does not quit the stage of action before the whole seven years are passed. It is during the *latter* half of the *seven*, then, beyond all reasonable question, that the sacrifice and oblations are suspended; and at the end of this, (as the remainder of v. 27 shows), the person who suspends them is cut off. Now this disagrees entirely with the Messianic chronology. According to the usual computation, our Saviour's ministry lasted but three and a half years, and this of course comes in the *first* part of the seven years, i. e. his death followed the *first half* of these. According to our text, the death of him, who made the covenant with many for seven years and suspended the temple-rites during the *last* half, took place after this suspension had continued three and a half years. It is impossible to reconcile the theory of Hengstenberg and Hävernick here, with the plain and obvious meaning of the writer.

He will make sacrifice and oblation to cease evidently means, in its connection, remove them by violence, forcibly suspend them. *He who destroys city and sanctuary* (v. 26); he who *treads down the sanctuary and its sacred retinue* (8: 13), is the person of whom this is said, and who actually did what is here described.

Nor is this all. He will carry his impiety to the daring length of introducing the symbols of the god whom he worships, into the holy temple; so that while they are worshipped by their appropriate rites, the sanctuary becomes desolate in regard to true worshippers and all their offerings. None will repair thither, because of the shocking abominations of idol-offerings and idol-images. So, or something like to this, does the following difficult clause seem to testify: וְעַל כְּנַף שִׁקּוּצִים מְשֹׁמֵם, *and over the winged-fowl of abominations shall be a waster.* I need not repeat the almost numberless conjectures about the meaning of this passage. כְּנַף seems to me to mean neither *summit*, *roof*, nor *pinnacle* of the temple. The word is often used for *borders* of a garment, a country, of the earth, etc. But to designate *height upward*, instead of *extension* or *breadth*, requires a very different word from כְּנַף. The *border* of a thing or object is not the *height* or *summit* of it. To compare it with πτερύγιον τοῦ ἱεροῦ (Matt. 4: 5), seems not to be much to the purpose, until we better understand the meaning of this phrase, which as yet remains somewhat uncertain. The *summit* of the temple was, we are told, filled with sharp pyramidical prominences to prevent the birds from lighting upon it. This would be no place, then, for שִׁקּוּצִים, i. e. *idol-statues.* Gesenius thinks, that the statue of Jupiter Olympius, (possibly of Antiochus), was placed conspicuously on the temple *roof.* The sense in itself is not an uninviting one; but we have to make two changes in order to bring it about. First we must read עַל כְּנָף וגו׳, *on the roof* [are] *idols;* and secondly, we must convert *summit* or *extremity*, into *roof* or *covering*. Figuratively this last would answer tolerably well for *wing*, כָּנָף. But besides all this, we are here met with still another difficulty, viz. that מְשֹׁמֵם which follows is in the *singular*. Cases of a *plural* with a part. or adj. *singular* there are, but only when the plural form designates a single agent or object, e. g. אֲדֹנִים קָשֶׁה. When *persons* are designated in the plural, and each individual is emphatically meant, the predicate may be in the sing., as in Prov. 3: 18. 27: 16. 28: 1. Gen. 27: 29. Ex. 31: 14. But neither of these cases is homogeneous with the one now before us. שִׁקּוּצִים is not a *pluralis majestaticus*, nor, so far as we can discover, is *individuality* designed particularly to be included in it, or expressed by it. We cannot accept, therefore, of such a solution of the difficulty; certainly not if we can find a better one.

The proposal of Hengstenberg, Hävernick, Lengerke, and others to apply שִׁקּוּצִים to the *temple*, which had been polluted by the Jews, is without parallel and contrary to all Heb. usage elsewhere. The prophets speak indeed of hypocritical offerings and incense as an *abomination* (תּוֹעֵבָה), Isa. 1: 13; they intimate that the doings of the dissembling and heathenish-minded Jews made Jehovah loathe his dwelling-place; but all this is far enough from vindicating such an appellation of the temple itself in Daniel, as שִׁקּוּצִים. Daniel calls it קֹדֶשׁ, 8: 13, 14; מְכוֹן מִקְדָּשׁוֹ, 8: 11. In 9: 26, also, he names it הַקֹּדֶשׁ, and in 9: 16 we have *thy city, thy sanctuary* and *thy people*. In most of these cases, also, he is speaking of the temple in the same circumstances as in our text. Comp. also Dan. 12: 7. Such an exegesis, then, makes against all usage elsewhere, and against the whole current of Hebrew feeling. *The holy city, the sanctuary*, is the indelible and eternal name stamped upon these objects. Down to the present hour, even the very Moslems call the city *El Qōds*, i. e. הַקֹּדֶשׁ. שִׁקּוּצִים then is a noun which qualifies or limits כְּנַף. It means always *idolatrous rites* or *abominations*, or else *idol-images* or *statues*. *Abominations*, in the general sense of *wicked deeds*, it never designates. Another word (תּוֹעֵבָה) is employed in such a sense. To suppose כְּנַף to mean *summit, pinnacle*, and then translate *over the pinnacle of idols* or *of idolatrous abominations is the destroyer*, and finally to apply this so as to designate the treading down and crushing the sacred edifice and its appurtenances, is even more strange than to use שִׁקּוּצִים as a designation of the temple. Where in all the Bible is such an image employed as being *over the pinnacle* of a thing, in order to designate the violence done to it by a conqueror, or to mark his sovereign control? *To tread down, to trample upon*, is indeed imagery everywhere employed; but *to be over a pinnacle*, or *a summit*, is an expression revolting both to good taste and to Heb. usage. To me, at least, it seems passing strange, to apply such expressions to the domineering sway of Antiochus in Jerusalem, or (with Hengst. and Häv.) to Titus and his final destruction of the temple.

But if the meaning *summit* and *roof* be denied to כְּנַף, only three other meanings remain, viz., that of *wing*, of *bird* or *winged-fowl*, and of *border* or *extreme limit*. To give to כְּנַף the meaning of *army-wings*, cannot well be conceded. Rosenmüller, indeed, gives the clause this turn: "Exercitui detestando vastator dux praeerit." He supposes that כְּנַף, like the Latin *ala*, may mean *the wing of an army*. But if an army is to be spoken of collectively, in this way, we should expect *wings* (כְּנָפַיִם), not *wing* (sing.) to designate it. Isa. 8: 8 and 18: 1, to which Rosenm. appeals, will hardly bear him out; for in both cases a different meaning of the word is more probable. In fact, the word כְּנַף does not seem to be employed in such a sense. Ezekiel employs אֲגַפִּים (plur. only) in the tropical sense of *army-wings*; see Lex. sub v. Besides, how flat it would be, after saying that the people, i. e. the army, of a prince who will invade Judea, have marred city and sanctuary, and after describing all the devastations which they had committed under his guidance and direction, to add that he had supremacy over them, or (in other words) was their leader. Not so Daniel. The discourse advances. First, the invader mars city and temple. Next, he prohibits sacrifices and oblations to Jehovah, on the part of the Jews. Then he sets up the statue and other insignia of his own chosen god, Jupiter Olympius, in the temple, where sacrifices abominable to the Jews were offered in conformity with the usages of the heathen. Lastly, comes the fearful end of him who has desolated the city and temple; for in his turn he becomes a שֹׁמֵם, i. e. *something to be desolated* or *destroyed*. Here all is climactic, and the tenor of the discourse, viewed in this light, becomes comparatively easy and probable.

If now we assume the second meaning, *winged-fowl*, how shall such a meaning be rendered probable? The fact is well known, that Antiochus devoted the temple at Jerusalem to the worship of Jupiter Olympius, and there offered the appropriate sacrifices. It is said of him, in 1 Macc. 1: 45 seq., that "he forbade burnt offerings and sacrifices and libations in the sanctuary, and [commanded] to profane the sabbaths and the feast-days, to defile holy places and persons, to build altars and sacred enclosures (τεμένη) and idol-apparatus, and to sacrifice swinish and unclean beasts . . . And whosoever would not obey the king's command, must be put to death." The word εἰδωλεῖα (v. 47) I have translated *idol-apparatus*, because it plainly does not mean *idol-temple* here, for such Antiochus had no need to build, when he had converted the temple of Jehovah into a place of worship to his god. The Syriac version reads εἰδῶλα here, which makes the sense required. But *εἰδωλεῖα* may be regarded as a mere neut. pl. adjective, and be rendered as above. Altars and sacred enclosures and sacrifices necessarily demanded idol representations of the god, to whom the offerings were made. So was it in all the Greek and Roman world. I do not see any reason to doubt, that Antiochus set up the statue of his god. " *They built* or *set up βδέλυγμα ἐρημώσεως by the altar*," says 1 Macc. 1: 54, i. e. הַשִּׁקּוּץ שֹׁמֵם. I understand this of a *statue* of Jupiter Olympius erected in the temple; and this statue, as is well known, usually stood over *an eagle at its feet with wide-spread wings.* Hence עַל כְּנַף שִׁקּוּצִים, *over a wing of abominations*, or rather *over an abominable winged-fowl, is a desolator.* That כְּנָף may mean *the possessor of a wing*, i. e. a winged fowl, as well as *wing*, is only in conformity with abundant analogies in Hebrew. Such a meaning it has in Gen. 7: 14. שִׁקּוּצִים qualifies כְּנַף, § 104. 1, and shows that the *winged bird* was a part of the heathen symbols. The plural seems here to be chosen in order that a connection with מְשֹׁמֵם may be avoided by the reader. The horror and disgust which such a spectacle would occasion to a pious Jew, can more easily be conceived of than expressed. But the wide-spread eagle-wings is not all. This is at the foot of an image that stands *over* it (עַל כְּנַף), which image is here characterized by the appellation מְשֹׁמֵם. Most critics have referred מְשֹׁמֵם to the *person* of the desolator, the "prince who will come," i. e. most of those who refer vs. 26, 27, to Antiochus. But in such a case, how could the *article* be dispensed with? It would not only be *renewed mention* of the person, but a case which would require special pains not to be misunderstood, and so demand specification. But as no article is prefixed to מְשֹׁמֵם, we may in this connection refer this word to the *statue* of the heathen god, which is very significantly named *a desolator*, from the effect which its erection in the temple produced upon the Jewish religious rites and those who performed them. In 11: 31, the שִׁקּוּץ (*idol*) has the same participle applied to it, and for the same reason. The temple was utterly forsaken by all but apostates to heathenism. Everything that pertained to the true God was trodden down and destroyed. In this case מְשֹׁמֵם should not have (as it has not) the article; for it is neither renewed mention of a thing, nor is it something of which the reader could be supposed to have formed an antecedent idea in his own mind. The single *statue* of Jupiter is spoken of in the sing. number; and thus the whole form of expression falls within the regular laws of grammar. The erection of such an image with its *winged symbolical bird*, is a consummation of impiety, which goes quite beyond the inhibition of the Jewish sacrifices and oblations. Iniquity is now *come to the full*, and therefore must be punished.

Hoffman (Die 70 Jahre) has proposed such an interpretation as that now suggested. In his Weissag. und Erfüll. (s. 308), he seems to give the preference to another and different explanation, which Steudel (ut sup. s. 47) has suggested. The verb כָּנַף means *to cover*. Of course כָּנָף may, as he thinks, retain this idea. He then refers it to a *covering* built on the Jewish altar by Antiochus, after the manner of the heathen; which was profane and abominable in the eyes of a Hebrew, who was commanded to construct his altar only with earth, Ex. 20: 24. On the profanely covered altar of Antiochus, heathen abominations were offered. Hence a *covering of abominations*. But how he disposes of מְשֹׁמֵם, in this case, he does not expressly tell us. He must refer it to כָּנָף. But this is hard. *Over the covering of abominations* is — what? מְשֹׁמֵם can hardly designate the sacrifices offered there. Is Antiochus, then, designated by it, as presiding *over* the heathen altar? If so, the *article* must be prefixed. An *altar-covering*, moreover, could hardly be regarded here, as answering to the *climactic* nature of the discourse. I deem his former opinion, therefore, to be much better grounded.

One other view of the case I will venture to suggest — a possible one if not probable — that I have nowhere met with. This would assume, in the present case, the frequent meaning of כְּנַף, viz. *border*, *extremity*, and then translate thus: *On the border of idols* or *idol-places*, *will be the destroyer*. The ground of this exegesis may be found in the history of Antiochus. After the ravages committed by him in Jerusalem, he went into the East (see Dan. 11: 44) to avenge himself there for offences; and in Persia he entered forcibly the great temple at Elymais, and robbed it of its treasures. The people of that region, exasperated by his sacrilege, rose *en masse* and forced him to retreat. On that retreat he was overtaken with the news of the destruction of his army in Palestine, and the victorious entrance of Judas into Jerusalem. Through fatigue, or exasperation and disappointment, or a combination of both, he fell into a raging fever, and died after a very short space in that condition. If now we may suppose our text to look to this, there is a regular progress in the narration: after all his outrages in Palestine, he goes to the *border* or *extremity of the idol countries*, robs an idol-temple there, and then the destruction, predicted in the next clause, hastens on. It is an augmentation of his woes, that he perishes in a distant land. *The destroyer* (מְשֹׁמֵם), to use the language applied to this very expedition in Dan. 11: 44, "went forth with great fury to destroy, and utterly to make away with many," and, in so doing, he himself becomes a שֹׁמֵם, i. e. is utterly destroyed. — If it be objected to this view of the subject, that it is too specific, let any one read Dan. xi. and he will no more insist on such an objection. It cannot be denied, moreover, that the prediction is thus regularly climactic, and that it is full of meaning. The only serious doubts would arise from another quarter. Would his eastern journey or expedition be described in language so obscure, and so alien from the usual methods of describing such events? And then, in case Antiochus is designated by מְשֹׁמֵם, how could the *article* be dispensed with in such a renewed mention of him? These two considerations occasion doubt and hesitation. There is somewhat less of difficulty in the solution given above; at least there is less of grammatical difficulty. But the general sense of the passage is plainly more striking, on the ground last assumed.

וְעַד כָּלָה, *but unto destruction.* Wieseler (Die 70 Wochen, s. 42 seq.) strenuously defends the position, that כָּלָה is a *verb* here, employed in its usual sense. He translates thus: *And until it* [the half-week] *is completed,* etc. His arguments are unsatisfactory. עַד must mean either *while* or *during,* or else *unto, even to.* Thus understood, it would make the death of the tyrant, which the next clause predicts, to happen *during* the half-week, or to be taking place until that was completed; so that Antiochus must, at all events, on such a ground, have died either before the end of the three and a half years, or just at that point. But neither of these positions is true. There can be no question as to the right to take כָּלָה as a *noun,* for such a usage is frequent. As little question can there be, as to its energetic meaning. The verb means *to consummate, to finish, to complete,* etc.; and of course the noun designates *consummation, a full end of, a finishing off with;*—a mode of expression stronger than that of mere *excision,* etc. Such was to be the end of the tyrant. The וְ in וְעַד is best rendered by *but.* The sentiment of the verse stands arranged thus: 'He will make a firm league with many apostate Jews; for three and a half years will he remove the sacrifices and oblations of the temple; he will even erect a statue of Jupiter there, accompanied by its usual eagle with expanded wings at its feet—but a dreadful reverse will overtake him; the overwhelming indignation of Heaven, that which is irreversibly decreed, will make an utter and final end of him.' Thus all is smooth and easy.

וְנֶחֱרָצָה תִּתַּךְ, *even that which is decreed, it shall be poured out,* or *even decreed* [destruction] *shall be poured out.* The accents follow the sense of the first rendering, and divide accordingly, putting a *Zākeph Qāton* on נֶחֱרָצָה. Of course, if we follow them, the verb is *impersonal,* or at least a kind of *constructio praegnans* which implies כָּלָה for its Nom., or else *wrath, indignation,* or *curse,* is implied. The verb נָתַךְ is not used in the literal sense, but only in the tropical one; and it is always joined with some subject like those just named, which makes the verb easy to be understood, if it be employed in an elliptical way. It is a kind of *terminus technicus* for the expression of such ideas; and being *intransitive*, it readily goes over into a *passive* sense. If we follow the accents, then, there is no serious difficulty in the construction. But if we depart from them, and take נֶחֱרָצָה as a participial noun, and as the Nom. to תִּתַּךְ, then all is easy and obvious. This member of the clause is an advance upon עַד כָּלָה. It designates a total end which is *definitely decreed* by Heaven, and this decree is beyond control and irreversible. The very same sentiment is developed in כָּלָה וְנֶחֱרָצָה in Isa. 10: 23. 28: 22. The accession of energy and definiteness to the threat, from the addition of וְנֶחֱרָצָה, must be obvious to every one familiar with the Hebrew. The imagery of *pouring out* originates here in וְקִצּוֹ בַשֶּׁטֶף of v. 26, and is therefore both natural and forcible.

עַל שׁוֹמֵם, *upon him who is to be made desolate.* Quite different from מְשֹׁמֵם (*the destroyer, waster*) is the participial intrans. form, שׁוֹמֵם. It has always a *passive* sense, and therefore means *delendus, vastandus, one who is* or *ought to be destroyed.* The first is the ὁ ἄνθρωπος τῆς ἁμαρτίας, and the second is the ὁ υἱὸς τῆς ἀπωλείας, of Paul in 2 Thess. 2: 3, who seems to have had his mind on the passage before us. In the expression is substantially couched the favorite παρανομασία of the Hebrews; the *desolator, waster* shall be שׁוֹמֵם (*wasted*).

Thus ends the second great national trial of the Jews. The tyrant who brought it upon them, falls in the midst of his contests and of his vengeance, and with his fall, the august drama closes, as in ch. vii. viii. xi.

It would be little to my present purpose, to give a minute history of all the interpretations that have been put upon the passage respecting the *seventy weeks*, and of the efforts made to sustain them. Most of them depend on some *a priori* conception of what Daniel ought to say, rather than on a philologico-historical deduction from what he has said. For my present purpose, I need to notice only two classes of interpretation; (1) The exclusively Messianic. (2) The exclusively Anti-Messianic. Of these, in their order, I shall speak very briefly.

(1) THE EXCLUSIVELY MESSIANIC. *An anointed one, a prince* (v. 25), is converted into *the Messiah, the Prince*, i. e. Christ the King of kings. The cutting off of *an Anointed One* (in v. 26) is the violent death of Jesus, *the Messiah;* וְאֵין לוֹ designates his vicarious suffering for sinners. The time when he entered on his public ministry, is the *terminus ad quem* of the sixty-two weeks and the seven weeks; and these two distinct periods are combined into one, which is made to commence, not with Cyrus' proclamation, nor yet with that of Darius, but with that of Artaxerxes in the twentieth year of his reign. Nor is this all that is assumed. Not only is the period of the *birth* of Christ arbitrarily set aside from the calculation, but in order to adjust the sixty-nine weeks to the period of his entrance on his public ministry, the reign of Artaxerxes is made ten years longer than

the most authentic histories make it, i. e. fifty-one years instead of forty-one, and so much is then taken from the reign of his father Xerxes. With all these assumptions, the sixty-nine weeks (62 + 7) or 483 years are at last adjusted to the period, when Jesus was baptized and entered on his official work. In this way two portions of the seventy weeks are summarily disposed of.

I need not here repeat the objections to most of these positions, which have already been made in the preceding pages. Most of these objections, to say the least, are founded in philology and in history, as well as in the analogy of the book in general. Enough of them, at all events, will abide the test, and are entirely unanswerable. But if not, what follows in respect to the *one* remaining *week*, is decisive of the whole matter.

According to v. 26, *an anointed one* is to be cut off at the *close* of the *sixty-two* weeks, and of course at the beginning of the *one week*, i. e. seven years. The interpreters in question, however, make his excision three and a half years later. But it is quite plain, that it is during the remainder of the week, i. e. during the next and latter three and a half years, that our text makes the principal desolations of the city and sanctuary to take place, and the invader perishes at the close of this period. The exclusively Messianic interpreters, however, make *Titus* the desolator, and the *Roman army* the people whom he leads on to waste the city and the sanctuary. But if Christ was crucified in A. D. 34, and Titus invested Jerusalem in A. D. 70, we have thirty-six intervening years instead of three and a half before his work of ruin; — a matter which, in such a book of accurate dates as the one before us, is inadmissible beyond all question. Besides, *how*, *where*, did *Titus* die? Under any special tokens of divine vengeance, such as 9: 27 predicts and threatens to the waster? We know not where to find these tokens. But further, *when* did he die? In A. D. 81. Instead of perishing then at the close of the noted *last week*, his death took place some forty-seven years afterwards.

In a word, history is at utter and irreconcilable variance with the scheme of interpretation in question. It is indeed wonderful that it ever could have been advocated by sensible men. According to this scheme, Jesus Christ and the *Roman* power are almost the only agents developed in the prophecy; whereas it lies upon the very face of v. 24, that *the seventy weeks* PRECEDE *the coming of the true Messiah*. The blessings there promised, are not bestowed until after those weeks are completed.

(2) THE EXCLUSIVELY ANTI-MESSIANIC INTERPRETATION. Wieseler (in his *Die siebzig Wochen*) has concentrated all that has been said, and I may add, all that can well be said, in favor of this. He possesses distinguished critical skill, and withal a discriminating knowledge of the Hebrew. All turns, however, on v. 24. Vs. 25—27 must undoubtedly be conceded to him, for reasons like to those already assigned above, in defence of the interpretation which I have given. I can not doubt, for a moment, that these verses refer to Antiochus. But for the reasons stated (in Comm. on v. 24), I can by no means concede to him the position, that the good there designated has respect only to the return from the Babylonish exile. Comparison of actual history with the splendid prospects and promises held out in v. 24, will show beyond all reasonable doubt, that the fulfilment of those predictions must be sought elsewhere than in the return from exile.

My leading reasons for choosing the *medium iter*, in this case, arise from no design to " split the difference" between the two conflicting views just stated. Long before I could obtain a sight of Wieseler and Hoffman on *the seventy weeks and years*, I had come, from the simple study of the text, substantially to the same conclusion that I have now developed. But some particulars of the prophecy continued still to be dark. On these, the two writers just named have cast some new light. All seems capable of reasonable illustration, and even of a good degree of certainty, with the exception of the beginning and end of the *seven weeks*, and the particular period which they designate, and perhaps the clause respecting כְּנַף שִׁקּוּצִים. The last seems, however, in some good measure, to be illustrated by historical facts respecting the worship of Jupiter Olympius at Jernsalem, and the statue with the usual symbol of the " winged-fowl." The seven weeks, I regret to say, remain for future efforts; which however need not be despaired of. In the meantime, I must try to console myself for my own ignorance, with a *Non omnia possumus omnes.*

All the close of this protracted examination of 9: 24—27, it may be useful to recapitulate summarily, and to compare the whole with the other predictions of Daniel.

The Babylonish exile was to continue seventy years; Jer. 25: 11. 29: 10. Dan. 9: 2. Near the close of these, Daniel betook himself to earnest prayer, that the fulfilment of the prediction that the Jews should return from their exile, might speedily be developed, Dan. 9: 2, 3. Gabriel is commissioned to make a new announcement to him, of what would take place after the exile and before the coming of the great deliverer. This he does, by still preserving the number seventy, but converting this into so many *weeks of years*, (lit. *seventy besevened*), instead of simple years which belonged to the prophecy of Jeremiah. The great question here is, or rather should be, (for in time past little or no attention has been paid to it) : Does the period of *seventy weeks* cover the *whole* ground, from the time of Daniel's vision to the coming of Christ? The greatest possible effort has been often made, to bring about a union of the end of the seventy weeks with the period of Christ's birth, or of his public ministry. Of course the *terminus a quo* has been the principal point of controversy; in as much as there has generally been at least a tacit concession, that the *terminus ad quem* must be one of the points just mentioned. But history baffles all attempts to accomplish the object in question. From Daniel's vision down to the birth of Christ, is some 538 years; and seventy weeks make but 490, i. e. forty-eight years less. Attempts to find the proclamation to *rebuild* in Jer. xxix; in Cyrus' edict, in that of Darius, or that of Artaxerxes; are all frustrated by history again; and this matter must be, after all, given up as impracticable by these means. But then, (if we may be permitted to ask the question), what need of all this trouble? *Is it any part of the angel's design to place the seventy weeks in such an attitude?* To me it seems plain, that it is not. In all the prophetic pages of the O. Test., or of the New, where does any prophecy assume the attitude of a book of *Annals?* The nearest approach is in Dan. xi.; but even here, there are merely touches on the fourth dynasty, until we come to the נִבְזֶה, the מְשֹׁמֵם, Antiochus. We have then only one prophetic history of one king, in all the Scriptures which is *annalistic;* and the Syrian tyrant is that king. For the rest; *great events*, and those only are described. When these cease, prophecy lays aside her pen, and keeps silence. The reason is obvious, viz. that only such events are adapted to instruct by making deep impressions. The ordinary course of events does not attract the prophetic eye; and so no sketch of them is drawn.

This consideration liberates us at once from all necessity of forcing the *terminus ad quem* of the seventy weeks into a union with the year of Christ's birth, or of his public ministry. All that the angel designs to communicate is, that as there had been seventy years of exile in regard to the Jews, seven times that number must pass away, before they would cease to be troubled in like manner, and before the Messiah would come. Sixty-two of these are "troublous times," but the following one week (= seven years) is to renew all the horrors of the Babylonish invasion, and even more, on the score of impiety and persecution. With these last seven years, times so hazardous to the nation and to religion are to cease, until the coming of Christ. So much, but no more, seems to be plainly within the design and scope of the angel's communication. And of course, we have, on this ground, no special interest to seek for a union of the *terminus ad quem* of the *seventy weeks* with the year of Christ's birth or of his entering on public office. We can leave it wherever it falls or terminates, as comprising all that was specially interesting for prophecy to disclose.

Inasmuch now as the period of sixty-two weeks has no *terminus a quo* expressly assigned to it, it would seem to be not inapposite, that it should be regarded as already virtually designated by the beginning of the seventy years in Jeremiah. So some have understood the matter. Then all that follows they consider as supported and illustrated by historical facts. Antiochus began to vex the Jews, in B. C. 171, (i. e. sixty-two weeks = 434 years after B. C. 606 when Jeremiah's seventy years begin); and in that year an *anointed one*, a lawful high-priest, Onias III., was cut off, and the people had no other legitimate officer of this rank until after the death of the tyrant. During the *week* (seven years) that followed, Antiochus laid waste the city and sanctuary; for three and a half years he took away sacrifice and oblation; he erected his altar and his idol-statue in the temple of God; and at the close of this period, and of course at the close of the seven years, he perished by a miserable death in a foreign land, whither he had gone to commit sacrilege again. How is it possible, they ask, (and with no small appearance of right), that all these periods should so exactly meet the *facts of history*, and at so many points, unless the exegesis that we have given is well grounded? To say the least, they add, *facts* make our exegesis altogether probable.

No one can refuse to acknowledge that the accordance of *dates* and *events*, in this case, is striking, and seemingly decisive at first view. But it must be remembered, that the sixty-two weeks are not the only period to be provided for. What is to be done with the seven weeks = forty-nine years, which constitute the first division of the seventy weeks? — No room is here left for them; or if any, they must be put *after* the sixty-two weeks, which seems to be at least an unnatural mode of exegesis. Then again as to the sixty-two weeks, the statement in Daniel (v. 25) is, that the city is to be in a course of rebuilding, during that period, and of rebuilding in a stinted and imperfect manner, by reason of troublous times. Yet, according to the scheme of interpretation which we are now examining, the first seventy years of the sixty-two weeks are those of the exile, when Jerusalem lay all the time in ruins. These two circumstances seem then, after all, to decide against the scheme in question. Could it be shown, or even made probable, that the seven weeks either follow the sixty-two weeks, or are coördinate and contemporaneous with a part of the latter, then all would be easy of explanation, and the whole paragraph might be enucleated, and placed in a clear and satisfactory light.

Desirable as it seems to be to bring this about, I cannot on the whole persuade my hermeneutical conscience to be reconciled to the plan. I see no satisfactory way of removing the impression which the text makes, of three *distinct* and *successive* periods, viz. of seven, sixty-two, and one weeks. The writer seems plainly to mean, not only that these are to be reckoned so as to make up the sum of seventy, but that each of the two latter periods begin, when the preceding one ends. How else can seventy weeks be made out ?

That there were events and persons corresponding to what the angel declares, I cannot well doubt. So many things strikingly correspond with facts known, that they seem to be a pledge for the certainty of the rest. At all events, my ignorance of facts, or inability to see how our text accords with those that we do know, cannot with propriety be regarded as decisive evidence against the correctness and truthfulness of the predictions. As history now lies before us, I am unable to find the *indicia* of the first period of seven weeks. Where I can easily make out a *terminus a quo*, I fail in my endeavors to find the *terminus ad quem* and so *vice versa*. And this is equally true, if I amalgamate, as many do, the periods of seven and sixty-two weeks. The beginning and end of the sixty-nine weeks thus made, i. e. 483 years, is no more discoverable in our histories, than the beginning and end of the seven years. At least the face of history is to be changed and remodelled, in respect to *time*, in order to make out any agreement between it and the sixty-nine weeks. Moreover the very amalgamation in question is, as has already been shown, against the tenor of the text, and against actual facts.

I have exposed myself, perhaps, to an accusation not very unfrequent, viz., that of pulling down without building up. But if I have endeavored to pull down, only where the foundations were tottering, and the building ready to fall by a slight touch, this is nothing that deserves reprobation. It is a first step toward a new and more stable edifice. If I am unable to erect it, others may succeed. May all prosperity (so do I devoutly wish) attend their efforts! But I will not pretend to know, what I feel conscious of not knowing to my satisfaction. I much prefer the confession of ignorance to a pretension of knowledge, specially when the means of acquiring that knowledge are not within our power.

A few words more, on the subject of applying vs. 25—27 to *Antiochus Epiphanes*, instead of the *Romans*, either heathen or Christian, and I have done.

Does the tenor of the book of Daniel, as to its prophecies, tend to support and confirm the exegesis which I have given ? The answer to this question must be in the affirmative. Antiochus does not indeed appear in a special manner, in chap. ii. But he is virtually there, in the crushing power of the fourth dynasty. His fall is involved in that of the dynasty, 2: 44. In 7: 7—11, 19—26, Antiochus specifically appears, in all his cruelty and blasphemy. In 8: 9—12, 23—25, he is still more graphically described, and as possessing the same characteristics. Chap. 11: 21—45 is even a kind of historical narration of him, which is particular beyond any example in all the Scriptures. His doings and his end are of the same character here as before. If language has any definite meaning, the identification of the same tyrant in all these prophecies and visions, is altogether certain. How comes it now, that all these prophecies should be uniform as to this trait, and the present one (in chap. ix.) be discrepant from all the rest? If the exclusively Messianic interpreters are in the right, then Antiochus is not at all the subject of the prediction in 9: 25—27. But if *analogy* has any force, it is quite plain that we might expect to find him there. That he is to be found there, we have seen, if any credit is to be given in this matter to historical facts and dates. It is utterly improbable that such a concurrence could exist between prediction and events and persons, unless there had been some actually designed and foreseen coincidence, i. e. unless the one were prediction and the other fulfilment, or unless, indeed, the book were written, as some have uncritically maintained, *post eventum*.

If one now will patiently go through with a comparison of the expressions and events in the prophecy before us, he will be forced to feel that there is a similarity very striking, which scarcely leaves any room for doubt. Compare the cutting off of the high priest in 9: 26 and 11: 22; the marring of the city and sanctuary in 9: 26, and in 11: 31, also in 8: 24; the final end of Antiochus in 9: 26 and 8: 25; the covenanting with many in 9: 27, and 11: 23, 30; and the removing of sacrifice and oblation in 9: 27, and in 8: 12. 11: 31. 12: 11. Even the עַד־כָּלָה וְנֶחֱרָצָה of 9: 27, has its parallel in 11: 35, 45. The 2300 days of 8: 13 should also be compared with the *one week* of 9: 27, with due allowance for the differences in the things presented; the 1290 and 1335 days of 12: 11, 12, in respect to the abolishing of sacrifice and oblation, are to be compared (with the like allowance) with the *half-week* (= three and a half years) of 9: 27, with which must also be joined 12: 7.

When all this is done, compare the development of the *Messianic kingdom* in chap. ii. vii. xii, with 9: 24. In this last case, the Messianic kingdom is indeed mentioned first; but still, it is arranged and spoken of as the *last in order*. It comes not until *after* the end of the seventy weeks; the other events in vs. 25—27 occur *during* that period, i. e. before it ends. Every where the monarchies predicted or brought to view fall, *before* the new and perpetual kingdom arises. How then can any of them be the dynasty of the *Romans?* Is there not throughout the whole book, a harmony so complete, that it amounts to nearly all but the repetition of the same things in the same words? In any case, where investigation should be made without any favorite theory to support, and without the aid of any *a priori* assumptions, would there or could there be any doubt, as to what conclusions we should adopt?

For the gratification of the reader's curiosity, and also for the sake of supplying him with the means of comparing different attempts to translate vs. 24—27, I shall here subjoin these verses in various translations, so that they may be compared with the original text and with each other. Perhaps, moreover, he who examines them will learn to estimate, in some good measure, the difficulty that attends the pasage in question, and cease to wonder at the diversity of translation and explanation that exists.

I. *The Hebrew.*

(24) שָׁבֻעִים שִׁבְעִים נֶחְתַּךְ עַל־עַמְּךָ ׀
וְעַל־עִיר קָדְשֶׁךָ לְכַלֵּא הַפֶּשַׁע וּלְחָתֵם
חַטָּאוֹת וּלְכַפֵּר עָוֹן וּלְהָבִיא צֶדֶק עֹלָמִים
וְלַחְתֹּם חָזוֹן וְנָבִיא וְלִמְשֹׁחַ קֹדֶשׁ קָדָשִׁים׃
(25) וְתֵדַע וְתַשְׂכֵּל מִן־מֹצָא דָבָר לְהָשִׁיב
וְלִבְנוֹת יְרוּשָׁלִַם עַד־מָשִׁיחַ נָגִיד שָׁבֻעִים
שִׁבְעָה וְשָׁבֻעִים שִׁשִּׁים וּשְׁנַיִם תָּשׁוּב
וְנִבְנְתָה רְחוֹב וְחָרוּץ וּבְצוֹק הָעִתִּים׃
(26) וְאַחֲרֵי הַשָּׁבֻעִים שִׁשִּׁים וּשְׁנַיִם יִכָּרֵת
מָשִׁיחַ וְאֵין לוֹ וְהָעִיר וְהַקֹּדֶשׁ יַשְׁחִית עַם
נָגִיד הַבָּא וְקִצּוֹ בַשֶּׁטֶף וְעַד קֵץ מִלְחָמָה
נֶחֱרֶצֶת שֹׁמֵמוֹת׃ (27) וְהִגְבִּיר בְּרִית
לָרַבִּים שָׁבוּעַ אֶחָד וַחֲצִי הַשָּׁבוּעַ יַשְׁבִּית ׀
זֶבַח וּמִנְחָה וְעַל כְּנַף שִׁקּוּצִים מְשֹׁמֵם
וְעַד־כָּלָה וְנֶחֱרָצָה תִּתַּךְ עַל־שׁוֹמֵם׃

II. *Translation.*

(24) Seventy weeks are decided
respecting thy people and thy holy
city, to restrain transgression, and to
seal up sin, and to expiate iniquity;
and to bring in everlasting righteousness, and to seal vision and prophecy,
and to anoint a holy of holies. (25)
Mark well and understand; from the
going forth of a command to rebuild
Jerusalem unto an anointed one, a
prince, shall be seven weeks; and sixty
and two weeks shall it be rebuilt, with
broad spaces and narrow limits, and
in troublous times. (26) And after
sixty and two weeks, an anointed one
shall be cut off, and there shall be
none for it [the people], and the
city and the sanctuary shall the people of a prince that will come destroy; but his end shall be with an
overwhelming flood, and unto the
end shall be war, a decreed measure
of desolations. (27) And he shall
firmly covenant with many, for one
week; and during half of the week,
shall he cause the sacrifice and oblation to cease; and a waster shall be
over a winged fowl of abominations;
but unto destruction, even that which
is decreed, shall there be an outpouring upon him who is to be destroyed.

III. *Version of the Septuagint.*

(24) Ἑβδομήκοντα ἑβδομάδες ἐκ-
ρίθησαν ἐπὶ τὸν λαόν σου, καὶ ἐπὶ
τὴν πόλιν Σιὼν συντελεσθῆναί τὴν
ἁμαρτίαν, καὶ τὰς ἀδικίας σπανίσαι,
καὶ ἀπαλεῖψαι τὰς ἀδικίας, καὶ
διανοηθῆναι τὸ ὅραμα, καὶ δοθῆναι
δικαιοσύνην αἰώνιον, καὶ συντελεσθῆναι τὰ ὁράματα καὶ προφήτην, καὶ εὐφράναι ἅγιον ἁγίων. (25)
Καὶ γνώσῃ, καὶ διανοηθήσῃ, καὶ εὑ-

IV. *Theodotion, (the usual text of our Sept. Bible).*

(24) Ἑβδομήκοντα ἑβδομάδες συ-
νετμήθησαν ἐπὶ τὸν λαόν σου, καὶ
ἐπὶ τὴν πόλιν τὴν ἁγίαν, ἕως τοῦ
παλαιωθῆναι τὸ παράπτωμα, καὶ
τοῦ συντελεσθῆναι ἁμαρτίαν, καὶ
τοῦ σφραγίσαι ἁμαρτίας, καὶ τοῦ
ἀπαλεῖψαι ἀνομίας, καὶ τοῦ ἐξιλά-
σασθαι ἀδικίας, καὶ τοῦ ἀγαγεῖν δικαιοσύνην αἰώνιον, καὶ τοῦ σφραγί-

φρανθήσῃ, καὶ εὑρήσεις προστάγματα ἀποκριθῆναι, καὶ οἰκοδομήσεις Ἱερουσαλὴμ πόλιν Κυρίῳ. (26) Καὶ μετὰ ἑπτὰ, καὶ ἑβδομήκοντα, καὶ ἑξήκοντα δύο ἀποσταθήσεται χρίσμα, καὶ οὐκ ἔσται, καὶ βασιλεία ἐθνῶν φθερεῖ τήν πόλιν, καὶ τὸ ἅγιον μετὰ τοῦ χριστοῦ· καὶ ἥξει ἡ συντέλεια αὐτοῦ μετ᾽ ὀργῆς, καὶ ἕως καιροῦ συντελείας, ἀπό πολέμου πολεμηθήσεται. (27) Καὶ δυναστεύσει ἡ διαθήκη εἰς πολλοὺς, καὶ πάλιν ἐπιστέψει, καὶ ἀνοικοδομηθήσεται, εἰς πλᾶτος, καὶ μῆκος, καὶ κατὰ σμντέλειαν καιρῶν· καὶ μετὰ ἑπτὰ καὶ ἑβδομήκοντα καιροὺς, καὶ ξβ ἐτῶν, ἕως καιροῦ συντελείας πολέμοῦ καὶ ἀφαιρεθήσεται ἡ ἐρήμωσις ἐν τῷ κατισχύσαι τὴν διαθήκην ἐπὶ πολλὰς ἑβδομάδας, καὶ ἐν τῷ τέλει τῆς ἑβδομάδος, ἀρθήσεται ἡ θυσία, καὶ ἡ σπονδὴ, καὶ ἐπὶ τὸ ἱερὸν βδέλυγμα τῶν ἐρημώσεων ἔσται ἕως συντελείας, καὶ συντέλεια δοθήσεται ἐπὶ τὴν ἐρήμωσιν.

σαι ὅρασιν, καὶ προφήτην, καὶ τοῦ χρῖσαι ἅγιον ἁγίων. (25) Καὶ γνώσῃ, καὶ συνήσεις, ἀπὸ ἐξόδου λόγων τοῦ ἀποκριθῆναι, καὶ τοῦ οἰκοδομηθῆναι Ἱερουσαλήμ, ἕως Χριστοῦ ἡγουμένου, ἑβδομάδες ἑπτὰ, καὶ ἑβδομάδες ἑξήκοντα δύο· καὶ ἐπιστρέψει, καὶ οἰκοδομηθήσεται πλατεῖα, καὶ περίτειχος, καὶ ἐκκενωθήσονται οἱ καιροί. (26) Καὶ μετὰ τὰς ἑβδομάδας τὰς ἑξήκοντα δύο ἐξολοθρευθήσεται χρίσμα, καὶ κρῖμα οὐκ ἔστιν ἐν αὐτῷ· καὶ τὴν πόλιν, καὶ τὸν ἅγιον διαφθερεῖ σὺν τῷ ἡγουμένῳ τῷ ἐρχομένῳ, καὶ ἐκκοπήσονται ὡς ἐν κατακλυσμῷ, καὶ ἕως τέλους πολέμου συντετμημένου ἀφανισμοῖς· [Καὶ δυναμώσει διαθήκην πολλοῖς ἑβδομὰς μία· καὶ ἥμισυ τῆς ἑβδομάδος καναπαύσει θυμίαμα, καὶ θυσίαν, καὶ σπονδὴν, και ἐπὶ πτερύγιον τάξει ἀφανισμοῦ, καὶ ἕως συντελείας, καὶ σπουδῆς τάξει ἀφανισμῷ.] (27) Καὶ δυναμώσει διαθήκην πολλοῖς ἑβδομὰς μία, καὶ ἐν τῷ ἡμίσει τῆς ἑβδομάδος ἀρθήσεται θυσία, καὶ σπονδὴ, καὶ ἐπι τούτοις, ἐπὶ τὸ ἱερὸν βδέλυγμα τῆς ἐρημώσεως καὶ ἕως συντελείας καιροῦ συντέλεια δοθήσεται ἐπί τὴν ἐρήμωσιν.

V. *Vulgate Version.*

(24) Septuaginta hebdomades abbreviatae sunt super populum tuum, et super urbem sanctam tuam, ut consummetur praevaricatio, et finem accipiat peccatum, et deleatur iniquitas, et adducatur justitia sempiterna, et impleatur visio et prophetia, et ungatur Sanctus sanctorum. (25) Scito ergo et animadverte, ab exitu sermonis ut iterum aedificetur Jerusalem, usque ad Christum ducem, hebdomades septem, et hebdomades sexaginta duae erunt; et rursum aedificabitur platea et muri in angustia temporum. (26) Et post hebdomades sexaginta duas occidetur Christus; et non erit ejus populus qui eum negaturus est. Et civitatem et

VI. *Syriac Version translated.*

(24) Seventy years shall rest upon thy people, and on thy holy city, to make an end of iniquity and to complete sin, to remit transgression, and to bring in righteousness which is eternal, and to complete prophetic vision, and to the Messiah the Holy of holies. (25) And know thou and understand, that from the going forth of the command to return and to rebuild Jerusalem, unto the coming of Messiah the king, there shall be seven weeks and sixty-two weeks; one shall return and rebuild Jerusalem, her streets and her broad places, unto the end of time. (26) And after sixty-two weeks, the Messiah shall be slain, and there shall be nothing to

sanctuarium dissipabit populus cum duce venturo; et finis ejus vastitas, et post finem belli statuta desolatio. (27) Confirmabit autem pactum multis hebdomadâ unâ; et in dimidio hebdomadis deficiet hostia et sacrificium; et erit in templo abominatio desolationis; et usque ad consummationem et finem perseverabit desolatio.

it. And the city of the sanctuary shall be laid waste, with a king who shall come; and its destruction shall be with a flood; and unto the end of the war which is a decree of destruction. (27) And he shall make firm his covenant with many, for one week, and a dividing of the week; and he will cause sacrifice and oblation to cease; and over the wing of abomination [shall be] a destroyer; unto the consummation of the decree it shall rest upon the destroyer.

VII. *Rosenmüller's Version.*

(24) Septuaginta hebdomades destinatae sunt tuo populo, tuaeque sacrae urbi, ad consummandum peccatum, ad obsignanda delicta, ad expiandam culpam, et ad inducendam aeternam justitiam, et ad obsignandam visionem et vaticinationem, atque ad unguendum Sanctorum Sanctissimum. (25) Scies igitur et intelliges, ab edito mandato de reditu, et de instauranda Hierosolyma usque ad unctum principem, fore hebdomades septem et sexaginta duas, quibus redibitur, et vici munimentaque instaurabuntur, idque in difficultate temporum. Post duas autem et sexaginta hebdomadas perimetur Unctus, nec amplius erit, urbemque et Sanctum perdet populus ducis venturi, eritque finis ejus subito, et usque ad finem belli decretae sunt desolationes. Confirmabit autem foedus multis per unam hebdomadam, et dimidia hebdomadâ sacrificium fertumque tollet, alaeque detestandae praeerit vastator; atque usque ad consummationem eamque praecisam super devastatorem effundetur.

VIII. *De Wette's Version.*

(24) Siebenzig Siebende sind bestimmt über dein Volk und über deine heilige Stadt, bis der Frevel vollbracht, und die Sünden besiegelt, und die Schuld gesühnet, und ewige Gerechtigkeit herbeigeführt, und Gesicht und Prophet besiegelt, und das Allerheiligste gesalbet wird. (25) Wisse also und merke: vom Ausgange des Wortes [das zu Jeremia geschah] daß Jerusalem wieder hergestellt und erbauet werden soll, bis auf einen gesalbten Fürsten, sind sieben Siebende; und binnen zwei und sechzig Siebenden wird es wieder hergestellt und erbaut werden mit Straßen und Graben, aber im Drucke der Zeiten. (26) Und nach den zwei und sechzig Siebenden wird ein Gesalbter weggerafft, und Keiner ist vorhanden, der ihm angehört, und die Stadt und das Heiligthum wird verwüsten das Volk eines Fürsten, welcher kommt, und dessen Ende [wie] in Fluth, und bis zum Ende Krieg, Beschluß von Verwüstungen. (27) Und er befestigt den Bund Vielen ein Siebend lang, und während der Hälfte des Siebends wird er Schlachtopfer und Speisopfer einstellen, und über der Zinne des Gräuels wird der Verwüster seyn, und zwar bis daß Vertilgung und Beschluß sich ergießet über den Verwüster.

For convenience' sake No. I. II. are here inserted. No. III. IV. speak for themselves. As to No. III., the author of this version plainly was perplexed about the meaning of the Hebrew, and has given some strange turns to the sentiment, even in vs. 24—26. But in v. 27 we are entirely lost. We can scarcely trace any certain resemblances. The clause in v. 26, " After seven and seventy years," is a guess that the time, here aimed at in the Heb. text, is the era of the Selucidae. This began 312 B. C., and the sum of the numbers named in the version is 139, which tallies with the time when Antiochus Epiphanes began his reign. What follows doubtless relates to him, but it is such a confused medley, that nothing can be made out of it. No wonder the ancient churches were discontented with such a version. I say *such a version*, because there are, in many parts of it elsewhere, characteristics of a similar nature. No. IV. is certainly a great improvement upon the Septuagint; but even this shows that the author of the version was at times quite uncertain in his own mind, about the meaning of the Hebrew. I need not point out particulars, as the reader can easily find them, and judge for himself. The part included in brackets is as it stands in the Romish edition of Theodotion, but it is omittted in Bos' edition of the Septuagint. It is palpably another version of v. 27, which was copied on the margin, and through carelessness was foisted into the text, by the copyist who wrote the Ms. used in the Romish edition. Both versions show in what perplexity the authors of them were. No. V. shows the deep acquaintance of Jerome with the Hebrew, and has come nearer to accuracy than any of ancient versions. Of the Targums of Daniel, we know nothing; not even whether any ever existed.

No. VI. deserves some special notice. The author of this plainly had a better knowledge of the Hebrew than any of his predecessors in translating, (fl. prob. Cent. II.); and in some points he has hit nearer the mark than even Jerome. The Latin translation of this Syriac Version is a miserable affair, and no dependence can be placed upon it. I have made a new and literal version, because it would be useless, or nearly so, to print it in Syriac. But this version deserves much more attention than it has yet received. Many a good hint may be got from it, to cast light on the difficult words or phrases in the Hebrew. The author was well grounded in the knowledge of that language.

As to No. VII. VIII., the object in presenting them lies upon the face of the thing. Two such scholars as Rosenmueller and De Wette may well excite the curiosity of the interpreter, to know how they understood the Hebrew text, in the passage before us. Most readers, I trust, will be glad of such a *conspectus* as that which is here submitted to their examination.

[It has already been said, that a great variety of interpretations have been proposed, of Dan. 9:24—27. The reader who is curious to know how much and what has been said, and what endless perplexity has attended all attempts to explain without the aid of a distinctive philology, is remitted for information to the following works, as exhibiting the ablest efforts of this nature. Some few of them, however, have been distinguished by philological effort.

Among the older writers, *Vitringa* stands preëminent, as usual, in his very learned discussion of the subject in Observatt. Sac. VI. 1—5. He is *exclusively Messianic*, and is the store-house from which Hengstenberg and Hävernick have drawn, in their discussions of the matter in question. Among the more respectable attempts to explain this matter may be reckoned *J. D. Michaelis* Versuch über die 70 Wochen Daniels, 1771. 8. *Eichhorn*, Bibliothek, B. III. s. 761 seq , has suggested many good hints, while he adopts a tortuous method of reckoning the respective classes of weeks. *Bleek*, Theol. Zeitschrift von Schleiermacher, De Wette, etc., 1819, Heft. 3, s. 171 seq. *Berthholdt*, Comm. zum Buche Daniel. II. Theil. *Hengstenberg*, Die 70 Wochen Daniels, in his Christol. Theil. II. s. 401 seq. 1831. *Hävernick*, Comm. über Daniel, in loc. 1832. *Scholl*, Comm. exeget. de 70 hebdom. Danielis, 1829. *Hitzig*, Recension in Theol. Stud. et Krit. 1832. s. 143 seq. *Rösch*, Die 70 Wochen des Daniel, ib. Jahr 1835. *Lengerke*, Comm. über Dan. in loc. As distinguished greatly from all the preceding efforts, remain to be noted, *J. C K. Hoffman*, Die 70 Jahre des Jeremias, 1836; and his later and highly important work, Weissagung und Erfüllung, 1841, Th. I. s. 296 seq., which is filled indeed with mere hints, but they are exceedingly significant, and are the result of much thought and profound study. The recent exclusively *Anti-messianic* interpreter is *Wieseler*, Die 70 Wochen und die 63 Jahrwochen, 1839, a book pregnant with thought and interesting matter, and giving evidence of great acuteness in philology; but exhibiting some inconclusive reasoning, and a strong leaning to preconceived theory. Substantial progress in philology has been made by these two last named writers. It would be easy to subjoin scores of other writers; but they would add little or nothing to the apparatus of the reader who has access to those named above.]

[The preceding vision was seen in the *first* year of Darius the Mede, 9: 1. The one now before us is dated in the *third* year of the reign of Cyrus, which would make it some seventy-two years from the time that Daniel was carried to Babylon by Nebuchadnezzar, 1: 1—3, and about four years later than the preceding vision. The vision is prefaced by a narration of Daniel's special fasting and prayer, for the space of three weeks, vs. 1—3. The *occasion* of this is not directly and explicitly stated. But we may gather hints from the book of Ezra, which will give some probable illustration. Soon after the building of the temple was commenced, "the adversaries of Judah and Benjamin" began their opposition to it by active measures. During all the remainder of Cyrus' reign, and even down to that of Darius, i. e. from B. C. 536 down to 519, (Ezra 4: 4, 5. 6: 1—15), opposition was continued. If Daniel was uncertain in his mind, whether the שָׁבֻעִים שִׁבְעִים of 9: 24 meant seventy weeks of *days* or seventy weeks of *years*, (and considering the ellipsis in this case of שָׁנִים, we may easily suppose him to have been in doubt for a time), then must he have felt greatly perplexed with such a state of things as existed in the third year of Cyrus' reign. Nothing of consequence had yet taken place, excepting the bare return of a company of exiles to Palestine. The temple-building was at a stand. The city-building must have been in a very embarrassed and perplexing state. If Daniel had hitherto indulged the hope that only seventy *weeks of days* were appointed for the restoration of the city and sanctuary, he must now be greatly in doubt what to think. The time of seventy *weeks of days* had more than passed, yea double that time, and yet there were no indications of successful progress at Jerusalem. The close of v. 1 indicates the deliverance which the mind of the prophet experienced, by the new revelation which he was about to record. It also contains an indication, tacit but yet intelligible, that he had not before satisfactorily understood the communication made to him in 9: 24—27. In 10: 12 is an intimation, moreover, of the fear which had oppressed Daniel, when he considered the then-present state of the holy city and temple. The events which are disclosed in the prophecy that follows, show that one could not reasonably suppose them all to happen in the course of seventy weeks of *days;* the time therefore of 9: 24, must be weeks of *years*.

Daniel had fasted and prayed, from the first day of the first [Heb.] month until the close of the twenty-first, 10: 3. Three days after this, viz. on the twenty-fourth, he was on the banks of the Tigris, and there saw his last and very instructive vision, 10: 4. An angel appears in splendid costume, and addresses him in a voice like that of a great multitude, vs. 5, 6. To Daniel alone was this heavenly messenger visible; but his attendants were stricken with great fear and fled, probably because of some audible and preternatural sound, v. 7. Daniel remained alone, and he grew pale with terror, and sunk down in great weakness, v. 8. In a kind of trance, while on the ground, he heard the angel speaking to him, who came near and partially lifted him up, vs. 9, 10. The angel then addressed to him words of great kindness, and bade him attend carefully to what he was about to communicate, by which he was somewhat revived, even so as to stand erect, although with trembling, v. 11. He assures Daniel, that his prayers had been heard, and his solicitude to understand more fully what had been addressed to him on a former occasion, was favorably regarded, v. 12. The angel discloses a reason why there had been some delay, in bringing his message. The angel of the Persian kingdom had withstood him for twenty-one days, until Michael came to his aid, when he was left alone to exercise his good influence over the Persian dynasty. [His object seems to have been, to give a turn to the Persian affairs which would be favorable to the Hebrews], v. 13. The next verse (14) discloses the special object of the angel's mission; which was, to instruct Daniel what would befal his people at a future period, for the vision had respect to a prolonged period. When this was mentioned, Daniel cast down his eyes to the earth, and remained silent, v. 15. In this plight, an angel under the appearance of a man touched his lips, and enabled him to speak; which he did by stating, that the terror caused by the vision had deprived him of the use of his bodily powers, vs. 16, 17. An angel in human form then touched him again, and his strength was somewhat restored, v. 18. He bade Daniel not to fear, for he was greatly beloved, and peace would be given him; after which Daniel requested him to proceed, inasmuch as he was fully revived, v. 19. The angel begins his communication by asking the seer, whether he knew for what purpose he had come? Taking his answer for granted, (as indeed he might, if we compare v. 14), the angel goes on to say, that he shall return [to Persia] in order to contend with the prince of Persia; that when he departs, the prince of Grecia will come, [when he abandons the Persian court, the king of Greece, Alexander, will come against the country], v. 20. What is written in the book of truth respecting the future, will now be disclosed. Only the angel Michael assists him against his antagonists; — but this same Michael is the special guardian of the Hebrews.]

CHAPTER X.

(1) In the third year of Cyrus king of Persia, a message was revealed to Daniel, whose name was called Belteshazzar; the message was truth, and the warfare great. And he understood the message, for understanding was given to him in the prophetic vision.

In 1: 21 it is said, that *Daniel was*, i. e. continued, remained, until the *first* year of Cyrus; which some have maintained to be a contradiction to the verse before us, which asserts that Daniel was living and active some two years after the period named in 1: 21. But (as above explained in Comm. on 1: 21) I understand the object of this last-mentioned passage to be, to show that as Daniel saw the *beginning* of the exile, so he also lived to see the *end* of it; which end came about in the first year of Cyrus' reign. As the object of that passage seems not to be to state the full extent of Daniel's life, so the passage before us is no contradiction, nor even a discrepancy, in respect to 1: 21. The *third* year of Cyrus was B. C. 534. — *King of Persia* means king of the united Medo-Persian empire; for the sacred writers reckon the dominion of Cyrus from the commencement of his reign as son-in-law and heir of Darius the Mede. — דָּבָר, *a communication* or *message;* for the word is generic in a sense like to that of these English words; comp. Isa. 2: 1. — נִגְלָה has reference to a supernatural revelation. — *Whose name was called Belteshazzar*, see 1: 7. The object of this is to specify, that he is the same Daniel to whom the preceding portion of the book relates. — וֶאֱמֶת is predicate — *the message was truth* — and is put first for the sake of emphasis; comp. Rev. 22: 6. 21: 5. 19: 9, as to the assertion. — צָבָא, lit. *warfare*, tropically (as here), *trouble, hardship, severe trial with suffering.* A reference is by implication here made to the *contents* of the message about to be imparted. These disclose trials very severe, and much (גָּדוֹל) suffering to the Hebrew nation. — *And he understood the message;* comp. 8: 27, which asserts that he did not at that time fully comprehend what had then been said to him. Comp. also 10: 12, which appears to refer to 9: 24—27, and to imply the like sentiment. The present message is so much in detail and so particular, that the prophet ceased to doubt. — *Understanding* [of the message] *was given to him by the vision*, viz. the vision to which the preceding נִגְלָה refers. Hence the *article* before מַּרְאֶה. What he means to say is, that the manner of the vision which follows was such, that he attained to a satisfactory understanding of it — such an understanding as he had not had in respect to either of the three preceding visions; see 7: 15, 28. 8: 27. 10: 12. Lengerke takes בִּין and בִּינָה as Imperatives; and so the accent might seem to decide, בִּינָה having a penult accent, § 71. 6. But I apprehend this to be only an accidental case of accentuation. The verb has a penult accent, because of the immediate sequency of a monosyllabic word which takes an accent, § 29. 3. b. C. B. Michaelis and Lengerke, (who make the word Imper. on the ground of the accentuation), have both failed to recognize this. Lengerke says, also, that בִּין must be in Hiph., and that הַ praefix-formative is dropped by aphaeresis. But this cannot well be. The usual Imper.

Hiph. is הֵבֵן, and the apocopate (made by aphaeresis) would be בֵּן, not בִּין. That Kal has two forms in the Praeter, בָּן and בִּין, seems clear, § 72. 1. e. g. The sense of the passage (as I understand it) I have given in the version above. Lengerke says, that such a meaning is incompatible with 12: 8. But I understand what is there said (וְלֹא אָבִין), to relate only to what is said of the resurrection and its sequel in 12: 1—4. The reader will observe, that the *third* person is employed by the writer in this verse, after which he goes over into the *first.* This is the usual method; see Isa. 1: 1 seq. 2: 1 seq. Jer. 1: 1 seq. Ezek. 1: 3, 4. Hos. 1: 1, 2, (comp. 3: 1), and so in the other prophets, comp. §134. 3. N. 3.

(2) In those days I Daniel was mourning three weeks of days.

Those days belong to the time mentioned in the preceding verse, viz. during the third year of Cyrus. The probable occasion of Daniel's mourning has already been stated in the introduction to this chapter. — *Three* שְׁבֻעִים יָמִים, lit. *three days besevened,* i. e. twenty-one days. The word יָמִים is here added, so as to avoid being misunderstood; for שָׁבֻעִים in 9: 24 means *year-weeks,* i. e. years is implied after it, as being the ordinary measure of time. But to show that the case is different here, יָמִים is employed, and put in the Acc. as designating time, § 116. 2, and for the *adverbial* use, see § 116. 3. Three weeks' fasting, in the absolute and highest sense of the word, cannot be supposed without a miraculous interposition. Does the next verse so represent the fast, as to make such an interposition necessary?

(3) Pleasant bread I ate not, and neither flesh nor wine came into my mouth, nor did I anoint myself, until the completion of three weeks of days.

לֶחֶם חֲמֻדוֹת, lit. *bread of delights,* i. e. choice bread, such as was furnished for the tables of the wealthy and the honorable. The implication of course is, that Daniel sustained himself with coarse bread, such as was eaten by the lower class of people. But as to *flesh* and *wine,* which were not necessary to his sustenance, but to be regarded merely in the light of a comfort or luxury, he did not at all partake of them. Nor did he resort, as usual, to the place of bathing and anointing. The סוֹךְ here is Inf. abs., rendering intense the expression, viz. *I did not at all anoint myself.* This verb is never used for ceremonial anointing to office, but for anointing the body after bathing. Among the upper classes, oils highly perfumed were employed for this purpose. The *fasting* of Daniel was extended to abstinence from every convenience and luxury, and no more than a bare support of coarse bread was admitted. With this, however, he could easily sustain himself, so that nothing wonderful as to the length of the fast need be supposed. Why it was *three weeks* rather than some other period, we are not told. But the last week of this period, v. 4 (it being in the *first* month), would include the passover with its seven days of fasting. The light in which the number *three* was regarded by the Hebrews, may have had its influence in regard to the period, which was three times as long as the passover-fast. At all events, the length of the fast betokens deep humiliation.

(4) And on the twenty-fourth day of the first month, I was near by the great river, that is, the Hiddekel [the Tigris].

His presence on the banks of the river named, is to be regarded here as actual or physical, and not merely in vision. There is nothing in the circumstances of the case, or in the manner of the language, which requires us to give any other than a literal interpretation. It deserves remark, that the angel does not appear to him, until the third day after his fasting was ended. In the sequel, the reason of his delay is stated. For לַחֹדֶשׁ, see § 113. 2. *d.* *The first month* is reckoned in the Hebrew manner.

(5) And I lifted up my eyes, and behold a man clothed in linen garments, and his loins girt about with fine gold of Uphaz.

אִישׁ אֶחָד, *a man*, lit. *one man;* for אֶחָד in the sense of our indefinite article *a*, see Lex. אֶחָד, 4. The expression shows, that the angel assumed a *human* form, in addressing the prophet. — בַדִּים, *linen* or *cotton vestments.* Here it means the long white mantle which covered the whole person, and was girt around the waist, in order to adjust and render firm its position. — אוּפָז, here and Jer. 10: 9, probably the same as אוֹפִיר, for which see Lex. The ז and ר are sometimes exchanged; see Lex. in v. — *Fine gold of Uphaz*, i. e. having his girdle adorned with the most precious gold.

(6) And his body was like the topaz, and his face like the appearance of lightning, and his eyes like flaming lamps, and his arms and his feet were like the appearance of polished brass; and as to his voice, his words were like the shout of a multitude.

In a word, he appeared in dazzling splendor and magnificence throughout. כְּתַרְשִׁישׁ, first, the name of a place [now Guadalquiver] in Spain; then, the name of a yellowish gem found there, which the Greeks called χρυσόλιθος, and recent chemists name *topaz.* The *resplendence* is the main point of the comparison here. The *yellowish* hue is in conformity with the color of the oriental skin. — *His visage like the lightning, and his eyes like flaming lamps*, is exceedingly vivid description, and conveys the mingled idea of the *splendid and the terrible;* comp. Rev. 1: 13—15, which closely resembles the present passage. The *splendor of the arms and feet* seems to be the result of the ornaments attached to them, which were exceedingly lustrous; for such was the appearance of *polished brass* among the ancients. — עַיִן, lit. *eye*, but also *look*, *appearance*. נְחֹשֶׁת is here used as masc.; so in Ezek. 1: 7. — *Like the shout of a great multitude*, a vivid and strong conception. John, in Apoc. 1: 15, "His voice was like the sound of *many waters*," i. e. like the roaring of the ocean-waves. It is difficult to decide which is the most vivid and powerful expression. Comp. also Rev. 14: 2, where "loud thunder" is added. In all respects, as to majesty, splendor, and power, the angel appears preëminent. How deep the impression made by his majestic appearance and costume was, the sequel serves to show.

(7) And I Daniel alone saw the vision; and the men who were with me saw not the vision, but great terror fell upon them, and in secreting themselves they fled away.

If the men who accompanied Daniel saw *not* the vision, perhaps it was not visible to the natural physical eye, but only to the *mental* eye of the prophet. But something must have been either seen or heard, in order to excite so much terror. It may be, therefore, that the sound of the voice was audible by Daniel's attendants. — חֲרָדָה is placed before its verb, for the sake of emphasis. — בְּהֵחָבֵא *in secreting themselves*, i. e. either they fled clandestinely, so as to evade their master's notice, or (more probably) the idea of the last two words is: *They fled away in secreting themselves*, i. e. in finding, or in order to find a hiding place, they fled away. The verb is in Niph. Inf., the הִ prefix going over into הֵ because the following guttural excludes the Dagh. forte.

(8) And I was left alone, and then I saw that great vision, and there was no strength left in me, and my glowing ruddiness was changed upon me to a marred state, and I retained no strength.

לְבַדִּי, lit. *in my loneliness*; וָאֶרְאֶה, *and then I saw*, § 152. I. B. 1. — הַגְּדֹלָה in the sense of *grand, sublime, majestic*. — וְהוֹדִי, lit. *and my splendor*, means the natural bright and glowing color of the skin of a healthy person. — עָלַי, *upon me*, or rather perhaps *over me*, i. e. throughout my person, for not the cheek only grew pale, but the whole body. The sequel shows that the *surface* of his person became *marred* in its appearance, for מַשְׁחִית indicates such a *marring* as sickness or death brings upon the natural color of the skin. — *I retained no strength* indicates, that he fell down to the earth as lifeless; see v. 9.

(9) And I heard the voice of his words; and when I heard the voice of his words, then was I in a deep sleep upon my face, and my face was on the ground.

This also shows, that the communication with the prophet was more in a mental, than in a physical way. Otherwise a *deep sleep* would have prevented his hearing the voice. Comp. 8. 17. Ezek. 1: 28. 3: 23. Zech. 4: 1. Rev. 1, 17.

(10) And lo! a hand touched me, and it raised me upon my knees and the palms of my hands.

The touch of the hand seems to have partially restored sensation, so that he could perceive it. — וַתְּנִיעֵנִי, from נוּעַ *to nod* or *vacillate*, so that the true and exact meaning here seems to be: *Placed me in a vacillating state upon my hands and knees.* The vacillation doubtless proceeded from terror and the loss of strength. — וְכַפּוֹת, lit. כַּף means *curve, hollow;* hence applied to the palms of the hands, and the soles of the feet. There is no necessity of finding here the hand of another angel, different from the one so splendidly clad, as described in vs. 5, 6. Indeed, since the one who touched Daniel, and raised him partly up, declares in v. 11, that he has been sent to make communications to the seer, it must be one and the same personage.

(11) And he said to me: Daniel, a man greatly beloved, mark well the words which I shall speak to thee, and stand upright; for now am I sent to thee. And while he was uttering these words, I stood up, trembling.

חֲמֻדוֹת, see in 9:23. The Imper. form הָבֵן here and elsewhere in this book, makes against the position, that בִּין in v. 1 is Imper. — דֹּבֵר, it is peculiar, that in *Kal* this is the only form (Part.) to which the meaning *speak* is attached. — עָמְדֶךָ, Ges. renders *locus, place;* well enough as to the general sense of the passage, but not sufficiently specific. I understand the word here as indicating either what is equivalent to our English word *stand*, or *station*, or else the *means* or *instrument of standing*, viz. *the feet.* Such a tropical use is by no means impossible or improbable. The reason which the angel gives for the command is, that he is about to solve the doubts or difficulties of Daniel, on account of which he had been fasting and praying. In obedience to his requisition Daniel *stood up* (עָמַדְתִּי); which seems to explain the preceding command. *Stand fast in thy place* is the meaning which Lengerke gives to the command; which, to say the least, is doubtful as to *fast* or *firm.* What I deem to be the shade of the idea, I have given in the version above. — מַרְעִיד, Hiph. intrans. *trembling.* See the like meanings in Hiph. § 52. 2. *Remarks.*

(12) And he said unto me: Fear not, Daniel, for from the first day when thou didst apply thy mind to understand, and to humble thyself before God, thy words were heard, and I am come on account of thy words.

There is an intimation in לְהָבִין, that a leading part of Daniel's solicitude had arisen, from his doubts as to the exact meaning of some things in the previous communications made to him. לִבְּךָ, in its predominant sense, this noun means *mind.* — לְהִתְעַנּוֹת, Hithp. reflex. *to humble thyself.* — *Thy words* mean, the words uttered in his prayers before God.

(13) And the prince of the kingdom of Persia stood against me, twenty-one days; and lo! Michael, one of the chief princes, came to my aid, and I was left there near the kings of Persia.

That שַׂר here designates an *angel* of some sort, and not a *king* of Persia, seems to be clear from v. 21. מִיכָאֵל שַׂרְכֶם, *Michael your prince*, i. e. your guardian angel. Whether the angel in question was *good* or *bad*, has been disputed. That the heathen nations, as such, should have guardian angels assigned them who were good, seems hardly to comport with the Hebrew views of their character and desert. Yet that good angels might receive commission to watch over their concerns in some general way, is sufficiently in accordance with the dispensations of Him, "who maketh his sun to rise on the evil and on the good, and sendeth rain on the just and on the unjust." The only serious difficulty is, that of *contest* between the guardian-angel of the Jews and that of Persia. Such, it would seem, must have taken place; for when the communicating angel says, that "he was left near the kings of Persia," the implication of course is, that the victory was accorded to him, for the Persian שַׂר had withdrawn. — In the phrase *kings of Persia*, the plural number appears to be used in order to designate collectively the *supreme dynasty* of that country. When Lengerke asserts, that the idea of *guardian-angels* was borrowed from Parsism and Zoroaster, one cannot but feel prompted to ask: Whether the Hebrews, specially the pious, would be likely to borrow from such a source? And then, secondly, Whether Josh. 5: 13. Ex. 23: 20, where the same idea is plain, were in his view written after the times of Zoroaster? לְנֶגְדִּי, lit. *before me;* but the particle has sometimes an *adversative* sense, and then may be translated *against.* It would seem that the narrator was one of the guardian-angels of the Jews, who had been striving to procure favorable measures for them on the part of the Persian government. There is a plain intimation, in the phrase *Michael one of the chief princes*, of *different orders* of angels. This idea, however, is not often brought to view in the O. Test.; but in the New it is somewhat familiar, Eph. 3: 10. 1 Thess. 4: 16. Jude v. 9. Rev. 1: 4. 8: 2. 12: 7. The very name שַׂר tacitly conveys the same idea.

(14) And I have come to make thee know what shall happen to thy people in later times; for the vision is yet for some time.

לַהֲבִינְךָ has reference to the same word in v. 12. — יִקְרָה from קָרָה with the vowel points of its equivalent יִקְרָא, see § 74. Note 22. *b.* Here it is followed by a לְ; but usually it subjoins the simple Acc. of person. — בְּאַחֲרִית הַיָּמִים is not necessarily restricted to the latter or final portion of time before the end of the world, but it may mean the latter part of any period particularly in the mind of the speaker, specially when this can be understood by those who are addressed. Here it evidently means, the latter part of the period which precedes the coming of the Messiah; for so the sequel of the vision shows it to mean. Indeed, the speaker himself explains his own declaration, by saying that *the vision* is לַיָּמִים lit. *for days*, i. e. for a considerably long and undefined period.

(15) And while he was speaking with me after the tenor of these words, I placed my face on the ground, and was silent.

כַּדְּבָרִים shows that Daniel does not repeat verbatim, but only for substance, the words of the angel. — אַרְצָה, with ־ָה, local, which shows that the word is in the adverbial Acc. — נֶאֱלַמְתִּי, Niph., differs slightly from Kal, in that it is reflexive = *I kept myself silent.*

(16) And lo! one like the sons of men touched my lips; and I opened my mouth, and spake, and said to him who stood before me: My lord, by the vision my comeliness upon me is changed, and I retain no strength.

כִּדְמוּת implies before it some one who is the object of comparison; but since no Nom. or subject is expressed, the indefinite Nom. אִישׁ, *one, a man*, i. e. in appearance a man, is to be supplied. *One in human form* is the plain meaning of the whole phrase. — *Touched my lips*, i. e. in order that he might *speak*, for he had just said, that previous to this he remained *dumb.* The effect was immediate. The power of speech was restored; and his first words apologize for his continued silence, which he thought might seem to betoken a want of respect or comity. — צִירַי I feel constrained to interpret differently from most critics. It is neither *terrors* (Leng. Maurer), nor *pains, distresses* (Ges. al.). Etymology forbids the first, and the nature of the passage the second meaning. *Terror* is very different from *dolores.* The verb צוּר means, among other things, *to form, fashion*, etc.; and from this comes צִיר *idol*, and also *form*, Ps. 49: 15. I take צִירַי, therefore, in a sense like that which הוֹדִי bears, in v. 8 above. It is an easy transition from *form* to *comeliness;* just as the Latin *forma* designates both ideas. הוֹדִי marks the shining appearance of the skin in a healthy person, in v. 8; and צִירַי here marks the simple idea of *comeliness* or *fair appearance.* As to the plur. form of the noun, see § 106. 2. *a.*, where many parallels will be found. For עָלַי, see under v. 8 above.

(17) And how shall the servant of this my lord speak with this my lord? And as for me — at present no strength remaineth in me, nor is there any breath left in me.

The servant of my lord = I. This is the usual mode of address among the Hebrews, in all cases where an inferior addresses an acknowledged superior. — הֵיךְ = אֵיךְ, the usual Heb. form. The first form *Chaldaizes.* — יוּכַל, Hoph. lit. *be made able, become able*, which is equivalent to our simple *can* or *be able.* — זֶה is a demonstrative and intensive = *this here*, i. e. how can I address such a personage as now stands before me? — וַאֲנִי, Nom. abs. — מֵעַתָּה, lit. *from this very time*, viz. from the time when the angel appeared, and addressed himself to Daniel, he had been in a kind of swoon, and incapable of employing his bodily organs to any effectual purpose. I have given the idea in our usual idiom, in the version.

(18) And one having the appearance of a man again touched me, and he strengthened me.

וַיֹּסֶף, lit. *and he added*, shows that the same personage repeated the touch, who had first given it, as related in v. 16. In the first case, the power of speech was restored; in the second, the strength of the whole frame. For the idiom of the verbs וַיֹּסֶף וַיִּגַּע, see § 139. 3. יִגַּע from נָגַע.

(19) And he said: Fear not, O man greatly beloved; it will be well for thee; be of good courage! And while he was speaking with me, I felt myself strengthened, and said: Let my lord speak, for thou hast strengthened me.

שָׁלוֹם לָךְ is often employed as a mere form of greeting, like *salus tibi!* The phrase might here be regarded as *optative*, but is more energetic when rendered as the Indicative. — חֲזַק וַחֲזָק, *take good courage*, or *be very strong!* The repetition marks intensity of expression. The Hiph. הִתְחַזַּקְתִּי has a shade of the reflexive in it, which I have endeavored to express in the translation.

(20) And he said: Dost thou know why I have come to thee? And now I must return, in order to contend with the prince of Persia; and I shall depart, and lo! the prince of Greece will come;

The question asked in the first part of the verse, seems rather designed to call attention, than to make inquiry. In v. 14 is a declaration of the purpose of the angel in coming. What follows shows, that the *prince of Persia* (guardian-angel), although he had departed when Michael came to the aid of the speaker, would return and resume his former course, or had already returned. The guardian of the Jews, therefore, goes back to Persia, in order to prevent the effects of his influence. — יוֹצֵא, when coupled as here with בָּא, means to *depart*, while בָּא in such a position means *to come, accedere, ἐπέρχεσθαι.* But from what place does the narrator expect to *depart?* And does the prince of Grecia design to *come, arrive*, at the same place? Questions somewhat difficult to answer. From the last clause of v. 21, we may conclude, that *prince* of Persia and of Greece means *guardian* or *superintending angel.* To this conclusion the tenor of the discourse would also lead. Guided by this, we may reasonably conclude that the angel means to say, that sometime after his return to Persia to contend there for the interests of the Hebrews, he will again leave that country, that the prince of Greece may seek and obtain a preëminence there for Grecian rule. Against the inclination of the Persian court to treat the Jews with neglect, he has first to strive, and when Grecian power usurps the place of the Persian, he has the like difficulty to overcome. Hence he speaks, in the next verse, of Michael's aiding him עַל־אֵלֶּה *against these,* viz. against the *princes* of Persia and Greece. I do not see how the text will well bear any other construction. That *going* and *coming* are used here in a *military* sense, i. e. indicate mutual strife between the two parties, is assumed by Häv. and Leng.; but this is not strictly the case. *Going away* (יוֹצֵא) denotes the departure from, and relinquishment of, the Persian court, giving place to Grecian rule. The *coming* of Grecian rule, as connected with what is related in the following verse, indicates that there would be a *hostile bearing* toward the Jews, so that the guardian angel of the Hebrews must needs be strengthened by Michael עַל־אֵלֶּה, i. e. against both countries or sovereignties. To such a view as is here given, Hoffman gives his assent, (Weissag. etc. s. 312).

(21) (But I will tell thee what is written in the book of truth), and there is no one who putteth forth his strength with me against those, except Michael your prince.

The first clause I have put in parenthesis, because it is plainly thrown in so as to interrupt the regular train of thought. When the speaker had intimated, that the princes of Persia and Greece would be hostile to the Jews, and thus excited an alarm in the feelings of the hearer, he employed means to quiet this by telling him, that whatever of suffering or of deliverance awaits the Jews, it amounts only to so much as heaven had wisely decreed, and cannot pass these bounds. — רָשׁוּם is a later Heb. word, taken from the Chaldee, instead of the more ancient כָּתוּב. — *Book of truth* is the book of God's decrees, the book which contains what will truly come to pass; comp. the like in Deut. 32: 34. Mal. 3: 16. Ps. 139: 16. Rev. 5: 1. This is different from the *book of life*, which is so frequently mentioned; for this is so named by allusion to the register of the names of the living in a city or town; but the *book of truth* is the book which records what is or will be *true*, i. e. *verified.* — וְאֵין אֶחָד, *and there is no one,* connects with בָּא at the close of v. 20. The angel means to say, that in the successive aggressions upon the Jews by the Persian and Grecian dynasties, he has no one to aid him but the guardian Michael. The intimation seems to be, that without more helpers not a little of suffering and trial must be expected, and thus to prepare Daniel for the disclosures of the sequel. — מִתְחַזֵּק, *to put forth* or *show one's strength*. — עַל־אֵלֶּה, *against those,* viz. those princes of Persia and Grecia. — שַׂרְכֶם, *your prince*, can mean nothing more nor less here, than *your leading guardian-angel.*

[It is common for interpreters to assume here, that the angel *Gabriel* was the one who appeared to Daniel, and made communications on the occasion before us. Analogy from a comparison of Dan. 8: 16. 9: 21, where he is named, might naturally lead to such an opinion; which might also be strengthened by Luke 1: 19. The apocryphal books, both of the O. Test. and of the New, frequently name this angel, and also many others; specially does the book of Enoch abound in the names of angels. But still, the opinion about Gabriel in the present case must be conjectural; for there is no name assigned to the angel-communicator, in chap. x. xi.

The question: How much of the representation of chap. x. is *costume*, and what is *historical reality?* is more difficult than one might at first suppose. If the princes of Persia and Grecia be *good* angels, how, it is asked, 'can contention arise between them and the guardians of the Jews? Each would bow in submission to the divine will, and so, when that was known, there could be no differences of opinion.' But angels are not *omniscient;* and a good being, with limited faculties, who is set to watch over a particular king or country, may very naturally contract some partiality for the object of his attention, and may not always see clearly what his duty is. In a case of this kind, it is easy to see, that something like an opposition to another good being may arise, who is commissioned to interfere with the object of guardianship. Somewhat in this light, I think, we must regard the narration in the present chapter, provided we consider it as based on simple historical facts.

'But may not the whole be in the way of allegorical representation, i. e. so as to represent the activity of the enemies of the Jews, and the stumbling-blocks which they threw in the way of those who had returned from exile; and also the opposition of the Grecian kings of Syria and Egypt, after the death of Alexander? In such a case, guardian-angels of the holy land would represent the kind care which heaven bestowed upon the Hebrews; and the opposing *princes* of Persia and Grecia would indicate the counsel unfriendly to the Jews, which those dynasties were inclined to follow.'

That it is possible to regard the whole representation in this light, *salva fide et salva ecclesia*, I would not deny; but the angelology of the Scriptures prevents me from admitting this. I feel the difficulty presented by an account of *contest* between good angels; and specially the difficulty of supposing that these good beings would excite the Persian and Grecian chiefs against the Hebrew nation. But is it the design of the writer to communicate any thing more, than the general idea of the angel-guardianship of nations, and of that zeal for their respective interests, which springs from a feeling that is natural to such a relation? If he designs more than this, we are at least left in the dark, as to the manner in which his views can be reconciled with the character of angels, as beings perfectly holy and obedient to the will of God, and also beings of superior, although not of perfect, knowledge. The Apocalypse is through and through of the same tenor, in regard to angels and their offices, as the present book.]

CHAPTER XI.

[This chapter should not have been separated from the preceding one; for it is a mere continuance of the address to Daniel, which was begun in the close of that chapter. V. 1 informs him, that the angel-narrator, now engaged in behalf of the Hebrews, had for some time before, at the Medo-Persian court, been engaged in like manner with Darius the Mede. He then goes on to sketch some of the events of the Persian dynasty, the invasion of Greece by Xerxes; the spirit of hostility which will be roused up by this; the rise and fall of Alexander the Great; and the subsequent division of his broken empire into four dynasties, vs. 2—4. After this, the dynasties of Egypt and Syria are selected, doubtless because they are the only ones with which the Jews were to be concerned. The mutual alliances, attacks, and defences, of the kings of these countries, are next detailed with almost historical minuteness, vs. 5—20. We come next upon Antiochus Epiphanes, whose history (as we may almost name it) occupies the rest of the chapter. It is a prophetic representation so ample and particular, as to be without a parallel in all the Scriptures. Something in the aspect of the times, or in the feelings and views of the Jewish people, was probably the immediate occasion of this. The expectation of no more trial and suffering may have been too confident among the Hebrews, and have needed a check. Or we may suppose another ground: *Forewarned, forearmed.* But whatever was the cause of the peculiar *form* of the prediction before us, there can be but one view as to its actual character. As has already been said, Porphyry in ancient times, and not a few critics in recent times, have strenously asserted that it was written *post eventum*, and is therefore nothing more than real history. The assertion is grounded mainly on its historical minuteness; but partly (by the new school of criticism) on the alleged impossibility of a miricle. A real *prediction*, so minute and circumstantial, must of course be the result of a miraculous interposition; and the *a priori* assumption is, that a miracle is impossible. Therefore the author of the book of Daniel must have written *post eventum*.

But the assumption in this case is too great, reasonably to claim assent on the part of the sober-minded; and the critical history of the book of Daniel, as also the internal evidence of the book itself, throw obstacles in the way of supposing a very late composition that seem to be insuperable. But this is not the place to pursue the illustration and confirmation of these suggestions. The matter, however, must necessarily be investigated, in a critical introduction to the book.]

(1) Moreover, during the first year of Darius the Mede, I stood to strengthen and confirm him.

Lit. 'And as to me, in the first year of Darius the Mede, my standing was to strengthen etc.' the וַאֲנִי at the beginning of the verse shows how closely the present chapter stands connected with chap. x. I have rendered עָמְדִי *stood*, for we cannot possibly imitate the Heb. Infin. with a suffix, in our language, but are compelled to choose a definite verb. Forms like the present are by no means unfrequent in Heb.: e. g. הֲרִיחוֹ, Is. 11: 3, the exact literal version of which would be *the to delight of him*, which we cannot tolerate, but must simply say, *he delights;* so Job 9: 27, אִם אָמְרִי, *if the to say of me*, the same as *if I say*. Hence אֲנִי ... עָמְדִי *I... stood.* But עָמְדִי is followed by לְ before the object to be accomplished by his standing, in which case the idiom makes it to mean the offering of aid or assistance. In the same way is קוּם לְ employed in Ps. 94: 16.—לוֹ, *him* .... whom? Darius or Michael? The reader most naturally refers the aid to Darius; and so some of the commentators. But this will hardly bear the test of examination. The angel had just declared, that Michael was to him a מִתְחַזֵּק, when he went to Persia; and now he says, that on a former occasion, under the reign of Darius, he then in like manner helped Michael. Mutual aid, then, as it would seem, had been given respectively when needed. Hävernick thinks such an idea to be incongruous. But if angels are beings of *limited* powers and capacities, I do not see what incongruity there is in these declarations as above explained.

(2) And now I will tell thee what is true. Behold! three kings of Persia shall yet stand up, and the fourth shall be abundantly rich above all; and when he shall grow strong by his riches, he will rouse up all — even the kingdom of Greece.

The hint given in the parenthesis of 10: 21 ("written in the book of of truth"), is here repeated as a preface to the prediction which he is about to utter. אֱמֶת (apoc. of אֱמֶנֶת, § 19. 2. *b.* Note 1), *truth*, may omit the article by virtue of its being abstract and of a somewhat generic nature; for it is equivalent here to the phrase, *that which is true.* Plainly the meaning is not *all truth*, which would demand the article; nor truth in opposition simply to *falsehood*, which also would take the article; but merely the positive idea that what he communicates is *true*, i. e. belongs to truth.—עוֹד, *yet*, so qualifies the clause as to make it mean, that three kings more *besides* (עוֹד, *yet*) the one then in power (Cyrus), should rise up, before a fourth would invade the country of Greece, and thus sow the seeds of destruction to the Persian dynasty. But how shall we count the three? Very diversely have they been reckoned. E. g. Cyrus, Cambyses, Pseudo-smerdis, (so Polychronius); Cyrus, Cambyses, Darius Hystaspis, (C. B. Mich.); Cyrus, Darius, Xerxes, (Hitzig). I cannot see room for doubt. It is certain that the fourth is Xerxes who invaded Greece; and the עוֹד makes it certain, that Cyrus is excluded. Of course we have the intermediate kings; and these are Cambyses, Pseudo-smerdis, and Darius Hystaspis. Lengerke and Maurer maintain that הָרְבִיעִי means the *fourth* including the then reigning king (Cyrus), so that the last of three yet to come, would be the *fourth* here adverted to. I see no good reason for this, in the appeal which they make to the article. Lengerke says, that if the *fourth* after Cyrus be meant, the article must be omitted; which Maurer approves. I regard the case in quite a different light. After saying that *three* kings would arise, whose history he wholly passes by, he comes to another in distinction from them, a part of whose history he gives. The distinction intended, and the emphasis demanded, would either of them call the article to its aid. It is even not uncommon in respect to *ordinals*, to append the article to them when the noun connected with them omits it; e. g. יוֹם הַשִּׁשִּׁי, Gen. 1: 31. Whenever the *ordinal* is to be specially distinguished from other preceding things, it follows of course that the article is congruous. The natural and obvious meaning of הָרְבִיעִי, in the present case, is the *one* that next follows after the *three*. So Jerome, Theodoret, Bertholdt, Rosenmüller, Hävernick, and others. Besides, this accurately agrees with historical facts. If Pseudo-smerdis is to be left out, because he was a *usurper*, and had a short reign — what was Darius but a usurper? The article therefore seems to me quite in place, and we need seek no strained exposition, since history so well supports the most obvious exegesis.

He shall be abundantly rich. The fame of Xerxes' wealth is well known. Darius his father, a great statesman and conqueror, mostly acquired it for him. See in Herod. III. 96. VII. 27—29. Justin II. 10. Diod. Sic. XI. 3. Plin. Hist. Nat. XXIII. 10. Ael. XIII. 3. — מִכֹּל *above all*, מִ comparative after גָּדוֹל. — In בְּחֶזְקָתוֹ there is an indication of *time* by means of the בְּ, *when he is strengthened.* Lengerke refers the word to Xerxes' state of mind, *when he encourages* or *props up himself.* To me the obvious meaning seems to be, 'when he increases or makes strong his power, by riches which can call great armies into the field;' for "money is the sinews of war." — בְּעָשְׁרוֹ simply *by his riches.* — יָעִיר, Imperf. Hiph. of עוּר, *he will rouse up, excite, provoke,* viz. by attacking and injuring, as Xerxes did. — הַכֹּל, *the whole,* τὸ πᾶν, equivalent to the whole world, i. e. all the countries around him; and so, in this sense of universality, the article is demanded, as in Greek. — Such hyperbole is common in describing extensive dominion; comp. Dan. 2: 38, 39. 4: 1, 22. 6: 25. 8: 5. — אֵת מַלְכוּת יָוָן is in apposition with הַכֹּל, and specifies the leading country against which the forces of Xerxes would be directed.

Because only four kings of Persia are here adverted to, Lengerke concludes that the writer knew of no more, and therefore regarded Xerxes as the end of the Persian series or dynasty, inasmuch as he has placed him in contiguity with Alexander the Great; see v. 3. This would ill agree, however, with the minute and extensive knowledge of history displayed in the remainder of the chapter. Besides, who does not at once see, that the plan of the book of Daniel comprises only great and marked events or characters; and that nothing like a book of *annals* is either designed or attempted. Quite to the purpose is the remark of Jerome here: "Non curae fuit prophetali spiritui historiae ordinem sequi, sed praeclara quaeque perstringere." Comm. in loc.

(3) And a mighty king will rise up, and he shall rule with extensive sway, and do according to his pleasure.

The sequel shows that Alexander the Great is here meant. To him גִּבּוֹר applies with peculiar force. — מִמְשָׁל רַב, Acc. of manner here = extensively, or it may be translated *an extensive dominion*, making the noun the Acc. of object. It is singular that Curtius X. 5. § 35, should use the same phraseology respecting Alexander, as the angel does in the present case: "By the aid of his good fortune, he seemed to the nations *agere quidquid placebat.*"

(4) And when he is risen up, his kingdom shall be broken in pieces, and it shall be divided according to the four winds of heaven; but not to his posterity, and not according to the dominion with which he ruled, for his kingdom shall be plucked up, and shall be for others besides those.

וּכְעָמְדוֹ, if referred to the עָמַד in the preceding verse, must be regarded as simply expressing the general idea: *when he shall have risen up.* Rosenm. and Häv. connect with the word the idea of attaining to the height of his power; which might answer well enough out of such a connection. But as the word is now connected, it would seem to be urging more significance upon it than properly belongs to it. — תִּשָּׁבֵר, lit. *shall be shivered,* (our English word being merely a repetition of the Hebrew one.) The same word is used in 8: 8, where it is applied to the *great horn,* and well fits the nature of the expression there. It was natural to retain it here. But how to save the dynasty from *ending* with Alexander, after what is said in this verse, I do not well see. Lengerke and others who make the empire of the four dynasties that follow, a part of the same dynasty with that of Alexander, are obliged to do actual violence to the language. —

Shall be divided toward or *according to the four winds of heaven* has reference to the four great divisions, into which, some years after the death of Alexander the Great, his empire was mainly divided. The Hebrews name only four of the cardinal points; but here the mere direction of these points is not the main thing aimed at. The number *four* has a special significancy; and the general idea of being situated in different parts of the great empire, constitutes the remainder of what is designated by *the four winds of heaven.* וְתֵחָץ, Niph. apoc. of חָצָה, with *Tseri* under the praeformative (instead of short Hhireq) because of the following Guttural. — *But not to his posterity,* i. e. the kingdom shall not be for his offspring. Alexander had two sons; one named Hercules, by Barsine the daughter of Darius, who was assassinated soon after his father's death by Polysperchon; the other, by Roxana, who was named Alexander, and with his guardian Philip Aridaeus was shortly cut off in the same manner. The universal empire was soon seized upon by the leading spirits of Alexander's army, and after many and bloody contests, finally was partitioned among four of the leaders. This is merely adverted to in our text; for in itself it little concerned the Jews, and there is no intention of communicating the history of foreign nations which does not concern them.

And not according to the dominion with which he ruled, i. e. These four kingdoms shall none of them be so powerful in itself as his empire was. Alexander's dominion embraced the whole, theirs only a part. — מָשָׁל Rosenmüller takes for a participial, like חָכָם, because, as he alleges, the *Zaqeph* over it has no power to prolong the last vowel, in מָשַׁל; a singular reason, since cases of prolongation by this accent are sufficiently frequent, see v. 27 below, תִּצְלָח; also Ezek. 18: 12, and the like in Amos 3: 8. Lev. 5: 18, al saepe. The noun and verb of the same root are here employed in the usual manner of the Hebrews, § 135. 1. Note 1. — כִּי, *for,* is to be referred back to the clause, *but not to his posterity.* It stands before the ground or reason why the empire was not given to his offspring. — תִּנָּתֵשׁ, *it shall be plucked up, eradicated.* The very nature of the image employed shows the *utter destruction* of the great empire. I see not how stronger language could well be selected. — The אֲחֵרִים, *others,* are such as belong not to his posterity. So the sequel: מִלְּבַד אֵלֶּה, lit. *of the separation from these,* (as we must express it), מִלְּבַד being a compound of מִן, לְ, and בַּד, and means *besides, separate from,* or *than,* according to the nature of the passage. All is plain in view of the historic facts related above. Rosenm. and Leng. give a different turn to מִלְּבַד אֵלֶּה, but without good reason, see Maurer in loc.

To these simple outlines the speaker limits himself, in giving an account of the fourth dynasty in general. He proceeds, in the sequel, to notice only those divisions of the great kingdom, which concerned the welfare of the Jews, and were in their neighborhood. The king of the *south* is the king of Egypt, and the *north* means Syria.

(5) And the king of the south shall wax strong, but one of his princes shall become more powerful than he, and shall become a king, an extensive domain shall his kingdom be.

The *king* here noticed is Ptolemy Lagi or Soter, the first Grecian king of Egypt, and one of Alexander's generals. He gave the Jews much trouble for a time, but afterwards treated them with more mildness; Jos. Ant. VII. 1. — וּמִן שָׂרָיו, *but one of his princes;* וּ I translate *but*, because contrast is here intended. That מִן may signify *one* as well as *some of* (plur.), see Lex. מִן 1. *a.* Ezek. 6: 25. Gen. 28:11, comp. v. 18. Ps. 137: 3. But to whom does שָׂרָיו refer by its suffix? Rosenm. refers it back to Alexander (v. 4), and he applies שַׂר to Ptolemy thus: "Et is quidem unus ex ducibus ejus" (i. e. Alexander), so that the affirmation has respect merely to the rank or condition of Ptolemy. More correctly, as I apprehend, do Leng., Maurer, Ges., and others refer the suffix to Ptolemy, and regard *Seleucus Nicator* as the person designated. He was first a satrap and commander under Ptolemy; then he declared himself independent, proclaimed himself a king, subdued for himself all the country east of the Euphrates, and formed the powerful Syrian dynasty which goes under his name. From him comes the era of the Seleucidae, B. C. 312. He was by far the most powerful of all Alexander's followers. Hence יֶחֱזַק עָלָיו, *he shall be strong above* or *beyond him*, i. e. beyond Ptolemy Lagi. — וּמָשַׁל, *and shall rule*, a verb, not a participial as Rosenm. maintains. The extent of his dominion is indicated by מִמְשָׁל רַב. See Arrian Exped. Alex. VII. 22. Appian de Reb. Syr. c. LV.

(6) And at the end of some years, shall they form alliances, and the daughter of the king of the South shall come to the king of the North, in order to make conciliation; but she shall not retain the power of aid, nor shall he stand, nor his aid, but she shall be given up, and they who sent her, and he who begat her, and he who received her, in those times.

שָׁנִים, used in this way without limitation, means *some time.* יִתְחַבָּרוּ refers not to Ptolemy Lagi and Seleucus Nicator, but to the kings of the North and South after some years; for Antiochus Soter, who followed Nicator, is passed by, without any mention. The southern king here adverted to seems plainly to be Ptolemy Philadelphus (not Lagi). Philadelphus gave his daughter Berenice in marriage to Antiochus Theos of Syria, in hope of putting an end to the contests between the two countries. —

תָּבוֹא אֶל indicates more than mere *journeying*. The meaning is, that she shall go to the king of the North as his wife, implying an entrance into his palace. — מֵישָׁרִים, lit. *recta*, i. e. to make *straight* things that were crooked or perverse; but here it stands for *conciliation*, *peace*, inasmuch as before this marriage the two kingdoms were at war. — In כּוֹחַ הַזְּרוֹעַ, *she shall not retain the power of an auxiliary*, I take the article to belong to the first word in reality, § 109. 1. כּוֹחַ has here a peculiar sense, being applied to the ability of an *ally* or *helper*, i. e. helping power (זְרוֹעַ), and being made definite in this case by this latter word, it becomes a proper subject to be qualified by the article. Lengerke supposes the article to refer to the marriage of Berenice with Antiochus, thus making virtually a *repeated* mention of this occurrence in the word זְרוֹעַ. I deem the other view of the subject to be more correct; see the like in § 109. *Arm*, being the leading member of the body employed in the accomplishment of any work, is naturally enough employed in the tropical sense of *aid*, *help*, or (abstract being put for concrete) in the sense of *aider*, *helper*. — וְלֹא יַעֲמֹד, the sense of the passage demands that we should refer it to the king of the South, the father of the *helper* or *aid*. — וּזְרֹעוֹ, nor *his helper*, וּ, after a negative in the preceding connected clause, is equivalent to וְלֹא, i. e. = *nor*. Here the *helper* is of course Berenice. — *But she shall be given up*, refers to the violent death of Berenice, who, after the death of her father Ptolemy Philadelphus, was rejected by Antiochus, who then resumed his former wife Laodice. The latter, jealous of Berenice, caused her and her child to be put to death. — וּמְבִיאֶיהָ, *and those who sent her* or *caused her to go*, viz. to the Syrian king; see תָּבֹא in the first part of the verse. I take this not to mean mere *way-conductors*, i. e. servants, but the court of Egypt making the alliance. The *plural* is preserved by all the ancient Versions; but many Codices (some thirty) read מְבִיאָהּ, i. e. the sing. number, referring to *him who introduced her* to Antiochus, i. e. her husband. But there is no need of this change in the text. The plural will designate the court of Ptolemy, who were doubtless concerned with the negotiation of the marriage. Moreover, in case we adopt the singular here, and then refer the word to Ptolemy, then there will be a kind of tautology, inasmuch as the next word describes Ptolemy as the *father* of Berenice.

וְהַיֹּלְדָהּ, *and him who begat her*. This is the only construction the text as now pointed will bear. When a Part. is employed in the sense of a verb, (and it is so here), then the prefixing of the article is the regular construction, even when a suffix-pronoun is appended, Ewald Krit. Gramm. s. 582. In reality the so called article, in such a case, is a relative demonstrative, § 109. 2. *a*. On the contrary, the reading proposed by Dathe, Bertholdt, Dereser, Rosenmüller, and De Wette, viz. הַיַּלְדָּה (suff. state of יֶלֶד *child*, with the article), is contrary to the *usus loquendi;* for *nouns* having a suffix pronoun *omit* the article, § 108. 2. The sense of the word thus pointed would indeed be good; for the child of Berenice was murdered with its mother. This would well agree with תִּנָּתֵן, which here signifies *to give over* or *give up* to death. The difficulty with the text as it is, seems to be principally this, viz. that neither Ptolemy nor his court were given up to a violent death. But breviloquence in animated discourse, not unfrequently leads the writer to the omission of verbs which must be mentally supplied; as in all cases of *Zeugma.* Besides, the difficulty is just the same as it respects מְבִיאֶיהָ, (whether one reads it as plur. or sing.), so that no relief is gained from this by reading הַיַּלְדָּה in the case before us. The text must therefore be regarded as *breviloquence*, and the appropriate verb must be supplied by the reader, in respect to the nouns which follow הִיא. — וּמַחֲזִקָהּ, Part. Hiph. with suff., the Yodh between the second and third radical letter omitted, i. e. written *defectivè;* lit. *him who took hold on her*, i. e. Antiochus Theos. In order to marry Berenice he rejected his former wife Laodice; and doubtless, in order to propitiate the king of Egypt, he put on the appearance of eagerness for the new connection. Hence the strong word here employed, not meaning simply to *take* or *receive*, but *to take with a grasp*, and so (at least to appearance) with eagerness. However, soon after the death of Ptolemy Philadelphus (in some two years), Antiochus resumed his former wife Laodice; but she, jealous of his constancy, administered poison to him, by which he died. Soon after this event, in order to secure the crown to her own son, Laodice, procured the death of Berenice and her infant child. Inasmuch then as Philadelphus himself died in some two years after the alliance formed with Antiochus, it follows that all the parties here concerned speedily perished, with the exception of the מְבִיאֶיהָ, in regard to whom, we do not know whether such was the case or not, because we have no particular history of their times. But after the test of history, to which we have put the rest of the text, we may trust the writer for this, and believe that he has described things as they were. The whole affair was marked with insidious and treacherous designs, and also with perfidy and blood. — בָּעִתִּים, *during those times*, the article (in the prefix בָּ) here referring to *the end of some years* (לְקֵץ שָׁנִים) at the beginning of the verse, and of course being equivalent to the pronominal *those.*

(7) And one of the shoots of her roots shall rise up in his place, and he shall come to his army, and enter into the fortified places of the king of the north, and he shall do [his pleasure] in them, and bring [them] into his grasp.

מִנֵּצֶר, here מִן has a partitive sense = *one of;* see under מִן שָׂרָיו in v. 5. As נֵצֶר is singular, it would make the best sense to regard it as *generic* here, meaning *posterity, progeny.* — Of שָׁרָשֶׁיהָ (*sho-rā-she-hā*), the same expression in Isa. 11: 1; lit. *the roots* or *source of her*, i. e. of the daughter of the king of the South (v. 5), means her father or her parents. The נֵצֶר or *offshoot*, is Ptolemy Euergetes, the brother of Berenice, and son and successor of Philadelphus. To avenge the death of Berenice, he marched with a large army against the king of the North, slew Laodice, and swept over the whole country even to the Tigris, everywhere exacting contributions at his pleasure. — בְּמָעוֹז may be taken in a generic sense = *fortifications*, (I have translated it as a noun of multitude), since בָּהֶם in the sequel indicates a plur. number, either in respect to strongholds, or possibly in respect to the Syrians. Indeed, considering the extent of Ptolemy's conquests, it would seem necessary to give מָעוֹז such a generic sense, at any rate. — עָשָׂה is here, as elsewhere in this book, a *constructio praegnans*, רְצוֹנוֹ being understood after it. — בָּהֶם may be applied, as before noted, to the *strongholds* generically considered, or to the Syrians belonging to the north country. I incline to the former, on the ground that the following הֶחֱזִיק is better suited to the *taking fast possession* of them than of the people. This whole invasion by the Egyptian king was conducted with great skill and power, and had not Euergetes been summoned back to Egypt by tumults there, it seems quite probable he would have made a complete conquest of Syria, and brought the Syrian dynasty to a close.

(8) And moreover their gods, with their molten images, with their costly vessels, silver and gold, will he carry into captivity to Egypt; and then will he stand aloof, for some time, from the king of the North.

Their gods with their molten images is an expression in accordance with the views of the conquerors. Idolaters generally suppose, that the god whom they worship dwells in his image or statue. When the guardian-gods of any country were carried away, it was supposed that no one would protect them against aggressors. On such a ground the Philistines seem to have carried away the ark of the covenant, 1 Sam. 5: 1 seq. The Romans carried the gods of conquered countries in triumphal procession at Rome. There can be no doubt, that Ptolemy Euergetes did the like, in his victorious Syrian war. — נְסִכֵיהֶם, participial from נָסִיךְ, means *images made by fusion and casting.* The suff. ־ֵיהֶם must relate to the Syrian nation or people. — עִם כְּלֵי חֶמְדָּתָם, lit. *with their vessels of desire*, which of course indicates those that were made of the precious metals, and such as were adorned with jewels, or were of curious workmanship; and the like. — *Silver and gold* may be an explanatory clause, put in apposition with *vessels of desire*, designed to show the *materials* out of which the vessels were made. This seems to be the most obvious construction. But these words may indicate the *precious metals* over and above the statues and the vessels. One would hardly expect, however, the omission of וְ before כֶּסֶף, if this were the design of the writer. On this account, I must prefer the preceding interpretation. — בַּשְּׁבִי יָבִא *into exile shall he carry*. But שְׁבִי generally applies only to *persons*, not to things. Instances, however, may be found, of its being applied to things; e. g. Ps. 78: 61, and so to beasts, Amos 4: 10. Ex. 12: 29. Here, however, as the *gods* are also carried away, שְׁבִי may be employed without doing any violence to propriety. — יַעֲמֹד מִן seems plainly to mean *stand off* or *aloof, abstain from*, and the like; although Berth. Ges., Winer, De Wette, and others, render the phrase *stand before*, that is *withstand*, the king of the North. But the idiom does not seem to admit of this. Jerome (in loc.) says, that Ptolemy "brought back with him from Syria, 40,000 talents of silver, costly vessels, and 2,500 statues of the gods, among which latter were those which had been carried away by Cambyses from Egypt to Persia." The idolatrous Egyptians were so elated at this, that they gave to Ptolemy the surname of εὐεργέτης, *the beneficent.*

(9) And he shall come to the kingdom of the king of the South, but he shall return to his own land.

וּבָא, viz. the king of Syria, Seleucus Callinicus, who is the immediate antecedent. — וְשָׁב, וְ *but*, for here is contrast, § 152. B. *b*. Callinicus, after some two years from the withdrawal of Ptolemy from Syria, reclaimed some of the provinces in Asia Minor, and attacked the Egyptian domain by sea and land, on both of which he was utterly defeated.

Under Ptolemy Euergetes much favor was shown to the Jews; and it seems to be on this account, that so much is here said of him; for after this, Egypt comes into view only as connected with or opposed to the Syrian kings.

(10) And his sons shall make war, and they shall collect a multitude of large armies; and he shall move onward, and overwhelm, and pass through; and he shall return, and shall carry on the war even to his strong hold.

וּבָנָו, (the י after נ being omitted), *and his sons*, i. e. the sons of Seleucus Callinicus (for he is the immediate antecedent), whose names were Seleucus Ceraunus and Antiochus Magnus. The former of these two began the war against Egypt, in Asia Minor where Egypt had tributary or allied provinces. He perished in the contest there. Antiochus Magnus then led on his army toward Egypt; and hence וּבָא בוֹא in the singular. The Inf. being after the definite verb here denotes the *continued* advance of the army under Antiochus, § 128. 3. *b.* — וְשָׁטַף borrows its imagery from the overwhelming of a mighty and irresistible stream; as also does עָבַר. — וְיָשֹׁב, *he shall return* here means, that he shall come a second time to renew the contest. After the first attack, in which Antiochus had much success, and advanced even to Pelusium, the Egyptians, then under Ptolemy Philopator the son of Euergetes, persuaded him to a truce of four months. During this he prepared for renewing the contest, which he did with much energy, and was for awhile victorious. — וְיִתְגָּרוּ, (so it should be pointed, if we follow the *Kethibh*), and not (as the Qeri) יִתְגָּרֶה in the singular. The subjects of the verb (plur.) seem to be Antiochus and Ptolemy Philopator. But the *Qeri* seems here to be preferable, and this points to Antiochus, who, by constantly pushing onwards, penetrated even to the fortification of Raphia on the border of Egypt; which our text designates by מָעֻזּה, (ה– suff. for ו–), *his fortress*, viz. the fortress of the Egyptian king; for the nature of the case shows, that the king of the North is attacking the domain of the king of the South, and of course the reference of *his* to the Egyptian king in this case becomes plain. When the verb גָּרָה is followed by בְּ or עַד before an object, the verb implies after it a noun designating *war*, *attack*, etc., and so the expression here is breviloquent, or a *constructio praegnans*.

(11) And the king of the South will become exceedingly embittered, and he will go forth and fight with him, the king of the north, and he will raise up a large multitude, and that multitude shall be given into his hand.

Philopator was aroused from his sloth and voluptuous habits by the attack upon Raphia, so near the proper borders of Egypt, and under the sway of its king. He assembled a large army, 70,000 foot, 5,000 cavalry, and seventy-three elephants, Polyb. c. 86. Ptolemy himself took the command of these forces, or (to use the literal language of our text), *they were put into his hand*, meaning that they were under his control; for it is plain that the same multitude which he raised up, is the one committed to his direction.

(12) And the multitude shall be lifted up, and his mind become elated, and he will cast down myriads; but he shall not become powerful.

Favorable occurrences, as Polybius relates, excited hope and ardor in the Egyptian army, and of course in their leader. The Kethibh must be read יָרוּם, and thus make the construction *asyndic*. For this reason

I prefer, in this case, the Keri (וְרָם), because it gives the bond of connection. The destroying of *myriads* was the consequence of a severe battle, in which a great victory was won over Antiochus. — וְלֹא יָעוֹז, *but he will not be powerful.* Ptolemy, content with repelling the invasion, made a treaty with Antiochus, and failed to take advantage of his victories. He then hastened back to the enjoyment of his usual sloth and debauchery. This occasions the prophet to say, that *he would not become powerful.*

(13) And the king of the North shall return, and he will raise up a multitude greater than the first one; and at the end of some time, [after] several years, he shall come with a great army and with much wealth.

At the end of times, הָעִתִּים, with the article. I take this, however, not as qualifying עִתִּים, but the whole phrase, § 109. 1; and in accordance with this, the word שָׁנִים, which is in apposition with הָעִתִּים and exegetical of it (§ 111), has no article. שָׁנִים is a common phrase to designate the idea of *some years*, i. e. some moderate and not exactly defined period. And the like as to עִתִּים = *some time.* But the word *end* is specific, and admits qualification by the article; which however must be placed before the noun that follows in the Genitive, (§ 109. 1). As to facts, Antiochus Magnus waited some thirteen or fourteen years, before he again invaded Egypt. Philopator was then dead (†203 B. C.), and his son, Ptolemy Epiphanes, (four years of age) reigned in his stead. Antiochus had then just returned from his splendid conquests and triumphs in Persia, Bactria, and Asia Minor, and was at the very height of his power and wealth. His army must have been very large, and the plunder which he had collected in so many countries must have made him very rich. Hence בִּרְכוּשׁ רָב, *with much wealth.* The mention of this in connection with his march of invasion, יָבוֹא בוֹא, would seem to indicate, that his troops, returning from their conquests, had marched in the direction of Egypt, before returning to Syria and depositing their wealth there. — בְּחַיִל *with force*, but this, like our English word *force*, is often applied to the power of an *army.*

(14) And in those times, many will stand up against the king of the South, even the most violent of thy people will lift themselves up, so as to establish prophetic vision, but they shall fall.

On the return of Antiochus from his victories in Egypt, a portion of the Jews welcomed him with his army, provided for them, and assisted in reducing the Egyptian garrison in Jerusalem, Jos. Antiq. XII. 3. 3. By calling the party who thus allied themselves to Antiochus, בְּנֵי פָּרִיצֵי עַמְּךָ, the speaker has shown his strong disapprobation of their conduct.

פָּרִיצֵי is the const. of a *forma dagessanda*, פָּרִיץ = פַּרִּיץ, the Qamets being of course immutable. The meaning is *violent*, *disruptive*, which may be spoken in a literal or in a *tropical* sense. The latter sense, (which belongs to this passage), would probably have relation to their breaking either the sacred covenant of the Jews, or more probably the treaty with the Egyptian king; for Egyptian dominion the Jews had acknowledged for more than a century. In thus rising up, they do but establish the prophetic vision, חָזוֹן, viz. the prophecies respecting the troubles of the Jews under the fourth dynasty: see 7: 19—25. 8: 9 seq. 9: 26, 27. — וְנִכְשָׁלוּ, for the form with Qamets, see § 29. 4. *b*, *but they shall fall*, i. e. they shall perish, or at least be disappointed in their hopes and expectations.

(15) And the king of the North shall come, and he shall cast up a mound, and take a strongly fortified city; and the forces of the South shall not stand, even his choicest troops — there shall be no power to stand.

The Egyptian king sent Scopas, one of his ablest warriors, to reclaim the cities of Palestine and Coelesyria. Antiochus met him in contest, near the sources of the Jordan, and drove him back, until he took refuge in Sidon, a fortified place. Antiochus there besieged the remnant of the Egyptian troops, and of course *cast up* (יִשְׁפֹּךְ), or (lit.) *poured out*, a mound by which he might storm the city. The verb here employed refers to the method of raising artificial mounds, by bringing in and *pouring down* the earth necessary to construct them. Scopas was finally reduced by famine, and gave up the city and his army, with liberty for the latter to depart without their arms and other possessions. — עִיר מִבְצָרוֹת, *a city of fortifications*, which was taken by Antiochus. The latter noun is a *pluralis intensivus*, having the meaning given to it in the version, § 106. Note 2, with *Remark*. — זְרֹעוֹת, plur. fem., but plainly designating the idea of *forces*, like חֲיָלִים, and so the masc. verb יַעֲמֹדוּ is joined with it. — וְעַם מִבְחָרָיו, the word עַם is not confined to designating a *nation* or *tribe*, but is applied to any large collection of *citizens*, *servants*, *soldiers*, etc.; lit. then, *the company of his choice ones*, i. e. his *Corps d'Elites* or chosen troops, the best of his army. Such doubtless were those soldiers who had accompanied Scopas. *They had no power to stand*, i. e. to maintain their post against the aggressions of Antiochus. But not improbably the *chosen men* refers to the army sent by Ptolemy to relieve Scopas during the siege, which of course were *picked men*, and were led by three of the best Egyptian officers. But they were defeated, and were unable to save Scopas from capture. The phrase וְעַם מִבְחָרָיו is in the Nom. absolute, *as to his chosen bands*, etc.

(16) And he who cometh shall do to him according to his pleasure, and none will stand before him, and he will take his position in the goodly land, and it shall be entirely in his hand.

הַבָּא, *he who cometh* refers to the leading agent in the preceding verse, viz. to Antiochus. — וְיַעַשׂ, *apoc.* form of the verb without a *Vav consecutive* (which would be וַיַּעַשׂ), and yet with the like narrative sense as the common Imperfect, although a *jussive* sense properly and usually belongs to the apoc. form, § 48. 2, and 4. *a.* We have the like in this chapter, in v. 10. וְיָשֹׁב, in v. 17 וְיָשֵׂם, and in v. 18 וְיָשֵׁב; in all of which cases, although the form of the verb is apoc., yet the meaning is such as the normal form gives. — אֵלָיו *to him*, i. e. to the person whom he invades, viz. the King of the South. — עוֹמֵד, *stands firmly*, i. e. keeps his place. — וְיַעֲמֹד *shall occupy a standing*, i. e. shall establish his position. בְּאֶרֶץ הַצְּבִי, lit. *in the land of beauty*. So in 8: 9 above; and so in Ezek. 20: 6, 15, where the reason of the appellation is given, viz. that it excels all other lands, comp. Jer. 3: 10. The article stands before צְבִי, as often before *abstract* nouns. — וְכָלָה בְיָדוֹ seems to demand the meaning: *And he shall utterly destroy with his hand* or *by his power*. But this would disagree with historic facts. Antiochus was gratified with the submission and aid of the בְּנֵי פָּרִיצִים (v. 14), and treated the Jews with kindness. We must give to כָּלָה, then, the other sense that it bears, viz. that of *completion*, and render the word (for so we lawfully may) as a noun, lit. *completion shall be in his hand*, i. e. in his power. The *complete possession* or *sovereignty* of the country must, in such a connection, be the idea meant to be conveyed, for *destruction* is not the idea here conveyed by כָּלָה. This word, moreover, might be rendered adverbially: "And entirely shall [it] be in his hand."

(17) And he shall set his face to enter upon the strength of all his kingdom, and pacification with him shall he make, and the daughter of women shall he give to him, that he may destroy it; but it shall not stand, neither shall it take place for him.

תֹּקֶף, *power*, *strength*, apparently abstract for concrete, i. e. *strength* for the strong places and populous parts of Egypt. As *war* is not described in this verse, the translation *with the might of all his kingdom*, i. e. with the hosts of Syria, will not fit the passage. What Antiochus is aiming at, is to have a *predominance* in Egypt, so that he may resist the Roman aggressions. מַלְכוּתוֹ, then, refers to the kingdom of Ptolemy. — וִישָׁרִים has occasioned much perplexity among interpreters. To apply this appellation to the apostate Jews, the בְּנֵי פָּרִיצִים of v. 14, seems a mere contradiction. The really *upright* Jews, on the other hand, were not the persons to break covenant, and join with Antiochus. I cannot hesitate, therefore, with Maurer, to regard the word in the same light as I do מֵישָׁרִים in v. 6, and to translate it *pacification* or *conciliation*, i. e. a treaty of peace and concord. The objection of Lengerke, that the word is not used as a *noun*, does not seem to be very solid. Are not Hebrew adjectives, in numerous cases, employed as *nouns*, just as in Greek and Latin? Having the same root then as מֵישָׁרִים, and being used in a connection altogether of the same nature, I see no serious difficulty in the interpretation now given. It is certain, that a general appellation of the Jews as יְשָׁרִים, is no where else to be found; and we have seen, indeed, that the *Jews* are really out of question in this case. The sense given, then, is the only tolerable one that remains.

The daughter of women is idiomatic, (like *son of man* for *man*), and designates, in this case, Cleopatra the daughter of Antiochus, whom he gave to the Egyptian king as a wife, with a promised dowry of Coelesyria and Palestine, and in this way made יְשָׁרִים, *conciliation.* — לְהַשְׁחִיתָהּ, not *to destroy her*, but *to destroy* the מַלְכוּתוֹ, i. e. Ptolemy's *dominion.* Not so much the *country* as the *domination* over it, is designated by מַלְכוּת here, and so the ־ָהּ suffixed to the verb, refers to this מַלְכוּת. The whole plan was to bring Ptolemy within the power of the Syrian king, and put him at the disposal of the latter. But in all this, as the sequel asserts, Antiochus was entirely frustrated. לֹא תַעֲמֹד, fem., i. e. it, viz. his counsel, purpose, shall not be executed or established.

(18) And he shall turn his face toward the isles, and seize many; but a chieftain shall cause his reproach to cease; besides that he will turn back his reproaches upon himself.

Soon after the events in Egypt, related in the preceding verse, Antiochus engaged in new undertakings. Already had he won from the Roman grasp several islands and coast-towns, along the shores of Asia Minor. After wintering at Ephesus, he set out to pass over to the European side of the Greeks. In Lycia, at Magnesia, he was met by the Roman general Lucius Scipio, after a series of preceding losses and defeats on the part of Antiochus, and the final battle was fought, in which, of some 75,000 men in the Syrian army, at least 55,000 were left dead on the field, and the rest scattered to the winds ; all of which was achieved by about 30,000 Romans. Antiochus was then forced to give up all claims to any domain beyond the Taurus, and to pay the Romans 15,000 talents of Attic silver. Thus ruined both as to his forces and his treasury, he soon came to an unhappy end, as v. 19 indicates. — קָצִין, *a chieftain*, anarthrous because it is not designed to specificate a particular individual. — חֶרְפָּתוֹ may be either active or passive, i. e. it may indicate the *reproach* which one utters, or which is uttered against him, § 112. 2. The first is the meaning here. When the Romans sent ambassadors to request Antiochus to desist from his incursions, he treated them with haughtiness and reproach, Polyb. XVIII. 34. The Roman chieftain not only put a stop to this, but most effectually turned back the reproaches on Antiochus himself, whose defeat and disgrace were almost without a parallel. — לוֹ . . . הִשְׁבִּית, *stilled for him, brought to silence in respect to him.* — בִּלְתִּי, *besides*, or *besides that*, אֲשֶׁר being implied after the particle, as it often is; see Lex. — *Turn back on himself*, i. e. Scipio not only reduced the haughty and reproachful king to silence, but he brought him into disgrace and contempt. Appian (de Reb. Syr. c. 37) says, that men were wont to say of him: ἦν βασιλεὺς Ἀντίοχος ὁ μέγας, i. e. Antiochus the Great *was* a king. לוֹ, in this last case, is *Dativus incommodi.*

(19) And he shall turn his face toward the strong holds of his country, and he shall stumble, and fall, and shall no more be found.

After a pledge to pay such an enormous sum to the Romans, Antiochus found no way to provide for it except by military exactions of tribute and presents from his subjects. He robbed even the temples, in order to furnish the stipulated sum. He made an excursion for this purpose into the East, and undertook, by the aid of his soldiers, to plunder by night the temple at Elymais in Persia. But the inhabitants rose *en masse*, and destroyed both him and his soldiers. — לְמָעוּזֵּי refers to the garrisoned places east of the Taurus, which Antiochus fortified partly for defence and partly for the sake of giving power and energy to the military exaction of tribute. His sudden and violent death is predicted by the last clause: *He shall stumble and fall, and shall no more be found.*

(20) And there shall stand up, in his place, one who will make an exactor of tribute to pass through the glory of the kingdom; and after some time, he shall be destroyed, but not by anger, nor yet by war.

Seleucus Philopator, the eldest son of Antiochus, succeeded him. The tribute stipulated by his father was 1000 talents each year, for twelve years. In order to pay this, the most rigid system of exacting money became necessary. Hence the exactor that passes through *the glory of the kingdom*, i. e. Palestine; for here is the same idea as in אֶרֶץ הַצְּבִי of v. 16. Bertholdt makes הֶדֶר to mean the same as the Greek τιμή, *tribute, honorary gift.* But as there is no other example of this nature in the Scriptures, and as another explanation is easy and obvious, there is no need of such an interpretation. Palestine was regarded and spoken of by the Hebrews as the most glorious of all countries. — בְּיָמִים אֲחָדִים, *after some time*, for בְּ, before words of time, occasionally, indicates the *close* of that time, Lex. בְּ. A. 3. — וְלֹא בְאַפַּיִם, *but not in anger*, for the dual form is used in this *tropical* sense, because the nostrils are affected by anger. What the speaker means, is that Seleucus would not be cut off in a *quarrel*, where the passions were heated; and *not in war*, i. e. not in battle. He seems to have been poisoned by one of his courtiers, Heliodorus, who endeavored to usurp his place, but was speedily ejected from it.

(21) And there shall stand up in his place a despicable person, on whom they have not put the splendor of dominion, and he shall come quietly, and lay hold upon the kingdom by flattery.

The נִבְזֶה is Antiochus Epiphanes, the brother of Philopator, and son of Antiochus the Great, one of the most extraordinary characters exhibited on the pages of history. He was both avaricious and prodigal, excessive in his indulgences and prone to violent passions, a compound of the veriest folly and weakness in some respects, and of great cunning and dexterity in some others, specially in regard to flattery. At one period of his reign, there was a prospect of his becoming quite powerful. But reverses came upon him, and he died at last nearly as his father had done before him, and on the like occasion. Indeed his extravagances and follies and cruelty were so great, that his contemporaries gave him the nickname of *ἐπιμανής* (madman), instead of the title which he assumed, viz. *ἐπιφανής* (illustrious). This will explain the ground of the characteristic in the text, נִבְזֶה, *despicable.* — נָֽתְנוּ, 3 plur. impers. = pass. voice, so that we may translate thus: *the splendor* or *dignity of dominion was not put upon him*, viz. was not voluntarily given to him by the Syrians. The regal dignity descended regularly, on the death of Seleucus Philopator, to his son *Demetrius Soter ;* but Antiochus, then on his return from Rome, (where he had been as a hostage given by Antiochus Magnus, to secure the fulfilment of the treaty he had made with the Romans), seized upon the kingdom in spite of Demetrius; who had been sent to Rome in the room of Antiochus. He was at Athens on his return from Rome, when the news reached him of the death of Seleucus Philopator. On his way thence to Antioch, he visited Eumenes and Attalus, kings of Pergamus, and by his cunning and flattery led them to espouse his cause. Overawed by them the Syrians yielded peaceably to the claims of Antiochus, although they did not voluntarily place him on the throne. To this last circumstance נָֽתְנוּ וְגוֹ׳ alludes. In like manner וּבָא בְשַׁלְוָה, *he shall come peaceably*, alludes to his coming without the tumult and alarm of war. Lengerke, and even Gesenius, translates בְּשַׁלְוָה by *inopinato* i. e. *suddenly, unexpectedly ;* but this seems rather an improbable meaning here. It was doubtless known publicly, that Demetrius, the lawful heir of the throne, had gone to Rome, as a hostage in the room of Antiochus, and that the latter was on his return. *Unexpectedly*, then, could hardly apply to his return. That there was no civil war and no contests worth recording, on the occasion of his accession to the throne, seems to be matter of fact. That part of the Syrians, who were opposed to the usurper Heliodorus, would of course favor the claims of Antiochus. They and the forces of Eumenes and Attalus, ready for action, would naturally overawe the faction of the usurper ; and thus Antiochus seated himself on the throne without any war, i. e. בְּשַׁלְוָה. — *Lay hold upon the kingdom by flatteries*, in which, as it would appear from history, and from various declarations of this book, he exceeded most men. His antagonists, and all the different partizans for Heliodorus, Demetrius, and Ptolemy of Egypt, were, as it would seem, conciliated and won over by such means.

(22) And overwhelming forces shall be overwhelmed before him, and be broken in pieces, even a covenanted prince.

When Antiochus seated himself on the throne of Syria, Ptolemy Philometor, a minor, was on the throne of Egypt. The latter was the son of Cleopatra, daughter of Antiochus the Great, and sister of Antiochus Epiphanes. The guardians of the young Philometor demanded of Antiochus Epiphanes, that he should give up Coelesyria and Palestine to Egypt, inasmuch as Antiochus the Great had agreed, that these should be a part of the dowry that would be given by him to his daughter Cleopatra, who was married to Ptolemy Epiphanes. Antiochus Epiphanes refused to make the required concession, and even denied that there was any promise or obligation to make it. The Romans interfered between the parties, for the purpose of conciliation, but in vain. The matter came at last to active contest. In B. C. 171, Antiochus met the forces of the Egyptian king, between Pelusium and the Casian mountain, and routed them. In B. C. 170, the contest was again renewed, but with the like results. Hence the declaration of the text: *Overwhelming forces shall be overwhelmed before him.* — הַשֶּׁטֶף, lit. *of overwhelming*, employed to qualify the preceding noun, § 104. 1; the article stands, as often, before the noun as *abstract*, § 107. Note 1. *c.* — וְיִשָּׁבְרוּ, lit. *shall be shivered*, being a word that is sometimes employed to designate total or utter destruction, and sometimes an entire frustration or overthrow of purposes or designs. The imagery is borrowed from the dashing in pieces of an earthen vessel of pottery. — *And even a covenanted Prince* [shall be broken in pieces]; for יִשָּׁבֵר is unquestionably implied in this case. — נְגִיד בְּרִית, not the high-priest, Onias, the prince of the Jewish covenant, as Rosenm. maintains, for then הַבְּרִית would of course be employed. בְּרִית is designed for a mere adjective of quality or condition here, and so the article is omitted, as it more generally is in such cases. The design of the speaker is, to render the description of overwhelming battle more intensive by adding the circumstance, that it was with a prince who had a covenant or treaty of amity with the conquering king. — וְגַם implies accession, advance, in description. For the like modes of expression, see Gen. 14: 13. Neh. 6: 18. Obad. v. 7. If Rosenm. be in the right, the order of time would be inverted, and a ὕστερον πρότερον must consequently be admitted in the course of the narration; which is improbable.

(23) And from the time of connecting himself with him [or of joining himself to him], he will practise deceit, and he will go up, and prevail with a small company.

Usually מִן drops the ן and is united with the following word, when the latter has no article; but occasionally it is retained in some other cases, e. g. in Ps. 18: 4, 49. 2 Sam. 22: 14, Joel 1: 12, and so here. — הִתְחַבְּרוּת, an Inf. *nominascens* of Hithp., constructed after the manner of Aramaean Infinitives, i. e. with וּת — added to the ground form. After the battle near Pelusium, Antiochus made a league with Ptolemy, under pretence of guarantying to him his kingly rights and claims; his real object however was, to get possession of all Egypt. To do this peaceably, he took with him only a small army, rightly suspecting that but little resistance would be made to a force insignificant with regard to strength. He took possession of Memphis, the old capital; thence he went with his fleet to Naucratis, (at one of the mouths of the Nile), and afterward encamped, in hostile attitude, before Alexandria. Here, as we shall see, his progress was arrested. — עָלָה is often employed to designate a march to a country with hostile designs. — גּוֹי, not merely *nation*, but any body of people, as *soldiers, servants,* etc.

(24) Quietly shall he come upon the richest provinces, and he shall do what neither his fathers, nor his fathers' fathers did, plunder and spoil, and wealth shall he distribute to them, and against fortified places will he form devices, even unto a limited time.

בְּשַׁלְוָה is transferred to the preceding verse by Leng., and Rosenm. translates it *a friendly land.* There is no need of either expedient. The word means *a state of tranquillity.* Joined with what follows, it seems to show, that Antiochus contrived to come upon the richest provinces, before their fears had disturbed them, or caused any excitement among them. Perhaps the idea is simply: *with peaceable pretensions.* מְדִינָה, being of the singular, must be understood generically, = *each province.* — *Do what neither his fathers,* etc., *have done,* i. e. take possession of a whole country with a few soldiers and by crafty policy. — לָהֶם, *to them,* to whom? To the rich provinces, says Lengerke; which is at least highly improbable. It was not his object to make the rich more rich. Others take לָהֶם as the *Dat. posses.*, indicating to whom the wealth, etc., belonged; in which case it should either have אֲשֶׁר before it, or else stand before the nouns. Maurer: "Ad milites Antiochi referendum esse, sole clarius;" in which light it appears to me. גּוֹי of the preceding verse is the true antecedent. — *Form devices against fortified places;* it was the *richest* places, those where plunder was to be had, that Antiochus had thus far got within his grasp. The strongly fortified ones still held out for Ptolemy. Against these Antiochus now formed designs. — עַד־עֵת, designates a *limited time;* for the speaker throughout keeps in sight the decrees of Heaven, beyond which men cannot go.

(25) And he shall rouse up his force and his courage against the king of the South, with a great army; and the king of the South shall be roused up to contest with an army great and very powerful, but he shall not stand, for they shall form devices against him.

There is some difficulty here, as to the order of relation. Lengerke supposes vs. 23, 24, to mention what took place in 169 B. C., and that v. 25 seq. is a resumption of what is said in v. 22, and an account of what took place in 171, 170 B. C. In a war which was so often renewed, and interrupted by pacificatory truces or leagues, and which continued for several years, at least parts of years, in succession, it is hardly to be supposed that the speaker means minutely to arrange in order the chronology of events. The effort to get quiet possession of Egypt by employing only a *few soldiers*, and thus not exciting any military alarm, as presented in v. 23, is no contradiction to the *great army* mentioned in the verse before us. The two passages are an account of what took place at different times and under different circumstances. As the histories of Antiochus are confessedly imperfect, instead of an effort to obtain from them the exact order of events, (which is vain), I prefer following the statement of the text; and I regard v. 22 as a kind of summary introduction to what follows. The preceding verse informs us, that Antiochus was meditating designs against the fortified places of Egypt, i. e. to make a military seizure of the whole kingdom. The present one shows that he had determined to execute those designs. — כֹּחוֹ, *his force*, i. e. his military force; or does it mean *rousing up his own energy?* I incline to the latter, because his *army* is mentioned at the end of the clause. It saves repetition. לְבָבוֹ, *his heart*, i. e. courage to engage in the contest. — *With a great army*, which of course is entirely a different case from the one above, where he goes only בִּמְעַט גּוֹי — יִתְגָּרֶה, Hithp. of גָּרָה, *to enter into contest*, or *to rouse up*, here in the latter sense, because of לַמִּלְחָמָה. The article in the latter word points to the warfare already indicated by the first clause. — *He shall not stand*, i. e. the king of the South, who is the agent that next precedes. *They shall form devices against him*, where *they* of course means an opposing party, or else, (which is the more probable), the Syrians in connection with some of his own courtiers who were corrupted by bribes. The 3d plur. verb might therefore be rendered passively: *Devices shall be formed*, etc. The next verse seems plainly to confirm this view of the matter.

(26) And those who eat of his own choice food shall crush him, and his army shall rush impetuously on, and many shall fall down wounded.

Probably *those who eat of his choice food* means Lennaeus and Eulaeus, the guardians and state-ministers of the young Ptolemy. — יִשְׁבְּרוּהוּ is to be taken in a modified sense. His treacherous guardians did not literally destroy him, but they *ruined his purposes* or *designs* as to opposing Antiochus. — *His army*, i. e. that of Ptolemy, who is the nearest agent named. — יִשְׁטוֹף, *rush on like a flood*, i. e. madly, or impetuously, to danger or ruin. So in Jer. 8: 6, in respect to the horse which rushes impetuously and inconsiderately into the battle, not to victory as the context shows, but to destruction. So in the present case. The sequel of the verse shows the consequence of their impetuous rushing. — חֲלָלִים of itself means nothing more than *wounded*, but in connection with נָפְלוּ it designates *mortally wounded.*

(27) As to those two kings, their intention is to do mischief; at one table do they utter falsehood. But it will not succeed, for the end is still at the appointed time.

וּשְׁנֵיהֶם, lit. *and the two of them* = they two; after which follows the explanatory הַמְּלָכִים, being put in apposition. Both are in the Nom. abs., and so are they translated above. — מֵרָע, derivate of רָעַע, a kind of Inf. noun, (like the Aramaean Inf.), see § 84. II. 14. We might translate *for the doing of evil.* Final *Qamets* because of the pause-accent. — *At one table* designates the dissembled amity and intimacy of the parties, who did and said all that they could in order to mislead each other. — *It will not succeed*, וְלֹא תִצְלָח, fem. impersonal = there shall not be success, namely, to the falsehood which they utter. *Qamets* in pause. The reason of failure follows. *The end*, viz. of the contest in which they are engaged, is not to be brought about by their wishes, devices, or deceit, but Providence has a מוֹעֵד for it, i. e. an appointed or determined time, which all their craftiness cannot change. As a recognized time it takes the article. Here, as throughout, the hand of an overruling power is distinctly recognized.

(28) And he shall return to his land with great wealth; and his mind shall be

against the holy covenant, and he shall accomplish [his purpose], and shall return to his land.

As to the *spoils* or *wealth* which Antiochus carried back to Syria, see 1 Macc. 1: 19 seq., ἔλαβε τὰ σκῦλα τῆς Αἰγύπτου. — עַל בְּרִית קֹדֶשׁ, lit. *against the covenant of holiness.* We might, perhaps, expect הַקֹּדֶשׁ, just as we have אֶרֶץ הַצְּבִי in v. 16. But first, abstract nouns are continually varying in respect to the insertion or omission of the article; and secondly, הַקֹּדֶשׁ would naturally designate *the holy place*, which is not the design of the speaker. *Holiness* is a quality here, which makes an adjective for בְּרִית, § 104. 1. *The holy covenant* here stands for the people who have entered into that covenant, i. e. the Hebrews. For an account of the hostile visit of Antiochus to Jerusalem, see 1 Macc. 1: 20 seq.

(29) At the appointed time shall he again invade the South; but the latter time shall not be like the former.

The מוֹעֵד here is probably the same which is mentioned in v. 27; hence the article. When the time to bring the controversy between the two kings to an end shall come, *he will invade*, etc. — יָשׁוּב merely denotes *repetition* here of the action designated by the verb that follows; see Lex. — וְלֹא תִהְיֶה וגו׳, lit. *but it shall not be, as at the first so at the last.* In the version above, I have abbreviated the mode of expression, in conformity with our idiom. The two fem. nouns, or rather adjectives, אַחֲרוֹנָה and רִאשֹׁנָה, are therefore the Acc. of time. We have no need, then, with Lengerke, to account for the omission of בְּ before them. The meaning is, that Antiochus shall no more be successful, as in former times.

(30) And there shall come against him the ships of Chittim, and he shall be disheartened, and he shall return, and rage against the holy covenant, and accomplish [his purpose]; and again shall he have an understanding with those who forsake the holy covenant.

צִיִּים, *ships;* כִּתִּים, properly *Chittaei*, i. e. *inhabitants of Citium*, the capital of Cyprus. Hence the word sometimes stands for the island itself, and sometimes (like אִיִּים) for the sea-coast countries, or the West generally. Josephus (Antiq. 1. 6. 1) says: "All the islands, and most of the maritime coasts, are named Χεθίμ (כִּתִּים) by the Hebrews." In respect to this last contest of Antiochus with Egypt, the two brothers there, Ptolemy Philometor and Euergetes, both suspecting and fearing Antiochus, agreed on a joint-sovereignty, and a union against him. They sent for help to Rome; and when the consul Aemilius Paulus had finally conquered Macedonia then under Perseus, the Romans dispatched the Macedonian fleet to Alexandria, with three ambassadors to Antiochus, in order to enjoin peace. Caius Popilius, who was the head of the embassy, with his colleagues, met Antiochus near Alexandria, and tendered to him, before salutation, the decree of the Roman Senate, which enjoined upon him to desist and return. Antiochus took and read it, and replied, that he would consult with his friends what he should do. Popilius then drew a circle around him in the sand, with his staff, and told him that he must give a final answer, before he left that circle. Antiochus astonished and intimidated, assented to the Romish decree, and bound himself to obedience. Popilius, who, although familiar with Antiochus while he was at Rome as a hostage, had before refused to give him his hand, now courteously saluted him, as did also his colleagues. No wonder that he went back *enraged*, as our text declares. For some reason he owed the Jews a peculiar grudge; he, therefore, on his way home, sent a detachment to pillage Jerusalem under Apollonius. The excesses which they committed, are related in 1 Macc. 1: 30 seq.— בְּרִית קֹדֶשׁ as in v. 28.— עָשָׂה has an implied complement in the meaning of the preceding זָעַם, i. e. *he carried out* or *executed* the promptings of his anger, or רְצוֹנוֹ may be supplied, (as in the version), which comes to the same thing.— וְשָׁב, before וְיָבֵן, seems to mean *again*. A *return* to Syria would here be inapposite. *To have an understanding*, etc., *again*, implies a former transaction of a similar nature; and this is mentioned in v. 28.— עֹזְבֵי בְרִית designates *apostates from Judaism*, see vs. 32, 33, also 9: 27, and 1 Macc. 1: 11 seq. A considerable party from the first, had labored to introduce heathenism. In v. 32 they are called מַרְשִׁיעֵי בְרִית very significantly, i. e. *apostates from the covenant.*

(31) And forces from him shall stand up, and they shall profane the sanctuary, the strong place, and they shall remove the perpetual offering, and set up the abomination that maketh desolate.

מִמֶּנּוּ, *from him*, refers to the detachment mentioned above, under Apollonius. יַעֲמֹדוּ designates the taking of a position ready for active effort, in opposition to *sitting* which is the attitude of quiet and remission. 1 Macc. i. gives a full account of all the shocking deeds of Antiochus. — הַמָּעוֹז, the *stronghold*, should be compared with בָּמוֹת *high-places*, so often designated as the locality of temples. There was a fort and a garrison attached to the temple-grounds; and this Antiochus took possession of. Hence *the strong-hold.* It is doubtless mentioned, because of the peculiar annoyance which this enabled the tyrant to give to the temple-service and the worshippers. So 1 Macc. 1: 37, "And they shed innocent blood round about the sanctuary, and they defiled the sanctuary." —*Remove the perpetual offering;* comp. 8: 11, 13. 9: 27. 12: 11; and for the facts, see 1 Macc. 1: 45 seq. — הַשִּׁקּוּץ מְשֹׁמֵם, I take in substantially the same sense as in the controverted עַל כְּנַף שִׁקּוּצִים מְשֹׁמֵם in 9: 27. But in this last passage, the plural designates *idol-abominations*, and serves merely as an adjective to כְּנַף, while מְשֹׁמֵם, *the desolator*, probably designates the image of Jupiter Olympius, which stood over the eagle with out-spread wings at its feet. In the passage before us, הַשִּׁקּוּץ means, as I apprehend, *the abomination* or *abominable idol*, i. e. the image of Jupiter, which, being placed near the altar on which sacrifices to that heathen divinity were offered, made the sanctuary desolate, as to all true worshippers and legal sacrifices and rites. None but apostate Jews would frequent such a place. See the graphic history of this, in 1 Macc. 1: 37 seq. The article is here appropriately employed, inasmuch as 8: 13 and 9: 27 had already made the reader familiar with the abomination now adverted to. What is ascribed to הַשִּׁקּוּץ here is, in 9: 27, ascribed to the *bird of abominations* in connection with the image standing over it. The article might be employed before מְשֹׁמֵם, because it is a renewed mention of the word; but if the speaker meant not so much to point out here an individual image to which this name was appropriately and peculiarly given, as to designate the kind of quality it possessed, or agency which belonged to it, i. e. the causing of desolations, the article might well be omitted. To translate by *the abomination of the desolator*, i. e. of Antiochus, is out of question; for the *construct state* does not admit the article before it. The law in respect to the participles having the article prefixed, is not equally stringent. If however אֲשֶׁר be supplied, (and in cases almost without number it is merely implied and not expressed), then מְשֹׁמֵם without the article would be the normal construction, inasmuch as the word is then a *predicate* of a relative clause.

(32) And the violators of covenant shall he render impious by flatteries; but the people who know their God shall wax strong and do prosperously.

מַרְשִׁיעֵי בְרִית, *transgressors* or *violators of covenant;* what covenant? If simply the *holy* covenant were intended here, should we not have בְּרִית קֹדֶשׁ, as above in vs. 28, 30? Or, at all events, as it would seem, הַבְּרִית, that is, with the article appended. But as we have neither of these, we may presume that the speaker meant to be understood in a generic way, without nicely defining the whole class as such; which last would also demand the article between the two words. I take the meaning to be *covenant-violators*, where the word *covenant* designates a quality or rather characteristic of the מַרְשִׁיעֵי. We say familiarly, *covenant-breakers;* and so the Hebrews. As these, however, are here placed in contrast with יֹדְעֵי אֱלֹהָיו in the sequel, it must include the violators of the holy covenant. But the expression would seem not to be limited merely to the holy covenant, but, inasmuch as the apostate Jews who joined with Antiochus, not only broke the covenant of the Hebrews, but also the covenant with Egypt, which had been in existence more than a century, it designates this characteristic also. Hence the *omission* of the article in order to give latitude to the expression. Comp. נְגִיד בְּרִית, in v. 22 above. — Antiochus flattered, as usual, the Jewish party who favored him, and thus prepared them for all the impieties of the heathen, יַחֲנִיף. — אֱלֹהָיו with sing. suff., because it relates to עַם. I have translated it by the plural, because its antecedent is a noun of multitude. By *those who know God* is meant Mattathias and his party, as described in 1 Macc. ii.; who resisted the decrees of Antiochus with success, for awhile, and were joined by many of the pious Jews. — וְעָשׂוּ denotes the success which attended their first efforts, the verb, as usual in this book, being a *constructio praegnans.* — יַחֲזִקוּ designates the accessions that were made, and the strength thus acquired by the party of the pious.

(33) And the wise of the people will give instruction to many, but they shall fall by sword, and by flame, by exile, and by plunder, for some time.

The wise of the people here means those who are intelligent in matters of religion. *Wisdom*, in the scriptural idiom, often means *the true knowledge of God.* — לָרַבִּים, with the article, *the many*, has reference to the *strength* of the party (which implies considerable numbers) who are said *to know God*, in v. 32; or it may mean *the mass of the people*, the οἱ πολλοί. Mattathias and his sons used great efforts to enlighten those, who attached themselves to the cause which they espoused. Persecution of course followed, on the part of Antiochus, in all the various ways here mentioned. — בְּחֶרֶב without the article, and so of the following nouns. In such cases, usage is divided between admitting and rejecting it. — יָמִים, as before, a moderate undefined period of time.

(34) And when they shall fall, they will be aided by a little help, and many will join themselves to them with flattering pretences.

When persecution was going on with severity, a spirit of opposition to it was of course awakened among the people, and many were moved to join the party of Judas Maccabaeus and his brethren. But among these were not a few who acted hypocritically, desirous of saving their credit as zealous Jews, but ready to desert when danger pressed hard upon them. Mattathias punished severely the apostate Jews (1 Macc. 2: 44), as did also Judas (1 Macc. 3: 5—8); and of course many through

30

fear would dissemble before them, who still would not abide by them in the hour of trial.

(35) And some of the wise shall fall, to make trial of them, to purify, and to cleanse, unto the time of the end; for it will yet be at the appointed time.

מִן partitive, as often before = *some of.* In the three verbs in the Inf., there is a gradation of meaning. צְרוֹף is properly applied to the *smelting* of silver ore; בָּרֵר to *purifying* it from the dross; and לַלְבֵּן (Hiph. for לְהַלְבֵּן) to *whitening* the metal and freeing it from all specks. The tropical meaning is obvious. — בָּהֶם, who? the wise, or the רַבִּים? It seems to me that the nature of the case decides for the latter. Here is a large accession to the party of the pious. Some of them are hypocrites. Persecution puts them to the test. Such among them as are true-hearted, are purified and shine brighter; such as are not, become known by their shrinking from trials. — בָּרֵר Inf. Piel. — *Time of the end* means the end of Antiochus' reign or life. The end, however, is not to come immediately after the success of the pious party, alluded to in vs. 33, 34; but still, it will come at a *time appointed* (מוֹעֵד) by an overruling Providence. The pious may be assured, that the evils in question will not go beyond this set time.

(36) And the king shall do according to his will, and he will exalt and magnify himself above every god; and against the God of gods will he speak wonderfully; and he will prosper until the indignation is completed, for that which is decreed will surely be done.

The king is of course Antiochus, pointed out in the preceding context. The next verse shows that he had no regard to his country's gods; and his whole course of life, his plundering the temple at Jerusalem, and finally in Elymais, show the reckless and impious character of the tyrant. — *The God of gods* is the supreme God, i. e. Jehovah. How striking the traits of Antiochus as to *haughtiness.* and *blasphemy* were, may be seen by comparing 7: 8, 11, 25. 8: 25. — נִפְלָאוֹת, participial plur. fem. used adverbially, § 98. 2. *c.* *Wonder* or *surprise*, arising from the singularity or strangeness of any thing, are expressed by this Hebrew word. — נֶעֱשָׂתָה, Niph. Praet., thus indicating the *certainty* of the event decreed, § 124. 4. — *The accomplishment of indignation* means the indignation of God against the apostatizing and heathenish Jews.

(37) To the gods of his fathers will he have no respect, nor to the delight of women; to no god will he have any respect, but he will magnify himself above all.

יָבִין, when it means *attend to* or *pay regard to* anything, may take

אֶל or עַל after it, which, specially in the later Hebrew, are often coincident in meaning. See Lex. under Kal of בִּין. The intimation here given, of *disregarding the gods of his fathers*, shows that the previous Grecian kings of Syria had adopted the gods of the Syrian nation; while Antiochus, who had lived some years at Rome, had learned to despise the Syrian gods, and to prefer the Jupiter Olympius and Xenios of the Romans and Greeks. The establishment at Jerusalem of the worship of the first, and at Samaria of the second, shows that Antiochus was ambitious at times of imitating the Greeks and Romans. That he did not regard the Syrian gods, seems to be implied in 1 Macc. 1: 41 seq., where it is said, that "Antiochus wrote to all his kingdom, that they should be one people; and that each one should forsake its customs," in order to accomplish this. The passage has a special respect to religion. — חֶמְדַּת נָשִׁים, in this connection, where the objects of religious veneration or contempt are spoken of, very clearly seems to mean the famous goddess of the Syrians, *Astarte* or *Ashtoreth*. Both names come from the old Persian ستارة *(stārt)* the fem. form of the word *star* or *ʿstar*= our English *star*, and are only different modes of pronouncing the same word. This female deity, under different names, was worshipped in Africa, Syria, Phenicia, Cyprus, Greece, Rome, Babylonia, Persia, and some other countries. The *Mylitta* (=Heb. מוֹלֶדֶת, *generatrix*) of the East was the Venus of the West, the Neith of Egypt, the Astarte of the Syrians, the Anais or Anaitis of the Armenians; all uniting in the worship of the power who represented maternal productiveness. In different countries, some of the rites were different; but there seems to have been an extensive agreement, in the shocking practice of obliging every virgin to sacrifice her chastity, as the most acceptable offering to such a goddess. Herodotus speaks with disgust of this, as practised at Babylon, I. 199. In Syriac the name is written ܥܣܬܪܘܬ, i. e. עַסְתְּרוּת. By turning to Jer. 7: 18. 44: 17, 18, 19, 25, the reader may see with what eagerness the Heb. women engaged in the worship of this *queen of heaven*, as the goddess is there called. The *King* of heaven was *Baal* = the sun. Syria seems to have first brought forward this divinity; at least, if we may pay any deference to the account given by Ctesias. We may well suppose, therefore, that the worship of it was zealously kept up there. Antiochus, it seems, paid little or no regard to this idol, viz. Astarte. Near the close of his life, he made an effort to plunder the temple of this same goddess (Anaitis) in Elymais, but was repelled by a rising of the people *en masse*, and forced to fly in disgrace, soon after which he died. In 1 Macc. 6: 1—4 is an account of this expedition; and in 2 Macc. 1: 13—16 is another account, in which the goddess in question is called *Ναναία*, (an appellative formed, as it seems to me, from Anaitis by vulgar pronunciation.) All these facts seem to make clear this much contested phrase, חֶמְדַּת נָשִׁים. The description is progressive; Antiochus not only despised the common gods of the Syrians, but even that divinity which most of all was worshipped by them, specially by females.

The third clause: *To no God will he have any respect*, is designed to go beyond either of the preceding declarations, which only show that Antiochus paid no regard to any of the national Syrian gods. The third clause asserts that the same was true in respect to all other gods. That he set up the worship of Jupiter Olympius at Jerusalem, and of Jupiter Xenios at Samaria, and began to build a most magnificent temple to Jupiter Olympius at Athens, and promised to build one to Jupiter Capitolinus in Antioch (Liv. XLI. 20), only shows his foolish ambition to imitate the Romans, and perhaps to surpass them in their own way. It still remained true, as the last clause declares, that *he magnified himself above every* [god.]

(38) But to the god of strong holds upon his pedestal, will he render honor, even to the god whom his fathers knew not will he render honor, with gold, and silver, and precious stones, and costly things.

מָעֻזִּים, not a proper name, (Theodotion Vulg. Luther), but a noun of quality which serves as an adjective to the preceding noun. *The god of strong holds* is the god who has power over them; and as it is plain, from a comparison of the preceding verse, that Antiochus overlooked his country's gods, and consequently that the deity now in question must be some foreign *war-god* unknown to the Syrians, it is altogether probable that Jupiter Capitolinus is meant; for to him did he undertake to build a temple at Antioch, adorned with every species of expensive ornaments.—בְּזָהָב וגו׳, all four nouns that follow are *anarthrous*, although the names of substances more usually have the article, § 107, 3. Rem. 1. b. But in such cases practice varies. For the sake of show, the Syrian tyrant most lavishly squandered his money in the building and adornment of temples.

(39) And he shall do (his will) in respect to fenced strong-holds with a strange god; whoever shall acknowledge he will greatly honor, and he will make them to rule over many, and land will he distribute as a reward.

A difficult verse, which has occasioned many discrepant interpretations. Lengerke makes *the fenced strong-holds* to mean *temples*, and the sentiment to be, that the tyrant will do for temples and their foreign gods the same thing that v. 38 says he will do in respect to the *god of strong-holds*, i. e. he will bestow many liberal presents upon them; a very improbable thing, except in a case where his vanity was concerned, as in the case of building a temple for Jupiter at Athens. Then this critic is obliged to supply כֹּה *(so)* before עָשָׂה, which here seems to be a forced construction. Continually in this book, as we have already seen, and specially in chap. xi., we have עָשָׂה in the sense of *effecting* or *accomplishing one's wishes* or *designs;* and this, in cases where no noun follows the verb. Occasionally רְצֹנוֹ follows; and this discloses the true filling up or complement of the brachylogical עָשָׂה. I take the word in the same sense here. An ellipsis of *so* (כֹּה) cannot be rendered probable by like examples. Maurer interprets thus: "And so shall he do to fortified holds with a strange god, i. e. he will enforce upon them the worship of Jupiter Capitolinus." The *so* is here to be supplied by the reader; but it is too important a word to be omitted. I understand the declaration to be, that, since Antiochus exalts peculiarly the *god of strong-holds*, he does this because of his success in attacking such places. The *strange god* here mentioned means a god which differs from that of Antiochus, or at least from the Syrian gods; in other words, he will conquer the fortified strong-holds of foreigners who worship a god different from his. Then follows אֲשֶׁר יַכִּיר (as the Qeri reads), i. e. *whoever acknowledges* him, his sway, or perhaps his *war-god*, shall recieve much honor. יַכִּיר is used absolutely in 2 Sam. 3: 36. Ps. 142: 5. We might render, in accordance with the Hebrew, *makes acknowledgment.* That he often liberally rewarded those who attached themselves to his cause, there is no doubt. That he bestowed the government of provinces or cities on leading men of this character, there can be no good ground to doubt. בָּרַבִּים with the article, as twice before, meaning οἱ πλείονες, or the mass of people within any particular limits. That an apportionment of *land* is mentioned in the next clause, is explained by his directions to Lysias, one of his generals, to root out Israel, and divide their lands among his friends, 1 Macc. 3: 32—36. That his adherents were to be thus rewarded, seems to have resulted from the poverty of his treasury at the time of making this arrangement; which is related in 1 Macc. 3: 29.

The clause *with a strange god* is not mainly designed for the description of a foreign strong-hold, but, while it imports this, עִם is employed to show that the strange god is included with the strong-holds, in regard to being within the grasp of Antiochus. Both *fortified place* and *strange god* are subject to his pleasure; see Lex. עִם, 1. *e.*, which explains the word by *communio sortis.* — בִּמְחִיר, *as a reward*, or *in the way of reward;* for the meaning of the noun, comp. Mic. 3: 11. Deut. 23: 19. For בְּ before a word indicating *price, reward,* see Lex. B. 9. *Our* mode of expressing the idea, I have given in the version above.

(40) And at the time of the end, the King of the South shall make war with him, and the King of the North shall rush forth like a storm against him, with chariots, and with horsemen, and with many ships, and he shall march into countries, and shall overwhelm and pass onward.

All history, says Lengerke, is silent respecting this last war of Antiochus, nor was he able to command the money and the forces to carry it on, specially in the face of the Romans who had forbidden him to intermeddle with Egypt. To the like purpose Maurer; and most of the earlier commentators assign vs. 40—43 to the category of *recapitulation.* They suppose a general summary of the whole of Antiochus' reign to be here introduced, before the conclusion of his history. This is not impossible, inasmuch as v. 29 seq. seems to repeat what had been said in v. 24. But I must regard it as very improbable. The repetition at so much length here of events so minutely related as the preceding, is at least inopportune, and not often the manner of the author. Lengerke asserts the entire improbability of another and fourth invasion of Egypt and Palestine, on the ground that Antiochus was too weak and too poor to collect forces enough to carry on such a war with success. But 1 Macc. 1: 27 seq. shows us, that after Antiochus had heard of the notable defeat by Judas of his general, Seron, "he was enraged, and gathered together all the forces of his Kingdom *παρεμβαλὴν ἰσχυρὰν σφόδρα, an exceedingly great encampment.*" These he paid profusely, while in an attitude of preparation for active service, and thus exhausted his treasury, 1 Macc. 1: 28, 29. To Lysias, his general, he left one half of his troops (1 Macc. 1: 34), which amounted to 47,000 (v. 39), with orders to subdue and partition out Palestine, (vs. 35, 36). *Weak,* then, Antiochus was not, at that time. It is indeed true, that neither Appian, nor Polybius, nor Justin, nor Livy, nor Josephus, have given us any particulars about this latest war of Antiochus; but who that has read their Syrian histories, does not know that mere summaries, scraps, and fragments, are all that remain of these writers in respect to Antiochus? Josephus depends on 1 Macc.; and this is mainly confined to the exploits of Judas and his brethren. Rosenmueller very appositely remarks: "Caremus omnino integra aliqua et continua de rebus Antiochi narratione, quae a suae aetatis scriptore aliquo fide digno literis sit mandat." The *argumentum a silentio,* specially in respect to ancient history, is far from being cogent and satisfactory. On the other hand, the accuracy of the statements in the book of Daniel, respecting the domain of Alexander's successors, is on all hands admitted in other cases. Here it has narrated the events of an expedition in vs. 40—43, with its usual minuteness, and apparently in regular order. Why should this testimony be rejected? Nor does it stand alone. Jerome refers to Porphyry, who wrote against the book of Daniel, as saying with respect to vs. 40—43, that they relate to the last war of Antiochus, near the close of his life. Jerome's words run thus: "These things Porphyry refers to Antiochus, because (quod) he fought, *in the eleventh year of his reign*, against Ptolemy Philometor, his sister's son, who having intelligence that Antiochus was coming, collected many thousands of troops. But Antiochus, like a mighty tempest, with chariots, and horsemen, and a numerous fleet, entered many countries, and laid waste every thing as he passed along; and he came to Judea, and fortified a tower there from the ruins of the city walls, and then proceeded to Egypt." Let it be remembered, that Jerome does not say a word to contradict this statement, although it made for his favorite object to do so if he could, inasmuch as he might then refer the passage to his favorite *Antichrist*. I do not see why the testimony of the book before us, the full confirmation of it by Porphyry, and the apparently consenting attitude of Jerome, do not place the matter before us fairly out of the reach of *destructive* criticism.

The time of the end is here, as repeatedly before, the time in which the reign of the tyrant was to come to its end. It need not be limited to a few days, or even months, but cannot reasonably be extended to a period far back from the death of Antiochus.—הִתְנַגַּח, lit. *thrust at*, borrowed from the action of horned beasts in their contests. Tropically, *to attack, make war upon.*—וְיִשְׂתָּעֵר, Hithp. of שָׂעַר, with transposed שׂ. It is a very expressive word, שַׂעַר meaning *tempest, storm.* וּבָאֳנִיּוֹת, read *u-bho-ᵒnĭy-yōth*, for there is no *article* here, (both the preceding nouns are anarthrous), but בָּ is a prep. and conforms its punctuation to the Hateph Qamets that follows, § 28, 2. § 9, also p. 35 note 2. The ships belonged to the Syrian fleet.—בָּא בְּ, *march into, invade.*—בָּאֲרָצוֹת, i. e. *divers countries* under Egyptian sway, in Coelesyria and Palestine. *Shall overwhelm and pass onward*, an image borrowed from the overflowing of a mighty stream, which sweeps away every thing opposed to it.

(41) And he shall march into the goodly land, and many shall fall, but these shall be delivered from his hand, Edom, and Moab, and the chief part of the sons of Ammon.

אֶרֶץ הַצְּבִי, see on 8: 9. 11: 16. — רַבּוֹת plur. fem. taken substantively, =

multitudes. The *masc.* verb that follows is simply *constructio ad sensum,* inasmuch as *multitudes of men* are meant. — יִכָּשְׁלוּ does not here so much import excision as defeat, subjugation. It would seem, therefore, that this last invasion of Palestine, by Antiochus, was not of so severe and bloody a character as his former ones. The reason is obvious. The country was mainly subdued, and held in slavish subjection under his oppressive military government, and he had a large party of heathenish Jews in his favor from mercenary and other considerations. The few that still resisted were overborne and prostrated. In the great battle with Gorgias (1 Macc. iv. B. C. 165), Judas had but 3000 men, and these but ill equipped, 1 Macc. 4: 6. The last invasion of Antiochus, therefore, is merely touched here, but not dwelt upon, because its effects could not well be compared with those of former invasions. *Edom, and Moab, and the chief part of the sons of Ammon,* dwelt in the south, and south-east of Palestine, and out of the range of Antiochus' direct march to Egypt. But why are they noted here? The implication seems to be, that they then belonged to the domain of Egypt, and would naturally have been overrun and subjugated by Antiochus, had they been within the line of his march. The אֲרָצוֹת, *some countries,* of the preceding verse, designates those countries subject to Egypt, through which the Syrian invader passed on his march into that country. There seems to be another implication, also, in what is here said, viz. that Antiochus, in his former victorious expeditions, had taken possession of those countries, through which, on the present occasion, he did not march. We can hardly see any motive for particularizing the countries in question, unless these circumstances were as they are here supposed to be. The countries of themselves were of little significance in the time of Antiochus. But if the speaker, on this occasion, is describing an invasion by Antiochus later than the others and different from them, and has added this apparently minute circumstance which we are now considering, in order to specificate and make a distinction, then all is not only plain but also significant. Evidence of the attention of critics to these circumstances, I have not indeed been able to find; but to my own mind they appear to be important to the explanation of the text. How else can we account for such a mention of the petty nations in question? And indeed, as *Moab* was no more a nation at the actual time of Antiochus, how could a writer of the book of Daniel, living (as the Liberalists will have it) after the death of Antiochus, have thought of inserting Moab here? If he did, it was from a set purpose to mislead his readers respecting the time in which he lived. This however does not accord with the views respecting him, which even

Lengerke professes to entertain, Einl. z. Comm. s. LXXXV. seq. The sketch before us exhibits one of those minute touches, which seem to point to the hand that must have drawn it. — רֵאשִׁית does not mean the *better part* in the sense of larger portion (Rosenm.), but the *chief part* in the sense of the *leading* or *predominant part.*

(42) And he shall thrust forth his hand against several countries, and the land of Egypt shall not escape.

אֲרָצוֹת, *some* or *several countries;* like יָמִים, *some time.* These, from the order in which they are mentioned, are different from those in v. 40, and probably are those countries lying on the eastern border of Egypt, through which Antiochus would pass in his line of march. — מִצְרַיִם, as a *country*, takes the fem. verb sing. after it. That the invasion of Egypt was an actual and a successful one for a time, seems to be indicated by the next verse.

(43) And he shall rule over the treasures of gold and silver, and over all the costly things of Egypt, and the Libyans and the Ethiopians shall wait on his footsteps.

The treasures of Egypt were doubtless what he was in quest of, for he was now straitened in respect to money; comp. 1 Macc. 3: 29. — הַזָּהָב וגו׳ with the article, as is the more common usage before the names of substances, § 107. 3. Remarks, *b.* — The Libyans on the northwest, and the Ethiopians on the South of Egypt were attached to the Ptolemaean dynasty; comp. Ezek. 30: 5. The possession of Egypt gave Antiochus dominion over those countries. — בְּמִצְעָדָיו, lit. [shall be] *in his steps*, i. e. shall follow on after him as their leader.

(44) And with tidings from the East and from the North shall they disturb him, and he shall march forth in great wrath to destroy and to lay waste many.

While Antiochus was in the attitude of inflicting a final blow upon Judea, tidings reached him, that the Parthians in the East, and the Armenians in the North, had rebelled and refused to pay tribute; Tacit. V. 8. Appian. c. 45. 1 Macc. 3: 37. Armenia he soon subdued, and marching thence to Elymais, in order to replenish his treasury by robbing temples, he there met with a signal repulse, that was soon followed by his death. — As to שְׁמֻעוֹת, fem. plur., it seems to be associated with a verb plur. *masculine.* Lengerke here accuses the writer of negligence. Does he not know, that the Hebrew is susceptible of another translation than that which he gives it? What difficulty in making the noun the Acc. of instrumentality, and translating thus: *With* [evil] *tidings shall they terrify* or *agitate him*, the verb being the third pers. plur. with the indef. Nom.? I apprehend the true pointing however, to be יְבַהֲלֻהוּ, i. e. it is a verb singular = *one shall terrify him* = he shall be terrified.

(45) And he shall plant his lofty regal tent between the sea and the holy and beautiful mountain, and he shall come to his end, and none shall help him.

אַפֶּדֶן, like the Arab. *padan*, means *lofty palace;* suff. form אַפַּדְנוֹ. What the text means is, that the tent of Antiochus was a splendid structure, like that of a palace, made *lofty* as the rallying point of the whole army. — יַמִּים, lit. *seas*, but the plural of nouns designating great and extensive masses, is often employed in preference to the singular, § 106. 2. *a*. The Mediterranean sea I take to be meant here. — The usual construction, בֵּין . . . לְ is here employed, as marking the intermediate ground between two objects ; see Lex. לְ. A. 2. — *Beautiful holy mountain* is so named, because that mountain is meant on which the holy temple was built. קֹדֶשׁ as taking the place of an adjective, does not well admit the article, since of itself it merely marks here an abstract quality. *Omission* of the article before pure abstracts, is the predominant, but not exclusive, usage in Hebrew.

The fearful end of Antiochus is again predicted, as in 7: 26. 8: 25. 9: 27. But why is the mention of Antiochus' encampment between the Mediterranean and Jerusalem here brought again to view, after the speaker had already followed him to the East? For the purpose of *impression*, I should say, rather than from any necessity of the case. 'Look at the contrast,' (the speaker would seem to say) ; '*now*, Antiochus encamps in his lofty tent like a palace, meditating the overthrow of the holy city and temple ; *next*, we see him in disgrace — and even in the agonies of death, stricken by an invisible and an irresistible hand.' The interest with which a Hebrew would survey this picture, may be imagined, but cannot well be described.

CHAPTER XII.

[Nothing can be plainer, than that the beginning of this chapter belongs to the prophecy which precedes. It is not only a continuation of the address of the same speaker, but evidently a sequel of the same subject. The division, if made at all, should have been made at the end of 12: 3.]

(1) And at the same time, Michael, the great prince who protects the sons of thy people, shall stand up, and there shall be a time of distress which never was since the existence of any nation until that period; and at that time thy people shall be delivered, every one whose name is found written in the book [of the living].

וּבָעֵת הַהִיא cannot well be made to mean either *at some future time*, or *at some* [indefinite] *time*. הַהִיא means *that, that same ;* and when the question is asked: The *same* as what? the answer of course must be: The same which the preceding context has already indicated. Hävernick's labored arguments to show that a Messianic period, i. e. either before the first or second period of Christ's yet future coming, is meant, have failed to make any convincing impression upon my mind, because I cannot abandon the plain meaning of the words, and accept of a conjectural interpretation in the room of it. Nor, when he refers to Theodoret, Calov, Cocceius, L'Empereur, Geier, and Roos, as being of the same opinion, does this satisfy me. These interpreters applied the preceding chapter, at least the latter portion of it, to *Antichrist* instead of Antiochus, and therefore, consistently with their views, they interpreted the passage before us in a corresponding manner. Not finding it *exegetically* possible for me to take the same course, I cannot follow them in relation to בָּעֵת הַהִיא. The appeal to Matt. 24: 21, 22, by Hävernick, gives as little satisfaction as the preceding view, notwithstanding he calls it *entscheidend* (decisive). It remains yet to be shown, that this passage does not apply merely to the destruction of Jerusalem by the Romans. Hoffman (Würdig. etc. s. 313) finds fault with the exegesis which Hävernick and others of the like opinion suggest; but he has substituted another in its room, which seems, at least to me, to be no better. He refers בעֵת הַהִיא first to the period of Antiochus' death; and then immediately proceeds to say, that what follows refers to a period at the close of the history of nations, i. e. to a time of trouble and distress which shall come at a distant period upon all nations, while the Jews shall be defended and delivered by their guardian angel. Are the Jews then to be a *separate* people to the end of time? And this too, after Paul has decided that under the gospel "there is neither Jew nor Greek," that "there is one and the same God of the Jew and of the Gentile," and also that "they who are of the faith, [whether Jews or Gentiles], are the children of Abraham," and Israelites in the true and highest sense. The idea is inconsistent with that of a truly Messianic period. Besides, if we closely connect (as we must) v. 1 with its first clause, how can the phrase *at that time* fail to designate the time when the events there described will take place? But how are they to take place near the time when Antiochus died, and yet take place near the end of the world? There is an utter inconsistency in this. With Maurer, then, and Rosenmüller, I follow the simple grammatical interpretation; and that can have but one meaning, i. e. *that time* means the same period mentioned in the preceding context, and this is the time at or near the close of the reign of Antiochus. — *Michael your great prince;* this angel has already been brought to view in 10: 21. The epithet *great* seems to import one of the rank of ἀρχἄγγελος, i. e. an angel of superior rank or dignity. — הָעֹמֵד עַל, *stand over*, designates an attitude of *defending* that over which one stands; or, which is equivalent, *a guardianship over* any person or thing. Hence the whole phrase amounts simply to *Michael, your guardian archangel.* The meaning is, that when all the distresses come upon the nation that will take place near the period of Antiochus' death, (for בָּעֵת הַהִיא is not a strictly definite or limited period, although it cannot extend farther back than the context allows), then will Michael interpose and deliver the Jewish people, at least all of them who shall not have been destroyed by previous oppression and persecution. — נִהְיְתָה means somewhat more than simply *was.* It appears like the passive of a Hiphil = *was caused to be*, i. e. *took place, happened.* — מִהְיוֹת, *since the being of*, Inf. nominasc. in the const. state. — The repetition of the words *at that time* before the last clause, gives definitiveness to the expression, making it more specific. — Not all of the Jews are to *escape*, for many will fall martyrs to the cause. That the expression here is strong, and even hyperbolic, is clear. Yet how many hundreds are like it, in the Scriptures and in all oriental writings! — But *all who are found to be recorded in the book* [of the living], will be saved by the interposition of Michael. — בַּסֵּפֶר, *in the book*, i. e. in the well known *book of life*, or rather *of the living.* The metaphor is taken from city registers, where the names of all the citizens were enrolled; and as soon as any man died, his name was erased. *The book of the living*, therefore, is God's book, in which those who are to outlive the Antiochian persecutions stand recorded as survivors. Who will escape, none knows but he in whose book the destinies of all are recorded. That there is an ellipsis of חַיִּים in the text, is plain from the nature of the case, and from a comparison with the passages in Ex. 32: 32. Isa. 4: 3. Ps. 56: 8 (9). 69: 28 (29). In a little different sense is the phrase used in Ezek. 13: 9. Phil. 4: 3. Rev. 3: 5. 13: 8. 17: 8. 21: 27. 22: 19. but still in one altogether analogous. Sentiment: Be not overwhelmed with sorrow, at the prospect of times such as those of Antiochus; when they come, your guardian angel will protect and save all, whom the counsels of Heaven have determined shall escape.

(2) And many of those who sleep in the dust of the earth, shall awake, some to everlasting life, and some to shame and everlasting contempt.

Our English translation, and that which I have given, runs thus: *And many of them who sleep in the dust.* But this seems contrary to the accents, for these join מִיְּשֵׁנֵי וגו׳ with the verb יָקִיצוּ; and the sense thus given compares well with the N. Test. ἐγείρεσθαι ἐκ νεκρῶν, 1 Cor. 15: 12, 20. Comp. John 5: 29. But this is not important as to the general meaning of the clause. — As to רַבִּים, I cannot regard it as designed to contrast with *few*, i. e. with some, or a few, who do not rise, but as an expression equivalent to our word *multitudes*. Ezekiel, in respect to the valley of dry bones, says of them when raised up : חַיִל גָּדוֹל מְאֹד מְאֹד. There is no intimation in the context of a party *not to be raised up*. רַבִּים cannot mean the *good* only, for *all* of them are to be restored to life in the way of reward, and in order to be made happy ; nor can it mean the *evil* only, for they are raised up to suffer the retribution due to them, *shame and everlasting contempt;* which plainly is not affirmed of all. In Rom. 5: 15, 17, *οἱ πολλοί* is used by Paul in the like manner ; i. e. as equivalent to *multitudes, the mass*. Leng. stoutly denies the application of these last passages to the present case. But he first assumes an *a priori* ground, by asserting that a *general* resurrection cannot be meant. He says, that " the whole spirit of the book, so hostile to all other religions, makes against the admission of a general resurrection." The Jews only, he further says, are represented by the book before us, as capable of such a blessing. Yet, under another head of objections, he says, that " the author of our book expected *all nations to be converted to Judaism*." Where then are those to be found, who are *not Jews* at the time of the resurrection ? But dismissing this, who are they that come forth to *the resurrection of damnation?* If the Jews are all to be saved, and the heathen are not to be raised up at all, who are those that are to be raised up to condemnation ? These questions force us upon another and a different exegesis. — לְחַיֵּי עוֹלָם, frequent in the N. Test. ; but nowhere else in the Old. It shows progress in the clearness with which a future state of happiness was discerned, in the time of Daniel.— לַחֲרָפוֹת, plur. of intensity, sing. חֶרְפָּה. — דִּרְאוֹן, const. form of דְּרָאוֹן, *aversion, contempt*. This also is united with עוֹלָם; and with this clause is to be compared John 5: 29. Matt. 25: 46.

It should be noted, that the softened word *sleep* is here employed for *death ;* an image which could hardly become current, excepting among those who believe in a future state, and in the resurrection of the body.

The great and difficult question about this passage is : Does it relate to a period *immediately succeeding* the death of Antiochus, or to a *subsequent* and *undefined* period? The difficulty which some critics have had, about conceding a belief in a resurrection to the ancient Hebrews, seems now to be in the main removed. It is conceded, even by most of the so-called *liberal* critics, that Is. 26: 18, 19, to which some add Ezek. 37: 1—14, (and to which I should be disposed to subjoin Ps. 16: 11. 17: 15), recognize the doctrine in question. Daniel stands not alone, in this respect. The allegation that this was only a later doctrine of the Hebrews, borrowed from the system of Zoroaster, even Lengerke confesses has been refuted by Hävernick, in his Comm. s. 509—519. On the question now before us, in respect to the application of vs. 2, 3, in the present chapter, I would, with diffidence, make some suggestions, which are the result of my own reflections.

It seems to me, that *analogy* of the prophecy before us with other prophecies in the book of Daniel, may help to satisfy the mind of an inquirer. In chap. ii. we have the four monarchies, which are followed by a fifth that is Messianic, 2: 44, 45. Immediately following the same four monarchies, and after the death of Antiochus, the Messianic kingdom is predicted again, 7: 26, 27. In chap. viii., the last three kingdoms out of the four are again described, and the death of Antiochus is represented as before; while, in this particular case, the vision goes not beyond the death of the same Antiochus, (the little horn, 8: 9, 25). In the present case, the analogy of the prophecies in chaps. ii. vii. is followed with the exception, that inasmuch as the vision took place in the third year of Cyrus, and of course *after* the Babylonish empire was destroyed, the latter empire is omitted. The death of Antiochus, and the troubles of the Jews at and near that period (11: 45. 12: 1), precede, as in chaps. ii. vii., the prophecy respecting the Messianic kingdom. Verses 2 and 3 I regard, therefore, as having reference to the Messianic period and its ultimate results. No notation of time, however, is here made, at the beginning of the second verse. The prophetic vision looks forward to the distant future, but it is undefined as to any particular time. Just the same is the case in chap. 7: 27; for there is simple prediction of events, without any definite limitation as to the time when they will take place. In 2: 44, however, there is an *indefinite* notation of time, in passing to a description of the Messianic kingdom. The words are, בְּיוֹמֵיהוֹן דִּי מַלְכַיָּא אִנּוּן, *in the days of those kings*, (viz. of the four kingdoms before mentioned), shall the God of heaven set up a kingdom, etc. I have said *indefinite notation of time*, because, although strictly considered בְּ would mean *in*, i. e. *within* or *during*, yet as merely the word *days* is here joined with it, there are of course no definite limits drawn, and the writer is not confined to particular years. It is evident, moreover, that if the strict meaning of בְּיוֹמֵיהוֹן be urged, it would bring the prophecy connected with it to mean, that the Messianic kingdom should commence *during the time of the four monarchies*, or at all events during the fourth monarchy. This would be contrary to the whole tenor of the prophecies in chap. ii. vii. and viii.; for these all represent the dynasties as *successive* and not contemporaneous. Matter of fact shows that such was the case. The *fifth* kingdom, therefore, i. e. the Messianic one, is in like manner *successive*. But the intervals of time are no where distinctively marked, in respect to the succession. I am aware that Lengerke and some others have strenuously maintained, that the writer of the book of Daniel expected the Messianic kingdom *immediately* to succeed the death of Antiochus. But how they can insist on this, when they date the rise of the book *after* the death of that tyrant, I am unable to see. Did the writer shut his eyes against all the signs of the times? for they surely indicated nothing of this sort. And could he rationally expect that others would give credit to such a representation, in spite of those signs? Both of these suppositions are incredible. If an earlier writer, say in or near the time which is usually regarded as the period of Daniel, could predict all that is related in chap. xi., one may well suppose that he might know whether the Messianic kingdom was to follow in quick and immediate succession, or not.

The result seems to be, that the phrase, *in the days of those kings*, like ἐν ἐκείναις ταῖς ἡμέραις, is a general expression of a somewhat indefinite period of time, which however is not to be greatly extended. In most cases, it occupies some considerable time for one empire to fall and another to rise. The phrase in question must therefore be understood according to the reason and nature of such cases.

In the text now before us, we are embarrassed by no designation of time. Verse 1, indeed, has a limitation. But I understand v. 2, as making the transition, after the death of Antiochus and the vindication of the Jewish cause by Michael, to the new Messianic kingdom. Instead of repeating the description of the power and greatness of that kingdom, as in chaps. ii. vii., the speaker here utters what more resembles the view taken in 9: 24. He refers us to the consequences that would ultimately follow under a new dispensation; and to such of those consequences as are intimately connected with his preceding theme. Chap. 11: 33 shows the ravages of the tyrant among the faithful Jews. It is natural to ask: Is there no adequate future reward for the noble martyrs in question? And equally natural to ask: Is there no adequate future retribution for the tyrant? The gospel, i. e. the principles of the Messianic kingdom, "brings life and immortality to light." In due time all the faithful martyrs will be rewarded, and their persecutors adequately punished. Thus much the new dispensation makes certain. And it is because of the immediate connection of this subject with the preceding account of the tyrant's cruelties, that this great truth is here placed before that which is announced in the third verse. In common cases, the sentiment of v. 2 would naturally *succeed* the matter brought to view in v. 3. It was more directly to the speaker's purpose in the present case, to reverse this order.

What objection now of any serious importance can be raised against this view of vs. 2, 3? That the prophecy in xi. xii., viewed in the light of *analogy*, may in all probability be interpreted in the manner now proposed, is clear. Such a method is characteristic of the prophecies of Daniel. That all attempts to accommodate vs. 2, 3, to mere moral or political changes or revolutions, which occurred after the renewed dedication of the temple by Judas Maccabaeus, or after the introduction of Christianity, have proved to be failures, scarcely needs to be said. They are so evidently against the plain deductions of philology, and they do such violence to the language, that no one can easily satisfy himself with them, unless he has some preconceived plan or theory to maintain. The only difficulty that seems to press upon us, is that resulting from the want of words appropriate to the designation of time. On this point one can make the appeal only to thorough and practised readers of the other prophetic parts of the O. Test., who must often have met with the like difficulty. It is easy to point to examples. Isa. ii. iv. is a comminatory prophecy against the Jews then living, i. e. the Jews of Isaiah's time. In 4: 2—6 is (as I cannot well doubt) a Messianic passage, following immediately a description of the evils to be suffered by the rebellious Jews then living, and joined to that description even by a בַּיּוֹם הַהוּא, vs. 1, 2. But if any refuse to regard Isa. iv. as Messianic, how can they dispose of chap. viii. ix.? Surely the threatenings, and the execution of them, uttered in chap. viii., have respect to the Jews of Isaiah's time. Yet in making the transition from this period to the Messianic sequel in chap. 9: 1—7, not a word is said as to the interim of more than seven centuries which actually elapsed. Here all are constrained to acknowledge a prediction truly Messianic; and yet the case is the same, as in the passage under consideration.

Let us now advance another step in the examination of Isaiah, and we shall see the same arrangement of prophecy, still preserving the same characteristic. Chap. x. is a splendid description of the progress, the desolating power, and the overthrow of the Assyrian king. Chap. xi. is a continuation of the same prophecy, (as the וְיָצָא at the beginning clearly indicates), and this contains one of the most signal of all the Messianic predictions. Yet an unpractised or uninformed reader would never suspect, that the Messianic day was to be seven centuries after the fall of the Assyrian invader, since the prediction of it stands in direct contact with that respecting the fall of the same Assyrian. In chap. xix. the smiting and fall of Egypt is predicted, vs. 1—22; while vs. 23—25 seem plainly to recognize a Messianic reign, which is to be universal. This, be it also noted, is introduced with a בַּיּוֹם הַהוּא, which is apparently stronger and more specific than the בְּיוֹמֵיהוֹן אִנּוּן of Dan. 2: 44. In chap. xxvi. xxvii., the same thing is virtually repeated, for I take Isa. 27: 13 to refer to a Messianic period. In Isa. xxxi. is reproof of the Israelites, who sought foreign aid, and a prediction, that when they become penitent, the Messianic king shall arise to execute justice, and the Spirit also be poured out, chap. xxxii. Here the time is not specified; but the latter prediction is in continuity with the former one respecting Jewish disobedience. For the rest of Isaiah, chap. xl.—lxvi., whether we assign it to the prophet whose name it bears, or to a later writer, makes no difference with the point before us. The continual intermingling and junction of the return from the Babylonish exile, and that from the exile of sin, shows that the writer has not taken the least pains to throw into his composition any distinctive notes of time. He has left this unrevealed; and so much so, that one is strongly moved, in view of his whole composition, to repeat the declaration of the Saviour: "The *times* and *seasons* hath the Father put in his own power," Acts 1: 7.

The like result would follow a scrutiny of the other prophets. But I deem this to be superfluous, after all that has been said above. I may safely assume, for the present, that the want of any notation of time, in a transition to the later Messianic period, is no bar at all against regarding vs. 2, 3, as being connected with that period. These verses open the prospect of the future and final destiny of men, both the righteous and the wicked, and show us the final result of the Messianic period.— As to the question, whether רַבִּים should be referred only to the *pious* Jews, there is no need of a moment's delay. No such Jews surely will be raised up to *everlasting contempt*. I do not see any good reason, why רַבִּים should be limited merely to Hebrews, excepting that the martyrs of the preceding chapter belong to that nation. Undoubtedly the general truth before us, respecting a future restoration, is *introduced* because it comes in appropriately as connected with the subject in hand. And inasmuch as a *general* resurrection is here taught, it can be no other than that which will take place, at the end of the gospel dispensation.

(3) And the wise shall shine as the splendor of the firmament, and those who turn many to righteousness, as the stars forever and ever.

That מַשְׂכִּלִים designates such men as are described in 11: 33, 35, seems undeniable. But I would not limit the meaning merely to the Jewish leaders and martyrs, nor to the pious Jews in general of Antiochus' time, but, while it includes those and shows what their reward will be, the leading object seems to be to say, that the influence and success of such men at a future period, shall be greatly augmented. The truth is here distinctly taught, that all such will have a glorious reward, in the resurrection of the just.—זֹהַר, as a noun, is confined to the later Hebrew, but is frequent in the Rabbinic and Arabic. *The splendor of the firmament* designates the shining appearance of the welkin, with all its suns and stars. So the last clause of the verse has explained it.—The article is inserted before כּוֹכָבִים, because it comprises a whole class.

Such then is the nature and character of the Messianic period; these are truths which it will reveal and inculcate. The sequel of all the adversity of the Hebrews and of their trials, will be marked by their elevated happiness, and by retributive justice to their persecutors; which is a state of things that every pious Hebrew must anxiously have desired.

If after all any one is not satisfied with this view of vs. 2, 3, there is another view, not more analogical, but perhaps more simple, which he can take. This is, that vs. 2, 3, merely declare the doctrine of *a general resurrection and retribution*, in and by which retribution, the martyrs and the faithful will meet with ample reward, and persecutors and faithless men will meet with condign punishment. In this simple view no serious difficulties are to be met with, on the supposition that the clause וּבָעֵת הַהִיא extends its influence only over v. 1; and the examples above given show that we may assume this position in full conformity with usage elsewhere. This position being taken, all serious difficulty is removed indeed with respect to both of the last proposed interpretations. The first of them can appeal to analogy in its defence; the second may lay claim to being unembarrassed by any lack of Messianic traits in vs. 2, 3. The positions assumed are religious truths, appropriate indeed to every age, but specially revealed here for the consolation of the oppressed and the persecuted. The appropriateness of the sentiments to the place which they occupy, none can reasonably deny.

[The strong resemblance between what follows and Rev. 22: 6—21, must be apparent to every attentive reader. The object of the closing part of Daniel is, to render secure the record of the preceding prophecy; to reassure the mind of the prophet in respect to the *limited* continuance of the severest trials predicted; and finally to cheer him with the certain prospect of his own final and personal reward.]

(4) Moreover do thou, Daniel, close up these sayings, and seal the book, until the time of the end. Many shall make diligent search, and knowledge shall be increased.

The same direction in respect to *closing up* is given in 8: 26, with regard to the prediction which there precedes. See the remarks on the passage. Each is a plain case. *Close it up and seal it*, that no additions or subtractions may be made, nor anything changed or tampered with. The truth and credit of prophecy will then be established, when it is seen that facts strictly accord with it. In 8: 26, however, a specific reason is given for *closing up* the prophecy, which is, that *it is for a long time*, i. e. has respect to a distant period, and so is not a matter of immediate concern in respect to any duty to be presently performed. Just the reverse of this is the case in Rev. 22: 10, "Seal *not* up the words of the prophecy of this book, *for the time is* NEAR," i. e. it is wanted for immediate use, inasmuch as the fulfilment of what is predicted speedily commences. What those can do with this direction and the reason for it, who pertinaciously adhere to the system of interpretation, which refers the Apoc. mainly to the *papacy*, when this papacy scarcely began its rise in half a thousand years from the time when the book was written, — is a question that no one has yet been able satisfactorily to answer. Enough for the case in hand, that *the time of the end* was more than three and a half centuries after the period named in 10: 1. — הַדְּבָרִים, with the article, must refer to the narration and predictions in x. xi.; and strictly speaking only to those, for the command has respect to sealing up what had been revealed during the interview described in chap. x. — הַסֵּפֶר, with the article for the same reason as before; *the book*, viz. that in which the words just adverted to are recorded. — *The time of the end* is the same as the קֵצו in 9: 26, also in 11: 35, 45, viz. the end of Antiochus' reign and life, for he is the principal character in the preceding picture. The prophecy mainly concentres in him, and has respect to him; therefore, when he makes his appearance, the time for perusing it, and meditating upon it, will come. — So we are taught by what follows: *Many* יְשֹׁטְטוּ, *shall make diligent search*, i. e. this is the tropical meaning of the word; the literal one is: *shall run to and fro in search* of something. It does not mean *to run through, percurrere*, a book, i. e. to glance over its pages, but to *make diligent search* after its contents. Much less does it mean, (as it is often interpreted), *to run hither and thither* in respect to localities, i. e. to travel about, as the means of increasing knowledge. The speaker designs to say, that the book, when the time of the end draws nigh, shall be sedulously studied and investigated, and that the knowledge of duty, and of what God designs to do, will be greatly increased by such an investigation. — הַדָּעַת, *the knowledge*, viz. of the prophecy in question. To put סְתֹם and חֲתֹם into the form of a prediction, and to give them a mere tropical sense, i. e. make them to signify, that the prediction must be kept secret and no disclosure of it made, nor understanding of it acquired, until the events take place which it predicts, (as Hengstenberg and Hävernick do), seems to be a forced and unnatural process. How is *knowledge to be increased*, if the prophecy means nothing intelligible, until after it becomes *history*? If this be indeed so, then Daniel, or at any rate the angel who communicated with him, must have differed widely from Paul, who says: "I had rather speak five words in an intelligible manner, so that I may instruct others, than ten thousand words in an unintelligible language."

(5) And I Daniel looked, and behold! two others were standing, the one on this side on the bank of the river, and the other on that side on the bank of the river.

Two others — other than who? The answer must be: Other than the angel mentioned in 10: 5 seq., 10, 16, 18, who made communications to him. These two additional angels now appeared, to render more impressive the closing scene. — הֵנָּה ... וְהֵנָּה, lit. *here and here,* which is the Hebrew method of expressing *here and there,* or *on this side and on that side.* To make Gabriel one of these *other* angels, who had all along been the speaker, as Lengerke does, seems foreign to the simple meaning of the text.

(6) And [one] said to the man clothed in fine linen, who stood over the waters of the river: Until how long shall be the end of these wonderful matters?

Evidently these new actors in the scene are introduced, partly in order to give more explicitness to the designation of time in the prophecy. Daniel, as we have seen (10: 8, 9, 15—17), was greatly affected with the appearance of the heavenly messenger. Out of compassion to his weakness, an angel here appears, and asks the question which Daniel doubtless was desirous should be put. One of the two *other* angels, therefore, is represented as addressing the question to him who had made the communication, 10: 11, 19, comp. also 10: 5 seq. — We express the idea of עַד מָתַי by the simple *how long?* I have translated a little differently, in order to imitate the Hebrew. — *The end of the wonderful matters* is the death of Antiochus, in whom centres the wonderful disclosures of the preceding vision. So the article before פְּלָאוֹת indicates. We shall see that such is the design of the question, by the answers that follow. — That the man *clothed in fine linen* was *over the waters of the river,* i. e. stood on the banks that rose over the river, is plain from 10: 4, 5, 6 seq.

(7) And I heard the man clothed in white linen, who was over the waters of the river, and he lifted up his right hand and his left to heaven, and he sware by him who liveth forever, that [it shall be] at a time, and times, and a half, even when the crushing of the power of the holy people shall be completed all these things shall be accomplished.

The latter half of the verse parallelizes with the first half, but expresses the time of completion by referring to *events,* rather than to portions of time. The lifting up of *both hands* toward heaven indicates unusual solemnity; for commonly only one was lifted up, Gen. 14: 22.

Ex. 6: 8. Deut. 32: 40. Ezek. 20: 5.—וַיִּשָּׁבַע, *he bound himself by an oath.*—בְּחֵי עוֹלָם, lit. *by the lives of eternity*, or *by the living one of eternity*, the adjective חַי being adopted in the latter case as the ground form. The sense is the same in both cases. God may be described by a noun abstract, as well as concrete; just as we say, *the Divinity*. The plur. of the noun is intensive, if we adopt the first mode of expression.—As to *the set time* (מוֹעֵד), *times, and a half*, we have merely to compare the Chaldee עִדָּן וְעִדָּנִין וּפְלַג עִדָּן, in 7: 25, with the notes there. The events and limitation of time, are the same there as here. The *three and a half years* in which Antiochus made the sanctuary desolate, is what is aimed at in this case. *Times*, thus used, means *years.*—וּכְכַלּוֹת נַפֵּץ וגו׳, lit. *and when there shall be a completion of breaking in pieces;* not with Ges., Win., De Wette, Leng., *when the dispersion shall be completed of a part of the people*, etc. יַד, in this case, is not *part, portion*, but *power*, as often elsewhere. The idea is, that when the power of the Jewish nation is as it were crushed or broken in pieces (נַפֵּץ), then the death of Antiochus shall take place, and the fulfilment of the last and leading part of the preceding prophecy shall be accomplished.—קֹדֶשׁ again without the article, being used in the sense of an adjective, i. e. as designating an abstract qualification.—אֵלֶּה, *these things* has a verb plur. *fem.*, for this is the more usual construction with the names of things that are of a *neuter* gender.

(8) And I heard, but I understood not; and I said: My lord, what is the latter end of these things?

Still benumbed as it were in the use of his senses, Daniel heard indeed the voice of the angel, but did not fully comprehend his meaning, either as to the exact measure of the time, or as to the nature of the events which would make up the crisis or consummation of the whole. Consequently, on somewhat recovering himself he asks for more special information. By אַחֲרִית cannot be meant, as some have maintained, a time subsequent to the three and a half years; it must be the latter part of those years.

(9) And he said: Go, Daniel, for these things are closed up and sealed, until the time of the end.

לֵךְ in the sense of *depart*, viz. from life = *die*, cannot be meant here, for what has the closing and sealing up of the prophecy to do with Daniel's death? But if we understand it in the sense of *go away*, (which the phrase often has), the connection shows it to be a request or command to *desist* from making further inquiries. The reason given is, that the revelation is already completed, it is closed up and sealed, until the time when men shall be interested to make diligent inquiry for its meaning.

(10) Many will purify themselves, and become clean, and make trial of themselves; but the wicked will do wickedly, and none of the wicked will understand, but the wise shall understand.

This is a mere summary of the events comprised in the prediction, by which the angel means to say, that Daniel should acquiesce in these general views, without seeking further minute explanations. — יִתְבָּרְרוּ, Hithp. of בָּרַר. — וְיִצָּרְפוּ, Hithp. with assimilated ת, § 53. 2. *b.* It is unusual for ת to assimilate with צ, as here; comp. § 53. 2. *a.* — *None of the wicked will understand*, viz. the words of the prediction, so as to be restrained by it from doing wickedly. They will go on in spite of its threats and predictions, despising the idea of consulting it or of listening to it. — On the other hand, the wise, near the time of the end, will make diligent inquiry (יְשֹׁטְטוּ), both for the sake of instruction and consolation, and they will attain to a right understanding of the predictions.

(11) And from the time of removing the continual sacrifice, and of setting up the abomination that shall be made desolate, will be a thousand, two hundred, and ninety days.

הוּסַר Inf. Hoph. as a noun in the Gen. — לָתֵת, also Inf. of נָתַן in the Gen. after מֵעֵת implied. The לְ is put before it to indicate its Genitive condition, § 113. See the very same verbs and nouns in 11: 31, and comp. 8: 11—13. In 11: 31, שִׁקּוּץ is described as מְשֹׁמֵם, *causing desolation;* here as שֹׁמֵם, i. e. *that which is to be destroyed*, or *ought to be destroyed*, which is more apposite to the present tenor of the discourse. *The* 1290 *days* are more specific than the phrase, *time, times, and a half*, in v. 7 and also in 7: 25. The latter (*time*, etc.) is as it were a round number, three and a half first equalling the one half of the sacred number *seven*, and the fractional part equalling the half of one year. In such a case, minute exactness of course is not to be expected. But the thirty additional days here (over 1260 days = forty-two months = three and a half years), are doubtless designed as an *exact* account of time during which the detestable abomination continued in the temple. The *terminus a quo* is the time when Antiochus first removed the daily sacrifice, which was probably near the end of May or at the beginning of June in B. C. 168. Judas Maccabaeus removed this שִׁקּוּץ, and purified the temple, Dec. 25 of B. C. 165, making the time in question, i. e. three and a half years, as nearly as history will enable us to compute it. There can hardly be room for doubt that the statement in our text is minutely exact. The work of Judas, then, is the *terminus ad quem* of the period in question.

(12) Blessed is he who waiteth, and attaineth to one thousand three hundred and thirty-five days.

I must refer the reader to the historical facts stated in the Notes on 7:

25 above, for information in regard to the course of events near the end of Antiochus' reign. It appears from 11: 40—44 above, that Antiochus made another and final invasion of Egypt, near the close of his life, after which he marched against Palestine. Mattathias and his sons, in the mean time, had been organizing the party of the pious, and Antiochus was exceedingly indignant at the efforts which they had made and the success with which they were attended. In 1 Macc. 2: 26—37, we have an account of the situation of Antiochus, while in the "glorious land." His treasury was empty. He had already robbed the temple of all which it contained that was of any value, and he was necessitated to look to another quarter. He left half of his army, therefore, with Lysias, one of his favorite officers, and passed over the Euphrates in order to rifle the countries of the East. First he went through and subdued Armenia (τὰς ἐπάνω χώρας, v. 37), and then turned off to rob the temple in Elymais, where he met with disgrace, and finally with death. Not long after the departure of Antiochus, Lysias began the contest in Palestine in serious earnest; but Judas uniformly triumphed in all his encounters; and so decisive was one of them over Lysias, that Judas proceeded to purify the temple, and to restore its worship, 1 Macc. 4: 36 seq. All this must have occupied some months; and the consecration of the temple took place the 25th of Dec. 165 B. C. Of course Antiochus had had sufficient time for his conquest in Armenia and for his advance to Elymais, before the winter had far advanced. It was in early spring that he undertook the robbery of the temple in Elymais; after which, on his retreat, the news met him of total defeat in Palestine, and helped to increase the malady under which he was then laboring. In 1 Macc. 6: 1 seq. is an account of the close of the life of Antiochus, and of his failure at Elymais. If now we count onward, from the consecration of the temple by Judas, to the time when Antiochus deceased, we shall perceive, at once, that the period of 1335 days is in all probability the period of Antiochus' death. From the time that the daily burnt offering was removed by Apollonius, at the command of Antiochus, to the time of reconsecration, were 1290 days. From the same *terminus a quo* to the death of Antiochus, were 1335 days, i. e. forty-five days more than is included in the preceding period. History has not anywhere recorded the precise day of Antiochus' death; so that we cannot compare the passage before us with that. But we are certain as to the order of events, and as to the season of the year, as well as the year itself, in which the death of this king took place. Of the *general* accuracy there can be no doubt; and such are the chronological designations of this book, that we may safely rely, in this case, on its minute accuracy.

Blessed is he that waiteth, more exactly: *O beatitudines expectantis!*

— הַֽמְחַכֶּה, Dagh. omitted after the article, § 20. 3. *b*. The lexicon gives us only *expecto* as the meaning of חָכָה, i. e. to wait with hope or expectation. This may be the shade of meaning here; but if so, it will imply a knowledge, on the part of those who wait, of the predictions before us, and a looking for their accomplishment. This is not a bad sense. But still, I apprehend the meaning of the speaker here to be: 'Blessed are those who *continue* in life, and attain to the happy period of Israel's liberation!' No one, in view of the horrid cruelties and impieties of Antiochus, can wonder that those are congratulated, who had been subject to his dominion and are now delivered from it. On the ground assumed above, all is congruous and well adapted to complete the symmetry of the whole prophecy.

(13) But as for thee, go onward to the end [of life]; and thou shalt have rest, and stand up for thy lot at the end of time.

I take לֵךְ to be used here, in a somewhat different shade of meaning from that which the word has in v. 9. Here it is equivalent to our: *Depart in peace.* In other words, it is a courteous method of dismissing an auditor, when all is told which was designed to be communicated. Otherwise expressed it would be: *You now have leave to retire.* The tone of voice, in such a case, would decide whether one was dismissed in anger or in peace. Here the latter is quite certain. — לַקֵּץ, *to the end*, i. e. the end of Daniel's life, and hence the article, which in such a case is equivalent (as in Greek) to the pronoun-adjective *thy*. — תָּנוּחַ, *rest* in a peaceful grave. — וְתַעֲמֹד, the opposite of *resting*, viz. *standing up*. The meaning seems plainly to be: *Thou shalt obtain a resurrection, rise up* (= קוּם, as עָמַד often does in the later Hebrew). תַּעֲמֹד has also the adsignification of *stand up firmly*, being placed in a permanent condition. V. 3 above entitles us to make all these conclusions in respect to the meaning here. — For the illustration of the גֹּרָל, comp. Acts 26: 18, κλῆρον; Col. 1: 12, τὴν μερίδα τοῦ κλήρου; Rev. 20: 6, μέρος ἐν τῇ ἀναστάσει. The allusion is to the *lot* or *inheritance* given to the Hebrew tribes, who took possession of Palestine. Daniel's part is in the heavenly Canaan. — לְקֵץ הַיָּמִין, lit. *at the end of the days.* The word *days* means undefined or unlimited time, and the whole expression exactly meets our English phrase, *at the end of time.* The article stands before the noun as comprising a *totality*, *at the end of time.* A comparison of this with v. 3 shows at least that there is here no new or strange doctrine. Daniel is to have a place, among those "who have been wise and turned many to righteousness." An assurance full of comfort to him, who was now very far advanced in life; and full of comfort to all who walk in his steps, and are animated by his spirit.

CRITICAL HISTORY AND DEFENCE

OF

THE BOOK OF DANIEL.

---

§ 1. *Personal History of Daniel.*

THE only authentic source whence we can draw this, is the book which bears his name. His character and the peculiar incidents of his life have indeed given occasion to many apocryphal narrations respecting him; but these mostly belong to a later period, and are unworthy of critical confidence.

According to the statement in Dan. 1: 1—3, Nebuchadnezzar the king of Babylon besieged and took the city of Jerusalem, in the third year of Jehoiakim king of Judah, i. e. B. C. 607. With many of the vessels of the temple which he sent to Babylon, there were also, as the sequel of the narration shows us, a company of young Hebrews of royal or princely origin brought to the capital of the conqueror. Among these, Daniel and his three friends, Hananiah, Mishael, and Azariah, were the most comely and conspicuous. These, therefore, were given in charge by Nebuchadnezzar to his master-courtier, Ashpenaz, to be supported at the expense of the king, and instructed in the language and sciences of the Chaldees, in order that they might be fitted in due time, to become the personal waiters and attendants of the monarch.

The age of Daniel, when he was carried into exile, is no where stated in his writings; but he and his friends are called יְלָדִים, (v. 4). This word, in Hebrew, characterizes the period from the age of childhood up to that of manhood, and might be translated *boys, lads,* or *youth.* Ignatius (Ep. ad Magn.) says, that Daniel was twelve years of age when he went into exile; Chrysostom (Opp. VI. p. 423) says that he was eighteen; Epiphanius says: ἔτι νήπιος ὤν; Jerome (adv. Jovin. III.) calls him *admodum puer.* Of course, these are but mere guesses, or at best but floating traditions. Still they cannot be far from the truth. The nature of the case, and the usual custom of Oriental monarchs to prepare for themselves the most active and sprightly waiters from the highest classes of society, are sufficient vouchers for the probability, that Daniel was not more than some twelve or fourteen years of age, when he was brought to the court of Nebuchadnezzar.

That Daniel was of *regal* descent, is by no means improbable. According to Dan. 1: 3, the captives whom Nebuchadnezzar had sent away were either of *regal* or of *princely* extraction. The history of that period, in Kings and Chronicles, seems to warrant the supposition, that the Jewish lads in question were *hostages*, who were drawn from the upper classes of society at Jerusalem, in order to secure the quiet and submission of the Jewish king and his nobles, in their tributary condition.

Daniel's first developments of character showed that he was possessed of sincere and ardent love for the law of God as contained in the sacred books of his country, and also of great firmness and integrity. Nor did the early buddings of his youth disappoint the expectations which they raised; for they ripened into precious and abundant fruit in his maturer age. Daniel declined to feed on the luxurious viands of the Babylonish monarch; and in order to shun such food as the law of Moses had prohibited, he sought and obtained leave of his guardian, for him and his companions to live on a vegetable diet. With signal success they pursued this mode of living, until the time came for them to be called into the service of the king; Dan. 1: 5—18. To attribute, as some do, the conduct of Daniel on this occasion of abstinence to excessive superstition, seems neither candid nor equitable. The laws of Moses were simply obeyed, and nothing more. The least that can be said of these laws is, that certain kinds of food are absolutely prohibited by them, in all cases where abstinence is feasible, and life and health are not endangered by it.

It appears from 1: 17, that Daniel and his friends became acquainted with all the knowledge and science and wisdom of the Chaldees; while Daniel himself was distinguished from the others by the power of understanding and interpreting dreams and visions. In relating this fact, however, the prophet is careful to declare, that God, and he only, had bestowed these gifts upon him and upon his companions.

When called before Nebuchadnezzar, at the end of their three years' course of education, he and his companions were found by that monarch to be far more skilled in all science and wisdom, than the Babylonian astrologers and sacred scribes; 1: 20.

Not long after this, Nebuchadnezzar had a dream, which occasioned him great agitation of mind and disquietude. But the particulars of that dream had eluded his memory. In this state, he summoned all the Babylonish Magi and soothsayers before him, and demanded of them, on pain of death, to disclose to him both the dream itself and its interpretation. This they felt to be impossible; and they therefore sought for delay, in order that in some way the king might be either pacified or deluded. The king refused to grant the delay sought for, and ordered the whole mass of this order of men to be destroyed. In this state of things, Daniel interposed, having first sought by earnest supplication of himself and his friends that God would reveal to them the matter in question, and having obtained a favorable answer to his prayer. The Jewish prophet repaired to Nebuchadnezzar's audience-chamber, and there disclosed all the particulars of the dream, and gave the significant and ominous interpretation thereof. Nebuchadnezzar, stricken with awe and astonishment, commanded oblations to be made to him, made him ruler or satrap over the province of Babylon, and placed him at the head of the Magi and all the learned men of his capital; ch. ii.

In this exalted station, Daniel did not forget or neglect his friends, with whom he had so long and so intimately been associated. He requested the king to bestow some office upon them; who, in compliance with his wishes, made them overseers of his affairs in the province of Babylon.

It lies on the face of Daniel's narration, that he had little or nothing of the spirit of jealousy and self-exaltation. Most heartily did he rejoice in the honor done to his companions. They, as well as he, were found by the king to be far more skilled "in all matters of wisdom and understanding," than the Magi and astrologers, (1: 20). They made common cause with him, as to the decree that the Magi should be cut off; and their supplications, as well as his, went up before the throne of mercy, that the secret of the king's dream might be revealed. And although Daniel was the chosen instrument of disclosure, they participated with him in the honors and emoluments that ensued.

Nor is this all. Daniel has perpetuated the memory of his friends, as taking a place among the noblest martyrs for truth that stand recorded on the pages of sacred history. The third chapter of his work is wholly devoted to an account of their martyrdom, and its results. They refused to do homage before the gigantic idol of Nebuchadnezzar; and by his command were cast into a furnace of fire, heated far beyond the customary degree. There they were accompanied and protected by an angel of God, who assumed a radiant and dazzling appearance. When Nebuchadnezzar saw him, he was terrified, and commanded the objects of his vengeance to quit the furnace. Once more, as in the case when his first dream was interpreted, this passionate and haughty monarch was constrained to give glory to the God of the Hebrews. He even issued a proclamation, forbidding his subjects to speak any word of reproach against that God; chap. iii. Thus has Daniel consigned to perpetual remembrance, admiration, and heart-felt applause, his three pious and distinguished companions.

We have no designation of the time when these events happened. In all probability, however, it was not until some time after Nebuchadnezzar had finished his conquests, and amassed an almost boundless store of wealth. Usher names 580 B. C. as a probable period, i. e. eight years after the destruction of Jerusalem and the temple.

It is a singular circumstance, that Daniel is not at all mentioned, in connection with the affair on the plain of Dura, but only his companions. But to make this a serious objection against the truthful narrative of the book, as Lengerke has done, is hardly just or generous. Was not Daniel prime minister of the king? And could not a man, "who was ruler over the whole province of Babylon," be so busied with some special duties of his office, as to be unable to attend the dedication of the image? And might he not, for some good reason which respected the affairs of the State, have been excused by the king himself from attendance on that occasion? These suppositions are neither unnatural nor improbable; and if they are well grounded, they account satisfactorily for the absence of Daniel.

Sometime after this, (Usher supposes some ten years, i. e. B. C. 570), Nebuchadnezzar had another dream, which gave him deep anxiety. He applied in vain to the magicians and astrologers to interpret it. His application first to them, was not improbably a measure dictated by policy, so as to save Daniel from the envy that would be excited by a primary application to him. It would seem that the king had already seen enough of their impotence, to convince him that they could do nothing in such an exigency. The issue of this application was like that in the case of the former dream; although the king had not now forgotten his dream, but related it. Daniel was at last introduced. The king told him what he had seen, in the visions of the night. The prophet was deeply affected with it, and out of kind feeling and gratitude to the king was reluctant to give the explanation. But the king insisted on it. He therefore told him plainly, that the dream foreboded the loss of his throne and of his reason, for seven years. This came upon him. At the end of this period his reason returned, and he was again welcomed by his nobles and his people to the throne so long vacant. On this occasion he issued a proclamation narrating all these facts, and extolling and honoring the

Most High, who had thus abased and chastised him, and also had mercy upon him. Dan. iv. is occupied with this proclamation.

It seems to be quite probable, that Daniel retained his place during the *interregnum*, and as chief of the Magi, he was of course the temporary viceroy of the king. He too would be most likely to keep the throne in abeyance for Nebuchadnezzar, because he was confident of his being ultimately restored to his reason and his place. In other hands, the government would, in all probability, have gone over to some son of Nebuchadnezzar, or some fortunate aspirant to the vacant throne.

Not improbably the death of Nebuchadnezzar occurred soon after this. He reigned forty-one years; or, inasmuch as the Jews reckoned from the time of the first invasion of Palestine by him, he reigned, according to their reckoning, forty-three years. If Usher is in the right, the end of the seven years' mania, would be in the forty-first of his reign.

Our next account of Daniel has reference to some thirty years after the period just named. In B. C. 538, Belshazzar is on the throne; and he was now at the close of the seventeen years of his reign. Inflated with pride and vain glory, he made a great feast to a thousand of his lords, and under the intoxicating influence of excessive banqueting, he sent for the vessels of the house of the Lord, which were deposited in the temple of Belus. These were brought, and subjected to the promiscuous use of the revellers, who, in honor of their idol-gods, drank from them, and chanted the impious praises of their deities, mixed (no doubt) with many reproaches to the God of Israel. In the midst of this Bacchanalian tumult, heathenish impiety, and contempt, a hand like that of a man, guided by some invisible being, appeared to the king and his companions, writing upon the wall some mystical letters which none could read. The Magi and astrologers were summoned; but all in vain. Finally, the king's mother addressed the terrified assemblage, and told them what had been done by Daniel in the way of interpretation, during the days of king Nebuchadnezzar. Daniel is forthwith sent for, and large promises of reward are made to him, in case he should read and explain the writing upon the wall. He did so; and the explanation was, that the death of the king, and the extinction of his dynasty, was near at hand. In that very night, Cyrus made himself master of the city, and the king was slain; chap. v.

It would seem that Daniel, under this last monarch, had retired to private life; for the king seems to have, at that period, no particular knowledge of him. Nothing is more common in the East, than the entire change of the civil ministry after the death of a king. The new king is usually jealous of the old ministers on account of their acquired influence, and prefers for his confidants those whom he has well known and with whom he is familiar. It is quite probable, therefore, that Daniel withdrew from the high public station which he had occupied, after the death of Nebuchadnezzar. But still, that he might have been employed in minor affairs, and in the provinces, seems to be made probable by 8: 2, 27. We find him in Elam, as there stated, when his second vision occurred; and here he did the king's business, v. 27. Belshazzar, however, in accordance with his promise, bestowed costly decorations upon him, and made him third ruler in the kingdom. But this honor lasted only for an hour. The death of Belshazzar, and the destruction of his dynasty, followed immediately after the elevation of the prophet.

Darius the Mede, who had long been leagued with Cyrus in the subjugation of Asia Minor, now assumed the throne of Babylon. Under him Daniel held a most conspicuous place, being the first of three presidents or viceroys of the kingdom; 6: 1, 2. But the splendid acquisitions and talents and honors of Daniel greatly disturbed his colleagues in office, and they, moved by envy, sought to destroy him. By appeals to the pride and ambition of Darius, they obtained a decree from him, that no one should, during thirty days, ask either God or man for anything, except the king himself. Daniel, who was a man of prayer, disobeyed this decree. As usual, he repaired to his *sanctum* in the upper story of his house, and there, as he was wont, prayed three times every day. He was watched, and reported to the king. The latter was greatly distressed at the intelligence, because of his attachment to Daniel; but he was obliged to yield to the demand of his nobles, that the penalty of the decree should be inflicted. Daniel was cast into a den of lions. But there he was kept in safety, by an angel commissioned for this purpose. The king, on discovering this, ordered him to be taken out of the den, and also that the men who had maligned him, with their wives and children, should be cast into the same den. There they were instantly torn in pieces.

We have no further authentic particulars of the life of Daniel. We know merely, from the dates of his prophetic visions, that the first of these occurred in the first year of the reign of Belshazzar, about 555 B. C. The second was in the third year of Belshazzar's reign, i. e. during 553 B. C. In both these cases he was deeply affected in body and mind, the matter of the visions being portentous of much coming evil. His third vision was in B. C. 538, in the first year of Darius the Mede. In this case, an attentive perusal of the prophecies of Jeremiah had brought him to see, that the seventy years of exile which had been predicted, were near their close. With fasting and prayer, he besought the Lord most earnestly to forgive his offending people, and to accomplish his promises in respect to their return from exile. On this occasion, the angel Gabriel was sent to make some new and portentous communications to him. They respected the laying waste of Jerusalem the profanation of the temple, and the persecution of the godly. The famous period of seventy weeks is a part of what Gabriel declared on this occasion; which was probably understood by Daniel, but has hardly been explained or agreed upon in any after age. This is undoubtedly among the most difficult passages in all the Bible.

Down so late as 534 B. C., i. e. in the third year of Cyrus' reign, we meet with the most peculiar of all Daniel's prophetic visions, including chaps. x.—xii. The larger part of chap. xi. seems more like a history of what had past, than a prediction of the future. So Porphyry understood it; and he grounded his main objection to the *prophetic* nature of the book, on this view of the chapter in question. In this particular he has had not a few followers, within a recent period. There is truly nothing like it, in all the Bible. Even our Saviour's prediction respecting the destruction of Jerusalem, will not compare with it in respect to minute historical detail. The terrible catastrophe that followed the quarrel of Antiochus Epiphanes with the Jews, seems to have been the principal burden of all Daniel's prophetic annunciations; and in this last vision, he has advanced far beyond any example of minuteness in his earlier disclosures.

The vision closes, appropriately, with kind and comforting assurances to Daniel, in a personal respect. He needed them. His bosom had beat so high and so long with patriotic feeling, that now, when liberation from the Babylonish exile was at hand, it was very trying to look forward and see the future miseries and vexations of his people. Never did that people raise up a truer patriot, or possess a warmer and more faithful and constant friend.

At the time of this last vision, Daniel must have been some 84 years of age. There is nothing uncommon, however, in this; for not a few persons of temperate and abstemious habits attain such an age, with little or no diminution of mental vigor. But as we find not his name among those Jews who returned to Palestine, it is probable that his age, and perhaps his offices, prevented him from undertaking such a journey.

It is singular enough that the existence of such a man at Babylon, during the exile, should have recently been doubted, and even denied. Besides Moses, there is hardly any one of the Hebrew prophets that has obtained so much celebrity. There are none whose wisdom, and dexterity, and elevation, and influence, have been more celebrated among the Jews. It would be as reasonable to deny that David or Solomon were real personages, as that Daniel was. That he was *such* a man as the book that bears his name represents him to have been, may indeed be denied by skeptical criticism; but that a distinguished man, of such a name, lived and flourished at Babylon, during the exile, cannot be denied with any more probability than the existence of Nebuchadnezzar can be denied. None of the Greek historians mention such a king as Nebuchadnezzar at Babylon. Are we then to conclude that there was none? We might as well do so, yea do so with even a better face, than we can deny the existence and offices of Daniel.

That Daniel has ever been placed by the Jews among the foremost rank of their prophets, is quite clear. Josephus, near the close of his Antiq. Jud. Lib. x., after giving a summary of all the historical parts of Daniel, concludes by saying that "the merits of this man must excite the wonder of all who hear of them. Everything succeeded to admiration with him, as *one of the greatest prophets*. Not only during his lifetime, was honor and glory bestowed on him by kings, and by the multitude, but after his death he is held in perpetual remembrance. For his writings, which he left behind him, are now read by us, and through them we believe that Daniel held converse with God, for he not only predicted things to come, like other prophets, but definitely limited the period when they should take place." Such was the view which this most distinguished historian and learned priest of the Jews, took of the person and work of Daniel; a view common to all his countrymen at that period, and to nearly all ever since that time. The author of 1 Macc. (2: 59,60) has expressly referred to Daniel and his companions, and ranked them with other Jewish worthies of the highest note. The apocryphal books of Susannah and of Bel and the Dragon, make Daniel the hero of their romantic tales; and the former speaks of him as deciding the case of the adulterous judges, when he was yet a youth. Finally, Ezekiel, the contemporary of Daniel, and like him in exile, speaks of him (about B. C. 584) as a shining example of uprightness and of wisdom, ranking him with Noah and Job, 14: 13, 18, 20. In another passage (28: 3) he refers to Daniel as a preëminent examplar of wisdom. The Saviour himself calls Daniel a prophet, and quotes his words as such; Matt: 24: 15. Mark 13: 14. Paul (Heb. 11: 33, 34) alludes to him; and John has taken him as a kind of model, throughout the Apocalypse.

The question, then, whether there was such a man as Daniel, conspicuous above most men, and beloved and honored of God, seems to be sufficiently vouched for by all these testimonies.

The attentive reader of the Scriptures will perceive, that the part which Daniel had to act, was not only conspicuous, but singular and very difficult. What other Hebrew prophet was ever called to such a course of action, at a heathen court, yea a court which then governed, as it were, the world? Jonah, indeed, had a short mission to the Ninevites; but briefly and grudgingly was it performed. Daniel, although a mere lad when brought to Babylon, preserved an incorruptible integrity of character as a true disciple of Moses, and ever lived uninfluenced by the luxury and splendor and honors of the Babylonish court. That he was a man of a most fearless spirit, is evident from the whole tenor of his life. That he did the duties of his station in the most able and faithful manner, is evident from the length of time in which he was prime minister of State. That he cherished the warmest emotions of patriotism toward his own country and people, is inscribed in high relief upon his whole book; but above all, upon his intercessions in their behalf, as developed in chap. ix.

Of Daniel's characteristics as a writer, and of the object, style, and qualities of his work, we shall have occasion to speak in the sequel.

§ 2. *Nature and Design of the Book.*

It is difficult to make a greater mistake in regard to these, than to suppose that he designed to write a continuous and regular history, either of himself, of the Jews, or of the kings of Babylon. So much of his early history is developed, as serves to cast light on the manner in which he became qualified to act the important part which fell to his lot. When this is accomplished, he is brought to view only on some great occasions, where his interposition seems to make a signal display of divine power and goodness. E. g. he interprets Nebuchadnezzar's first and second mysterious dreams. He explains to the impious Belshazzar the ominous hand-writing on the wall. He is elevated to the post of viceroy under Darius the Mede, and had a marvellous escape from the den of lions, into which he had been cast by the malignant artifices of envious courtiers. It appears probable from 6 : 28 and 10 : 1, that he retained a high post of honor, at least for some three years of the reign of Cyrus. These are all the incidents recorded of a life of some seventy years, in connection with the Babylonish court. To speak of a regular *biography*, then, as undertaken by Daniel, would indicate a very singular notion of what belongs to his book.

As to the Jews, not one word is said concerning them, either as to the good or evil that befel them, during their state of exile. What was their condition, and what their demeanor, the writer of the book of Daniel has not undertaken at all to inform us.

In regard to the native kings of Babylon, the names of only two of them occur, viz. of Nebuchadnezzar and of Belshazzar. Nebuchadnezzar reigned more than forty years, and made many conquests. But it is only on the occasion of his two dreams, and the consecration of his colossal idol, that he is brought to view, after Daniel becomes a member of his court. Belshazzar appears only on the last day of his life; and his Medo-Persian successors are brought to view in such a way, that we have only a single glance at them. Darius' sad mistake in yielding to the artifices of his courtiers to destroy Daniel, is graphically placed before us; but nothing further is disclosed respecting him. That Cyrus succeeded him in the throne of Babylon, is all that is said concerning him, excepting that he was the friend of Daniel.

The rest of the book is made up of four prophetic visions, seen between B. C. 555 and 534, i. e. in the later part of Daniel's life. These are *sui generis* both in respect to form and matter, to a certain extent; although in several respects they strongly resemble other visions of other prophets during the exile, e. g. those of Ezekiel and Zachariah. The main object of them is, to show the future condition and destiny of the Jewish people, after the exile and before the period when their great Deliverer should come.

Some critics have assumed, that Daniel undertook to write his own history and that of Babylon; or at least, that he ought to have done so; and then they take him to task for having performed his work so imperfectly and unskilfully. Others, perceiving how slender is the foundation on which all this is built, proclaim *(adunco naso)* that the whole book has a mere paraenetic or hortatory object in view; and that this design is reached just as well by romance or allegory as by facts. They compare the narratives in Daniel with the parables in the Evangelists, and aver, that in both cases the end is reached equally as well by romance as by facts. In this way, all investigation as to actual events or occurrences is superseded, or rendered a matter of indifference, and it comes out that we have before us, in the book of Daniel, a mere fiction or allegory, a part of which has pretended facts for its basis, and the other part is underlaid by supposed prophetic revelations and visions.

When the question is asked: What book in the Old Test. or the New stands on such a basis? it becomes difficult to give a satifactory answer. Strauss, indeed, and those who sympathize with him, have no difficulty in answering the question; for they take the same position as the objectors before us, with regard to the Gospels themselves, viz. that they are but a tissue of allegories and romance. But men of more sober minds can find but little satisfaction, in the assumption of positions such as these.

When it is said (as it sometimes has been), that the design of the author of the book of Daniel is wholly *paraenetic*, the assertion plainly goes too far. The *prophetic* parts of this book have surely but a slight tinge of this cast. But still, if I might be permitted to define the word *paraenetic*, I should not wish to deny that the book at large has this characteristic, even in a high degree. I understand this word to designate something that is *edifying*, and this in the way of *warning* and *exhortation* or excitement. Most surely the occurrences related by Daniel are deeply interesting in their nature, and highly adapted to make a deep impression on all minds, of the power and goodness and holiness of the Supreme Being. Could Daniel, or any other prophet, preach more impressive sermons to Nebuchadnezzar and his court, than the explanation of the monarch's dreams, and the defeat of his murderous purposes on the plains of Dura? Was there ever a more impressive scene, than that in Belshazzar's palace, on the night of his death? Could a thousand books or addresses have made an impression so deep and awful, on the riotous and idolatrous courtiers of the king, as the mysterious hand writing on the wall, and the interpretation of the same? Or was there any means of securing to Daniel his place in the court of Darius, and afterwards in that of Cyrus, so stringent and effectual, as the deliverance of the Heb. prophet from the den of lions? All this undoubtedly is *paraenetic*, and is so in a high degree. Indeed the mind cannot well conceive of occasions that would command a more thrilling interest, than those related by Daniel. Nothing trifling, nothing indifferent, nothing *mediocre*, is connected with them. They far exceed, in point of real interest, the renowned tales of oriental fiction so long current and popular in the West as well as the East. The reason is, that the events with which they are concerned are of the highest magnitude and importance; and while there is enough in them of the marvellous to gratify this craving of the human mind, there is still nothing of the monstrous, the absurd, the puerile, and the impossible. I speak of course as a believer in the possibility of miracles; but even those who deny this, cannot deny the thrilling interest of the narrations, nor their adaptedness to excite a deep religious feeling. What could be devised better to show the heathenish court and city, that their "idol gods were a lie, and that those who make them are like unto them?"

The prophetic parts of the book are designed more for believing

Jews, than for the heathen. Yet even here there is matter which might well instruct the heathen, and specially those of that period. The succession of the four dynasties was a thing that could be nothing more than guessed at, without the aid of inspiration. The character and demeanor of the Syrian dynasty were matters in the dark, and also, as yet, in the distant future. Supposing Daniel to have written all the predictions in his book respecting this dynasty, how is it possible to deny that he had a foresight altogether supernatural? Josephus (Antiqq. x. ad. fin.) argues, from this book of Daniel, the certainty of an omniscient and omnipotent overruling Providence. The argument is sound and conclusive; unless indeed we assume, with many recent critics, that a miracle is an utter impossibility.

But let us view the book before us in another light. The Jews were in exile, in different parts of Babylonia; many of them near the metropolis. All captives in war were universally considered, at that time, as the *slaves* of the conquerors. In this state, they must naturally have been exposed to many injuries, insults, and severities. Slavery is but a bitter draught, even when the potion is sweetened. But a slavish subjection of the people of God to a highly superstitious and idolatrous nation, must, in the usual course of things, have exposed them to many indignities and cruelties. Was it nothing, then, to this degraded and suffering people, that one of their own nation was the highest officer at court, the king excepted? Was it nothing, that Daniel and his three friends managed all the concerns of Babylonia? Could they not, in many ways, and without exciting the suspicion or displeasure of the king, modify and allay the severities to which the exiles were exposed, and lighten the yoke that was on their neck? And if the God of heaven meant to preserve his people, in the midst of their chastisement and humiliation, and finally to restore them to their country, was it not worthy of him to interpose as he did, and order matters in such a way that the Jews would be kept quiet until the appointed time, and would be protected from special insult and injury? One can scarcely believe that the miracles wrought under Moses in the wilderness, were more important to the existence and welfare of the Jews, than those which were wrought in Babylon.

Nor is this all. Babylon was to change masters. What then would the new sovereigns do, in regard to the Jews? Would they oppress them, as other slaves were usually oppressed? Or would they treat them kindly, and give them their liberty? When Darius came to the throne of Babylon, this was a deeply interesting question. The time of deliverance, as predicted by Jeremiah, was near at hand.

Much was to be done. Darius, therefore, and after him Cyrus, were to be won over to the cause of the exiles. Daniel's standing and relation to these kings doubtless accomplished this important work. No sooner had Cyrus become seated on his new throne, than he set the whole Jewish nation free. All the sacred vessels of the temple were given up to the returning exiles, and all persons were called upon to encourage them, and contribute to their holy and patriotic undertaking.

If now the events related in the book of Daniel have evidently such important ends in view, and are well adapted to accomplish them, who will deny the importance of recording them for the instruction of all future ages? Facts like these, which exhibit the power and glory of God, and show his tender care for his people even when erring from his ways, are, I readily concede, *paraenetic* even in the highest degree. But they are far indeed from detracting from the value of the book, or from being unworthy of the sacred records.

It has been made an objection against the book before us, that it is a mixture of history and prediction, and thus exhibits itself as alien from the Hebrew prophetic writing in general. But this objection has little ground to support it. Is not Isaiah in part historical? See chap. xxxvi—xxxix. Is not almost one half of Jeremiah historical? Are not parts of Haggai and Zechariah historical? How is it any objection to Daniel, then, that it contains historical narrations, when all that is related has a most evident and intimate connection with the welfare of the people, and is adapted to impress deeply on their minds, what God had done in their behalf?

In respect to the *prophetic* parts of the book, there is no portion of them which does not point the Jews to the great Deliverer, who was yet to appear among them. In regard to *Messianic* views, no prophet introduces them so often; although some, e. g. Isaiah, have dwelt longer on the detail. In regard to the times of distress and danger that were yet to come, we may apply the common apothegm: 'Forewarned, forearmed.' Daniel and others might, of themselves, have hoped that liberation from the Babylonish exile would secure the lasting and uniform prosperity of the Jews. But his visions warn him and them not to rely on false hopes. Still further chastisement would be needed, and still more would be inflicted. Rejoice indeed they might; but they were warned to rejoice with trembling.

One other characteristic of the book deserves special notice. A portion — a large one — of its prophetic parts relates to a period between the return from exile and the coming of the Messiah. No other prophecy has occupied this ground. With the exception of the Messianic period itself, all other prophetic books close, as to any future, either with the exile itself, or with return from it. Has Isaiah, Jeremiah, or Ezekiel gone beyond this, excepting in what is Messianic, much as they have said about the exile and the return from it? And is there no special propriety in Daniel's occupying the highly important ground in question? Ezra and Nehemiah and the book of Esther have indeed related some important occurrences, within the first century after the return from Babylon. But even the latest of the Hebrew prophets, Haggai, Zechariah, and Malachi, leave more than four centuries unoccupied by prediction, and equally so by history. The great misfortunes and sufferings of the Jews, even such as in some respects surpassed those of the Babylonish captivity, were yet to come, and the Jews, as a nation, had as yet no warning of them. Is no important object accomplished, then, when Daniel fills up this gap? At least it will be acknowledged, that the Jews had, and must have, a deep interest in such predictions as disclosed to them other times of trial and of danger. It cannot be charged upon the prophecies of Daniel, therefore, that they are insignificant or unimportant.

'But why (the Messianic period excepted) do his predictions stop short with the death of Antiochus Epiphanes? The Jews had many troubles *after* his time; why not predict and specify them in like manner?'

To these questions one might reply, by asking why all the other prophets have, with the exception of the Messianic prophecies, a *terminus ad quem* short of Daniel's? Why did they not go beyond the exile, and the return from it? But, passing this, I would remark, that, as has already been stated, neither Daniel, nor any other prophet, undertakes to write *annals* of the Jewish nation. Ordinary events and occurrences are omitted in prophecy. Daniel stops with those occurrences which were not inferior, in point of interest, to the Babylonish captivity itself. There was even more danger to the religion of the Jews under Antiochus' reign than under Nebuchadnezzar's. Let us see moreover, for a moment, whether there is not a natural turn (so to speak) given to the mind of the prophet. When the seventy years were near to a close, Daniel prays most earnestly for the promised deliverance. Gabriel then appears to tell him, that although one period of seventy had now come near its close, yet another period of seven times seventy awaited his people, one of deep and thrilling interest. The city and temple would indeed be rebuilt; but this would be accomplished in troublous times; and at last another crisis in their affairs would come, not unlike that through which they had just passed. Jeremiah had occupied his book with the crisis which had just passed; Daniel might very naturally occupy his with the one that was yet to come.

'But why not go beyond this?' I answer again by asking: Why did not Jeremiah go beyond the end of the exile? There must be some stopping place, unless prophecy necessarily becomes a book of continuous annals. Enough for Daniel, that he looked forward to the second exile as it were, and predicted it. The Jews had indeed many troubles after that period; but they bore no comparison with those of the reign of Antiochus. They were temporary. They always had their own kings and priests. Even the conquest of Pompey (B. C. 63) did not seriously interrupt the independence and prosperity of the Jews. He left the temple untouched, with all its sacred untensils. It is no objection then to the book before us, that its predictions close with a second horrible catastrophe. And surely it is no unimportant object to be accomplished by it, to disclose a sad catastrophe which no other prophet had foretold.

Even those interpreters (who are quite numerous), that look upon the book of Daniel as having named a specific period of seventy weeks of years which reaches down to the Messiah, are obliged to confess its silence respecting *events* after the reign of Antiochus, and even until the Messianic period. But for the 490 years which these weeks contain, there has been found by those interpreters no apposite *terminus a quo;* as we have already seen in the Comm. on 9: 24—27. That they *end* with the reign and death of Antiochus, I cannot doubt; although I am unable to make the commencement of them clear. But as I shall not here renew the discussion of this topic, I merely remark, that any *a priori* prescription of the metes and bounds of prophecy must be inapposite and irrelevant. *Everything* is not predicted, nor designed to be predicted. We must leave the matter of judging where to stop, and what to include, to the prophet himself. Enough in the present case, that analogy drawn from other prophets justifies Daniel in stopping with a signal catastrophe.

A class of objectors to the contents of the book of Daniel, different from those whom I have noticed, make the allegation, that 'the book has no important *moral* object in view. It never preaches, never denounces, never threatens, and never promises. It is therefore unlike any other of the prophecies.'

But if we should suppose the alleged histories in the book to be romance, or allegory, even then there would be little force in this objection. Does not our Saviour teach, yea preach, and threaten, and promise, and exhort, in his parables? Daniel was not by regular office a prophet; i. e. he was not sent to the Jewish people in the capacity of a public teacher. He does not address them at all, in a direct manner, like Isaiah, Jeremiah, and others. But are not his narrations full of most important instruction? Are they not comminatory to idolaters, and encouraging and soul-stirring to the pious? Are any more lofty ideas of God, and his superintending and remunerating providence, anywhere disclosed? Are not the events then future, which are disclosed in the predictions of Daniel, of thrilling interest and importance? And with all this before us, are we entitled to make such an objection as that in question?

On another extreme are those who assert that 'the object of the book is that of a narrow-minded and superstitious Hebrew. According to him, there is no God but Jehovah; and no people but the Jews. Everything is purely national and selfish; or else it savors of superstition and closely adheres to the Jewish ritual.'

To the accusation, that Daniel makes Jehovah supreme and all in all, and the Jewish people his then only chosen people, I plead *guilty* in his behalf. But if there be culpable guilt or superstition in this, then all the Heb. prophets lie under the same condemnation — yea, all the O. Testament. But on *such* points, accusation is eulogy. God be thanked, that there are many millions who have thought with Daniel, and who still think and believe with him, as to Jehovah and his chosen people! In regard to *superstition* and *selfishness*, I am unable to find either of them in the pages of Daniel. A more pious, devoted, noble minded man never lived. How could he have been so long in the Babylonish court, without a liberality and courteousness of mind and manners of which there are but few examples?

Lengerke and others, who assign the book to the period of Antiochus' persecutions, represent 'the main object of it to be, to encourage the Jewish people who were suffering under them, and to hold up to them, in the example of Nebuchadnezzar, the probable fate of their tyrannical oppressor. Everything throughout the book, it is alleged, is written with such a purpose in mind, and to this both the historical part and the predictions have a constant reference. It was, moreover, this *a propos* character and quality of the book which procured for it, at so late a period, a place in the Jewish canon.'

I do not feel disposed in any measure to call in question the fact, that the book of Daniel was highly adapted to admonish, to comfort, and to quicken the righteous sufferers, under the cruel persecutions of Epiphanes; nor that it is a book adapted peculiarly to seasons of distress and trouble, at all times and in all countries. But that the book was written for the purpose of making Nebuchadnezzar an allegorical personage, whose real antitype was Antiochus, I must be permitted to call in question. Some features of mutual resemblance indeed there are, as there always must be between men who are tyrants and oppressors and plunderers. But beyond the facts, that both of these kings overran and subdued Palestine, and took possession of its capital city; that both of them rifled the temple of many of its treasures, and destroyed many of the Jews in war — beyond these facts, there is little in common between Nebuchadnezzar and Antiochus. Nebuchadnezzar was no persecutor for the sake of religion. With the exception of the three Jewish worthies who were cast into the furnace of fire, (and this because they publicly refused to obey the king's orders to prostrate themselves before his idol, and thus, as he viewed the matter, showed him disrespect), we read of no persecution for the sake of religion in Nebuchadnezzar's time. We are told indeed by Jeremiah (29: 22), that the king of Babylon roasted Zedekiah and Ahab in the fire. But it appears from the context, that these were false prophets and preachers of sedition among the Hebrew captives. In all probability it was for reasons of State, that they were sentenced to death. But in all the accounts we have of Nebuchadnezzar's demeanor in respect to the Jews in exile, we have nothing to excite suspicion that he was a bigoted persecutor, or even a persecutor at all. In accordance with the war-usages of the times, Nebuchadnezzar, when provoked by the frequent rebellion of the Jews, made havoc among their leaders, after they had been conquered in battle. But none of the prophets, during the exile, have told us of anything which he did to the Jews, which resembled the furious and bloody and long-continued persecutions of Antiochus. Nebuchadnezzar destroyed the temple, because he knew it would be a rallying point for the Jewish nation. But Antiochus, the מְשֹׁמֵם, made it desolate and polluted it by his abominations, his statue of Jupiter with his eagle, and his offerings of swine's flesh on the altar. He also sought to destroy every copy of the Jewish sacred books, and punished with death those who concealed them from him. He bribed apostate Jews to practise the heathen rites, and deluged with blood the holy city for several years. We have no account that Nebuchadnezzar did anything like to this. We do not read of his prohibiting the Jews to retain their Scriptures, or of his obliging them to desist from their worship and rites. It is impossible to suppose, with any probability, that Nebuchadnezzar had any bitter and bigoted resentment against the Jews as such. If so, how could he have constituted a *Jew* his prime minister, and his three intimate friends satraps in Babylonia? It lies on the face of the whole narration, that the state of the Jews at that period must have been rendered quite tolerable, in a civil and social respect, under such a viceroy and such governors. The advice which Jeremiah gives them (ch. xxix), shows that the exiles were far from being in a very degraded state, or destitute of many important privileges.

Compare now with all this, the doings of Antiochus as related in

1 Macc. i. seq. In common, both the king of Babylon and the king of Syria were conquerors, and masters of Judea for a time. But the demeanor of Nebuchadnezzar toward the vanquished, and that of Antiochus, was as discrepant as we can well imagine.

Why then should a writer, in the time of Antiochus, go about inventing a fictitious exemplar of that tyrant, and yet make it so widely diverse, that one can scarcely find any analogy between the two cases, excepting that of original conquest and pillage? A very unskilful writer of fiction he must have been, not to make the prototype more like the antitype. Even as to temper and character, the two kings were very unlike. Nebuchadnezzar was indeed haughty, and passionate, and during his passion he was cruel. But he had his seasons of deep relenting, and could be made to feel the force of an appeal to that God who alone is supreme. It seems even probable from Dan. iv., that he died at last a penitent and a believer. But Antiochus had all his bad qualities, without any of his good ones. He was relentless, bigoted to the last degree, cruel beyond any precedent where his anger had been excited, and irascible to an extreme. Well was he nicknamed ἐπιμανής. Besides all this, he was avaricious, debauched beyond all measure, mean, contemptible, (נִבְזֶה as Daniel very appropriately calls him), and withal very arrogant and ambitious. It would be difficult to find his parallel, even in a Tiberius, a Caligula, or a Nero.

To me it would appear a matter of wonder, that a writer having such an object in view as that of making out a prototype for Antiochus, should have succeeded so ill, since he has manifested, in many parts of his book, ideas and emotions that are truly sublime and striking. That a man of even *mediocre* talent, should not better succeed, must be a matter of surprise to all, in case we make the main object of the book to be what Lengerke asserts it to be.

But this is not all. Lengerke and his *liberal* friends declare unhesitatingly their disbelief of all miracles. Of course, they deny that *prediction*, in a truly prophetic sense, is any where to be found in the Bible. Of course Daniel could really predict nothing. But as his book contains many things, which if written during the exile, must be considered as real predictions, it follows of course, as they conclude, that the book could have been written only after the events described had taken place.

But here is some substantial disagreement with the positions that we have just been examining. Daniel, they say, was written in the time of the Maccabees, to encourage and comfort the Jews under persecution. Of course, if this were the object, it must have been written when the persecution was going on, i. e. during the life of Antiochus. But how then did the writer come to know so much about the *death* of Antiochus? How did he know that this would happen at the end of the last week of the 70 weeks? To fill this gap, Bleek alleges, that chaps. x—xii. were written *after* his death, so that it is *prophecy post eventum.* But unluckily for this subterfuge, Dan. 7 : 24—26 predicts his death after a *definite* period, viz. after the last half of the final week of years. It is also again predicted in Dan. 8 : 23—25, where it is explicitly stated, that Antiochus shall be crushed, not in war, nor by human power, but by the mighty hand of the Prince of princes, without human aid. Dan. 9 : 26, 27, repeats the same declarations. Here then the time and manner of Antiochus' death are both explicitly declared. How now could a writer under his reign, foresee all this, without the spirit of prophecy? And of what use is it to tell us, that chap. x—xii. at least were written *post eventum?* If we concede it, it does not in the least remove our difficulty with the theory in question.

At all events, then, those who reject *prophecy* as an impossibility, must maintain that the whole book of Daniel (comp. 2 : 40—43) was written *after* the death of Antiochus. But here again we have a *ὕστερον πρότερον.* If such were the case, then what need of the *parænetics* addressed to the persecuted? Antiochus was dead; Judas was triumphant; Judea was free; her temple was cleansed and reconsecrated, and all its holy rites and privileges renewed. Did the Jews need the exhortation and consolation addressed to the persecuted, when it was with them a time of feasting, and of keeping their national thanksgiving? Rather, we should suppose, did the times call for something like Ex. xv., or Ps. lxviii., or Is. xiv.

And then, (I cannot help asking the question): How were the Jews of that period, led on by such men as Mattathias, and Judas, and Simon, to be convinced that a book just written, and never before heard of, was the work of a man who lived more than four centuries before, and deserved a place in their sacred canon, now rendered doubly dear by persecution, and by the efforts to destroy it? Believe all this who may, I must regard it as a stretch of credulity far beyond that belief which others cherish, who are accused of an *a priori* faith, and are treated with so much scorn on account of it.

That the book of Daniel may profit the people of God at all times and in all places, I have fully conceded. But that it was written in *Antiochian* times, and for such a specific purpose as is alleged, and was foisted at that time into the Jewish canon, are assertions which require better evidence to establish them than has yet been adduced.

Enough has been said, to show the moral, religious, and, I may add, political or civil designs and objects of the book before us. It does not, like most of the prophets, contain *preaching* or *hortatory addresses*. But both its narratives and its predictions are full of interesting and important instruction. In one particular it differs from most of the other prophetic books. It contains predictions that relate to a series of successive empires, in middle and hither Asia. The like is not elsewhere to be met with. But it is not of these empires because they are such, or rather, it is not of them *historically* regarded as empires, that it treats. It is of them only as standing in relation to or in connection with the Jews, that it speaks. When it was written, the first of the four great empires had attained its height of power. The prophet follows on to sketch very briefly the fall of all the four great dynasties, until he comes to the last, on which he dwells more than on all the others, merely because the Jews were more affected by it than by all the rest. It lies upon the very face of his predictions, that such is the nature of his design. Having brought his people to what we may call their second exile, (for multitudes did in reality become exiles and fled to the caves and deserts), he breaks off here, with the exception of disclosing a future great Deliverer and Saviour, whose kingdom is to be universal. It was not to his purpose, to pursue the detail of historic facts any further.

That he has left behind him a book of the deepest interest, to all who admit the miracles of the Bible, none I think will question. We should lose an important link in the golden chain of revelation, if this were struck out. My belief is, that all the efforts of unbelieving and sneering criticism will not be able to remove it from its place.

§ 3. *Style and aesthetical character of the book.*

No one can pass from the reading of such books as Isaiah, Nahum, Habakkuk, and some other of the Minor Prophets, to the study of Daniel, without perceiving a great change. The characteristic, and (when well understood) delightful poetic parallelism which pervades them, is here unfrequent and but faintly marked. The like may be said of most of Jeremiah, Ezekiel, the first eight chapters of Zechariah, Jonah, Haggai, and Malachi. The prophetic parts of all these books are often prosaic in their form, even when animated by a poetic spirit. Above all, Daniel approaches nearest to Ezekiel and Zechariah in manner and style, although not in matter. Like these prophets, he deals everywhere with symbols and visions. They were, the one his contemporary, and the other but little after him; and all three formed their style and their modes of thinking and expression in a foreign land, where symbol, and imagery, and vision, and dreams, were greatly relished and admired. The ruins of the oriental cities recently brought to the light of day, as well as those which have ever remained exposed to view, are replete with symbolic forms and images which once gave play and delight to the fancy. Nothing is more certain, than that the exiled prophets were strongly influenced in their style, by the training which their condition necessarily gave them. Hence the great dissimilitude between them and (for example) such a writer as Isaiah. *Our* aesthetical judgment is strongly biassed in favor of such writers as Isaiah, and Nahum, and Habakkuk; perhaps justly. But this cannot prove, that the Jews in exile would not have a higher relish for the manner of Ezekiel and Zechariah. It may indeed be taken for granted that such was the case; for otherwise, we can hardly suppose these prophets would have so far departed from the ancient models. That they possessed talents competent to writing in another style, cannot well be doubted by any one who has studied their works.

In the narratives of Daniel, there is a copiousness and exuberance of diction, approaching that of Ezekiel. There is also a strong tinge of the dramatic, in the change of scenes, and of persons and their respective addresses. It cannot be denied, that the impression on the reader is strong and vivid. The writer never tires us, nor suffers his narrative to halt and delay. If the story, in some cases, might be more simply and briefly told, it is quite doubtful whether it would not lose in interest, what it might gain in normal rhetoric.

In the narratives are frequent bursts of feeling which give much additional interest to the pious mind. For example, in 2: 19—23. In the interpretation of dreams and visions, there are many passages that attain to the true sublime; e. g. 2: 27—45. 4: 19—27. 5: 17—28. In fearless and unshaken fidelity and boldness, these last two passages are no where surpassed; while at the same time all becoming respect and courteousness are duly observed. In the prophetic portions, there are passages which reach the height of sublimity; e. g. 7: 9—12. 8: 23—25. 10: 5—9. 11: 40—45 with 12: 1—3. Not unfrequently, do many passages here approach near to the manner of the older prophets, and border upon the higher poetry. The *spirit* of poetry, indeed, mingles itself more or less with nearly all parts of the work. The whole tone is solemn, grave, elevated, and adapted to produce serious, lively, and deep impressions. That the manner and style are *oriental*, may be readily acknowledged; for how could the book well be supposed to be genuine, if they were not so? That none of the visions will aesthetically compare with Is. vi. or Ps. xviii., we may easily concede; but then where are the compositions that will compare with those theophanies? But the reader of Ezekiel, or Zechariah, or Malachi, or Haggai, or Jonah, will concede to Daniel a place in aesthetics decidedly above theirs. The book contains in itself no good reason, why the Masorites should have ejected it from its place among the prophets, and none that render it unworthy of a place in the Canon.

That the book is not of the same stamp as the older prophets, may be readily conceded; but this only puts it on the same ground with Ezekiel and some four or five of the Minor Prophets. That it was adapted to the taste of the later Jews, is abundantly evident from the numerous writings that have attempted to imitate it, near the beginning of the Christian era. Besides, of all books in the Old Test., John in his Apocalypse has most closely followed this. As the standard of taste, in various respects, is not absolute and unlimited, it would be difficult to decide with much positiveness, that Daniel is not entitled to most respectful consideration, in regard to manner as well as matter; at any rate, to decide that he was not so considered among his own people, and in ancient times. Cicero and Tacitus are exceedingly unlike; but a scholar may admit both to a high place in his regard. Daniel and Isaiah are very unlike; but I know of no offence against the laws of taste, when one relishes them both. God, in his wisdom, has introduced all kinds of style into his word; so that all varieties of taste may be gratified. When God speaks to men, he speaks *more humano.* We should love and prize the Bible the more for this. It bears internal marks in abundance, of having been composed by different persons, in different ages and countries. This to us is an evidence, that it is what it claims to be.

In regard to the *idiom* of the book, I shall have something to say in the following section. Its style and aesthetical character are little, if any, affected by this. It is the *matter* of the book, its narratives and course of thought, that create an interest in the mind of the reader. The mass of religious readers are, as I apprehend, more interested in it than in almost any other prophetic composition. There are indeed many things in the prophetic part, which they do not well understand. And this is true of nearly all the prophets. But still, these are fraught with such a spirit of piety and reverence for God, that they are not without interest even to them. The more intelligent reader, who is familiar with oriental manners and customs and objects, cannot fail to read all parts of the book with much interest. The God who guides the affairs of nations and rules over all, is every where supreme, and every where prominent. His providential care and guardianship over his true worshippers and chosen people, stand in high relief upon its pages, and cannot fail to interest and instruct the pious and docile reader.

§ 4. *Language and Idiom of the Book.*

The language is nearly half Chaldee, and the other half Hebrew. Chap. ii. 4, and on to the end of chap. vii., is the *Hebrew-Chaldee.* I give it this name, because of the many conformities to the Hebrew in orthography, and also in the use of particular conjugations (e. g. Hiphil instead of Aphel), which it exhibits. The use of הָ‎ final, instead of the later Chaldee אָ‎ every where abounds. Still, we are not secure in the position, that the Chaldee of the time of Daniel was not different, in the respects mentioned, from that in the Targums of Onkelos and Jonathan. It is by comparison with these last named writings, that we come to the conclusion that Daniel is *Hebrew-Chaldee.* But it may be, that in the time of Daniel, the Chaldee of the Babylonish court was much nearer to that in his book, than the Chaldee of the Targums. Indeed, this is not at all improbable.

At all events, we have convincing evidence that Daniel wrote such Chaldee as was current among the Hebrews of that period. The book of Ezra, which contains several chapters of Chaldee, exhibits the same language in all characteristic respects, as the Chaldee part of Daniel. It is a striking testimony in favor of the position, that these two books were nearly coetaneous. Later Hebrew writers of the Chaldee must have approached nearer to the idiom of the Targums. If the original Hebrew of the son of Sirach, or of Tobit, were extant, we could better judge what the state of the Chaldaizing Hebrew of their day was, and thus obtain many illustrations of the Chaldee at that period, i. e. about 180 B. C. We can hardly believe that such men as Daniel and Ezra were half learned in the Chaldee of their time; and therefore when we speak of their books as containing *Chaldaic-Hebrew*, we say this merely by referring to the Chaldee of the Targums as a standard.

As to the *Hebrew* part of Daniel, it has been charged with deep declension from the early and pure Hebrew. Nay, it is even insisted on, that it is a farrago of Aramaean and Talmudico-Rabbinic; Knobel, Heb. Prophet. § 40. 4. Lengerke makes similar charges. With all becoming deference to these critics, I venture to deny this charge. The production of some 8 or 10 words, which are of the character in question, has but little weight in such a matter. Where is the book in the

Bible, of any considerable length, which could not be proved to be Aramaic or Rabbinic, if some few words approaching or conforming to these idioms constitute a proof? It does not follow, most surely, that such words as are *ἅπαξ λεγόμενα*, are of course *late* Hebrew. What Hebrew writer has not some such words?

The truth is, that all the usual laws of the Hebrew, both as to syntax and to forms, reign throughout the Hebrew of this book. The Hebrew itself approaches nearer the golden age than that of Ezra, or of Ezekiel; I might almost say, than that of Jeremiah. But if the book be genuine, then should the Hebrew belong to the *silver* age; like that of nearly all the later Hebrew writers. *Coheleth* was, not long since, put down to a very late age, on the ground of the like charge. But since Hirtzfeld published his commentary on this book, I believe little has been said against the book of Coheleth on this ground. At least, there can but little be justly said.

That the book of Daniel contains Hebrew words used in the sense of a *later age*, can surely not aid the objector to its genuineness. On the contrary, that fact helps to establish its genuineness. Daniel, when a child, was brought to Babylon and instructed in the language and learning of the *Chaldees* by the court-teachers. That he wrote and spoke both Hebrew and Chaldee with ease, and equally well, is proved from the manner of his diction throughout. With the exception, that the reader finds himself passing into a Chaldee element, or rather, that he meets the author in Chaldee costume, all is the same. The very same person is actor and speaker through and through. If he addresses us in his Chaldee costume to-day, tomorrow he comes in a Hebrew dress, but with the same face and manners as before. This is all the difference that is perceivable, between the two parts of the book. There is not a composition in all the Bible, that bears stronger marks of unity and identity of authorship. The peculiarities of the writer are so many and so striking, that it is impossible to overlook them or lose sight of them. We know nothing more of passing from Hebrew to Chaldee, and then from Chaldee to Hebrew, than that we are reading different dialects indeed, but not different compositions. Never was there an author who is more completely himself, and *semper idem* throughout.

It is the *matter*, not the manner or style, of Daniel, which makes it a difficult book for readers. The sentences are not particularly involved or intricate. Ellipsis is not so frequent as in some other Hebrew books. But the symbols are sometimes of such a nature that they do not interpret themselves, and need the interposition of the *angel-interpreter* who holds intercourse with the prophet. To make a proper application of his predictions to events in history, an extended knowledge of history is needed. But this does not result from any fault in the diction, or from want of skill in the language. It results from the nature of prediction, when it is clothed in symbols and trope.

It has been objected to the genuineness of the book, that it contains *two* different languages. Why not reject the book of Ezra then, if such a ground be tenable? With as little, or perhaps less, apparent reason, this latter book passes more than once from Hebrew to Chaldee. I do not undertake to give a specific reason why Daniel wrote in two languages. But this is plain, viz., that he is equally at home in both. Another thing also is plain, viz., that when his book was written, the great mass of the Jews in Babylon must have been more familiar with Chaldee than with Hebrew. Still the Hebrew as a *written* language was, if I may so speak, a living one. All learned or well instructed persons could read it with ease. Recent experience among Missionaries to the Arabians in Palestine, shows that it is mere pastime for them to learn the Hebrew. So it must have been with the second generation of the Hebrews in exile.

That Daniel had reasons for the exchange of languages, which satisfied his own mind, it is needless to suggest, since he has done it. But if his work be supposititious, as so many recent critics allege, and if it belongs to the age of the Maccabees, what inducement could the romancer have to write in two languages? If it be said, (as it has been), that this might help to palm off his book on the public as a more ancient one, the reply is, that there are prophets contemporaneous and subsequent, who had lived in Babylonia, but whose books are not bilingual. It would have been no matter of supicion, then, if all of Daniel had been composed in Hebrew. But that a Jew of the *Maccabaean* period could write such Chaldee, or such Hebrew, as Daniel has written, is much against all probability. Would that Jerome had given us Sirach and Tobit in the originals! It would then be more easy to decide. But that the Chaldee remained so exactly of the same type as that in Ezra, down to the period of the Maccabees, is against probability. The present Chaldee of the book is an evident pledge for its more advanced age. All the later Chaldee that we know of, is discrepant in many important respects from that in Daniel and Ezra. Whence then can the probability be made out, that a writer of the Maccabaean period, should be able, or be induced, to write in the older Chaldee?

Knobel objects to the Chaldee part of Daniel, that it contains *Persian* words. His inference would be, that the Persian, in Daniel's time, could not have influenced the Chaldee, and therefore the book must have been written at a later period. But of these so called Persian words, he has produced only three, viz. כְּרַז, נְבִזְבָּה and פִּתְגָּם. The *Persian* origin of the two first is altogether doubtful (see Ges. Lex.); and as to the third, Fuerst (Heb. Concord.) decides strongly against the Persian origin, as he also does against that of the other two; and seemingly with good reason. On what a slight and sandy foundation, then, does Knobel take his station, when he assails the genuineness of the book on such a ground! Even if the words were Persian, or rather *Parsi*, how could it be shown that the Chaldeans who came from the country of the Parsis, did not incorporate some of the words of their vernacular with the language which they spoke in the time of Daniel?

Finally, the resemblance of Daniel to Ezekiel is so striking as to the use of many words peculiar to the later Hebrew, that Lengerke maintains a *designed imitation* of the latter, by the late writer of the former. Yet what there is of argument in this, to prove the lateness of the book of Daniel, I cannot see. Lengerke first assumes that the book of Daniel is supposititious, and then accounts for its resemblance to Ezekiel with regard to diction, by asserting that it is an *imitation*. But what hinders us from reversing the process, and reasoning thus: Daniel was first written, and Ezekiel copied after him? If Lengerke reasons correctly, then we may go a step farther, and make another syllogism thus: The *Ascensio Isaiae* has many things in common with the scriptural Isaiah; therefore the author of the latter must have copied from the former. It may be convenient, for certain purposes, to argue in such a way, where a point is to be carried at all adventures, and one commences with a — *delenda est Carthago*. But it makes not much in favor of a cause, to employ such argumentation in its behalf. After all, moreover, the resemblances between Ezekiel and Daniel by no means prove copying in either. They show *contemporaneousness* in the writers, beyond fair doubt; but not the dependence of either upon the other.

§ 5. *Unity of the book or sameness of Authorship.*

Bertholdt was the first, I believe, to divide the book of Daniel into *nine* parts, and assign to it so many different authors. This was such an extravagance in criticism, that it has had but few if any advocates or imitators. Eichhorn contented himself with *two* authors, one for the history, and another for the prophecies. The conclusion of both these writers is, that the book is a *mish-mush*, made up by some later writer in the way of compiling fragments from different compositions. But this ground has long since been abandoned, even by the so called liberal critics. Bleek, who is one of them, first gave this criticism a death-blow; and it is not probable that it will ever attain to a resurrection; (Theol. Zeitschr. No. 3. s. 242. ff.). It is needless, therefore, to discuss this matter at any length. I shall merely advert to some of the arguments by which the unity and sameness of the book are established.

(1) There is an evident *plan* in the arrangement of the book. The *historical* part is orderly and chronologically arranged. The different kings brought to view succeed each other in the order of time, as well as of the occurrences under their reign. In the *prophetical* part, the same arrangement is regularly observed. The book as a whole has an appropriate introduction in chap. i., and an appropriate ending in chap. xii.

(2) There is, as has already been said above, a resemblance of character through and through, so exact as can scarcely be found in any other book in all the Bible. Even in passing from Hebrew to Chaldee, and *vice versâ*, the difference in style and character cannot be at all discerned. The difference is simply *linguistic*, and nothing more. It seems to me impossible for any one at all skilled in discerning the characteristics of writing, to read the book through attentively in the original, without an overwhelming conviction that the whole proceeded from one pen and one mind.

(3) The several portions of the book, both in history and prophecy, stand related to each, and are similar, in a variety of respects.

E. g. 2: 47 and 3: 29.* — 4: 1—3 and 4: 37. 6: 29. — 3: 30 and 6: 28, and generally chaps. iii. and vi. — Comp. the latter part of ii. with corresponding parts of vii. viii. So 8: 26 seq. with 12: 4, 9. — 9: 3 with 10: 2, 3. — 8: 16 with 9: 21. — 8: 18 with 10: 9. — Compare, moreover, 2: 49 with 3: 12. — 5: 1, 2 with 5: 23. — 5: 11 with 2: 48. — 5: 18 seq. with 4: 22 seq. — 6: 1—3 with 6: 28, — 8: 1 seq. with 7: 1 seq. — 9: 21 with 8: 15 seq. — 10: 12 with 9: 23.

Besides these affinities, there are others still more decisive, because they have respect to peculiarities of phraseology which belong only to this book.

Compare the comminations in 2: 5. 3: 29. — Compare also the idiomatic phrases, חֶזְוֵי רֵאשׁ in 2: 28. 4: 2, 7, 10. 7: 1, 7. — קָרָא בְחַיִל, 3: 4. 5: 7. 4: 14 — זִיו שְׁנָא, 5: 6, 9. 7: 28, comp. 10: 8. — אֲכַל קַרְצֵי דִי, 3: 8. 6: 24. — רַעְיוֹנֹהִי יְבַהֲלֻנֵּהּ, 4: 16. 5: 6, 10. 7: 28. — עַמְמַיָּא אֻמַּיָּא וְלִשָּׁנַיָּא, 3: 4, 7. 4: 1. 5: 19. 6: 25. — Also the designation of time by a peculiar use of יָמִים, 8: 27. 10: 3. — לַמּוֹעֵד, 8: 19. 11: 27, 35. — The peculiar

* The references are conformed to the division of chapter and verse in our English Bible, for the sake of more easy comparison. The Hebrew can be easily found, in cases where it differs in its notation.

נִרְדָּם, 8: 18. 10: 9. — שִׁקּוּץ שֹׁמֵם, 9: 27. 11: 31. 12: 11. — צְבִי for Palestine, 8: 9. 11: 16, 41. Compare also the various cases in which Daniel is mentioned and commended, 2: 26. 4: 8, 18. 10: 1. 5: 11. 9: 23. 10: 11, 19. The repetition of more or less of passages in nearly the same words, may be seen in 3: 7, 10, 15. 4: 10 seq. and 20 seq. al.

These are by no means all the resemblances and affinities of different parts of the book. Nothing can be more palpable, than that these different parts, both historical and prophetic, come from the same source, and that in the whole there is a unity and completeness of design. There is not a structure on the whole area of sacred ground, in which the parts are more homogeneous, better fittèd to each other, or more firmly dovetailed together, than the one before us. That Bertholdt should imagine the book to comprise nine or even seven authors, would be unaccountable in any ordinary case — but still it is nothing very strange for him.

§ 6. *Genuineness and Authenticity of the Book.*

I join these two categories together, because it is difficult to treat of them separately, without making many repetitions. If the book be *genuine*, i. e. if it be the production of Daniel the *prophet*, then is it of course *authentic*, and has a fair claim to a place in the Canon.

The objections made to the genuineness of the book are numerous, and are urged with great confidence and earnestness, by nearly the whole corps of neological critics. They have even shaken the faith of some, who receive most of the other sacred books as authentic. Indeed it has of late been confidently and somewhat frequently declared, that *fuit Ilium* will soon be written on this supposed monument of ancient times; and that ere long it will come to a state of desuetude as complete as that of the devoted Trojan city, while its pretended remains will attract far less of the curiosity of scholars. Or, (to use another of the *decent* comparisons that have lately been made), it will take its place, with general acquiescence, along with Amadis de Gaul and Jack the Giant-killer.

We shall inquire, by and by, whether there is any good reason for such sweeping condemnation and excision as this. But I deem it preferable first to bring under notice, the reasons which may be urged in favor of the genuineness of the book. It is incumbent on those who admit the valid claims of the book to a place in the canon, to produce the grounds or reasons of their belief. The *affirmative* of a controverted claim, specially where the claim has long been made, naturally demands our first attention, when we are about to examine its validity.

It is not my design to enter into and dwell upon all the *minutiae* of this subject. It is enough, when points are established, which must settle, or ought to settle, the controversy. In what I do say, my design moreover is to be as brief as perspicuity and the nature of the case will allow.

Several writers divide the proofs of the genuineness of Daniel, into those which are *external*, i. e. arise from the testimony of others; and those which are *internal*, i. e. arise from a view of the contents. I do not deem it of any importance to confine ourselves within these technical limits of order; for I regard it as more convincing and satisfactory, to produce the arguments in some natural consecution, and so that their relation to each other may be easily apprehended.

As an argument, then, in favor of the genuineness of the book, I would mention, (1) *The testimony of the writer himself to this fact.* In 7: 28. 8: 2, 15, 27. 9: 2. 10: 1. 12: 5, the writer speaks of himself as *I Daniel*, i. e. the same Daniel whose history is given in chap. i. I do not indeed regard this as conclusive evidence; for the forger of a book may insert the name of another person as the author, and be constant in maintaining that he is so. But when we find the name of Thucydides, or of any Greek or Roman classic author, apparently inserted by himself as the writer of this book or of that, we regard it at least as *prima facie* evidence of the fact, and credible until something shall be produced which contradicts it. This must be either what the book itself contains, which will show that it belongs to another age or country; or else it must be contradicted by other credible witnesses, who lived at the alleged author's time, or soon after; or finally it must bear evident marks of designed fraud, or at least of designed fiction. Nothing of *testimony* against the genuineness of the book, by competent and cognizant witnesses of ancient times, has been or can be produced. From the time in which it made its appearance down to the last quarter of the eighteenth century, among Jews and Christians, the book held an uniform and undisputed rank as a genuine book. No one, except men like Porphyry, who rejected all the sacred books of the Old and the New Test., rose up to call it in question. That it bears *evident* marks of fraud or of fiction, would seem to be sufficiently contradicted by the simple fact of universal reception for at least 2000 years. *Evident* — to whom? Not to men who for more than this long period were its serious and enlightened readers — men too of all classes and conditions, hostile to each other on many speculative points of religion, but all agreed in conceding to the book before us the place that it occupies.

It is vain to say, that the Talmudists who assigned it a place among the *Kethubim*, meant to degrade it thereby, whatever other reasons they might have had for this proceeding. The Talmud itself says of Daniel:

"If all the wise men of the Gentiles were put in one scale, and Daniel in the other, he would outweigh them all; see in Carpzov. Introd., p. 228, 230. Josephus, as we have seen above (p. 380), ranks Daniel above all the prophets. Jerome says, that "none of the prophets have spoken so plainly respecting Christ;" Pref. in Dan. Augustine says, that "no one in the O. Test. has written so expressly concerning the rewards of the kingdom of heaven." Even Lengerke does not venture to impute *fraud* to it, but charges it with *romantic fiction*. He and others charge it, moreover, with inconsistencies, with parachronisms, with lack of historical knowledge, and with various whimsies and excesses which render it suspicious. But what if these last charges, when examined, turn out to be more *subjective* than *objective*? If so, (and of this, after having traversed the ground, I cannot doubt), then there can be no valid objection to admitting the author's testimony to his own authorship.

Why do we admit the testimony of Ezekiel, Haggai, Zechariah, Malachi, and indeed of all the prophets, to their own authorship, and reject that of Daniel? Why do we give credence to like testimony of Thucydides, and other Greek and also Roman writers? *Prima facie* then, the repeated declarations of Daniel respecting his authorship, are evidence in favor of it — evidence of importance, unless it can be rebutted.

The fact that he so often exchanges the first person for the third, or *vice versa*, is no evidence against this, for such is the custom of all the prophets. It is the frequency with which he introduces himself, that Lengerke charges with being a suspicious circumstance. 'None but a supposititious writer,' he says, 'would be so anxious to reassert so often his claims and the credibility of his book.' And yet if we look into Jeremiah, Ezekiel, and several other prophets, we find the authors of the book brought to our notice at every new revelation. — What could be more natural? Why should Daniel only be required to depart from this common usage?

(2) The sacred writers of the O. Test. and the New, and also the Saviour himself, have testified to the personage and to the book of Daniel, in such a way as fully to establish the claims made by that book in behalf of Daniel as a true prophet.

We begin with Ezekiel, a contemporary of Daniel, and like him living in exile. When threatening the Jews, still remaining in Palestine just before the final captivity, with thorough excision because of their sins, he says, as the messenger of God authorized to repeat his message to them: "Though these three men, Noah, Daniel, and Job, were in it [Jerusalem], they should deliver but their own souls [lives] by their righteousness;" 14: 14. This is twice more repeated in vs. 18, 20. Again in speaking of the prince of Tyre (28: 3), he says, in the way of chastising his insolence and self conceit: "Behold, thou art wiser than Daniel; there is no secret that they can hide from thee!" The cutting irony of this is quite plain. Equally plain is the high elevation given to the wisdom of Daniel. It is as much as saying to the prince: 'Thou comparest thyself with one of the wisest of men, and thinkest thyself his equal.' The manner in which this is said, shows that the prophet appeals to the common sentiment, respecting Daniel, of the Jews of his time whom he addressed. And the like may be said of the preceding testimony. Daniel is classed, as a preëminent example of a just and holy life, with Noah and Job. What can render any testimony more impressive, in respect to the character of Daniel?

In vain are we told, that there are other Daniels in the sacred volume; for they are at least nothing to our purpose. One of them was a son of David, 1 Chron. 3: 1, of whom nothing but his name is known. The other was a son of Ithamar, one of the leaders of a company, who went up to Jerusalem with Ezra, some seventy years after Daniel's death, and more than that after the death of Ezekiel, Ezra 8: 2. Comp. Neh. 10: 6. Of course he is out of question. Besides these we know of no Daniel but the one before us. It is no objection of any weight, in the question as to his person, that he was *young* when Ezekiel wrote the passages cited. The first passages were written about B. C. 594, and the second passage about 588. When the first were written, Daniel must have been some twenty-five or twenty-seven years of age, if we allow that he was some twelve to fourteen when he was carried into exile; (יֶלֶד he is called in Dan. 1: 4). When the second was written, he was some thirty-one to thirty-three years old. He was indeed very young to acquire such a reputation for holiness and wisdom. But the solution of the problem is made by the history of him in ch. i. ii. of his book. The testimony of Ezekiel is in strict conformity with all that history, and is indeed a notable comment on it and voucher for it. Considering the publicity and conspicuous nature of his station as prime minister of the Babylonish court, even when he could have been but some eighteen or nineteen years of age, there can be no doubt that his fame had spread far and wide, at the time when Ezekiel bore testimony concerning him.

In vain are we told by Bleek and others, that the Daniel of Ezekiel must have been a more ancient and probably a mythical person. Ezekiel classes him with *scriptural* personages, *real* ones, not with mythical abstractions. He would not have been intelligible to his readers, if he did not. Such then being the case, we cannot avoid the conclusion, that when Ezekiel wrote, the condition and character of Daniel was altogether such as his book asserts or describes it to be. It is indeed a signal testimony, and such an one as is scarcely given elsewhere in any part of the Scriptures, by one prophet in respect to another.

Thus much then for Daniel's person and character. And thus much, be it remembered, from the pen of a distinguished prophet of God, contemporary with Daniel, and a companion in exile. Let us now see what is the testimony of the N. Test. in relation to the same personage.

First of all, then, we appeal to the testimony of Christ himself, in Matt. 24: 15, "When ye, therefore, shall see the abomination of desolation, *spoken of by Daniel the prophet*, stand in the holy place, (whoso readeth let him understand), then let them that are in Judea flee, etc." The same is repeated in Mark 13: 14; excepting that some critical editions now omit one clause there, viz. "spoken of by Daniel the prophet". But this omission alters not the nature of the case. The Saviour quotes written words from Daniel, and refers the *reader* (*ὁ ἀναγινώσκων*) to them for reflection upon them. In these passages then, or rather in the Saviour's discourse, he bears explicit testimony to two things; first, that Daniel was a *prophet;* and secondly, that his words, when attentively perused and understood, give warning to his disciples to escape by flight from the then impending fate of Jerusalem. Now as we must concede that Jesus spoke the words of truth and soberness, yea that he spake them as never man did speak, what can we make of such testimony, except that he believed, as well as the disciples whom he addressed, that Daniel was a *true prophet,* and his book worthy of all honor and credit? To suppose the Saviour of the world to make such an appeal to a book that was the comparatively recent work of an impostor — or at least a forger of romances — although the book had been lucky enough to gain a place in the sacred canon, is to suppose Christ himself to be either ignorant of the state of facts, or else willing to foster the false regard which was paid to the book by the Jews. My views of that sacred, that divine teacher, will not permit me to believe either. Of course I must, on his authority, regard the book as sacred.*

* I have assumed in my remarks the position, that the parenthetic *ὁ ἀναγινώσκων νοείτω* are the words of *Christ*, and not a suggestion of the evangelist. I know not where to find warnings of this nature, inserted by the evangelists themselves, on their own authority, in the discourses of Christ. But with the Saviour such warnings are frequent. E. g. "He that hath ears to hear, let him hear," and the like. In the case before us, Jesus cites the words of Daniel, and warns his hearers to give to them deliberate consideration, *νοείτω*, *revolve them in mind.* The labored attempt of Wieseler (Ausleg. u. Krit. d. Apoc. Lit. s. 173 ff.) to show that the parenthesis belongs, in both Matthew and Mark, to these evangelists themselves, has entirely failed to convince me. The design of such an effort is, to remove the impression that Christ has himself referred to Daniel as conclusive authority. The burden of such an allegation some recent critics would rather lay upon the apostles, whom they regard as undoubtedly liable to mistaken apprehensions.

That at that period the book was in the Jewish canon, no one worthy of any regard will deny. That it was what it now is, through and through, is quite certain. Josephus follows κατὰ πόδα the narrative part, in Antiq. X. He also refers to the contents of the prophecies. And so, as we shall soon see, do the writers of the N. Test. But what we have already seen, viz. that Christ himself has expressly sanctioned this book, and named the author as *Daniel the prophet*, settles the great question with every believing mind, both as to its genuineness and its authenticity. Still, this is not all the testimony of Christ. He calls himself very often *the Son of Man*; an appellation which would seem, at first view, to detract from his dignity, and place him on a level with men at large, or at most on a level with those prophets (e. g. Ezekiel) who are often addressed in this way. But John 5: 27 solves the mystery. There Christ represents himself to be the appointed judge of the world and the giver of life both spiritual and natural, *because he is the Son of Man.* The allusion is so palpable to Dan. 7: 13, 14, that none can well mistake it. There we find ascribed to the Son of Man supremacy and power, like that which is asserted in the Gospels. It is because he is the Son of Man in the sense of the book of Daniel, that he claims the prerogatives in question. Again, if we compare Dan. 7: 13, 14, and 26, 27 with Matt. 10: 23. 16: 27, 28. 19: 28. 24: 30. 26: 64, the conclusion seems inevitable that Christ has applied the words of Daniel to the description of his own dominion and reign — so carefully applied them as to follow, as often as practicable, the very diction of the prophet. Once more; in John 5: 28, 29, Christ has employed the words of Dan. 12: 2, which contains the most peculiar statement that exists in the O. Test., respecting the doctrine of a general resurrection.

Thus much for the testimony of him who was the Truth and the Light of the world. Let us now see what some of his leading apostles and disciples have said.

(*a*) In Heb. 11: 33, 34, "stopped the mouths of lions; quenched the violence of fire, escaped the edge of the sword," seem very plainly to refer to the history in Dan. vi. iii. and ii. Daniel's escape in the den of lions; the deliverance of his three companions from the power of the fiery furnace; and the liberation of him and them, from the impending decree of Nebuchadnezzar to destroy all the wise men; must have been distinctly before the mind of the writer. (*b*) Paul's second epistle to the Thessalonians (ch. ii. iii.) seems to contain an evident reference to Daniel's description of Antiochus Epiphanes; comp. 2 Thess. 2: 4 with Dan. 11: 36. Also 2 Thess. 2: 8 with Dan. 11: 45. 8: 25. I cannot think however, as Hengstenberg does, that Daniel and Paul both refer to the same individual. I regard the apostle as describing such a character as he brings to view, under the new dispensation, in the same way as Daniel has described a similar one under the ancient dispensation. The instance before us, however, is not produced as one of a character altogether decisive, but only as one which shows the estimate which Paul put upon the book of Daniel, by employing language taken from him in respect to a very grave matter. More decisive seems to be 1 Cor. 6: 2, "Know ye not that the saints shall judge the world;" when compared with Daniel 7: 27, "And the kingdom and dominion, and the greatness of the kingdom under the whole heaven, shall be given to the people of the saints of the most High." The manner of the apostle's inquiry implies, that his readers are already in possession of the knowledge in question. Where else could they obtain it so directly and easily as in the passage of Daniel just cited?

(*c*) In Acts 7: 56, it is related of Stephen that he said: "I see the heavens opened, and the *Son of Man* standing on the right hand of God." How exactly this tallies with Daniel 7: 13, every reader may easily see. That Stephen had his mind on that passage in Daniel, and has employed its peculiar language, cannot well be doubted. No where else does any disciple ever speak of the Saviour as *the Son of Man*. It is hardly to be supposed that Stephen would, in this case, have departed from universal usage, unless his mind had been distinctly on the passage in Daniel, which he has quoted as to its most distinctive particular.

(*d*) Finally, if we take up the Apocalypse, and read it through with care, we shall find that the general arrangement of this work, and a multitude of passages in it, are altogether after the manner of Daniel. It begins with a historical part, chap. i—iii., and the rest is prophecy. The kind of imagery employed, the symbols chosen for representation, the intervention of angel-assistants and angel-interpreters, and even the designation of times, are all after the model of Daniel throughout, although far from a plagiarist's imitation. It is no small testimony to the estimation in which Daniel was held, that John has thus preferred in general his manner of communication to all others. To cite instances, in a case so palpable and so generally if not universally acknowledged, would be useless on the present occasion. The two books stand side by side, the one describing the approaching end of the *Ante*-Messianic dispensation, the other describing the sequel and the end of the Messianic one.

In review of the facts presented under our present category, let me ask: What prophet in all the Old Test. is more expressly, or (taking the New Test. all in all) more amply recognized and authenticated, than Daniel? Isaiah is indeed very frequently quoted; but, if the Apocalypse be taken into the account, he does not so often appear in the New Test. as Daniel does. No other prophet, at all events, can make claim to so much reference as Daniel. But how, now, and why is this? If we are to believe the mass of recent critics, the book of Daniel is a *supposititious* work — a romance forged during the persecution of Antiochus Epiphanes — how then came Christ to appeal to, and to treat, Daniel as a true prophet? And how came those disciples, to whom he had promised that "the Holy Ghost should teach them all things, and bring all things to their remembrance" (John 14: 26), to regard and treat one who was an impostor, or at all events a forger and a romancer, as a prophet of God, whose work was worthy of all confidence and reverence?

The answer to these and the like questions is, that 'a miracle is an impossibility; that if Daniel was written before the time of Antiochus, a miraculous inspiration must be conceded, and therefore it could not have been written so early as the book pretends; and lastly, that the disciples of Christ often conformed to Jewish notions and prejudices, and were not conversant with critical matters, and moreover that even Jesus himself sometimes assumed the Jewish views without contradiction, because he did not wish to excite their prejudices by opposition to them.' But let those think and say all this who may and will, it is perfectly evident that when these positions are assumed, all confidence in the unvarying truth and authority of the New Test. is gone, and can never more be defended. Even this, however, would be of small account in the eyes of such men as Strauss, and Lengerke, and Knobel, and many others. But the sincere lover of gosj el-truth can never be led to regard the Saviour of the world, or his holy apostles, as deceived in regard to the book of Daniel, or as giving currency by their authority to forgery and imposture. Nothing can be plainer, than that the principle assumed in regard to miracles, in order to show that the book of Daniel is a late and supposititious book, would show with equal force, that all the miracles of the Saviour and of his Apostles are mere figments of the imagination, and that the books which describe them are the mere productions of fiction and of superstition. Well may the sober believer say: *Quod probat nimium, probat nihil.*

(3) Various other works of antiquity besides the sacred volume, bear testimony more or less directly to the ancient and venerated character of the book of Daniel.

(*a*) Josephus (Antiqq. xi. 8. 4. seq.) relates, that Alexander the

Great, when besieging Tyre, sent to the Jews for aid; which was declined on the ground of the fealty of the Jews to Darius the Persian king. The Grecian conqueror was highly exasperated, and as soon as Tyre was taken, marched his army against Jesusalem. The Jews were in the utmost consternation, and betook themselves to prayers and offerings in the temple. Josephus states (loc. cit.), that the high priest Jaddua was warned, in a dream, to go out with the priests in their sacred robes, and the leading civilians in white garments, and meet and propitiate the conqueror. This they did, when Alexander drew near to the city; and he was appeased, and did reverence to the high priest, and repaired to the temple, and offered sacrifices there. When questioned by Parmenio, one of his generals, how he, who made all other kings and princes do homage to him, could himself do this to the Jewish high-priest, his reply was, that it was not to the *man* that he did reverence, but to the *God* whom the man adored. He then added, as Josephus tells the story, that he, while at Dios in Macedonia, had seen in a dream this very man (the high-priest), who told him to go forward in his Persian expedition, for he would be victorious. In the temple, the same historian tells us, the passages in Daniel (8: 3—7. 11: 2, 3) were shown to Alexander, i. e. interpreted to him, which predicted his success. In the sequel, Alexander gave full liberty to the Jews to follow their own religion, and freed them from taxes during the Sabbatical year. All this happened in 332 B. C.

This account by Josephus has, of course, been attacked and called in question as fabulous. But as to the main historical facts, they are vouched for by other writers. That Alexander was personally in Judea, Pliny testifies; Hist. Nat. xii. 26. That Palestine voluntarily surrendered to him, is testified in Arrian's history of Alexander, ii. 25. That he was met by the high-priest and his brethren dressed in turbans, is testified by Justin (xi. 10), who says: "Obvios cum *infulis* multos orientis reges habuit." Hecataeus Abderita, a historian contemporary with Alexander, testifies that there were Jews in Alexander's army; (cited in Josephus cont. Apion. ii. 4). And finally the Talmudists often, specially in *Tract. Taanith*, eulogize the liberality of Alexander.

What now if we allow, (as I should be disposed to do), that tradition had added something to the report of Alexander's invasion, which will not bear critical scanning? Does this prove that the narration has no basis in matter of fact? Surely not. What would become of most of the Greek and Roman histories, on such a ground? We may, if we please, reject the dreams as being special and divine monitions. Indeed, that of Alexander seems to bear evident marks of cunning forgery on his part. That of the high-priest might very naturally have taken place, in his agitated state of mind. It seems to have been conformed, however, to the dictates of prudential policy; and whether he really had such a dream, or not, it was an easy and ready expedient to induce the Jews to follow his peace-making counsel. For the rest, that Alexander was pacified and flattered by the honors paid him, there can be no room to doubt. That such passages in Daniel as those above referred to were shown him, in order to secure his favor and protection, is perfectly natural. Hitzig himself declares, that "if indeed the book existed at that time, it was undoubtedly shown to him;" Heid. Jahrb. 1832, s. 135. But why the *if?* I know of no historical testimony against its existence at that period. All the objections to its antiquity are founded on the *a priori* assumption, that prophecy and miracle are impossible. No one can doubt that Josephus fully believed in its existence at the close of the Babylonish exile. No man in the Jewish nation had a better opportunity than he, to know the history of his own people. He was of high descent — a priest himself, and the son of an eminent priest on the paternal side, and of the royal Hasmonaean race on the maternal, being of the fourth generation from the Maccabaean family. If we can suppose any person among the Jews to be cognizant of their history, he was the most probable man. That he has honestly chronicled the story respecting Alexander, there can be no good reason for doubting. That he has told it with some of the appendages, which tradition and a love of the marvellous had affixed to it, forms no serious objection to the credible and probable facts contained in it. Nor can I see, how an *a priori* assumption about the book of Daniel can be made to discredit it; unless we assume the position, that whatever may contradict a favorite theory of our own philosophy, must be regarded as false. After all, the question of prediction, i. e. of miracles, is one that depends on credible testimony, not on *a priori* assumption.

Taking the ground, then, that the narration of Josephus is substantially true, it follows that the book of Daniel, as it now exists, was current among the Jews as a sacred book, at least some 168—170 years before the time when, according to the critics of the skeptical school, the book could be written. If so, then *prediction* must be conceded.

(*b*) The first book of Maccabees (2: 59, 60), written in all probability not long after the death of Simon the brother of Judas Maccabaeus, and during the reign of his son John Hyrcanus (i. e. about 125—130 B. C.), represents the father of the Maccabees, the venerable priest Mattathias, on his death bed, as warning his friends and encouraging them by appeal to the example 'of the three worthies who were saved from the furnace of Nebuchadnezzar, and of Daniel who was rescued from the den of lions,' (Dan. iii. vi.) If he did actually make such an appeal, then the position of the doubting critics has no good foundation. It is necessary to the success of their cause, that the book should have been written, at least completed, *after* the death of Antiochus. Otherwise, according to their views, neither the *time* nor the *manner* of that death could have been designated; for both of these are specially declared, and are prominent on the face of the record.

How now is this conclusion, which the advocates of its antiquity make, avoided? Bleek tells us (p. 183), that the historian of a later period may have put these words into the mouth of Mattathias, although he did not himself employ them. We cannot disprove this; but we may well say, that unless the book is destitute of support in other quarters, the assertion of Bleek is not entitled to much credit. At all events, let the book have originated when it might, it was, in the time of Hyrcanus when 1 Macc. was written, regarded as sacred. In what way a book not written by a prophet, (for 1 Macc. repeatedly declares that prophets were then no more), could obtain a place in the Canon, and be regarded as a prophetic work, during the period between the death of Antiochus and the writing of the Maccabaean history, is for those to explain and show, who assert the late origin of that book. No tolerable solution of this very difficult problem has yet been offered.

(*c*) The Sept. Version of the Pentateuch is the oldest part of the Greek translation. It is a controverted question, when this version was made. But after all, I see not how the testimony of Aristobulus and of Hecataeus Abderita can be set aside, viz. that at least this part of the Sept. was completed during the reign of Ptolemy Lagus, or at all events of his son Ptolemy Philadelphus, i. e. some 315—295 B. C. Hävernick (Einleit. ins A. Test. I. § 70) has discussed this subject in an able, and (on the whole) satisfactory manner. Now in the Sept. (Deut. 32: 8) is a passage, which seems plainly to owe its origin to Daniel 10: 13, 20, 21. 11: 1. The original Hebrew in Deuteronomy runs thus: "When the most High divided to the nations their inheritance . . . he set the bounds of the people *according to the number of the children of Israel.*" This last clause the Sept. have rendered: *κατὰ ἀριθμὸν ἀγγέλων θεοῦ*. Again, in Isa. 30: 4, the prophet in speaking of the king of Egypt, says: "His princes were at Zoan, and his ambassadors came to Hanes." The Sept. translates thus: *εἰσὶν ἐν Τάνει ἀρχηγοὶ ἄγγελοι πονηροί*. The version of Isaiah was doubtless somewhat later than that of the Pentateuch, but not so much so as to interfere with the present argument. Here, in both of these passages, there seems to be a distinct recognition of the doctrine, that nations have their *presiding angels*; a doctrine taught nowhere else in the O. Test., save in the passages of Daniel above referred to. I am aware of the allegation, that the Seventy may have drawn this doctrine in respect to presiding national angels, from the Parsis and the religion of Zoroaster. But I am also aware, that no such doctrine can be shown to have existed among the Parsis; as Hengstenberg and Hävernick have indeed sufficiently shown. Nor is this a very probable source from which the Jews would deduce their religious notions. Much more easy and natural is it to suppose, that the Seventy drew from the book of Daniel. It will hardly be contended, that their version in general originated so late as the time of the Maccabees. At all events we know that the composition of Jesus Sirach was antecedent to the reign of Antiochus; and here (17: 17) we find it written: *Ἑκάστῳ ἔθνει κατέστησεν* [*θεὸς*] *ἡγούμενον*; which looks very much like being drawn from Daniel. The possibility of some other origin we may readily acknowledge; but the *probability* of such an one cannot well be made out.

If any one of the instances of resemblance now produced did in fact take its rise from Daniel, then is the theory of a Maccabaean or post-Antiochian origin of the book out of question. It must have existed earlier; and if so, then is the edifice of the objectors undermined. They may as well concede the book to the true Daniel, as to any one between his time and the death of Epiphanes. It cannot be said, that the facts in question do not seriously embarrass the antagonists of the book.

(*d*) The *Septuagint version* of Daniel, however, bears evident marks of coming from the hand of some one who lived during the Maccabaean period. It contains several explanatory clauses, which appear to have been occasioned by events then recent, the accurate knowledge of which enabled the translator to make his historical commentary. E. g. in 11: 30, where the Heb. has: "The ships of Chittim shall come against him, and he shall be disheartened," the Sept. runs thus: *ἥξουσι Ῥωμαῖοι, καὶ ἐξώσουσιν αὐτόν*, i. e. *the Romans shall come, and expel him*. This evidently refers to the interference of the Roman embassy with Antiochus, when he was ready to seize upon the capital of Egypt; for he was stopped by them in his career, and to his great chagrin was obliged to quit the country. Again, in Dan. 9: 26, the Hebrew runs thus: "After sixty-two weeks an anointed one shall be cut off," while the Sept. translates thus: *καὶ μετὰ ἑπτὰ καὶ ἑβδομήκοντα καὶ ἑξήκοντα δυὸ, ἀποσταθήσεται χρίσμα*, i. e. after seven and seventy and sixty-two [years], anointing shall cease. The sum of these numbers = 139; and this, no doubt, means the 139th year of the era of the Selucidae, which began 312 B. C.

This would bring the period for the anointing to fail or cease, down to 173 B. C.; and it was at this period, or within a few months of it, that the high priest Onias III. was ejected from his office by Antiochus, and soon after murdered by his lieutenant in Syria. It is to this event, doubtless, that the version refers, when it says: *ἀποσταθήσηται χρίσμα.* Now all this shows a minute and accurate knowledge of those times, which renders it probable that the writer lived at that period. At all events, if the comparison be made of the loose and erroneous manner of stating facts in 2 Macc. (a later and an Alexandrian composition), one must feel that the translator was unusually and accurately cognizant of the history of those times. But if his *version* was then made, how could it be, in case the original had just then made its appearance, that such alterations would be introduced, and such comments inserted? We may well suppose the author of the *Hebrew* Daniel to be then living, if we hearken to Lengerke and others of like views. Would or could a translator take such liberties with a recent composition? I do not say that it is impossible; yet I may venture to say that such a thing seems to be quite improbable. But if we suppose Daniel to have been written in the sixth century B. C., then there was time for a book, so obscure in some of its passages, to have been subjected to traditional explications, and to efforts for the purpose of rendering it more intelligible.

Beyond all this, it should be observed, that the whole Sept. version of Daniel is a *paraphrastic* one, departing so often and so widely from the original, that even in the early ages of Christianity, with all their reverence for the Sept. in general, this book was thrown aside, and the version of Theodotion, more literal and exact, was taken in the room of it. Even at that period, the Sept. version had attached to it several apocryphal appendages, e. g. the Hymn of the three Martyrs in the furnace, the story of Susanna, and of Bel and the Dragon. At least so the matter stands, in the Sept. of the Chisian Codex as published at Rome. All this argues an age for the book of Daniel back of the Maccabaean period. Such stories and legends are usually attached to books of a more ancient period, and not to recent productions. That so many of them came into the Sept. version, would help to confirm the position, that the book of Daniel is older than recent liberal criticism allows it to be.

Finally the writer of the 1 Macc., has quoted the Sept. version, beyond all reasonable doubt. It must then have enjoyed full credit in his time. But could a book written after the death of Epiphanes have already been translated, and this translation have become a source of citation and appeal, unless the original book was written earlier than the death of that tyrant? Such a view of the matter is at least quite an improbable one.

(*e*) The *Sibylline Oracles* bear testimony to the antiquity of the book. That portion of them to which I refer, is Lib. III. vs. 319 seq. Bleek himself has shown, that this book in all probability originated from an Alexandrine Jew, in the time of the Maccabees. But it exhibits an evident effort to imitate the book of Daniel, even transferring some of its imagery to itself. E. g. (in loc. cit.), we find Antiochus described as *ῥίζαν ἴαν γε διδούς — ἐκ δέκα δὴ κεράτων παρὰ δὴ φυτὸν ἄλλο φυτεύσει —καὶ τότε δὴ παραφυόμενον κέρας ἄρξει*, comp. Dan. 7: 7, 8. 8: 9, 10. 11: 21. This is so plain, that Bleek acknowledges the agreement between the two, but says that we must account for this, by the supposition that both had for their source one common and older tradition. But where are we to stop, in assumptions of such a nature? It would be easy, on such ground, *deducere aliquid ex aliquo*. If the matter be as stated above, it follows that the book of Daniel is older than the time of the Maccabees; for in their time it already had currency as a *prophetic* writing, inasmuch as the design of the Sibyllist is to show the fulfilment of prophecy by Antiochus.

(*f*) The book of Baruch was evidently written during the period of the Jewish persecutions by the Syrian tyrant, and written like the Macc., for the sake of consoling the Hebrews under their distresses. It assumes the attitude of assurance that the tyrant will fall, and that the Jews will regain their liberty and privileges. It seems to have drawn these views from the book of Daniel; and if this be admitted, it follows that at that time the book of Daniel was received and regarded as a prophetic writing.

(*g*) To come down somewhat lower; it lies upon the whole face of Josephus' narration of matters comprised in the book before us (in Antiq. X.), that he had not only regarded Daniel as a prophet, but the greatest of all the prophets. That the Jews of his day universally cherished the same sentiment, no one acquainted with their history will attempt to deny. But how comes it, now, that such productions as the Sibylline Oracles, the book of Enoch, and the like, never gained any such credit among the Jews as did the book of Daniel. If the Hebrews of that period were so credulous and easily deceived about books, as the newer criticism now in fashion represents them to have been, then how comes it that all the other productions of a like nature, i. e. designed to resemble it, were rejected as apocryphal and unworthy of a place in the sacred Canon?

(4) The reception of Daniel into the *Jewish Canon* bears strong testimony to its genuineness and authenticity.

(*a*) I need not here go into any detail of argument, to show that the Heb. Scriptures were the *same*, in the time of Christ and the apostles, that they now are. This is conceded even by those who attack the genuineness of the book before us. Nor is there any necessity here of showing at length, that the N. Test. writers in common with the Jews, attributed a divine origin and authority to the O. Test. Paul says (2 Tim. 3: 16), that "all Scripture is given *by inspiration of God*, and is profitable for doctrine, for reproof, for correction, for instruction in righteousness." Peter (2 Pet. 1: 21) declares, that "prophecy came not in old time by the will of man, but that holy men of God spake as they were moved by the Holy Ghost." It were easy to quote abundance of passages of the like tenor, not only from the N. Test., but from the Son of Sirach, Wisdom, 1 Macc., and other apocryphal books, written before the N. Test., as well as from Josephus, Philo, and other later Jewish writers. There was but one voice in all antiquity, among both Jews and Christians, in relation to this matter.

This of itself shows, that a wide difference was made at that period, between sacred and other books. But by what criterion were the two classes distinguished and separated? The only answer that can be given is, by that of *inspiration*, i. e. of inspiration supposed and believed to exist, in the writers of the respective books. But what was the evidence of this? What led the ancients to give credit to this alleged inspiration? The answer must be, that they gave credit in any particular case, because they deemed the author to be a *prophet*, either by virtue of a regular prophetic office, or by being endowed with some of the highest qualities which belonged to a regular prophet. The Jews, beyond all doubt, as the Talmud shows us (Bava Bathra, fol. 13. 2), attributed Joshua, Judges, Ruth, 1 and 2 Samuel, to Joshua and Samuel. The properly prophetic books testified for themselves; and the rest were distributed among David, Solomon, Jeremiah, Ezra, and Nehemiah. There are, indeed, some strange conceits mixed up with the Talmudic tradition. But they do not affect the point in question. On all hands it is and must be conceded, that however and whenever the book of Daniel came into the canon, it must have gained admittance as the supposed work of a real personage and a true prophet.

When then did the order of prophets cease? We have testimony in 4: 46 of the first book of the Maccabees, (written some 125—130 B. C. and very near the time when neological critics suppose the book of Daniel to have been written), that Judas Maccabaeus and his companions, when they reconsecrated the temple, after the defeat of the Syrian army and just before the death of Antiochus, pulled down the altar and removed the stones thereof to a place appropriate for keeping them, "until a *prophet* should come who would give directions concerning them," i. e. should order the manner in which they were to be disposed of. This transaction, according to the decision of *liberal* criticism, preceded only some months the composition of the book of Daniel. At that period, then, there was no *prophet* in Israel to settle such a question; much less to write a canonical book. Again, in 1 Macc. 9: 27, the same writer says: "There was great affliction in Israel, such as never occurred from the time when a *prophet* was no more seen;" which, from the very nature of the reference, implies a long period antecedent. Once more, in 14: 41, the same author says, that Simon was appointed governor and perpetual high priest, "until there should arise a *prophet worthy of credit*," (πιστόν). Of course there was no such prophet at that period.

Josephus says in the most express terms: "We have only *twenty-two* books, containing the history of every age, which are justly accredited. . . . From the time of Artaxerxes until our present period, all occurrences have been written down; *but they are not regarded as entitled to the like credit with those which precede them, because there was no infallible* (ἀκριβῆ) *succession of prophets*;" Cont. Ap. I. 8. All Jewish writings so far as we know, both earlier and later, consider the period of Malachi as the close or end of the succession of the prophets.

Adopting then the position, that the Jews never admitted any book to their sacred Canon, which they did not believe to be inspired, and to have originated from a prophet or a prophetical man in respect to gifts, our first inquiry has been, whether any such men were extant at the Maccabaean period. We have the direct testimony of a writer, at the very close of that period, (and a writer he is, moreover, of distinguished candor and fidelity, and by general consent worthy of credit), — we have his testimony, not only that there were no prophets, at that time, but that for a long time there had been none. The passage 1 Macc. 9: 27 (already quoted above) cannot mean less than this. Besides all this, the manner in which Jesus Sirach speaks of the ancient prophets, in 46: 15. 48: 22, shows that he considered the πιστοὶ ὁράσεως as belonging to the days of yore. Nor is there a syllable of history to contradict this. Certainly the Jews had national pride enough, to maintain the existence of prophets and the continuance of inspiration among them long after the death of Malachi, if there existed any fair or even tolerable ground for pretensions of this sort. The loss of the prophetic order was considered by them as a severe chastisement, and also as a great degradation. There cannot be, then, even the remotest probability, that the Jews would have given up such a claim, if it had been possible to support it.

(*b*) The next question that occurs then is: How came the book of Daniel to be inserted in the canon, if it were composed, as the Neologists assert, during the Maccabaean period, or rather, during that part of it which followed the death of Epiphanes? Who was the man to introduce a book unknown and unheard of before, and to procure a place for it in the sacred canon? Not any prophet; for such an one there was not. How then were the priests and elders and magistracy among the Jews persuaded to admit it? The forger of the book must have been a consummate manager as well as skilful writer, to persuade the Sanhedrim to such a measure; or else they must have been deplorably ignorant of their national usages in regard to Scripture, or so superstitious as to lay hold greedily of every book which made claims to sanctity. From what we know, and so far as we know, of the men of that period, there was no such dexterous forger in existence among the Jews; and even if there were, there was little likelihood of his success. The men of that day were far enough from being ignorant, stupid, or indifferent. There was among them a *συναγωγὴ γραμματέων*, whose business it was to attend to holy things; so 1 Macc. 7: 12. To the same purpose testifies Sirach (38: 24), who lived and wrote before Antiochus' reign, i. e. about 180 B. C. He speaks of the *σοφία γραμματέως* as being attained only by leisurely study, implying that there was such an order of men who were devoted to the study of sacred things. Again, in 39: 1, he speaks of the *γραμματεύς* as "seeking after the wisdom of all the ancients (*πάντων ἀρχαίων*), and diligently employing himself with the study of the prophecies" (*ἐν προφετείαις*). Beyond this, we are brought by 1 Macc. to an intimate acquaintance with Mattathias, the noble priest at Modin, who indignantly refused to obey the mandate of Epiphanes to sacrifice to idols; and also with his talented, heroic, and excellent sons, Judas, Jonathan, and Simon, who regained the freedom of their country. All these chose to die, rather than yield up anything belonging to their religion. Is it reasonable, now, to suppose that such men could have been entrapped and deceived, by a forger of a book at that period, claiming indeed to be much older, but never having before been heard of? And with all the rigorous attachment of such men to their ancient Scriptures and customs, so rigorous that it exposes them now to the accusation of superstition and severity, on the part of the Neologists, — with all their zeal and jealousy for the honor of their religion and their holy books, could they have been persuaded by a writer of their own time to add to their sacred canon? How obvious the questions they would ask, viz. If this book be as old as the time of Daniel, where has it been for these nearly four hundred years? How comes it to pass, that a book of such high import, as this seems to be, and so honorable to our nation, should have lain in utter neglect and forgetfulness during all that period? And to these questions, what possible answer that would be satisfactory, could be given by the forger of the book? I cannot even imagine what could have been his reply — I mean what reply could be such as would have given them satisfaction about the *age* and *authenticity* of the book. They all knew, of course, that until the forger presented this book, it was, and had for time immemorial been, unknown.

If now we unite all these considerations in one general view, it seems impossible that any one well acquainted with Jewish antiquity, can seriously maintain the probability of such a book being forged and forced into the Jewish canon, at that period. I should as soon have expected that Judas and his brethren would yield to the demands of Antiochus, in relation to sacrificing to idols, as that they would have altered the canon, when confessedly no prophet was extant, and for a long time there had been none. What says Josephus, himself a priest of a distinguished order, and a descendant of the Maccabees? In Cont. Ap. I. 8 he says: "Although so many ages have passed away, [viz. since the Scriptures were written], no one has dared to add to them, nor to take anything from them, nor to make alterations. In all Jews it is implanted, even from their birth, to regard them as being the instructions of God; and to abide steadfastly by them; and if it be necessary, to die gladly for them." Such are the genuine words of a genuine Jew, one of the most learned and enlightened of all Jews, as to the affairs and customs of his nation. Indeed, one cannot well conceive of a greater improbability, than that the book of Daniel was added to the sacred canon in the time of the Maccabees.

In truth, the representations of the Neologists are very inconsistent with themselves and contradictory, in regard to this period. As often as convenience dictates, the book of Daniel is assailed, on the ground that it exhibits rigorous fastings and praying and obstinate adherence to Jewish rites and opinions, which are characteristic only of such a period as that of the Macc., and therefore the book could not have been written by the enlightened ancient Daniel. Yet this very Maccabaean age of severe and superstitious adherence to the rites and usages and opinions of the fathers and elders, is the very one, according to our opponents, which not merely forges a new book, under a distinguished prophet's name, but gives credit without any hesitation to the antiquity and authority of a book pretending to be sacred, that had been unknown and unnoticed, from the time when the alleged author lived, down to their own time, i. e. about four centuries. Was there ever such a strange mixture of character as this, in the same age and among the same people? They are all rigor and severity and superstitious adherence to patristical tradition, on the one hand; and on the other, they are ready to welcome with open arms the imposture of a forger, who would fain put off his romantic and fantastic fictions, for the work of an ancient and holy prophet! In my humble opinion, it requires more real credulity to believe all this, than to believe that the book is ancient and genuine. How can we believe that such an age as that of the Maccabees, which produced so many noble patriots, such excellent statesmen, such enlightened and zealous priests, and withal such works as the Wisdom of Sirach and the first book of the Maccabees, not to name other productions of the time — how can we believe that an age, so zealous for the word of God and the honor of religion as to hold fast and adhere to even the minutest traditional opinions and usages, should commit a sacrilege on one of the holiest parts of the sacred domain, viz. on that of the most highly revered Scriptures? If it is not impossible, it is utterly improbable.

We are often told by the advocates of the Maccabaean period, that 'the age was too uncritical and undistinguishing, and indeed too ignorant, to detect the imposture in regard to the book of Daniel;' and we are now and then assured, by some of the bolder spirits among these advocates, that 'any book written in Hebrew, and on a religious subject, was of course added to the canon, if the writer desired it. In this way, the book of Daniel gained admittance into the sacred enclosure.' — But such a view of the subject is encompassed with difficulties. First of all, how came the writer of the book before us to hit upon the plan of writing one half of it in the Chaldee language? Other prophets of the exile period, viz. Ezekiel, Haggai, Zechariah, and Malachi, all wrote in *Hebrew*. Only Ezra exhibits any Chaldee in his composition; and here the occasion of so doing was the transcription of Chaldee documents. But Ezra is *history*, not prophecy. What advantage, then, in regard to the reception of the book of Daniel, could a writer of a late period anticipate, from writing in *Chaldee?* None. Moreover, the Chaldee of the Maccabaean period was very different from that in the books of Daniel and Ezra. Whence then did he get his skill in the old Hebrew-Chaldee? There was no model of a mixture of languages among the prophetic books of the O. Test. Why then should he choose such a method of writing? I see no good answer that can be made to this question. On the other hand; if the true Daniel wrote the book, all difficulty is easily solved. Daniel was equally at home in both languages, as his work fully testifies. He introduces Chaldee very naturally, when he comes to represent Nebuchadnezzar and his courtiers in mutual conference. He then continues it until the Chaldee history is completed, and even onward in ch. vi. vii. And why? Because he well knew, that those whom he addressed, would understand the Chaldee quite as well, or even better than they would the

Hebrew. A forger in the Maccabaean times had no inducement to mix languages. It was contrary to prophetic usage ; and therefore it would subject his book to suspicion.

In the next place, it is not true that other books of that period, written on religious subjects, were received into the Canon. The work of the Son of Sirach was written in *Hebrew*, as the preface of the translator testifies. This work, moreover, is not without strong claims on the pious mind. Some parts of it seem to be not unworthy of an inspired pen, and would do no disgrace to the sacred Canon. Nor is this all. The writer himself makes high claims to consideration. In 24: 33, 34 he says; "Further, I beam forth instruction as the morning light, and disclose those things even to distant ages. I moreover pour forth instruction as *prophecy* (προφητείαν), and leave it for future ages." Again in 33. 19, he represents himself as the last of the wise men, and compares himself with Solomon ; ἔσχατος ἠγρύπνησα are his words. In 30: 17, 18 he says: "Consider that I have not labored for myself alone . . . Hear ye rulers of the people, and give ear ye leaders of the congregation" (ἐκκλησίας). At the close, he assays to make strong impressions on the reader of his high claims: "In this book I have written the instruction of wisdom and knowledge . . . Blessed is he who is conversant with these things, and he who lays them up in his heart shall be wise; for if he do these things, he will be powerful in all respects, for the light of the Lord is on his footsteps," 50: 27—29. We must consider now, not only these high claims, but that the book was written *more prophetico*, i. e. in Hebrew and in *parallelisms*. Moreover, it was written in Palestine. In respect now to poetic parallelisms, they are almost entirely wanting in the book of Daniel, although there are some approaches to them. Why then was not the claim of Sirach admitted? Plainly because the canon was already closed. No other satisfactory reason can be given. The spirit and tenor of the book are certainly not unworthy of a very high place. But Sirach came too late. The Canon was completed and sealed as such. And all this, too, *before* the Maccabaean period or the reign of Antiochus began. The lowest point assignable to the composition of the book is 180 B. C. ; and it remains to this day a disputed question, whether it was not written a century earlier.

Here then is a fair specimen of the manner in which the Jews thought and acted, during the Maccabaean period. So little impression did the work of Jesus Sirach make in Palestine, where it was written, that his grandson, when he came to translate it into Greek, was obliged to go to Egypt in order to find a good copy of it, worthy of study. See Prol. ad Lib.

Nor is this all. There is the book of Tobit, in all probability earlier than that of Sirach, which was written also in *Hebrew*, and abounds in such fictions as the Maccabaean period is accused of fostering and approving. Did the Jews ever receive it into their Canon? This is not even pretended by any party.

The first book of the Maccabees, also, was written soon after the close of the limited Maccabaean period, (limited to the sons of Mattathias), the writer of it having evidently been himself conversant with a good part of that period. This too was written in *Hebrew*, as Jerome (Prol. Gal.) expressly testifies. Nothing could be more acceptable or interesting to the Jews of that time, than such a book. It is a very sober and veracious book for the most part, written with all becoming gravity and earnestness. Yet this never had any place in the Jewish Canon.

I say nothing of several other books, whose claims and age are doubtful. Enough that the asserted principle of easy reception into the Canon, and of inability in the Maccabaean age to distinguish the respective claims of books, are most glaringly contradicted by facts such as these. THAT AGE DID DISTINGUISH. It set aside Sirach, Tobit, 1 Macc., and doubtless many other books, and never thought of adding them to the Canon. Neither the Hebrew, nor the parallelisms, nor the pious matter, nor the lofty claims of Sirach, made any impression on the Jewish Sanhedrim of a just claim to a place in the Canon.

Enough has now been said respecting the character and design of the age of the Maccabees, in regard to religious things and religious books, to show the utter improbability of a book being foisted into the Canon at that period. But we have not done with the subject. Proof direct and positive of a defined and completed Canon, *before* the Maccabaean period, can be produced — proof that candor and impartiality can hardly reject.

The grandson of Jesus Sirach, who translated his work into Greek, says that his grandfather "gave himself very much to the reading of *the Law, the Prophets, and the Other Books* of his country." By this study, he was excited to write his own work. This *triplex* division is mentioned, in the preface to the Greek Version, not less than *three* times. (1) The Law, the Prophets, and the *other* (τῶν ἄλλων) books following them of the like tenor" (κατ' αὐτοὺς). (2) "The Law, the Prophets, and *the other* Books of his country," (τῶν ἄλλων πατρίων βίβλίων). (3) "The Law, the Prophecies, and *the rest of the Books*" (τὰ λοιπὰ τῶν βιβλίων). Nothing can be plainer, than that the translator here employs language in describing the sacred books which had been long and familiarly current. He expects his readers of course to apprehend readily and definitely, what books are meant. And what are they? Certainly not *all* other books; for then the article before *the other* or *the rest* (τῶν ἄλλων, τὰ λοιπά), must of necessity have been *omitted.* But now in every case, *the article is inserted.* This then makes a *definite, well-known* collection of sacred books which J. Sirach studied. And this collection was so defined, beyond any reasonable doubt, before the time of Sirach; for in his own work, we have evidence of this. In 45: 5, he speaks of the νόμος ζωῆς as given by Moses. In 44: 3, 5, speaking of ancient celebrated men, he says: "They gave counsel with intelligence, and delivered messages *in prophecies* (ἐν προφητείαις) ... They sought out musical songs, disclosing *maxims in writing*" (μέλη μουσικῶν ... ἔπη ἐν γραφῇ). Here then are plain traces of the triplex division of the Hebrew Scriptures; even more specific than the declarations of Sirach's grandson in his preface. Here the classification as to *matter* is essentially made. We have the Law, the Prophets, and virtually *the Psalms and Proverbs*, i. e. the leading and principal books in the Hagiography. That μέλη μουσικῶν means *Psalms*, and ἔπη *maxims*, (a frequent later classical use of this word), there can be no good room to doubt. Jesus Sirach and his grandson, then, are united in proclaiming the existence of a *definite* third division of the Hebrew Scriptures at that period. If so, then as Sirach *preceded* the Maccabees, the Canon was not open in the time of the latter to any new comer, but already definitely completed.

Let us follow this matter down to a later period. Our next witness is Christ himself. In Luke 24: 44, we have his words thus: "All things must be fulfilled, which are written in *the Law of Moses, and the Prophets, and the Psalms,* concerning me." V. 27 of the same chapter is substantially of the like tenor. Here, then, is the same thing, viz. triplex division, that we have already found in Sirach; excepting that the *Kethubhim* is designated only by its leading and principal book, viz. the *Psalms.*

We come next to Philo Judaeus (flor. circa 40 A. D.), who, in describing the Essenes, says of them, that "they receive the *Law*, and the Oracles uttered by the *Prophets*, and the *Hymns* and *the other* [books], by which knowledge and piety are augmented and perfected;" De Vita contemplat. ii. p. 475, edit. Mangey. Here then is Sirach's view reproduced; for here are his μέλη μουσικῶν and ἔπη. And so also the Ψαλμοί of Luke, plainly correspond to the ὕμνους of Philo.

Josephus is more graphic still. In Cont. Ap. i. 8, he says: "We have not a countless number of books, discordant and arrayed against

36

each other, [like those of the heathen], but only *two and twenty* books, containing the history of every age, which are justly accredited as divine. Of these *five* belong to Moses, containing laws and history... From the death of Moses, moreover, until the reign of Artaxerxes, king of the Persians after Xerxes, the Prophets who followed have described the things, which were done during the age of each one respectively, in *thirteen* books. The remaining four contain *Hymns to God, and rules of life for men.*" He then goes on to say, that other books have been written to describe occurrences subsequent to the time of Artaxerxes, but that "*they are not regarded as entitled to the like credit with those which precede them, because there was no certain succession of the Prophets.*" He declares, in the sequel, that "No addition to, or substraction from, them has ever been made, during the lapse of so long a period." Now here is, as we might expect, the identical division of Sirach, the New Testament, and Philo. All the difference is, that Josephus has been more specific in describing the third division, by averring that it consists of *Hymns to God and rules of life for men.* That the Psalms, Proverbs, Ecclesiastes, and Canticles are plainly included in this last division, cannot with any show of reason be denied. It appears indeed on the very face of the record. To make out the twenty-two books of Josephus, we have the Pent. = 5 ; the *thirteen* are Josh., Judg. with Ruth, 1 and 2 Sam., 1 and 2 Kings, 1 and 2 Chron., Ezra with Neh., Esth., Job., Is., Jer. with Lam., Ezek., Daniel, and twelve minor Prophets, = 13. *Four* books are still left; and these of course must be Psalms, Prov., Ecc., and Canticles. That the books of Solomon were counted in this manner by the Jews, Origen explicitly states, (in Euseb. Hist. Ecc. IV. 25). In no other way can the number twenty-two be made out. The description of the contents of the last four, puts it beyond a doubt, moreover, that the Psalms, Prov., Ecc., and Canticles, belonged to this division. Of course, therefore, the book of Daniel was included by Josephus in the division of the Prophets. And Josephus' description, moreover, is in perfect accordance with all that is said of the same third division in Sirach, the New Testament, and Philo Alexandrinus.

(*d*) This brings us to say something in regard to the Masoretic and Talmudic divisions of the Hebrew Scriptures, which place Daniel among the *Kethubhim* or third division. The place thus assigned to the book of Daniel, (and now occupied by it in our common Hebrew Bibles), has been a matter of much speculation and discussion, and has been regarded by most of the neological critics, as decisive of the *late* composition of the book. This circumstance stands in the very front of their arguments adduced against the antiquity of the book; and it may be as well, or better discussed here, than in any other place.

The course of argument, fairly drawn out and yet compressed, stands thus: (1) 'A miracle is an impossibility; and of course, real prediction of minute future events is impossible, for this would be a miracle. (2) The book of Daniel contains such a minute account of the Syrian and Egyptian (Macedonian) kings, that it is *history*, and not prophecy. It could have been written only *post eventum*. (3) The Canon, of course, could not have been closed until after the death of Antiochus, since Daniel is comprised in it. (4) This last position is confirmed by the fact, that Daniel stands near the close of *Kethubhim*, separated from all his prophetical brethren, who are honored with a place among the *Prophets*. No good account can be given of this, except the *lateness* of its composition. We must therefore conclude, that the division of the Prophets had been *closed*, while that of the *Kethubhim* was kept open for later books.'

Such is the course of argument by which Daniel is to be degraded from his rank, and his work held up as a supposititious book of fiction and of mere pretension to an oracular character. I shall not follow this view of the subject *seriatim*, nor attempt a separate refutation at length of each assertion. I shall first make a few remarks on some of the positions, and then proceed to inquire *when* and *how* Daniel came into its present position among the sacred books.

On the first argument I have nothing more to say, than that it sets itself immediately in direct array against the often repeated declarations of the Saviour himself, that the Old Test. prophets had *predicted* his coming, his work, and his sufferings; and also against Paul, and Peter, and John, who all testify to the same things, and to the divine inspiration of the Old Test., as well as the *prophetical* powers of those who wrote it. Secondly, that the book of Daniel contains prophecies of events so minute and circumstantial, that it has the appearance of history, yea is (as it were) veritable history, I doubt not. I fully accede to this. But that it was written *post eventum*, is another matter; a matter to be decided by *testimony*, not by fore-gone *a priori* conclusions. The *when* is as much a matter-of-fact inquiry, as the *when* of the Æneid, or the Iliad, or of Livy's History. Had there been one scrap of positive evidence to prove the *lateness* of the composition of Daniel, its opponents would not have failed to adduce it. But not finding a syllable of this nature in all antiquity, the only resort must be to the *a priori* argument. But this unhappily goes too far. If followed out, it would inevitably convict the Saviour of the world of being an impostor or an ignoramus;

and prove that all his apostles must be rânked under the same category. Such men as Lengerke and Knobel and Hitzig may not start at this, probably would not; but God be thanked, there are many thousands and millions throughout Christendom, who shrink back with shuddering from such fearful conclusions.

Thirdly, as the Canon actually contained Daniel, it remains to inquire, as a matter of fact, *when* and *how* it came into its present place. The assertion of neologists, that the Canon was kept open until after the death of Antiochus, has already been sufficiently examined. Scarcely any thing belonging to the criticism of antiquity, can be made clearer or more certain, than that before the time of Sirach the Canon was definite and complete. This alone, if regarded as true, completely overturns the neological edifice. A *post eventum* Daniel could, of course, have been written only after the death of Antiochus. If the Canon was complete so early as the time of Sirach, then Daniel must be *prophecy;* as entirely so, and as much so, as if we assign it to the true Daniel.

The last refuge of our opponents, then, is the *position* of Daniel in the Hagiography, viz. its being dissociated from the other prophets. How came the book there, we are asked, unless the division of the prophets was closed, and the *third* division yet left open? What else could induce the Rabbies to assign such a place to it? To these questions many different answers have been attempted. I shall notice only some of the leading ones.

It has been matter of surprise to me, that Hengstenberg (Auth. des Daniel, s. 27 seq.) assumes as the basis of his solution of the question, the opinion of Maimonides and other Rabbies, viz. that the triplex division of the Old Test. was occasioned by the different *grades of inspiration* in their authors. Rabbinic speculation and phantasy has made three degrees of inspiration, as it would seem, viz. (1) That of Moses, who talked *face to face* with Jehovah. That was peculiar and special, for no other prophet ever did the same. (2) That of the prophets proper, who were rapt into such an ecstasy, that their bodily powers were affected and suspended, and their minds guided entirely and solely by divine influence. Such men as these wrote the *prophets* or second division of the Scriptures. (3) Such as were quickened and illuminated and guided indeed, but who still retained and used their bodily and mental powers. These wrote the Kethubhim. I do not understand Hengstenberg as intending to vouch for the soundness of this assumed distinction in the grades of inspiration, but as maintaining that the Talmudists, or the older Rabbies, who assigned to Daniel its present place, were guided by such a rule.

Perhaps this may be so. They seem to have held, that a prophet could not write a sacred book abroad, and yet enjoy the same degree of aid as one in Palestine. In the Talmud. Bab. Megill. fol. 10. c. 2, they assert that "the men of the great Synagogue *wrote out* (כָּתְבוּ) Ezekiel, Daniel, and Esther." This, if we are to believe Rabbi Sol. Jarchi (Comm. in Bava Bathra), they did "because prophecy is not given for any one to write *in a foreign land*." It is unnecessary to examine seriously and minutely refute all this. It is enough to ask a few questions. *(a)* If Daniel was at all admitted to the Canon, (which no one denies), it must have been on the ground that it was believed to be a true book, and worthy of credit. None will deny this. Yet Daniel claims what the Rabbies call the *middle grade* of inspiration, like that of Is. in 6: 5, 6; of Ezekiel in 1: 28. 2: 1, 2. 3: 24; comp. Dan. 7: 28. 8: 18, 27. 10: 7—10. Why then was he not put among the *prophets?* *(b)* The Talmudic ground is self-contradictory, as it respects the Kethubhim. Who are the Moses and David, who appear in the Psalms, and the Solomon in the Proverbs? Is not their high inspiration admitted on all hands? Jeremiah, moreover, as a prophet, is ranked with the other prophets; how then came his *Lamentations* into the Hagiography? Besides, the Talmud says, that Moses wrote the book of Job; how then came it to be put into the *third* division? And as to any power on the part of the Talmudists, to distinguish the gradations of inspiration, how shall this be illustrated or authenticated? How could Ps. ii. xxii. xlv. cx., not to name many others, be supposed to exhibit less of inspiration than the works of Haggai, or Malachi, or Obadiah, or Jonah? Christ and his apostles make no gradations of authenticity for the Old Test. Paul says, that "all Scripture is given by inspiration of God." The whole matter, then, of the Rabbinical distinction, is a figment; and a very inconsistent one besides. I do not say that it is impossible to suppose the Talmudists to have been influenced by it; for what conceit is there, which they have not broached, and brought their authority to support? I only say, that there is not the least solidity or consistency in the ground here assumed for putting Daniel among the Kethubhim.

Havernick retreats from this untenable ground, but assumes another, which I deem to be equally unsafe and unsolid. He avers (Einleit. § 11), that 'the classification is grounded on the distinction between נָבִיא and חֹזֶה or רֹאֶה.' The first of these, he says, 'was *officially* a prophet; the second might have the gift and power of prediction, but was not properly a prophet. The second class of scriptural books belong to *the official prophets;* the third to the *seers.* Daniel was put in the third division because he was only a *seer*. He never claims to hold the proper office of prophet among the Hebrews; nor was he sent to address the Jews.' He avers, moreover, that 'the Hebrew Scriptures throughout keep up the distinction in question;' although he allows that the Septuagint and the New Test. have usually rendered both classes of words by *προφήτης*. How easily might he have avoided such an ungrounded statement, had he consulted his Hebrew Concordance! Indeed, 1 Sam. 9: 9 of itself shows, that all the difference between נָבִיא and רֹאֶה is, that the latter is the old name, and the other the new one just come into vogue in the time of Samuel. *Etymologically* the words are different; both designate the same person. No assignable distinction of any importance can be made out between רֹאֶה and חֹזֶה. That these latter words are often applied to the same prophet, who is elsewhere styled נָבִיא, sufficiently denotes identity of meaning in both words. E. g. the collective body of those more usually styled *prophets*, are called *seers*, in 2 Kings 17: 13. 2 Chron. 33: 18. Is. 29: 10. 30: 10. Mic. 3: 7. Then Samuel is נָבִיא in 1 Sam. 3: 20. 2 Chron. 35: 18, and רֹאֶה in 1 Sam. 9: 11, 18, 19. 1 Chron. 9: 22. 26: 28. 29: 29. Gad is a *prophet* in 1 Sam. 22: 5. 2 Sam. 24: 11, and a *seer* in 1 Chron. 29: 29. Iddo is *prophet* in 2 Chron. 13: 22, and *seer* in 9: 29. Jehu is *prophet* in 1 Kings 16: 7, 12, and *seer* in 2 Chron. 19: 2. The *prophet* Amos is also called חֹזֶה *seer* in Amos 7: 12. That נָבִיא, which in the time of Samuel began to thrust out רֹאֶה, was afterwards much more frequently employed than the other appellations, is readily admitted. But that any important distinction was made between the two classes of words, is palpably a mistake. Of course, the whole superstructure erected upon this distinction falls with the distinction itself. Whatever may have been the reason or ground of the Talmudic arrangement, it was plainly not the one in question.

Omitting to canvass other less probable theories, and also mere phantasies, in relation to the matter before us, I shall resort to a shorter method of settling the controversy; and this is, to show that *the book of Daniel, from the time of the earliest testimony concerning it,* WAS NOT PLACED AMONG THE KETHUBHIM, BUT OCCUPIED ITS PROPER PLACE AMONG THE PROPHETS, *down to the time of Jerome and the compiling of the Talmud.* After all that has been exhibited above, the proof is short and easy.

We have seen that the triplex division of *Law, Prophets,* and *Other Books* is at least older than Sirach, and that he describes the third division (in 44: 5), as consisting of *μέλη μουσικῶν* and *ἔπη ἐν γραφῇ*, i. e. *poetry to be sung*, and *written maxims*. He does not define more minutely; but this method of expression does of itself exclude Daniel from said division. The next testimony, in Luke 24: 44, designates the third division by the word *Psalms*, making out the title, as was frequently the custom, from the leading book. But *Daniel* has nothing to do with *Psalms*. Then comes Philo, (in Vit. Contempl. II. p. 475), who says of the Kethubhim, that "*they are hymns, and other writings designed to increase knowledge and piety*;" which last clause is descriptive of Proverbs and Ecclesiastes. That he includes *Daniel* in this last class, there is not a shadow of proof. Certain it is, that Josephus, his contemporary in part, and who wrote a few years after him, (in Cont. Ap. I. 8), beyond all question *excludes* Daniel from the Kethubhim. He assigns, as we have seen, five books to Moses, thirteen to the Prophets, and four to the third division, which, like all his predecessors, he describes as consisting of "*hymns to God and rules of life for men.*" His *second* division can by no possibility be made out by the Jewish mode of reckoning, without the aid of *Daniel*. Of course, Psalms, Proverbs, Ecclesiastes, and Canticles, in his time, made out the Hagiography.

But how stood the matter afterwards? The first catalogue, *seriatim* and with the names of the books, we find in Melito bishop of Sardis, fl. A. D. 170. It is copied entire into Euseb. Hist. Ecc. IV. 26. He disregards the order of succession in our Heb. Bibles, and follows in the main that of the Septuagint. He places Daniel after Jeremiah and before Ezekiel, i. e. between them. Origen, that great lover and master of the critical study of the Scriptures, (as preserved in Euseb. Hist. Ecc. IV. 25), assigns to Daniel the same place. The Council of Laodicea, (between A. D. 360—364), in their canon (59) put Daniel among the Prophets, and next after Ezekiel, as in our English Bibles. Cyril of Jerusalem, (fl. A. D. 350), in his Catechesis IV, says expressly that Daniel belongs to the *prophetical* books, and he ranks him next after Ezekiel. Gregory Nazianzen, (fl. A. D. 370), in his Carmen. XXXIII. (Opp. II.), ranks Daniel in the same way. Athanasius (fl. 326), in his festal Epistle (Opp. I. p. 961), in his list of sacred books, ranks Daniel next after Ezekiel. The Synopsis Scrip. Sac., by an anonymous writer who was his contemporary, (in Athanas. Opp. II. p. 126), gives to Daniel the same place. The same does Epiphanius (fl. A. D. 368), in his De Mens. et Ponder. 23. II. p. 180. The Council of Hippo, (the *magnus Apollo* of the Romish canon), in A. D. 393, in their list of the holy books, placed Daniel between Jeremiah and Ezek., just as Melito and Origen had done. The Council of Carthage, held in A.D. 397, (Mansi, III. p. 891), follow the same order. Hilary of Poictiers (fl. A. D. 254) also arranges Daniel in the same order. Rufinus (fl. 390 A. D.), the distinguished friend and also opponent of Jerome, puts Daniel next after Ezekiel, and before the twelve

Minor Prophets; Expos. in Symb. Apost., ad calcem Opp. Cyp. p. 26, edit. Oxon.

Thus *every regular catalogue of scriptural books in all antiquity, puts Daniel among the Prophets,* and nearly one half of them put him before Ezekiel. In this way we come to see, that the division asserted by Josephus, and by his predecessors, Sirach and the N. Test. and Philo, is fully and abundantly vindicated.

There is an additional witness, as yet only alluded to, whom we must now bring upon the stand. This is the *Septuagint.* It is all but certain, that this version was completed as early at least as 130 B. C. In this, the whole Talmudical arrangement is utterly disregarded, and *Daniel appears between Ezekiel and the Minor Prophets;* see Bos' edition.

One thing more should be remarked, before we advert to Jerome and the Rabbies. This is, that in all the catalogues of scriptural books throughout all antiquity, which have now been brought to view, the arrangement in regard to the books of the *Kethubhim,* which Josephus discloses, is substantially preserved. In all those catalogues, the Psalms, Proverbs, Ecclesiastes, and Canticles, are brought into *successive and immediate continuity;* nor are they in a single instance separated, as they are in the Masoretico-Talmudic arrangement. There can be no good reason to doubt, that before the Talmudists meddled with the Kethubhim, no separation of the four books in question was known or thought of. Even Jerome, with all his deference to the Talmud, holds fast to this continuity; and in some other respects he has varied from the Talmud, as we shall see in the sequel.

We are now prepared for the testimony of Jerome. He makes (in Prol. Gal.) twenty-two books, five belonging to the Law, eight to the Prophets, and nine to the Hagiography. But still he puts Ruth into one book with Judges, and Lam. into one with Jeremiah; whereas the Talmud separates both of these, and throws them into the Kethubhim; and of course it makes twenty-four books. Jerome closes the third division in the following order: "Daniel, Chron., Ezra, Esther." In this arrangement of Daniel he stands unsupported by a single witness in all antiquity, excepting the Talmud. Jerome spent twenty years among the Rabbies of Palestine; and although the Talmud was not written until some time after his death, yet the elements of it were then concocting, and from the Masorites of Tiberias he learned to arrange the Kethubhim in the main, in the manner stated. It was natural for him to follow in such a matter his masters in Hebrew; although he has not after all made, as they did, *twenty-four* books, nor thrown either Ruth or Lam. into the third class.

But the Jewish doctors themselves — are they agreed? By no means; the Talmud puts Isaiah *after* Jeremiah and Ezekiel, while the Masorites place Isaiah at the head of the Prophets proper; and besides this, there are some other discrepancies in arranging some of the smaller books. The reason given by the Talmudists for their preposterous arrangement, presents a good specimen of their skill in *critique*. 'Isaiah,' say they, 'is full of consolation, Jeremiah of woe, and Ezek. of woe first and consolation afterwards. It was meet that woe should be joined with woe, and consolation with consolation.' Such was a sufficient reason, in the view of their phantasy, for committing a real ὕστερον πρότερον in the arrangement of these books.

How much deference now is due, to such Jewish authorities as these of the fifth and sixth century? Much less, truly, than has been paid to it. Independent of this, however, there is not one scrap of evidence in all antiquity to prove that Daniel was disconnected from the other prophets; but all of it goes in a solid phalanx to establish the position, that he held a place immediately before or after Ezekiel. The whole affair of ejecting him from his proper heritage, was got up and carried through about the time of Jerome, i. e. near A. D. 400, and therefore about the time when Talmudism was concocting.

But *why* did the Rabbies do this? To this question we can give only a conjectural answer. The theories of Hengstenberg and Hävernick, designed to account for this transaction, have already been examined. I have not said, and would not say, that the Talmudists never entertained such views. My aim has been to show how insufficient and unsatisfactory and inconsistent they are. Bertholdt, as others had done before, suggests that the ground of Talmudic arrangement was the dispute between the Rabbies and the Christians, in which the latter continually appealed to Daniel for proof that the Messiah had already come. They designed, he supposes, to abridge the credit of Daniel, by dissevering him from the prophets. But although this seems rather plausible, yet it will not bear the test of rigid scrutiny; for surely the Kethubhim were not regarded by the Rabbies as *uninspired* books. It is even quite doubtful, whether they could have supposed that such books as the Psalms, Proverbs, and Job, were less inspired than the Law and the Prophets. In fact, the Talmud (Bab. Megill. fol. 10. c. 2.) says that "*Moses* wrote the book of Job." David and Solomon are exceedingly elevated by the Talmudists. Still, Job, Psalms, and Proverbs, are comprised in their Kethubhim. So is Lam., while Jer. is in the second division. The *degree* of inspiration, then, as a principle of division, seems fairly to be out of question. Jarchi, perhaps, has hit on one reason which might have influenced them in the separation of Daniel from his fellow-prophets. This Rabbi says (Comm. on Bava Bathra), that "prophecy is not given for any one to write it in a foreign country." But even here they are inconsistent. Did not Ezekiel write in Babylonia? Did not Jeremiah write a part of his book in Egypt? See chap. xlvi. seq.

All attempts then, to solve this question respecting the principle of division with any certainty, appear to be ineffectual. We must leave it, as we are obliged to leave a multitude of other Rabbinic conceits and inventions, as neither accounted for nor supported.

But Neology has found, as stated above, a new reason for Daniel's place, at least one surely unknown to the Rabbins. It assures us, that 'the first and second divisions were *closed* before Daniel was written, and that the third division was kept open purposely in order to add the later books.'

Lateness of composition, then, is here assumed as the principle which guided the combination of books in the Kethubhim. But will this hold? Was *Moses* a late writer? for the 90th Psalm they have always attributed to him. Were David and Solomon *late* writers? And the book of Job — was this a *late* production, in the view of Jewish Rabbies, who attributed it to Moses? No; such an account of the matter is unsatisfactory and inconsistent with plain facts. Besides this, we have seen, that the Canon was closed before the Maccabaean age; and that there was no opening for Daniel at that period, not any more than there was for Sirach, Tobit, and the first of Maccabees.

Besides; what shall we say to the latest edition of neology, which, in the person of Hitzig, one of its chief exponents, declares that Jonah and Obadiah were both written by the same person, and written in Egypt during the Maccabaean age? (Hitz., Jona Orakel üb. Moab, s. 36 ff.) But how is this? If Daniel was put into the Kethubhim, because it was written so late as that time, why was not the author of Jonah and Obadiah assigned to the same location for the same reason? Is neology consistent, then, with itself?

I trust that enough has now been said, to show beyond all reasonable doubt or contradiction, that Daniel was never put among the Kethubhim, until near the close of the fourth century; and then only by the Rabbies, from whom Jerome received his account of the number and order of the sacred books, as he himself declares. From him and his teachers has been derived that classification of the Hebrew Scriptures, which has been prevalent since that period, and which appears in most if not all of our printed Hebrew Bibles. That this is against the testimony of the Sept., Sirach, N. Test., Philo, Josephus, Melito, Origen, the Council of

Laodicea, Cyrill of Jerusalem, Gregory Nazianzen, Athanasius, Synop. Scrip. Sac., Epiphanius, the Council of Hippo, and that of Carthage, Hilary, and Rufinus, has been shown above.* I do not know of a single error, in regard to ancient critical matters, which has been so long and generally admitted as the one in question, nor scarcely any one of the like nature, which has been so little examined. It would seem, that confidence in Talmudic doctors, as to the point before us, has been as complete and as general as they could desire; and it has been even more implicit than that of Jerome.

Such being the actual state of the case, we may know what answer to give to neological assertions respecting Daniel's place in the Canon. The main external argument against the genuineness of the book, is derived by the *liberal* critics from the *location* of Daniel among the books of the Hagiography. The simple answer is, that *facts contradict the assumption* that Daniel was ever ranked in this way, before the close of the fourth century of the Christian era. Within the last half of that century, we have a cloud of witnesses that such an arrangement was unknown in the churches; for the Council of Laodicea, Cyrill of Jerusalem, Gregory Nazianzen, Athanasius, the author of the Synopsis Scrip. Sac., Epiphanius, the Councils of Hippo and of Carthage, Hilary, and Rufinus, all testified during this period, and every one of these, as well as Melito and Origen, puts Daniel immediately before or after Ezekiel. It was only those that had opportunity to pry into the Kabbala of Rabbinism, who had any cognizance of Daniel as being separated from his fellow-prophets; and Jerome was the only man among them all, who was conversant with Rabbinical lore, and all that he does is, to tell us how the Rabbies of his day classified the sacred books. The fact we do not deny. But we assert, because we think we have fully proved, that such a classification of Daniel as the one in question, was a *recent* conceit, produced in the concoction of Talmudism.

In confirmation of the opinion that the Canon (Kethubhim) was open to addition, in the time of the Maccabees, our opponents appeal to the so-called *Maccabaean Psalms*, and ask: 'How came these into the Canon? The answer is simple and easy, viz. that this is only proving the amount of an unknown quantity by reference to another equally unknown. The *Maccabaean* Psalms! We have often enough heard this decantated, and have sought in vain for a single proof, external or internal, of origin in the Maccabaean age, but have never been able to find any. Even De Wette, whose proclivity to critical suspicions is everywhere prominently

* See all the passages relating to this subject, at full length, in the appendix to my little work on the Canon of the Old Testament.

developed, pronounces the matter in question to be *doubtful* (zweïfelhaft), Einl. ins Alt. Test. § 271, edit. 3. Rosenmüller, who once held the opinion in question, has given it up in his last edition of the Psalms. How any one can examine the Comm. Crit. de Psal. Maccab. (4to 1827) of Hassler, and yet persevere in this opinion, I am unable to see. One specimen of argumentation will suffice. Of all the Psalms (xliv. lxxiv. lxxvi. lxxix. lxxxiii. cxix.) said to be Maccabaean, it will be acknowledged that the seventy-ninth has much the strongest claims to be so considered. Yet in 1 Macc. 7: 17, the second verse of this very Psalm is quoted, and applied as a prediction of the slaughter of the sixty priests described in the context.

Some other books have here and there been assigned to a Maccabaean period. But no serious impression has been made by such an assignment, and the arguments employed in its favor are too unimportant to need notice.

We have now seen on what a sandy foundation the structure of opposition to the book of Daniel is built, so far as it respects the *place* which it holds in the Canon. We have seen that all antiquity, down to about A. D. 400, assigned the book to the division of the *Prophets*, and not to the Hagiography. We have also seen, that the Canon was closed before the period of Antiochus. Our general position under our *fourth* head, then, that the *canonicity* of the book goes to establish its genuineness, is illustrated, and (as we believe) amply confirmed.

But we have not yet done with this matter concerning the *antiquity of a definite Canon.* There is another argument, which, although I do not remember to have seen it anywhere adduced, seems to me to be of great if not absolutely conclusive weight. It is this. The well known sects of the *Pharisees* and *Sadducees* were in existence long before the Christian era. The Jewish tradition ascribes the name and origin of the Sadducees to one צָדוֹק, i. e. *Zadok*, who flourished in the time of Ptolemy Euergetes, about 240 B. C. The probability is, that they were still more ancient; but be that as it may, this is enough for our purpose. The matter in dispute, which brought out or raised up the two sects just named, was the simple but very important question: *Whether the Scriptures were the sufficient and only rule of faith and practice?* The Pharisees maintained the authority of *tradition*, and agreed with what the doctors of the Mishna afterwards taught. The Sadducees were strict and rigid *Scripturists;* just as the *Karaites* (קָרָאִים) among the Jews of modern times are. That the accusations brought against the Sadducees, of rejecting all the books of the O. Test. except the Pent., are utterly groundless, has often been shown of late. Winer has done a good service in regard to this matter, in his Bibl. Real-Wörterbuch, art. Sadducäer. Free and skeptical notions about some things, the Sadducees of our Saviour's time entertained, as we know by the N. Test.; but of the assertion that they ever rejected any portion of the Jewish Scriptures, there is not any proof at all. Nay, there is, as Winer has shown, abundant evidence of the contrary.

It is quite probable, that the sects in question date back to the time of the Persian domination in Palestine, or very near to it. At all events, we find them fully developed, and in the most heated contest, in the days of John Hyrcanus, the nephew of Judas Maccabaeus, and son of Simon his brother. This man was, as we have seen, the most distinguished of all his illustrious house, being prince, high priest, and (as Josephus thinks) favored with some divine communications. He began life as a most zealous Pharisee. In the sequel he took offence at the reproaches of one Eleazer, a turbulent man of the same sect, and because the Pharisees would not mete out adequate punishment to the offender, Hyrcanus went over to the Sadducees, and had no more connection with his former associates. Josephus has told the whole of this story, in Antiq. XIII. 10. 3, 5—7. The whole narration of the matter makes an impression on the reader, that the sects had then been formed for a long time, and were most inveterately divided and hostile. The Pharisees did all they could to put down John Hyrcanus, after he quitted them. In Antiq. XIII. 10. 6 and XVIII. 1. 4, Josephus states very explicitly, that the great point in dispute between the two parties, was *the sufficiency of the Scriptures alone*, the one defending this position, and the other appealing to *tradition* as well and as much as to Scripture.

This state of matters and of opinions, then, necessarily implies several important things; (1) That the Scriptures were already a definite, well known, and authoritative collection or code. The Pharisees conceded this as fully as the Sadducees. But they clung also to *traditional oral laws* or *maxims*, as designed to be a supplement to the Scriptures. Yet they never undertook to intermingle and combine the two. Indeed it was not until more than 200 years after the birth of Christ, that the traditional laws of the Pharisees were embodied in writing, i. e. when the *Mishna* was composed. Of course the matter of the Mishna could never intermingle with the genuine Scriptures. If these, moreover, had not been definite, there could have been no quarrel about extraneous additions. (2) The quarrel having first arisen on the very point of *the exclusive authority of the Scriptures*, neither party could ever add any thing to the Scriptural books, and cause it to be acknowledged by the other. The thing was impossible. Nor did either party ever attempt, so far as we know, to add to the number of the sacred books. Every attempt must evidently have been futile. The case is just such an one, in its main aspect, as the question between the Jews and the Romanists, in regard to the *Apocrypha*. The latter acknowledge and defend it as a *deutero-canon*, as they eulogistically call it; while the Jews have ever looked on the Apocrypha with disdain and contempt, in respect to any claims set up for it as a part of their sacred volume. They never have acknowledged it, and probably never will acknowledge it. Yet even the Romanists do not pretend, that the apocryphal books were attached by the Jews to their Scriptures. And so it was with the Pharisees and and Sadducees. Neither party ever tried to enlarge the sacred volume itself. Right glad we may naturally suppose, might a thorough Pharisaical devotee have been, to give his traditional law all the authority of Scripture, and to attach, it may be, some book like the Mishna to his Bible. But he well knew the effort would be vain. The scriptural books must therefore continue to remain by themselves, and have no new associates.

All this now has its basis in historical facts. The opposing sects did exist. The question that raised up the sects, was, whether any addition could be made to *scriptural* authority. Moreover, the sects arose, most plainly, some considerable time before the reign of John Hyrcanus; and very probably near the close of the Persian, or at the beginning of the Macedonian, domination in Palestine. After the sects arose, such was the nature of the quarrel, that *all addition to, or diminishing from, the Scriptures then extant was morally impossible.* It follows, then, as an inevitable consequence of all this, that the Jewish Canon was completed before the Maccabaean period. Of course, the book of Daniel belonged to it *before* that period, for it could not have been added *after* it; and if so, then is its place in the Canon strong testimony in favor of its antiquity and authority. Our opponents do not even pretend, that between the time of the real Daniel and that of the supposititious one at the Maccabaean period, there was any occasion for writing the book, or any person who could write it. If indeed any such person did write it in that intervening period, then he must plainly have been a *prophet* in the true sense of that word; but the possibility of this Neology denies.

(*e*) In confirmation of what has been said above, to show that the book of Daniel was written and belonged to the Canon, before the Maccabaean period, and not at that time, may be adduced several striking discrepancies as to some important doctrines, between the books of the Maccabaean age and the book of Daniel. (1) It is acknowledged, on all hadns, that the *Christology* of the book of Daniel is peculiar for its amplitude and its speciality. Indeed, Lengerke himself appeals to it as a proof, that the book could not have been written at an early period; and this because none of the earlier prophets exhibit a Christology so fully developed. But he has ignored the Christology of the Maccabaean age, and has not led us at all to see whether Messianic expectations are developed in that age, in a manner kindred to that of Daniel. Whether this proceeds from haste or design in Lengerke, is not my present task to inquire. Thus much I have learned by studying the pages of this author, (who is the Coryphaeus of Daniel's opponents), viz. that he needs looking after, and that it is better to trust to one's own researches, than to his representations.

How then does this whole matter stand? It stands thus: Daniel exhibits more *Messianic* matter in proportion to the length of his book, than any other writer of the Old Test. One may truly say, that the Messianic development constitutes the very kernel or essence of the whole book. The first dream of Nebuchadnezzar brings out, on the part of the interpreter, a striking development of the fifth or Messianic universal and perpetual empire, 2: 44, 45. The first vision of Daniel does this more amply still; see 7: 13, 14, 27. In 7: 13 the human nature and person of the Messiah is specifically developed, and he is called by the very name *(Son of Man)* which he so often bestowed on himself. The characteristics of his dominion and empire are the same here, as in the preceding case. His coming and atonement are again declared in 9: 24. In 12: 1—3 we have the events that will ensue after his coming, viz. the resurrection of the dead, and the retributions of eternity. What prophet in the Old Test. has so plainly revealed these several particulars?

But how was this matter in the time of the Maccabees? In the book of Tobit, we find two passages which seem to be built on some vague and floating Messianic ideas. They are in 13: 7—18. 14: 4—7, and exhibit a probable reference to the prophets, who had predicted the return of the Jews from all foreign countries, the building up and adorning of Jerusalem, and the submission of the nations to the Jewish dominion. But all these are plainly understood in their literal sense. No *spiritual* Messianic kingdom is even hinted at. In 1 Macc. 2: 57 and Sir. 47: 11, are two passages which pertain to the splendor and perpetuity of David's throne, i. e. they refer to Ps. 89: 36 literally interpreted. In Sir. 32: 19, there is a passage which asserts the future general prosperity of the Jewish nation. In 1 Macc. 14: 41, *a prophet* yet to come is adverted to; but plainly it is a prophet of the ordinary stamp, for the word is προφήτην, i. e. it is without the article, whereas, if the Messiah had been meant, the insertion of the article was plainly necessary.

These are all that look like *Messianic* predictions in the whole of the Apocrypha. What a striking contrast between Sirach, Tobit, and 1 Macc. on the one hand, and the prophecies of Daniel on the other! In the Apocrypha, what little it contains of this nature is mere generalization, and altogether of a temporal and civil aspect. Not a single passage has respect to a *spiritual* kingdom, and a *spiritual* redemption. All is purely national, merely Jewish, limited to one people, or extended to others only in proportion as they submit to the Jews. In Daniel, on the other hand, the kingdom is universal; the views of a future period are most extensive and cosmopolitan. He tells us of "making reconcilation for iniquity, of bringing in everlasting righteousness, and of confirming vision and prophecy," 9: 24. He discloses to us a *personal* Messiah; also a resurrection, and a general judgment; but the Apocrypha has nothing of all these. Only 2 Macc., (a late production, and far from being authentic), in 7: 9 seq. speaks of a resurrection; but even here, it speaks only of the *just.* Nor has this any connection with the Messiah. This is all that the Apocrypha yields, in regard to these momentous topics. How barren, how poor, how frigid, in comparison with the soul-stirring declarations of Daniel!

It is a fair question now to ask: How came all this? The writer of Daniel, in the midst of the Maccabaean time and partaking of the common views of his contemporaries, as we should naturally suppose — this writer makes a more ample Christological development than any other prophet of the Old Test., while all his contemporaries are either profoundly silent on these great topics, or, if they are not silent, they say nothing of the same tenor and significancy as the words of Daniel! And all this too, from a *forger* of a book — a singular person, one would think, to cherish and develop such views! No; the thing is not credible. It is wholly opposed to the state of opinion in the Maccabaean age. It is on the very face of the whole Apocrypha, that nothing but obscure and floating and general conceptions were entertained at that time, about a Messiah, or a Messianic kingdom. The Daniel before us stands much more nearly connected with Is., and Micah, and Jer., and Joel, and other ancient prophets, than with the writers of the Maccabaean period. It is on that account that he merits, and has obtained, a place in the ancient Canon; and the fact that he did, pleads strongly for the genuineness and authenticity of his book.

Besides these striking discrepancies between the spirit and tenor of

Daniel's book and the productions of the Maccabaean period, there are several other circumstances which serve to show how incongruous it is to attribute Daniel to that late age. For example; would a Maccabaean Jew ever have thought of giving to Daniel and his companions names compounded with those of *idol-gods*, as in Daniel 1: 7? Would he have thought of placing Daniel at the head of the heathen Magi? 2: 48. At least, would he not have thrown some qualifying or mitigating circumstance into the account, which would show how Daniel escaped participating in the rites of the heathen priests? And further, at the Maccabaean period, would a writer have thought of making Daniel the subject of such sympathy for an idolatrous king, and a tyrant and an oppressor of his own people, as is exhibited in Daniel 4: 19?

But leaving circumstances of this nature, which might easily be multiplied, let us take into view the *aesthetical character* of the book. What composition of the Maccabaean age can compare with it in this respect? What is there in all the Apocrypha, that approaches the lofty, animated, independent spirit and tone of Daniel? What apocryphal narrations approach the vivid and deeply exciting narratives found in his book? Some of the apocryphal histories are pleasantly written; and some of them seriously and pretty accurately, e. g. 1 Macc.; but they are tameness itself compared with those of Daniel. Well has Fenelon said: "Read Daniel, denouncing to Belshazzar the vengeance of God all prepared to burst upon him, and then search the most sublime originals of antiquity, and find if you can any thing which will bear comparison with these passages." What well informed reader, capable of appreciating style, will not applaud this sentiment? Painters have chosen the narration respecting Belshazzar, as presenting an admirable subject for the highest efforts of their skill and powers. As men of taste they have chosen well.*

I freely grant, that the evidence on which I have been insisting, under this last head, is more of a *negative* than positive character. In other words, it suggests as a reason why we ought not to attribute the book of Daniel to the Maccabaean age, that there were in that age no other productions of the like character and contents. I know that this will not prove conclusively, that Daniel was not written then; for it is within the bounds of possibility, that such a man might rise up, distinguished in

---

* Who among us does not remember, with unfeigned regret, the half finished picture of our greatest historical painter, who was arrested by sudden and unexpected death, in the midst of his favorite, his last, and his greatest undertaking, *the Feast of Belshazzar*?

so remarkable a manner from all his contemporaries. But is it probable? If a book should now come to light in England, and bear upon its title page the assertion, that it was written in the time of Henry the eighth, and that book should have all the qualities of Addison's style, or of Goldsmith's, would any one believe the title-page? Not one, is the ready answer. Then why *(mutatis mutandis)* should the book of Daniel be assigned to the Maccabaean age, which is as discrepant from it in respect to style and manner of thinking, as Addison or Goldsmith is from the writers under Henry the eighth? If the existence of such a Maccabaean writer is possible, it is to the last degree *improbable.*

(5) The accurate knowledge, which the writer of the book of Daniel displays, of ancient history, manners and customs, and oriental-Babylonish peculiarities, shows that he must have lived at or near the time and place, when and where the book leads us to suppose that he lived.

A great variety of particulars might be adduced to illustrate and confirm this proposition; but I aim only to introduce the leading and more striking ones.

(a) In drawing the character of Nebuchadnezzar, and giving some brighter spots to it, Daniel agrees with hints of the like nature in Jer. 42: 12. 39: 11. If a writer in the Maccabaean age had undertaken, as is asserted, to symbolize Antiochus Epiphanes by drawing the character of Nebuchadnezzar, it would be difficult to conceive how he would have been persuaded to throw into the picture these mellower tints.

(b) In drawing the portrait of Belshazzar, the last king of Babylon, Daniel agrees very strikingly with Xenophon. In this latter writer, he appears as a debauched, pleasure-loving, cruel, and impious monarch. Cyrop. iv. v. represents him as killing the son of Gobryas, one of his nobles, because he had anticipated him, while hunting, in striking down the game. When the father remonstrated, he replied, that he was sorry only that he had not killed him also. In Lib. v. 2, he is styled *haughty* and *abusive.* One of his concubines spoke in praise of Gadates, a courtier, as a handsome man. The king invited him to a banquet, and there caused him to be seized and unmanned. It is all in keeping with this, when he appears in Daniel v. In his intoxication and pride, he orders the sacred vessels of the Jerusalem-temple to be profaned; and Daniel is so disgusted with his behaviour, that he does not, as in the case of Nebuchadnezzar (chap. iv.), disclose any strong sympathy for him, but denounces unqualified destruction. Xenophon calls this king, *ἀνόσιος.*

(c) Cyaxares (*Darius the Mede* in Dan.) is drawn by Xenophon as

devoted to wine and women (Cyrop. IV.). In Dan. 6: 19 it is mentioned of Darius as an extraordinary thing, that after he saw the supposed ruin of Daniel, he neither approached his table or his harem. Xenophon speaks of him as indolent, averse to business, of small understanding, vain, without self-restraint, and easily thrown into tears; and then moreover as subject to violent outbursts of passion (iv. v.). In Daniel he appears as wholly governed by his courtiers; they flatter his vanity and obtain the decree intended to destroy Daniel. Daniel's supposed impending fate throws him into lamentation, and he betakes himself to fasting and vigils; and when he learns the safety of his Hebrew servant, he sentences his accusers, with all their wives and children, to be thrown into the lions' den, 6: 18—24.

Now as there was no history of these times and kings among the Hebrews, and none among the Greeks that gave any minute particulars, in what way did a *late* writer of the book of Daniel obtain his knowledge?

(*d*) When in Dan. 1: 21 it is stated, that Daniel continued until the *first year of Cyrus*, without any specification when this was, the writer seems plainly to suppose his readers to be familiar with this period. It is true, that from the book of Ezra a knowledge of that time, the period of Jewish liberation, might be gained; but the familiar manner of the reference to it, indicates that the writer feels himself to be addressing those, who were cognizant of matters pertaining to the period.

(*e*) In ch. i. and ii. we are told that *king* Nebuchadnezzar besieged Jerusalem, took it, and sent Daniel and his companions to Babylon. There they were taken under the care and instruction of learned men among the Chaldees, and trained up for the personal service of the king. The period of training was *three* years. At the close of this, they were examined and approved by the king; and soon after this occurred Nebuchadnezzar's first dream, which Daniel was summoned to interpret. This dream is said to be in the *second* year of Nebuchadnezzar's reign. Here then is an apparent *parachronism*. How could Daniel have been taken and sent into exile by *king* Nebuchadnezzar, educated *three* years, and then be called to interpret a dream in the *second* year of Nebuchadnezzar's reign? The solution of this difficulty I have already exhibited in an Exc. at the end of the commentary on ch. i. I need not repeat the process here. It amounts simply to this, viz. that Nebuchadnezzar is called *king* in Dan. 1: 1, *by way of anticipation*; a usage followed by Kings, Chron., and Jeremiah. Before he quitted Judea he became actual king by the death of his father; and the Jews, in speaking of him as commanding the invading army, always called him *king*. But in Dan. 2: 1, Nebuchadnezzar is spoken of in the Chaldee mode of reference to his actual reign. This leaves some *four* years for Daniel's discipline and service. But to those who were not familiar with the Jewish mode of speaking in respect to Nebuchadnezzar, it would naturally and inevitably appear like a parachronism, or even a downright contradiction of dates. Yet the writer has not a word of explanation to make. He evidently feels as if all were plain to his readers; (as doubtless it was). But a writer of the Maccabaean age would plainly have seen and avoided the difficulty.

(*f*) In Dan. 5: 30, it is stated that Belshazzar was slain; but not a word is said descriptive of the manner in which this was brought about, nor even that the city of Babylon was taken. The next verse simply mentions that Darius the Mede took the kingdom. All this brevity seems to imply, that the writer supposed those whom he was addressing to be cognizant of the whole matter. Had he lived in the Maccabaean age, would he have written thus respecting events so interesting and important? — In like manner Dan. 10: 1 seq. tells us, that in the third year of Cyrus, Daniel mourned and fasted three weeks. But not a word is said to explain the occasion of this peculiar and extraordinary humiliation. If we turn now to Ezra 4: 1—5, we shall find an account of a combination among the enemies of the Jews to hinder the building of the city walls, which was successful, and which took place in the *third* year of Cyrus' reign, i. e. the same year with Daniel's mourning. There can scarcely be a doubt that this was the occasion of that mourning; for certainly it was no ritual, legal, or ordinary fast. The manner now in which ch. x. is written, plainly imports that the writer feels no need of giving explanations. He takes it for granted that his readers will at once perceive the whole extent of the matter. But how, in the Maccabaean age, could a writer suppose this knowledge within the grasp of his readers?

(*g*) In Dan. ii. the dream is interpreted as indicating the destruction of the Babylonish empire by the Medo-Persians. Abydenus, in his singular account of Nebuchadnezzar's last hours (given on p. 122 above), represents this king as rapt into a kind of prophetic ecstasy, and in this state as declaring his fearful anticipations of the Medo-Persian conquest. How came such a coincidence?

(*h*) In 4: 27 Nebuchadnezzar is introduced as saying: "Is not this *great* Babylon which I have built?" Recent critics allege this to be a mistake. 'Ctesias,' they tell us, 'attributes the building of Babylon to Semiramis (Bähr Ctes. p. 397 seq.), and Herodotus (I. 181 seq.) ascribes it to Semiramis and Nitocris.' — My answer is, that Ctesias follows the Assyrian tradition, and Herodotus the Persian. But Berosus and Abydenus give us the *Babylonian* account; which is, that Nebuchadnezzar added much to the old town, built a magnificent royal palace, surrounded the city with new walls, and adorned it with a vast number of buildings. Well and truly might he say that he had built it, meaning (as he plainly did) its magnificent structures. It was not any falsehood in his declaration, which was visited with speedy chastisement, but the pride and vain-glory of his boasting gave offence to Heaven. But how came a writer of the *Maccabaean* period to know of all this matter? No Greek writer has told anything about Nebuchadnezzar or his doings. To Berosus and Abydenus, a writer of the Maccabaean age could hardly have had access. Herodotus and Ctesias told another and different story. Whence then did he get his knowledge of the part which Nebuchadnezzar had acted, in the building of the city? And yet the account of it in Daniel accords entirely with both Berosus and Abydenus. Even the account of Nebuchadnezzar's madness is virtually adverted to in these writers; see above, p.122 seq.

(*i*) In Dan. 5: 10—12 is introduced a personage styled the *queen*, not because she was Belshazzar's wife, for the latter was already in the banqueting-room (5: 3, 23), but probably because she was a queen-mother. Not improbably this was the Nitocris of Herodotus; and Berosus, Diod. Sic. (II. 10), and Alex. Polyhist. (in Chron. Armen.), all say that Nitocris was a wife of Nebuchadnezzar. If so, she might have had much to do with ornamenting the city both before and after Nebuchadnezzar's death; and this will account for the great deference paid to her by Belshazzar, as related in 5: 10—12. It is one of those accidental circumstances, which speaks much for the accordance of Daniel with the narrations of history. It is, moreover, a circumstance, about which a writer of the Maccabaean age cannot well be supposed to have known anything.

And since we are now examining ch. v., it may be proper to note another circumstance. We have seen, that at *Babylon* the wives and concubines of the king were without any scruple present at the feast. But in Esth. i. we have an account of the positive refusal of queen Vashti, to enter the guest-chamber of Ahasuerus. In other words, this was, and is, against the general custom of the East. How came a writer of the Maccabaean period, to know this distinction between the customs of Babylon and of Persia? The author of the Sept. Version, a contemporary of this period, knows so little of such a matter that he even leaves out the passage respecting the presence of women at the feast. Why? Plainly because he thought this matter would be deemed incredible by his readers. In Xen. Cyrop. (V. 2. 28) is an account of a feast of Belshazzar, where his concubines are represented as being present. Not only so, but we have elsewhere, in Greek and Roman writers, abundant testimony to usages of this kind, in their accounts of the Babylonish excesses. But how comes it about, that the forger of the book of Daniel whose familiarity with those writings is not credible, should know so much more of Babylonish customs than the Sept. translator?

(*j*) Of the manner in which Babylon was taken, and Belshazzar slain, Daniel has not given us any minute particulars. But he has told us that the *Medes* and *Persians* acquired the dominion of Babylon (5: 28), and that *Darius the Mede* succeeded Belshazzar. The manner in which he announces the slaying of Belshazzar (5: 30), shows that the event was altogether sudden and unexpected. Now Herodotus (in I. 190), and Xenophon (Cyrop. VII.), have told us, that Cyrus diverted the waters of the Euphrates, and marched in its channel into the heart of Babylon, and took the city in a single night. They tell us that the Babylonians were in the midst of feast-rioting that night, and were unprepared to meet the enemy who were not expected in the city. How entirely all this harmonizes with Daniel, is quite plain. Gesenius himself acknowledges that this is *sehr auffallend*, i. e. very striking. He has even acknowledged, in a moment of more than usual candor and concession, that Isa. 44: 27 has a definite reference to the stratagem of Cyrus in taking the city. In connection with a prediction concerning Cyrus, Jehovah is here represented as "saying to the deep, *Be dry;* yea, I will *dry up thy rivers.*" So in Jer. 50: 38, "A drought is upon her waters, and they shall be dried up;" and again 51: 36, "I will dry up her sea [river], and make her springs dry." If the book of Daniel is to be cast out as a late production, and as spurious, because it seems to predict the sudden capture of Babylon in one night, by the Medes and Persians, what is to be done with these passages of Isa. and Jer.? Even the Neologists, although they maintain a later composition in respect to those parts of the prophets which have just been cited, still do not venture to place that composition *post eventum*. If not, then there is *prediction;* and this too of a strange event, and one so minute and specific, that *guessing* is out of question. If then Isa. and Jer. *predicted*, why might not a Daniel also *predict?*

Another circumstance there is also, in which all three of these prophets are agreed. According to Dan. vi., Babylon was feasting and carousing, on the night of its capture. In Isa. 21: 5 we have the like: "Prepare the table . . . Eat, drink; arise ye princes, and anoint the shield," i. e. rise up from your feast-table, and make ready for assault. So Jer. 51: 39, "I will prepare their feasts, and I will make them drunken, that they may rejoice, and sleep a perpetual sleep, and not wake, saith the Lord."

If now a writer of the Maccabaean period had undertaken to write the story of the capture of Babylon, is there any probability that he would have hit upon all these circumstances, so peculiar and so concordant?

Conversant with the native Greek historians we cannot well suppose him to have been; for Greek literature was regarded as reproachful by the Jews of that period, and even down to the time of Josephus, who speaks strongly on this subject.

(*k*) Daniel 5: 30 relates the *violent death* of Belshazzar, when the city was taken. In this particular he is vouched for by Xenophon, Cyrop. VII. 5. 24, 30. So do Isa. 21: 2—9. 14: 18—20. Jer. 50: 29—35. 51: 57, declare the same thing. But here Berosus and Abydenus dissent, both of them representing the Babylonish king as surrendering, and as being treated humanely by Cyrus. How comes it, if the forger of the book of Daniel wrote about B. C. 160, that he did not consult those authors on Babylonish affairs? Or if, (as was surely the fact in regard to most Jewish writers at that period), he had no familiarity with Greek authors, then where did he obtain his views about the death of Belshazzar? For a full discussion of this matter, see p. 147 seq. above. There can scarcely be a doubt, that the account of Daniel and Xenophon is the true one.

Xenophon relates, that the party which assailed the palace, who were led on by Gobryas and Gadatas, fell upon the guards who were carousing πρὸς φῶς πολὺ, i. e. *at broad daylight;** Cyrop. VII. 5. 27. In other words, the Persians did not accomplish their onset upon the palace, until the night was far spent, and daylight was dawning. How now are matters presented in the book of Daniel? First, there is the feast, (of course in the evening); then the quaffing of wine; then the hand-writing on the wall; then the assembling of all the Magi to interpret it; then the introduction of Daniel, whose interpretation was followed by his being clothed with the *insignia* of nobility, and being proclaimed the third ruler in the kingdom. All this must of course have taken up most of the night. Here then one writer confirms and illustrates the other. A Pseudo-Daniel would not have risked such a statement as the true one has made; for at first view, the matter seems incredible, and it is charged upon the book as such. But Xenophon has freed it from all difficulties.

Dan. vi. also declares, that Belshazzar was a son, i. e. a descendant of Nebuchadnezzar. An appeal is made to Berosus and Megasthenes, to show that this was not true. Yet they do not so testify, but only that Belshazzar was *not of the regular line* of heirs of the throne. He might still have been a younger son of Nebuchadnezzar, or a son of

---

* Singular, that in a critical edition and commentary on Xenophon, now before me, this is rendered *before a good fire*. First, the Greek words do not allow this. Secondly, the Babylonians need and have no fires for warmth. Thirdly, Cyrus would not have drained the Euphrates and marched his army in its channel, at a time when fires were needed for warmth.

Nebuchadnezzar's daughter. Now Herodotus agrees with Daniel, I. 188, I. 74. So does Xenophon. And as the other authors have not in reality contradicted this, what reason is there for refusing to believe? See the discussion of this topic at large, p. 144 seq.

It certainly deserves to be noted, that in part the book of Daniel is on the side of the Greek writers, and against Berosus and Abydenus, where the representations of the latter may be justly regarded as designed to save the honor and credit of the Babylonians; in part also is Daniel on the side of the latter, and against the Greek writers, i. e. in cases where there is no reason to suppose the native historians to be partial. The *media via* appears in this case to be hit upon, by the simple pursuit of historical truth in the narratives of the book before us.

Again, in Dan. 5 : 31, we have an assurance, that *Darius* the *Mede* assumed the throne of Babylon. Here Herodotus and Ctesias are silent; but here Xenophon fully confirms the account given by Daniel. Herodotus himself states (I. 95), that there were two other modes of telling the story of Cyrus, besides that which he follows; and that of Xenophon and Daniel is probably one of these. This is confirmed by Is. 13 : 17, where the *Mede* is declared to be the leading nation in destroying Babylon, and the same is also said in Jer. 53 : 11, 28. In Is. 21 : 2, both Media and Persia are mentioned. The *silence* of Herodotus and Ctesias can not disprove a matter of this kind. See a full discussion of the topic, p. 148 seq.

Dan. 6 : 1 states, that Darius set over his kingdom 120 satraps. Xenophon (Cyrop. VIII. 6, 1 seq.) relates, that satraps were set over all the conquered nations, when Cyrus was in Babylon. He speaks of the appointments as made by Cyrus; and doubtless they were, since he was the only *acting* governor of Babylon, and *vice-gerent* of the king. No less true is it, that to Darius also, as supreme, may the appointment be attributed. How came the alleged *late* writer of Daniel to know this? Xenophon mentions no express number. The book of Esther (1 : 1) mentions 127 satraps. Why did not our late writer copy that number, in order to remove suspicion as to so great a number of those high officers? And how is it that 120 in Daniel is objected to as an incredible number, when the empire was actually as large at the time of their appointment, as it was in the time of Xerxes, as exhibited in Esth. 1: 1? The Septuagint translator of Daniel, who belonged to the Maccabaean age, did not venture to write 120, as it seems, but 127, (so in Cod. Chis.), thus according with Esth. 1: 1, and leaning upon that passage. He seems evidently to have felt that the story of so many satrapies must be supported by the book of Esther, in order to be believed. He even, in his ignorance of history, translates 5: 31 thus: "And Artaxerxes, the Mede, took the kingdom," probably meaning the Persian Artaxerxes Longimanus!

(*l*) It is worthy of remark, that the order of the two nations, *Medes and Persians*, is to be found in strict accordance with the idiom of the times. Thus in 6: 8, 12, 15, we have the *Medes and Persians;* but after Cyrus comes to the throne, the order is invariably *Persians and Medes.* So in the book of Esther, *the law of the Persians and Medes* shows the same change of *usus loquendi.* Would a Pseudo-Daniel have been likely to note such a small circumstance?

It is also noted (Dan. 5: 31), that when Darius took the kingdom, he was threescore and two years old. From his history, his reign, and his descent from Ahasuerus (9: 1), this seems altogether probable. But no other author states his age. The fact that it is done in Daniel, betokens a familiarity of the writer with the *minutiae* of his history. So does the mention, that in the *first* year of his reign, Daniel took into most serious consideration the prophecy of Jeremiah, respecting the 70 years' exile of the Hebrews.

Thus far, then, all is well. All seems to be in conformity with true history, so far as we can ascertain it. It is not upon one or two particulars, that we would lay stress. We acknowledge that these might have been traditionally known, and accurately reported. It is on the *tout ensemble* of the historical matters contained in the book, that stress is to be laid. And certainly it would be very singular, if all these circumstances should be true and consistent, and yet the book be written in the Maccabaean period.

How is it with the best historical books of that period? The first book of the Maccabees is, in the main, a trustworthy and veracious book. But how easy it is, to detect errors in it, both in respect to geography and history! In 7: 7 it is related that the Romans took Antiochus the Great prisoner alive. But this never happened. They gained a great victory over him, and took away many of his provinces; but he himself escaped their grasp. In 7: 8 it is said, that they took from him the land of *India*, *Media*, and Lydia. But neither India nor Media ever belonged to him. The efforts to show that Mysia was originally written instead of Media, are of course but mere guesses; and if true, *India* still remains. More likely is it, that the author himself put Media for Mysia, and if so, then this does not mend the matter. In 7: 9, 10, it is related, that 'the Greeks resolved to send an army to Rome and destroy it; but that the Romans learning this, sent forth an army, who slew many, carried away numerous captives of their women and children, laid hold of their strong places, and took possession of their lands, and reduced the people of Syria to servitude *unto this day*.' Now nothing of all this ever happened. There was indeed a fracas between the Aetolians and the Romans at that period; but it was soon made up, without any ravages of war, or any servitude. Further, the author in 7: 15 represents the Roman Senate as consisting of 320 members, continually administering the government. He goes on to state (v. 16), that they choose a ruler annually, and that all obey this one. Every tyro in Roman history knows how unfounded all this is. And what shall we say of the very first sentence in the book, which tells us, that Alexander the son of Philip smote Darius king of the Persians and Medes, and then reigned *in his stead* over Greece? In 1: 6, he states that the same Alexander, about to die, made a partition of his empire among his chiefs — a thing that took place some considerable time afterwards, partly by mutual agreement and partly by force. In 6: 1 he makes Elymais a *town* instead of a province.

Such are some of the specimens of this writer's errors in geography and history. That he was a grave, enlightened, and veracious writer, in the main, is conceded by all. But if in things so plain, and transactions so recent, he commits so many errors as have been specified, what would he have done, if the scene had been shifted from near countries to the remote places where the book of Daniel finds its circle of action?

As to the *second* book of the Maccabees, it is so notorious for errors and mistakes, that very little credit has been attached to it, on the part of intelligent critics. It is not once to be named, in comparison with the book of Daniel. It must have been written, when a knowledge of historical events was confused, and at a very low ebb. The book of Tobit, which originated in or near the Maccabaean period, exhibits not only a romantic and as it were fairy tale, but contains historical and geographical difficulties incapable of solution; also physical phenomena are brought to view, which are incredible. It is needless to specificate them here. De Wette's Einleit. presents them, § 309.

We have dwelt hitherto, under our 5th head, mainly on things of a *historical* nature, i. e. events and occurrences. Let us now examine a number of things that are of a miscellaneous nature, which it would be somewhat difficult if not useless to classify throughout, but most of which are connected with manners, customs, demeanor, etc.

(m) Daniel makes no mention in his book of prostration before the king, in addressing him. *O King, live forever!* was the usual greeting. Arrian (iv.) testifies, that the story in the East was, that Cyrus was the

first before whom prostration was practised. It is easy to see how this came about. With the Persians, the king was regarded as the *representative of Ormusd*, and therefore entitled to adoration. Nebuchadnezzar was high enough in claims to submission and honor; but not a word of exacting adoration from those who addressed him. How could a Pseudo-Daniel know of this nice distinction, when all the oriental sovereigns of whom he had any knowledge had, at least for four centuries, exacted prostration from all who approached them?

(*n*) In mere prose (Dan. 1: 2), Babylon is called by the old name *Shinar* (Gen. 11: 2, 14: 1); and as an old name, it is poetically used once by Isaiah (11: 11), and once by Zechariah (5: 11). Now *Shinar* was the vernacular name of what foreigners call *Babylonia;* and it was easy and natural for Daniel to call it so. But *how* or *why* came a Pseudo-Daniel to such a use of the word? *Babylon* he would naturally and almost with certainty call it.

(*o*) Dan. 1: 5 tells us, that the Hebrew lads were to be fed from the king's table. Such a custom, even in respect to royal prisoners, Jer. 52: 33, 34, discloses. Among the Persians this was notorious, and extended to the whole *corps d'elites* of the soldiery. Ctesias tells us, that the king of Persia daily fed 15,000 men. How came the *late* writer of Daniel to be acquainted with a minute circumstance of the nature of that before us?

(*p*) Daniel and his companions receive Chaldee names, some of which are compounded of the names of their false gods. In 2 Kings 24: 17, Nebuchadnezzar is reported to have changed the name of king Mattaniah into *Zedekiah.* How did the late forger of the book come by the notion of assigning to his Hebrew heroes the names of idol-gods? The rigorous attachment to all that was Jewish, and the hearty hatred of heathenism by all the pious in the time of the Maccabees, makes it difficult to account for his course.

(*q*) In Dan. 2: 1, the Babylonish mode of reckoning time is introduced, viz. the second year of Nebuchadnezzar. Where else, unless in Ezek. 1: 1, is this employed? How came the late interpolator of the sacred books to betake himself to this mode of reckoning; and especially since it apparently contradicts 1: 1, 5, 18? See the solution of the difficulty, in Exc. I. p. 19 seq.

(*r*) In Dan. 2: 5, 3: 29, one part of the threatened punishment is, that the houses of the transgressors should be turned into a *dung-hill,* or rather a *morass-heap.* Here an intimate acquaintance with the Babylonish mode of building is developed. The houses were mostly constructed of *sun-baked* bricks, or with those slightly burned; and when once demolished, the rain and dew would soon dissolve the whole mass, and make them sink down, in that wet land near the river, into a miry place of clay, whenever the weather was wet.

(*s*) In Dan. 3: 1, the plain of *Dura* is mentioned; a name found no where else, yet mentioned here as a place familiar to the original readers of the book, inasmuch as no explanation is added. Whence did the *Pseudo-Daniel* derive this name?

(*t*) In Dan. 2: 5 and 3: 6, we find the punishment of hewing to pieces and burning in ovens mentioned. Testimony to such modes of punishment may be found in Ezek. 16: 40. 23: 25 and Jer. 29: 22. But such a mode of punishment could not exist among the Persians, who were *fire-worshippers;* and accordingly in chap. vi. we find casting into a den of lions as substituted for it.

(*u*) In Dan. iii. we find not only a huge idol (in keeping with the Babylonish taste), but also a great variety of musical instruments employed at the dedication of it. Quintus Curtius has told us, that when Alexander the Great entered Babylon, 'there were in the procession singing Magi . . . and artists playing on stringed instruments of a peculiar kind, accustomed to chant the praises of the king.' (v. 3.)

(*v*) According to Herod. I. 195, the Babylonish costume consisted of three parts, first the wide and long pantaloons for the lower part of the person; secondly, a woollen shirt; and thirdly, a large mantle with a girdle around it. On the cylinder rolls found at Babylon, Münter (Relig. d. Bab. s. 96) discovered the same costume. In Dan. 3: 21, the same three leading and principal articles of dress are particularized. Other parts of clothing are merely referred to, but not specificated; but these garments being large and loose, and made of delicate material, are mentioned in order to show how powerless the furnace was, since they were not even singed. How did a Pseudo-Daniel obtain such particulars as these?

(*w*) Dan. 6: 16 shows, that the regal token of honor bestowed, was a collet or golden chain put around the neck. Brissonius, in his work on the Persian dominion, has shown the same custom among the Persian kings, who, not improbably, borrowed it from the Babylonians.

(*x*) In Dan. 6: 8, "the laws of the Medes which change not" are mentioned. In Esth. 1: 19 and 8: 8, we have repeated mention of this same peculiar custom. The reason of this probably was, that the king was regarded as the impersonation of Ormusd, and therefore as infallible.

(*y*) In Dan. 7: 9, we have a description of the divine throne as placed upon *movable wheels.* The same we find in Ezekiel i. and x.; which renders it quite probable, that the Babylonian throne was constructed in this way, so that the monarch might move in processions, with all the insignia of royalty about him.

(*z*) It deserves special remark, that Daniel has given individual classifications of priests and civilians, such as are nowhere else given in Scripture, and the knowledge of which must have been acquired from intimate acquaintance with the state of things in Babylon. In Dan. 2: 2, 10, 27, the various classes of diviners and literati are named. In Dan. 3: 2, 3, the different classes of magistrates, civilians, and rulers, are specifically named. On this whole subject, I must refer the reader to Exc. III. *on the Chaldees*, p. 34 seq. above. Whence a *Maccabaean* writer could have derived such knowledge, it would be difficult to say. It is one of those circumstances which could not well be feigned. Several of the names occur nowhere else in the Heb. Bible, and some of them are evidently derivates of the Parsi or Median language; e. g. סָרְכִין in 6: 3, a name unknown in the Semitic. On the other hand, several of them are exclusively Chaldean; e. g. Dan. 3: 3, אֲדַרְגָּזְרַיָּא, תִּפְתָּיֵא, of which no profane writer has given the least hint. How came the Pseudo-Daniel to a knowledge of such officers?

Finally, the passages in 3: 10, 20, in respect to the WATCHERS, is most decisive proof of an intimate acquaintance of the writer with the Parsi or Zoroastrian system of religion. If the reader will turn to the Remarks on p. 103, he will see how well grounded this statement is. According to that system, the planets were inhabited by *Amshaspands*, and were guardians and *watchers* placed over the universe by Ormusd, and running to and fro to discharge the duty of their office. The *watchers* were included among the *Dii Minores* of the Parsis, and Nebuchadnezzar speaks of them as celestial beings, announcing to him the decrees of heaven. This view, beyond all doubt, belonged to and constituted a part of the Chaldaic religion; and if not indigenous, it came into Babylonia with the northern Chaldee invaders and their Magi. How came the Pseudo-Daniel by knowledge such as this imports?

It were easy to add many more minute circumstances to show the *historical* agreement of the book of Daniel with the history of those times, and specially its accordance with the manners, customs, civil and hieratical officers and arrangements, etc., of the Babylonish capital. But I deem it superfluous. All the great oriental antiquarians — such men as Heeren, Münter, Schlosser, Herder and others — concede an intimate knowledge of oriental objects and matters to the writer of Daniel. Heeren and Münter and Herder do this very heartily and fully; and even Schlosser, cold and skeptical as he was in respect to revelation and everything miraculous, does not hesitate to speak thus: "Truly we find in the Aramaean part of the book [2: 4—vii.], matter of great importance for ancient history. In Daniel, we believe that the only remains of the modes of thinking and the customs of the Babylonish period, together with the remains of their ancient language, are preserved; while the Greeks have given us only a *Grecian* view, or at most, (like that of Berosus), only a Babylonish view transformed by the Greek one. The whole way and manner of interpreting signs and dreams, the organization of the priestly caste, and the fashion of living among the later Babylonish monarchs, and also some hints respecting the Medo-Persian period, one finds in these remains," (Welt-Geschichte). A noble concession for a cold skeptical historian; yet, as all acknowledge, he was a man of distinguished talent and of extensive research. An *expert* in oriental history, manners, customs, arts, governments, geography, and the like, cannot but be struck with the apparent ease of the writer of Daniel in the midst of such matters, and the entire unconcern he shows about being detected as lacking in exact knowledge. Truly it is something, to write such a book in such a way — something, moreover, that transcends the ability of a forger in the Maccabaean day. There were no sources whence he could derive all the knowledge displayed in this work. It requires at least a greater stretch of the *credulous* to believe in such a Pseudo-Daniel, than it does to believe in the real one.

(6) The prophet Daniel had contemporaries, who were companions in office, and who, if not personally acquainted with him, at least were living in a condition which was like his own, some peculiarities of a court-life excepted. Ezekiel was probably older than he; Zechariah and Haggai younger. Malachi, also, was a century younger; but he does not seem to have been born or to have lived abroad; and therefore he cannot be brought fairly into the comparison. But Ezekiel and Zechariah remain; and it becomes a matter of much importance to inquire whether the book of Daniel bears any striking resemblance to the productions of the two last-named prophets. It is in this way, that we undertake to judge of the claims of an author to any particular age. We compare him with other like men of that age, and see whether he has the stamp of the period in question impressed upon him. If so, it is strong circumstantial testimony in favor of the claims which are made for the age and genuineness of his production.

It is proper to remark, here, that the book of Haggai, also a prophet of the exile-period, is a very short one, and has only one specific object in view. This is to urge on the lagging work of temple-building. Of course the book is paraenetic or hortatory. One or two short sentences only are *predictive*, viz. 2: 6—9, 21—23. We may therefore lay this book out of our present account, and apply ourselves to a summary comparison of the others with the book of Daniel.

It was characteristic of the Chaldees, to use *symbolical representations* beyond any other nation with which we are acquainted. But it was common also for the Medes and Persians to make an abundant use of the like imagery or pictorial representations. All the monuments of Middle Asia, on the great Mesopotamian plain, those heretofore discovered, and those recently disinterred, are filled with symbols of various kinds, and specially of beasts that are of gigantic and grotesque forms. In no part of the world has the taste for the huge and the grotesque been carried so far. In no part, has the attachment to symbol developed itself in so many and such singular ways.

It is striking to note, how much a familiar view of those persons and things which surrounded Ezekiel, Zechariah, and Daniel, impressed itself on their minds in the way of shaping their taste, and gave a coloring to their style. In Ezekiel, the king of Babylon is a huge eagle, who crops off the top branches of the cedars in Lebanon, and carries them to Babylon; and the king of Egypt is symbolized in the same way, *mutatis mutandis*, chap. xvii. In chap. xix. Judah is presented under the image of a lioness. In chap. xxxii., the king of Egypt is likened to a crocodile of the Nile. In xxxi., the Assyrian, who had been prostrated, is symbolized as the loftiest of the trees in Lebanon in the day of his exaltation. All the fowls of the air built their nests in its boughs; under its branches did the beasts find repose; and under its shadow all the great nations of the earth dwelt, 31: 6, comp. Dan. 4: 12, 21. Even Schlosser (Welt-Geschichte, s. 240) fully admits the oriental costume of Ezekiel: "In his compositions, a Chaldaeo-Babylonian tone is so predominant, that he speaks out the character of his age in a striking manner. This symbolical style, that thunder-chariot, those terrible horses of thunder which draw it, that sapphire-throne, that covering arch decked with the colors of the rainbow, belong to the Babylonish court in a Babylonish temple; and symbolism is as much more predominant in Ezekiel, than in Isaiah, as the poetry of the latter transcends that of the former." This is a striking picture; but not more striking than true.

How stands the matter, in respect to Zechariah? I include in the work of Zechariah, the returned exile, only the first eight chapters of the book that bears his name. I do so, because I deem the arguments for the composition of the last six chapters by an older prophet, (probably of the same name), to be on the whole unanswerable. Even our common authorized English version has taken such a ground, dating the first eight chapters 520—518 B. C., and the last six 587 B. C. It is indeed possible, on such a ground, that the same man may have written both parts of the book; but the discrepancy of style and matter is too great to admit of any considerable probability.

How is it, then, with the prophet Zechariah who came out of exile? Ezra 5: 1. That renowned antiquarian, bishop Münter, has given his opinion thus: "The prophet Zechariah has shown, in his visions, a coloring altogether foreign to the Jews, and which could take its origin only in Chaldea. He speaks of a stone with seven eyes (3: 9); of a golden lamp with seven branch-lights, symbols of the seven eyes of Jehovah which look through the whole earth (4: 2, 10); of four chariots, spirits of heaven, which come from the four quarters of the world, and take their station before the Most High," (Relig. d. Bab. s. 89). But this is far from all. In chap. i., we have four horses of different colors, emblems of the angelic watch-guard placed over Judea. An angel appears with a measuring line to mete out Jerusalem, chap. ii. Joshua the high priest, in filthy garments, with Satan at his right hand, next appears in vision; and the significance of the vision is explained by an *angel interpreter*, chap. iii. The two olive-trees that supply the lamp mentioned above with oil, are described in chap. iv. In chap. v., a flying roll of thirty feet in length and half as much in breadth, is seen moving through the air, written with the doom of the wicked on both sides, and on it is the personification of wickedness, thrust into an ephah, and covered with a sheet of lead; and all are borne to the land of *Shinar* (comp. Dan. 1: 2), by two women with the wings of a stork. Then comes the vision of the chariots, as stated by Münter in the passage above quoted.

Who now that has read these books and compared them with that of Daniel, can fail to discern the likeness of style, manner, and imagery? When I say this, I would limit my remark to the general features of style, and the general circle of thought and representation. Where else, in all the Hebrew Scriptures, is there anything that compares with these prophets, either in the frequency of symbols, or in the kinds of them? Compare the Theophany in Isa. vi. with that in Ezek. i. and Dan. vii. The difference is very striking. Then compare the monsters in Dan. vii. viii. with those in Ezek., and the frequency with which these occur. The like are now found on the Babylonish cylinders and tapestry. Even the strange beast in Dan. 7: 5, of which it is said לְשְׂטַר חַד הֳקִימַת, (a phrase that has nonplussed all commentators until recently, and which has been very diversely and wildly explained), has now been presented to our view among the ruins of Persepolis and elsewhere, in the very attitude described by the prophet, and is one of the symbols of the Persian dynasty, as Daniel describes it in 7: 5. (See the Comm. above on this passage.)

How comes it, now, that these three writers of the exile-period, should resemble each other so strikingly in general taste and manner and circle of imagery, and in the frequency of it? How comes it that all of them are so manifestly out of the Palestine circle of action or description? One feels himself *abroad*, the moment he begins to read them. They are indeed animated by the same spirit; but they are far from wearing the same costume. May not one almost take it for granted, that the images of things seen in a dream or trance-vision are copies in the main of those seen in a waking state, and only formed into new combinations, or placed in new positions? It would seem, now, that all these contemporaries of the exile-period had seen the originals of their symbols on the Babylonish walls and houses and temples. The grotesque, the gigantic, everywhere met their eyes. Even their descriptions partake of the usual *hyperbole* of the remoter East. 'All men, all the beasts of the field, and the fowls of the air, are subject to king Nebuchadnezzar,' Dan. 2: 38. So 'the tree in the midst of the earth, whose height reached to heaven, and was seen to the ends of the earth — this tree nourished all flesh, and afforded shelter for all birds and beasts and men,' Dan. 4: 7 seq. Just such a tree is presented to view as an image of the Assyrian king, in Ezek. 31: 3—8. So much are the two passages alike, that the writer of Daniel has been accused, by Lengerke, of *copying* from Ezekiel. If either is a *copy* of the other, then why are we not at liberty to guess that Ezekiel copied from Daniel? But a close and minute attention to the diction and style of each, shows manifestly that neither is copied from the other. Both merely drew from a source of imagery familiar to both. Other examples, moreover, of *hyperbole* are frequent in both writers, and are found on all sides. They are even more frequent in Ezekiel, than in any other of the Hebrew writers. Partaking of this same character are such passages in Daniel, as speak of the furnace of Nebuchadnezzar as being heated *seven times* hotter than was customary (3: 19); and bordering almost on the grotesque is the description of Nebuchadnezzar's mania: 'He eats grass like the ox; the hair of his body becomes like eagles' feathers; and his nails like the claws of birds,' 4: 33.

Like Ezekiel, Daniel sees visions on the margin of great rivers. Ezekiel was on the Chebar (Chaboras), 1: 1, 3. 3: 15, 23. 10: 15, 20, 22. 43: 3. Daniel was, in like manner, on the borders of a great sea (river) 7: 2; and again on the banks of the Ulai, 8: 2, 16; and lastly on the great Hiddekel (the Tigris), 10: 4. In a country abounding in such large rivers, it would seem that Daniel and Ezekiel lived; and hence the easy and natural reference to them. But we find nothing of the like kind in the Palestine prophets.

Thus it appears, that the writers of Ezekiel, Daniel, and Zechariah, were of like taste, like age, and like country. Their taste, either formed in Mesopotamia as in the case of Daniel, or *conformed* to it by long residence there as in the case of Ezekiel and perhaps of Zechariah, has developed itself in a similar style and circle of imagery in all of them. Individually distinct indeed they are; fully enough to show their independence on each other. Yet there is a general Mesopotamian, Chaldean hue diffused over all their works; and they stand out quite distinctly, as to manner, from all the Palestine writers. No one familiar with the original Scriptures, and who is well versed in critical matters, can help the distinct feeling, that Daniel, Ezekiel, and Zechariah, are writers *sui generis* in comparison with the Palestine authors, and yet altogether of a kindred spirit among themselves. Where, in all the Hebrew prophets, is there anything like Ezek. i. x. xl—xlviii, Dan. vii—xii, and Zech. i—vi?

How came it, now, that a *pseudo-Daniel* should lean on Ezekiel and Zechariah, when there were other late prophets whom he might have imitated without suspicion, i. e. Jeremiah, Haggai, and Malachi? How could a native of Palestine, in the Maccabaean period, even if he travelled to Babylon (then in a ruinous condition), acquire such an intimate knowledge of Babylonish manners and customs and objects; since these had long been done away under the Persian and Grecian dynasties? And even if he could in any way have become acquainted with these things, how could it have had influence enough to give to his style a costume so Babylonish?

(7) There are traits in the book of Daniel, which are connected with his life at court, and his management of state affairs, which are altogether peculiar to him and congruous with his place and character, but which belong to no other Hebrew writer.

If the word had not been so much abused, I should characterize what I aim at, by calling it *cosmopolitism*. With all the deep and unaffected reverence which Daniel cherishes for the God of the Hebrews and the laws of Moses; with all his ardent and dauntless piety and exemplary humility; there is a freedom in his book from Jewish *rigorism*, which is very remarkable. Where is the passage which exalts and cries up the Jews, at the expense and degradation of the heathen? And yet, where is there one word or action, that shows approbation of heathenism, or indifference to it? Jehovah God is GOD ALONE; all idols are nothing and vanity. His name, his servants, the vessels even of his temple, cannot be profaned and abused, without a signal and awful retribution; ch. v. Yet Daniel forms no conspiracies to deliver the Jews from their conqueror's hand. He never sacrifices his allegiance or fidelity to Nebuchadnezzar. He keeps his place as prime minister nearly forty years, in spite of all the native nobles and Magi of the realm. Indeed, he never, as it would seem, gave offence to them, or had a quarrel with them. And how could he be *head Magian* all this time, and yet escape the infectious influence of Parsism, and keep himself clear from its polytheistic rites? That he did, cannot be doubted, if his book is to be believed. Truly he must have been a magnanimous, a discreet, a liberal, and a wary courtier to accomplish all this! And such is his bearing in his whole history. Look at him, when a mere youth, before Nebuchadnezzar and his court, interpreting the dreams of the haughty and powerful monarch. See him before Belshazzar and his thousand lords, announcing the judgments of Heaven, when that awful invisible hand inscribed the doom of that tyrant and his capital on the wall before his eyes! Is this an ordinary man? In truth I know not where to look for examples of such a kind. A most sagacious, independent, enlightened and fearless man he must have been, to have filled such a place, so long, and with so much approbation.

We should also take into view the nature and general course of his prophetic annunciations. What are they? Not denunciation against Tyre, or Sidon, or Syria, or Philistia, or Moab, or Egypt. No, they are views of *dynasties;* of powers that influence the destiny of the world; of the four great empires which all history celebrates. Who does not see the *statesman* here, whose elevated thoughts and conceptions dwell on the mighty changes among the mass of nations? The circle in which he moves, and the thoughts which are inspired by his position, are all plainly stamped upon the productions of his pen.

There are some other traits of the book of Daniel, which seem to result from the *literary* character and habits (if I may so speak) of the writer. How comes it, that everywhere so much attention is paid to *chronology?* A careful *designation of dates* accompanies all his prophecies, and for the most part his historical narrations. This is frequent in Ezekiel, and found more than once in Zechariah; but it is not so uniform as in Daniel. Every one who knows the history of the Magi, knows that astronomy and the observation of times and periods were their leading occupation. A familiarity with such reckonings seems to have formed the taste of Daniel respecting them. We might even venture to suggest it as probable, that those occult sciences had an influence on the introduction of so many new and peculiar periods in his book. Take for example, "the time, times, and half a time;" the mysterious seventy weeks; and then the seven weeks, the sixty-two weeks, and the one week. It is indeed no new thing, that *definite* periods should appear in his prophecy;

for other prophets furnish us with examples of the like kind. What is new, however, or at least peculiar, is the *frequency* of this definiteness, and the *peculiar costume* with which some of the designations are invested. Where else is the like to be found? And how came the Pseudo-Daniel to hit upon such a method of conveying his ideas? On the other hand, how could the real Daniel, the real רַב מָג, avoid a familiar acquaintance with all the mathematical and astronomical sciences of the order to which he belonged? Was there not something in this training, which had, it may be, an insensible influence on his manner of designating and reckoning time?

At any rate, there is the man, distinct from all other prophets in several respects, inferior to none in power, influence, integrity, holiness, and piety; and withal he is a statesman and civilian of a rank above any of the others. There is the man, in a full length portrait, whom Ezekiel classes with *Noah* and *Job;* whom the Saviour calls a *prophet;* whom the angel Gabriel thrice pronounced to be one *greatly beloved* of God (9: 23. 10: 11, 19); and who, though a captive and a Jewish foreigner, regulated the concerns of Babylon for almost half a century. Did any conception of such a man ever enter the brain of a forger — a Pseudo-Daniel — during the Maccabaean period? At least we are certain, that nothing among the known writers of that period makes any approach to such a picture as this.

Lastly, we should look at the characteristics of his *Messianic periods.* In other prophets, we find as it were a great struggle to throw off their Jewish feelings and partialities. The brightest part of their pictures is the coming glory of the *descendants of Abraham.* The Gentiles are represented as coming to them laden with contributions; they acknowledge the prior right and the loftier position of the Jews; and the full glory of the Millennial day itself is described in language that often has a strong Jewish coloring. Even Isaiah partakes of this deep Hebrew feeling. When (in chap. lxvi.) he opens to our view "the new heavens and the new earth," he tells us of offerings brought by all nations to the holy mountain at Jerusalem, and that "priests and Levites" will be selected from the Jews to present them. Nor is this all. "At every new moon, and on every Sabbath," all flesh shall repair to Jerusalem, in order to worship in the temple there. And the like of this might be produced from many a passage in the Hebrew Palestine prophets; e. g. Jer. 31: 31—40, et al. saepe. But not so in Daniel. Educated abroad, and unused to the regular Jewish ritual, its hold upon his mind seems to be less tenacious. Hence, the fifth glorious kingdom, as described by him, is universal, without any distinction of nation, and without any reference to Jewish rites. It is strictly cosmopolitan. "There is one God of the Jews and of the Gentiles." The *Son of Man*, who comes with the clouds of heaven to the Ancient of days, receives a dominion and glory and kingdom of such a nature, that "all people, nations, and languages serve him — a kingdom that will not pass away nor be destroyed." Daniel vii.

Whence now did the Pseudo-Daniel obtain such views? Above all, how could his *Messianic development* be so ample — so clearly the very kernel of the whole book — if this work came from his hand? His contemporaries exhibit no such views. The very little that they have said at all, is so worldly, so merely temporal and civil and social, that it seems quite plain, that all spiritual and elevated views in respect to this great subject were nearly extinct at that period. Did, I might even say, *could* any man in such an age as that of Sirach, and of the author of Tobit, and of the first book of the Maccabees, attain to views like those in Daniel? Even Lengerke confesses, that the *Messianic idea* is more developed here, than elsewhere in the Old Test., and in a more spiritual manner. If so, did the Maccabaean period produce any man adequate to make such a development? I will not say that the thing was impossible; but it is risking very little to say, that it is altogether improbable.

Let us now cast our view back, over the whole ground of the defence made for the book before us. What one thing is wanting to establish its genuineness, that we should deem important in proving the genuineness of any book so ancient? There is, first, the apparent testimony of the writer himself to his own authorship, which we are not entitled to distrust *a priori*, but must have some valid reason for rejecting it. There is, next, the testimony of a contemporary prophet (Ezek.) to his person and his worth. There is, then, the express testimony of our Saviour, that Daniel was a *prophet;* and that of Paul, and John, who in various ways acknowledge him as such, while John has built the Apocalypse, as it were, on the basis of Daniel. There is most decisive testimony of Josephus to the Jewish views, as well as his own, of the preëminence of Daniel as a prophet. There is, moreover, the perpetual and uninterrupted testimony of the Jews of all ages to the character and worth of the book, with which is united that of the whole Christian church, from the beginning down nearly to the 19th century. Not a voice was ever raised against the book, except by some Porphyry who scoffed at all revelation. There is moreover, most grave and weighty testimony, and this in constant succession, from the time of Sirach down to the present hour, that *the book of Daniel was a part of the Jewish*

Canon, and that this Canon was closed long before a Pseudo-Daniel is alleged to have written his work. The book is so written, moreover, viz. in two different languages, that we cannot well attribute it to a writer of the Maccabaean period. Add to all this, that the whole internal evidence is in its favor. Its references to historical facts, to manners, customs, natural and artificial objects, and the like, are all in keeping with the time when it professes to have been written. The character of the author in all respects is congruous with his alleged condition, qualities, and station. It bears the indelible marks of origin in a foreign land, and in that land where it claims to have been written. It is, down to the present hour, the best store-house of Babylonish antiquities which is extant. Why then reject its claims? Most philologers, even neological ones, would blush to disown a heathen book, which had half of these claims. Why should this book, then, be the object of such unrelenting persecution? Why subjected to so much contumely? There is, as it seems to me, but one honest answer to this; which is, that if the book be admitted to be genuine, then to deny *prophecy*, or even explain it away, is quite impossible. Porphyry saw this; and so do the skeptics of the present day. They can manage in their way to get round other prophetical books, because they have less distinctness in the narration of particulars. But here, there is no evading the history of Antiochus Epiphanes. Hence the conclusion is, that it must have been written *post eventum*. Miracles are first pronounced by an *a priori* process, to be impossible; and then it is averred, that Daniel could not have been written during the exile, because, if written then, we must admit the miracle of prediction. Of course, then, the Gospels, and the whole of the New Test. which admits the facts related in them, must be spurious productions; or if not spurious, they are at all events, and at best, but romantic fictions invented for the purpose of making men wonder, and of inducing them to listen to the precepts which they inculcate. All this, now, surely stands or falls together. Neology cannot stop with the overthrow of Daniel. The ground assumed here, sinks the whole Bible down to the level of the fabulous and the incredible. As Neology has not a single scrap of external evidence that will bear the test of examination, in support of the ground which it takes, so all degradation of Daniel depends on the *a priori* assumption of a principle, which equally degrades every book of the Old Test. and of the New.

§ 7. *Objections against the Genuineness of the Book.*

A large proportion of these have already been canvassed, in the course of the Commentary and in the preceding critical discussions. It is not my design to repeat these discussions at length, in any case where they were designed to be thorough. I shall therefore merely advert to such objections as have been canvassed, and remit the reader to the preceding pages, in which they have been respectively examined. It may perhaps strike the minds of some readers, that it would have been preferable to embody the objections into one mass, for the sake of a more convenient survey of them. But experience has taught me, in the reading and in the writing of Commentary, that discussions of difficulties engaged in upon the spot, at the very time and place where they occur, occasion a much higher interest in the reader, than will be felt when postponed to a distant time and place. It is on this account, that I have, in my Commentary, adopted the practice of discussing when the text called for discussion. I have, in consequence of this, but a moderate list of objections that now remain to be canvassed.

Lengerke's Commentary on Daniel (1835, Koenigs.) has been generally acknowledged, I believe, as the most complete exposition and defence of the neological views respecting this book, which have yet appeared. There is not much in it, indeed, which is strictly original; but the author is a most zealous, industrious, and pains-taking exponent and defender of the so-called *liberal* criticism. It is on this ground, that I have already so often referred to him; and on the same ground, that I follow him as my guide into all the recesses of skeptical criticism.

Lengerke, strenuous as he is in collecting all that can be said against the book of Daniel, admits (in his Introduction) that Josephus and all the Jews, the Talmudists and Masorites included, have acknowledged the genuineness and divine authority of the book, (s. iv. seq). He also concedes, that with Christ and his apostles this book was "in the highest credit;" and that "this view of the matter was not changed among the mass of Jews and Christians during the early ages of the Christian era." Yet he suggests, that in Theodoret's time there were some Jews, who doubted its place among the prophets. The passages of Theodoret, which he cites in confirmation of this, (viz. on pages 1056—57 and 1058—9, ed. Schulz), exhibit the writer as taxing the Jews with something *δυσσεβές* and *ἄδικον*, in removing Daniel from his proper place among the *prophets*. If Lengerke had studied out the order of the older Jewish Canon, as exhibited in the pages above, he would not have mistaken the object of Theodoret. This father lived, when the practice among the Jews of assigning Daniel to the *Kethubhim* was taking its rise. It was a *novelty* and was revolting to his feelings; and so he taxes them with great impropriety of conduct. This helps much, when rightly understood, to confirm the views taken above (p. 424 seq.), in respect to the original canonical place of Daniel.

Now and then a solitary doubt has appeared, in times comparatively recent, whether Daniel wrote *in propria persona* the whole of his book. The two different languages, and the two great divisions, viz. historic and prophetic, seem to have given rise to such doubts. Some have attributed one part to Daniel's own hand, and some to another's, e. g. Hobbes, I. Newton, Beausobre, Spinoza; whilst Edward Wells thinks the whole was reduced to writing, after the death of Daniel. J. D. Michaelis, (in his Anmerk. f. Ungelehrte. Th. 10), doubts the genuineness of chap. iii—vi.; and Eichhorn in his Einleit. (ed. 3 and 4) makes the work a mere copy of floating traditions. The first objector that handled the matter very seriously, was Corrodi, in his *Freimüthige Versuche.* The first works, however, that made any deep impression, were the Commentary of Bertholdt, and the Essay of Bleek on Daniel, (Theol. Zeitschrift von Schleiermacher etc.). Since that, Gesenius, De Wette, Rosenmueller, Hoffmann, Hitzig, Redepenning, Ewald, Knobel, and others, have followed in the track of Bleek. Lengerke has given to the world, in his Commentary, the substance of all which these and other writers have said, and for the purpose of consultation, therefore, his work is valuable to the student. Any one who wishes to examine the question of genuineness, will at least find all that has been, and I might almost venture to say, all that can be said against it, in the pages of Lengerke.

After a recently repeated and minute survey of all the objections against the genuineness of the book of Daniel that have been urged, I have been not a little surprised at the confident and triumphant air with which the objections are brought forward. The book is ejected from the creditable Scriptures with even a scornful air, and its claims to consideration are heard *adunco naso.* Nay, if some of the leaders in the new critical school are to be regarded, the story of Jack the Giant-killer or of Gulliver's Travels is altogether as veracious and as worthy of credit, as that of Daniel. What says Knobel, in his *Hebrew Prophets?* In § 40 he says: "In short, to an unprejudiced man no doubt can arise, that our narrations [viz. those of Daniel] are not strictly historical accounts," (s. 329). Again, speaking of the graphic specifications of Daniel's prophecies, he says: "The *special exactness* of these prophecies proves, in a striking manner, that they took their rise *after* the times respecting which they speak. *This is an incontrovertible argument against the genuineness of the book*," (s. 402). In like manner De Wette: "It is clear that Daniel was not the author of this book, from the fabulous contents of it, which are full of improbabilities, dazzling miracles, and historical inaccuracies, the like of which can be found in no other prophetical book of the O. Test.," (Einleit. § 255). In a note appended to this passage, he refers, in the way of example, to Dan. vi. (which gives an account of the lions' den), of which he says: "The representation is *ridiculous*," (lächerliche). Further proof than this, from two men usually so calm and sober, and who are so well informed, as Knobel and De Wette, is not needed in order to show with what *Turkish justice* the cause of Daniel has been heard and decided, by the neological court of late erected. But as we, in this land of liberty, are not yet under Turkish supervision or domain, we are quite inclined to take the liberty of appealing to the high court of *critical justice*, which decides *after* examination, and decides in accordance with facts and arguments. Daniel is indeed no *ridiculous* man, in our eyes; and *audi alteram partem* is yet current in our free land.

Meantime the book in question has not been without its advocates and defenders. Stäudlin, Beckhaus, Jahn, Sack, Hengstenberg, and Hävernick, with others of less note, have entered the lists, with various armour, and somewhat diverse skill in employing it. Hengstenberg's *Authentie des Daniel* is the most extensive discussion of the subject, and also the most able; with the exception, perhaps of Hävernick's *Neue Untersuchungen*, appended at present to his Commentary. In his general *Einleitung*, also, this last writer has presented a striking summary of the case of Daniel, as to the attacks make upon it and the defence set up for it. These two last named writers exhibit almost every thing, that has been advanced on both sides. I have not always followed either of them, however, in my defence of the book; and sometimes I have felt obliged to differ from and to oppose them both. But this abates little or nothing from the respect that I feel for them, nor from my gratitude for their very able and faithful services.* In several cases I have pursued investigations beyond the limits of theirs; and in some, I have assayed to make my way in tracks on which they did not enter. Each man who writes on a subject of so much moment as the one before us, ought to add something to the stock already on hand.

* A short time before the writing of this paragraph, I learned from the public Journals, that Hävernick has gone to his rest, in the very meridian of life and usefulness. Biblical criticism has experienced a great loss by his premature decease; for he was fast advancing on the high road to the very summit of the sacred Parnassus.

Opponents to the genuineness of the book of Daniel have, as yet, been able to find *only two grounds of an external nature*, on which they rest their cause.

(1) 'The book of Daniel is placed among the latest books of the *Kethubhim;* which shows, say they, that it must have been added to the Canon after the closing of the Law and the Prophets. Moreover, this Canon could not have been completed, until after the time of the Maccabees. Had the book been written in the exile-period, it would no doubt have been ranked with the other prophets.'

To this I have only to say, that the last assertion is not without good ground; but it in reality touches only a very small part of the case. As a matter of fact, it stands beyond any reasonable critical doubt, that *the book of Daniel was connected with the other prophets, and that it occupied, in the ancient Canon, a place immediately before or after Ezekiel, down to a period near to the fifth century.* The Talmudists of that day were the first to put it among the Kethubhim; and Jerome, at the same period, who spent many years in studying with them, gives us an account of the manner in which they divided the scriptural books, arranging Daniel among the Hagiography. Theodoret, as we have seen above (p. 459), tasks the Rabbies severely for this proceeding; and Jerome and the Rabbies of his day are the only men in all early antiquity, who have given to the Jewish Scriptures such an arrangement.

In § 6 (*d*) above, I have amply discussed this subject; and it would be superfluous here to do anything more, than I have already done by merely stating the results of my previous investigation. The answer to the allegation in question is, that the fact alleged, on which it is entirely grounded, is not only incapable of proof, but *the direct contrary has an overwhelming mass of evidence in its favor*. Such being the case, Daniel's *original* place in the Canon, (a fact clearly established), is one of the most cogent arguments in favor of its genuineness and antiquity; see § 6 ut supra.

(2) The only remaining *external ground* relied on is, that the 'Son of Sirach, in his *Eulogy of the Fathers*, (chaps. xliv—l.), has omitted to mention Daniel among these Fathers; which shows that the book of Daniel did not then exist.'

At most, however, this is only an *argumentum ex silentio* — nearly always a very weak and slippery one in matters of criticism. If there be any weight in it, on this occasion, it must result either from the fact, that the author's catalogue of worthies was designed to be complete, or at least from the fact, that he meant to include all canonical writers. But neither of these positions is true. Nearly one half of those whom he eulogizes, were not writers at all of any part of the Scriptures. On the other hand, he omits many of great name, while he inserts others who were clearly their inferiors. E. g. he inserts Phinehas, Caleb, Nathan, Zorobabel, and Joshua the high priest, while he omits many prophets, priests, and kings, of equal or greater celebrity. A glaring example is presented in the eulogy of Nehemiah, while Ezra (with his book also) is wholly omitted. Can there be any question as to the superiority of the latter over the former? But, what is more than all, *he omits the whole corps of the Minor Prophets.* The passage in 49: 10, which in the common Vatican text makes mention of them, is shown by Bretschneider (in loc.) to be clearly *spurious*, it having been copied verbatim from 46: 12, with merely the substitution of *τῶν δώδεκα προφητῶν* for *αὐτῶν*. Some partial friend of Sirach has plainly endeavored thus to fill up what was seemingly a gap in the *Αἴνησις*. This last circumstance shows most clearly, that the plan of Sirach was not all-comprehensive. He made a *selection;* and in this he did not confine himself to writers, or kings, or priests, or prophets. He has some, and only some, of all these classes. It would be difficult perhaps to say by what principle he was guided; but the general tenor of his selection justifies the position, that distinguished, active, influential, and pious men among the Jews, mostly before the exile, who had been signal benefactors, or deliverers, or moral and religious teachers, were the objects of his choice. But Daniel spent his life and wrote his book abroad, and never was either a hero or a prophet under the theocracy. Indeed, he never directly addressed the Jews at all. The plan of Sirach, therefore, so far as we can ascertain it, would hardly comprise him. Yet even when we assume this principle of selection, we find enough of the arbitrary in Sirach's eulogy, to show that he did not rigidly adhere even to this, or to any particular rule in selecting. How came he to omit Ezra, who did act in Palestine and who was a canonical writer, and yet insert Zerubbabel, and Jeshua, and Nehemiah? And can the circumstance, that Daniel is omitted in such a eulogy, where the selection manifests so little discrimination, and is confined within such narrow bounds — can this be alleged as a decisive reason against the existence of Daniel's book when Sirach wrote? If so, then it is equal evidence against the book of Ezra, and specially against the book of Esther. How came this last book, with the famous queen whose name it bears, and the renowned Mordecai, the great deliverer of the Jewish nation from universal massacre, to be passed over in silence? Why did Sirach omit *Job?* Ezekiel had held him up before the world as worthy of being associated with Noah and Daniel. Conspicuous also among the sacred writings, was the book of Job. Why should he be omitted? It is not even pretended, that Sirach had not a knowledge of these books and persons; and if he had that knowledge, on what ground, we ask again, were they omitted? And does the *silence* of Sirach, in this case, prove that these books and these personages did not exist? On the other hand, is it not plain, that the same principle led to the omission in this case, which governed in the omission of Daniel, viz. that the author intended to include only those who had been active in Palestine? At any rate, the whole argument is worthless, when such facts as these lie before us. Does any one regard it as a satisfactory proof, that no Nebuchadnezzar ever lived and reigned, and that he did not overrun Asia Minor and besiege Tyre, because none of the Greek historians, not even Herodotus, ever mention his name? (see p. 121 supra). Where, moreover, should we begin and where end, with this *argumentum a silentio?* What could be done with the *Gospels*, (where they differ from each other in their order, or where one or more of them keep entire silence as to certain facts), on such a ground as this? For my own part, I always feel suspicious either of a cause, or of the convictions of those who plead it, when they resort to such flimsy argumentation as this. Men do not commonly undertake to buttress a building with spalt and decaying timber, when they can obtain pillars of granite or of marble. De Wette, who at first welcomed this notable argument which Bleek has urged very strenuously, seems to have become rather shy of it in later times. He says with his usual *naiveté:* "To be sure, this circumstance *may be taken into consideration.*" I have endeavored to follow his advice; but I find a result quite different from that which he would seem to approve.

We have done with *external grounds.* And if the internal are not stronger than these, the opinion of Christ and his apostles respecting Daniel may still be regarded as quite safe and unshaken.

Let us now proceed to the INTERNAL GROUNDS alleged by the opponents of the book against its genuineness. For convenience' sake, I shall follow Lengerke as to the order of arrangement.

(3) Lengerke ranks at the head of these internal grounds, 'the testimony which he says is given by the *Greek words* in Daniel, inasmuch as they show the influence of the Greek on the real author of the book, i. e. the Pseudo-Daniel, who must have lived in the times of Greek domination.'

Most cases of this nature are taken from the name of musical instruments, in chap. 3: 5. I do not deem it important to repeat the discussion of this topic here, as the reader will find it in the Commentary on this passage, p. 81 seq. Whatever else Lengerke has of this nature, is also examined in the various passages where the words occur. The whole thing is so fanciful, and has so little foundation in true philology, that to particularize any further, would be a mere waste of time. At most, not more than three or four words are traceable to the Greek, and even these are of a doubtful origin.

(4) 'The diction of Daniel is of the very latest kind, such as we find in Ezra, Neh., Esth., and Chronicles, also in Ezekiel. It approaches very nearly to the Rabbinic of the later ages.' Thus Lengerke and Bertholdt.

Bleek, however, is candid enough to give up this entirely. He says very justly: "We have in general too few remains of the different centuries after the exile, to draw any conclusion as to the gradual depreciation of the language, and to determine with any certainty to what particular period any writer belongs," (Zeitschr., etc. s. 213). As to *Rabbinism*, no one has yet ventured to appeal to examples; and until the charge is sustained by some proof, we may rest content with the plea of *not guilty*. In respect to the other books named, I should deem it of no importance, to show that the Hebrew of Daniel was in general discrepant from that which they exhibit. So near were the writers to his time, that we may well suppose the idioms in general to be alike. All of them belong to a period closing with the exile, or occurring within a short time after it; and all of them are in some measure affected by the Chaldee dialect, which their authors spoke or wrote. Yet Daniel, in the judgment of Gesenius (Geschich. Heb. Sprach. s. 35), has decidedly a purer diction than Ezekiel; in which opinion, so far as I am able to judge after much time spent upon the book, and examining minutely every word and phrase in it many times over, I should entirely coincide. I should go still further, and say, it is more normal Hebrew than some portions of even Jeremiah, of Ezra, of Coheleth, and of Chronicles. As to the ἅπαξ λεγόμενα of the book, I feel no reluctance to admit them. But if there be any argument in adducing these, it will apply in an equal measure, to all the later books, and to not a few of the others. It proves nothing more, in general, than that the writer, having occasion to express ideas peculiarly his own, has used corresponding words not elsewhere found because the ideas are not. Besides, the argument is one of those which prove altogether *too much;* and therefore establish nothing. The examples which Lengerke produces are many of them mistaken and hasty ones; and the others are only of such a character as may be found in Ezekiel, in Jeremiah, in Zechariah, or in Coheleth.

(5) 'The expression הַסְּפָרִים, in Dan. 9: 2, shows that a definite well known collection of the Law and the Prophets had already been made,

which could not have been before Nehemiah's time. Moreover, the book of Daniel has copied many things from Nehemiah, which shows that it must have been later.'

As to the first, the Comm. on 9: 2 will supply the answer. It will not be denied, that each of Jeremiah's predictions in 25: 11 seq. 29: 10 seq. is called הַסֵּפֶר; of course, both of them, (for both relate to the seventy years), are rightly called הַסְּפָרִים. And these are plainly all the *closed canon*, that Daniel 9: 2 is concerned with. As to the assertion that Daniel has *copied* Nehemiah, I have only to guess that this matter may be regarded in the light of a ὕστερον πρότερον, and accordingly say, that Nehemiah copied Daniel; which, by the way, is much the more probable of the two, if there is any *copying* in the case. But of this, I see no satisfactory proof. Men in like circumstances, with like feelings, views, and wishes, and living at the same period, may easily be supposed to utter some things in relation to a matter of deep interest to both, that have a near resemblance. This is all that can be found in the case before us; and of this any critical reader of the originals may satisfy himself by minutely comparing Neh. ix. with Dan. ix., for these are the two passages mainly relied on. Both are *fast-day confessions;* both were poured forth from hearts deeply affected with the sins and the punishment of the Hebrews. After all, however, the general tenor of them is so different, that no one would suspect any copying in the case, unless put on the alert to find it by a famine of good arguments to suit his purpose.

(6) "The useless prodigality of miracles, which are improbable in themselves, and rest upon erroneous testimony, is a strong objection to the genuineness of the book." So Lengerke; and Knobel and others assert directly and fully, that the narration of such things demonstrates that the book is utterly unworthy of credit. De Wette, as we have seen above (p. 461), says that the story of the lions' den is *ridiculous.*

Of course, chap. iii, iv, v, vi, are all attacked with vehemence, and every kind of sneer and contumely and scorn is called into requisition, in order to show that they are utterly unworthy of credit. A few specimens may suffice. As to chap. ii., Lengerke says, that 'Nebuchadnezzar would never have permitted Daniel to speak of the overthrow of his dynasty; that he never would or could have demanded that a dream forgotten by himself, should be recalled by others; that the whole affair of dreaming and interpreting is only a mere imitation of Gen. xli, (Pharaoh's dream and Joseph's interpretation); that Daniel makes out a *Median* dynasty, which never existed; that he makes the Messianic kingdom immediately to follow that of Alexander's successors, and finally, that it was of no use to Nebuchadnezzar to know who would succeed him, and therefore the whole matter was unimportant, and unworthy of any miracle to carry it through.'

Chap. iii. comes in for its full share. 'The idol is monstrous and incredible; and Daniel — where was he, so that no mention is made of him, when he of all men was most expected to be present? The Babylonians were no persecutors for the sake of religion, and yet this book represents them as such; during the exile no miracles were performed or heard of; Nebuchadnezzar was favorable to the Jews, and would heat no furnaces seven times hotter than usual to destroy *them*, (I say *them*, for of course he did not expect his own heathen subjects to disobey him); every where there is an effort to introduce the wonderful and to magnify it; and finally, Hitzig is quoted as having *strikingly* (treffend) said: "As to the miraculous escape [in the furnace], Hengstenberg must here fall back on his *a priori* faith. Forsooth a miracle which changes the very nature of an element, is a great one! It is the greatest in the Old Testament; but not, therefore, the most probable." In conclusion Lengerke remarks, that "the story considered as a matter of fact, contradicts the regular and sublime movements of the Godhead as developed in history, and his manner of dealing with his people." (s. 105 seq).

Chap. iv. has also its full share of difficulties. 'Nebuchadnezzar's madness is the strangest and most incredible of all things, and no historian takes notice of it; we can never suppose, with any probability, that he would have published his own shame and degradation to the world; and what became of his kingdom during seven years of mania? How comes it that he "built great Babylon," when other historians ascribe this to Semiramis and Nitocris? And who can believe in his restoration to the throne, and in his thanksgiving to the God of the Jews?

Chap. v. is said to 'exhibit many a contradiction and improbability; Daniel appears as a stranger to the son of Nebuchadnezzar; and this so-called son was not even of the royal progeny; if the writing on the wall was *hieroglyphical*, then the Magi could interpret it; if it was *demotic*, all could read it; if it was neither, Daniel could interpret it no more than the Magi; such a tyrant as Belshazzar would neither have suffered Daniel to threaten him with judgments, nor have rewarded him; the profanation of the sacred vessels of the temple was a thing unheard of in all ancient heathendom. Daniel contradicts himself, for one moment he refuses a bribe, and the next he receives it; and finally, it is altogether improbable, that, during one and the same night, the feast could be celebrated, the writing interpreted, the city taken, and Daniel proclaimed the third officer in the kingdom, (s. 238 ff).

Against chap. vi. it is alleged, that there was no Darius the Mede; that the division of the realm into three great Satrapies is unsupposable; that the silly statute, forbidding all to ask any thing of God or man for thirty days, is altogether incredible; that there are internal *indicia* in this statute of its being a *Jewish* composition; that Daniel could never have been fanatic enough to believe in his escape from punishment; that the lions could not have lived without being smothered, in such a den as the book describes, and that the whole story is manufactured out of the account of the pit into which Joseph's brethren cast him (Gen. 37: 24); that the edict of Darius, commanding all his subjects to worship the God of Daniel, is the most atrocious and incredible intolerance; and finally, that the preservation of Daniel in such a den, was, like all the other wonders of this book, not only a useless affair, but against the divine economy.'

Thus Lengerke; with whom Knobel fully sympathizes, and De Wette, as we have seen, calls the whole story *ridiculous*. As a standing accusation, scattered here and there throughout the whole commentary of Leng. on these chapters, it is declared, that the writer every where seeks to paint every thing in the most glaring colors, and is excessively prone to make every thing into a stupendous miracle, so often as he can find an occasion.

I need not here repeat an investigation of any of these charges. In my Commentary and Excursus on the chapters in question, I have said all that I deem necessary or expedient. It would seem that the mind of any one must be full of bitterness, as well as unbelief, to treat the lofty scenes of this book in such a manner. I should deem it a difficult task, to find specimens of the moral sublime superior to those exhibited in the conduct of Daniel. A deeper vein of ardent piety and humility, more lofty and inflexible integrity, and less of the fear of man where the honor of God and the claims of duty demand action or speaking, I think could be found only in him "who knew no sin, and in whose mouth guile was not found." How different are impressions which different persons may receive, in reading the very same book! There is some evidence, however, that in this case I am in the right, because our Saviour, and his apostles, and the prophet Ezekiel of old, have given plain and incontrovertible evidence of the same impressions in respect to Daniel that I have expressed.

One thing is clear; which is, that if the principles assumed and urged by Lengerke and his friends are correct, then are the *Gospels* as much more incredible than the book of Daniel, as the number of miracles related in them is greater than those in the prophet's book. This is a consequence inevitable and utterly undeniable. Unbelief as to miracles is the simple basis of all this seemingly imposing structure of the Neologists; and this, maintained with consistency, brings us just where Strauss has invited us to go, or puts us under the same category with Bruno Bauer.

(7) Parachronisms, or errors in chronology, are alleged against the book; e. g. in 1:1, (the *third* year of Jehoiakim); 1: 5 and 2: 1; 1: 21 and 10: 1; also historical contradictions respecting the Magi in ch. ii.; and respecting the lions' den in ch. vi. It is alleged, moreover, that there was no Shushan in the time of Belshazzar, as stated in 8: 2; that there were no *Satrapies* in the time of the Babylonish dynasty, nor even among the Medes and Persians when Babylon was taken; that Nebuchadnezzar was not the father of Belshazzar; that there was no king of this latter name; that such king, whatever was his name, was not slain at the capture of the city; that Darius the Mede (as king of Babylon) never had any existence; and that in 11: 2, the writer shows himself wholly ignorant of the history of the Persian kings, making only four.

All these allegations have been discussed, in my remarks on the passages respectively concerned, and to them I refer the reader for what I have deemed proper to say in respect to the objections just mentioned.

(8) A great multitude of improbable and suspicious *assertions* or *declarations* are put to the account of Daniel. The rigorous ascetics of the young Jews in ch. i.; the foolish demand of Nebuchadnezzar in ch. ii.; the description of the image in ch. iii.; the absence of Daniel at the consecration of the idol (ibid.); the religious persecution of Nebuchadnezzar, and "the despicable obstinacy and fanaticism of the Jewish officials" (ibid.); the seven years' madness of Nebuchadnezzar; his publishing this to the world; his praying, before his madness left him; the definite marks of not being authentic contained in his edict itself; that Daniel did not appear with the Magi before Belshazzar; the kindness of this king to Daniel; that the latter was made third ruler the same night in which the feast was held; the profanation of the holy vessels (ch. v.); the foolish decree of Darius; the fanaticism of Daniel; the incredible intolerance of the king, and marks of *Jewish* composition in his edict (ch. vi.); all these are alleged against the book of Daniel. But nearly every one of these has already been produced by Lengerke under preceding heads, and therefore need not have been again repeated. But he seems to feel, that his cause depends somewhat on the *number* as well as the quality of the testimonies which he reckons up; and if the same witness is twice brought upon the stand, it helps to increase the *number* of testimonies, if not their weight.

I have only to subjoin, that all these topics have already been discussed, as our text has presented occasion; and therefore I shall not follow him in repeating over again the same arguments.

(9) 'The dogmatic views of the book differ widely from those that belong to the exile-period, and agree with those in the times of the Maccabees. (*a*) The *Christology* in Daniel is far more perfected than in Ezekiel. In ch. vii., the Messiah appears as a super-human being; even a divine nature is attributed to him, (which occurs nowhere else except in those Sibylline Oracles which were written at the Maccabaean period); and in general, the Messianic views in Daniel find numerous parallels in the apocryphal books, but nowhere else.'

That the Messianic development is more clear and full in Daniel than in Ezekiel, I am as fully persuaded as Lengerke is. But what of that? Is it any strange thing, that the last great prophet, employed to predict the state of the Jewish nation after their return from exile, and when they come under the domain of some of the great dynasties which he foresaw — is it strange that he, who has developed the fifth or universal Messianic empire with a true catholic and cosmopolitan spirit, rejecting even the usual Jewish costume in his picture — that he should have gone on in advance of Ezekiel? So far is this from being strange, that I should say, it is altogether congruous with what we should expect of him situated as he was, and with that peculiar measure of special prophetic foresight, which his other predictions develop. How is Lengerke to show, that *progress* is impossible or improbable?

As to the assertion that a *divine nature* is nowhere else in the O. Test. Scriptures attributed to the Messiah — that is a matter which belongs to Lengerke's *subjective* views of exegesis. It is quite possible, as we find by frequent experience, for men "to have eyes and see not." But if a man, shutting his eyes at mid-day with a clear sky, should deny that it is light, we should not feel bound to disprove his assertion. Still we may advert to some of the passages which make against the declaration of Lengerke. Ps. 2: 7 calls him the *Son of God*, which, as Hengstenberg and others insist, must be understood in a *literal* sense. This I do not believe; for if he is a *literal Son*, then could he be neither self-existent nor independent, and therefore could not be *truly God*. The word *Son* has an *official* sense. But in Ps. 45: 7, 8, he is called God, and God's throne is assigned to him. Ps. cx., compared with our Saviour's commentary in Matt. 22: 41—46, plainly shows his higher nature. Isa. 9: 5 calls him *the mighty God*. Isa. 11: 2—4 ascribes to him supreme power of chastising the wicked. Micah 5: 2 makes his "goings forth to be everlasting." Ps. lxxii. attributes to him an eternal reign. Mal. 3: 1 represents him as

Jehovah coming to his temple. Isa. 6 :1—4, if we may trust the apostle John as an expositor (John 12: 41), shows that Christ is *Jehovah of hosts.* By implication, many other passages might be brought to bear on the same point. But I forbear. Lengerke has a way in which he disposes of each, and which makes them give very different testimony from that which I must believe they were intended to give.

In respect to the remaining declaration of Lengerke, viz. that the Christology of Daniel, so advanced and completed as it is, can 'find its like only in the *apocryphal* books, it is the most unfortunate of all. We have already seen, (pp. 435 seq.), that a spiritual and personal Messiah and moral and spiritual kingdom are not once adverted to in all the apocryphal books. In all there are not half a dozen passages, which even advert to the subject of a future deliverance; none to a specific Deliverer. A general indistinct belief of future prosperity, in respect to Jerusalem and the Jewish commonwealth, with the perpetuity of the Davidic race of kings, is all that we can gather from the *tout ensemble* of the Apocrypha. Where then is the *advanced* view of the Messianic reign, with which Daniel is said to harmonize? So far from this, all the spirit and soul of the earlier prophets is entirely evaporated, and we have in their room only the tame surmisings of a narrow Jewish spirit, disclosing only the expectation of worldly civil preëminence and prosperity. And while Lengerke himself alleges, that Daniel above all Heb. prophets has developed a personal Messiah, divine and human, he cannot find a trace of such a Messiah in any or all the apocryphal books put together. Yet he asserts that Daniel is a late book, because his Messianic views are the same as those in the Apocrypha. In this only is he in the right, viz. that the Sibylline Oracles of the Maccabaean period contain like views. But, as we have seen (p. 413 above), these compositions contain the most indubitable marks of borrowing from Daniel; and so they prove the higher age and credit of that book.

(*b*) 'The views of the resurrection and general judgment that follow the Messianic development,' Lengerke says, 'are too definite and specific to belong to an earlier period.'

If this proves anything to the purpose, it must be by virtue of assuming, that the Daniel of the exile could have had no views in advance of his brother-prophets who had preceded him. But how is this to be shown? When it is admitted that his *Messianic views* are much more specific, and more catholic in spirit, than those found elsewhere, how is it unreasonable to suppose, that his views on the subjects just named may be in advance of his predecessors' views? For other considerations, I refer the reader to the Comm. on Dan. 12: 1—3.

(c) 'But the *angelology* of the book is altogether in the form in which the Jews received it from the later Parsism. Here is first found a distinction between the higher and lower angels; also the doctrine of *guardian* angels; and moreover the names of individual angels.'

Lengerke has not ventured on the assertion (often made by some), that the whole angelology of the O. Test. comes from the Parsis. As nearly every book of the Heb. Scriptures is full of the mention of angels, it would be difficult to render this plausible. But the *distinctions*, he says, are from the Parsis. And is this really so? Who are the Seraphim, the presence-angels, in Isa. vi.? Gesenius acknowledges these to be *angel-chieftains*, Comm. on v. 2. Ex. 32: 34 speaks of a special guardian angel, comp. 33: 2. Deut. 33: 2 speaks of *ten thousand holy ones* in the retinue of Jehovah. In Josh. 5: 14, a *captain of the Lord's host* appears to Joshua. Apparently the same leader reappears in Judg. 2: 1. In Job i. ii., the angels assemble on special occasions, before the throne of God, to render an account of their respective watch-stations. In Job 33: 23, an *angel interpreter* appears as the monitor of men. In 1 Kings 22: 19—23, an angel of chastisement appears before the Lord. In Ps. 68: 17, the chariots of God are twenty thousand, even thousands of angels. What is more than all, Ezekiel and Zechariah introduce angel-interpreters, in the same way as Daniel, being his contemporaries. Does this prove the *late* origin of their works also? As to the *names* of good angels, I grant that these are peculiar to Daniel; but in Job and in Zechariah we have a *Satan* among the evil angels. If it be said that this is no *proper* name, but only an *appellative*, cannot the same be said of *Gabriel* and *Michael*? Both are of appellative significance. But what is still more against Lengerke is, that no one has yet shown that the Babylonians or Persians entertained the idea of *national* guardian angels. In the Zend-Avesta one may seek in vain for it. He will find merely, that Bahman, the first of the Amshaspands, is a subordinate to Ormusd, in watching over the good in general; but of *national* angels there is not a word.

Indeed, if any one will carefully go through the Zend-Avesta, he will find the whole system of Zoroaster as to *Amshaspands* and *Izeds*, as well as to *Devs* and *Archdevs*, to differ so widely from the Heb. angelology, that derivation of the latter from the former is out of fair question. And finally, the idea that the rigid Jews would borrow from Heathenism and Dualism, and introduce this into their own Scriptures, is one that a sober man, well acquainted with their history, cannot readily admit — cannot at all admit.

(10) 'The *dogmatic ascetic views* of Daniel savor strongly of Pharisaism.

Excessive representations about the efficacy of prayer are manifest, in 2: 18. 6: 11. 9: 3. 10: 2. Revelations even are made to him in consequence of prayer, chap. ix. Then we have ascetic abstinence from profane food, 1: 12; a three weeks' fasting, 10: 2; prayer three times a day, 6: 11; and seeking and curiously prying into (grübeln, *grubbing into*) former prophecies.'

Subjective, I trow, rather than objective, are most of these objections. Lengerke, it would seem, deems all special faith in prayer as Pharisaism; all belief in an answer to prayer, as superstitious credulity; all strict conscientious obedience to the plain and express laws of Moses concerning unclean food, even on the part of a *Jew*, as foolish ascetic severity; and searching with eagerness into prophecies, which were of the highest possible interest to a Jewish patriot mourning over the exile of his nation, is an incredible and unprecedented affair. Unfortunate prophet! If he complies with heathen customs, even so far as to belong to the order of the Magi, then forsooth, he is no Jew, much less a *Daniel;* and if he adheres with unshaken constancy and fidelity to the laws of his country and his God, he is a bigot and a Pharisee. It is difficult, amidst all this, to see what course Daniel could have steered, in order to satisfy Neology.

For the rest, I have said all that I wish to say, in commenting on the passages to which appeal is made.

(11) 'Certain representations in the book lead us down to the latest, i. e. the Maccabaean period, as the time of its composition. The author unwarily speaks of the prophets as far distant from him,' 9: 6, 10, 24.

But in these passages there is not a word about the *antiquity* of the prophets, excepting merely that such are alluded to as addressed the Jews previous to the exile. On the contrary, if the words be rigidly construed, they imply that Daniel was himself a hearer of the prophets alluded to: "*We* have not hearkened to thy servants, the prophets, who spake in thy name." In reality I suppose this to be a mere κοίνωσις in speaking; but at all events, there is not the remotest ground for any supposition such as Lengerke makes.

(12) 'The writer of the book, although studious of concealment, betrays at times the Maccabaean period. Thus in 9: 19 he says: "Accomplish and delay not." Here the writer shows that he partook of the expectation of the Maccabaean period, viz. that the Messiah was immediately to come. The writer reckons time, moreover, according to *Sabbath-years*, 9: 24; and so did the Maccabees. The temple is also supposed to be extant, 9: 24.

But what is it, in 9: 19, that is not to be delayed? Simply compassion on the desolated and ruined holy city; see v. 18. There is not a word here of the Messiah. Then where does the writer get an account of the Maccabaean reckoning by *Sabbath-years?* He does not tell us; and I have sought in vain for it. And even if it be found, how can it be proved that this mode of reckoning first commenced so late as that period? Of the *extant* temple, moreover, in 9: 24, I find no traces. I find only, that when the Messiah has come, he will, as the great high priest, anoint a *Holy of Holies* to be consecrated to his service. Paul was of the same opinion, Heb. 7: 20, 26. 8: 1, 6. 9: 11—14. And when Leng. says: "Dan. 9: 8 shows that the book does not stand on a *historical* basis;" the reply is, that this passage merely represents Daniel as confessing, that the kings, princes, and fathers of the Jews had sinned, and ought to be penitent for it. Is there, then, no *historical* basis for this?

(13) 'The writer lets drop his mask, when he makes such frequent assertions that his words are true;' e. g. 2: 45. 8: 26. 10: 1. 11: 2.

But are not such assurances frequent in Isa., Jer., Ezekiel, and other prophets, and especially in the Apocalypse? And how often does the Saviour preface his discourses with ἀμήν, ἀμήν, and declare to the Jews and to his apostles, that his words are true. It is needless to accumulate references here, to what is in the memory of every intelligent and careful reader. In Apoc. 1: 7. 19: 9. 21: 5. 22: 6, will be found passages sufficient for the purpose of comparison.

Lengerke further asserts, that 'the writer has betrayed himself, by remarking that his oracles must be *sealed* and *secret*, until the time of fulfilment,' 8: 26. 12: 4. — But I do not see how sealing and secreting would be to his purpose, in gaining credit for his book. If this is to be entirely *secreted*, then his object in publishing it must be defeated. Or did he expect, on his mere pretension to have discovered an ancient writing, to satisfy the Jewish Sanhedrim of its genuineness by having it sealed up? No; Leng. has mistaken the design of *sealing* in both cases, which is not for *concealment*, but for *safe preservation*. Prophecies thus carefully kept could not be tampered with.

(14) 'The writer's repeated eulogies on himself can never be supposed to have come from the real ancient Daniel.'

But why? 'Because regard to modesty forbids us to suppose this of such a man,' is the answer. Very well; then if the case is so plain and striking, how came the shrewd, cunning, sharp-sighted forger in question, (as neologists now and then allow him to be), not to know better than to put such suspicious things into his book, which would so obviously betray him? He could not, if objectors are in the right, have had but a small portion of the shrewdness and cunning that are often attributed to him. But bating all this, how much real foundation is there for the allegation, that he is taxable with excessive eulogy? In 1: 19, 20, Daniel includes his three friends as well as himself, when he says they were found greatly superior to the magicians and astrologers, in matters of wisdom and understanding. This was assuming no very extravagant position. They were *pretenders* in recondite matters, and nothing more. But the wisdom of these Hebrews, whatever it is, is all attributed (v. 17) to the special gift of God, and not to their own talents. When before Nebuchadnezzar, and about to disclose the king's dream, Daniel says expressly, that this power comes not from any superior wisdom in him, but only because God has willed that this secret shall be revealed, 2: 29, 30. In 5: 11, 12, 13, what is said of his wisdom, is said by the queen-mother of Belshazzar, and not by him, and it is said to induce the king to send for Daniel and seek his counsel. It is related plainly to the honor of God, and not of himself. What is said in 6: 4, relates merely to his *official* conduct, in respect to which his envious fellow-courtiers could find no ground of inculpation before the king. In 9: 23 and 10: 11, the assurance that he is *greatly beloved* comes from the angel, in order to comfort and strengthen him when he was sinking. And what is there of vanity and extravagance in all this? If we desire to see Daniel in his real attitude of mind with respect to himself, we must look at him in chap. ix. and x. Throughout his book there is unequivocal evidence of decorum and deep humility. He never claims either praise or reward. And why should he not be permitted to relate kind words addressed to him, as well as Moses be permitted to say, that he was *meek* above all other men? Num. 12: 3. Why not, as well as Paul to say, that he was "a wise master-builder?" 1 Cor. 3: 10. Paul, like Daniel, attributes all to the grace of God. What forbids his magnifying that grace even when extended to himself? In 2 Cor. 3: 5, he speaks of his *sufficiency;* but he attributes it all to God. He tells us that he was caught up into the third heaven (2 Cor. 12: 2), and heard unspeakable words; yet he is careful to say, that he glories not in himself, but in an enraptured Paul. John tells us of "a disciple, whom Jesus loved, and who leaned on his bosom" (John 13: 23), evidently meaning himself. He tells us again (21: 21) of the same beloved disciple, who leaned on his Master's bosom. Was John assuming and vain? Finally, is there no difference between a man who is conscious of divine illumination, and one who is not? May not the former speak truly, yea modestly of the *fact*, and yet, when he does this to exalt the grace of God, be acquitted of vanity and of self-gratulation? I trust this may be so. I will not bring into comparison the claims which Jesus makes for himself, for he spake as never man spake, and was what never man was. Truth obliged him to speak as he did. But is not the testimony concerning Daniel *true?* So thought Ezekiel, who ranks him with Noah and Job. So thought Christ and his apostles, who place him among the prophets. So thought John, who has made his work the basis-model of his own Apocalypse. So thought the Jewish doctors who put him into one scale, and all the wise men of the world into the other, and made him outweigh them all. So thought Josephus, who places him at the very head of all the prophets. So thought the Christian Fathers, one and all. And so all the church of God have thought, until Neology came forth to correct a mistaken world, and chastise it for its credulity.

(15) 'In Daniel is one and the same uniform tone throughout. In every paragraph the same things happen over and over to Daniel and his friends. The Magi are at their wits end and stupid, that Daniel may have the chance of surpassing them. So is it in chap. ii. iv. v. The three friends of Daniel, moreover, are thrown into the furnace, that an angel may interpose in their behalf. So is it with Daniel in the lions' den, vi. Daniel fasts (ix. x.), that an angel may intervene. Daniel every where gets new honors for himself, 2: 48, 49. 3: 30. 5: 29. 6: 29. Chapters ii—vi. all conclude with praises of the Jewish God, wrung from heathen despots. All the book, from chap. vii. to the end, has but one *exitus* and one object, viz. the death of Antiochus and the commencement of the Messianic reign. The heathen kings all issue edicts commanding that Jehovah be universally worshipped. And all this is said over and over, in nearly the same words and expressions.' So Lengerke, p. lxxiv. seq.

I feel the difficuly of the task, when undertaking to answer declamation instead of argument. Supposing the facts related in Daniel to be true, how could Daniel do otherwise than he has done? The Magi were impostors, when they claimed the power of predicting and interpreting dreams. The simple story of their failure and disgrace is told. Is there any thing to be inculpated here? God preserves his faithful servants in the midst of dangers; is there any thing in this which is incredible to any one who does not, like Lengerke, deny the possibility of miracles? As to *angelic interposition,* if the mention of this be evidence of a forged book, then is all the rest of the Old Test., and the whole of the New, to be regarded as forged. That all the narrations conclude with ascribing glory to God, is an evidence of the genuineness of the book, instead of the contrary. The true Daniel was just such a man as would do this. That *heathen* despots are compelled to praise the God of Israel, was a matter of serious moment to the poor exiled Jews, who were at their mercy. Was there no important end to be answered in softening and humbling the hearts of kings, in whose power the lives and fortunes of the Hebrew nation were? Lengerke can see nothing in all this, except Daniel's exalting himself, and the Jews, and their national God (Jehovah), at the expense of the poor heathen. The divinities of the Chaldees seem to him to be as good, and to have as valid claims, as the God of the Jews. But Daniel was of a different mind; and so, as I hope, will most of his readers be. As to *sameness* in the writer of the book — the echoing and reëchoing of the same thing in nearly the same language — nothing can be farther from the truth, than such a charge. Read chap. ii—vi., and then say, whether any two of these narrations are alike. A greater diversity of circumstances can no where be found, in events which have one common culminating point, viz. a display of the supremacy, glory, and mercy of Jehovah. Go into the prophecies of this book. Every one is different from all its associates. Chap. ii. exhibits symbols entirely different from all the others. Chap. vii. has monsters altogether *sui generis*. Chap. viii. has another set of symbols, entirely differing from these. Chap. xi. drops symbol altogether, and becomes (as one might almost say) simple narrative, or takes the form of mere historical prose. The passage in 9: 24—27 is *toto coelo* different from all other parts of the book. While the same hand is every where plainly cognoscible in the coloring of the style, yet the variety in description is as great as we can well conceive it could be, where the same great events are described in all. "A tame dull sameness," in such a book as this? We might as well accuse Isaiah of sameness, when he prophesies so often concering Assyria and Babylon; or Jeremiah, or Ezekiel, when they say so much, and speak so often, respecting the ruin of the Jewish State and capital. No; there is scarcely a book in the Old Test., that is more free from *sameness*, or from *tameness*. A veritable witling — a great bungler — he must have been who wrote this book, if Lengerke's accusations are true. But this unsparing critic should have taken better care, and not been off his guard so as to attribute to the Pseudo-Daniel so much shrewdness and tact as he has. After all, however, no book is read with more eagerness than Daniel, when a reader is intelligent enough to understand him; and one simple and considerate perusal of it, with a candid and serious mind, will scatter to the four winds such objections as those which we have now been canvassing.

(16) 'An independent prophet, like the pretended Daniel, could never have busied himself in groping after the meaning of almost contemporary prophecy, [that of Jer. respecting the 70 years]; nor did any one before the time of Ezra think of *interpreting* the prophets.'

We have had this same thing once before to deal with, (p. 473); but the number of times that a testimony is repeated, seems to add corresponding increase to its weight and value, in the view of Lengerke. The idea that Ezra was the first man, who ever thought of *interpreting* the prophets, is novel. We have usually supposed, that so many as thought it a duty to read them, endeavored at least to interpret them, i. e. they gave some particular sense to the words of prophecy. And as to Ezra's *new* employment or discovery, I do not know where to find any account of it. I find in Neh. 8: 1—3, that Ezra brought the *law of Moses* before the people, and read and expounded it; but not a word is said about the *prophets*. If any more need be said on the objection before us, it has already been said, *(ut supra)*. Does it not sound strangely in our ears, to hear Daniel taxed with singular conduct, with superstition, because he read Jeremiah's predictions concerning the Babylonish exile with the highest interest and keenest scrutiny? Unfortunate man! we are tempted to exclaim again; if he does not read the prophets, he is no Jew; if he does read them with anxious scrutiny, then he is a bigot and an enthusiast.

(17) 'If the book is authentic, it must have been written by a Daniel contemporary with Ezek., and the same that Ezek. mentions in 14: 14—20. 28: 3. But as the writer has so often quoted Ezekiel, the supposition of identity with the ancient Daniel is directly contradictory.'

But this *contradiction* I can not see. How can it prove that the Daniel of Ezekiel's time could not write the book that bears his name, because this book quotes Ezekiel? What hindered his quoting a contemporaneous writer, if he had occasion to do so? I do not and cannot see the point of Lengerke's argument. However, as we have had the subject of quoting Ezekiel upon the tapis before (p. 453), it is unnecessary to discuss it again. If either has quoted, (which I see no evidence of), then it seems more probable that Ezekiel is the borrower. This would not be strange, after what he has said of Daniel. The reader will hardly fail to notice how industriously arguments are multiplied, even by the repetition of *idem per idem*. Lengerke seems to adopt the maxim: "Non refert vim, sed multum."

(18) 'Most convincing of all that the book is not genuine, is the character of its predictions in regard to *definiteness*. The prophets of the Old Test., when they speak of the *future*, give only hints and generic descriptions. Whenever they do *individualize*, it is in a mere poetical way; and those few predictions which are *special*, are either not fulfilled at all, or are so only in part. Of such an indistinct and

general nature are all the other Messianic predictions. They usually describe nothing more than a flourishing political condition. Isa. vi. predicts the destruction of the Jewish people by the *Assyrians;* but it happened only by the Chaldeans. In Isa. 8: 4 and 17: 1—3, the contemporaneous fall of Damascus and Samaria is predicted, and that this will take place in 65 years. Neither of these predictions was fulfilled. Isa. xiii. and xiv. predict the destruction of Babylon by the Medes and Persians, and the slaying of the last Babylonish king when the city was taken. Neither happened; for Cyrus spared both the city and its king. Isa. xxix. predicts a *siege* of Jerusalem by the Assyrians; but chap. xxxvi. xxxvii. show us the contrary. Nearly all the prophets foretell the utter destruction of the Edomites, (see Isa. chap. xxxiv. xliii. and Jer. chap. xlix., also Obadiah); yet this did not take place, for the Edomites ravaged Palestine during the Babylonish exile, and Herod, the king of Judea, sprung from them. In Isa. xxiii. and Ezek. xxvi. xxviii. the seizure of Tyre by Nebuchadnezzar is predicted; but Nebuchadnezzar marched to Egypt, and left the matter of the seige unaccomplished. According to Isa. xl. xlv. xlvi., after the return from exile, Jerusalem will be built up and adorned in the most magnificent manner, and all nations will go up to it, and offer their richest presents. Was there any thing like to this, as a matter of fact? Hos. 9: 3. 11: 5 declares that the ten tribes shall go into Egypt as captives; a thing that never happened. In fact, in all cases where seemingly future events actually take place, the alleged predictions are spurious and written *post eventum*, or a wrong exegesis is put upon them, in order to make them correspond with historical facts; e. g. Jer. l. li.; and for what may be done by exegesis to make out fulfilment, see Hengst. on Zech. 9: 1—8. If neither of these principles will solve any particular case, then the pretended prophet does nothing more than describe what is present before his vision; as in Isa. xiii. xiv. and xxi. 1—10. Of what concerns foreign heathen nations, in their mutual relations and strifes, the Hebrew prophets say nothing; so that Daniel is a perfect *ἅπαξ λεγόμενον* among them, on any other ground than that the book was written *post eventum*. Indeed this is the only possible way in which it could be written.' Thus Leng. § 14.

Here again I am puzzled to know the drift of the argument. Isaiah, and all the prophets besides Daniel, have predicted things, it is said, that never came to pass. Be it so then, for the sake of argument. How does this prove the book of Daniel to be spurious? This book, it is said, has predicted things in the same manner as the others; e. g. the coming of the Messiah's kingdom immediately after the death of

Antiochus. But allowing the correctness of this statement, what bearing has it on the genuineness of the book? If the other prophets did but *guess*, and if they sometimes failed to guess rightly, yet the fact that they wrote the books assigned to them by universal consent, is not at all disproved thereby. Now Daniel's case is just the same. If he *guessed wrong*, it does not prove that he did not write the book which bears his name. Whether his predictions were fulfilled or not, has no concern with the question whether he wrote the book; excepting that, in case of actual fulfilment, it would prove that some prophetic man, at all events, wrote the book. According to Lengerke himself, then, Daniel stands on as good ground as any of the other prophets.

On the other hand, when it becomes convenient, Daniel's *definiteness* and *certainty* or *exactness* is made the ground of confident conclusion, that all was written *post eventum*. Why? Because a miracle is impossible; and prediction in its proper sense would be a miracle. The interposition of a *Pseudo-Daniel*, then, becomes a matter of necessity, and of course must be admitted. But this process of logic we have examined in the preceding pages, and therefore need not repeat the examination here.

As to that part of Lengerke's objection, which asserts that predictions concerning the future are always clothed in general and indefinite expressions, conveying no idea of any thing definite and tangible, the answer is short and easy. Jeremiah (in chap. xxv. xxix.) predicts 70 years' exile. Bleek, Lengerke, and others say, that this is only a mere round number. But Zech. 1: 12 and Ezra 1: 1, both written after the exile, when it must of necessity have been exactly known how long it had lasted, declare that it had continued 70 years. Besides, is not the time definite in Isa. 7: 14—16; 8: 1—4; 16: 14, three years for the crushing of the Moabites; 17: 14, destruction of the Assryian host between evening and morning; 20: 3, three years for the subjugation of Egypt and Ethiopia; 21: 16, exactly one year for the humbling of Kedar; 38: 15. (comp. 2 K. 20: 6), life of Hezekiah prolonged 15 years. To these, others might be added; but I deem it unnecessary. Lengerke asserts that most of these predictions failed, and those which did not, were written *post eventum*. Was Jeremiah's prediction, then, of 70 years' exile, written *post eventum?* If so then he must have lived some 115 years, and have written after this. Comp. Jer. 1: 2 and Ezra 1: 1. But enough. I might follow all his assertions as to *failure* in the fulfilment of definite predictions, by showing that he has either done violence to the exegesis, or presented a distorted view of historical facts. But this would lead me quite away from my present object. The thing moreover, has already been done by others; and it will be easy, either in Calvin, or Vitringa, or Hengstenberg, to find a refutation of such assertions.

Truly I do not wonder, that those who reject the possibility of *prediction* should be so anxious to show the *lateness* of Daniel's book. It is so definite in many cases, so graphic, and in chap. xi. so historically minute and true, that all possibility of being explained away is out of question. And hence the confident and often repeated assertions of its being written *post eventum*. But as this whole subject has already been discussed, it need not be again repeated here.

(18) 'In no other book of the Old Testament is any nation or kingdom ever spoken of, which did not exist at the time of the prophet. In Daniel, future kingdoms and nations are brought before our view in abundance; a thing impossible before history had actually developed them.'

Yet in Num. 24: 14—24, in Balaam's prophecy, there seems to be a distant and then unknown nation in view. Ezek. (chap. xxxviii. xxxix.) brings to view, in Gog and Magog, the incursion of nations then seemingly unknown. At all events, the *fifth* kingdom in Daniel, viz. that which is named the Messianic reign elsewhere, and which is future and distant, is often spoken of. Lengerke avers, however, that the prophets had very erroneous views as to the time of this, and that they expected it after a short period. But this is a result of his own special exegesis. In my apprehension, however, it is not of much moment to find parallels here in other prophets. Who of all these prophets, except Daniel, was called to disclose the state of the Jews after their return from exile, and before the appearance of the Messiah? No one has undertaken it. If Daniel then occupies a ground, in his book, which is *not* occupied by others, why should it be strange that he has predicted things unlike what is found in other prophets. The last great *national* prophet had views extending beyond those of his predecessors. His situa ion fitted him for it. Hence he brings dynasties to view, as yet unknown. They are intimately connected with the chosen people of God. Hence he was commissioned to describe them. Who now can show, that one prophet may not have had different and more extended views than another? Who shall set the metes and bounds of individual prophecy? There is the book of Daniel, at all events, a part of it written almost with the minuteness of historical narrative. If it was actually written during the exile, then it certainly contains *prediction*. Whether it was or was not then written, is a question of course dependent on testimony as to *facts* — and it is altogether a mere question of *fact.* How can such a question be decided by an *a priori* theory? Such a theory is irrelevant, and a mere *petitio principii.*

(19) "That the writer lived in the Maccabaean age, is evident from the fact that he every where represents the Messianic reign as commencing immediately after the death of Antiochus." (p. 81 pref.).

On this Lengerke has often insisted, in his commentary; and yet I have never been able to see any force in this argument. According to Lengerke, the writer must have known the time and manner of Antiochus' death, as things already developed in fact and in history. Granting, for the present, that the author did live at that late period, how came he by an expectation of the *immediate* appearance of the Messiah? In the latter part of the very year of Antiochus' death, Lysias, the self-appointed regent of Syria and guardian of Antiochus' son, attacked the Jews with an army of 80,000 foot, 80 elephants, and a large body of cavalry. He was repulsed; but the Syrian garrison at Jerusalem held out, and continually annoyed the Jews; and in a short time Lysias rallied and sent a much larger army than before against them. Bethsura was taken, and Jerusalem besieged. Fortunately Philip, the real regent appointed by Antiochus, at that time invaded Syria with oriental troops, and took possession of Antioch. In order to expel him, Lysias was obliged to make peace with the Jews, and withdraw his army. But even after the treaty of peace, when he was admitted into Jerusalem, he caused the walls of the city to be thrown down. In 161 B. C., Demetrius Soter then on the throne of Syria, sent another army to Palestine, in order to enforce upon the Jews the renegado Alcimus as high priest. But soon afterwards the Jews rallied under Judas, and expelled Alcimus. He fled to Syria, and excited and persuaded Demetrius to send another army, in order to establish his official dignity as high priest. It was sent, commanded by Nicanor; the country was ravaged, the inhabitants killed, and Judas was proscribed. But Judas collected his patriot soldiers around him, encountered Nicanor, slew him and utterly routed and dispersed his army. However, only a few months of peace followed; for in 160 B. C., another large army of Demetrius was sent against Judea; and it was in attacking the 22,000 troops of which it was composed, that Judas, at the head of only 800 men lost his life. Thus much for the first three years after the death of Antiochus: How was it in the sequel?

It was still worse. The Syrian army, headed by Bacchides, gave full power to the *apostate* heathenized Jews, who behaved with unbounded insolence and ferocity. To heighten calamity a famine occurred; the apostates monopolized all the provisions of the land, and Bacchides ravaged the country, and massacred the friends of Judas. It was only after the death of Alcimus (159 B. C.), that the country had a good degree of quiet for nearly two years. Again in 158 B. C. Bacchides came up against the Jews, with a large army. The war did not last long; but all the treaties and truces of the Jews with the Syrian despots were utterly disregarded, whenever it appeared to be for their interest to disregard them. Thus until some 30 years afterwards, the Jews were subjected continually to petty vexations and occasionally to violent attacks. It was not until a generation had passed away, not until the reign of John Hyrcanus (135—106 B. C.), that peace and independence were wholly achieved.

Such are the exhibitions of history. What now is there in all this, to induce any man in his senses to say, that the *Messianic* period had come? What was there to encourage even a hope of it, during the whole generation that succeeded the death of Antiochus? Nothing — if possible, less than nothing. How then could the shrewd Pseudo-Daniel think of uniting the death of Antiochus with the introduction of the Messianic reign? The thing is absolutely incredible. No man of sense could say that such a period was ominous of an immediate Messianic reign, or that it was ushering in a peaceful and universal kingdom.

Nothing then can be more improbable, than Lengerke's assertions in regard to this matter. The thing is critically and rationally impossible.

'But,' I shall be asked, 'is it not matter of fact that Daniel has joined the advent of the fifth or Messianic dynasty, with the destruction of the last of the other four? Yes, I reply, *prima facie* his words would seem to import this. But any one well acquainted with the tenor of Old Testament prophecies, will find nothing strange or peculiar in this. It is merely treading in the steps of all the other prophets. Peter has given us an opening in respect to this matter. He tells us (1 Pet. 1: 11), that the ancient prophets "sought both *what time*, and also *what manner of time*, the spirit that was in them did signify, when it testified of the sufferings and the glory of Christ." In other words, their curiosity was greatly excited to know *when* Christ would come; and *in what manner* he would develop himself. But was this curiosity gratified? Peter has told us (v. 12), that only so much was revealed as would show that a *distant* future period was intended—"not unto *themselves*, but unto us, they ministered, etc." So it is in fact. Not one prophet has marked the *tempus in quo*. We have seen above, that the famous period of 70 weeks accomplishes no such object; and surely it will not be said that it is to be found any where else, if not found there.

I grant that in *the order of disclosure*, the Messianic times, as represented in Daniel, follow on immediately after the death of Antiochus. But such is the case, also, in all the prophets, whatever the events may be. In Isa. iii. the Messianic day follows the severe punishment of the then offending Jews. With the Assyrian invasion, in ch. vii. viii., is connected one of the most striking of all the Messianic prophecies, Isa. 9: 1—7. With the end of the Assyrian invasion, in ch. x., is united another magnificent prediction of the same nature, in ch. xi. With the overthrow of Idumea, ch. xxxiv., is united a Messianic prediction, ch. xxxv. In ch. xl—lxvi. the return from exile is constantly connected with the Messianic times. In Jeremiah, promises of gospel-times are attached to the penitence of Israel then backsliding, ch. iii. In ch. xxiii., the BRANCH is to reign, after the scattered Jews are called in. In. ch. xxxi. xxxii. xxxiii., substantially the same things are repeated, in the like connection. The same is the case in Ezek. xxxiv. and xxxvii. In Joel ii., gospel-times are predicted, in connection with a recovery from drought and locusts. In Joel iii., the Messianic period follows the defeat of the surrounding nations who attack Jerusalem. In Amos ix., the same period follows punishment and repentance. In Micah iv. v., it follows a time of punishment and desolation. In Hag. ii. it follows the finishing of the temple, "after a little while." In Zech. ii., it follows the return from exile. In ch. iii. xii. xiv., it follows the subjugation of foreign enemies who had afflicted the Jews. But in Mal. iii. iv., and almost only there in the prophets, it hardly stands related to specific occurrences.

Such is the view which the prophets afford us. To say now that Daniel is strange or peculiar, in regard to associating the Messianic times with definite historical events, is to say what is plainly against the whole tenor of the prophets. We have just seen this. If Daniel is in the wrong, they are equally so. If he has mistaken or misrepresented the matter, so have they; and some of them, e. g. Isaiah, have misrepresented it even more abundantly than he. If they are all in the wrong, that is another affair. My present business is, to show that Daniel stands on the same platform as his brethren.

If it be a fact, then, (and we have seen that it is), that Daniel's Messianic predictions are in conformity with those of all the other prophets as to arrangement, how can the matter of arrangement be adduced as an argument for the *later* composition of the book? And what shall we say, moreover, when we find that the Saviour himself has spoken in like manner of his *second* coming? In Matt. xxiv. xxv., his coming, and even his final coming, seems, at first view, to be linked with the destruction of Jerusalem by the Romans. So is it, too, with Paul and other writers of the

N. Test. The coming of the Lord is seemingly put in connection with certain events, or personages, of apostolic times. So in the Apocalypse, the Millenium is linked with the destruction of the beast which has seven heads and ten horns, i. e. Pagan and persecuting Rome. So the general judgment seems to follow on, as soon as the Millennium is concluded.*

What now are we to conclude from all this, in respect to Lengerke's allegations? And more especially, what are we to say, when we take a view of the Messianic developments at the Maccabaean period? We have seen (p. 435 above), that nothing but the most tame and anti-spiritual views of the Messianic period are to be found in Sirach, 1 Macc., Tobit, or Baruch, which are the writings of that period. There is not a word in all of them even of a *personal* Messiah, much less of a Redeemer who was immediately to come. Where then does Lengerke get *data*, from which he comes to the conclusion, that the Maccabaean times cherished the expectation of an *immediate* Messianic Deliverer? There is not a word in all history, nor in all the coetaneous writers of those times, which entitles him to make the conclusions which he has made. Directly the contrary; for, as we have seen above (p. 435), Daniel differs heaven-wide in his Messianic developments from the writers of the Maccabaean age. Lengerke's argument, then, is altogether groundless; and even if he could show that the Maccabaean period cherished hopes of the immediate advent of the Messiah, it would prove nothing. The representations of Daniel are in strict conformity with the method and arrangement of all the older prophets.

It is a different question, how the phenomena before us are to be accounted for. Is it, as has often been alleged, because prophets and apostles really thought the advent of the Messiah was immediately to take place, that they have thus spoken? Believe this who may or can; I cannot in any measure accede to it. When Paul wrote to the Thessalonians in the usual manner about *the coming of Christ*, even his last coming (1 Thess. 4: 13—18, comp. ch. v.), and they interpreted his words as Neologists and some others now interpret them — what did he do? He wrote another epistle, in which he corrected their mistake, 2 Thess. 2: 1 seq. And John — how was it with him? One coming of Christ was *speedily* to take place, John 21: 22, 23. Rev. 1: 1, 3, 7. 22: 7, 10, 20. What shall be said, then, of that exegesis, which, allowing only of *one* coming of Christ, makes it out from John, that he expected the end of the world during his day? Is this so? How then came John so fully and

* If Prof. Crosby had diligently surveyed this whole ground, he might have spared himself and others the enigmas which he has charged upon the N.Test. writers, in his little book on the subject of Christ's coming.

formally to declare, in Rev. xx., that a thousand years, yea, all this time moreover after the extinction of the beast and the false prophet (Rev.19: 20, 21), must needs be passed, during which the universal triumphs of the gospel were to continue? All this period must first pass away, before "the great white throne" (Rev. 20:11) will be occupied by the Judge of all. How then did John expect the *end of the world* during his own *life-time?* Did he really expect to live during all the period occupied by Messianic conquests, (which he has sung in his sublime epic with notes so loud and clear,) and then a thousand years more in addition; and then, no one knows how much longer before the end of the world? Or if he were to live so long, did he expect others whom he addressed, to live during all this period? One must think very differently of him from what I am disposed or able to think, if he believes all this. At all events, a man who can believe all this, has very little claim to tax others with *credulity.*

We are not at liberty, then, to charge the sacred writers of the N. Test., (who have thus developed their views), with a belief in the immediate and final coming of the Messiah. As little are the O. Test. prophets chargeable with a belief that his first coming was to be immediate. Such a supposition is opposed by the consideration, that the same prophets, who speak apparently of his immediate coming, have predicted other events, the happening of which must occupy many years, yea a long period, before that coming. How can we suppose them to be so grossly and palpably inconsistent with themselves?

Thus far then, we have no satisfactory solution of the problem before us. In what does this solution lie, or how can we explain the usage in question? Only in the way, I would answer, in which Peter (1 Pet. 1: 11) has taught us to go. He says, that although prophets sought most anxiously to know the *when* of the Messianic development, yet they were merely taught that it would be at a distant day, even at the period in which Peter lived. "The times and the seasons hath the Father kept in his own power." Hence no prophet, not even Daniel, specificates the time of the advent. The fact then, everywhere apparent, that the prophets have connected the coming of the Messiah with events of their time, is to be regarded in quite a different light from that in which Lengerke and others have placed it. It results from a connection and sequency of *order* and *arrangement,* not from an immediate sequency of time. After predictions of evil of any kind, and of devastation and destruction, words of *comfort* are next subjoined. The pious are thus led to the cheering hope of better times and a future Deliverer. This saves them from a despairing attitude of mind. If they know not, and are not permitted to know, the day nor the hour of the promised good, yet they are permitted to cherish the animated hope which the certain futurition of good inspires.

In contemplating their position, I imagine to myself a spectator, from an elevated station, looking to a distant mountain-prospect. Behind each other are ridges of mountains, with intervening vallies or table-lands. The latter he cannot see; but the ridges heaved up to a great altitude are perfectly visible, while at the same time they appear quite proximate to each other. The eye can discern nothing between them, and the inexperienced seer is ready to affirm that they are in close proximity; while the experienced observer knows how fallacious such a conclusion may be. So is it with the prophets. According to Peter the specific time of the Messiah's advent was not revealed. But the advent itself loomed up into distinct visibility. The prophets wrote according to the appearance of things; or rather, they wrote according to the train of thought in their own minds. While they were seeing visions of calamity and deep distress, they were filled with gloom. Daniel and others tell us that they were sick, and fainted, in the midst of such visions. But the scene soon changes. Their fainting spirits are revived. They see the Sun of righteousness arising upon the darkness. They are cheered with his light. How long the darkness will endure, it may be that they know not; but that light and peace and hope and joy will follow, they feel assured. Their pens follow the visions and emotions of their minds. These are in immediate succession; and they describe them accordingly. But the *times* and *seasons* are not specifically limited. *Events only* are made definite and certain, while *chronology* stands silently by. The prophets are not writing *annals*, but they simply foretell events of thrilling interest.

In this way I should account for the striking phenomena in question. As these phenomena are so uniform and all but universal, there must be one common principle at the basis of the whole. I see no other so probable and satisfactory as the one just stated.

But enough of Lengerke, and of objections. I have not canvassed every thing which he has said, or rather declaimed; but I have omitted no one thing to which a reasonable and sober man can attach any importance.

And now, at the conclusion of this protracted discussion, let me merely glance at some of the leading reasons for receiving the book of Daniel as genuine, and I shall dismiss the topic.

I will not insist on the writer's own declaration of his authorship, although such an argument has weight, when there are no particular grounds of suspicion. But that such a man as Daniel existed, is testified repeatedly by Ezekiel; that he was a *prophet*, is asserted by Christ and his apostles who quote from his book; that his book was in the Canon before the Maccabaean period, is clear from the testimony of Sirach (at least 180 B. C.), of the N. Test., of Philo, of Josephus, of Melito, of Origen, and of all the Christian Fathers and Jewish Rabbies down to the fifth century; what I mean is, that all of them tell in substance the same story, without a dissenting voice. That Daniel was ranked with the prophets, and stood *immediately before* or *after Ezekiel*, is clear from the description of the nature of the Canon in Sirach, the N. Test., Philo, and Josephus; and from Melito down to Jerome, by the catalogues of the O. Test. books where each is named *seriatim*. Jerome was the first who learned from the Rabbins, that they in his time, ranked Daniel among the writers of the Hagiography or Kethubhim. For this dislocation, Theodoret, of that same period, taxes them with impudent audacity. Then the *internal* evidences in favor of the antiquity of the book are of the most conclusive kind. Whether we make inquiries in reference to history, or customs, or manners, or laws, or natural objects, or political *regime*, or the language or dialects of the book — to whatever quarter we direct our scrutiny, all — all is as it should be, all is as we might expect it would be, in case the book is genuine and ancient. Not a solitary voice for more than 2200 years was ever raised against it, except by some Porphyry who denied all revelation. What more do we want? What more can we reasonably ask for? Indeed, I feel prepared to aver with open face, and without fear of confutation, that there is no book in the O. Test. whose antiquity and genuineness are better vouched for than that of Daniel.

Lengerke thinks there is no good evidence that David wrote the Psalms, or Solomon a good part of the Proverbs, certainly not Canticles or Ecclesiastes. He believes that Moses did not write the Pentateuch, nor Isaiah the most of what goes under his name; and so of several of the prophets. So in the New Testament. Matthew is rejected by one critic; Mark by a second; Luke by another; John by another; all the Gospels are assigned to the second century by others; many of Paul's writings are wrested from him; the 2 Peter is lopped off; Jude is supposititious; the Apocalypse is the work of an enthusiastic Millenarian of the second century. Such are the heights to which the new criticism climbs, or rather, the deep abysses into which it plunges. The stopping place, I suppose, is where Bruno Baur has found his rest, viz. that the whole is a fiction and a fraud, got up by superstitious priests in order to sway and manage the vulgar. But if this be not the *ultima Thule*, then it may be thought by some, that Kant and Hegel have proposed a more inviting region. Christianity, and its predecessor, Mosaism, were but stepping stones in our way to the top of the mountain. Reason, pure reason, reason absolute, instinctive, godlike, indeed the Divinity itself—this sits in judgment on all revelations and on all religions, and enthroned high above them all looks down on all and says: 'Before due place was given to me, you were of some account; but now I have no further service for you to perform; take your humble place at my footstool, and there await my pleasure.'

Such is the *ultimatum* of neological criticism in religion and philosophy. And as to the book before us, nearly every objection which is urged against it converges to, and centers in, one single *a priori* maxim, viz. 'A miracle is an impossibility; *prediction* would be a miracle; if the book of Daniel be ancient and genuine, prediction must inevitably be admitted; and because this cannot be admitted, the book must be from the hand of a Pseudo-Daniel, and have been written *post eventum*.'

Such are the positions, such the objections, and such the spirit, that a sober inquirer is called to meet with and to oppose. But if he will have patience, and examine the whole matter, he need not fear a challenge to combat. He enters the lists with prophets, and apostles, and the whole church of God in past ages, and the Saviour himself, on his side, and ready to support him. Neology has indeed raised a loud outcry against the book before us. It has contradicted; it has poured out contumely; it has haughtily looked down with contemptuous sneering. And yet, after all, there is not a single argument on which it can place any reliance, which will not prove the Saviour of the world to have been an impostor, in pretending to work miracles; and his apostles to have been enthusiasts or impostors, in believing in them and also pretending to work them. The arguments that eject Daniel from the Canon, cast out with equal violence the writings of the evangelists and the apostles.

It is time to pass on to remaining topics. They are but few, and will require but a little space to canvass them.

§ 8. *Ancient Versions of the book of Daniel.*

(1) That an Alexandrine or Septuagintal Version of Daniel was extant, in the latter part of the Maccabaean period, is quite certain; for 1 Macc. has quoted it in a number of places: e. g. comp. Sept. Daniel, 11: 31 with 1 Macc. 1: 46; Sept. 11: 25 with Macc. 1: 17, 18; Sept. 11: 26 with Macc. 1: 18—20, 24, 28, 36, 54, et al. That it continued to be used until the time of Theodotion (2nd century), is plain. Justin Martyr (Dial. c. Tryp. p. 128) clearly quotes it; and so in other passages. Tertullian (De Jejun.) quotes Daniel 2: 19, according to the same Version. Origen had it included in his Hexapla. But from that time down to

A. D. 1772, nothing more was heard or known of it, so far as can now be discovered, excepting what Jerome says respecting it. In the year last named, this LXX. Version was published at Rome, from the Codex Chisianus in the Vatican library, in a folio volume. The important parts of this volume were republished by J. D. Michaelis, 1774; and by Segaar at Utrecht soon after, accompanied by his own annotations.

Jerome's testimony mostly respects the desuetude into which the Version had fallen, even long before his time. Origen himself, in his Commentary, uses the Version of Theodotion, then but recently made. Jerome seems to be in some perplexity, about the cause of the neglect exhibited toward the Sept. Version. In the preface to his own version of Daniel, in speaking of this neglect, he says: "Hoc cur accidit nescio." After suggesting various conjectures respecting the matter he adds: "Quod multum a veritate discordet, et recto judicio repudiata sit." In commenting on Dan. iv., he adverts to a remarkable departure of the Sept. version from the Hebrew original, and then adds: "Unde judicio magistrorum ecclesiae editio eorum in hoc volumine repudiata est;" and to this he subjoins the remark that "the version of Theodotion is read in the churches, which agrees better with the Hebrew and with other translators." Probably the version of the Sept. went gradually into desuetude; for that of Theodotion was, on account of his alleged heresy, somewhat slow in coming into usage. Michaelis (in Bib. Orient. Th. 4.) has given a most minute and circumstantial account of this version, having examined every word and letter in it. Its historical worth is not much. It shows an effort at an ornate style and purity of Greek, and often sacrifices to these the exactness required in a version. Not a few arbitrary omissions and additions are made; the notions of the times are sometimes developed, and historical facts, then recent, are alluded to. The wonderful in the book is augmented in the version. The same spirit which led to this is exhibited by the apocryphal additions to the book, which are described in § 9.

There are many specific departures from the Hebrew. By consulting Michaelis (ut supra), the student may find them all enumerated. Here and there a happy rendering occurs, which assists the intelligible reading of the original.

(2) The Greek of Daniel, in our common Septuagint, is the translation of Theodotion, made in the second century of the Christian era. It is much more literal and exact than the Sept. version. There can be no doubt, however, that the translator had this before him. Yet he has extended his corrections further than was necessary. However, it is beyond any reasonable doubt, that many of these have been interpolated since the time of Theodotion; for some of them hardly consist with the

general character of his version. There is no good reason to believe, that the long addition to Dan. iii., viz. the prayer of Azarias and the hymn of the three martyrs, also Dan. xiii. xiv. (as appended to the book since Theodotion's time), were originally attached to his version; for he merely translated the Hebrew Daniel. The prayer and hymn, the story of Susanna, and the history of Bel and the Dragon, were doubtless composed in Greek; but at an early period. We find Origen defending them; the Alexandrine church very partial to them; and the Romish church admitting them into the canon, as incorporated with the book of Daniel. But Jerome denounces them all as mere fables; and even Origen admits that the Hebrews never had them. It is remarkable, that our oldest MSS. of the Sept. in general, exhibit these apocryphal books as connected with the Daniel of Theodotion. That this was originally the case, there is not, as has been said, the slightest probability. The whole thing was brought about by the fondness of the Alexandrine churches for the marvellous, and their unscrupulous reception into the canon of many books that did not belong there, and which even the Romish church named *deutero-canonical.*

On the whole, not much important aid can be drawn from the version even of Theodotion. Now and then there is a happy rendering of a Hebrew word or phrase; but not unfrequently, also, one which shows that the translator had no very exact view of the meaning of the Hebrew text. Great caution is needed, in reading such a version; one moreover, which has beyond all doubt been considerably interpolated and sometimes abriged. It is sound advice to the student of the book of Daniel that he should consider the Greek version as merely adventitious *aid,* but never as an *authority.*

(3). The Syriac version of this book, as already intimated (p. 312 above), exhibits a knowledge of the Hebrew, which renders it well worth the attention of the enquirer. As Daniel has no Targum or Chaldee version, it performs a valuable service in the explanation of Hebrew words. In the Chaldee part of Daniel, however, it exhibits some strange misconceptions of the meaning of the author. The apocryphal additions made to the book, as before noticed, are appended to this version; but probably by interpolation in the third century. The student may find in this version, something of the same assistance, which is rendered to other books by the Targums.

(4). The Vulgate. This is, as a whole, superior to any other ancient version, and shows a more thorough knowledge than any of them in respect to the tenor and nature of the book. An invaluable service has Jerome done, by this translation of Daniel and by his commentary upon the book. As received by the Romish church, it has the apocryphal additions, translated from the Greek as appended to the version of Theodotion. Jerome evidently bestowed much time and pains upon these works.

(5) Some other versions, or fragments of versions, are extant. (*a*) A Greek version, out of St. Mark's Library at Venice, published by Villoison, A. D. 1784; a slavishly literal translation. (*b*) Fragments out of Theodotion by Jacob of Edessa, in Syriac. (*c*) A Hebrew version of the Chaldee in Daniel and Ezra, printed in Kennicott's Bible, from a manuscript of 1327 in the Vatican.

§ 9. *Apocryphal additions to Daniel.*

Already we had occasion to advert frequently to them, in describing the ancient versions. It will be proper here to descant on them with somewhat more of particularity.

(*a*) In the midst of the third chapter (after v. 24,) is inserted, first the prayer of Azarias (Abednego), who, for himself and his friends, made confession and supplication. The prayer is plainly made up of fragments from Dan. ix. and Neh. ix. It abounds in the confession of Jewish national sins, and supplications for pardon and restoration. There is scarcely anything in it which is appropriate to the condition of Azarias and his friends. It is such a prayer as we could well suppose might have been uttered in a fast-day-assemblage of exiled Jews. But there is one feature in it, that seems to betray the fact that a *later* hand has been meddling with the original composition. In v. 40, Azarias prays thus: "As in the offering of rams, bulls, and thousands of fat lambs, so let our sacrifice in thy sight to day make propitiation for us!" This savors strongly of a Romish Christian hand. I know not where to find any parallel in the Hebrew Scriptures. I could with a good degree of confidence say, that some such man as wrote Hermas' Pastor, must have written this. The prayer includes vs. 25—45, and vs. 46—51 are then occupied with narrative, stating how the furnace was heated, that the flame mounted up 49 cubits, and how an angel descended into the furnace and made the air like a dewy blowing wind. Forthwith the martyrs burst into a song of praise, which is contained in vs. 52—90. The model of the writer was Ps. 148, where the different creatures of God, animate and inanimate, are called on to praise him. But here the matter is extended to a wearisome length; for the same objects in different combinations are repeatedly introduced. There is a kind of chorus to nearly every verse, like that in Ps. 136. For the rest — some of the thoughts are expressed in a pleasing manner, but on the whole there is great tameness and want of vital energy. It is but a sorry composition, when compared with the Psalms which it attempts to imitate. From v. 91 to 100, the original Chaldee of Daniel is followed although with not a few of minor departures from the original. The days of abounding zeal for litanies and liturgies, must have given birth to such a composition; and only such a period sanctioned the addition of it to the Jewish canonical Daniel.

(*b*) THE HISTORY OF SUSANNA. This is quite an attractive *novelette.* Most children and young persons read it with great pleasure. The narration is simple, and the style indicates a writer more expert in Greek than Hebrews in general were. Vs. 54, 55, also 58, 59, betray a Greek original beyond all doubt, by the paronomasias which they exhibit. The object of the narration is, to exalt the early youth of Daniel. Dan. i. ii. gave rise, no doubt, to the story. The modesty, virtue, and piety of Susanna form an attractive picture; and the dexterity of Daniel in bringing out the concealed guilt of the elders, is not unworthy of the man. One is inclined to ask, however, in what way a youth came by authority to sit in judgment, as Daniel does, upon elders; but the writer has solved the *nodus*, by telling us (v. 45), that he had a special divine commission. The narrative ends, in imitation of several passages in the genuine Daniel, with bringing to view the elevation and influence of the prophet. If apocryphal writers had never composed anything worse than the history of Susanna, we might feel quite favorably disposed toward them. I add merely that Jer. 29: 23 seq. appears to have suggested material to the author for the plan of his work.

(*c*) BEL AND THE DRAGON. Somewhat inappropriately has the writer introduced *Bel* here, as the object of religious worship under Cyrus. The older Magi had no temples, no altars, no idol-statues. Xenophon, indeed, makes Cyrus oftentimes speak and act like a Greek, in relation to Grecian divinities. This is the greatest mistake in his book, and shows that he knew little of the religion of the Parsis. But he was writing for *Grecian* readers; and they probably felt but little interest in *Parsism.* The writer of the story under review has brought Cyrus before us as a worshipper of *Bel,* who was a *Babylonian* god. The story itself is composed with some adroitness, and is attractive to readers in general. The exposure of the imposture of the heathen priests, in providing such sumptuous feasts for Bel, while they themselves secretly consumed the whole by night, is very well managed, and in itself would present nothing incredible. But the latter part of the story spoils the credit of the whole. Daniel is cast into the lions' den by Cyrus, who was forced by the priests to give him up to their vengeance. While there, the spirit of God bids the prophet Habakkuk, in Judea, to go to

42

Babylon, and furnish Daniel with food. On the suggestion of difficulties by the prophet about obeying this command, an angel takes him by the hair of his head, and carries him through the air to the lions' den at Babylon, with the food in his possession, and there Habakkuk feeds and comforts Daniel. The angel then transports him back to Judea. After seven days Cyrus comes to mourn for Daniel; he finds him living and well; and causes him to be taken out of the den, and his persecutors to be thrown into it, who were instantly devoured.

The transportation through the air is an exact imitation of Ezek. 8: 3. But in Ezekiel's case, all is done merely in a *trance* or *prophetic vision.* The rest of the last paragraph is all taken from Daniel vi. One escape of Daniel from lions was not enough for the author of this fiction. He seems to have practised upon the maxim: "The *more* of a good thing, the better."

The two last named works compare well with some of the Jewish (Rabbinic) Haggadoth, i. e. חַגָּדוֹת, *pleasant stories.* They seem to be of Jewish origin, whether Christian or not it would be difficult to say. There is nothing decisive of this point, in the narratives themselves. Be this as it may, no one can imbue himself with the spirit of the canonical Daniel, without feeling that he is transported to a foreign region, when he begins to open his eyes upon these romances. It is indeed a difficult task, to imitate such a writer as Daniel. Full surely, the apocryphal writers have attempted it with very little success. My belief is, that a Pseudo-Daniel of the Maccabaean period would have won few, if any, more laurels than they have won.

§ 10. *Leading Commentaries and Critical Disquisitions on the Book of Daniel.*

Among the ancients, is the Commentary of Ephrem Syrus, and is of importance principally as leading to an understanding of the Peshito or old Syriac Version. The four monarchies are ill understood, and the exegesis tasteless and adventurous. Among the Greeks, Theodoret has left behind him a Commentary on the Greek version of Theodotion. Few of his remarks are grammatico-exegetical, but he has some historical data that are of value. Jerome (in Latin) stands preëminent above all the ancients, for tact in exegesis, and for historical and Rabbinical learning. Specially has he given us the views of Porphyry, which otherwise would have been wholly lost. Among the moderns stands conspicuous the great Genevan, John Calvin, whose work is rich in psychological and doctrinal remarks. A critical examination of the Hebrew in a *grammatical* way, was a thing not begun in his day, and must not be looked for in him. But many a fine remark will be found, and a deep insight into the spiritual meaning of the author is every where manifest.

The most considerable Commentators after him, are Grotius, and C. B. Michaelis in the Notae Uberiores. Bertholdt (1806—1808) published an extensive work on Daniel, in two parts. He exhibits many useful explanations of a historical nature; but he has not a few tasteless conceits, and abounds every where in rationalistic views. Rosenmueller on Daniel; Maurer's brief Commentary; Hävernick on Daniel, and Lengerke on the same, all contain useful things, although in different measures and in a diversity of ways. The first two and the last are pretty thoroughly neological; specially as to all critical and literary matters; but Lengerke especially, as we have already seen, goes all lengths in the *destructive* criticism. But in the explanation of words and phrases, he is not inferior to any of the others; for he evidently possesses a good knowledge of the Hebrew and the Chaldee.

In regard to the *literature* of the book, we have an abundance of writers. Among those who have called in question the genuineness of the book, are Corrodi, in his Freimuthige Versuche and Beleuchtung des Bibelkanons, the oldest opponent of the book, who is really in earnest and at all formidable; Eichhorn, in his Einleitung; Bertholdt, in his Einleitung und Commentär; Griesinger, in his Neue Ansicht des Daniel, Gesenius, in Allgem. Litt. Zeitung (Halle), Erganz. Blätter No. 80; De Wette in his Einleit.; Bleek in Theol. Zeitschrift von Schleiermacher etc. Heft iii. s. 171 seq.; also Rosenmüller in Comm.; Lengerke in Comm.; Hitzig, in Heidelb. Jahrb. Heft ii.; Redepenning, in Theol. Studien und Kritiken, 1833 and also 1835 (review of Hävernick); Ewald, in Berliner Jahrb. 1831; and Knobel, Hebrew Propheten, ii. § 40, brief, but full of matter, and full of neology.

In defence of the genuineness of the book, may be mentioned Lüderwald, die 6 ersten capp. Daniel's geprüft, 1787; Staudlin, Neue Beiträge; Beckhaus, Integrität prophet. Schriften; Jahn, Einleit.; Sack, Apologetik; and, preëminent above them all, Hengstenberg, Authentie des Daniel, altogether the most thorough, fundamental, and discriminating performance, yet not free from some inadmissible exegesis, specially in regard to the fourth monarchy and the 70 weeks. Hävernick's Commentar defends, in the introduction, the genuineness of Daniel, with a good degree of critical ability; but his Neue Untersuchungen, written after the work of Lengerke, is a great advance upon his former defence, and in many respects even upon the work of Hengstenberg. He has thoroughly dissipated not a few of Lengerke's skeptical conclusions.

This last work is now usually appended to his Commentary. Besides this, in his Einleitung he has put the last hand to what he desired to do, for the book which he had so long and earnestly defended. But he also believes in a *Roman* empire, as predicted by Daniel; yet in his Excursus on the fourth monarchy, at the close of his Commentary, he has altogether failed to satisfy the reasonable demands of historico-grammatical exegesis.

More recent still are some very valuable remarks of Oehler, in Tholuck's Lit. Anzeiger, 1842, Nos. 49—51.

I have not referred to English writers, who, although some of them have valuable remarks on the book before us, have almost *en masse*, gone in the old road of a *fourth Roman empire*, and entirely neglected grammatico-historical exegesis. Nearly all have made out an exposition *a priori*, and harmonize Daniel and the Apocalypse together, as if the main object of both books were one and the same. There may be some writing with which I am unacquainted, which has undertaken the historico-grammatical interpretation of the book; if so, I regret that I have not had access to it. England now has men fitted for such labor, but hitherto the study of Daniel has been pursued in quite a different way. A recent work of Mr. Birk's on Daniel I have seen, and examined to some extent; but I find no attempt to cast light on the book by the aid of interpretation grounded on philology, nor even the slightest evidence of any knowledge of the original language of the book. Of course it must follow, that Daniel is explained by the process which the Germans name *hineinexegesiren*, i. e. throwing an *a priori* explanation *into* it, instead of getting one out of it. I cannot conceive, how any valuable light can be thrown on the Scriptures in this way of writing.

So far as I know, all the books written in the U. States on the subject of Daniel's prophecies, (none of them are running Commentaries on the book), are of the same character as the English ones, excepting a like book of the Rev. Ira Chase, D. D., and another of the Rev. Mr. Folsom. These reject the idea of a *Roman* monarchy, and show that the writers of them had discovered the fallacies in the older modes of interpretation, with regard to this subject. They can find no *Pope* in the book, other than Antiochus; and for this *heresy* (?), they have found the usual retribution from those interpreters, who make Daniel to speak out their own views, instead of laboriously searching after his. It requires no prophetic views that are profound, to predict that such a method of interpretation as the last cannot continue to be current long, with an enlightened ministry now coming on the stage of action.

www.ingramcontent.com/pod-product-compliance
Lightning Source LLC
LaVergne TN
LVHW021318110826
845150LV00003B/605

* 9 7 8 1 4 2 5 5 5 6 9 1 4 *